FOUNDATIONS OF MARKETING

DAVID JOBBER
2ND EDITION
JOHN FAHY

FOUNDATIONS OF MARKETING
Second Edition

David Jobber and John Fahy

The **McGraw-Hill** Companies

London   Boston   Burr Ridge, IL   Dubuque, IA   Madison, WI   New York   San Francisco   St. Louis   Bangkok   Bogotá   Caracas   Kuala Lumpur   Lisbon   Madrid   Mexico City   Milan   Montreal   New Delhi   Santiago   Seoul   Singapore   Sydney   Taipei   Toronto

Foundations of Marketing
David Jobber and John Fahy
ISBN-13 978-0-07-710918-9
ISBN-007710918x

Published by McGraw-Hill Education
Shoppenhangers Road
Maidenhead
Berkshire
SL6 2QL
Telephone: 44 (0) 1628 502 500
Fax: 44 (0) 1628 770 224
Website: www.mcgraw-hill.co.uk

British Library Cataloguing in Publication Data
A catalogue record for this book is available from the British Library

Library of Congress Cataloging-in-Publication Data
The Library of Congress data for this book has been applied for from the Library of Congress

Acquisitions Editor: Kirsty Reade
Development Editor: Rachel Crookes
Marketing Manager: Marca Wosoba

Text design by Hard Lines
Printed and bound in Spain by Mateu Cromo

ISBN-13 978-0-07-710918-9
ISBN-10 007710918x

Dedication

For Mary Jobber

David Jobber

To Sarah, September 2004, *No Frontiers . . . .*

and

in memory of Pat Cahill,

a dedicated marketer and great friend

John Fahy

The authors

David Jobber is an internationally recognized marketing academic. He is Professor of Marketing at the University of Bradford School of Management. He holds an Honours Degree in Economics from the University of Manchester, a Masters Degree from the University of Warwick and a Doctorate from the University of Bradford.

Before joining the faculty at the Bradford Management Centre, David worked for the TI Group in marketing and sales, and was Senior Lecturer in Marketing at the University of Huddersfield. He has wide experience of teaching core marketing courses at undergraduate, postgraduate and post-experience levels. His specialisms are industrial marketing, sales management and marketing research. He has a proven, ratings-based record of teaching achievements at all levels. His competence in teaching is reflected in visiting appointment at the universities of Aston, Lancaster, Loughborough and Warwick in the UK and the university of Wellington, New Zealand. He has taught marketing to executives of such international companies as BP, Crude International, Allied Domecq, the BBC, Bass, Royal and Sun Alliance, Rolls-Royce, and Rio Tinto.

Supporting his teaching is a record of achievement in academic research. David has over 150 publications in the marketing area in such journals as the *International Journal of Research in Marketing*, *MIS Quarterly*, *Strategic Management Journal*, *Journal of International Business Studies*, *Journal of Business*

Research, *Journal of Product Innovation Management* and the *Journal of Personal Selling and Sales Management*. David has served on the editorial boards of *the International Journal of Research in Marketing*, *Journal of Personal Selling and Sales Management*, *European Journal of Marketing* and the *Journal of Marketing Management*. In 2001, David was appointed Special Adviser to the Research Assessment Exercise panel that rated research output from business and management schools throughout the UK.

John Fahy is an internationally recognized academic and one of Ireland's leading marketing thinkers. He is currently Professor of Marketing at the University of Limerick. Prior to this he lectured at Trinity College, Dublin; he holds a Masters Degree from Texas A&M University and a Doctorate from Trinity College.

His research interests are in the areas of marketing strategy, global competition, services marketing and electronic commerce. He is the author of three books and over 60 articles on these topics in journals including *Journal of Marketing, Journal of International Business Studies, Journal of Business Research, Journal of Market-Focused Management, European Journal of Marketing, International Business Review* and *Sloan Management Review*. He is the winner of several major international research awards such as the AMA Services Marketing Paper of the Year Award and the Chartered Institute of Marketing Best Paper Award at the Academy of Marketing Annual Conference. He is also a distinguished case study author and the winner of several case competitions.

He has a distinguished teaching record at all levels including undergraduate, postgraduate and executive, where he specializes in marketing strategy. He also has extensive international experience having held visiting appointments at Senshu University, Japan, Texas A&M University, USA, and Monash University, Australia. He retains close links with industry through consulting assignments and his involvement in executive training programmes, and is regularly invited to speak on business issues.

Brief table of contents

Detailed table of contents

Case list

Vignette list

Marketing Spotlights

Marketing in Action

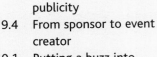

e-Marketing

Preface to the second edition

Marketing is a field that is evolving all the time and often at a very dramatic rate. Witness, for example, the changes taking place in advertising. Media are rapidly fragmenting with a multitude of television and radio channels trying to reach consumers, many of whom are moving more of their leisure time to the Internet and their mobile phones. This presents real challenges for both the media owner and the advertiser trying to catch up with an ever more elusive audience.

This book is about marketing in the modern world. Marketing is a real-life, exciting activity that everyone is exposed to on a daily basis. Therefore, with its emphasis on including a vast array of marketing applications and examples, this new edition aims to bring this reality to life for the reader. In all there are a total of 76 new inserts detailing issues of marketing practice. A special effort has been made to include marketing topics that fit within the realm of the modern student. Therefore, for example, the book includes features on the Apple iPod, promotional messaging, tattooing, male grooming, MTV, Madonna, Diesel and Sony PlayStation, to name but a few.

The range of features achieves other objectives as well. The e-Marketing vignettes point to up-to-the minute trends that may change aspects of marketing practice in the future. Interactive television, weblogs, RFID tags and web analytics are cases in point. Care has also been taken to ensure a wide geographic spread. As well as the UK and Ireland, there are fea-tures on companies and brands from Finland, Sweden, Denmark, Germany, France, Spain, The Netherlands and the USA. Additional examples are included throughout the text from companies in the rest of Europe and around the world. The vignettes also feature many smaller firms, such as Naty (Sweden), Fopp (UK), Riverford (UK) and Lily O'Brien's (Ireland), as well as the better-known global organizations such as Boeing, Nokia, Manchester United and Singapore Airlines.

The structure of the book

Despite the pace of change, the fundamentals of mar-keting remain the same. Therefore this book retains its original goal of focusing on these fundamentals. While most of the existing marketing principles text-books have become ever longer and more detailed, this book aims to be concise, returning to and exam-ining the core foundations of marketing. For this reason it will appeal, in particular, to instructors who teach 'Introduction to Marketing' as a half-year course or one-semester module.

We have removed the separate sections of the last edition and now have 12 chapters that broadly equate with the marketing planning framework shown in Figure 1. The early chapters deal with understanding the nature of customers and markets—the starting point of any marketing activity. We then move on to

Stages in the planning process	Relevant chapters in the book		
Business mission			
Marketing audit			Chapters 2, 3 and 4
SWOT analysis			
Marketing objectives			
Strategic thrust	Strategic objectives		
Core strategy			Chapter 5
Target markets	Competitive advantage	Competitor targets	
Marketing mix decisions			Chapters 6, 7, 8, 9, 10 and 11
Organization and implementation			Chapter 12
Control			

Figure 1 The marketing planning process

discuss the marketing mix for both products and services. And we close by pulling all of this together within a detailed discussion of marketing planning and strategy.

New to this edition

The book retains many of the popular features of the first edition, such as the Learning Objectives and Marketing Spotlights at the start of each chapter, the Internet Exercises, Key Terms and Study Questions, as well as suggested additional readings. The chapter summaries have been changed to a bullet-point format for ease of review. As in the previous edition, key topics such as Internet marketing and marketing ethics run as core themes throughout the book.

The following is a description of some of the new content in this edition.

Services marketing

One of the observations on the first edition was that the coverage of services marketing was too limited so this time a full chapter has been devoted to the topic. Services are a key driver of economic growth in most developed economies and the chapter addresses all the core issues such as the unique characteristics of services, the services marketing mix, service quality and service productivity. The chapter closes with a case study on one of the UK's most exciting services marketing enterprises, Pret a Manger.

Integrated marketing communications

Due to the breadth and diversity of communications tools being used by modern organizations, the discussion of IMC can become unwieldy. In this book, what we have done is to distinguish between mass communications techniques, such as advertising and public relations, and direct communications techniques such as personal selling and direct marketing. A specific chapter is devoted to each. In a break with the practice of other textbooks and to reflect how mainstream it has become, Internet marketing is incorporated with the other direct communications techniques due to its potential for customization and interactivity. The material covered has been significantly updated with an emphasis on the marketing potential and power of the Internet. Finally, throughout the two chapters in question, expanded coverage is given to those types of integrated marketing communications that are growing in popularity such as sponsorship, product placement and mobile marketing.

Pricing

Significant changes have been made to the pricing chapter to put a greater focus on the marketing rather than the economic aspects of pricing. Several new sections have been added, such as those on product-line pricing, pricing in distribution channels and pricing in international markets, while some, such as the impact of pricing on positioning, have been expanded.

Relationship marketing

The importance of building relationships with customers is a theme that runs throughout the book. Specific attention is also devoted to it in the services marketing chapter, which describes the benefits of customer relationships and how they can be built and maintained. In the direct communications chapter, a special section is devoted to the advances in customer relationship management (CRM).

International marketing

The treatment of international marketing issues has been expanded throughout the book. For example, in Chapter 2, there is a new section on the impact of exchange rates on businesses, which is discussed under the economic forces in the macroenvironment. The product chapter discusses the growth in pan-European and global brands, while the pricing chapter includes a new section on pricing in international markets.

Branding

In a world that is becoming increasingly dominated by power brands, or superbrands, several changes have been made to the discussion on branding in the product chapter. The benefits of branding are explored in detail. A new section has been added on the growth of co-branding initiatives between companies and the emerging topic of brand communities is examined.

Case studies

The book contains 11 brand new award-winning cases, as well as an updated version of the Ryanair case included in the first edition. Once again, many have been student tested and fit perfectly within the world of the modern student, such as those on online music distribution, fast fashion and Absolut vodka. They have also been expanded in length and include more data to permit intensive analysis and discussion.

Supplementary resources

In addition to the features included in the book to help students learn and lecturers teach, extra support can be found on the Online Learning Centre for this text, details of which can be found on page xxiii.

Acknowledgements

A special word of thanks to Sinead Moloney, University of Limerick, for her tireless research work and for her contributions to this book.

Picture acknowledgements

The author and the Publishers would like to extend thanks to the following for allowing the reproduction of company advertising and/or logos:

Exhibits

1.1 With thanks to Polaroid, BBH, Noelle Pickford and Dave Stewart; 1.2 With thanks to Cisco Systems; 1.3 With thanks to BUPA; 1.4 With thanks to IKEA; 1.5 With thanks to Cancer Research UK and OgilvyOne worldwide; 2.1 With thanks to Alliance and Leicester; 2.2 With thanks to Lexmark; 2.3 Reproduced by kind permission of Beiersdorf UK; 2.4 With thanks to British Heart Foundation; 2.5 With thanks to Toyota and M&C Saatchi ; 3.1 With thanks to Cow & Gate, and Ogilvy Mather; 3.2 With thanks to Unilever and DDB London; 3.3 With thanks to Gillette; 3.4 With thanks to Anchor and Clemmo Hornby Inge; 3.5 With thanks to SEAT. Photography: Fergus Stothart; 3.6 With thanks to easyCruise; 3.7 With thanks to Storm; 3.8 With thanks to ICM; 4.1 With thanks to The Daily Telegraph; 4.2 These materials have been reproduced with the permission of eBay Inc. Copyright Ebay Inc. All rights reserved; 4.3 With thanks to McAfee; 5.1 With thanks to Ercol and HDM Total Communication; 5.2 With thanks to Nokia; 5.3 With thanks to Kellogg's; 5.4 With thanks to Neville Johnson; 5.5 With thanks to Lexus and M&C Saatchi; 5.6 With thanks to Cross Pens; 6.1 With thanks to Mercedes Benz and Campbell Doyle Dye; 6.2 With thanks to Bertolli and Unilever; 6.3 With thanks to Virgin Mobile, Rainey Kelly Campbell Roalfe/Y&R; 6.4 With thanks to Green & Black's and Brave; 6.5 With thanks to Pernod Ricard UK; 7.1 With thanks to the AA; 7.2 With thanks to Champneys; 7.3 With thanks to Bank of Scotland and T3; 7.4 With thanks to ABN AMRO Bank NV; 7.5 With thanks to Royal Mail and Proximity London; 8.1 With thanks to Magnet; 8.2 With thanks to TK Maxx; 8.3 With thanks to Boots; 8.4 © 2005 Dell Inc. All rights reserved; 9.1 With thanks to Eurostar; 9.2 With thanks to Orange and Mother; 9.3 With thanks to Hovis and British Bakeries; 9.4 With thanks to Specsavers; 9.5 With thanks to Boots; 10.1 With thanks to MSB&K; 10.2 With thanks to Axa Insurance; 10.3 With thanks to La Redoute; 10.4 With thanks to the Viral Factory ; 10.5 With thanks to FBD Insurance plc; 11.1 With thanks to Wm Morrisons Supermarkets plc; 11.2 With thanks to O'Briens; 11.3 With thanks to La Senza; 11.4 With thanks to Sainsbury's Banking; 12.1 With thanks to Dyson; 12.2 With thanks to British Airways and M & C Saatchi; 12.3 Under permission by V&S Vin & sprit AB (publ). ABSOLUT®VODKA. ABSOLUT COUNTRY OF SWEDEN VODKA & LOGO, ABSOLUT, ABSOLUT BOTTLE DESIGN AND ABSOLUT CALLIGRAPHY ARE TRADE-MARKS OWNED BY V&S VIN & SPRIT AB (PUBL) © 2005 V&S VIN & SPRIT AB (PUBL). Michel Dubois is also credited for this work; 12.4 With thanks to GE Healthcare. Case study 5 With thanks to Pret A Manger; case study 9 Under permission by V&S Vin & sprit AB (publ). ABSOLUT®VODKA. ABSOLUT COUNTRY OF SWEDEN VODKA & LOGO, ABSOLUT, ABSOLUT BOTTLE DESIGN AND ABSOLUT CALLIGRAPHY ARE TRADEMARKS OWNED BY V&S VIN & SPRIT AB (PUBL) © 2005 V&S VIN & SPRIT AB (PUBL); case study 11 With thanks to Zara and INDITEX; [Marketing spotlights] chapter 1 ©Apple Computer, Inc. Used with permission. All rights reserved. Apple® and the Apple Logoi are registered trademark of Apple Computer, Inc; chapter 2 With thanks to Cafédirect; chapter 3 Tim Robberts/Getty images; chapter 4 With thanks to easyGroup; chapter 5 Evan Agostini/Getty images; chapter 6 Frank Micelotta/Getty images; chapter 10 Paul Barker/Getty images; chapter 11 Dave M. Benett/Getty Images.

Every effort has been made to trace and acknowledge ownership of copyright. The publishers would be pleased to make suitable arrangements to clear permission with any copyright holders whom it has not been possible to contact.

Guided tour

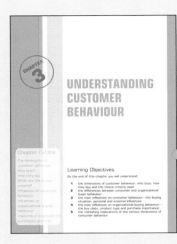

Chapter Outline and Learning Objectives

The topics covered and a set of objectives are included at the start of each chapter, summarising what to expect from each chapter.

Marketing Spotlight

A lively vignette begins each chapter to introduce the main topic and show how marketing works in real life.

Key Terms

These are highlighted throughout the chapter, with definition re-caps at the end of each chapter for quick and easy revision.

Ads, Figures and Tables

We've included a hand-selected array of contemporary ads to show marketing in action. Key concepts and models are illustrated using figures, tables and charts.

Marketing in Action and e-Marketing boxes

In each chapter you'll find these fun and useful examples of Marketing in Action and e-Marketing; they show how the issues covered in the chapter affect real-life companies and products.

Chapter Summary

This briefly reviews and reinforces the main topics you will have covered in each chapter to ensure you have acquired a solid understanding of the key topics.

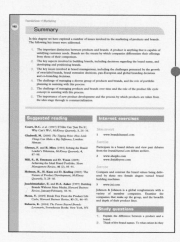

Study Questions and Internet Exercises

These questions encourage you to review and apply the knowledge you have acquired from each chapter.

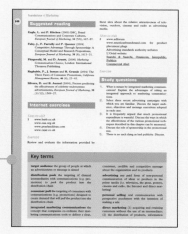

Suggested Reading and References

We've hand selected the best secondary sources for each topic, along with all of the references you'll need – find these at the end of each chapter.

Case Studies

Every chapter has its own case study, directly relating to the issues discussed and designed to bring the theories to life. See page xiv for a full list of companies and issues covered. Questions are included for class work, assignments and revision.

Technology to enhance learning and teaching

Visit www.mcgraw-hill.co.uk/textbooks/jobber today

Online Learning Centre (OLC)

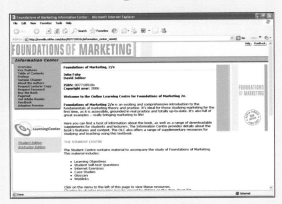

After completing each chapter, log on to the supporting Online Learning Centre website. Take advantage of the study tools offered to reinforce the material you have read in the text, and to develop your knowledge of marketing in a fun and effective way.

Resources for students include:

- New case studies
- Self-test questions
- Internet exercises
- Glossary

Also available for lecturers:

- Lecturers' manual
- Testbank in EZTest format
- PowerPoint slides
- New case studies
- Image bank

For lecturers:
Primis Content Centre

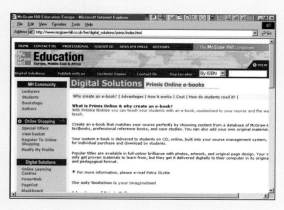

If you need to supplement your course with additional cases or content, create a personalised e-Book for your students. Visit www.primiscontentcenter.com or e-mail primis_euro@mcgraw-hill.com for more information.

Study Skills

We publish guides to help you study, research, pass exams and write essays, all the way through your university studies.

Visit **www.openup.co.uk/ss/** to see the full selection and get £2 discount by entering promotional code **study** when buying online!

Computing Skills

If you'd like to brush up on your Computing skills, we have a range of titles covering MS Office applications such as Word, Excel, PowerPoint, Access and more.

Get a £2 discount off these titles by entering the promotional code **app** when ordering online at www.mcgraw-hill.co.uk/app

CHAPTER 1

THE NATURE OF MARKETING

Learning Objectives

By the end of this chapter you will understand:

1 the development of marketing and the marketing concept
2 the nature of customer satisfaction and value
3 the scope of marketing
4 the relationship between adopting a marketing philosophy and business performance
5 the role and importance of marketing planning.

The success of iPod

The activities of companies both reflect and shape the world that we live in. For example, some argue that the invention of the motor car has defined the way we live today because it allowed personal mobility on a scale that had never been seen before. It contributed to the growth of city suburbs, to increased recreation and to an upsurge in consumer credit. It gave us shopping malls, theme parks, motels, a fast-food industry and a generation of road movies.

Not all inventions have such a long-lasting impact, but almost every year some new product or service comes along that captures the imagination of the marketplace and succeeds on an unprecedented scale. One such recent launch has been Apple's portable digital music player, the iPod. When it was brought on to the market in 2001, Apple was a struggling company as, over the years, its share of the computer market had been eroded by Microsoft. So it launched the iPod as an upmarket accessory to its personal computers in the hope of boosting sales of the latter. Instead it was the iPod that became the star of the show. Already, 10 million of them have been sold—so many that it has become the dominant manufacturer in the sector by a wide margin with over 60 per cent of the US market alone. Such is its dominance that 'iPod' is fast becoming the generic name for this type of device in the same way as 'Walkman' did for personal cassette/CD players.

The iPod has caught the wave of change in how consumers enjoy their music. MP3 players are seen as superior to more traditional formats such as cassette and CD. They are capable of storing a great deal more music and also allow users to bypass traditional record shops and download songs from various online suppliers. And they fit seamlessly into modern lifestyles characterized by long commuting times, outdoor activities, and the dominance of the personal computer as both a work and recreation device. Apple has stolen a march on its competitors due to the superior design of the iPod with its sleek appearance, ease of use and functionality, its excellent storage capability and its adaptability in terms of integration into cars, etc. And with the launch of the iTunes online music store, holding over a million songs, sales of the device were boosted hugely as it became easy and legal for consumers to download music. The premium pricing of the iPod helped Apple generate a net income increase of 300 per cent in 2004 and its stock price has risen over 600 per cent since 2003.

It will not be able to rest on its laurels, however. A new generation of smaller, sleeker and cheaper MP3 players have begun hitting the market since 2004 as competitors like Sony, Rio and GoVideo seek to capture some of this rapidly growing business. And, given that the only online site the iPod is capable of downloading songs from is the iTunes music store, the growth in other legal online music sites has given a boost to its rivals and raises problems for Apple. It has responded quickly however, bringing out the iPod Shuffle, which retails at US$99 and is targeted at young consumers and the economy end of the market, as well as a new, enhanced iPod (the iPod Photo) with the capacity to store 25,000 photographs.

The success of the iPod to date demonstrates the power of innovation and market awareness. Companies need to be sensitive to the subtle changes that take place every day in the marketplace. Sony dominated the first wave of portable music players with its hugely successful Walkman but has ceded the advantage to Apple this time around. Being able to anticipate the next need, and deliver a response to it, is the challenge facing the marketer, and that is what this book is about.[1]

In the exciting world of business, there are new successes and failures every day. For example, towards the end of the 1990s, there were many predictions that the future was online and that a new wave of e-businesses was about to obliterate many of the more established enterprises. Thousands of new companies were started, billions of euros of investors' money was spent and the vast majority of these start-ups have already disappeared. At the same time, there are many young and old businesses that continue to thrive and grow. Unlike their fellow dotcoms, companies like eBay and Google have enjoyed a meteoric rise in the past decade. Venerable brands like Coca-Cola, Virgin, IKEA and Nokia continue to command big shares of their markets, though others—such as Marks & Spencer, Sony and Volkswagen—struggle. And everywhere around the world there are small, local enterprises that thrive on the support of local customers.

At the heart of all of this change is marketing. Companies succeed and fail for many reasons but very often marketing is central to the outcome. The reason for this is that the focus of marketing is on customers and their changing needs. If you don't have customers, you don't have a business. Successful companies are those that succeed not only in getting customers but also in keeping them through being constantly aware of their changing needs. The goal of marketing is long-term customer satisfaction, not short-term deception or gimmicks. This theme is reinforced by the writings of top management consultant Peter Drucker, who stated:[2]

> Because the purpose of business is to create and keep customers, it has only two central functions—marketing and innovation. The basic function of marketing is to attract and retain customers at a profit.

What does this statement tell us? First, it places marketing in a central role for business success since it is concerned with the creation and retention of customers. The failure of many products, particularly those in sectors like information technology, is often attributed to a lack of attention to customer needs. Second, it is a reality of commercial life that it is much more expensive to attract new customers than to retain existing ones. Indeed, the costs of attracting new customers have been found to be up to six times higher than the costs of retaining old ones.[3] Consequently, marketing-orientated companies recognize the importance of building relationships with customers by providing satisfaction and attracting new customers by creating added value. Grönroos stressed the importance of relationship building in his definition of marketing, in which he describes the objective of marketing as to establish, develop and commercialize long-term customer relationships so that the objectives of the parties involved are met.[4] Third, since most markets are characterized by strong competition, the statement also suggests the need to monitor and understand competitors, since it is to rivals that customers will turn if their needs are not being met. The rest of this chapter will examine some of these ideas in more detail, and provide an introduction to how marketing can create customer value and satisfaction.

The marketing concept

The modern marketing concept can be expressed as 'the achievement of corporate goals through meeting and exceeding customer needs better than the competition'. For example, the mantra at Procter & Gamble, one of the world's leading consumer products companies, is that it must win at the first and second moments of truth—that is, in the shop where the consumer decides which brand to select and in the home when he/she uses it. Three conditions must be met before the marketing concept can be applied. First, company activities should be focused on providing customer satisfaction rather than, for example, simply producing products. This is often not an easy condition to meet. For example, Adidas's significant fall in sales in the US market in 2003 was put down to a failure to meet US consumer tastes.[5] Second, the achievement of customer satisfaction relies on integrated effort. The responsibility for the implementation of the concept lies not just within the marketing department but should run right through production, finance, research and development, engineering, and other departments. Finally, for integrated effort to come about, management must believe that corporate goals can be achieved through satisfied customers (see Figure 1.1). Some companies are quicker and better at recognizing the importance of the marketing concept than others. For example, the computer company Dell is still relatively young, but through a better understanding of the direction in which the industry was moving it overtook several well-established rivals such as HP/Compaq and IBM.

In essence, the marketing concept is a philosophy of business that puts the customer and customer satisfaction at the centre of things. For example, through implementation of the marketing concept, the Body Shop grew rapidly from a small cosmetics retailer in the south of England to a well-known global brand. Senior management were committed to an alternative

Figure 1.1 Key components of the marketing concept

approach to the marketing of cosmetics, and all activities within the company were focused around meeting customer needs. Companies like the Body Shop also exemplify what has become known as the 'societal marketing concept', which holds that companies should deliver customer satisfaction in a way that improves both the consumer's and society's well-being. We will examine this issue in greater detail in the next chapter.

Exhibit 1.1 This advertisement for the Polaroid One humorously demonstrates the benefits provided by an instant camera

The development of marketing

The origins of modern marketing can be traced to the Industrial Revolutions that took place in Britain around 1750 and in the USA and Germany around 1830.[6] Advances in production and distribution, and the migration of rural masses to urban areas created the potential for large-scale markets. As business-people sought to exploit these markets, the institutions of marketing such as advertising media and distribution channels began to grow and develop. Marketing as a field of study began in the early part of the twentieth century, growing out of courses that examined issues relating to distribution.[7] The focus of marketing courses in the 1950s and 1960s was on 'how to do it', with an emphasis on the techniques of marketing.[8] In more recent times, attention has been paid to the philosophy of marketing as a way of doing business, and to the nature and impact of marketing on stakeholders and society in general.

Despite this long tradition, there is no guarantee that all companies will adopt a **marketing orientation**. Many firms today are characterized by an inward-looking stance, where their focus is on existing products or the internal operations of the company (see Marketing in Action 1.1). Figure 1.2 illustrates **production orientation** in its crudest form. The focus is on current production capabilities. The purpose of the organization is to manufacture products and sell them aggressively to customers. A classic example of the catastrophe that can happen when this philosophy drives a company is that of Pollitt and Wigsell, a steam engine producer that sold its products to the textile industry. It made the finest steam engine available and the company grew to employ over 1000 people on a 12-hectare site. Its focus was on steam engine production, so when the electric motor superseded the earlier technology it failed to respond. The 12-hectare site is now a housing estate. Similarly, a report on the funds management industry in the UK found that, in general, the sector was characterized by a lack of customer focus and a lack of effective market segmentation, with the result that many products being offered were unsuitable and potential sales were being lost.[9]

Companies that are marketing-orientated focus on customers' needs. Change is recognized as endemic, and adaptation considered necessary for survival. For example, dry cleaning used to be a big industry but changing consumer behaviour patterns mean that it is now less attractive. Research has found that 46 per cent of people in the UK never use a dry cleaner—up from 38 per cent five years ago—and, as a result, the number of dry-cleaning outlets has fallen from 5300 in 2000 to about 4500 in 2005.[10] Changing needs present potential market opportunities, which drive the company. Market-driven companies seek to adapt their product and service offerings to the demands of current and latent markets. This orientation is shown

in Figure 1.3. Because marketing-orientated companies get close to their customers, they understand their needs and problems. When personal contact is insufficient or not feasible, formal marketing research is commissioned to enable the companies to understand customer motivations and behaviour. Part of the success of German machine tool manufacturers can be attributed to their willingness to develop new products with lead customers—those companies that, themselves, were innovative.[11] This contrasts sharply with the attitude of UK machine tool manufacturers, who saw marketing research only as a tactic to delay new product proposals and who feared that involving customers in new product design would have adverse effects on sales of their current products.

In short, the differences between market-orientated businesses and internally orientated businesses are summarized in Table 1.1. Market-driven businesses display customer concern throughout the business; they understand the criteria customers use to choose between competing suppliers; they invest in market

Marketing in Action: Gillette moves to a market orientation

It is often felt that the only companies that are still product-orientated are small, local and unfashionable, but one of the world's largest consumer brand companies, Gillette, also stands accused, by its current chief executive, of having been very inward-looking. Gillette is a company with sales of over US$9 billion in 2003 and with operations throughout the world. Its product range includes shaving products, oral care products (including the Oral B brand), skincare products and moisturizers, the Braun range of kitchen and haircare appliances, and Duracell batteries.

When Jim Kilts took over as CEO of Gillette in 2001, he found that the company had a very different approach to doing business than he had been used to. Gillette had a product culture, relying on its technical expertise and innovative capabilities to bring out new products, like the three-blade razor, which were launched with a big splash. The prevailing view seemed to be that consumers may not know that they need a better shave but once they try a superior Gillette system they will 'trade up' and pay a premium for it. This strategy had worked well, creating breakthrough innovations like the Mach3 razor for men and Venus for women. However, it had also led the company to make a terrible mistake with the purchase of battery maker Duracell in 1996. Gillette applied the same strategy of 'build a better battery and they will come'. A new brand, Ultra, was launched, but it failed badly. It became apparent that what consumers wanted was not a better battery but a cheaper one.

With a background at Kraft Foods, Kilts is a strong believer in using consumer research to guide key strategic decisions. Innovations are now driven by a combination of Gillette's core competencies in new product development along with a sensitivity to market needs. For example, in its oral care division, Gillette now has a staged toothbrush range for children of different ages. In terms of management, it has a more open and integrative style, which emphasizes communication between managers and with the CEO. And, in January 2005, Gillette announced a merger with Procter & Gamble to create the world's largest consumer products manufacturer.

Based on: Griffith (2003);[12] Moss Kanter (2003)[13]

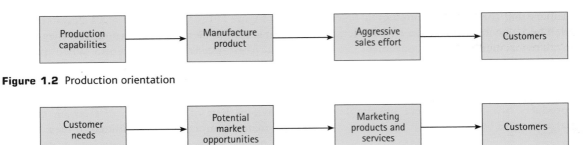

Figure 1.2 Production orientation

Figure 1.3 Marketing orientation

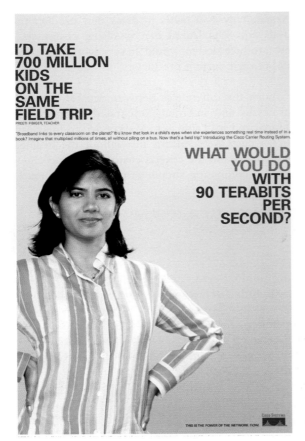

I'D TAKE
700 MILLION
KIDS
ON THE
SAME
FIELD TRIP.

PREETI PIBIGER, TEACHER

"Broadband links to every classroom on the planet? You know that look in a child's eyes when she experiences something real time instead of in a book? Imagine that multiplied millions of times, all without piling on a bus. Now that's a field trip." Introducing the Cisco Carrier Routing System.

WHAT WOULD
YOU DO
WITH
90 TERABITS
PER
SECOND?

THIS IS THE POWER OF THE NETWORK. NOW.

Exhibit 1.2 This Cisco Systems advertisement makes a powerful statement regarding customer benefit.

research, and track market changes; they regard marketing spend as an investment, and are fast and flexible in terms of their pursuit of new opportunities.

Creating customer value and satisfaction

Those companies that are marketing-orientated aim to create customer value in order to attract and retain customers. Their intention is to deliver superior value to their target customers and, in doing so, they implement the marketing concept by meeting and exceeding customer needs better than the competition. One of the great benefits of having satisfied customers is that they tell others of their experiences, further enhancing sales. For example, recent research has shown that the experience of other customers with a product or service has a significant impact on purchase decision in sectors like automobiles and financial services.[14]

No matter how famous your brand is, failure to implement the marketing concept can have severe consequences for the business, as shown in Marketing in Action 1.2. In contrast, Ritz Carlton has developed an enviable reputation in the luxury hotel market. One of the company's mottos is that staff 'only have permission to say yes'.[15] This is a clear signal to everyone in the company that no effort should be spared in responding to the needs of its discerning customers. Customer value is dependent on how the customer perceives the benefits of an offering and the sacrifice that is associated with its purchase. Therefore:

$$\text{customer value} = \text{perceived benefits} - \text{perceived sacrifice}$$

Perceived benefits can be derived from the product (for example, the hotel room and restaurant), the associated service (for example, how responsive the hotel is to the specific needs of customers) and the image of the company (for example, is the image of the company/product favourable?). Conveying benefits is a critical marketing task and is central to positioning and branding, as we shall see in Chapters 5 and 6. *Perceived sacrifice* is the total cost associated with buying the product. This consists not just of monetary costs, but also the time and energy involved in the purchase. For example, with hotels, good location can reduce the time and energy required to find a suitable place to stay. But marketers need to be aware of another critical sacrifice in some buying situations; this is the potential psychological cost of not making the right decision. Uncertainty means that people perceive risk when purchasing. Top hotels like the

Ritz Carlton and the Marriott aim for consistency so that customers can be confident of what they will receive before staying there.

The key to marketing success is to exceed the value offered by competitors. Consumers decide on purchases on the basis of judgements about the value offered by suppliers. Once a product has been purchased, customer satisfaction depends on its perceived performance compared to the buyer's

Table 1.1 Marketing-orientated businesses

Market-driven businesses	Internally orientated businesses
Customer concern throughout business	Convenience comes first
Know customer choice criteria and match with marketing mix	Assume price and product performance key to most sales
Segment by customer differences	Segment by product
Invest in market research (MR) and track market changes	Rely on anecdotes and received wisdom
Welcome change	Cherish status quo
Try to understand competition	Ignore competition
Marketing spend regarded as an investment	Marketing spend regarded as a luxury
Innovation rewarded	Innovation punished
Search for latent markets	Stick with the same
Be fast	Why rush?
Strive for competitive advantage	Happy to be me-too

Marketing in Action: The demise of Rover

1.2

The importance of customer satisfaction is aptly demonstrated by the decline and ultimate demise of the Rover car brand. Once the third largest car producer in the world, and pride of British car manufacturing, Rover has been on a downward spiral for the last four decades. Several different owners and a series of government interventions have tried, without success, to save the company. It finally went into receivership in 2005 following a government-backed purchase by the Phoenix Group just three years earlier. Phoenix, made up of just four men, paid £10 to BMW for control of Rover. The management group caused public outrage when it emerged that its members had been awarding themselves extravagant salaries, pensions and loans while the company was sustaining serious losses. While it is easy to blame the demise of Rover on the greed and incompetence of the Phoenix group, industry experts believe Rover's decline was inevitable. In fact, had it not been for numerous government interventions, the company would most likely have fallen much sooner.

Troubles began for Rover as far back as 1968 with the merger of Leyland, parent company of Rover, and BMC (British Motor Company) to create British Leyland. This merger signalled Rover's move into the mass market, where it never succeeded in getting a solid foothold. Its R&D budget was a fraction of that of larger competitors, resulting in outdated models. Evidence of Rover's failure to satisfy customers is obvious from the most recent JD Power customer satisfaction survey. The study placed Rover fifth from bottom of the 32 car marques surveyed. Only Land Rover, Peugeot, Fiat and Alfa Romeo scored lower. As a result of low customer satisfaction and low sales, Rover has been producing a paltry 150,000 cars a year, compared with approximately 3 million for the large mass-market car makers. As a result, it had neither the economies of scale to compete on cost nor the product quality to compete with luxury niche car makers, leaving it stuck in the middle and in danger of its ultimate demise.

Based on: Guha, Guthrie, Griffiths and Eaglesham (2005);[16] Mackintosh, Guthrie and Griffiths (2003)[17]

health insurance   care homes   hospitals   health assessments

feel better

BUPA

0800 600 500   bupa.com

Exhibit 1.3 This advertisement for BUPA helps to reduce the perceived sacrifice by highlighting a reduction in social costs such as worry and stress.

expectations. Customer satisfaction occurs when perceived performance matches or exceeds expectations. Expectations are formed through pre-buying experiences, discussions with other people and suppliers' marketing activities. Companies need to avoid the mistake of setting customer expectations too high through exaggerated promotional claims, since this can lead to dissatisfaction if performance falls short of expectations.

In the current competitive climate, it is usually not enough simply to match performance and expectations. Expectations need to be exceeded for commercial success so that customers are delighted with the outcome. In order to understand the concept of customer satisfaction, the Kano model (see Figure 1.4) helps to separate characteristics that cause dissatisfaction, satisfaction and delight. Three characteristics underlie the model: 'must be', 'more is better' and 'delighters'.

Those characteristics recognized as 'must bes' are expected and thus taken for granted. For example, in a hotel, customers expect service at reception and a clean room. Lack of these characteristics causes annoyance but their presence only brings dissatisfaction up to a neutral level. 'More is better' characteristics can take satisfaction past neutral and into the positive satisfaction range. For example, no response to a telephone call can cause dissatisfaction, but a fast response may cause positive satisfaction or even delight. The usability of search results is an example of 'more is better' and has become a key differentiating factor in the search engine industry, as shown in e-Marketing 1.1. 'Delighters' are the unexpected characteristics that surprise the customer. Their absence does not cause dissatisfaction, but their presence delights the customer. For example, a UK hotel chain provides free measures of brandy in the rooms of their adult guests. This delights many of its customers, who were not expecting this treat.

Over time, however, such 'delighters' become expected, and this is a problem that marketers must tackle. For example, some car manufacturers provided small, unexpected delighters such as pen

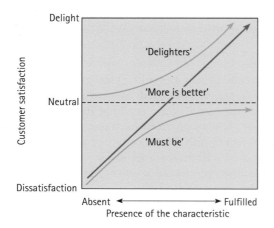

Figure 1.4 Creating customer satisfaction
Source: Joiner, B.L. (1994) *Fourth Generation Management*, New York: McGraw-Hill

e-Marketing: Making your web search worthwhile

Competition among Internet search engine providers is hotting up. Ever since the phenomenal success of Google, newcomers have been flooding into the market hoping for similar good fortune. Microsoft is the latest high-profile company to get in on the act. But as Internet users become increasingly more sophisticated and demanding, providers are finding that returning a list of website addresses in response to a search query is no longer enough to guarantee success. This is now a 'must be' in this market. The battle for advantage is now being fought on the basis of making it easier and quicker for web surfers to find and use information that they want.

The organization of search results, in a user-friendly format, is just one means of gaining a competitive edge. Yahoo! and Amazon both allow users to create histories of the websites they have found useful in previous searches. This could eventually allow them to create a personal directory of the web that can then guide future searches. Microsoft's approach to improving the relevancy of results has been to prioritize websites that have a geographic link with users. Linking search results to particular activities users conduct online is another means of adding value. Yahoo! is currently building a search function into web services such as online shopping or job hunting, which they hope will reduce the need for users to visit specialized search engines.

The quality of information provided is another basis for advantage. Tools under development by players in the market include the facility to keep track of everything one has seen on his/her PC, 'active folder technology' (which continuously keeps track of information related to the user's interests), and 'implicit query' (which searches for information related to the work the user is currently undertaking on their PC). As many of these tools are embedded in the PC, it could give the operating systems companies, as opposed to the search companies, the upper hand. Could Microsoft, a latecomer to this market, be the ultimate winner against more established players such as Google and Yahoo!? Only time will tell.

Based on: Waters (2004)[18]

holders and delay mechanisms on interior lights so that there is time to find the ignition socket at night. These are standard on most cars now and have become 'must be' characteristics because customers have come to expect them. This means that marketers must constantly strive to find new ways of delighting; innovative thinking and listening to customers are key ingredients in this.

The effects of these kinds of changes can be seen in the case of Marks & Spencer. M&S became one of the most admired companies in the world on the back of its marketing and innovation. In its clothing section, it provided well-made, adequately stylish, reasonably priced women's and men's wear. In terms of the market, it was delivering 'more is better'. In food, it delighted its customers with its innovative range of ready-to-eat gourmet meals. But the failure to maintain these leads hit the company severely. Its clothing began to be seen as dated and its service poor, while even its innovative food was matched by rapidly improving supermarkets like Tesco and Safeway. M&S was no longer delivering the 'must bes'; now its sales and profits have fallen dramatically and in recent years it has become the subject of takeover bids.

Similarly, Microsoft is a leading computer company that does not have a great reputation for its quality of attention to customer needs. However, it has recognized that it needs to change and, in a bid to improve the customer orientation of the company, has implemented a programme whereby the bonus pay of 600 senior executives is based on customer satisfaction measures.[19]

Delivering customer value

As well as being a philosophy that puts the customer at the centre of the business, marketing is also a business function that encompasses the variety of activities that must be conducted in order to deliver customer value. These include conducting marketing research to understand customer needs and their behaviour, segmenting markets into submarkets to be targeted by the company, developing products and brands, and positioning these in the marketplace, making pricing decisions, deciding on a **promotional mix**, selling and distributing products, and marketing planning and management. These are the kinds of issues that will be introduced briefly in the

Marketing in Action: The success of Walkers Sensations

Adult luxury snacking is a growing sector in the snack market. Valued at £237 million in 2002, this sector has undergone substantial growth of over 26 per cent since 1988. Walkers' foray into the evening snack market followed research that identified lunchtime and dinner as the most popular snacking times. This presented an opportunity for evening salty snacking, a gap that Walkers filled with the highly successful launch of Doritos Dippas in 2000. Fresh from this success, the company was keen to further develop evening snacking.

Qualitative research found that price and indulgence were key attributes consumers' used when choosing between potato crisp brands. Consumers perceived everyday crisps to fall into the low-price, low-indulgence category, while speciality crisps were seen as high-price, high-indulgence. Herein lay an opportunity to develop a reasonably priced, high-indulgence brand for the evening snack market. Walkers grasped this opening in the market and began developing the mainstream premium brand, Walkers Sensations.

Walkers decided to target this new luxury brand at an adult audience, principally 25–45-year-old parents of young children. In terms of usage occasion, it envisaged the brand to be consumed as part of evening relaxation. Extensive qualitative and quantitative research further refined their positioning strategy, product and price. It was decided to offer the crisps in an array of flavours, from the familiar to the exotic. Packaging was key to creating an augmented product that would appeal to the target customers. Photographs were used to convey its premium nature and a reduced Walkers banner also succeeding in differentiating the product from the Walkers master brand. It was priced in line with its mainstream premium positioning, at 20 per cent above a large pack of Walkers crisps.

The launch of Walkers Sensations was also critical to reinforcing its distinctive brand values. TV and print advertising initially used celebrity endorsers such as Gary Lineker and Victoria Beckham. Later, 'it girl', Tara Palmer-Tomkinson replaced Victoria Beckham as one of the brand's celebrity faces. The ads have given the brand a sense of fun while effectively communicating the indulgent nature of the product. Walkers succeeded in achieving complete saturation of the market through intensive distribution. First appearing in stores in 2002, this new brand achieved phenomenal sales levels of £78 million in its first year.

Based on: Goldstone (2002);[20] Murphy and Goldstone (2003)[21]

next section on the marketing mix and will be the focus of later chapters in this book. For now we can see how important some of these activities were for the successful launch of Walkers Sensations (see Marketing in Action 1.3). Markets and marketing are constantly changing, and new methods of delivering value—such as **customer relationship management** (CRM)—are being developed. These new techniques, along with issues of importance to the marketing profession such as marketing ethics, will also be discussed throughout this book.

Marketing, therefore, is an exciting and multifaceted profession. Marketing managers are responsible for ensuring that the organization delivers value to customers; but in doing so they may avail themselves of the services of researchers, salespeople, communication specialists, advertising agencies and retail specialists. The wide range of careers that fall

within the realm of marketing is outlined in Appendix 1.1 at the end of this chapter.

The marketing mix

A key marketing activity is the management of the company's **marketing mix**. The marketing mix consists of four major elements: **product**, **price**, **promotion** and **place**. These '4-Ps' are four key decision areas and form a major aspect of marketing concept implementation. Later, we will look at each of the 4-Ps in considerable detail. At this point, however, it will be useful to examine each element briefly so that we can understand the essence of marketing mix decision-making.

Product

The choice of what products/services and benefits should be offered to a group of customers is known as

To design my Van den Puup bed creation, I journeyed into the forest for a month. I slept by day and lived by night so I could watch animals, birds and even trees sleeping. When I returned from the forest, I added my learning to my

"Why it's right to pay £5000 for one of my bed creations and not £109 for this one."

genius to create a bed with the boldness of a tangled wood and the calmness of a sleeping doe. I called it Kaka and priced it at £5000. This IKEA bed may have style but at £109 it is so sickeningly shallow. How can anyone sleep on anything so meaningless?

£109

IKEA

Van den Puup, Elite Designer

ELITE DESIGNERS AGAINST IKEA

Exhibit 1.4 Price is a key component of IKEA's marketing mix as demonstrated by this advertisement

the 'product decision'. An important element is new product/service development. As technology and tastes change, products become out of date and inferior to those of the competition, so companies must replace them with features that customers value. For example, when Microsoft launched Windows XP in 2001, it offered home users new features such as Windows Movie Maker for editing and organizing home movies, and a Network Set-up Wizard so that all the computers in a home can share printers, files and an Internet connection. Product decisions also involve choices regarding brand names, guarantees, packaging and the services that should accompany the product offering. Guarantees can be an important component of the product offering. For example, the operators of the AVE, Spain's high-speed train, capable of travelling at 300 kmph, are so confident of its performance that they guarantee to give customers a full refund of their fare if they are more than five minutes late.

Price

Because price represents, on a unit basis, what the company receives for the product or service that is being marketed, it is a key element of the marketing mix. All the other elements represent costs—for example, expenditure on product design (product), advertising and salespeople (promotion), and trans-

portation and distribution (place). Marketers, therefore, need to be very clear about pricing objectives, methods and the factors that influence price setting; they must also take into account the necessity for discounting and offering allowances in some transactions.

Promotion

Decisions have to be taken with due attention to the promotional mix: advertising, personal selling, sales promotions, public relations, direct marketing and Internet marketing. By these means, the target audience is made aware of the existence of a product or service, and the benefits (both economic and psychological) it confers to customers. Each element of the promotional mix has its own set of strengths and weaknesses, and these will be explored later. A growing form of promotion is the use of the Internet as a promotional tool. A key advantage of this medium is that small local companies can expand the scope of their market at a relatively low cost.

Place

The aspect of place is to do with those decisions concerning the distribution channels that are to be used and their management, the location of outlets, methods of transportation, and the inventory levels to be held. The objective is to ensure that products and services are available in the proper quantities, at the right time and in the right place. Distribution channels consist of organizations such as retailers or wholesalers through which goods pass on their way to customers. Producers need to manage their relationships with these organizations well because they may provide the only cost-effective access to the marketplace.

An effective marketing mix (see Figure 1.5) is composed of four main features. Initially, the mix must be designed to match the needs of a target customer

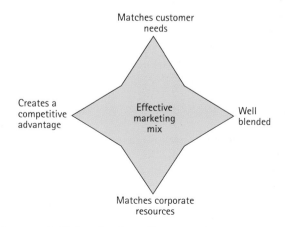

Figure 1.5 Hallmarks of an effective marketing mix

group. Second, it must contribute to the creation of a **competitive advantage**, which is a clear performance differential over the competition on factors that are important to customers. Third, the marketing mix must match the resources that are available to the firm. Certain media—for example, television advertising—require a minimum threshold investment before they are regarded as feasible. In the UK a rule of thumb is that at least £1 million per year is required to achieve impact in a national advertising campaign. Clearly, those brands that cannot afford such a promotional budget must use other less expensive media (for example, posters or sales promotion) to attract and hold customers. Finally, an effective marketing mix should be well blended to form a consistent theme. For example, the use of exclusive outlets for upmarket fashion and cosmetic brands—Armani, Christian Dior and Calvin Klein, for example—is consistent with their strategic positioning.

Thinking of the marketing mix simply in terms of the 4-Ps has been the subject of some criticism in recent years. For example, in service businesses like hair salons, the hairdresser is a key part of the service itself, while the décor of a restaurant or café is an important aspect of the enjoyment of that experience. Consequently, service marketers have argued for a '7-Ps' approach to incorporate (in addition to the original 4-Ps) the *people*, *process* and *physical evidence* aspects of services.[22] Whatever framework is used, the important issue is not to neglect decision-making areas that are critical to effective marketing. The strength of the 4-Ps approach is that it represents a memorable and practical framework for marketing decision-making, and has proved useful in the classroom and in practice for many years.

Managing marketing activity

Though the reasons why a company should be marketing orientated may be easy to understand, achieving this in practice is often much more difficult. A combination of factors is required to successfully drive a customer focus, as shown in Figure 1.6. First, shared values and beliefs are a necessary prerequisite for successful marketing implementation;[23] achieving this can be a problem for long-established companies

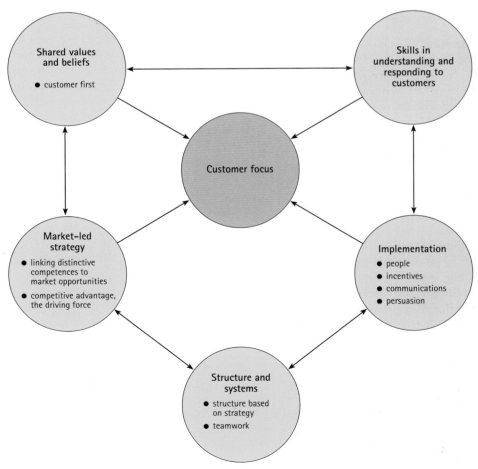

Figure 1.6 Key dimensions of market-driven management

that hitherto did not put the customer first. In general, success in changing attitudes is a hard-won battle.

The second dimension concerns the skills in understanding and responding to customers, or what Peters and Waterman call 'getting and keeping close to the customer'. A study by Kohli and Jaworski[24] found that the starting-point of market orientation was intelligence gathering, which included not only customers' needs and preferences, but also an analysis and interpretation of the factors that influence those needs and preferences. Furthermore, they found that information gathering was not the exclusive responsibility of the marketing department and that individuals (such as engineers at conferences) and departments (such as R&D) often gathered information informally. Next, information needs to be disseminated throughout the company by formal and informal means. Kohli and Jaworski tell how marketing managers in two consumer products companies developed and circulated periodic newsletters to facilitate the spread of information, while in another manufacturing company a manager encouraged the process of dissemination by 'storytelling'. She told stories about customers, their needs, personalities and even their families. The idea was to have secretaries, engineers and production personnel get to know customers. Finally, responsiveness highlighted the need to select target markets, design and offer products and services that cater to current and anticipated needs, and to produce, price, distribute and promote these products and services in a way that customers value.

Third, a customer focus implies market-led strategies and the desire to meet needs better than the competition. However, as Davidson points out, the reality of the marketplace should be aligned with the assets (distinctive competencies) of the company.[25] When looking to enter new markets, companies should be aware of their inherent corporate strengths and weaknesses. Fourth, organizational structure must reflect marketing strategy. As markets change, marketing strategy changes, and the structure and systems may require modification to implement new strategies. This may involve, for example, using new distribution systems, the breaking down of barriers between departments to foster innovation, or the formation of new alliances.[26]

The last dimension of market-driven management is implementation, which requires clear communication of strategy so that it is not undermined by those who deal with the customer at first hand. For example, an inability to get salespeople or distributors to buy into the marketing strategy is likely to result in its failure.

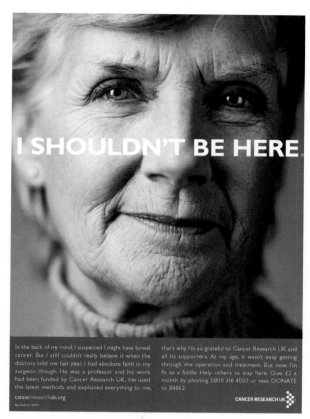

Exhibit 1.5 This ad for Cancer Research demonstrates the use of marketing in a not-for-profit context

The scope of marketing

Up to now our focus has been on the application of marketing in commercial contexts—that is, its use by companies with products or services to sell. But it is clear from simple observation that the marketing concept, and marketing tools and techniques, are in evidence in many other contexts too. For example, political parties are often criticized for their over-use of marketing. They are heavy users of marketing research to find out what the views of the voting public are; the candidates they put forward for election are often carefully selected and 'packaged' to appeal to voters. They are also extensive users of advertising and public relations to get their message across.

Evidence of the application of marketing can be found in many other contexts. Educational institutions have become more market-led as demographic changes have given rise to greater competition for students, whose choices are increasingly being influenced by the publication of performance-based league tables. Universities are responding by developing new logos and rebranding themselves, conducting promotional campaigns, and targeting new markets such as mature students and those from other countries around the

Marketing in Action: The challenge facing Catholicism

The Catholic Church has been likened to a global brand. It has 980 million followers around the world but is facing a number of challenges. First, its interpretation of the Bible is seen by many as being overly conservative. Its teachings on social issues like abortion, divorce and homosexuality are divisive in many countries, and it has also been attacked for its handling of a series of sex abuse cases involving members of the clergy. Second, church attendances have been falling steadily in recent years, particularly in the West. And, third, it is faced with the rise of competing religions, including major belief systems like Islam and Buddhism as well as more fundamentalist interpretations of the Catholic faith.

Finding the appropriate responses to these changes has been difficult. In the past, the Roman Catholic Church has relied heavily on public service broadcasters to carry its message, but the fragmentation of the media and the rise in digital television means that it has become increasingly difficult for it to communicate its message to a mass audience. Conversely, other religions have used these changes for their own benefit—for instance, the growth in dedicated religious channels in the USA, such as the Christian Broadcast Network and the Trinity Broadcast Network. To date, the Catholic Church's forays into the media have been restricted to Radio Vaticano in the Vatican and to low-cost FM stations in Africa, Asia and Latin America.

The Vatican also sees the Internet as an increasingly important means for spreading its message to younger audiences, and it now has its own website: www.vatican.va. However, the site has been criticized for its European rather than global appeal. Visitors are welcomed to the site in six European languages and most of the content on the site is in Italian. Compared with other religions, the Catholic Church has been less active in using mass advertising. However, this is starting to change. In Italy, it has run a television campaign produced by the global advertising company Saatchi & Saatchi to encourage Italians to use a tax incentive to make donations. And, in 2000, a group of Italian bishops also asked Saatchi & Saatchi to create 30-second advertisements based on three parables in the gospel to communicate the fundamental values of the Catholic faith.

Based on: Brandchannel.com (2003);[29] Tadida (2004)[30]

world. The use of marketing takes many forms in the arts and media. It has been argued that many media vehicles, such as newspapers and television channels, are being 'dumbed down' in order to appeal to certain market segments and to maximize revenues, in the same way many artistic organizations would be criticized for putting revenues ahead of quality and originality by producing art that appeals to a mass audience. The use of marketing can be found in almost all walks of life, including religion, as shown in Marketing in Action 1.4.

The range of potential applications for marketing has given rise to much debate among marketing scholars regarding the scope of marketing.[27] In particular, the challenge has been to find a core concept that effectively integrates both business and non-business or social marketing. For example, initially the idea of a transaction was put forward, but not all marketing requires a transaction or sale. Kotler then put forward

the notion of exchange, implying that any exchange between two parties can be considered marketing.[28] However, this is also clearly problematic as many exchanges, such as favours given by family members, are not marketing activities. For our purposes, the core of marketing is the notion of a customer and the need to understand and respond to the customer's needs.

Marketing works!

Does marketing work? Surprisingly this is a controversial question, with many people arguing that, yes, of course it does, while others are less sure. The difficulty surrounds the intangibility of marketing. It is very difficult to predict in advance whether a marketing or promotional campaign is going to work. Sometimes campaigns like those for Levi's 501 jeans are stunningly successful. On the back of the famous ad featuring Nick Kamen in a launderette, sales of Levi's 501s rose 800 per cent. Not only that but sales of all jeans (even those of competitors) went up.

Similarly, recent developments in retail banking in the UK demonstrate the importance and power of effective marketing. Loyalty to particular providers has been decreasing and in the five-year period 2000–04, the number of people switching current accounts has doubled from 500,000 to 1 million. In response, HBOS has begun adopting marketing practices more usually associated with the retail trade than with banks, such as offering value-for-money products and introducing comparative advertising showing the different rates of interest charged by the big banks. The strategy has worked. The bank attracted 1 million new bank account customers and 1.2 million new credit card customers in 2004, and profits rose by 22 per cent.[31]

In other companies, marketing is seen as the central engine of business growth. For example, Nestlé is a huge global company with 8000 products (a figure that grows to 20,000 when local variations are included) and an annual marketing budget of US$2.5 billion. The company's chief executive has a marketing background and the head of marketing is responsible for each of the company's seven strategic business units. This structure is designed to ensure that marketing thinking is central to the company's strategic decisions.[32]

But, for some, the issue is not whether marketing works but rather that it works too well. In recent years, marketing has been the subject of a great deal of criticism.[33] It has been equated with trickery and deception, and with persuading people (often those on low incomes) to buy products they do not really need. Significant concerns have been raised about marketers targeting children, often employing the skills of child psychologists to find more and more novel ways to instil brand preferences in very young children.[34] Others are critical that marketing has invaded every aspect of our lives, from the home to the classroom and entertainment like sports and concerts.[35] Like all professions, marketing has its unscrupulous practitioners. Throughout this book we will discuss the ethical dilemmas surrounding various marketing topics.

In short, marketing works. Succeeding in making it work in any particular situation is the challenge. In that regard some issues relating to the nature and impact of marketing need to be borne in mind.

Efficiency versus effectiveness

We can gain another perspective on customer orientation if we understand the distinction between **efficiency** and **effectiveness**. *Efficiency* is concerned with inputs and outputs. An efficient firm produces goods economically—it does things right. The benefit is that cost per unit of output is low and, therefore, the potential for offering low prices to gain market share, or charging medium to high prices and achieving high profit margins, is present. However, to be successful, a company needs to be more than just efficient, it needs to be effective as well. *Effectiveness* means doing the right things. This implies operating in attractive markets and making products that consumers want to buy. Conversely, companies that operate in unattractive markets or are not producing what consumers want to buy will go out of business— the only question is one of timing. The link between performance and combinations of efficiency and effectiveness is illustrated in Figure 1.7.

A company that is both inefficient and ineffective will go out of business quickly because it is a high-cost producer of products that consumers do not want to buy. This was the case with many web-based businesses that were formed during the dotcom boom of the late 1990s. A company that is efficient and ineffective may last a little longer because its low cost base may generate more profits from the dwindling sales volume it is achieving. Firms that are effective but inefficient are likely to survive because they are operating in attractive markets and are marketing products that people want to buy. The problem is that their inefficiency is preventing them from reaping the maximum profits from their endeavours. It is the combination of both efficiency and effectiveness that leads to optimum business success. Such firms do well and thrive because they are operating in attractive markets, are supplying products that consumers want to buy and are benefiting from a low cost base.

Virgin Atlantic is an example of a company that is both effective and efficient. It is effective by being innovative in terms of service delivery (for example,

	Ineffective	Effective
Inefficient	Goes out of business quickly	Survives
Efficient	Dies slowly	Does well Thrives

Figure 1.7 Efficiency and effectiveness

personal televisions built into the seating on its planes) as well as efficient in keeping costs low (for example, promotional expenditures are kept in check by Richard Branson's capacity to generate publicity for the airline). The essential difference between efficiency and effectiveness, then, is that the former is cost-focused while the latter is customer-focused. An effective company has the ability to attract and retain customers.

Marketing and business performance

The adoption of the marketing concept will improve business performance—that is the basic premise. Marketing is not an abstract concept, its acid test is the effect that its use has on key corporate indices such as profitability and market share. Fortunately, in recent years, studies in both Europe and North America have sought to examine the relationship between marketing and performance. The results suggest that the relationship is positive.

Narver and Slater, for instance, looked closely at the relationship between business performance and marketing orientation.[36] They collected data from 113 strategic business units (SBUs) of a major US corporation. In the main, their study found that the relationship between market orientation and profitability was strongly linear, with the businesses displaying the highest level of market orientation achieving the highest levels of profitability, and those with the lowest scores on market orientation having the lowest profitability figures. As the authors state: 'The findings give marketing scholars and practitioners a basis beyond mere intuition for recommending the superiority of a market orientation.'

A study by the consultants Bain & Company in the USA looked at the performance of 500 consumer brands in 100 categories between the years 1997 and 2001. It found that brands that belonged to companies that innovated and advertised were likely to see higher revenues. Companies that drew at least 10 per cent of their 2001 sales from new products introduced during the period were 60 per cent more likely to post higher sales growth. Also, those companies reporting double-digit revenue increases were 60 per cent more likely to out-spend other brands in their category on advertising. An example is Old Spice, a brand that is over 50 years old. It introduced sub-brands such as High Endurance deodorant in 1994 and Red Zone in 1999. Both products accounted for more that 75 per cent of Old Spice sales in 2001 and helped the brand to grow by 13 per cent that year, in a category that grew at an average of 1 per cent.[37]

A study published in the UK by Hooley, Lynch and Shepherd[38] sought to develop a typology of approaches to marketing, and to relate those approaches to business performance. They identified four groups of companies, namely 'marketing philosophers', 'sales supporters', 'departmental marketers' and 'unsures'. The marketing philosophers saw marketing as a function with prime responsibility for identifying and meeting customers' needs and as a guiding philosophy for the whole organization; they did not see marketing as confined to the marketing department, nor did they regard it merely as sales support. The sales supporters saw marketing's primary functions as being sales and promotion support. Marketing was confined to what the marketing department did, and had little to do with identifying and meeting customer needs. The departmental marketers not only shared the view of the marketing philosophers that marketing was about identifying and meeting customer needs, but also believed that marketing was restricted to what the marketing department did. The final group of companies—the unsures—tended to be indecisive regarding their marketing approach.

The attitudes, organization and practices of the four groups were compared, with the marketing philosophers exhibiting many distinct characteristics, as summarized below.

1   Marketing philosophers adopted a more proactive, aggressive approach towards the future.
2   They had a more proactive approach to new product development.
3   They placed a higher importance on marketing training.
4   They adopted longer time horizons for marketing planning.
5   Marketing had a higher status within the company.
6   Marketing had a higher chance of being represented at board level.
7   Marketing had more chance of working closely with other functional areas.
8   Marketing made a greater input into strategic plans.

Significantly, the marketing philosophers achieve a significantly higher ROI (return on investment) than the remainder of the sample. The departmental marketers performed at the sample average, while the unsures and sales supporters performed significantly worse. Hooley *et al.*'s conclusion was that marketing should be viewed not just as a departmental function but as a guiding philosophy for the whole organization.

It is surprising, then, that marketing has not had the influence in corporate boardrooms its importance would seem to justify. A recent study in the UK found that only 21 per cent of CEOs in the FTSE 100 had worked in marketing before going into general management, and only five of the FTSE 100 companies had dedicated marketing directors on their boards.[39] Research in the USA shows that the majority of chief executives in recent decades have had a finance background.[40] Doyle argues that the reason for marketing's relatively low status is that the links between marketing investments and the long-term profitability of the organization have not been made clear.[41] Too often, marketers justify their investments in terms of increasing customer awareness, sales volume or market share. Doyle proposes the concept of **value-based marketing**, where the objective of marketing is seen as contributing to the maximization of **shareholder value**, which has become the overarching goal of chief executives in more and more companies. This approach helps clarify the importance of investment in marketing assets such as brands and marketing knowledge, and helps to dissuade management from making arbitrary cuts in marketing expenditure, such as advertising, in times of economic difficulty.

Planning marketing activity

Finally, in many organizations, marketing can be a haphazard activity often done in response to particular opportunities or in times of difficulty or crisis. But attention to marketing must be consistent as markets change and nothing lasts for ever. For example, who would have thought it would be necessary to market gold? It is. Demand for gold has been falling as consumers switch their spending to luxury brands like Cartier and Louis Vuitton, and its image has been tarnished by its use on everything from biscuits to credit cards. In response the World Gold Council has developed an advertising campaign for gold jewellery.[42]

For marketing efforts to be effective, it is essential that a planned approach is taken. Planning is about deciding where we want to go and how we are going to get there. The process of **marketing planning** involves analysing the environment and the organization's capabilities, and deciding on courses of action and ways to implement those decisions. Having a plan gives managers a focal point for decisions and actions. It also stimulates achievement by giving the organization clear targets to aim at, which can be helpful in generating change in an organization.

The marketing planning process is shown in Figure 1.8 and we will revisit the issue of marketing planning in more detail in Chapter 12.

Stages in the planning process	Relevant chapters in the book		
Business mission			
Marketing audit			Chapters 2, 3 and 4
SWOT analysis			
Marketing objectives			
Strategic thrust	Strategic objectives		
Core strategy			Chapter 5
Target markets	Competitive advantage	Competitor targets	
Marketing mix decisions			Chapters 6, 7, 8, 9, 10 and 11
Organization and implementation			Chapter 12
Control			

Figure 1.8 The marketing planning process

Summary

This chapter has introduced the concept of marketing and discussed how and why organizations become market-oriented. In particular, the following issues were addressed.

1. What is meant by the marketing concept and a market orientation. The key idea here is that it is a business philosophy that puts the customer at the centre of things.

2. The idea of customer value, which is the difference between the perceived benefits from consuming a product or service and the perceived sacrifice involved in doing so.

3. That customer value is delivered through the basic marketing mix of product, price, promotion and place.

4. That there are five key actions involved in managing marketing activity: shared values, skills in understanding customers, a market-led strategy, structures and systems, and implementation activities.

5. That the scope of marketing is broad, involving non-business as well as business contexts.

6. That marketing works and there is a strong relationship between a marketing philosophy and business performance.

7. That marketing planning is an important activity to ensure marketing effectiveness.

Suggested reading

Brown, S. (2001) Torment Your Customers (They'll Love It), *Harvard Business Review*, October, 83–8.

Gummesson, E. (1987) The New Marketing: Developing Long-term Interactive Relationships, *Long Range Planning*, **20** (4), 10–20.

Levitt, T. (1960) Marketing Myopia, *Harvard Business Review*, **38**, 45–56.

McGovern, G., D. Court, J.A. Quelch and **B. Crawford** (2004) Bringing Customers into the Boardroom, *Harvard Business Review*, **82** (11) 70–81.

Vandermerwe, S. (2003) Achieving Deep Customer Focus, *Sloan Management Review*, 45 (3), 26–35.

Internet exercises

Sites to visit

1 www.knowthis.com
www.cim.co.uk
www.marketing.about.com

Exercise

Visit these websites and familiarize yourself with the kinds of marketing intelligence that is available to you.

Sites to visit

2 www.careers-in-marketing.com

Exercise

Visit this site and learn about the various career options available to you in marketing.

Study questions

1. Discuss the differences between marketing as a philosophy and marketing as a set of business activities. How are the two ideas related?

2. Identify two examples of organizations that you consider provide customer satisfaction, and describe how they do it.

3. Marketing is sometimes considered to be an expensive luxury. Respond to this claim by demonstrating how a marketing orientation can have a positive impact on business performance.

4. Marketing is everywhere. Discuss.

5. Describe and explain the five dimensions of market-driven management.

Key terms

marketing concept the achievement of corporate goals through meeting and exceeding customer needs better than the competition

marketing orientation companies with a marketing orientation focus on customer needs as the primary drivers of organizational performance

production orientation a business approach that is inwardly focused either on costs or on a definition of a company in terms of its production facilities

efficiency a way of managing business processes to a high standard, usually concerned with cost reduction; also called 'doing things right'

effectiveness doing the right thing, making the correct strategic choice

customer value perceived benefits minus perceived sacrifice

customer satisfaction the fulfilment of customers' requirements or needs

shareholder value the returns to a company's shareholders, which grow when the company increases its dividends or its share price rises

customer relationship management (CRM) the practice of using information technology to build customer profiles with the objective of identifying, serving and retaining the 'best' customers

marketing mix a framework for the tactical management of the customer relationship, including product, place, price, promotion (the 4-Ps); in the case of services, three other elements to be taken into account are process, people and physical evidence

product a good or service offered or performed by an organization or individual, which is capable of satisfying customer needs

price (1) the amount of money paid for a product; (2) the agreed value placed on the exchange by a buyer and seller

promotional mix advertising, personal selling, sales promotion, public relations and direct marketing

place the distribution channels to be used, outlet locations, methods of transportation

competitive advantage a clear performance differential over the competition on factors that are important to target customers

value-based marketing a perspective on marketing which emphasizes how a marketing philosophy and marketing activities contribute to the maximization of shareholder value

marketing planning the process by which businesses analyse the environment and their capabilities, decide upon courses of marketing action and implement those decisions

References

1. **Anonymous** (2003) Beyond the Model T: How Henry Ford's Legacy Has Shaped Modern Life, *Financial Times*, 16 June, 19; **Bulik, B.S.** (2004) The iPod Economy, *Advertising Age*, 18 October, 1; **Lillington, K.** (2005) Apple Goes for Bigger Bite with Low-cost Products, *Irish Times*, Business, 14 January, 8; **Pesola** (2004) Music Rivals Look to Bite Apple, *Financial Times*, 19 November, 13; **Schlender, B.** (2005) How Big Can Apple Get?, *Fortune*, 28 February, 38–45.

2. **Drucker, P.F.** (1999) *The Practice of Management*, London: Heinemann.

3. **Rosenberg, L.J.** and **J.A. Czepeil** (1983) A **Marketing Approach to Customer Retention**, *Journal of Consumer Marketing*, 2, 45–51.

4. **Grönroos, C.** (1989) Defining Marketing: A Market-oriented Approach, *European Journal of Marketing*, **23** (1), 52–60.

5. **Harnischfeger, U.** (2003) Failure to Meet US Tastes Cuts Sales at Adidas, *Financial Times*, 7 August, 25.

6. **Fullerton, R.** (1988) How Modern is Modern Marketing? Marketing's Evolution and the Myth of the 'Production Era', *Journal of Marketing*, **52**, 108–25.

7. **Jones, D.** and **D. Monieson** (1990) Early Development of the Philosophy of Marketing Thought, *Journal of Marketing*, **54**, 102–13.

8. **Benton, R.** (1987) The Practical Domain of Marketing, *American Journal of Economics and Sociology*, **46** (4), 415–30.

9. **Davis, P.** (2005) Attack on 'Outdated'

Marketing, *Financial Times*, Fund Management Supplement, 30 May, 1.

10. **Moules, J.** (2005) Spotless Service Undermined by Shrinking Revenues, *Financial Times*, 5 July, 5.

11. **Brown, R.J.** (1987) Marketing: A Function and a Philosophy, *Quarterly Review of Marketing*, **12** (3), 25–30.

12. **Griffith, V.** (2003) How Gillette's Media-shy Boss Led it Back to the Cutting Edge, *Financial Times,* 7 May, 11.

13. **Moss Kanter, R.** (2003) Inspire People to Turn Round Your Business, *Financial Times*, 25 August, 11.

14. **Satterthwaite, C.** (2004) Trust Me, and Martin and Sophie and the Boys, *Financial Times*, Creative Business, 16 November, 10.

15. **Freemantle, D.** (1998) *What Customers Like About You*, London: Nicholas Brealey Publishing.

16. **Guha, K., J. Guthrie, J. Griffiths** and **J. Eaglesham** (2005) The Wrong and Winding Road: Decades of Blunders that took Rover to Ignominy, *Financial Times*, 13 April, 17.

17. **Mackintosh, J., J. Guthrie** and **J. Griffiths** (2003) Rover's Returns: As Five Directors Pay £12.9m into their Pension Funds, the Unions that Backed Them Cry Foul, *Financial Times*, 20 November, 19.

18. **Waters, R.** (2004) On the Look-out for the Next Search Engine Change, *Financial Times*, 17 November, 14.

19. **Skapinker, M.** (2003) Wanted: Customers Who Know What they Want, *Financial Times*, 6 August, 10.

20. **Goldstone, J.** (2002) Posh Nosh, *Brand Strategy*, May, 34.

21. **Murphy, C.** and **J. Goldstone** (2003) And for my Next Trick ..., *Marketing*, 30 October, 22–3.

22. **Booms, B.H.** and **M.J. Bitner** (1981) Marketing Strategies and Organisation Structures for Service Firms, in **Donnelly, J.H.** and **W.R. George** (eds) *Marketing of Services*, Chicago: American Marketing Association, 47–52.

23. **Peters, T.J.** and **R.H. Waterman Jr** (1982) *In Search of Excellence: Lessons from America's Best Run Companies*, New York: Harper & Row.

24. **Kohli, A.K.** and **B.J. Jaworski** (1990) Market Orientation: The Construct, Research Propositions and Managerial Implications, *Journal of Marketing*, **54** (April), 1–18.

25. **Davidson, H.** (1998) *Offensive Marketing*, Harmondsworth: Penguin.

26. **Saunders, J.** and **V. Wong** (1985) In Search of Excellence in the UK, *Journal of Marketing Management*, Winter, 119–37.

27. See, for example, **Foxall, G.** (1984) Marketing's Domain, *European Journal of Marketing*, **18** (1), 25–40; **Kotler, P.** and **S. Levy** (1969) Broadening the Concept of Marketing, *Journal of Marketing*, **33**, 10–15.

28. **Kotler, P.** (1972) A Generic Concept of Marketing, *Journal of Marketing*, **36**, 46–54.

29. Brandchannel.com (2003) The Holy See, *Nubibus*, 27 October.

30. **Tadida, M.** (2004) Making Roman Inroads into the Mass Media, *Financial Times*, Creative Business, 30 November, 8–9.

31. **Croft, J.** (2005) Banks Shop Around to Set Out their Stalls, *Financial Times*, 5 April, 23.

32. **Benady, A.** (2005) Nestlé's New Flavour of Strategy, *Financial Times*, 22 February, 13.

33. **Klein, N.** (2001) *No Logo*, London: Flamingo Press.

34. **Linn, S.** (2004) *Consuming Kids: The Hostile Takeover of Childhood*, The New Press.

35. **Klein, N.** (2001) *No Logo*, London: Flamingo Press.

36. **Narver, J.C.** and **S.F. Slater** (1990) The Effect of a Market Orientation on Business Profitability, *Journal of Marketing*, **54** (October), 20–35.

37. **Terazono, E.** (2003) Spending Money to Make Money, *Financial Times*, Creative Business, 17 June, 4–5.

38. **Hooley, G., J. Lynch** and **J. Shepherd** (1990) The Marketing Concept: Putting the Theory into Practice, *European Journal of Marketing*, **24** (9), 7–23.

39. **Terazono, E.** (2003) Always on the Outside Looking In, *Financial Times*, Creative Business, 5 August, 4–5.

40. **Fligstein, N.** (1987) Intraorganisational Power Struggles: The Rise of Finance Personnel to Top Leadership in Large Corporations, 1919–1979, *American Sociology Review*, **52**, 44–58.

41. **Doyle, P.** (2000) *Value-based Marketing*, Chichester: John Wiley & Sons, Ltd.

42. **Morrison, K.** (2005) Into a New Golden Age, *Financial Times*, 6 January, 10.

Appendix 1.1

Careers in marketing

Choosing a career in marketing can offer a wide range of opportunities. The following table outlines some of the potential positions available in marketing.

Marketing positions	
Marketing executive/co-ordinator	Management of all marketing-related activities for an organization.
Brand/product manager	A product manager is responsible for the management of a single product or a family of products. In this capacity, he or she may participate in product design and development according to the results of research into the evolving needs of their customer base. In addition, marketing managers develop business plans and marketing strategies for their product line, manage product distribution, disseminate information about the product, and co-ordinate customer service and sales.
Brand/marketing assistant	At the entry level of brand assistant, responsibilities consist of market analysis, competitive tracking, sales and market share analysis, monitoring of promotion programmes, etc.
Marketing researcher/analyst	Market researchers collect and analyse information to assist in marketing, and determine whether a demand exists for a particular product or service. Some of the tasks involved include designing questionnaires, collecting all available and pertinent information, arranging and analysing collected information, presenting research results to clients, making recommendations.
Marketing communications manager	Manages the marketing communications activity of an organization manager such as advertising, public relations, sponsorships and direct marketing.
Customer service manager/executive	Manages the service delivery and any interactions a customer may have with an organization. Role can be quite varied, depending on industry.
Sales positions	
Sales executive/business development	Aims to develop successful business relationships with existing and potential customers. Manages the company's selling activities to existing customers and identifies potential sales prospects.
Sales manager	Plans and co-ordinates the activities of a sales team, controls product distribution, monitors budget achievement, trains and motivates personnel, prepares forecasts.
Key account executive	Manages the selling and marketing function to key customers (accounts). Conducts negotiations on products, quantities, prices, promotions, special offers etc. Networks with other key account personnel influential in the buying decision process. Liaises internally with all departments and colleagues in supplying and servicing the key account. Monitors performance of the key account.
Sales support manager	Provides sales support by fielding enquiries, taking orders and providing phone advice to customers. Also assists with exhibitions, prepares documentation for brochures and sales kits, and commissions market research suppliers for primary data.
Merchandiser	Aims to maximize the display of a company's products in assigned retail outlets. Ensures that point-of-sale displays are stocked and maintained correctly.
Sales promotion executive	Aims to communicate product features and benefits directly to customers at customer locations through sampling, demonstrations and the management of any sales promotion activities.
Telesales representative	Takes in-bound or makes out-bound calls, which are sales related.
Advertising sales executive	Sells a media organization's airplay, TV spot or space to companies for the purpose of advertising.

Table A1.1 continued

Retailing positions

Retail management	Plans and co-ordinates the operations of retail outlets. Supervises the recruitment, training, conduct and work of staff. Maintains high levels of customer service. Manages stock levels.
Retail buyer	Purchases goods to be sold in retail stores. Manages and analyses stock levels. Obtains information about the range of products available. Manages vendor relations.

Advertising positions

Account executive	Helps devise and co-ordinate advertising campaigns. Liaises with clients, obtaining relevant information from them such as product and company details, budget and marketing goals, and marketing research information. Briefs other specialists in the agency (such as creative team, media planners and researchers) on client requirements, to develop the details of a campaign. May present draft campaign suggestions to clients along with a summary of the expenditure involved, and negotiate and arrange for modifications if required. May supervise and co-ordinate the work of the relevant production departments so that the campaign is developed as planned to meet deadlines and budget requirements.
Media planner/buyer	Organizes and purchases advertising space on television, radio, in magazines, newspapers or on outdoor advertising. Liaises between clients and sellers of advertising space to ensure that the advertising campaign reaches the target market.

Public relations positions

Public relations executive	Helps to develop and maintain a hospitable, friendly public environment for the organization. This involves liaising with clients, co-ordination of special events, lobbying, crisis management, media relations, writing and editing of printed material.
Press relations/ corporate affairs	Develops and maintains a good working relationship with the media. Creates press releases or responds to media queries.

Case 1 Managing the Guinness brand in the face of consumers' changing tastes

1997 saw the US$19 billion merger of Guinness and GrandMet to form Diageo, the world's largest drinks company. Guinness was the group's top-selling beverage after Smirnoff vodka, and the group's third most profitable brand, with an estimated global value of US$1.2 billion. More than 10 million glasses of the world's most popular stout were sold every day, predominantly in Guinness's top markets: respectively, the UK, Ireland, Nigeria, the USA and Cameroon.

However, the famous dark stout with the white, creamy head was causing some strategic concerns for Diageo. In 1999, for the first time in the 241-year history of Guinness, sales fell. In early 2002 Diageo CEO Paul Walsh announced to the group's concerned shareholders that global volume growth of Guinness was down 4 per cent in the last six months of 2001 and, more alarmingly, sales were also down 4 per cent in its home market, Ireland. How should Diageo address falling sales in the centuries-old brand shrouded in Irish mystique and tradition?

The changing face of the Irish beer market

The Irish were very fond of beer and even fonder of Guinness. With close to 200 litres per capita drunk each year—the equivalent of one pint per person per day—Ireland ranked top in worldwide per capita beer consumption, ahead of the Czech Republic and Germany.

Beer accounted for two-thirds of all alcohol bought in Ireland in 2001. Stout led the way in volume sales and accounted for 40 per cent of all beer value sales. Guinness, first brewed in 1759 in Dublin by Arthur Guinness, enjoyed legendary status in Ireland, a national symbol as respected as the green, white and gold flag. It was by far the most popular alcoholic drink in Ireland, accounting for nearly one of every two pints of beer sold. Its nearest competitors were Budweiser and Heineken, which held 13 per cent and 12 per cent of the market respectively.

However, the spectacular economic growth of the Irish economy since the mid-1990s had opened up the traditional drinking market to new cultures and influences, and encouraged the travel-friendly Irish to try other drinks. Beer and in particular stout were gradually losing popularity compared with wine or the recently launched RTDs (ready-to-drinks) or FABs (flavoured alcoholic beverages), which the younger generation of drinkers considered trendier and 'healthier'. As a Euromonitor report explained:

> Younger consumers consider dark beers and stout to be old fashioned drinks, with the perceived stout or ale drinker being an old, slightly overweight man and thus not in tune with image conscious youth culture.[1]

Beer sales, which once accounted for 75 per cent of all alcohol bought in Ireland, were expected to drop to close to 50 per cent by 2006, while stout sales were forecast to decrease by 12 per cent between 2002 and 2006.

Giving Guinness a boost in its home market

With Guinness alone accounting for 37 per cent of Diageo's volume in the market, Guinness/UDV Ireland was one of the first to feel the pain caused by the declining popularity of beer and in particular stout. A Euromonitor report in February 2002 explained how the profile of the Guinness drinker, typically men aged 21-plus, was affected:

> The average age of Guinness drinkers is rising and this is bringing about the worrying fact that the size of the Guinness target audience is falling. The rate of decline is likely to quicken as the number of less brand loyal, non-stout drinking younger consumers increases.[2]

The report continued:

> In Ireland, in particular, the consumer base for Guinness is shrinking as the majority of 18 to 24 year olds consistently reject stout as a product relevant to their generation, opting instead to consume lager or spirits.

Effectively, one-third of young Irish men and half of young Irish women had reportedly never tried Guinness.[3] A Guinness employee provided another explanation.

Guinness is similar to coffee in that when you're young you drink it [coffee] with sugar, but when you're older you drink it without. It's got a similar acquired taste and once you're over the initial hurdle, you'll fall in love with it.[4]

In an attempt to lure young drinkers to the somewhat 'acquired' Guinness taste (40 per cent of the Irish population was under the age of 24) Diageo had invested millions in developing product innovations and brand building in Ireland's 10,000 pubs, clubs and supermarkets.

Product innovations

Until the mid-1990s most Guinness in Ireland was drunk in a pint glass in the local pub. The launch of product innovations in the form of a new cooling mechanism for draft Guinness and the 'widget' technology applied to cans and bottles attempted to modernize the brand's image and respond to increasing competition from other local and imported stouts and lagers.

'A perfect head' for canned Guinness

In 1989, and at a cost of more than £10 million, Guinness developed an ingenious 'widget' device for its canned draft stout sold in 'off-trade' outlets such as supermarkets and off-licences. The widget, placed in the bottom of the can, released a gas that replicated the draft effect.

Although over 90 per cent of beer in Ireland was sold in 'on-trade' pubs and bars, sales of beer in the cheaper 'off-trade' channel were slowly gaining in importance. The Guinness brand manager at the time, John O'Keeffe, explained how home drinkers could now enjoy a smoother, creamier head similar to the one obtained in a pub thanks to the new widget technology:

> When the can is opened, the pressure causes the nitrogen to be released as the widget moves through the beer, creating the classic draft Guinness surge.

Nearly 10 years later, in 1997, the 'floating widget' was introduced, which improved the effectiveness of the device.

A colder pint

In 1997 Guinness Draft Extra Cold was launched in Ireland. An additional chilled tap system could be added to the standard barrel in pubs, allowing the Guinness to be served at 4°C rather than the normal 6°C. By serving Guinness at a cooler temperature, Guinness/UDV hoped to mute the bitter taste of the stout and make it more palatable for younger adults, who were increasingly accustomed to drinking chilled lager, particularly in the summer.

A cooler image for Guinness

In October 1999 the widget technology was applied to long-stemmed bottles of Guinness. The launch was supported by a US$2 million TV and outdoor board campaign. The packaging—with a clear, shiny plastic wrap, designed to look like a pint complete with creamy head—was quite a departure from the traditional Guinness look.

The objective was to reposition Guinness alongside certain similarly packaged lagers and RTDs and offer younger adults a more fashionable way to drink Guinness: straight from the bottle. It also gave Guinness easier access to the growing number of clubs and bars that were less likely to serve traditional draft Guinness, which could be kept for only six to eight weeks and took two minutes to pour. The RTDs, by contrast, had a shelf-life of more than a year and were drunk straight from the bottle.

However, financial analysts remained sceptical about the Guinness product innovations, which had no significant positive impact on sales or profitability:

> The latest news about the success of the recently introduced innovations suggests that they have not had a notably material impact on Guinness brand performance.[5]

Brand building

Euromonitor estimated that, in 2000, Diageo invested between US$230 and US$250 million worldwide in Guinness advertising and promotions. However, with a cost-cutting objective, the company reduced marketing expenses in both Ireland and the UK by up to 10 per cent in 2001 and the number of global Guinness agencies from six to two.[6]

Nevertheless, Guinness remained one of the most advertised brands in Ireland. It was the leading cinema advertiser and, in terms of outdoor advertising, was second only to the national telecoms provider, Eircom.[7] Guinness was also heavily promoted at leading sporting and music events, in particular those that were popular with the younger age groups.

The ultimate tribute to the brand was the opening of the new Guinness Storehouse in Dublin in late 2000, a sort of Mecca for all Guinness fans. The Storehouse was also a fashionable visitor centre with an art gallery and restaurants, and regularly hosted evening events. The company's design brief highlighted another key objective:

> To use an ultramodern facility to breathe life into an ageing brand, to reconnect an old company with young (sceptical) customers.[8]

As the Storehouse's design firm's director, Ralph Ardill, explained:

> Guinness Storehouse is a way to get in touch with a new generation to help young people re-evaluate Guinness.[9]

Within a year, the Storehouse had become the top tourist destination in Ireland, attracting more than half a million people and hosting 45,000 people for special events and training.

The Storehouse also had training facilities for Guinness's bartenders and 3000 Irish employees. The quality of the Guinness pint remained a high priority for the company, which not only developed pub-like classrooms at the Storehouse but also employed teams of draft technicians to teach barmen how to pour a proper pint. The process involved two steps—the pour and the top-up—and took a total of 119.5 seconds. Barmen also needed to learn how to check that the pressure gauges were properly set and that the proportion of nitrogen to carbon dioxide in the gas was correct.

The uncertain future of the Guinness brand in Ireland

Despite Guinness/UDV's attempt to appeal to the younger generation of drinkers and boost its fading image, rumours persisted in Ireland about the brand's future. The country's leading and respected newspaper, the *Irish Times*, reported in an article in July 2001:

> The uncertainty over its future all adds to the air of crisis that is building around Guinness. Sales of the famous stout in Ireland, still its single most important market, are falling ... The decline in Irish sales triggered a review process at Guinness Ireland Group four months ago ... The review is not complete and the assumption is that there is more bad news to come.[10]

In the pubs across Ireland, the traditional Guinness drinkers looked on anxiously as the younger generation drank Bacardi Breezers, Smirnoff Ices or Californian wines. Could the goliath Guinness survive another two centuries? Was the preference for these new drinks just a fad or fashion, or did Diageo need to seriously reconsider how it marketed Guinness?

A quick solution?

In late February 2002, Diageo CEO Paul Walsh revealed that the company was testing technology to cut the waiting time for a pint of Guinness from 1 minute 59 seconds to 15–25 seconds. Ultrasound could release bubbles in the stout and form the head instantly, making a pint of Guinness that would be indistinguishable from one produced by the slower, traditional method.

'A two-minute pour is not relevant to our customers today,' Walsh said.[11] A Guinness spokeswoman continued, 'We have got to move with the times and the brand must evolve. We must take all the opportunities that we can. In outlets where it is really busy, if you walk in after nine o'clock in the evening there will be a cloth over the Guinness pump because it takes longer to pour than other drinks.'[12] Aware that some consumers might not be attracted by the innovation, she added 'It wouldn't be put everywhere—only where people want a quick pint with no effect on the quality.'

Although still being tested, the 'quick-pour pint' was a popular topic of conversation in Dublin pubs, among barmen and customers alike. There were rumours that it would be introduced in Britain only; others thought it would be released worldwide.

Some market commentators viewed the quick-pour pint as an innovative way to appeal to the younger, less patient segment in which Guinness had underperformed. Others feared that the young would be unconvinced by the introduction, and loyal customers would be turned off by what they characterized as a 'marketing u-turn'.

Questions

1. From a marketing perspective, what has Guinness done to ensure its longevity?
2. How would you characterize the Guinness brand?
3. What could Guinness do to attract younger drinkers? And to retain its older loyal customer base? Can both be done at the same time?

4. Is the quick-pour concept a good or bad idea? Why?

References

This case was written by John Walsh, International Institute for Management Development, Lausanne, Switzerland. Copyright © 2002, IMD.

1. **Euromonitor** (2002) *Alcoholic Drinks in Ireland*, February.

2. **Euromonitor** (2002) *Diageo Profile*, February.

3. **Anonymous** (1996) Making Stout Profits: In Black and White: Roderick Oram Explains Why Guinness Believes Cold Porter Is Hot, Companies and Finance, *Financial Times*, II, 15 June.

4. **Creevy, J.** (200) Interview, April.

5. **Winston, C., A. Spielman** and **N. Schaufele** (2002) *Diageo: In the Grip of Momentum*, Schroder Salomon Smith Barney, 2 April.

6. **Euromonitor** (2002) *Diageo Profile*, February.

7. **Euromonitor** (2002) *Alcoholic Drinks in Ireland*, February.

8. **Kirsner, S.** (2002) Brand Marketing: Guinness Storehouse is a Way to Get in Touch with a New Generation, *Fast Company*, May.

9. **Kirsner, S.** (2002) Brand Marketing: Guinness Storehouse is a Way to Get in Touch with a New Generation, *Fast Company*, May.

10. **McManus, J.** (2001) Future Plans for Guinness Business Remain Uncertain, *Irish Times*, 21 July.

11. CNN (2002) *Waiting Time Cut for Guinness*, www.cnn.com, 25 February.

12. **Anonymous** (2002) Guinness Considers Quick-pour Solution in Britain, www.ireland.com

CHAPTER

2

THE GLOBAL MARKETING ENVIRONMENT

Learning Objectives

By the end of this chapter you will understand:

1 what is meant by the term 'marketing environment'
2 the distinction between the microenvironment and the macroenvironment
3 the impact of economic, social, political and legal, physical, and technological forces on marketing decisions
4 the growing importance of social responsibility and ethical marketing practices
5 how companies respond to environmental change.

The Fairtrade Movement

Through improvements in technology and communications in the past three decades, business has become truly global. Products may be produced in China or in small factories in Vietnam, and within a period of 24 to 36 hours they are hitting the shelves of stores in London or New York. But a concern for many is that not every player in this sequence of events is reaping a fair share of the rewards. In particular, there are instances where the primary producers, such as the farmers in Latin America growing coffee, are getting meagre returns while restaurants and cafés sell lattes and cappuccinos at significant margins.

It is against this background that the Fairtrade movement has grown from modest beginnings in 1992 to an international labelling organization endorsing brands in 19 markets around the world. The largest market for Fairtrade products is the UK, where sales of items carrying the label rose to £100 million in 2004, up by 50 per cent on 2003. Significant sales levels have also been attained in markets like Switzerland, France, Italy and the USA. The Fairtrade mark is controlled by the Fairtrade Foundation, a non-profit organization that was set up by a group of development organizations such as Oxfam, Christian Aid and Traidcraft Exchange.

The Fairtrade movement has a number of guiding aims. These include to enhance the livelihoods of producers by improving market access and paying a better price, to promote development opportunities for disadvantaged producers such as women and indigenous peoples, and to make consumers aware of the negative effects of international trade on producers. Fairtrade standards ensure that the price covers producers' costs and that it includes a premium for producers to invest in their communities in areas like clean water, healthcare, education and the environment.

Volatility and downward pressure on the prices of major commodities such as coffee, tea, bananas, cotton, rice and sugar have often had a devastating effect on producer communities around the world. These are the product categories where the Fairtrade mark is usually to be found, but it has also expanded very successfully into other arenas such as flowers, wines, oils and footballs. Companies like Green & Black and Cafédirect in the UK have been very successful through their adoption of the Fairtrade philosophy. Cafédirect sells four major tea and coffee brands, namely Cafédirect, 5065, Teadirect and Cocodirect through the major supermarket chains, and has become Britain's third largest ground and roasted coffee brand. Fairtrade coffee brands now have 18 per cent of the roast and ground coffee market in the UK, worth £5.9 million.

Many of the leading retail groups have recognized the potential of Fairtrade products. Tesco carries 60 Fairtrade products and was the first retailer to sell Fairtrade flowers. The Co-op began switching its own-label range to Fairtrade products in 2002 and saw sales of its block chocolate rise by 21 per cent as a result. Others, like Asda and Safeway, are increasing the space devoted to the brand. Succeeding in getting retailers to carry the products has been crucial as Fairtrade products are now positioned alongside competitors in the food sector rather than being located in a niche category. In 2005 Nestlé launched their own Fairtrade coffee under the Partners' Blend label.

Many Fairtrade brands have had limited promotional budgets so they have had to market themselves creatively, placing an emphasis on sampling, events, public relations and packaging rather than on advertising. However, this has been effective as unprompted recognition of the Fairtrade mark in the UK rose from 12 per cent in 2000 to 25 per cent in 2003. And the Foundation and its brand have been very successful in raising consumer awareness of the impact on producers of the choices that are made in the supermarket.[1]

A market-orientated firm looks outward to the environment in which it operates, adapting to take advantage of emerging opportunities and to minimize potential threats. In this chapter we shall examine the **marketing environment** and how to monitor it. In particular, we shall look at some of the major forces acting on companies such as the economic, social, legal, physical and technological issues that affect corporate activities.

The marketing environment is composed of the forces and actors that affect a company's ability to operate effectively in providing products and services to its customers. It is useful to classify these forces into the **microenvironment** and the **macroenvironment** (see Figure 2.1). The microenvironment consists of the actors in the firm's immediate environment or business system that affect its capabilities to operate effectively in its chosen markets. The key actors are suppliers, distributors, customers and competitors. The macroenvironment consists of a number of broader forces that affect not only the company, but also the other actors in the microenvironment. These can be grouped into economic, social, political/legal, physical and technological forces. These shape the character of the opportunities and threats facing a company, and yet are largely uncontrollable.

This chapter will focus on the major macroeconomic forces that affect marketing decisions. Four forces—namely economic, social, political/legal and technological—have been the focus of most attention, with the result that the acronyms PEST or STEP are often used to describe macroenvironmental analysis. The growing importance of the impact of marketing activity on the physical environment means that this issue, too, will be a focus of attention. Later in the chapter we will introduce the four dimensions of the microenvironment, which will then be dealt with in greater detail throughout the book. The changing nature of the supply chain and customer behaviour will be dealt with in detail in the next chapter. Distribution will be examined in Chapter 11 and competitive forces in Chapter 12.

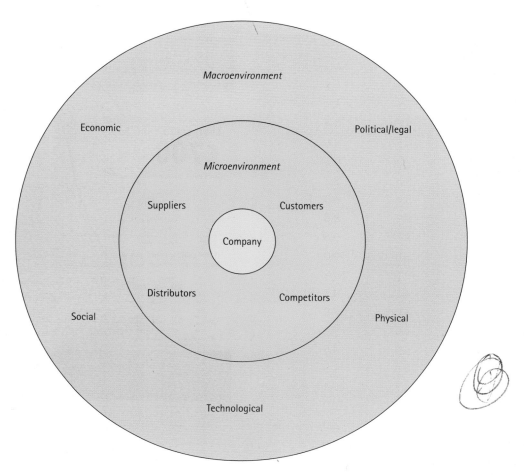

Figure 2.1 The marketing environment

Economic forces

Through its effect on supply and demand, the economic environment can have a crucial influence on the success of companies. They must choose those economic influences that are relevant to their business and monitor them. We shall now examine three major economic influences on the marketing environment of companies: economic growth and unemployment; interest rates and exchange rates; and the development of economic areas.

Economic growth and unemployment

The general state of both national and international economies can have a profound effect on an individual company's prosperity. Economies tend to fluctuate according to the 'business cycle'. Most of the world's economies went through a period of significant growth from the mid-1990s, driven mainly by productivity gains brought about by developments in computing and telecommunications technologies. The fortunes of many sectors, such as retailing, services and consumer durables, closely mirror this

economic pattern. In Ireland, which had very strong growth during the late 1990s, new car sales rose from a level of about 70,000 per year in the early part of the decade to over 200,000 in 2000. Similarly, the current buoyant growth of the Chinese economy is resulting in a boom in demand for cars, housing and

Table 2.1 Unemployment rates (per cent) in selected countries

Country	2004	2005
Canada	7.2	6.8
United States	5.5	5.2
Australia	5.5	5.1
Japan	4.7	4.4
Austria	4.5	4.6
Belgium	7.8	8.0
Czech Republic	8.3	8.2
Denmark	5.4	4.9
Finland	8.9	8.6
France	9.7	9.8
Germany	9.6	10.0
Greece	10.5	N/A
Ireland	4.5	4.3
Italy	8.0	7.8
Netherlands	4.6	5.0
Norway	4.4	4.6
Poland	18.8	17.9
Portugal	6.7	7.1
Spain	10.9	10.0
Sweden	6.4	6.3
United Kingdom	4.6	4.6
Euro Area	8.9	8.9

Source: OECD

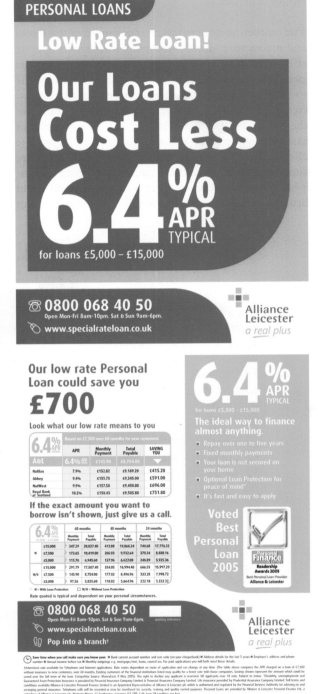

Exhibit 2.1 For banks like Alliance & Leicester, interest rates are an important marketing tool

consumer durables. A major marketing problem is predicting the next boom or slump. Investments made during periods of high growth can become massive cash drains if customer spending falls suddenly. The problems facing most of the world's leading technology firms, such as Cisco Systems, Compaq and Intel, in 2001 were partly caused by this trap.

Low growth rates are reflected in high unemployment levels, which in turn affect consumer spending power. Unemployment levels throughout some of the world's major economies are shown in Table 2.1. In times of economic recession, consumers tend to postpone spending and/or become more cost conscious, shifting more of their spending to discount stores.

Interest and exchange rates

One of the levers that the government uses to manage the economy is interest rates; the interest rate is the rate at which money is borrowed by businesses and individuals. Throughout the world, interest rates are at historically low levels. One of the results of this has been a boom in consumer borrowing. House prices have been growing at double-digit rates in many countries, which has meant significant sales and profit rises for construction companies and global furniture retailers like IKEA. There has even been a surge in the number of television programmes dealing with property acquisition, purchasing holiday homes abroad and home improvement. While taking on debt to buy homes and cars has traditionally been considered acceptable, what is worrying policy-makers now is the high levels of consumer debt arising particularly from the over-use of credit cards. For example, in the UK, the level of personal debt is over £1000 billion with credit card debt at a record level of £56 billion.[2] In Ireland the amount of personal debt outstanding in 2004 was close to €85 billion, which was well above the estimated level of disposable income for the country in that year.[3] All loans

Marketing in Action: Falling dollar hits profits at Waterford-Wedgwood

2.1

Waterford-Wedgwood, a luxury lifestyle company best known for its crystal and ceramic tableware, has four key brands: Waterford, Wedgwood, Rosenthal and Royal Doulton. The company was formed in 1986 following the merger of premium brands Waterford Crystal, the producer of Irish crystal, and Wedgwood, an English fine china manufacturer. In 1998, it acquired German company Rosenthal AG and in 2005 bought rival UK-based firm Royal Doulton. Primarily an export company, the USA is its number one market, accounting for over 70 per cent of all sales. Consequently this dependence on the USA means that Waterford-Wedgwood is very vulnerable to dollar/euro exchange rate volatility.

The uncontrollable events of 11 September 2001 sent shock waves around the world and led to a weakening of the US dollar. Since the end of 2002 the dollar has lost one-third of its value against the euro, making products coming from Europe more expensive in the USA. So, a few years ago, a vase yielding US$100 in the USA was worth €100 to Waterford's bottom line in Europe. Now the same vase is worth just €80. This has had a disastrous impact on the company, which has gone from being profitable in 2001 to recently announcing an annual loss of €149 million. Its share price has dropped from a high of €1.15 in 2000 to around 5 cents. As Waterford has a range of luxury brands in one main market, its options are limited. It cannot cut prices as this damages the brand's image and raising prices is only likely to further alienate US consumers. Therefore, it has had to cut costs and closed one of its plants in Ireland in 2005 with the loss of 500 jobs, and another in Germany with the loss of 160 jobs.

To add to its woes there has been increasing evidence that its products are becoming less fashionable and less of a 'must have' gift item than has heretofore been the case. Dining today is a much more casual affair with no place for traditional ornate tableware, and consumers are demanding more practical dishwasher-proof stemware and less elaborate styling. These are difficult times for the luxury goods maker and demonstrate how the uncontrollable forces of the macroenvironment, such as exchange rates, can have a significant impact on the fortunes of companies.

Based on: Jones and Mackintosh (2005);[5] Murray Brown (2005);[6] Sheridan (2005)[7]

eventually have to be paid back and, should interest rates rise, repayment costs will rise too. This is likely to result in a drop in consumer spending, possibly leading to difficulties for some companies.

Exchange rates are the rates at which one currency buys another. With the formation of the European Union, exchange rates between most European countries are now fixed. However, the rates at which major currencies like the US dollar, the euro, sterling and the yen are traded are still variable. These floating rates can have a significant impact on the profitability of a company's international operations. For example, during 2004, the value of the US dollar fell amid concerns about the widening US trade deficit and the cost of the Iraq War, losing about one-third of its value against the euro. This in turn meant both British and European goods became more expensive in the United States. For example, it is estimated that Heineken's operating profits in the United States will have fallen from €357 million to €119 million between 2002 and 2006.[4] From the point of view of some American businesses, the falling dollar has brought very positive results. For example, the number of UK tourists visiting Florida reached a record 1.65 million in 2004. Luxury goods companies like Waterford-Wedgwood have been particularly hard-hit by the fall in the value of the dollar, as shown in Marketing in Action 2.1.

The growth of economic areas

In the past, the basic economic unit has been the country, which was largely autonomous with regard to the decisions it makes about its economy and levels of supply and demand. But for the past three decades all this has been changing rapidly, driven mainly by the globalization of business. The world's largest companies, like Microsoft, General Electric, Wal-Mart and others are now larger than most countries in economic terms. At the same time, countries have been merging together into economic areas to more effectively manage their affairs. Most European countries are now part of the European Union (EU), the North American countries have grouped together into an economic area known as NAFTA, and the Pacific Rim countries are part of an economic area known as the ASEAN.

The European Union

The advent in 1986 of the Single European Act was the launch pad for a free-flowing internal market in the EU. The intention was to create a massive deregulated market of 320 million consumers by abolishing barriers to the free flow of products, services, capital

and people among the then 12 member states. More recently, the Maastricht Treaty (1992), the Nice Treaty (2000) and the introduction of the euro (2002) have all been further steps towards the development of full economic union. Another significant milestone for the EU was the admission of a further 10 new countries in May 2004, bringing the total to 25. The current EU members are Austria, Belgium, Britain, Czech Republic, Cyprus, Denmark, Estonia, Finland, France, Germany, Greece, Hungary, Ireland, Italy, Latvia, Lithuania, Luxembourg, Malta, Netherlands, Poland, Portugal, Slovakia, Slovenia, Spain and Sweden. The common currency, the euro, is in use in 13 countries, making travel, price comparisons and cross-border trade easier. The development of the EU has had a number of business implications.

Scale building

For Europe, the development of an economic union has created an internal zone of 320 million consumers, compared with 220 million in the United States and 120 million in Japan. This offered European industry the opportunity to organize itself on a scale large enough to enable it to compete with its main rivals in the USA and Japan. Many European high-tech industries suffer from a fragmented structure, making it difficult for them to keep pace with the research and development expenditures of their foreign competitors. For example, in 1990 there were 11 companies battling for the US$8 billion European market for central office telephone exchanges, compared with only four in the USA.[8] In order to compete, European companies are forming strategic alliances to reduce the effects of fragmentation. Olivetti, for example, acquired Telecom Italia in 2001 in a deal worth almost US$12 billion, while French car manufacturer, Peugeot-Citroën has formed a joint venture with Toyota, manufacturing cars in the Czech Republic.

Reorganization

A second feature is the move towards new organization structures in anticipation of a unified Europe.[9] For example, Philips reorganized its consumer electronics business by replacing its 60-year-old structure of autonomous national subsidiaries—a Dutch Philips, a British Philips, etc.—with Europe-wide, product-based businesses. Pilkington, Europe's second largest glass manufacturer, relocated its headquarters from St Helens in north-west England to Brussels and, at the same time, reduced its head office staff numbers from 500 to 130.[10] Electrolux rationalized its production of white goods, manufacturing all front-loading washing machines in

Pordenone, Italy, all top loaders in Revin, France, and all microwave ovens in Luton, England.[11]

Pan-European marketing

There has been a great deal of discussion about just how much the single European market will advance the level of pan-European marketing. On the one hand, the increasing mobility of European consumers, the accelerating flow of information across borders and the publicity surrounding the introduction of the euro has promoted a pan-European marketing approach; on the other hand, the persistence of local tastes and preferences means that the elimination of formal trade barriers may not bring about standardization of marketing strategies between countries. Standardization appears to depend on product type. In the case of many industrial goods, consumer durables (such as cameras, toasters, watches, radios) and clothing (Gucci shoes, Benetton sweaters, Levi's jeans) standardization is well advanced. However, for many fast-moving consumer goods (fmcg), standardization of products is more difficult to achieve because of local tastes. Even a pan-European brand like Garnier, owned by the French cosmetics group L'Oréal, has adapted its promotional campaign for its hair-colouring product Garnier Nutrisse. Because it felt that trust was an important element in selling hair-colouring products it sought to identify suitable celebrities in each market. In the UK, *Big Brother* host Davina McCall was chosen, while similarly appropriate local television presenters and actresses were chosen in France, Italy, Germany and Spain.[12] Each element of the marketing mix may be affected by the changes accompanying the arrival of the single European market.[13]

1 *Product:* manufacturers should benefit from the harmonization of standards, testing and certification procedures, by avoiding expensive product modifications and avoiding market entry delays (e.g. in pharmaceuticals) due to different country-specific requirements. For example, Philips will no longer have to produce seven types of television set to cope with different national standards in Europe. As cross-border segmentation of markets develops, new 'Eurobrands' may be launched, targeted at newly identified pan-European consumer segments. The patenting of products may become even more important because of the larger potential market.

2 *Price:* the price of goods and services throughout the EU could decrease by as much as 8 per cent according to European Commission estimates. The introduction of the euro has increased levels of price transparency, enabling consumers to easily and accurately compare prices across the 13 countries currently using the currency. Therefore, the potential for parallel importing, whereby goods sold in different countries at varying prices are exported from low- to high-price countries, is increased and this may also serve to depress price levels. A countervailing force may be that, as European consumers become wealthier, quality rather than price becomes the major strategic weapon for producers.

3 *Promotion:* despite the obvious attractions of potentially being able to use a single advertising campaign (with different voiceovers) to reach 320 million Europeans, variations in tastes, attitudes and perceptions restrict such an application. Even Coca-Cola, the ultimate 'one sight, one sound, one sell' global brand, modifies the advertising of its other drinks, such as Fanta, to national markets. A study of advertising standardization practices by Whitelock and Kalpaxoglou[14] concluded that many fast-moving consumer goods do not lend themselves readily to standardization, except for products that are not culture bound (cosmetics, for example). Similarly, difficulties in sales promotional regulations mean that premiums (gifts), given as promotional items with products, and money-off vouchers are not allowed in Denmark or western Germany, but are perfectly acceptable in the UK or France.

4 *Place:* Franchising is likely to increase as global companies link with local franchises combining buying and marketing muscle with local know-how. European-wide competition between supermarkets is likely to increase. For example, companies like Ahold (the Netherlands), Aldi (Germany) and Carrefour (France) have been expanding rapidly throughout Europe.

Social forces

There are four social forces, in particular, that have had implications for marketing. These are: changes in the demographic profile of the population; cultural differences within and between nations; social responsibility and marketing ethics; and the influence of the consumer movement. We will now examine each of these in turn.

Demographic forces

The term demographics refers to changes in population. Three major forces are world population

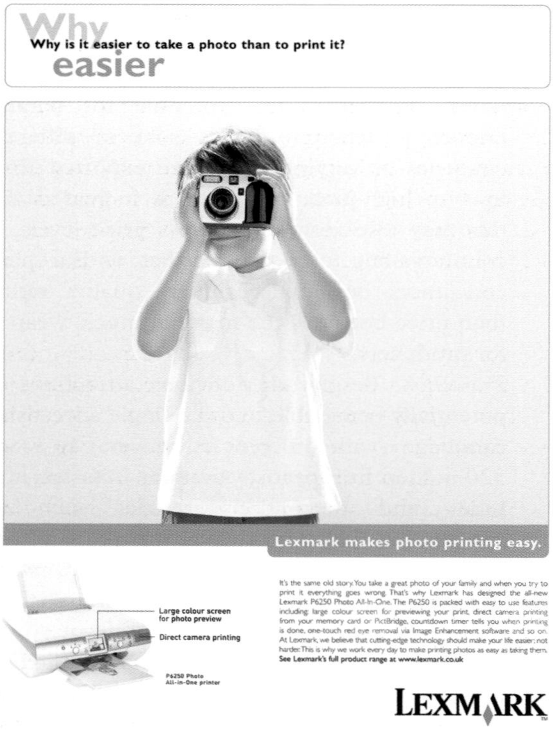

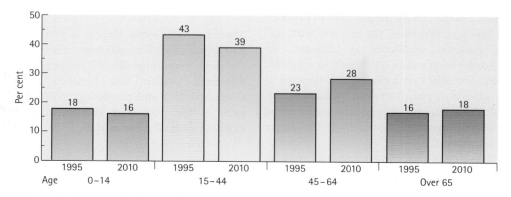

Why easier

Why is it easier to take a photo than to print it?

Lexmark makes photo printing easy.

Large colour screen for photo preview

Direct camera printing

P6250 Photo All-In-One printer

It's the same old story. You take a great photo of your family and when you try to print it everything goes wrong. That's why Lexmark has designed the all-new Lexmark P6250 Photo All-In-One. The P6250 is packed with easy to use features including large colour screen for previewing your print, direct camera printing from your memory card or PictBridge, countdown timer tells you when printing is done, one-touch red eye removal via Image Enhancement software and so on. At Lexmark, we believe that cutting-edge technology should make your life easier: not harder. This is why we work every day to make printing photos as easy as taking them. See Lexmark's full product range at www.lexmark.co.uk

LEXMARK

Exhibit 2.2 Many advertisements such as this one for Lexmark use images of children to demonstrate the ease of use of products

growth, changing age distribution and the rise in the number of two-income households. Most of the forecast world population growth is expected to occur in Africa, Asia and Latin America. Many marketers tend to ignore these countries because they are home to the bulk of the estimated four billion people worldwide that live in poverty (that is, survive on less than US$1500 a year). However, companies such as Hewlett-Packard, and Citibank are increasingly focusing their attention on these so-called 'premarkets' (i.e. not yet sufficiently developed to be considered consumer markets) and are recognizing that they can turn a profit while having a positive effect on the livelihoods of people. For example,

Hewlett-Packard aims to sell, lease or donate a billion dollars' worth of satellite-powered computer products and services to these under-served markets.[15]

A major demographic change that will continue to affect demand for products and services is the rising proportion of people over the age of 45 in the EU and the decline in the younger age group. Figure 2.2 gives age distribution trends in the EU between 1995 and 2010. The fall in the 15–44-year-old group suggests a slowdown in sales of products such as CDs, jeans and housing. However, the rise in the over-45-year-old group creates substantial marketing opportunities because of the high level of per capita income enjoyed by this group. They have much lower commitments in terms of mortgage repayments than younger people, tend to benefit from inheritance wealth and are healthier than ever before. In France, for example, the average per capita disposable income for households headed by a retired person is now higher than the average for all households, and people over 60 (who constitute 18 per cent of the population) consume more than 22 per cent of the French gross domestic product (GDP).[16] It is conceivable that the current trend for high-street clothing stores to target young and young-adult consumers will be replaced by shops catering for the tastes of the over-50s.[17] The overall implication of these trends is that many consumer companies may need to reposition their product and service offerings to take account of the rise in so-called 'grey' purchasing power (see Case 3, at the end of Chapter 3).

Finally, over half the couples with dependent children in the UK are dual-earner families. This is very different from the time when women were supported to work in the home and only men engaged in paid employment. The rise of the two-income household among professional and middle-class households means that this market segment has high disposable income leading to reduced price sensitivity and the capacity to buy luxury furniture and clothing prod-

Figure 2.2 Changes in European Union population

ucts, and expensive services (e.g. foreign holidays, restaurant meals). Also the combination of high incomes and busy lives has seen a boom in connoisseur convenience foods. As a result, the market for chilled foods in the UK is expected to grow from under £9 billion in 2001 to over £13 billion in 2006.[18] Companies like Northern Foods and Marks & Spencer, in particular, have catered for this market very successfully. Demand for child and homecare facilities has also risen.

Cultural forces

Culture is the combination of values, beliefs and attitudes that is possessed by a national group or subgroup. Cultural differences have implications for the way in which business is conducted. Humour in business life is acceptable in the UK, Italy, Greece, the Netherlands and Spain, but less commonplace in France and Germany. These facts of business life need to be recognized when interacting with European customers. Leadership patterns and organizational structure also vary significantly throughout Europe.[19] In southern European countries like Spain, business is typified by the family firm where the leadership style is autocratic and the organizational system informal. Communications tend to be vertical, therefore important purchasing decisions are

likely to be passed to top management for final approval, and good personal relations with middle management are vital to preventing the blocking of approaches at this level. In contrast, in the Netherlands, leadership is more democratic, and the organizational style is more formal and systematic. Buying, therefore, is characterized by large decision-making units and long decision-making processes as members attempt to reach agreement without conflict.

International marketers need to pay particular attention to the possible impact of culture. For example, the slower than expected take-off of the Euro-Disney (www.eurodisney.com) complex near Paris was partly attributed to French consumers' reluctance to accede to the US concept of spending a lot of money on a one-day trip to a single site. Once there, the French person—being an individualist—'hates being taken by the hand and led around'.[20]

Even within particular countries, however, it is important to bear in mind that many subcultures also exist. The rapid movement of global populations has meant that ethnically based subcultures have sprung up in most developed countries, creating potentially lucrative niche markets for products and services. For example, recent US census data estimates that there are 35.3 million Hispanics in America with a buying power of US$452.4 billion.[21] In addition, social trends and fashions give rise to their own particular subcultures, whose members dress and behave in certain ways—such as punk rock fans and football hooligans, for example. Where particular subcultures adopt a well-known brand as one of their signature items, this can cause difficulties for a brand manager, as the case of Burberry in Marketing in Action 2.1 demonstrates.

Corporate social responsibility and marketing ethics

Companies have a responsibility to society that goes beyond their legal responsibilities, and they need to recognize this. Corporate social responsibility (CSR) refers to the ethical principle that a person or an organization should be accountable for how its acts might affect the physical environment and the general public. Concerns about the environment and public welfare are represented by pressure groups such as Greenpeace (www.greenpeace.org) and ASH (Action on Smoking and Health) (www.ash.org).

Exhibit 2.3 Advertisements like this one featuring Martin Johnson work very well in the UK but may do less so in cultures where the rugby star is not as well known

Marketing managers need to be aware that organizations are part of a larger society and are accountable to that society for their actions. Such concerns led

Marketing in Action: Burberry's 'problem' customers

Burberry, the iconic English brand, was founded by Thomas Burberry back in 1856. By 1924 its distinctive check pattern appeared in the lining of its now famous trench coat. This trademark-registered design, which was to become the company's signature look, was later extended to umbrellas, scarves and luggage. A period of international expansion began in the 1980s for the, by then, fashionable clothing brand, marked by the opening of its first flagship store in New York. In 1997, the company turned to Rose Marie Bravo, previous head of Saks 5th Avenue to help revitalize the brand through a series of new design collections supported by glamorous advertising campaigns and the opening of further international retail outlets. Bravo succeeded in returning Burberry to its luxury status, embraced by the affluent and refined in society.

Unfortunately, unintended and much less desirable markets have also begun to adopt the brand. In the USA, a number of high-profile hip-hop artists have taken a fancy to wearing Burberry and mentioning the brand in their lyrics. This has prompted their legion of predominantly working-class, African-American fans to adopt the brand as a sign of loyalty to their idols. In the UK, Burberry's distinctive check has become the uniform of the 'chav', a term used in the media to deride a certain type of youth. Chavs are predominantly white, lower-class adolescents who like to sport numerous brands, often counterfeit, as a badge of aspirational cool.

The brand has also become particularly associated with football hooligans, who are often seen at matches sporting Burberry shirts and baseball caps. In 2004, two British pubs banned the wearing of Burberry on their premises, putting forward the argument that the brand had become a uniform for football hooligans and yobs. The story received huge media attention and this association with lower-class vulgarity and anarchy is in stark contrast to Burberry's adverts, which contain images of young, beautiful, well-heeled people who also tend to be mainly white.

The adoption of luxury brands by unintended markets can cause quite a headache for brand owners, who must decide how best to respond. While in the USA, Tommy Hilfiger has chosen to embrace the brand's unintended rapper audience, Burberry has decided to disassociate itself as much as possible from its new customers. In an attempt to discourage these new followers, it has stopped producing its baseball caps, though the strategy has had little impact as most Burberry caps owned by these customers are fake. While the brand has generally been performing well around the world, UK results reported for the quarter to January 2005 were disappointing, with Burberry reluctantly acknowledging that undesirable associations with 'chavs' may have played a role. Luxury brands must carefully manage their brand image and hope the fickleness of fashion will see their new 'problem' customers move on to their next unsuspecting victim.

Based on: Braddock (2003);[22] O'Brien (2003);[23] Sanchanta (2004);[24] Tomkins (2005)[25]

Perrier to recall 160 million bottles of its mineral water in 120 countries after traces of a toxic chemical were found in 13 bottles. The recall cost the company a total of £50 million, even though there was no evidence that the level of the chemical found in the water was harmful to humans. Perrier acted because it believed the least doubt in the consumers' minds should be removed in order to maintain its product's image of quality and purity. Companies are increasingly conscious of the need to communicate their socially responsible activities. The term 'Green marketing' is used to describe marketing efforts to produce, promote and reclaim environmentally sensitive products.[26]

The societal marketing concept is a label often used to describe how the activities of companies should not only consider the needs of customers but also society at large. This notion has given rise to movements like the Fairtrade Foundation discussed at the outset of the chapter and also to the formation of companies like Edun, the Dublin-based fashion company. Founded by U2's Bono and his wife Ali Hewson, the company manufactures a line of organic cotton shirts, jeans and hemp blazers. Its fashion line is made from non-subsidized cotton sourced in Peru and manufactured in Africa, while its second brand, Edun Live comprises mass-market clothes made from Tanzanian cotton and manufactured in Lesotho. The company's ethical goal is to support manufacturers in Africa and world farmers by championing organic, environmentally sustainable cotton products.[27]

Corporate social responsibility is no longer an optional extra but a key part of business strategy that comes under close scrutiny from pressure groups, private shareholders and institutional investors, some of whom manage ethical investment funds. Businesses are increasingly expected to adapt to climate change, biodiversity, social equity and human rights in a world characterized by greater transparency and more explicit values.[28] Two outcomes of these developments have been the growth in social reporting and **cause-related marketing**. Some of the corporate social responsibility (CSR) and cause-related marketing activities of leading companies operating in Ireland are shown in Table 2.2.

Social reporting is where firms conduct independent audits of their social performance. These audits usually involve surveys of key stakeholders such as customers and employees. Social audits normally take the form of printed reports, but these are increasingly being replaced by the Internet as the main communication medium. The advantages of the Internet are that it is easy to update, the distribution of information is cost effective, it is searchable, can be produced swiftly and is environmentally friendly. However, it is also the medium most favoured by those who wish to criticize big businesses. For example, www.ryan-be-fair.org features comments from people claiming to be Ryanair staff who are critical of the company and its practices, while the Professional Pilots Rumour Network (www.pprune.org) is a popular site on which pilots share information and gossip. Most comments on the site are negative towards Ryanair except one staunch defender who goes by the pseudonym of Leo Hairy Camel. His identity is a matter of speculation but Leo Hairy Camel is an anagram of Michael O'Leary, the name of the company's outspoken chief executive.[29]

Cause-related marketing is a commercial activity by which businesses and charities or causes form a partnership with each other in order to market an image, product or service for mutual benefit. Cause-related marketing works well when the business and charity have a similar target audience. For example, Nambarrie Tea Company, a Northern Ireland winner of the annual Business in the Community award for excellence in cause-related marketing, chose to sponsor the breast cancer agency Action Cancer. The company and the charity targeted women aged 16 to 60. In a two-month period, Nambarrie released 100,000 specially designed packs promoting its sponsorship of Action Cancer and covered media costs for a TV advertising campaign. This generated income of over £200,000.[30]

A related issue is that of marketing ethics. **Ethics** are the moral principles and values that govern the actions and decisions of an individual or group.[31] They involve values about right and wrong conduct.

Table 2.2 Corporate social responsibility activities of selected companies in Ireland

Company	CSR activities
Allied Irish Banks	The AIB Better Ireland programme focuses on helping disadvantaged children. AIB has donated over €10 million to 700 projects
Bank of Ireland	A member of the FTSE4Good Index; introduced an ethical business statement and environmental management system
Diageo	Developed Choice Zone to support education programmes to promote sensible drinking; contributed more than €3.5 million towards the Diageo Liberties Learning Initiative
IBM Ireland	A community volunteer programme registered over 12,000 volunteer hours in two years
Johnson & Johnson	Foundation of the Special Achievers Club in Janssen, Cork; mentoring programme in partnership with Tallaght Community School; CSR committee set up in 2004
KPMG	Training sessions for the ReadyforWork programme for the homeless; partner with Westland Row School in the Schools' Business Partnership
Marks & Spencer	Marks & Start is a community programme aiming to enable 2500 people each year to prepare for the world of work
O$_2$	Sponsored the O$_2$ Ability Awards; raising awareness of dyslexia with all employees
Tesco Ireland	Raised more than €2.6 million for national charities through a 'charity of the year' programme

Source: Responsible Business: Driving Innovation & Competitiveness, *Irish Times*, 27 May 2005, 12.

There can be a distinction between the legality and ethicality of marketing decisions. Ethics concern personal moral principles and values, while laws reflect society's principles, and standards that are enforceable in the courts.

Not all unethical practices are illegal. For example, it is not illegal to include genetically modified (GM) ingredients in products sold in supermarkets; however, some organizations (such as Greenpeace) believe it is unethical to sell GM products when their effect on health has not been scientifically proven. Such concerns have led to supermarket chains, such as Iceland and Sainsbury's in the UK, to remove GM foods from their own-label products. Similarly, mobile phone companies need to be responsive to the potential long-term risks posed by the use of these devices as some scientific studies have shown a link between mobile phone use and the development of brain tumours. Manufacturers are ensuring that handsets conform to international guidelines on the Specific Absorption Rate of radiation emissions and the industry has contributed millions of dollars to research on the issue.[32]

Many ethical dilemmas derive from a conflict between profits and business actions. For example, by using child labour the cost of producing items is kept low and profit margins are raised. Nevertheless, this has not stopped companies such as Reebok from monitoring the overseas production of, say, sporting goods to ensure that no child labour is used. Because of the importance of marketing ethics, many of the chapters in this book end with a discussion of ethical issues. For example, Chapter 4 ends with a discussion of ethical issues such as intrusions into privacy and selling in the guise of research.

The consumer movement

The 'consumer movement' is the name given to the set of individuals, groups and organizations whose aim is to safeguard consumer rights. For example, the Consumers' Association in the UK campaigns on behalf of consumers and provides information about products, often on a comparative basis, allowing consumers to make more informed choices between products and services. This information is published in the organization's magazine *Which?* (www.which.org).

As well as offering details of unbiased product testing and campaigning against unfair business practices, the consumer movement has been active in areas such as product quality and safety, and information accuracy. Notable successes have been the Campaign

Every cigarette we smoke makes fatty deposits stick in our arteries.

We'll help you give up before you clog up completely.   bhf.org.uk

British Heart Foundation

Exhibit 2.4 This advertisement by the British Heart Foundation graphically shows the dangers of smoking

Marketing in Action: McDonald's takes the healthy option

The rising level of obesity has become a major crisis across the developed world. In the USA, the fattest nation in the world, 61 per cent of citizens are overweight. One-quarter of Americans under the age of 19 are overweight or obese, which is double the amount reported 30 years ago. The epidemic is giving rise to serious healthcare problems, with 300,000 deaths a year being linked to obesity and US$117 billion being spent each year on treating obesity-related illnesses. Once smugly deemed a 'US problem', Europe is now facing similar growing obesity levels. A recent study by the NHS in Scotland found that one in five 12 year olds are clinically obese and ominously predicts that one-quarter of the British population could be clinically obese by 2010.

The rising levels of obesity are causing a major headache for the fast-food industry, which stand accused of being major contributors to the problem. Fast-food firms have been criticized for encouraging consumers to eat greater amounts of unhealthy, convenience food. The industry spends US$33 billion a year on advertising and promoting its product offerings with much of this effort being focused on children. Firms such as McDonald's, Pizza Hut, Coca-Cola and Pepsi have targeted schools with attractive financial incentives in return for allowing their product to be sold exclusively on school property, effectively guaranteeing a captive audience. Many fast-food firms have also engaged in the practice of 'supersizing' where products are sold in large portions and are also bundled together at a discounted price to encourage consumers to buy more.

2002 was not a good year for McDonald's. The company made its first quarterly loss since 1954 and growing health consciousness was also causing consumers to switch to restaurants with healthier menus. McDonald's needed to do something, and fast. It switched from an aggressive expansion programme to focusing on growing sales in existing restaurants through improving standards of cleanliness and service, and serving products more in tune with consumer tastes. This resulted in the introduction of a number of healthy options, including salads and fruit bags, sending a message to consumers that McDonald's was not just a 'burger company'. Marketing was overhauled with the introduction of the 'I'm Lovin' It' campaign—the first time McDonald's has used a single global advertising slogan.

The new 'back to basics strategy' has begun to work, with US sales increasing by 9.9 per cent in 2003 and its share price increasing by 80 per cent from the lows of March that year. McDonald's is currently experimenting with a new sandwich range on offer in selected American outlets. It is also promoting the importance of an active lifestyle with the introduction of an adult meal containing a salad, bottled water and a pedometer. The question is, can McDonald's, accused of being part of the obesity problem, become a credible part of the solution? Only time will tell if it can pull it off.

Based on: Anonymous (2004);[34] Buckley (2003);[35] Buckley (2004)[36]

for Real Ale (CamRA), improvements in car safety, the stipulation that advertisements for credit facilities must display the true interest charges (annual percentage rates), and the inclusion of health warnings on cigarette packets and advertisements.

Such consumer organizations can have a significant influence on production processes. For example, pressure from environmental movements in Finland and Germany on UPMKymmene, Finland's largest company and Europe's biggest papermaking firm, ensured that the number of new trees planted matched the number of trees felled. German customers (which constitute the firm's biggest market),

such as the publisher Springer, now have clauses on forest sustainability and biodiversity written into their contracts with paper companies.[33]

The consumer movement should not be considered a threat to business, but marketers should view its concerns as offering an opportunity to create new products and services to satisfy the needs of these emerging market segments. For example, growing concern over rising obesity levels in the developed world has led McDonald's to make significant changes to its menu items and marketing approach, as described in Marketing in Action 2.3.

Lower BIK taxation means £1800 saving over equivalent D segment diesels.

Happy New Year?
Drivers braced for further tax rises

New government drive to combat NOx emissions
See pa...

NOx emissions 96% lower than EURO IV diesel regulations.

Congestion charge:
London scheme has been so successful, will it roll out nationally?
See pag...

Congestion Charge exempt, saving up to £1250 per annum.

The headlines look bleak for company car drivers, but not with the new Toyota Prius. It's all good news because with its unique petrol-electric hybrid engine it delivers excellent tax savings and easily passes impending emissions regulations. To find out more about our headline-grabbing car call 0845 600 1461 or visit www.fleet.toyota.co.uk/startnow today. **TOYOTA**

Official Fuel Consumption Figures in mpg (l/100km): Urban - 56.5 (5.0), Extra-Urban - 67.3 (4.2), Combined - 65.7 (4.3), CO₂ - 104 g/km

Exhibit 2.5 This advertisement for the Toyota Prius describes how it easily meets emissions regulations

Political and legal forces

Marketing decisions can also be influenced by political and legal forces, which determine the rules by which business is conducted. Political forces play a major role in international markets, where decisions by governments can often have profound implications for companies, as shown in Marketing in Action 2.4. Close relationships with politicians are often cultivated by organizations, both to monitor the political mood and also to influence it. The cigarette industry, for example, has a vested interest in maintaining close ties with government whereby it hopes to counter proposals from pressure groups such as ASH, which demand that cigarette advertising be banned. Companies sometimes make sizeable contributions to the funds of political parties in an attempt to maintain favourable relationships. The closeness of big business and politicians is evident in the number of cases being pursued by the European Commission where it is examining instances of illegal state aid such as the alleged €9 billion bail-out of French Telecom by the government in France.[37]

Political action, then, in the form of legislation and less formal directives, can have a profound influence on business conduct. National laws governing advertising across Europe mean that what is acceptable in one country is banned in another. Toys, for example, cannot be advertised in Greece, tobacco advertising is illegal in Scandinavia and Italy, alcohol advertising is banned on television and at sports grounds in France, and in Germany any advertisement believed to be in bad taste can be prohibited. This patchwork of national advertising regulations means that those companies attempting to create a brand image across Europe often need to make substantial changes to their advertising strategy on a national basis. We shall now review some of the more important legal influences on marketing activities.

Monopolies and mergers

Formerly, the control of monopolies in Europe was enacted via Article 86 of the Treaty of Rome, which aimed to prevent the 'abuse' of a dominant market position. However, control was increased in 1990 when the EU introduced its first direct mechanism for dealing with mergers and take-overs: the Merger Regulation. This gave the Competition Directorate of the European Commission jurisdiction over 'concentrations with a European dimension'. Over the years, the Commission has blocked several proposed mergers on the grounds that they would give certain companies a dominant share of their markets, including, for example, General Electric's proposed take-over of Honeywell. European regulations are often supplemented by national bodies (for example, the Monopolies and Mergers Commission in the UK). This body has the authority to investigate monopolies and mergers that are thought to be anti-competitive.

Restrictive practices

Article 85 of the Treaty of Rome was, in Europe, designed to ban those practices 'preventing, restricting or distorting competition', except where these contribute to efficiency without inhibiting consumers' 'fair share of the resulting benefit' and without eliminating competition. A notable success for the Commission was the breaking of the plastics cartel involving Britain (ICI), France (Atochem), West Germany (BASF) and Italy (Montedison) among others. In addition to the work of the Commission, organizations such as the Bundeskartellamt in Germany and the Competition Council in France provide national protection against anti-competitive practices. Many countries in Europe supplement cross-border regulations with their own national laws.

Similarly, regulations from the Financial Services Authority in the UK are changing the way that financial products are sold there. High-street banks and building societies have been given the freedom to sell rivals' products such as mortgages and life assur-

Marketing in Action: Coping with anti-American sentiment

Major political events tend to also have significant economic consequences. For example, the American-led war in Iraq, which began in 2003, has had a significant impact on US companies operating around the world. A survey conducted in March 2003, showed that the USA's favourability ratings had fallen from 75 per cent to 48 per cent in Britain, from 63 per cent to 31 per cent in France and from 61 per cent to 28 per cent in Russia. In general, views on America are becoming increasingly negative, with another study taken in 2005 showing that people in countries like China, Germany, Spain, Indonesia, Pakistan, Turkey and Poland had more unfavourable than favourable attitudes to the country.

These negative sentiments in turn impact on the demand for American products. Worst affected tend to be brands that are seen as quintessentially American, such as Coca-Cola, McDonald's, Microsoft, Marlboro, MTV and others. During the Iraq War many of these brands were boycotted, particularly in the Middle East but also throughout Europe. For example, one German website, www.consumers-against-war.de, urged people to boycott 27 US companies from American Express to Walt Disney. Even more serious than boycotts are when commercial interests become the targets of terrorism such as the bombings of both the Marriott Hotel and McDonald's in Indonesia. Another symptom of the anti-US backlash is the launch of no fewer than three new brands of cola in France to compete with Pepsi and Coke. These new brands—Mecca-Cola, Arab-Cola and Muslim-Up—are popular not only with Muslims but also the wider community, and Mecca-Cola is already being sold in 22 countries.

The response of the multinational companies is to become as local as possible whether that involves acquiring local firms as part of their global expansion, leaving the names of local companies acquired in place, customizing products and services to local needs, or generally being sensitive to local attitudes to their brands. For example, when protests against the American-led strikes in Afghanistan increased during 2001, a McDonald's franchise owner in Indonesia displayed green (the colour of Islam) ownership banners, hired members of local Islamic organizations as security guards and played religious music in his restaurants. Across the globe, McDonald's is increasingly customizing its menus. The McArabia sandwich, which is a chicken sandwich in Arabic-style flatbread is available in the Middle East. Several other brands and chains are following suit. Coca-Cola now has a range of 200 products, some specific to regional markets in Asia and Africa, while Dunkin' Donuts provides green tea and mango versions of its Coolatta drink in Korea.

But perhaps the biggest challenge facing leading American multinationals is that America no longer symbolizes attributes such as freedom and individual self-expression, which were the kinds of positive images many brands attached themselves to. Conflicting views of what America stands for means that brands have to re-evaluate how much they promote their Americanism.

Based on: Anonymous (2005);[38] Murray (2004);[39] Silverman (2004);[40] Tomkins (2003)[41]

ance alongside their own in-house ranges. These changes are designed to give consumers more choice, and to increase the quality and availability of financial advice.[42]

Codes of practice

On top of the various laws that are in place, certain industries have drawn up codes of practice—sometimes as a result of political pressure—to protect consumer interests. The UK advertising industry, for example, has drawn up a self-regulatory Code of Advertising Standards and Practice designed to keep advertising 'legal, decent, honest and truthful'. Similarly, the marketing research industry has drawn up a code of practice to protect people from unethical activities such as using marketing research as a pretext for selling. However, many commentators are critical of the potential effectiveness of voluntary codes of conduct in industries like oil exploration and clothing manufacture.[43]

Marketing management must be aware of the constraints on its activities brought about by the political and legal environment. It must assess the extent to which there is a need to influence political decisions that may affect operations, and the degree to which industry practice needs to be self-regulated in order to maintain high standards of customer satisfaction and service.

Physical forces

As we have seen, the consumer movement aims to protect the rights of consumers; environmentalists, in turn, aim to protect the physical environment from the costs associated with producing and marketing products and services. They are concerned with the *social* costs of consumption, not just the *personal* costs to the consumer. Six environmental issues are of particular concern. These are the use of environmentally friendly ingredients in products, recyclable and non-wasteful packaging, protection of the ozone layer, animal testing of new products, pollution, and energy conservation. Marketers need to be aware of the

threats and opportunities associated with each of these issues.

Use of environmentally friendly ingredients

The use of biodegradable and natural ingredients when practicable is favoured by environmentalists. For example, ICI, the UK chemical group, has developed Biopol, which it claims is the first fully biodegradable commercial plastic. It states that the product's applications include disposable nappies, rubbish bags, and paper plates and cups coated with a thin plastic film. It is already being used in Germany to make bottles for Wella's Sanara shampoo, in the USA for Brocato International's Evanesce shampoo and in Japan for Ishizawa Kenkyujo's Earthic Alga shampoos and conditioners.[44] Similarly, Sanyo Electric has introduced the MildDisc, which is a brand of CD that can carry computer data, music and video but is made from a polymer derived from maize. One of the challenges

Marketing in Action: Naty: a sustainable enterprise

A growing niche market of ecologically conscious consumers is creating new business opportunities for the introduction of environmentally friendly products. Naty, a Swedish company, responded to the concerns that some consumers have regarding the social costs of their consumption activities with the introduction of a new brand of biodegradable disposable nappies: Nature Boy & Girl.

Naty was the brainchild of Marlene Sandberg, an environmentally conscious mother, who while pregnant with her second child was shocked to discover that, in Sweden, every baby creates several hundred kilos of nappy waste each year that does not decompose. The impact disposable nappies have on the environment is alarming. It takes approximately one cup of crude oil to make the plastic for every disposable nappy and almost two trees to make the pulp to fill the nappies of one child for one year.

She was so dismayed by this that she began to investigate the feasibility of creating an environmentally friendly disposable nappy, which could compete effectively on price and quality. With the assistance of a number of partners, she created a product that uses compostable biological maize instead of plastic. Each nappy consists of 70 per cent renewable and biodegradable materials compared to between 30 and 40 per cent for disposable nappies produced by large international manufacturers.

Naty began to produce its nappies in 1998; they were initially sold across Sweden and in Denmark. In the UK, Sainsbury's and Waitrose have carried the product since 2000, providing an alternative to conventional disposable nappy brands. Retailing at around £5.65, they are priced similarly to other non-biodegradable nappies. Sandberg is determined to expand into a number of other European markets and outside of Europe; the company has licensed the product for sale in the USA, Australia and New Zealand. It has recently expanded its range with new baby and feminine hygiene products, and has won the Good Environmental Choice Award from the Swedish Society of Nature Conservation.

Based on: Anonymous (2001);[46] Chandiramani (2003);[47] Houlder (2001)[48]

for the manufacturers of biodegradable products is the costs involved. Sanyo's MildDisc costs three times as much as a normal CD.[45] Many organizations, like the Swedish company Naty, specialize in making products from biodegradable materials (see Marketing in Action 2.5).

Recyclable and non-wasteful packaging

The past 20 years or so have seen significant growth in recycling throughout Europe. In Austria, used batteries, PCs, refrigerators and other products containing potentially dangerous wastes have to be returned by consumers and gathered by retailers; they are then recycled or treated centrally. Household waste is sorted into materials to be recycled: biological waste and the non-reusable rest. The fact that Austrians are environmentally conscious has led to an oversupply of recycled material, thus raising the price of waste disposal. As a result, consumers have put pressure on retailers and manufacturers to avoid overpackaging.[49] Recycling is also important in Sweden, where domestic industry has established a special company to organize the collection and sorting of waste for recycling, and in Finland where 35 per cent of packaging is recycled.[50] Cutting out waste in packaging is not only environmentally friendly but also makes commercial sense. Thus companies have introduced concentrated detergents and refill packs, and removed the cardboard packaging around some brands of toothpaste, for example. The savings can be substantial: in Germany, Lever GmbH saved 30 per cent by introducing concentrated detergents, 20 per cent by using lightweight plastic bottles, and the introduction of refills for concentrated liquids reduced the weight of packaging materials by a half.

The growth in the use of the personal computer has raised major recycling issues as PCs contain many harmful substances and pollutants. EU legislation is forcing manufacturers to face up to the issue of how these products are recycled, with some of the costs being absorbed by the companies and the rest by the consumer. Hewlett-Packard has set up a team to re-examine how PCs are made and to design them with their disposal in mind. The team has conducted projects such as using corn starch instead of plastic in its printers, redesigning packaging and cutting down on emissions from factories.[51]

Protection of the ozone layer

Concern about the depletion of the ozone layer has had a marked effect on the production of chlorofluo-rocarbons (CFCs), which are used in refrigerators and aerosols but are a major contributor to the breakdown of the ozone layer, allowing harmful radiation to pass through it. The Montreal Protocol Conference in 1990 ruled that the production of CFCs should be completely phased out by 2000, though this target was not achieved.

Animal testing of new products

To reduce the risk of them being harmful to humans, potential new products such as shampoos and cosmetics are tested on animals before launch. This has aroused much opposition. One of the major concepts underlining the initial success of UK retailer the Body Shop was that its products were not subject to animal testing. This is an example of the Body Shop's ethical approach to business, which also extends to its suppliers. Other larger stores, responding to Body Shop's success, have introduced their own range of animal-friendly products.

Pollution

The quality of the physical environment can be harmed by the manufacture, use and disposal of products. The production of chemicals that pollute the atmosphere, the use of nitrates in fertilizer that pollutes rivers, and the disposal of by-products into the sea have caused considerable public concern. In recent years, the introduction of lead-free petrol and catalytic converters has reduced the level of harmful exhaust emissions. Denmark has introduced a series of anti-pollution measures including a charge on pesticides and a CFC tax. In the Netherlands, higher taxes on pesticides, fertilizers and carbon monoxide emissions are proposed. Not all of the activity is simply cost raising, however. In Germany, one of the marketing benefits of its involvement in Green technology has been a thriving export business in pollution-control equipment.

Consumer groups can exert enormous pressure on companies by influencing public opinion. For example, environmentalist protests convinced Shell to abandon its plans to dump its obsolete North Sea oil installation, *Brent Spar*, at sea. Environmentalists are a key component of the wider movement that monitors business practices and generates pressure for change.

Energy conservation

Recognition of the finite nature of the world's energy resources has stimulated a drive to conserve energy. This is reflected in the demand for energy-efficient housing and fuel-efficient motor cars, for example. In

Europe, Sweden has taken the lead in developing an energy policy based on domestic and renewable resources. The tax system penalizes the use of polluting energy sources like coal and oil, while less polluting and domestic sources such as peat and woodchip receive favourable tax treatment. In addition, nuclear power is to be phased out by 2010. More efficient use of energy and the development of energy-efficient products (backed by an energy technology fund) will compensate for the shortfall in nuclear energy capacity.

Technological forces

People's lives and companies' fortunes can both be affected significantly by technology. Technological advances have given us body scanners, robotics, camcorders, computers and many other products that have contributed to our quality of life. Many technological breakthroughs have changed the rules of the competitive game. For example, the launch of the computer has decimated the market for typewriters and has made calculators virtually obsolete. Monitoring the technological environment may result in the spotting of opportunities and major investments in new technological areas. For example, ICI invested heavily in the biotechnology sector, and leads the market for equipment used in genetic fingerprinting. Japanese companies are investing heavily in areas such as microelectronics, biotechnology, new materials and telecommunications.

New potential applications for technology are emerging all the time. For example, the Piggy Wiggy

e-Marketing: Promotional messaging

The mobile phone has revolutionized the way we communicate today, with ownership in most developed countries reaching saturation point. According to research conducted in the UK, 86 per cent of 15–24 year olds own a mobile phone, making it the largest phone ownership age group. Despite warnings of the dangers of mobile phone usage, users are continuing to get younger, with 40 per cent of 7–11 year olds now having access to one. The number of services being offered is also undergoing explosive growth. According to Vodafone, its most popular services are text messaging, picture messaging, downloading of polyphonic ringtones, Java game downloads, downloads of logos and screensavers, and finally WAP browsing. It is those in the youth market that tend to be the early adopters of these services and the most avid fans.

For example, texting has become a way of life for today's youth, with 90 per cent of teenagers preferring texting to speaking on their mobile phones. It offers a more cost-effective option and is a way to chat with friends, allowing teens to keep abreast of the latest gossip. For the shy individual it offers a way to chat anonymously and initiate romance. With these teens spending more and more time on their mobile phones, marketers are finding them difficult to reach using traditional media and, as a result, have begun to use the short message services (SMS) of mobile phones as a marketing tool.

Numerous examples of SMS marketing now exist. In the UK, teen magazines are an example of just one sector that has enthusiastically embraced the new medium. The teen girls' magazine *Bliss* launched its first Valentine's SMS interactive campaign in 2004 to boost magazine readership. Here readers who registered to join the *Bliss* text club were asked to send in their star sign and the horoscope of the boy they liked. *Bliss* replied with a message on each girl's compatibility with her chosen boy. *Smash Hits*, another teen mag, has an opt-in poptxt club that allows members to receive hot gossip, avail themselves of special offers and enter competitions.

But marketers must beware when targeting young teenagers and children. They have an ethical responsibility to uphold the reputation of their profession and protect children from incurring excessive financial costs, exposure to unsuitable material and direct selling. Legally there are a number of industry regulations that must be adhered to. The 2002 European Commission's directive on privacy and electronic communication states that electronic communication must be on an opt-in basis—that is, prior consent is required before sending the message. The only exception to this is where a relationship already exists.

Based on: Anonymous (2004);[54] Budden (2003);[55] Tran (2003)[56]

supermarket chain in South Carolina has become the first US retailer to roll out a biometric payment system in its 120 stores. To pay, the customer places an index finger on a small screen, types in a number on an adjacent pad, selects an account from an electronic wallet and walks away. Cash, cheque books and credit cards are unnecessary.[52] The key to successful technological investment is, however, market potential, not technological sophistication for its own sake. The classic example of a high-tech initiative driven by technologists rather than pulled by the market is Concorde. Although technologically sophisticated, management knew before its launch that it never had any chance of being commercially viable.

One particular major technological change that is affecting marketing is the development of information technology. Information technology, or IT, describes the broad range of innovations within the fields of computing and telecommunications. Almost no aspect of marketing remains unaffected by developments in these areas. For example, many market research studies are being conducted via e-mail; the efficiency of salesforces is being improved through salesforce automation; and the ease with which international marketing can be conducted has been enhanced by technologies such as e-mail and video-conferencing. In Chapter 10 we will see that a whole new industry, called customer relationship management (CRM), has grown up in recent years; this uses database technologies to enable companies to improve their relationships with customers. The Internet is also having a profound effect on how business is conducted, despite the collapse of a wide range of internet-based businesses (so-called 'dotcoms') in the early years of this century. For example, we will see in Chapter 3 how more and more businesses are using the Internet as a medium for purchasing supplies.

Another technological area that is set to provide a wide range of marketing opportunities is that of mobile phones. Ownership in most developed markets is fast reaching saturation point, with all but the very young and very old already in possession of a mobile phone. Consequently, in an effort to boost sales, manufacturers are focusing on dimensions like fashion and innovation.[53] New phones are smaller and sleeker in design, and innovations like 3G (third generation) technology will allow users to have access to the Internet and enable them to download music and video on to their phones. Some of the marketing possibilities of using mobile phones being considered are described in e-Marketing 2.1 and discussed in more detail in Chapter 10.

The microenvironment

In addition to the broad macroeconomic forces discussed above, a number of microeconomic variables also impact on the opportunities and threats facing the organization. We shall introduce each of these in turn, and deal with them in greater detail throughout the book.

Customers

As we saw in Chapter 1, customers are at the centre of the marketing effort and we shall examine customer behaviour in great detail in the next chapter. Ultimately customers determine the success or failure of the business. The challenge for the company is to identify unserved market needs and to get and retain a customer base. This requires a sensitivity to changing needs in the marketplace and also having the adaptability to take advantage of the opportunities that present themselves.

Distributors

Some companies, such as mail-order houses, online music companies and service providers, distribute directly to their customers. Most others use the services of independent wholesalers and retailers. As we shall see in Chapter 11, these middlemen provide many valuable services, such as making products available to customers where and when they want them, breaking bulk and providing specialist services such as merchandising and installation. Developments in distribution can have a significant impact on the performance of manufacturers. For example, the growing power of grocery retailers such as Wal-Mart and Tesco has had a significant impact on the profitability of consumer foods manufacturers.

Suppliers

Not only are the fortunes of companies influenced by their distributors, they can also be influenced by their suppliers. Supply chains can be very simple or very complex. For example, the average car contains about 15,000 components. As a result the car industry is served by three tiers of suppliers. Tier-one companies make complete systems such as electrical systems or braking systems. They are served by tier-two suppliers, who might produce cables, for example, and are in turn supplied by tier-three suppliers who produce basic commodities such as plastic shields or metals. Just like distributors, powerful suppliers can extract profitability from an industry by restricting the supply of essential components and forcing the price up.

Competitors

Levels of competition vary from industry to industry. In some instances, there may be just one or two major players as is often the case in formerly state-run industries like energy or telecommunications. In others, where entry is easy or high profit potential exists, competition can be intense. For example, when Perrier launched its mineral water in response to a growing concern with healthy living, it spawned a rash of competitors in a rapidly growing industry. For example, the bottled water market in Ireland grew from 20 million litres in 1993 to 110 million litres in 2002.[57] To be successful in the marketplace, companies must not only be able to meet customer needs but must also be able to gain a differential advantage over competitors. We will examine the issue of competition in greater detail in Chapter 12.

Environmental scanning

The practice of monitoring and analysing a company's marketing environment is known as **environmental scanning**. Two key decisions that management need to make are what to scan and how to organize the activity. Clearly, in theory, every event in the world has the potential to affect a company's operations, but a scanning system that could cover every conceivable force would be unmanageable. The first task, then, is to define a feasible range of forces that require monitoring. These are the 'potentially relevant environmental forces' that have the most likelihood of affecting future business prospects— such as, for example, changes in the value of the yen for companies doing business in Japan. The second prerequisite for an effective scanning system is to design a system that provides a fast response to events that are only partially predictable, emerge as surprises and grow very rapidly. This has become essential due to the increasing turbulence of the marketing environment.

In general, environmental scanning is conducted by members of the senior management team, though some large corporations will have a separate unit dedicated to the task. The most appropriate organizational arrangement for scanning will depend on the unique circumstances facing a firm. A judgement needs to be made regarding the costs and benefits of each alternative. The size and profitability of the company and the perceived degree of environmental turbulence will be factors that impinge on this decision. Environmental scanning provides the essential informational input to create strategic fit between strategy, organization and the environment (see Figure 2.3). Marketing strategy should reflect the

environment even if this requires a fundamental reorganization of operations.

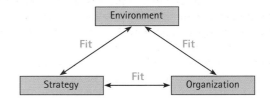

Figure 2.3 Strategic marketing fit

Companies respond in various ways to environmental change (see Figure 2.4).

Ignorance

If environmental scanning is poor, companies may not realize that salient forces are affecting their future prospects. They therefore continue as normal, ignorant of the environmental issues that are threatening their existence, or the opportunities that could be seized. No change is made.

Delay

The next response, once the force is understood, is to delay action. This can be the result of bureaucratic decision processes that stifle swift action. The slow response by Swiss watch manufacturers to the introduction of digital watches, for example, was thought, in part, to be caused by the bureaucratic nature of their decision-making. 'Marketing myopia' can slow response through management being product-focused rather than customer-focused. Management may believe that there will always be a need for made-to-measure suits, for example, and therefore delay responding to the growing popularity of casual wear. A third source of delay is 'technological myopia'; this

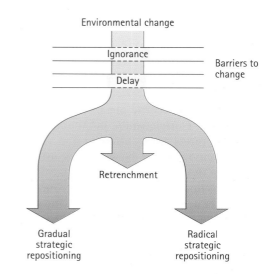

Figure 2.4 Responses to environmental change

occurs where a company fails to respond to technological change. The example of Pollitt and Wigsell—a steam engine manufacturer that was slow to respond to the emergence of electrical power—illustrates technological myopia. The fourth reason for delay is 'psychological recoil' by managers who see change as a threat and thus defend the status quo. These are four powerful contributors to inertia.

Retrenchment

This sort of response deals with efficiency problems but disregards effectiveness issues. As sales and profits decline, the management cuts costs; this leads to a period of higher profits but does nothing to stem declining sales. Costs (and capacity) are reduced once more, but the fundamental strategic problems remain. Retrenchment policies only delay the inevitable.

Gradual strategic repositioning

This approach involves a gradual, planned and continuous adaptation to the changing marketing environment.

Radical strategic repositioning

If its procrastination results in a crisis, a company could have to consider a radical shift in its strategic positioning—the direction of the entire business is fundamentally changed. For example, the UK clothing retailer Hepworths was radically repositioned as Next, a more upmarket outlet for women's wear targeted at 25–35-year-old working women. Radical strategic repositioning is much riskier than gradual repositioning because, if unsuccessful, the company is likely to fold.

Summary

This chapter has introduced the concept of the marketing environment. In particular, the following issues were addressed.

1. That the marketing environment is comprised of a microenvironment and a macroenvironment.
2. There are five key components of the macroenvironment: economic forces, social forces, legal/political forces, technological forces and physical forces.
3. There are four key components of the microenvironment: suppliers, distributors, customers and competitors.
4. That environmental scanning is the process of examining the company's marketing environment.
5. That firms exhibit a number of different responses to environmental change including no change through ignorance, delay and retrenchment, through to gradual or radical repositioning.

Suggested reading

Bakan, J. (2004) *The Corporation*, London: Constable & Robinson.

Brownlie, D. (1999) Environmental Analysis, in M.J. Baker (ed.) *The Marketing Book*, Oxford: Butterworth-Heinemann.

Economist (2005) The Good Company: A Survey of Corporate Social Responsibility, 22 January, 1–18.

Klein, N. (2000) *No Logo*, London: HarperCollins Publishers.

Schlosser, E. (2001) *Fast Food Nation*, London: Penguin.

Internet exercises

Sites to visit

1   www.walmartyrs.org
     www.mcspotlight.org
     www.ethicalconsumer.org
     www.studentagainstsweatshops.org

Exercise
Discuss the implications for firms of the existence of these organizations.

2   www.pg.com
     www.guidant.com
     www.statoil.com

Exercise

Identify and describe the corporate social responsibility initiatives being undertaken by these companies.

Study questions

1. Assume you are working for either Vodafone in mobile telecommunications or Sony in consumer electronics. Identify the major forces in the environment that are likely to affect your company's prospects in the next five years.

2. Assess the impact of the introduction of the euro on the prospects for motor car dealers.

3. What are the major opportunities and threats to EU businesses arising from the growth of China as one of the world's leading economies?

4. Discuss five business opportunities arising from the growth in the proportion of the population that might be classed as 'time poor and cash rich'.

5. Evaluate the marketing opportunities and threats posed by the growing importance of the socially conscious consumer.

Key terms

marketing environment the actors and forces that affect a company's capability to operate effectively in providing products and services to its customers

microenvironment the actors in the firm's immediate environment that affect its capability to operate effectively in its chosen markets—namely, suppliers, distributors, customers and competitors

macroenvironment a number of broader forces that affect not only the company but the other actors in the environment, e.g. social, political, technological and economic

social responsibility the ethical principle that a person or an organization should be account-able for how its actions might affect the physical environment and the general public

cause-related marketing the commercial activity by which businesses and charities or causes form a partnership with each other to market an image, product or service for mutual benefit

ethics the moral principles and values that govern the actions and decisions of an individual or group

environmental scanning the process of monitoring and analysing the marketing environment of a company

References

1. **Barnes, R.** (2004) Fairtrade Enters the Mainstream, *Marketing*, 4 March, 14–15; **Clegg, A.** (2005) Fairtrade: The Business of Ethics, www.brandchannel.com, 28 February; Doonar, J. (2004) Fighting a Fair Game, *Brand Strategy*, July/August, 24–7; **Moules, J.** (2004) Planting the Seeds of Fair Trade, *Financial Times*, 9 September, 13.

2. **Croft, J.** and **J. Moules** (2005) Personal Insolvencies Increase 31% to Record Debt, *Financial Times*, 5 February, 3.

3. **Kelly, J.** and **A. Reilly** (2005) Credit Card Debt in Ireland: Recent Trends, *Central Bank Quarterly Bulletin*, 1, 85–100.

4. **Jones, A.** and **J. Mackintosh** (2005) Taking the Hit: European Exporters Find the Dollar's Weakness is Hard to Counter, *Financial Times*, 3 May, 17.

5. **Jones** and **Mackintosh** (2005), op. cit.

6. **Murray Brown, J.** (2005) Waterford's Future is Less than Crystal Clear, *Financial Times*, 16 June, 24.

7. **Sheridan, K.** (2005) The Woes of Waterford, *The Irish Times*, Weekend Review, 19 March, 3.

8. **Friberg, E.G.** (1989) 1992: Moves Europeans are Making, *Harvard Business Review*, May–June, 85–9.

9. **Drucker, P.K.** (1988) Strategies for Survival in Europe in 1993, *McKinsey Quarterly*, Autumn, 41–5.

10. **Lorenz, C.** (1992) Transparent Moves to European Unity, *Financial Times*, 24 July, 16.

11. **Friberg** (1989), op. cit.

12. **Terzano, E.** (2004) A Campaign that Shows its Roots, *Financial Times*, Creative Business, 14 December, 12.

13. **Guido, G.** (1991) Implementing a Pan European Marketing Strategy, *Long Range Planning*, **24** (5), 23–33.

14. **Whitelock, J.** and **E. Kalpaxoglou** (1991) Standardized Advertising for the Single European Market? An Exploratory Study, *European Business Review*, **91** (3), 4–8.

15. **James, D.** (2001) B2–4B Spells Profits, *Marketing News*, 5 November, 1, 13.

16. Haut Conseil de la Population et de la Famille (1989) *Vieillissement et Emploi, Vieillissement et Travail*, Paris: Documentation Française, 31.

17. **Johnson, P.** (1990) Our Ageing Population: The Implications for Business and Government, *Long Range Planning*, 23 (2), 55–62.

18. **Politi, J.** (2003) Ready Money for Feeding Modern Lifestyles, *Financial Times,* 16 January, 24.

19. **Mole, J.** (1990) *Mind Your Manners*, London: Industrial Society.

20. **Writers, F.T.** (1992) Queuing for Flawed Fantasy, *Financial Times*, 13/14 June, 5.

21. **Authers, J.** (2003) US Grapples with 'Language of Love', *Financial Times*, 13 January, 9.

22. **Braddock, K.** (2003) When a Brand Becomes Guilty by Association, *Financial Times*, 17 July, 11.

23. **O'Brien, D.** (2003) Burberry Square, *brand-channel.com*, 16 June.

24. **Sanchanta, M.** (2004) Burberry Tailors a Fresh Image in Japan, *Financial Times*, 15 April, 13.

25. **Tomkins, R.** (2005) The Damage that the Wrong Kind of Customer can do, *Financial Times*, 18 January, 11.

26. For a discussion of some Green marketing issues, see **Pujari, D.** and **G. Wright** (1999) Integrating Environmental Issues into Product Development: Understanding the Dimensions of Perceived Driving Forces and Stakeholders, *Journal of Euromarketing*, 7 (4), 43–63; **Peattie, K.** and **A. Ringter** (1994) Management and the Environment in the UK and Germany: A Comparison, *European Management Journal*, 12 (2), 216–25.

27. **Carter, M.** (2005) Ethical Business Practices Come into Fashion, *Financial Times*, 19 April, 14.

28. **Elkington, J.** (2001) *The Chrysalis Economy*, Capstone.

29. **Hegarty, S.** (2005) So Who is Leo Hairy Camel?, *Irish Times*, Weekend Review, 2 April, 3.

30. **Anderson, P.** (1999) Give and Take, *Marketing Week*, 26 August, 39–41.

31. **Berkowitz, E.N., R.A. Kerin, S.W. Hartley** and **W. Rudelius** (2000) *Marketing*, Boston, MA: McGraw-Hill.

32. **Hunt, B.** (2005) Companies With Their Reputations on the Line, *Financial Times*, 24 January, 10.

33. Business Portrait (1997) Early Riser Reaches the Top, *European*, 17–23 April, 32.

34. **Anonymous** (2004) Big Mac's Makeover, *Economist*, 16 October, 67–8.

35. **Buckley, N.** (2003) Eyes on the Fries: Will New Products, Restaurant Refits and a Marketing Overhaul Sustain the Golden Arches?, *Financial Times*, 29 August, 15.

36. **Buckley, N.** (2004) Chains are Back in Shape, *Financial Times*, 16 June, 35.

37. **Guerrera, F.** (2003) Brussels Targets the Biggest Props, *Financial Times*, 6 January, 8.

38. **Anonymous** (2005) Still Not Loved, Now Not Envied, *Economist*, 25 June, 56.

39. **Murray, S.** (2004) Big Names Seek the Safety of Camouflage, *Financial Times*, 5 February, 11.

40. **Silverman, G.** (2004) America's New Brand of Anger and Resentment, *Financial Times*, 24 June, 15.

41. **Tomkins, R.** (2003) As Hostility Towards America Grows, Will the World Lose its Appetite for Coca-Cola, McDonald's and Nike?, *Financial Times*, 27 March, 19.

42. **Knight, R.** (2004) Tough New Regime for Savings Industry, *Financial Times*, 30 November, 5.

43. **Klein, N.** (2000) *No Logo*, London: HarperCollins Publishers.

44. **Cookson, C.** (1992) It Grows on Trees, *Financial Times*, 12 August, 8.

45. **Heavens, A.** (2003) Sanyo Tells Corny Tale of Disposable CDs, *Financial Times*, 25 November, 12.

46. **Anonymous** (2001) What's the Bottom Line on Nappies?, *Derby Evening Telegraph*, 20 April, 10.

47. **Chandiramani, R.** (2003) Naty Breaks into Sanpro Market with Green Range, *Marketing*, 13 March, 1.

48. **Houlder, V.** (2001) Green Nappy from a Green Entrepreneur, *Financial Times*, 4 January, 15.

49. **Muhlbacker, H., M. Botschen** and **W. Beutelmeyer** (1997) The Changing Consumer in Austria, *International Journal of Research in Marketing*, 14, 309–20.

50. See **Wilkstrom, S.R.** (1997) The Changing Consumer in Sweden, *International Journal of Research in Marketing*, 14, 261–75; **Laaksonen, P., M. Laaksonen** and **K. Moller** (1998) The Changing Consumer in Finland, *International Journal of Research in Marketing*, 15, 169–80.

51. **Harvey, F.** (2004) PC Makers Set to Face Costs of Recycling, *Financial Times*, 4 February, 13.

52. **Birchall, J.** (2005) US Supermarket Encourages Shoppers to Keep in Touch, *Financial Times*, 13 July, 22.

53. **Roberts, D.** (2001) An Industry in Search of a Ringing Endorsement, *Financial Times* Survey: Telecoms, 21 November, 1.

54. **Anonymous** (2004) *Bliss* to Launch Valentine's SMS Promotion, *Precision Marketing*, 13 February, 2.

55. **Budden, R.** (2003) Send, Send, Send, *Financial Times, Creative Business*, 6 May, 9.

56. **Tran, T.** (2003) How to Tap into the Teen Market, *Advertising and Marketing to Children*, July–September, 31–8.

57. **Pocock, I.** (2003) Clearly a Better Glass of Water, *Irish Times*, 21 January, 15.

Turn the page for a Case Study on Playing to a new beat

Case 2 Playing to a new beat: marketing in the music industry

Good old fashioned rock 'n' roll could be dead. If a mobile phone ringtone in the shape of the vocalizations of the animated Crazy Frog dominates the billboard charts for months on end, then it could well signal the death knell for the industry, and how it operates. If this ubiquitous amphibian's aurally annoying song, converted from a mobile phone ringtone, outsold even mainstay acts such as Oasis and Coldplay, why should music companies invest millions in cultivating fresh musical talent, hoping for them to be the next big thing, when their efforts can be beaten by basic synthesizer music? The industry is facing a number of challenges that it has to address, such as strong competition, piracy, changing delivery formats, increasing cost pressures, demanding primadonnas and changing customer needs. Gone are the days when music moguls were reliant on sales from albums alone, now the industry trawls for revenue from a variety of sources, such as ringtones, merchandising, concerts, and music DVDs, leveraging extensive back catalogues, and music rights from advertising, movies and TV programming.

The music industry is in a state of flux at the moment. The cornerstone of the industry—the singles chart—has been facing terminal decline since the mid-1990s. Some retailers are now not even stocking singles due to this marked freefall. Some industry commentators blame the Internet as the sole cause, while others point to value differences between the price of an album and the price of a single as too much. Likewise, some commentators criticize the heavy pre-release promotion of new songs, the targeting of ever-younger markets by pop acts, and the explosion of digital television music channels as root causes of the single's demise. The day when the typical record buyer browses through rows of shelves for a much sought-after band or song on a Saturday afternoon may be a thing of the past.

Long-term success stories for the music industry are increasingly difficult to develop. The old tradition of A&R (which stands for 'Artists & Repertoire') was to sign, nurture and develop musical talent over a period of years. The industry relied on continually feeding the system with fresh talent that could prove to be the next big thing and capture the public imagination. Now corporate short-term thinking has enveloped business strategies. If an act fails to be an immediate hit, the record label drops them. The industry is now characterized by an endless succession of one-hit wonders and videogenic artists churning out classic cover songs, before vanishing off the celebrity radar. Four large music labels now dominate the industry (see Table C2.1), and have emerged through years of consolidation. The 'big four' major labels have the marketing clout and resources to invest heavily in their acts, providing them with expensive videos, publicity tours and PR coverage. This clout allows their acts to get vital radio airplay and video rotation on dedicated TV music channels. Major record labels have even been accused of offering cash inducements or gifts to radio stations and DJs in an effort to get their songs on playlists. This activity is known in the industry as 'radio payola'.

Consumers have flocked to the Internet, to download, to stream, to 'rip and burn' copyrighted music material. The digital music revolution has changed the way people listen, use and obtain their favourite music. The very business model that has worked for decades, buying a single or album from a high-street store, may not survive. Music executives are left questioning whether the Internet will kill the music business altogether. The traditional music industry business model has been fundamentally altered. According to the British Phonographic Industry (BPI), it estimated that 8 million people in the UK are downloading music from the Internet—92 per cent of them doing so illegally. In 2005 alone, sales of CD singles fell by a colossal 23 per cent. To put the change into context, the sales of digital singles increased by 746.6 per cent in 2005. Consumers are

Table C2.1 The 'big four' music labels

Universal Music	Sony BMG
The largest music label, with 26 per cent of global music market share; artists on its roster include U2, Limp Bizkit, Mariah Carey and No Doubt	Merger consolidated its position; artists on its roster include Michael Jackson, Lauryn Hill, Westlife, Dido, Outkast and Christina Aguilera
Warner Music	**EMI**
Third biggest music group; artists on its roster include Madonna, Red Hot Chili Peppers and REM	Artists on its roster include the Rolling Stones, Coldplay, Norah Jones, Radiohead and Robbie Williams

buying their music through different channels and also listening to their favourite songs through digital media rather than through standard CD, cassette or vinyl. The emergence of MP3 players, particularly the immensely popular Apple iPod, has transformed the music landscape even further. Consumers are now downloading songs electronically from the Internet, and storing them on these digital devices or burning them onto rewritable CDs.

Glossary of online music jargon

Streaming: Allows the user to listen to or watch a file as it is being simultaneously downloaded. Radio channels utilize this technology to transmit their programming on the Internet.

'Rip n burn': Means downloading a song or audio file from the Internet and then burning the song on to a rewritable CD or DVD.

MP3 format: MP3 is a popular digital music file format. The sound quality is similar to that of a CD. The format reduces the size of a song to one-tenth of its original size allowing for it to be transmitted quickly over computer networks.

Apple iPod: The 'digital jukebox' that has transformed the fortunes of the pioneer PC maker. By the end of 2004 Apple is expected to have sold close on 5 million units of this ultra-hip gadget. It was the 'must-have item' for 2003. The standard 20GB iPod player can hold around 5000 songs. Other hardware companies, such as Dell & Creative Labs, have launched competing devices. These competing hardware brands can retail for less than £75.

Peer-to-peer networks (P2P): These networks allow users to share their music libraries with other net users. There is no central server, rather individual computers on the Internet communicating with one another. A P2P program allows users to search for material, such as music files, on other computers. The program lets users find their desired music files through the use of a central computer server. The system works like this: a user sends in a request for a song; the system checks where on the Internet that song is located; that song is downloaded directly onto the computer of the user who made the request. The P2P server never actually holds the physical music files—it just facilitates the process.

The Internet offers a number of benefits to music shoppers, such as instant delivery, access to huge music catalogues and provision of other rich multimedia material like concerts or videos, access to samples of tracks, cheaper pricing (buying songs for 99p rather than an expensive single) and, above all, convenience. On the positive side, labels now have access to a wider global audience, possibilities of new revenue streams and leveraging their vast back catalogues. It has diminished the bargaining power of large retailers, it is a cheaper distribution medium than traditional forms and labels can now create value-laden multimedia material for consumers. However, the biggest problem is that of piracy and copyright theft. Millions of songs are being downloaded from the Internet illegally with no payment to the copyright holder. The Internet allows surfers to download songs using a format called 'MP3', which doesn't have inbuilt copyright protection, thus allowing the user to copy and share with other surfers with ease. Peer to peer (P2P) networks such as Kazaa and Grokster have emerged and pose an even deadlier threat to the music industry—they are enemies that are even harder to track and contain. Consumers can easily source and download illegal copyrighted material with considerable ease using P2P networks (see accompanying box).

P2P Networks used for file sharing

Kazaa

Gnutella

Grokster

Morpheus

eDonkey

Imesh

Bearshare

WinMX

A large number of legal download sites have now been launched, where surfers can either stream their favourite music or download it for future use in their digital music libraries. This has been due to the rapid success of small digital media players such as the Apple iPod. The legal downloading of songs has grown exponentially. A la carte download services and subscription-based services are the two main business models. Independent research reveals that the Apple's iTunes service has over 70 per cent of the market. Highlighting this growing phenomenon of the Internet as an official channel of distribution, new music charts are now being created, such as the 'Official Download Chart'. Industry sources suggest that out of a typical 99p download, the music label gets 65p, while credit card companies get 4p, leaving the online music store with 30p per song download. These services may fundamentally eradicate the concept of an album, with customers selecting only a handful of their favourite songs rather than entire standard 12 tracks. These prices are having knock-on consequences for the pricing of physical formats. Consumers are now looking for a more value-laden music product rather than simply 12 songs with an album cover. Now they are expecting behind the scenes access to their favourite group, live concert footage and other content-rich material.

Big Noise Music is an example of one of the legitimate downloading sites running the OD2 system. The site is different in that for every £1 download, 10p of the revenue goes to the charity Oxfam.

The music industry is ferociously fighting back by issuing lawsuits for breach of copyright to people who are illegally downloading songs from the Internet using P2P software. The recording industry has started to sue thousands of people who illegally share music using P2P. They are issuing warnings to net surfers who are using P2P software that their activities are being watched and monitored. Instant Internet messages are being sent to those who are suspected of offering songs illegally. In addition, they have been awarded court orders so that Internet providers must identify people who are heavily involved in such activity. The music industry is also involved heavily in issue advertising campaigns, by promoting anti-piracy websites such as www.pro-music.org to educate people on the industry and the impact of piracy on artists. These types of public awareness campaign are designed to illustrate the implications of illegal downloading.

Small independent music labels view P2P networks differently, seeing them as vital in achieving publicity and distribution for their acts. These firms simply do not have the promotional resources or distribution clout of the 'big four' record labels. They see P2P networks as an excellent viral marketing tool, creating buzz about a song or artist that will ultimately lead to wider mainstream and commercial appeal. The Internet is used to create communities of fans who are interested in their music, providing them access to free videos and other material. It allows independent acts the opportunity to distribute their music to a

Table C2.2 The major legitimate online music providers

Name	Details	Pricing
Apple iTunes	Huge catalogue of over 750,000 songs; compatible with Apple's very hip iPod system; offers free single of the week and other exclusive material	79p per track, £7.99 per album
Napster	The now-legitimate website offers over 1,000,000 songs; offers several streaming radio stations too	Subscription based—subscribers pay £9.99 a month to stream any of the catalogue, plus another 99p to download on to a CD
Sony Connect	Over 300,000 songs from the major labels; excellent sound quality but compatible only with Sony products due to proprietary file formats	From 80p–£1.20 per track, and £8–£10 per album
Bleep.com	Small catalogue of 15,000 songs with a focus on independent music labels; high-quality downloads due to media files used	99p per track, £6.99 per album
Wippit	UK-based service; 175,000 songs to download; gives a selection of free tracks every month	From 30p to £1 to download; alternatively, users can subscribe to the service for £50 a year to gain access to 60,000 songs
OD2 System, used by: Mycokemusic.com HMV.com MSN.com TowerRecords.co.uk Big Noise Music	These online sites use the OD2 system for music downloads; they look after encryption, hosting, royalty management and the entire e-commerce system; provides access to nearly 350,000 tracks from 12,000 recording artists	Varying product bundles, typically 99p for track download, and 1p for streaming

wider audience, building up their fan base through word of mouth. Savvy unsigned bands have sophisticated websites showcasing their work, and offering free downloads as well as opportunities for audiophiles to purchase their tunes. Alternatively major labels still see that to gain success one has to get a video on rotation on MTV and that this in turn encourages greater airplay on radio stations, ultimately leading to increased purchases.

For traditional music retailers the retailing landscape is getting more competitive, with multiple channels of distribution emerging due to the Internet and large supermarket chains now selling music CDs. Supermarkets are becoming one of the main channels of distribution through which consumers buy music. These supermarkets are stocking only a limited number of the best-selling music titles, limiting the number of distribution outlets for new and independent music. Only charts hits and greatest hits collections will make it on to the shelves of such outlets.

Now consumers can buy albums from traditional Internet retailers such as Amazon.com, and also on websites that utilize access to grey markets such as cdwow.co.uk, as well as through legitimate download retailers. This has left traditional music retail operations with a severe conundrum: how can they entice more shoppers into their stores? The accompanying box highlights where typical shoppers source their music at present.

Where do people buy their music?

Music stores (*like HMV, Virgin Megastore*)	16 per cent
Chains (*like Woolworths, WHSmith*)	16 per cent
Supermarkets (*like Tesco, Asda*)	21.6 per cent
Mail order	3.9 per cent
Internet sales (*like Amazon.com*)	7 per cent
Downloads	Not yet measured

Source: British Phonographic Industry

The issue of online music retailers using parallel importing, such as CDWOW (www.cdwow.co.uk) is a concern. These retailers are taking advantage of worldwide price discrepancies for legitimate music CDs, sourcing them in low-cost countries like Hong Kong and exporting them into European countries. Prices for music in these markets are considerably lower than the market that they are exporting to, and

they don't even charge for international delivery. Yet technological improvements have led to revenue opportunities for the industry. Development such as online radio, digital rights management, Internet streaming, tethered downloads (locked to PC), downloads (burnable, portable), in-store kiosks, ringtones, mobile message clips, video clips and games soundtracks are great potential revenue sources. In an effort to unlock this potential the major labels have digitized their entire back catalogues. In the wake of these dramatic environmental changes the industry has had to radically adapt. The 'big four' music labels are consolidating even further, developing a digital music strategy, and re-evaluating their entire traditional business model. Mobile phones are seen as the next primary channel of distribution for digital music. High penetration levels in the market for mobile phones and the inherent mobility advantages make this the next crucial battlefield for the music industry.

The Internet may emerge as the primary channel of distribution for music, and the music industry is going to have to adapt to these changes. The move towards the online distribution of entertainment is still in its infancy, with more investment into the telecommunications infrastructure, such as greater Internet access, increased access to broadband technology, 3G technology and changing the way people shop for music will undoubtedly take time. The digital revolution will fundamentally change the way people purchase and consume their musical preferences. In forthcoming years the digital format will become more mainstream, leading to a proliferation of channels of distribution for music. However, as with most new channels or technology, catalogue shopping never surpassed regular high-street shopping, Internet shopping likewise, and 'video never really killed the radio star' . . . but will the Internet kill the record store?

Questions

1. Discuss the micro and macro forces that are affecting the music industry.
2. Based on this analysis, what strategic options would you recommend for both music publishers and music retailers in the current marketing environment?
3. Discuss the advantages and disadvantages associated with online distribution from a music label's perspective.

This case was written by Conor Carroll, Lecturer in

Marketing, University of Limerick. Copyright ©
Conor Carroll (2005). The material in the case has
been drawn from a variety of published sources.

When you have read this chapter log on to the Online
Learning Centre for *Foundations of Marketing* at
www.mcgraw-hill.co.uk/textbooks/jobber where you'll
find multiple choice test questions, links and extra online
study tools for marketing.

CHAPTER 3

UNDERSTANDING CUSTOMER BEHAVIOUR

Learning Objectives

By the end of this chapter you will understand:

1 the dimensions of customer behaviour, who buys, how they buy and the choice criteria used

2 the differences between consumer and organizational buyer behaviour

3 the main influences on consumer behaviour—the buying situation, personal and external influences

4 the main influences on organizational buying behaviour—the buy class, product type and purchase importance

5 the marketing implications of the various dimensions of consumer behaviour.

Tattoos become mainstream

Once the preserve of sailors, convicts and bikers, tattoos have now become commonplace. The art of tattooing is over 5000 years old but has only recently become fashionable again, driven by celebrities such as David Beckham, Robbie Williams, Julia Roberts, Britney Spears and the former Spice Girls. They are almost as important a fashion item for young ladies as Gucci bags or Dior sunglasses. With the advent of hipster jeans, many women want designs placed at the base of their spine so that they will show just above the waistband. Similarly, the popularity of cropped trousers has spawned a trend for small tattoos on the foot or ankle. Even Barbie now has a tattoo of a butterfly on her stomach and comes with temporary tattoos for the owner to add.

Chinese symbols are currently many people's first choice, along with Arabic writing for men and roses for women, but the most fashionable designs are based on Hindi lettering, popularized by David Beckham. Tattoos have become such a fashion statement that some people are asking for Louis Vuitton, Chanel and Gucci tattoos as well as the Nike 'swoosh'. Some of the more unusual requests have included the reproduction of labels from favourite wine and champagne bottles.

The number of tattoo parlours in Britain has reported to have soared from 300 five years ago to more than 1500 today. In addition, mainstream companies like Selfridges department store have picked up on the craze. As part of a month-long promotion entitled Body Craze, Selfridges asked Metal Morphosis, a Soho tattoo and piercing parlour, to open a concession in its Oxford Street branch. The promotion, which is part of a trend by some retailers to stage 'experiences', also included the supermodel Elle Macpherson and nude members of the public posing in elevators. During the promotion, more than 400 people were tattooed, leading Selfridges to decide that the parlour should become a permanent fixture. Many of the customers who took advantage of the promotion were middle-aged and unlikely to be those who would have visited a traditional tattoo parlour.

Of course a major problem for consumers is that now that tattooing has become mainstream, it risks losing its appeal and becoming subject to the whims of fashion. And those celebrities and others who have had the names of their partners tattooed on their bodies can often find that the tattoo lasts longer than the relationship, leading to the difficult and expensive task of having it removed.[1]

In Chapter 1 we saw that an in-depth knowledge of customers is a prerequisite of successful marketing; indeed, understanding customers is the cornerstone upon which the marketing concept is built. How customers behave can never be taken for granted and new trends emerge all the time, such as the demand for tattoos described above. There are a variety of influences on the purchasing habits of customers and these are constantly changing and evolving. As a result, products that may only recently have been seen as 'must haves' quickly go out of fashion to be replaced by something else. Successful marketing requires a great sensitivity to these subtle drivers of behaviour and an ability to anticipate how they influence demand. In this chapter we will explore the nature of customer behaviour; we will examine the frameworks and concepts used to understand customers; and we will review the dimensions we need to consider in order to grasp the nuances of customer behaviour and the influences upon it.

The dimensions of customer behaviour

At the outset, a distinction needs to be drawn between the purchases of private consumers and those of organizations. Most consumer purchasing is individual, such as the decision to purchase a chocolate bar on seeing an array of confectionery at a newsagent's counter, though it may also be by a group such as a household. In contrast, in organizational or business-to-business (B2B) purchasing there are three major types of buyer. First, the industrial market concerns those companies that buy products and services to help them produce other goods and services. Industrial goods include raw materials, components and capital goods such as machinery. Second, the reseller market comprises organizations that buy products and services to resell. Mail-order companies, retailers and supermarkets are examples of resellers. Third, the government market consists of government agencies that buy products and services to help them carry out their activities. Purchases for local authorities and defence are examples of this.

Understanding the behaviour of this array of customers requires answers to the following questions (see Figure 3.1).

- *Who* is important in the buying decision?
- *How* do they buy?
- *What* are their choice criteria?
- *Where* do they buy?
- *When* do they buy?

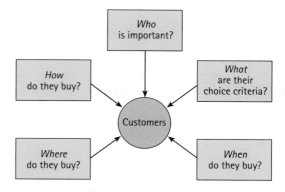

Figure 3.1 Understanding customers: the key questions

The answers to these questions can be derived from personal contact with customers and, increasingly, by employing marketing research, which we will examine in Chapter 4. In this chapter we examine consumer and organizational buyer behaviour. The structure of this analysis will be based on the first three questions: who, how and what. These are often the most intractable aspects of customer behaviour; it is usually much more straightforward to answer the last two questions, about where and when customers buy.

Who buys?

Blackwell, Miniard and Engel[2] describe five roles in the buying decision-making process.

1 *Initiator:* the person who begins the process of considering a purchase. Information may be gathered by this person to help the decision.
2 *Influencer:* the person who attempts to persuade others in the group concerning the outcome of the decision. Influencers typically gather information and attempt to impose their choice criteria on the decision.
3 *Decider:* the individual with the power and/or financial authority to make the ultimate choice regarding which product to buy.
4 *Buyer:* the person who conducts the transaction. The buyer calls the supplier, visits the store, makes the payment and effects delivery.
5 *User:* the actual consumer/user of the product.

Multiple roles in the buying group may, however, be assumed by one person. In a toy purchase, for example, a girl may be the initiator and attempt to influence her parents, who are the deciders. The girl may be influenced by her sister to buy a different brand. The buyer may be one of the parents, who visits the store to purchase the toy and brings it back

Exhibit 3.1 This advertisement for Cow & Gate Growing Up Milk is aimed at parents who are the buyers rather than the users

to the home. Finally, both children may be users of the toy. Although the purchase was for one person, in this example marketers have four opportunities—two children and two parents—to affect the outcome of the purchase decision. For example, Samsung has sponsored the European Computer Gaming Championships in a bid to build its brand image among young people, who are known to have a significant influence on the purchasing behaviour of adults when it comes to buying technology. While it does not have a very favourable image among over-40s, the company's research has found that positive attitudes towards the Samsung brand have increased by 25 per cent in the 18–29 age group since it changed its marketing focus.[3]

The role of children in influencing household purchasing is very significant. The expression 'pester power' is often used by advertisers to describe the process by which children subtly influence or more overtly nag their parents into buying a product. Young children are very brand aware. Studies show that over 80 per cent of children aged between three and six recognize the Coca-Cola logo.[4] Tweens—that is, children in the 8–12 age group—are estimated to

account for some 60 per cent of all household expenditure.[5] For example, as over two-thirds of households buying a new car are influenced in the decision by their children, Toyota in Australia has very successfully included chickens, puppies and kittens in its advertising[6].

The roles played by the different household members vary with the type of product under consideration and the stage of the buying process. For example, in the USA men now make more than half of their family's purchase decisions in food categories such as cereals, food and soft drinks[7] while women, however, still purchase the majority of men's sweaters, socks and sports shirts.[8] Women also have traditionally been big purchasers of male grooming products, though this is a trend that is clearly changing, as shown in Marketing in Action 3.1.

Men were faster to adopt the Internet as a shopping medium, but have recently been surpassed by women (see e-Marketing 3.1). Also, the respective roles may change as the purchasing process progresses. In general, one or other partner will tend to dominate the early stages, then joint decision-making tends to occur as the process moves towards final purchase.

Exhibit 3.2 Oral B's Stages toothbrushes is aimed at the children's market

Joint decision-making is more common when the household consists of two income-earners.

Most organizational buying tends to involve more than one individual and is often in the hands of a decision-making unit (DMU), or **buying centre** as it is sometimes called. This is not necessarily a fixed entity and may change as the **decision-making process** continues. Thus a managing director may be involved in the decision that new equipment should be purchased, but not in the decision as to which manufacturer to buy it from. The marketing task is to identify and reach the key members in order to convince them of the product's worth. This can be a difficult task as the 'gatekeeper' is an additional role in organizational buying. Gatekeepers are people like secretaries who may allow or prevent access to a key DMU member. The salesperson's task is to identify a person from within the decision-making unit who is a positive advocate and champion of the supplier's product. This person (or 'coach') should be given all the information needed to win the arguments that may take place within the decision-making unit.

The marketing implications of understanding who buys lie within the areas of marketing communications and segmentation. An identification of the roles played within the buying centre is a prerequisite for targeting persuasive communications. As we saw earlier, the person who actually uses or consumes the product may not be the most influential member of the buying centre, nor the decision-maker. Even when they do play the predominant role, communication to other members of the buying centre can make sense when their knowledge and opinions act as persuasive forces during the decision-making process.

Marketing in Action: The male grooming market booms

Outer beauty has long been seen to be a female preoccupation, but now it seems men are also becoming image-conscious, spawning a rapid growth in the male grooming market. Euromonitor reports that, in 2003, sales of male grooming products grew by 14.4 per cent, with almost one-quarter of total sales being generated in the USA. The demand for these products shows no sign of abating, with the market forecast to grow by a further 21.1 per cent between 2003 and 2008.

This radical shift in male attitudes towards grooming can be attributed to a number of factors. It appears that being part of an image-conscious society, where youth and beauty equate with success, has placed pressure on men to look good. They certainly don't have to go too far for inspiration with the dramatic growth in men's magazines, many devoting countless pages to looking good. Today's male icons are also very different from the more rugged, masculine icons of the past. Football international David Beckham epitomizes this new man. Unafraid to flirt with different fashions, including wearing a sarong and hair band, Beckham has made it permissible for men to spend time and effort on looking good. These icons have contributed to the rise of the 'metrosexual' male: an image-conscious heterosexual man with a positive attitude towards grooming. In the USA, the hit male-makeover programme *Queer Eye for the Straight Guy* has also been credited with making male grooming an acceptable mainstream activity.

Consumer product firms are now clambering over each other to get a piece of this very lucrative market. Gillette, Nivea, Avon, L'Oréal, King of Shaves and KoS have all launched affordable skincare ranges aimed specifically at mainstream men, while Clinique and Clarins are positioned at the premium end of the male grooming market. As well as general skincare products, such as face wash, aftershave and moisturizers, many of these ranges also offer products for the treatment of wrinkles, loss of skin firmness, and dark circles and puffiness under the eyes. Indeed it appears to be the anti-ageing products that are driving most of the growth in this market. Tinted moisturizers, fake tan and even make-up are available for the more adventurous man. The users of grooming products are split between younger men, with many desiring a high-fashion look and older men, who tend to be more interested in products that help to give a more youthful, healthy appearance. With the younger segment being the main user demographic, this market looks set to grow and grow.

Based on: Foster (2004);[9] Rigby (2004)[10]

e-Marketing: Women on the web

It is a well-known fact that women drive high-street shopping, yet surprisingly, until now, it has been men who have dominated the online shopping arena. One explanation for this is that, traditionally, surfing the net has been predominantly a male pursuit. But things are changing, with women now surpassing men as the biggest online spenders. Research conducted by Verdict, a UK retail consultancy firm, has reported that women spent an average of £495 online in 2003, a staggering 71.4 per cent increase from 2002. This is six times the growth rate of male spending, which was found to be £470 in 2003.

The increasing amount spent by women shopping online, which more accurately reflects their expenditure in bricks-and-mortar establishments, may be a sign that this virtual retail channel is coming of age. Whatever the reason for this growth, it comes as good news to e-tailers, who understand the importance of capturing a share of the female wallet in order to become a dominant channel. Women now account for just under half of online sales, spending more than men on groceries, furniture, health and beauty, clothing, footwear, homewares and books.

Firms wishing to appeal to women will have to invest in really understanding what it is that women want. Research has shown that women are very time conscious online. Therefore, it is important to keep the message simple and relevant. Also, cosmetics and haircare company, Revlon, found that for purchases of its products, women wanted a fun place where they could be creative. In response, it found imaginative ways to offer customized product information to customers. For example, the company's hair-colouring site allows women to experiment with different hair colours. This investment has paid off with traffic doubling on its hair-colouring site. One of the challenges facing online retailers is fully understanding and responding to the unique needs of women.

Based on: Oser (2003);[11] Voyle (2004)[12]

How they buy

The decision-making process for consumers and organizations is shown in Figure 3.2. This diagram shows that buyers typically move through a series of stages, from a recognition that a problem exists to an examination of potential alternatives to a purchase and the subsequent evaluation of the purchase. Organizational buying is typically more complex and may involve more stages. However, the exact nature of the process will depend on the buying situation. In certain situations some stages will be omitted; for example, in a routine rebuy situation such as re-ordering photocopying paper, the purchasing officer is unlikely to pass through the third, fourth and fifth stages of organizational decision-making (search for suppliers and analysis, and evaluation of their proposals). These stages will be bypassed as the buyer, recognizing a need, routinely re-orders from an existing supplier. In general, the more complex the decision and the more expensive the item, the more likely it is that each stage will be passed through and that the process will take more time.

Need recognition/problem awareness

Need recognition may be functional and occur as a result of routine depletion (e.g. petrol, food) or unpredictably (e.g. the breakdown of a car or washing machine). In other situations, consumer purchasing may be initiated by more emotional or psychological needs. For example, the purchase of Chanel perfume is likely to be motivated by status needs rather than by any marginal functional superiority over other perfumes.

Two issues govern the degree to which the buyer intends to resolve the problem: the magnitude of the discrepancy between the desired and present situation, and the relative importance of the problem.[13] A problem may be perceived but if the difference between the current and desired situation is small then the consumer may not be sufficiently motivated to move to the next step in the decision-making process. For example, a person may be considering upgrading their mobile phone from their existing model to a 3G phone. The 3G model may be viewed as desirable, but if the individual considers the difference in benefits to be small then no further purchase activity may take place. Conversely, a large discrepancy may be perceived but the person may not proceed to **infor-mation search** because the relative importance of the problem is small. A person may feel that a 3G model has significant advantages over an existing model, but that the relative importance of these advantages compared with other purchase needs (for example, a personal computer or a holiday) are small. The existence of a need, therefore, may not activate the decision-making process in all cases, due to the existence of 'need inhibitors'.[14] The marketing of mobile phones, with its emphasis on both the design features of new phones and their increased 'cool' factor is geared towards overcoming need inhibitors.

The need recognition stage has a number of implications for marketing. First, marketing managers must be aware of the needs of consumers and the problems they face. Sometimes this awareness may be due to the intuition of the marketer who, for example, spots a new trend (such as the early marketing pioneers who spotted the trend towards fast food, which has underpinned the global success of companies like McDonald's and Kentucky Fried Chicken). Alternatively, marketing research could be used to assess customer problems or needs (see Chapter 4). Second, marketers should be aware of need

inhibitors. For example, in the personal computer industry, fears of not being able to use a computer might suggest developing an easy-to-use computer. Apple Computers provided such opportunities through its 'Test drive a Mac' dealer promotion when it launched the Macintosh. Third, marketing managers should be aware that needs may arise because of stimulation. Their activities, such as developing advertising campaigns and training salespeople to sell product benefits, may act as cues to need arousal.

Not all consumer needs are immediately obvious. Consumers often engage in exploratory consumer behaviour such as being early adopters of new products and retail outlets, taking risks in making product choices, recreational shopping and seeking variety in purchasing products. Such activities can satisfy the need for novel purchase experiences, offer a change of pace and relief from boredom, and satisfy a thirst for knowledge and consumers' curiosity.[15]

Information search

The second stage in the buyer decision-making process will begin when problem recognition is sufficiently strong. In the case of an organizational buying decision, the DMU will draw up a description of

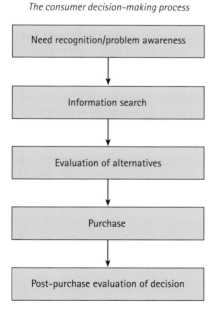

The consumer decision-making process

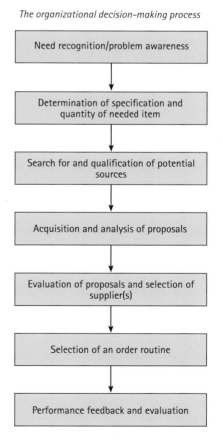

The organizational decision-making process

Figure 3.2 Buying – decision processes

what is required and then begin a search for potential alternatives. When marketers can influence the specification that is drawn up, it may give their company an advantage at later stages in the buying process.

In a consumer situation, the search may be internal or external. Internal search involves a review of relevant information from memory. This review would include potential solutions, methods of comparing solutions, reference to personal experiences and marketing communications. If a satisfactory solution is not found then an external search begins. This involves personal sources such as friends, family, work colleagues and neighbours, and commercial sources such as advertisements and salespeople. Third-party reports such as *Which?* reports, and product testing reports in print and online media may provide unbiased information, and personal experiences may be sought such as asking for demonstrations, and viewing, touching or tasting the product. A great deal of information searching now takes place on the Internet and one of the significant growth businesses has been intelligent agents—that is, websites such as buy.com and mysimon.com, which allow buyers to find out information about a wide range of products and compare online vendors. Many of these sites also provide product reviews and price comparisons free of charge. In addition, sites like Amazon.com provide ongoing product and service recommendations for their customers. The objective of information search is to build up the **awareness set**—that is, the array of brands that may provide a solution to the problem.

Evaluation of alternatives and the purchase

Reducing the awareness set to a smaller group of options for serious consideration is the first step in evaluation. The awareness set passes through a screening filter to produce an **evoked set**: those products or services that the buyer seriously considers before making a purchase. In a sense, the evoked set is a shortlist of options for careful evaluation. The screening process may use different choice criteria from those used when making the final choice, and the number of choice criteria used is often fewer.[16] In an organizational buying situation, each DMU member may use different choice criteria. One choice criterion used for screening may be price. For example, transportation companies whose services are below a certain price level may form the evoked set. Final choice may then depend on criteria such as reliability, reputation and flexibility. The range of choice criteria used by customers will be examined in more detail later in this chapter.

Exhibit 3.3 This Anchor Spreadable advertisement compares its natural ingredients to competitor products, which helps consumers to evaluate alternatives

Consumers' level of involvement is a key determinant of the extent to which they evaluate a brand. Involvement is the degree of perceived relevance and personal importance accompanying the brand choice.[17] When a purchase is highly involving, the consumer is more likely to carry out extensive evaluation. High-involvement purchases are likely to include those incurring high expenditure or personal risk, such as car or home buying. In contrast, low-involvement situations are characterized by simple evaluations about purchases. Consumers use simple choice tactics to reduce time and effort rather than maximize the consequences of the purchase.[18] For example, when purchasing baked beans or breakfast cereals, consumers are likely to make quick choices rather than agonize over the decision. Research by Laurent and Kapferer has identified four factors that affect involvement.[19]

1 *Self-image*: involvement is likely to be high when the decision potentially affects one's self-image. Thus purchase of jewellery, clothing and cosmetic surgery invokes more involvement than choosing a brand of soap or margarine.

2 *Perceived risk*: involvement is likely to be high when the perceived risk of making a mistake is high. The risk of buying the wrong house is much higher than that of buying the wrong chewing gum, because the potential negative

consequences of the wrong decision are higher. Risk usually increases with the price of the purchase.

3 *Social factors*: when social acceptance is dependent upon making a correct choice, involvement is likely to be high. Executives may be concerned about how their choice of car affects their standing among their peers in the same way that peer pressure is a significant influence on the clothing and music tastes of teenagers.

4 *Hedonistic influences*: when the purchase is capable of providing a high degree of pleasure, involvement is usually high. The choice of restaurant when on holiday can be highly involving since the difference between making the right or wrong choice can severely affect the amount of pleasure associated with the experience.

The distinction between high-involvement and low-involvement situations is important because the variations in how consumers evaluate products and brands lead to contrasting marketing implications. The complex evaluation in the high-involvement situation suggests that marketing managers need to provide a good deal of information about the positive consequences of buying. Print media may be appropriate in the high-involvement case since they allow detailed and repeated scrutiny of information. Car advertisements often provide information about the comfort, reliability and performance of the model. The salesforce also has an important role to play in the high-involvement situation by ensuring that the customer is aware of the important attributes of the product and correctly evaluates their consequences.

For low-involvement situations, the evaluation of alternatives is much more rudimentary and many purchases are made simply on impulse. In this case, attempting to gain 'top-of-mind awareness' through advertising, and providing positive reinforcement (e.g. through sales promotion) to gain trial may be more important than providing masses of information about the consequences of buying the brand. Furthermore, as this is of little interest, the consumer is not actively seeking information but is a passive receiver. Consequently, advertising messages should be short with a small number of key points, but with high repetition to enhance learning.[20] Television or radio may be the best media in this instance, since they facilitate the passive reception of messages. Also, they are ideal media for the transmission of short, highly repetitive messages. Advertising of many consumer products such as soap powder, toothpaste, tissue paper and the like follow this format.

Post-purchase evaluation of the decision

The creation of customer satisfaction is the real art of effective marketing. Marketing managers want to create positive experiences from the purchase of their products or services. Nevertheless, it is common for customers to experience some post-purchase concerns; this is known as **cognitive dissonance**. Such concerns arise because of an uncertainty surrounding the making of the right decision. This is because the choice of one product often means the rejection of the attractive features of the alternatives.

There are four ways in which dissonance is likely to be increased: due to the expense of the purchase; when the decision is difficult (e.g. there are many alternatives, many choice criteria, and each alternative offers benefits not available with the others); when the decision is irrevocable; and when the purchaser is inclined to experience anxiety.[21] Thus it is often associated with high-involvement purchases. Shortly after purchase, car buyers may attempt to reduce dissonance by looking at advertisements and brochures for their model, and seeking reassurance from owners of the same model. Rover buyers, say, are more likely to look at Rover advertisements and

Fuel consumption and CO_2 emissions for Ibiza Cupra range, measured in accordance with EU Directive 99/94. Urban: 25.7-40.4mpg / 7.0-11.0 ltr per 100km, Extra urban: 45.6-62.8mpg / 4.5-6.2 ltr per 100km, Combined: 35.3-52.3mpg / 5.4-8.0 ltr per 100km, CO_2: 146-192/km.

Exhibit 3.4 Advertisements like this one for the Seat Ibiza are often targeted at existing customers in order to reduce any potential post-purchase dissonance

avoid Renault or Ford ads. Clearly, advertisements can act as positive reinforcers in such situations, and follow-up sales efforts can act similarly. Car dealers can reduce this 'buyer remorse' by contacting recent purchasers by letter to reinforce the wisdom of their decision and to confirm the quality of their after-sales service.

The outcome of post-purchase evaluation, however, depends on many factors besides this kind of reassurance. The quality of the product or service is obviously a key determinant, and the role of the sales-person acting as a problem solver for the customer rather than simply pushing the highest profit margin product can also help create customer satisfaction, and thereby reduce cognitive dissonance.

What are the choice criteria?

The various attributes (and benefits) a customer uses when evaluating products and services are known as choice criteria. They provide the grounds for deciding to purchase one brand or another. Different members of the buying centre may use different choice criteria. For example, purchasing managers who are judged by the extent to which they reduce purchase expenditure are likely to be more cost con-

scious than production engineers who are evaluated in terms of the technical efficiency of the production process they design. Four types of choice criteria are listed in Table 3.1, which also gives examples of each.

Technical criteria are related to the performance of the product or service, and include reliability, durability, comfort and convenience. Reliability has become particularly important in industrial purchasing. Many buying organizations are unwilling to trade quality for price. For example, Jaguar cars under Sir John Egan moved from a price-orientated purchasing system to one where quality was central, and purchasing managers were instructed to pay more provided the price could be justified in terms of improved quality of components.

Economic criteria concern the cost aspects of purchase and include price, running costs and residual values (e.g. the trade-in value of a car). However, it should not be forgotten that price is only one component of cost for many buying organizations. Increasingly, buyers take into account life cycle costs—which may include productivity savings, maintenance costs and residual values as well as initial purchase price—when evaluating products. Marketers can use life cycle cost analysis to break into an account. By calculating life cycle costs with a buyer, new perceptions of value may be achieved.

Social criteria concern the impact that the purchase makes on the person's perceived relationships with other people, and the influence of social norms on the person. Choosing a brand of trainer may be determined by the need for social belonging. Nike and Adidas recognize the need for their footwear to have 'street cred'. Social norms such as convention and fashion can also be important choice criteria, with some brands being rejected as too unconventional or unfashionable. Products such as watches, phones and computers that, traditionally, were sold on the basis of technical and economic criteria are increasingly marketed on their fashionable attributes.

Personal criteria concern how the product or service relates to the individual psychologically. Emotions are an important element of customer decision-making. The rejection of new-formula Coca-Cola in 1985, despite product tests that showed it to be preferred on taste criteria to traditional Coca-Cola, has been explained in part by emotional reactions to the withdrawal of an old and well-loved brand.[22] Saab ran a two-page advertising campaign that combined technical and economic appeals with an emotional one. The first page was headlined '21 Logical Reasons to Buy a SAAB'. The second page ran the

Table 3.1 Choice criteria used when evaluating alternatives

Type of criteria	Examples
Technical	Reliability Durability Performance Style/looks Comfort Delivery Convenience Taste
Economic	Price Value for money Running costs Residual value Life cycle costs
Social	Status Social belonging Convention Fashion
Personal	Self-image Risk reduction Morals Emotions

headline 'One Emotional Reason'. The first page supported the headline with detailed body copy explaining the technical and economic rationale for purchase. The second page showed a Saab powering along a rain-drenched road. Personal criteria are also important in organizational purchasing. Risk reduction can affect choice decisions since some people are risk averse and prefer to choose 'safe' brands. The IBM advertising campaign that used the slogan 'No one ever got the sack for buying IBM' reflected its importance. Suppliers may be favoured on the basis that certain salespeople are liked or disliked, or due to office politics where certain factions within the company favour one supplier over another.

Marketing managers need to understand the choice criteria being used by customers to evaluate their products and services. Such knowledge has implications for priorities in product design, and the appeals to use in advertising and personal selling.

Influences on consumer behaviour

As noted above (in the discussion of the evaluation of alternatives), not all decisions follow the same decision-making process; nor do all decisions involve the same buying centre or use identical choice criteria. The following is a discussion of the major influences on the process, buying centre and choice criteria in consumer behaviour. They are classified into three groups: the buying situation, personal influences and social influences (see Figure 3.3). Later, we will look at the major influences on organizational buyer behaviour.

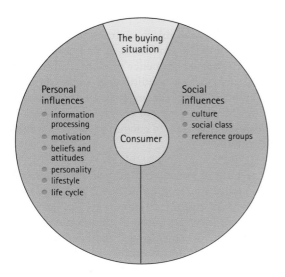

Figure 3.3 Influences on consumer purchasing behaviour

The buying situation

There are three kinds of buying situation: extended problem solving, limited problem solving and habitual problem solving.

The first of these, extended problem solving, involves a high degree of information search, as well as close examination of the alternative solutions using many choice criteria.[23] It is commonly seen in the purchase of cars, video and audio equipment, houses and expensive clothing, where it is important to make the right choice. Information search and evaluation may focus not only on which brand/model to buy, but also on where to make the purchase. The potential for cognitive dissonance is greatest in this buying situation. Extended problem solving is usually associated with three conditions: the alternatives are differentiated and numerous; there is an adequate amount of time available for deliberation; and the purchase has a high degree of involvement.[24] As we noted earlier, marketers can help in this buying situation by providing information-rich communications via advertising and the salesforce.

A great deal of consumer purchases come under the mantle of limited problem solving. The consumer has some experience with the product in question so that information search may be mainly internal through memory. However, a certain amount of external search and evaluation may take place (e.g. checking prices) before the purchase is made. This situation provides marketers with some opportunity to affect the purchase by stimulating the need to conduct a search (e.g. advertising) and reducing the risk of brand switching (e.g. warranties).

Habitual problem solving is what happens when a consumer repeat-buys a product while carrying out little or no evaluation of the alternatives. He or she may recall the satisfaction gained by purchasing a brand, and automatically buy it again. Advertising may be effective in keeping the brand name in the consumer's mind and reinforcing already favourable attitudes towards it.

Personal influences

The six personal influences on consumer behaviour are: information processing, motivation, **beliefs** and **attitudes**, personality, lifestyle and life cycle.

Information processing

The term 'information processing' refers to the process by which a stimulus is received, interpreted, stored in memory and later retrieved.[25] It is therefore the link between external influences including marketing activities and the consumer's decision-making process. Two key aspects of information processing are perception and learning.

Perception is the complicated means by which we select, organize and interpret sensory stimulation into a meaningful picture of the world.[26] Three processes may be used to sort, into a manageable amount, the masses of stimuli that could be perceived. These are **selective attention**, **selective distortion** and **selective retention**. Selective attention is the process by which we screen out those stimuli that are neither meaningful to us nor consistent with our experiences and beliefs. It has obvious implications for advertising as studies have shown that consumers consciously attend to only between 5 and 25 per cent of the advertisements to which they are exposed.[27] A number of factors influence attention. We pay more attention to stimuli that contrast with their background than to stimuli that blend in with it. The name Apple Computer is regarded as an attention-grabbing brand name because it contrasts with the technologically orientated names usually associated with computers. The size, colour and movement of a stimulus also affect attention. Position is also critical; objects placed near the centre of the visual range are more likely to be noticed than those on the periphery. This is why there is intense competition to obtain eye-level positions on supermarket shelves. We are also more likely to notice those messages that relate to our needs (benefits sought)[28] and those that provide surprises (for example, substantial price reductions).

When consumers distort the information they receive according to their existing beliefs and attitudes this is known as selective distortion. We may distort information that is not in accord with our existing views. Methods of doing this include thinking that we misheard the message, and discounting the message source. Consequently it is very important to present messages clearly without the possibility of ambiguity and to use a highly credible source. **Information framing** can affect interpretation. 'Framing' refers to ways in which information is presented to people. Levin and Gaeth[29] asked people to taste minced beef after telling half the sample that it was 70 per cent lean and the other half that it was 30 per cent fat. Despite the fact that the two statements are equivalent, the sample that had the information framed positively (70 per cent lean) recorded higher levels of taste satisfaction. Information framing has obvious implications for advertising and sales messages. The weight of evidence suggests that messages should be positively framed. Colour is another important influence on interpretation. Blue and green are viewed as cool, and evoke feelings of security. Red and yellow are regarded as warm and cheerful. Black is seen as an indication of strength. By using the appropriate colour in pack design it is possible to affect the consumer's feelings about a product.

Selective retention refers to the fact that only a selection of messages may be retained in memory. We tend to remember messages that are in line with existing beliefs and attitudes. Selective retention has a role to play in reducing cognitive dissonance: when reading reviews of a recently purchased car, positive messages are more likely to be remembered than negative ones.

Learning is the result of **information processing**; the term refers to any change in the content or organization of long-term memory.[30] There are numerous ways in which learning can take place. These include conditioning and cognitive learning. **Classical conditioning** is the process of using an established relationship between a stimulus and a response to cause the learning. Thus, in advertising, humour that is known to elicit a pleasant response may be used in the belief that these favourable feelings will be a condition of the product. The energy drink Red Bull uses humour in its advertising to appeal to its target market of young adults.

Operant conditioning differs from classical conditioning in terms of the role and timing of the reinforcement. In this case, reinforcement results from rewards: the more rewarding the response, the stronger the likelihood of the purchase being repeated. Operant conditioning occurs as a result of product trial. The use of free samples is based on the principles of operant conditioning. For example, free samples of a new shampoo are distributed to a large number of households. Because the use of the shampoo is costless it is used (desired response), and because it has desirable properties it is liked (reinforcement) and the likelihood of its being bought is increased. Thus the sequence of events is different for classical and operant conditioning. In the former, by association, liking precedes trial; in the latter, trial precedes liking. A series of rewards (reinforcements) may be used over time to encourage the repeat buying of the product.

The learning of knowledge, and the development of beliefs and attitudes without direct reinforcement is referred to as **cognitive learning**. The learning of two or more concepts without conditioning is known as **rote learning**. Having seen the headline 'Lemsip is for flu attacks', the consumer may remember that Lemsip is a remedy for flu attacks without the kinds of conditioning and reinforcement previously discussed. **Vicarious learning** involves learning from others without direct experience or reward. It is the promise of the reward that motivates. Thus we may learn the type of clothes that attract potential admirers by observing other people. In advertising, the 'admiring glance' can be used to signal approval of the type of clothing being worn or the alcoholic beverage being consumed. We imagine that the same may happen to us if we dress in a similar manner or drink a similar drink. **Reasoning** is a more complex form of cognitive learning and is usually associated with high-involvement situations. For example, some advertising messages rely on the recipient to draw their own conclusions, through reasoning. An anti-Richard Nixon ad campaign in the USA used a photograph of Nixon under the tag-line 'Would You Buy A Used Car From This Man?' to dissuade people from voting for him in the presidential election.

Whatever the type of learning that has taken place, the creation of product positioning is the result of the learning process. The market objective is to create a clear and favourable position in the mind of the consumer.[31] Some marketing companies are beginning to experiment with neuroscience, where brain activity is monitored while consumers are shown pictures of products, people and activities in order to try to better understand information processing and preference formation.[32]

Motivation

To understand **motivation** we must look at the relationship between needs, drives and goals.[33] The basic process involves needs (deprivations) that set drives in motion (deprivations with direction) to accomplish goals (anything that alleviates a need and reduces a drive). Motives can be grouped into five categories, as proposed by Maslow.[34]

1 *Physiological*: the fundamentals of survival, e.g. hunger or thirst.
2 *Safety*: protection from the unpredictable happening in life, e.g. accidents, ill-health.
3 *Belongingness and love*: striving to be accepted by those to whom we feel close and to be an important person to them.
4 *Esteem and status*: striving to achieve a high standing relative to other people; a desire for prestige and a good reputation.
5 *Self-actualization*: the desire for self-fulfilment in achieving what one is capable of for one's own sake, i.e. actualized in what one potentially is.

It is important to understand the motives that drive consumers because it is these that determine **choice criteria**. In Western markets, the first four stages of Maslow's hierarchy have largely been satisfied. Consequently, many brands now emphasize the need for self-actualization in their advertising.

Marketing in Action: *Psychologies* leads in France

Psychologies magazine is the second highest-selling title in France, above *Elle* and *Cosmo* and second only to *Marie-Claire*. Two years ago, it was a niche psychology title with annual sales in the region of 70,000. However, its publishers reckoned that it might have a much broader appeal. In their view, more and more women were fed up with the style and tone of women's magazines, which appeared to reduce their interests to sexuality, cooking and fashion. Their research showed that women considered existing titles to be 'unreal and prescriptive' and were looking for advice, empathy and solutions from their monthly magazine. These developments suggested that many consumers are moving away from a concern with the outer desires and towards a focus on their inner needs.

So *Psychologies* was re-launched providing a title that differed from existing brands by containing articles about health, self-fulfilment and well-being. It proved to be a huge success and quickly built up a base of 1.5 million readers. Its popularity spawned psychology sections within the pages of its competitors, and sections on well-being in mainstream newspapers. At the same time in the USA, several similar titles have been hitting the shelves, such as Oprah Winfrey's magazine *O* and others like *Real Simple* and *Eve*. They all mark a shift in the focus of women's magazines to more closely match changing attitudes in the marketplace. In September 2005, *Psychologies* was launched in the UK.

Based on: Conwy (2003)[35]

Beliefs and attitudes

A thought that a person holds about something is known as a 'belief'. In a marketing context, it is a thought about a product or service on one or more choice criteria. Marketing people are very interested in consumer beliefs because these are related to attitudes. In particular, misconceptions about products can be harmful to brand sales. Duracell batteries were believed by consumers to last three times as long as Ever Ready batteries, but in continuous use they lasted over six times as long. This prompted Duracell to launch an advertising campaign to correct this misconception.

An 'attitude' is an overall favourable or unfavourable evaluation of a product or service. The consequence of a set of beliefs may be a positive or negative attitude towards the product or service. The changing attitudes of women have created new opportunities in the women's magazine business, as shown in Marketing in Action 3.2.

Personality

Just from our everyday dealings with people we can tell that they differ enormously in their personalities. **Personality** is the sum of the inner psychological characteristics of individuals, which lead to consistent responses to their environment.[36] A person may tend

Exhibit 3.5 This easyCruise advertisement will appeal to extrovert, outgoing people

to be warm/cold, dominant/subservient, introvert/extrovert, sociable/a loner, adaptable/inflexible, competitive/co-operative, and so on. For example, luxury goods manufacturers are faced with the challenge of understanding and marketing to today's highly successful young businessmen, sometimes labelled 'alpha males'. While they too like to buy traditional luxury goods such as shoes, suits and gadgets, an increasing proportion of their spending is on the adrenalin buzz of experiences such as racing fast cars, private aircraft and gambling.[37] If we find from marketing research that our product is being purchased by people with certain personality profiles, then our advertising could show people of the same type using the product.

This concept—personality—is also relevant to brands. 'Brand personality' is the characterization of brands as perceived by consumers. Brands may be characterized as 'for young people' (Tommy Hilfiger), 'for winners' (Nike), or 'self-important' (L'Oréal). This is a dimension over and above the physical (e.g. colour) or functional (e.g. taste) attributes of a brand. By creating a brand personality a marketer may generate appeal to people who value that characterization. For example, one of the longest-running fictional brands is James Bond; a variety of car makers and technology companies have attempted to bring his cool, suave and sexy personality into their brands by placing them in Bond movies.

Lifestyle

Lifestyle patterns have been the subject of much interest as far as marketing research practitioners are concerned. The term 'lifestyle' refers to the pattern of living as expressed in a person's activities, interests and opinions. Lifestyle analysis (psychographics) groups consumers according to their beliefs, activities, values and demographic characteristics (such as education and income). For example, the advertising agency Young & Rubicam, identified seven major lifestyle groups that can be found throughout Europe and the USA.

1   *The mainstreamers*: the largest group. Attitudes include conventional, trusting, cautious and family centred. Leisure activities include spectator sports and gardening; purchase behaviour is habitual, brand loyal and in approved stores.

2   *The aspirers*: members of this group are unhappy, suspicious and ambitious. Leisure activities include trendy sports and fashion magazines; they buy fads, are impulse shoppers and engage in conspicuous consumption.

3   *The succeeders*: those that belong to this group are happy, confident, industrious and leaders.

Leisure activities include travel, sports, sailing and dining out. Purchase decisions are based on criteria like quality, status and luxury.

4   *The transitionals*: members of this group are liberal, rebellious, self-expressive and intuitive. They have unconventional tastes in music, travel and movies; and enjoy cooking and arts and crafts. Shopping behaviour tends to be impulsive and to involve unique products.

5   *The reformers*: those that belong to this group are self-confident and involved, have broad interests and are issues orientated. They like reading, cultural events, intelligent games and educational TV. They have eclectic tastes, enjoy natural foods, and are concerned about authenticity and ecology.

6   *The struggling poor*: members of this group are unhappy, suspicious and feel left out. Their interests are in sports, music and television; their purchase behaviour tends to be price based, but they are also looking for instant gratification.

7   *The resigned poor*: those in this group are unhappy, isolated and insecure. Television is their main leisure activity and shopping behaviour is price based, although they also look for the reassurance of branded goods.

Lifestyle analysis has implications for marketing since lifestyles have been found to correlate with purchasing behaviour.[38] A company may choose to target a particular lifestyle group (e.g. the mainstreamers) with a product offering, and use advertising that is in line with the values and beliefs of this group. For example, United Biscuits has brought out the McV a:m range, which is a range of cereal bars, muesli fingers and marmalade muffins designed for people who do not have time to eat a proper breakfast.[39] As information on the readership/viewership habits of lifestyle groups becomes more widely known so media selection may be influenced by lifestyle research.

Increasingly, even very niche lifestyles are the focus of marketing attention. For example, flash mobbing was a recent fad where groups of people in their 20s and 30s, mobilized by e-mail and text messages would gather in public places to engage in unconventional activities such as waving bananas in the air or speaking without the use of the letter 'O'. Record companies have adopted the approach in organizing concerts for some of their artists. Details of the location of the concert are kept secret until the last minute and revealed only to those who register at the Flash Fusion Concerts website.[40]

Life cycle

In addition to the factors we have already examined, consumer behaviour may depend on the 'life stage' people have reached. A person's life cycle stage is of particular relevance since disposable income and purchase requirements may vary according to life cycle stage. For example, young couples with no children may have high disposable income if both work, and may be heavy purchasers of home furnishings and appliances since they may be setting up home. When they have children, their disposable income may fall, particularly if they become a single-income family and the purchase of baby and child-related products increases. At the empty-nester stage, disposable income may rise due to the absence of dependent children, low mortgage repayments and high personal income. This type of person may make an excellent potential target for financial services and holiday companies.

Social influences

The three social influences on consumer behaviour are: culture, social class and reference groups.

Exhibit 3.6 This Storm advertisement has strong reference group imagery

Culture

As we noted in Chapter 2, **culture** refers to the traditions, taboos, values and basic attitudes of the whole society within which an individual lives. It provides the framework within which individuals and their lifestyles develop, and consequently affects consumption. The most notable trend in the past three decades has been the increased internationalization of cultures. Products and services that, previously, may only have been available in certain countries are now commonplace. For example, speciality cuisines like Japanese sushi, Korean barbeque and Cajun food can now be found in major cities throughout the world. Allied to this, though, is the growing domination of some cultures. For example, the successes of American fast-food chains and movie production companies represent a major challenge to smaller, local enterprises in many parts of the world.

Social class

Long regarded as an important determinant of consumer behaviour, in the UK the idea of social class is based largely on occupation (often that of the chief income earner). This is one way in which respondents in marketing research surveys are categorized, and it is usual for advertising media (e.g. newspapers) to give readership figures broken down by social class groupings. However, the use of traditional social class frameworks to explain differences in consumer behaviour has been criticized because certain social class categories may not relate to differences in dis-

posable income (for example, many self-employed manual workers can have very high incomes). The National Statistics Socio-economic Classification system (NS-SEC) in the UK aims to take account of this situation by identifying eight categories of occupation, as shown in Table 3.2. Consumption patterns are likely to vary significantly across these categories. For example, research on the social class of British grocery shoppers has found that the highest proportion of AB (managerial/professional) shoppers frequent Sainsbury's; Asda attracts a significantly higher share of people in lower supervisory and technical occupations; while Tesco's profile mirrored that of society in general.[41] However, some recent consumer trends would suggest that differences across the groups might be blurring, as illustrated in Marketing in Action 3.3.

Reference groups

A group of people that influences an individual's attitude or behaviour is called a **reference group**. Where a product is conspicuous (for example, clothing or cars) the brand or model chosen may have been strongly influenced by what buyers perceive as acceptable to their reference group; this may consist of the family, a group of friends or work colleagues. Some reference groups may be formal (e.g. members of a club or society) while others may be informal (friends with similar interests). Reference groups influence their members by the roles and norms expected of them. An opinion leader is someone in a reference group from whom other members seek

Table 3.2 Social class categories

Analytic class	Operational categories	Occupations
1	Higher managerial and professional occupations	Employers in large organizations; higher managerial and professional
2	Lower managerial and professional occupations	Lower managerial occupations; higher technical and supervisory occupations
3	Intermediate occupations	Intermediate clerical/administrative, sales/service, technical/auxiliary and engineering occupations
4	Small employers and own-account workers	Employers in small, non-professional and agricultural organizations, and own-account workers
5	Lower supervisory and technical occupations	Lower supervisory and lower technical craft and process operative occupations
6	Semi-routine occupations	Semi-routine sales, service, technical, operative, agricultural, clerical and childcare occupations
7	Routine occupations	Routine sales/service, production, technical, operative and agricultural occupations
8	Never worked and long-term unemployed	Never worked, long-term unemployed and students

Marketing in Action: The 'unpredictable' consumer

The largest population groups in the UK by disposable income are groups 2 and 3 in Table 3.2. Traditionally, this group, sometimes known as 'middle England', has been seen as quite homogeneous and easy to reach through a classic marketing mix of good product, competitive price and widespread distribution.

But recent research suggests that many consumers in this group no longer behave in such a predictable manner. They report that they are increasingly frustrated by the homogeneous nature of the mass market and are losing their loyalty to traditional brands and one-stop shops such as Marks & Spencer. As a result, many middle-market consumers are engaged by upmarket brands but are also just as willing to buy cheaper low-brow brands if they feel that the latter meet their needs. As a result, they regularly mix a variety of expensive and cheap brands in an effort to demonstrate their individualism and self-expression. An example would be a consumer who flies on a budget airline but then stays at a five-star hotel.

The motivation to behave in this way seems to be driven by a desire for a greater sense of individualism. Consumers are reacting to the ubiquity of brands; they argue that by buying certain clothing brands, for example, they know that they will see others wearing the same clothes as well. But unlike upmarket customers who want to flaunt their individuality, these customers don't want to be overtly conspicuous. Whether it is the purchase of fashion, food or interiors, the attitude of these consumers appears to be that they are willing to combine expensive and cheap brands in order to create a look that is both 'individual and makes you feel smart'.

What these developments demonstrate is that the marketing practices of today and yesterday may not be suitable tomorrow as how consumers react to and engage with brands is continually evolving. A further challenge for the marketer is that the distinction between 'mass market' and 'premium brand' begins to blur. For example, a number of mass-market brands, such as Tesco, have a premium dimension—for example, Tesco Finest—while at the same time some luxury brands, such as Ralph Lauren or Burberry, are seen by ordinary consumers as attainable.

Based on: Carter (2003);[42] Rigby (2005)[43]

guidance on a particular topic. This means that opinion leaders can exert enormous power over purchase decisions. For example, pop stars such as Jennifer Lopez, Britney Spears and Celine Dion have developed wide ranges of products ranging from music to clothes to perfumes, which are essentially aspirational brands selling the qualities of their celebrity and lifestyle.

In summary, the behaviour of consumers is affected by a variety of factors. The buying situation, a range of personal influences and some social influences all combine to make up the nature of the relationships that individuals have with products and services. We will now turn to the factors that influence the buying behaviour of organizations.

Influences on organizational buying behaviour

Organizational buying is characterized by a number of unique features. Typically, the number of customers is small and order sizes large. For example, Tesco, Asda, Sainsbury's and Morrisons account for over 70 per cent of supermarket sales in the UK, so getting or losing an account with these resellers can be crucial. Organizational purchases are often complex and risky, with several parties having input into the purchasing decision as would be the case with a major IT investment. The demand for many organizational goods is derived from the demand for consumer goods, which means that small changes in consumer demand can have an important impact on the demand for industrial goods. For example, the decline in the sale of VCRs will have a knock-on effect on the demand for VCR component parts.

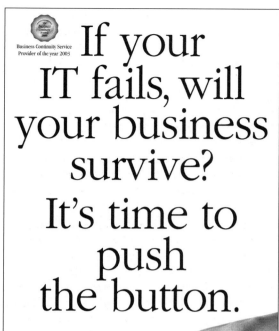

Exhibit 3.7 This advertisement for ICM Computer Group demonstrates how significant technology investments can be for client companies

When large organizational customers struggle, this impacts on their suppliers. Most major car manufacturers such as Ford, General Motors, Daimler-Chrysler and Volkswagen have all demanded significant price cuts from their suppliers

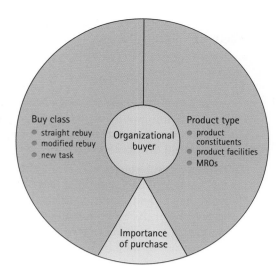

Figure 3.4 Influences on organizational purchasing behaviour

in recent years. However, at the same time suppliers have faced rising steel and raw material costs, which has affected profitability and forced some out of business.[44] Organizational buying is also characterized by the prevalence of negotiations between buyers and sellers; and in some cases reciprocal buying may take place where, for example, in negotiating to buy computers a company like Volvo might persuade a supplier to buy a fleet of company cars.

Figure 3.4 shows the three factors that influence organizational buying behaviour and the choice criteria that are used: the buy class, the product type and the importance of purchase.[45]

The buy class

Organizational purchases may be distinguished as either a **new task**, a **straight rebuy** or a **modified rebuy**.[46] A new task occurs when the need for the product has not arisen previously so that there is little or no relevant experience in the company, and a great deal of information is required. A straight rebuy occurs where an organization buys previously purchased items from suppliers already judged acceptable. Routine purchasing procedures are set up to facilitate straight rebuys. The modified rebuy lies between the two extremes. A regular requirement for the type of product exists, and the buying alternatives are known, but sufficient change (e.g. a delivery problem) has occurred to require some alteration to the normal supply procedure.

The buy classes affect organizational buying in the following ways. First, the membership of the DMU changes. For a straight rebuy possibly only the purchasing officer is involved, whereas for a new buy senior management, engineers, production managers and purchasing officers may be involved. Modified rebuys often involve engineers, production managers and purchasing officers, but not senior management, except when the purchase is critical to the company. Second, the decision-making process may be much longer as the buy class changes from a straight rebuy to a modified rebuy and to a new task. Third, in terms of influencing DMU members, they are likely to be much more receptive to new task and modified rebuy situations than straight rebuys. In the latter case, the purchasing manager has already solved the purchasing problem and has other problems to deal with. So why make it a problem again?

The first implication of this buy class analysis is that there are big gains to be made if a company can enter the new task at the start of the decision-making process. By providing information and helping with any technical problems that can arise, the company may be able to create goodwill and 'creeping commitment', which secures the order when the final decision is made. The second implication is that since the decision process is likely to be long, and many people are involved in the new task, supplier companies need to invest heavily in sales personnel for a considerable period of time. Some firms employ 'missionary' sales teams, comprising their best salespeople, to help secure big new task orders.

The product type

Products can be classified according to four types: materials, components, plant and equipment, and maintenance repair and operation (MRO):

1 materials—to be used in the production process, e.g. aluminium
2 components—to be incorporated in the finished product, e.g. headlights
3 plant and equipment—for example, bulldozers
4 products and services for MRO—for example, spanners, welding equipment and lubricants.

This classification is based on a customer perspective—how the product is used—and may be employed to identify differences in organizational buyer behaviour. First, the people who take part in the decision-making process tend to change according to product type. For example, senior management tend to get involved in the purchase of plant and equipment or, occasionally, when new materials are purchased if the change is of fundamental importance to company operations, e.g. if a move from aluminium to plastic is being considered. Rarely do they involve themselves in component or MRO supply. Similarly, design engineers tend to be involved in buying components and materials, but

not normally MRO and plant equipment. Second, the decision-making process tends to be slower and more complex as product type moves along the following continuum:

$$MRO \rightarrow components \rightarrow materials \rightarrow plant$$
$$and\ equipment$$

The importance of purchase

A purchase is likely to be perceived as being important to the buying organization when it involves large sums of money, when the cost of making the wrong decision, e.g. in terms of production downtime, is high and when there is considerable uncertainty about the outcome of alternative offerings. In such situations, many people at different organizational levels are likely to be involved in the decision and the process will be long, with extensive search for and analysis of information. Thus extensive marketing effort is likely to be required, but great opportunities present themselves to sales teams who work with buying organizations to convince them that their offering has the best pay-off; this may involve acceptance trials (e.g. private diesel manufacturers supply railway companies with prototypes for testing), engineering support and testimonials from other users. Additionally, guarantees of delivery dates and after-sales service may be necessary when buyer uncertainty regarding these factors is pronounced.

Features of organizational purchasing practice

A number of trends have occurred within the purchasing function that have marketing implications for supplier firms. The relentless drive for efficiency by businesses has been one of the key factors behind the growth of just-in-time purchasing, online purchasing and centralized purchasing. At the same time, these developments have often strengthened relationships between buyers and their suppliers, and we have seen a significant growth in relationship marketing and reverse marketing.

The **just-in-time (JIT)** concept aims to minimize stocks by organizing a supply system that provides materials and components as they are required.[47] The total effects of JIT can be enormous. Purchasing inventory and inspection costs can be reduced, product design can be improved, delivery streamlined, production downtime reduced, and the quality of the finished item enhanced. Very close co-operation is required between a manufacturer and its suppliers. An example of a company that employs a JIT system is the Nissan car assembly plant in

Sunderland in the UK. Nissan adopts what it terms 'synchronous supply': parts are delivered only minutes before they are needed. For example, carpets are delivered by Sommer Allibert, a French supplier, from its facility close to the Nissan assembly line in sequence for fitting to the correct model. Only 42 minutes elapse between the carpet being ordered and its being fitted to the car. This system also carries risks, however. For example, the Kobe earthquake in Japan shut down those car plant assembly lines in nearby regions that did not have parts in stock.

The growth in the use of the Internet has given rise to the development of online purchasing. Two main categories of marketplaces, or exchanges, have been created: **vertical electronic marketplaces** are industry specific, such as sites for the paper industry (e.g. www.paperexchange.com) or the automotive industry (e.g. www.covisint.com); **horizontal electronic marketplaces** cross industry boundaries and cater for supplies such as MROs (e.g. www.commerceone.com). Companies seeking supplies post their offers on these websites. Potential vendors then bid for the contracts electronically. Some companies report significant improvements in efficiency from managing their purchasing this way, through reducing the amount of procurement staff involved in processing orders and increasing the potential global spread of vendors. This heightened competition presents challenges for suppliers.

Where several operating units within a company have common requirements and where there is an opportunity to strengthen a negotiating position by bulk buying, centralized purchasing is an attractive option. Centralization encourages purchasing specialists to concentrate their energies on a small group of products, thus enabling them to develop an extensive knowledge of cost factors and the operation of suppliers.[48] For example, increasing concerns over the costs of healthcare has meant that many hospitals have centralized purchasing in procurement departments rather than devolving the activity to doctors and nurses as had been the case in the past. As a result, many contracts are put out to tender, often on a pan-European basis, with vendors selected on the basis of quality, cost and ability to deliver over a number of years. The net effect of this is that orders are much more difficult to secure but, once secured, are likely be more long lasting. At the same time, organizational buying has become increasingly characterized by very close relationships between buyers and sellers. **Relationship marketing** is the process of creating, developing and enhancing relationships with customers and other stakeholders. For example, Marks & Spencer has trading relationships with suppliers that stretch back almost a century. Such long-term relationships can have significant advantages for both buyer and seller. Risk is reduced for buyers as they get to know people in the supplier organization and know who to contact when problems arise. Communication is thus improved, and joint problem solving and design management can take place with suppliers becoming, in effect, strategic partners. Sellers gain through closer knowledge of buyer requirements, and many companies have reorganized their salesforces to reflect the importance of managing customer relationships effectively—a process known as key account management. New product development can benefit from such close relationships. The development of machine-washable lambs' wool fabrics and easy-to-iron cotton shirts came about because of Marks & Spencer's close relationship with UK manufacturers.[49] The benefits of a relational approach to dealing with suppliers are shown in Marketing in Action 3.4; the issue of relationship marketing will be dealt with in more detail in Chapter 7.

The traditional view of marketing is that supplier firms will actively seek out the requirements of customers and attempt to meet those needs better than the competition. However, purchasing is now taking on a more proactive, aggressive stance in acquiring the products and services needed to compete. This process, whereby the buyer attempts to persuade the supplier to provide exactly what the organization wants, is called **reverse marketing**.[50] Zeneca, an international supplier of chemicals, uses reverse marketing very effectively to target suppliers with a customized list of requirements concerning delivery times, delivery success rates and how often sales visits should occur. The growth of reverse marketing presents two key benefits to suppliers who are willing to listen to the buyer's proposition and carefully consider its merits: first, it provides the opportunity to develop a stronger and longer-lasting relationship with the customer; second, it could be a source of new product opportunities that may be developed to a broader customer base later on.

Finally in B2B contexts, a firm may not actually make a purchase but rather it simply leases a product. A lease is a contract by which the owner of an asset (e.g. a car) grants the right to use the asset for a period of time to another party in exchange for the payment of rent.[51] The benefits to the customer are that a leasing arrangement avoids the need to pay the cash purchase price of the product or service, is a hedge against fast product obsolescence, may have tax advantages, avoids the problem of equipment disposal and, with certain types of leasing contract, avoids some maintenance costs. These benefits need to be weighed against the costs of leasing, which may be higher than outright buying.

Marketing in Action: Working with suppliers in China

For the past decade, many of the world's global manufacturers have been shifting their production activities to low-cost locations such as Central Europe and Asia to take advantage of lower labour costs. But locating in these regions also means sourcing supplies locally and this can be troublesome. In some cases, the kinds of suppliers that companies are looking for simply do not exist. Where they do, many suppliers in these regions are small and are unable to produce in quantities large enough to generate economies of scale and pass these economies onto their buyers. Finally, the quality levels of many local suppliers does not come up to scratch, which means that they are often unable to manufacture to the specification level of their customers.

As a result, some global manufacturers are working hard at building close relationships with local suppliers in an effort to bring them up the learning curve. For example, Ingersoll-Rand, the diversified US industrial group, has 18 local component suppliers in China. It employs 20 engineers to work with suppliers and train them to meet its quality standards. The reward for this kind of investment is that the manufacturer gets quality supplies and at the same time benefits from the substantially lower labour costs currently available in China.

But where there are problems there are always opportunities. Many Western suppliers who already have good relationships with the manufacturers are following them to their new production locations. For example, Precision Technologies, a UK-based company, sends about 40 high-tech moulds per year to GKN's (the British vehicle parts manufacturer) China plant in Shanghai because the latter has failed to find Chinese companies that can make them to a sufficiently high quality. Similarly, Swissmatic, based in Motherwell, Scotland, which makes small components for industries such as telecommunications and defence has won several orders from electronics companies that have set up assembly sites in the Czech Republic and Hungary, because of its capability to make small volumes of very precise parts.

Based on: Marsh (2004)[52]

Summary

This chapter has examined the nature of customer behaviour and the key influences on customer behaviour. The following key issues were addressed.

1. The differences between consumer and organizational buying behaviour.
2. Who buys—the five roles in the buying decision-making process: initiator, influencer, decider, buyer and user.
3. The buying decision process, involving the stages of need recognition, search for alternatives, evaluation of alternatives, purchase and post-purchase evaluation.
4. The main choice criteria used in making purchase decisions—namely technical, economic, social and personal criteria.
5. The main influences on consumer buying behaviour: the buying situation, personal influences and social influences.
6. The main influences on organizational buying behaviour: the buy class, the product type and the importance of purchase.
7. The key features of organizational purchasing practice: just-in-time purchasing, online purchasing, centralized purchasing, relationship marketing, reverse marketing and leasing.

Suggested reading

Ford, D. (1997) *Understanding Business Markets*, London: Academic Press.

Jamal, A. (2003) Marketing in a Multicultural World, *European Journal of Marketing*, **37** (11/12), 1599–621.

Silverstein, M.J. and **N. Fiske** (2003) Luxury for the Masses, *Harvard Business Review*, **81** (4), 48–58.

Thompson, E.S. and **A.W. Laing** (2003), 'The Net Generation': Children and Young People, the Internet and Online Shopping, *Journal of Marketing Management*, **19** (3/4), 491–513.

Underhill, P. (2000) *Why we Buy: The Science of Shopping*, London: Texere.

Internet exercises

Sites to visit

1   www.shopping.com
www.shopping.yahoo.com
www.which.co.uk

Exercise

Pretend that you are about to buy a digital camera. Compare and contrast the information that is available on these three sites to help you make your buying decision.

Sites to visit

2   www.ubid.com
www.ebay.co.uk
www.auctions.yahoo.com

Exercise

Discuss the changes in consumer behaviour arising from the growth of online auction sites.

Study questions

1. What are the differences between organizational buying behaviour and consumer buying behaviour?
2. Choose a recent purchase that included not only yourself but also other people in making the decision. What role(s) did you play in the buying centre? What roles did these other people play and how did they influence your choice?
3. Review your decision to choose the educational establishment you are attending in terms of need recognition, information search, evaluation of alternatives and post-selection evaluation.
4. Review the choice criteria influencing some recent purchases such as a hairstyle, a meal, etc.
5. Describe the recent trends in just-in-time purchasing, online purchasing and centralized purchasing. Discuss the implications of these trends for marketers in vendor firms.

Key terms

buying centre a group that is involved in the buying decision; also known as a decision-making unit (DMU) in industrial buying situations

decision-making process the stages that organizations and people pass through when purchasing a physical product or service

information search the identification of alternative ways of problem solving

awareness set the set of brands that the consumer is aware may provide a solution to a problem

evoked set the set of brands that the consumer seriously evaluates before making a purchase

cognitive dissonance post-purchase concerns of a consumer arising from uncertainty as to whether a decision to purchase was the correct one

beliefs descriptive thoughts that a person holds about something

attitude the degree to which a customer or prospect likes or dislikes a brand

perception the process by which people select, organize and interpret sensory stimulation into a meaningful picture of the world

selective attention the process by which people screen out those stimuli that are neither meaningful to them nor consistent with their experiences and beliefs

selective distortion the distortion of information received by people according to their existing beliefs and attitudes

selective retention the process by which people retain only a selection of messages in memory

information framing the way in which information is presented to people

information processing the process by which a stimulus is received, interpreted, stored in memory and later retrieved

classical conditioning the process of using an established relationship between a stimulus and a response to cause the learning of the same response to a different stimulus

operant conditioning the use of rewards to generate reinforcement of response

cognitive learning the learning of knowledge, and development of beliefs and attitudes without direct reinforcement

rote learning the learning of two or more concepts without conditioning

vicarious learning learning from others without direct experience or reward

reasoning a more complex form of cognitive learning where conclusions are reached by connected thought

motivation the process involving needs that set drives in motion to accomplish goals

choice criteria the various attributes (and benefits) people use when evaluating products and services

personality the inner psychological characteristics of individuals that lead to consistent responses to their environment

lifestyle the pattern of living as expressed in a person's activities, interests and opinions

culture the traditions, taboos, values and basic attitudes of the whole society in which an individual lives

reference group a group of people that influences an individual's attitude or behaviour

new task refers to the first-time purchase of a product or input by an organization

straight rebuy refers to a purchase by an organization from a previously approved supplier of a previously purchased item

modified rebuy where a regular requirement for the type of product exists and the buying alternatives are known but sufficient (e.g. a delivery problem has occurred) to require some alteration to the normal supply procedure

just-in-time (JIT) the JIT concept aims to minimize stocks by organizing a supply system that provides materials and components as they are required

vertical electronic marketplaces online procurement sites that are dedicated to sourcing supplies for producers in one particular industry

horizontal electronic marketplaces online procurement sites that cross several industries and are typically used to source low-cost supplies such as MRO items

relationship marketing the process of creating, maintaining and enhancing strong relationships with customers and other stakeholders

reverse marketing the process whereby the buyer attempts to persuade the supplier to provide exactly what the organization wants

References

1. **Croft, C.** (2003) Getting the Needle, *Sunday Times*, Features, 29 June, 24; **Foster, L.** (2003) US Department Stores Launch Counter-Attack, *Financial Times*, 23 December, 8; **O'Donnell, F.** (2003) Top People's Store Offers an Arm to Take Tattoos into the Mainstream, *Scotsman*, 18 June, 3; **Rumbelow, H.** (2003) Ladies Who Lunch Get a Tattoo for Starters, *The Times*, 18 June, 9;

Voyle, S. (2003) Great Exhibition With A Nice Shop Attached, *Financial Times*, Creative Business, 17 June, 10–11.

2. **Blackwell R.D., P.W. Miniard** and **J.F. Engel** (2000) *Consumer Behavior*, Orlando, FL: Dryden, 174.

3. **Pesola, M.** (2005) Samsung Plays to the Young Generation, *Financial Times*, 29 March, 11.

4. **Jones, H.** (2002) What are they Playing At?, *Financial Times*, Creative Business, 17 December, 6.

5. **Shrimsley, R.** (2004) Children's Power is Out of Control: Blame the Parents, *Financial Times*, 26 November, 14.

6. **Lindstrom, M.** (2003) The Real Decision Makers, *Brandchannel.com*, 11 August.

7. **Donation, S.** (1989) Study Boosts Men's Buying Role, *Advertising Age*, 4 December, 48.

8. **Anonymous** (1990) Business Bulletin, *Wall Street Journal*, 17 May, A1.

9. **Foster, L.** (2004) Moisturiser Maketh the Man, *Financial Times*, 16 August, 9.

10. **Rigby, R.** (2004) Moisturiser Man Becomes a Market Force, *Financial Times*, 4 February, 12.

11. **Oser, C.** (2003) Marketing Well to Women Pays Off, *DIRECTnewsline*, 20 December.

12. **Voyle, S.** (2004) E-tailing Comes of Age as Women Spend More Than Men, *Financial Times*, 16 February, 5.

13. **Hawkins, D.I., R.J. Best** and **K.A. Coney** (1989) *Consumer Behaviour: Implications for Marketing Strategy*, Boston, MA: Irwin, 536.

14. **O'Shaughnessey, J.** (1987) *Why People Buy*, New York: Oxford University Press, 161.

15. **Baumgartner, H.** and **J.-Bem Steenkamp** (1996) Exploratory Consumer Buying Behaviour: Conceptualisation and Measurement, *International Journal of Research in Marketing*, **13**, 121–37.

16. **Kuusela, H., M.T. Spence** and **A.J. Kanto** (1998) Expertise Effects on Prechoice Decision Processes and Final Outcomes: A Protocol Analysis, *European Journal of Marketing*, **32** (5/6), 559–76.

17. **Blackwell R.D., P.W. Miniard** and **J.F. Engel** (2000) *Consumer Behavior*, Orlando, FL: Dryden, 34.

18. **Elliott, R.** and **E. Hamilton** (1991) Consumer Choice Tactics and Leisure Activities, *International Journal of Advertising*, **10**, 325–32.

19. **Laurent, G.** and **J.N. Kapferer** (1985) Measuring Consumer Involvement Profiles, *Journal of Marketing Research*, **12** (February), 41–53.

20. **Rothschild, M.L.** (1978) *Advertising Strategies for High and Low Involvement Situations*, Chicago: American Marketing Association Educator's Proceedings, 150–62.

21. **Hawkins, D.I., R.J. Best** and **K.A. Coney** (1989) *Consumer Behaviour: Implications for Marketing Strategy*, Boston, MA: Irwin, 30.

22. **Mowen, J.C.** (1988) Beyond Consumer Decision-making, *Journal of Consumer Research*, **5** (1), 15–25.

23. **Hawkins, D.I., R.J. Best** and **K.A. Coney** (1989) *Consumer Behaviour: Implications for Marketing Strategy*, Boston, MA: Irwin, 30.

24. **Engel, J.F., Blackwell, R.D.** and **P.W. Miniard** (1990) *Consumer Behaviour*, Orlando, FL: Dryden, 29.

25. **Engel, J.F., Blackwell, R.D.** and **P.W. Miniard** (1990) *Consumer Behaviour*, Orlando, FL: Dryden, 363.

26. **Williams, K.C.** (1981) *Behavioural Aspects of Marketing*, London: Heinemann.

27. **Hawkins, D.I., R.J. Best** and **K.A. Coney** (1989) *Consumer Behaviour: Implications for Marketing Strategy*, Boston, MA: Irwin, 275.

28. **Ratneshwar, S., L. Warlop, D.G. Mick** and **G. Seegar** (1997) Benefit Salience and Consumers' Selective Attention to Product Features, *International Journal of Research in Marketing*, **14**, 245–9.

29. **Levin, L.P.** and **G.J. Gaeth** (1988) Framing of Attribute Information Before and After Consuming the Product, *Journal of Consumer Research*, **15** (December), 374–8.

30. **Hawkins, D.I., R.J. Best** and **K.A. Coney** (1989) *Consumer Behaviour: Implications for Marketing Strategy*, Boston, MA: Irwin, 317.

31. **Ries, A.** and **J. Trout** (1982) *Positioning: The Battle for your Mind*, New York: Warner.

32. **Harford, T.** (2003) In Search of the Inside Story of Economics, *Financial Times*, 30 September, 16.

33. **Luthans, F.** (1981) *Organisational Behaviour*, San Francisco: McGraw-Hill.

34. **Maslow, A.H.** (1954) *Motivation and Personality*, New York: Harper & Row, 80–106.

35. **Conwy, S.** (2003) What Women Really Want, *Financial Times*, Creative Business, 22 July, 2.

36. **Kassarjan, H.H.** (1971) Personality and Consumer Behaviour: A Review, *Journal of Marketing Research*, November, 409–18.

37. **Silverman, G.** (2005) The Challenge is to Feed the Alpha Male's Insatiable Appetites, *Financial Times*, 5 July, 12.

38. **O'Brien, S.** and **R. Ford** (1988) Can We At Last Say Goodbye to Social Class?, *Journal of the Market Research Society*, **30** (3), 289–332.

39. **Urry, M.** (2003) United Biscuits' Biggest Breakfast Plan, *Financial Times*, 22 August, 21.

40. **Tomkins, R.** (2005) Flash Mobbing Gives Up its Wild Past and Goes Into Marketing, *Financial Times*, 26 July, 13.

41. **Anonymous** (2005) This Sceptred Aisle, *Economist*, 6 August, 29.

42. **Carter, M.** (2003) The Low-down on the Low-brow Consumer, *Financial Times*, 27 November, 13.

43. **Rigby, E.** (2005) Canny Consumers Dictate the In-store Trend, *Financial Times*, 12 July, 24.

44. **Simon, B.** (2005) Car Parts Groups Face a Depressed Future, *Financial Times*, 18 May, 31.

45. **Cardozo, R.N.** (1980) Situational Segmentation of Industrial Markets, *European Journal of Marketing*, **14** (5/6), 264–76.

46. **Robinson, P.J., C.W. Faris** and **Y. Wind** (1967) *Industrial Buying and Creative Marketing*, Boston, MA: Allyn & Bacon.

47. **Hutt, M.D.** and **T.W Speh** (1997) *Business Marketing Management*, 3rd edn, New York: Dryden Press, 40.

48. **Briefly, E.G., R.W. Eccles** and **R.R. Reeder** (1998) *Business Marketing*, Englewood Cliffs, NJ: Prentice-Hall, 105.

49. **Thornhill, J.** and **A. Rawsthorn** (1992) Why Sparks are Flying, *Financial Times*, 8 January, 12.

50. **Blenkhorn, D.L.** and **P.M. Banting** (1991) How Reverse Marketing Changes Buyer–Seller Roles, *Industrial Marketing Management*, **20**, 185–91.

51. **Anderson, F.** and **W. Lazer** (1978) Industrial Lease Marketing, *Journal of Marketing*, **42** (January), 71–9.

52. **Marsh, P.** (2004) A Little Local Difficulty in the Supply Chain, *Financial Times*, 23 June, 12.

When you have read this chapter log on to the Online Learning Centre for *Foundations of Marketing* at **www.mcgraw-hill.co.uk/textbooks/jobber** where you'll find multiple choice test questions, links and extra online study tools for marketing.

Turn the page for a Case Study on The Grey Market

Case 3 The grey market

Introduction

The over-50s market has long been ignored by advertising and marketing firms in favour of the youth market. The complexity of how to appeal to today's mature customers, without targeting their age, has proved just too challenging for many companies. But this preoccupation with youth runs counter to demographic changes. The over-50s represent the largest segment of the population, across western developed countries, due largely to the post-Second World War baby boom. The sheer size of this grey market, which will continue to grow as birth and mortality rates fall, coupled with its phenomenal spending power, presents enormous opportunities for business. However, successfully unleashing its potential will depend on companies truly understanding the attitudes, lifestyles and purchasing interests of this post-war generation.

Demographic forces

Following the Second World War many countries experienced a baby boom phenomenon as returning soldiers began families. This, coupled with a more positive outlook on the future, resulted in the baby boom generation, born between 1946 and 1964. Now beginning to enter retirement, this affluent group globally numbers approximately 532 million. In Western Europe they account for the largest proportion of the total population at 14.9%, followed closely by 14.2% in North America and 13.5% in Australasia.

Table C3.1 Global population aged 45–54 by region: baby boomers as a % of the total population 1990/2002

Baby boomers as a % of total population	1990	2002	% point change
Western Europe	12.9	14.9	2.0
North America	9.9	14.2	4.3
Australasia	10.4	13.5	3.1
Eastern Europe	9.7	13.0	3.3
Asia-Pacific	7.8	9.8	2.0
Latin America	6.6	8.4	1.8
Africa/Middle East	2.6	2.3	20.3
WORLD	7.9	9.5	1.6

Source: UN/Euromonitor

The grey market is big and getting bigger. Between 1990 and 2002 the global baby boomer population increased by 41%. This rate of growth is predicted to decrease to 35% between 2002 and 2015. Particularly noteworthy is the predicted increase in the proportion of baby boomers in many Western European countries, such as Austria, Spain, Germany, Italy and the UK. In developed countries, according to the United Nations, the percentage of elderly people (60+) is forecasted to rise from one-fifth of the population to one-third by 2050. The growth in the elderly population is exacerbated by falling fertility rates in many developed countries, coupled with a rise in human longevity.

The influences and buyer behaviour patterns of baby boomers

The members of the baby boomer generation are quite unlike their more conservative parents' generation. They are the children of the rebellious 'swinging sixties', growing up on the sounds of the Beatles and the Rolling Stones. Better educated than their parents, in a time of greater prosperity, they indulged in a more hedonistic lifestyle. It has been said that they were the first 'me generation'. Now, in later life, they have retained their liberal, adventurous and youthful attitude to life. Aptly termed 'younger older people' they abhor antiquated stereotypes of elderly people, preferring to be defined by their attitude rather than their age.

Baby boomers also tend to be very wealthy. Many are property owners and may have gained an inheritance from parents or other relatives. They have higher than average incomes or have retired with private pension plans. With their children having flown the nest they have greater financial freedom and more time to indulge themselves. Having worked all their lives, and educated their children, many baby boomers do not believe it is their responsibility to safeguard the financial future of their children by carefully protecting their children's inheritance. They are instead liquidating their assets, intent on enjoying their later life to the full, often through conspicuous consumption.

Based on research conducted by Euromonitor, the main areas of expenditure in the baby boomer market

Table C3.2 Population aged 45–54 in thousands by country: developed countries 2002–2015

Country	2002	2010	2015	% change 2002/2015
Austria	1,059	1,277	1,371	29
Spain	4,921	5,741	6,189	26
Germany	10,991	12,963	13,508	23
Italy	7,684	8,591	9,347	22
UK	7,786	8,731	9,388	21
New Zealand	521	607	613	18
Ireland	474	529	555	17
Switzerland	997	1,120	1,159	16
Australia	2,661	3,006	3,057	15
Greece	1,359	1,476	1,559	15
Canada	4,505	5,320	5,122	14
Netherlands	2,301	2,492	2,604	13
Portugal	1,334	1,438	1,511	13
Norway	612	640	678	11
Denmark	745	761	802	8
USA	38,951	44,140	42,207	8
Belgium	1,423	1,549	1,526	7
Sweden	1,206	1,179	1,233	2
Japan	18,344	15,661	16,459	−10
Finland	820	749	718	−12
France	8,266	7,626	7,292	−12

Source: UN/Euromonitor

are financial services, tourism, food and drink, luxury cars, electrical/electronic goods, clothing, health products, and DIY and gardening.

Unsurprisingly the financial services sector is the largest in this market. Baby boomers are concerned with being financially secure in their retirement. An ageing population, coupled with a rise in human longevity, is giving rise to a pensions crisis across Western Europe. Baby boomers are therefore right to be preoccupied with how they will maintain their lifestyle over the long term. They are actively engaging in financial planning, both before and after retirement. Popular financial services products include endowments, life insurance, personal pensions, PEPs and ISAs.

Baby boomers have adventurous attitudes with a desire to see the world. In their retirement foreign travel is a key expenditure. Given their greater levels of sophistication and education, baby boomers are much more demanding of holidays that suit their lifestyles. This group is very diverse, with holiday

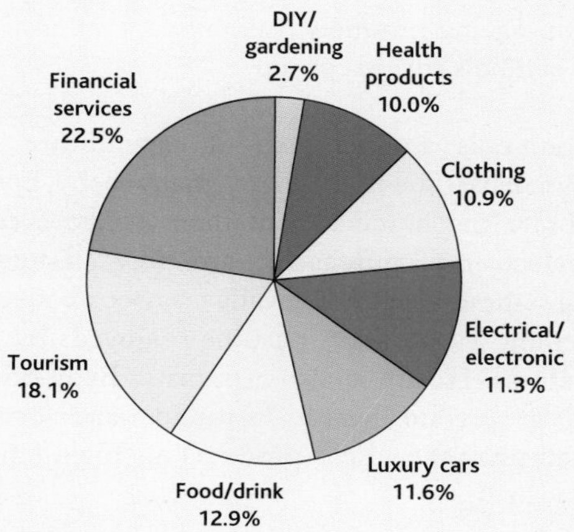

Figure C3.1 Global baby boomer market: % analysis by broad sector 2002 (% value)

Note: sectors valued on the basis of estimates by senior managers in major companies in each sector, consumer expenditure and industry sector data.
Source: Euromonitor

Figure C3.2

interests ranging from action-packed adventures to culturally rich experiences.

Baby boomers want to maintain a youthful appearance in line with their more youthful way of living. Fear of becoming invisible is a genuine concern among older generations. This image consciousness is reflected in their spending on clothing, cosmetics and anti-ageing products. Luxury cars are also a key status symbols for this group.

The home is another area of expenditure. Once children have flown the nest, many baby boomers redecorate the home to suit their needs. Electrical and electronic purchases are key indulgences among these technologically savvy consumers. Gardening is another pastime enjoyed by older generations. Health is also a priority. Baby boomers invest in private health insurance and over-the-counter pharmaceutical products to maintain their healthy lives.

Business opportunities

The sheer size of the grey market, which is getting bigger in many countries—characterized by consumers with high disposable income, ample free time,

interest in travel, concern about financial security and health, awareness of youth culture and brands, and desire for aspirational living—makes this market enormously attractive to many business sectors. Pharmaceuticals, health and beauty, technology, travel, financial services, luxury cars, lavish food and entertainment are key growth sectors for the grey market. However, successfully tapping into this market will depend on companies truly understanding the attitudes, lifestyles and purchasing interests of this post-war generation. Communicating with this group is a tricky business but, done right, it can be hugely rewarding.

When targeting the older consumer it is important to target their lifestyle and not their age. Older people do not want to be reminded, in a patronizing way, of their age or what they should be doing now they are at a certain stage in life. With an interest in maintaining a youthful way of life these consumers are interested in similar brands to those that appeal to younger generations. The key for companies is to find a way of making their brands also appeal to an older consumer without explicitly targeting their age. One tried-and-tested method of targeting this group is to use nostalgia. Mercedes Benz used the Janis Joplin song 'Oh Lord won't you buy me a Mercedes Benz' to great effect despite the obvious irony in that the song was written to highlight the dangers of materialism! Volkswagen's new retro-style Beetle has also been popular among this group.

In the tourism sector Saga Holidays, the leader in holidays for the over-50s, has changed its product offering to reflect changing trends among this group. In line with the more adventurous attitudes of many older consumers it now offers more action-packed adventure holidays to far-flung destinations.

More recently, Thomas Cook has rebranded it over-50s 'Forever Young' programme to reflect the diverse interests of its target customers. Its new primetime brochure targets five distinct groups with the following holiday types: 'Discover', 'Learn', 'Relax', 'Active' and 'Enjoy Life'.

Conclusion

The over-50s represent the largest segment of the population across Western developed countries. This affluent market is big and getting bigger. Having ignored it for so long marketers are finally beginning to see the enormous opportunities presented by the grey market. But conquering this market will not be easy. The baby boomer generation is quite unlike its predecessors. With a youthful and adventuresome spirit these 'younger older people' want to be defined by their attitude and not their age. Only time will tell whether today's marketers are up to the challenge.

Questions

1. Why is the grey market so attractive to business?
2. Identify the influences on the purchasing behaviour of the over-50s consumer.
3. Discuss the challenges involved in targeting the grey market.

This case was prepared by Sinéad Moloney and Professor John Fahy, University of Limerick, as a basis for classroom discussion.

References

The material in this case was drawn from the following sources:

1. **Byrne, C.** (2003) Middle Age Spreads Out, *Guardian*, 18 August, 4.
2. FT Reinventing Retirement (2004) *Financial Times*, Special Report, 17 November.
3. Global Market Information Database (2003) Baby Boomers in World, *Global Report*, 20 June.
4. **Harkin, J.** (2004) Please Don't Call me Baby, *Financial Times*, 22 July, 11.
5. **Jones, D.** (2004) Targeting the Grey Market is not a Simple Process, *Marketing* (UK), 3 November, 22.
6. **Malkani, G.** (2004) Affluent Over-50s Accuse Advertising Industry of Ignoring the Grey Pound, *Financial Times*, 26 April, 5.
7. **Prior, L.** (2004) Go Grab the Grey Market, *Travel Trade Gazette*, 8 October, 28.
8. **Prior, L.** (2005) Cook Rebrands Over-50s Brochure, *Travel Trade Gazette*, 11 March, 22.

CHAPTER 4

MARKETING RESEARCH AND INFORMATION SYSTEMS

Learning Objectives

By the end of this chapter you will understand:

1 the importance of marketing research
2 the different types of marketing research available
3 the approaches to conducting research
4 the stages in the marketing research process
5 the nature and purpose of marketing information systems.

Searching for 'Cool'

Trend spotting is one of the biggest marketing research challenges facing companies marketing to the 16–34 age group. It is sometimes described as the search for 'cool', which is an invisible, intangible but very valuable commodity. Marketers know that if 'cool' people start talking or eating or dressing or shopping in a certain way, then 'non-cool' people will follow them. Understand what cool people are doing today and you can see what everyone else will be doing a year from now.

But cool is an elusive quality. And it will not be discovered through conventional market research techniques such as surveys or focus group interviews. Many leading companies employ professional trend spotters ('cool hunters') to seek it out. In what might sound like the ideal job, trend spotters, who are usually in their 20s, spend their time going to parties, making new friends online, travelling to far-flung destinations and hanging out in 'cool' places like New York's Soho district. They are then responsible for providing regular reports on the latest happenings in music, fashion, lifestyle and technology. Perhaps the biggest challenge for both the trend spotter and their employer is to sift

through the mass of information that is available to truly identify the drivers of youth behaviour. Separating fads from real trends is not easy, as the obsession with everything online demonstrated in the late 1990s. In addition, there are now a variety of boutique research firms providing trend-spotting services—including, for example, the Zandl Group and www.trendwatching.com.

One company that uses trend spotters to maintain its cool positioning in the marketplace is the urbanwear brand, Diesel. The Diesel brand started out in Italy in 1975 and has since grown to annual global sales levels in the region of US$680 million. The company employs 50 25-year-old trend spotters from around the world who travel wherever they want to research and seek out new trends and ideas. Maintaining its cool image is extremely important to a brand that is now so large that it has become mainstream. Therefore it must constantly seek to be innovative in its product design—for example, producing a new line like 55 DSL, which targets skateboarders and snowboarders, as well as being creative in its advertising and online marketing (www.diesel.co.uk).[1]

The importance of marketing research

We saw in Chapter 1 that the core philosophy of marketing is one that puts the customer at the centre of the organization's activity. As such, the focus of marketing is, or should be, outward, towards markets, customers and the environment. One of the largest research areas in marketing in the past 15 years has been market orientation,[2] which looks at the extent to which organizations are market-led in their activities and marketing capabilities;[3] considered to be critical to organizational success. **Marketing research** is the organizational activity that translates this philosophy of being market-led into day-to-day actions. Figure 4.1 shows how the outward philosophy of marketing funnels through a concern with the environment and customer behaviour to the activity of marketing research.

Marketing research is enormously important. Truly market-led companies recognize that they need to always be in touch with what is happening in the marketplace. Customer needs are continually changing, often in ways that are very subtle. For some companies, no major strategic decisions are made without first researching the market. But this activity goes far beyond commercial organizations. For example, organizations ranging from political parties to record companies are heavy users of marketing research and often stand accused of over-dependence on it to shape everything from manifestos to new albums. Marketing research can play a role in many different activities. Research can be useful to help

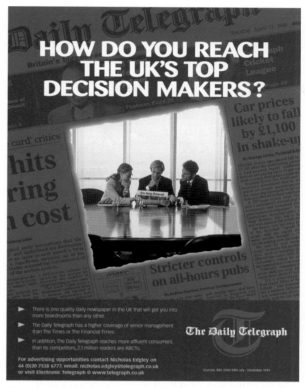

Exhibit 4.1 Marketing research output such as circulation figures by market segment are crucial for newspapers

understand what customers want, to decide whether to launch a new product or not, to get feedback from customers about ongoing levels of service, to measure the effectiveness of a sponsorship campaign, and so on.

The marketing research industry is massive, estimated to be worth over US$19 billion globally and

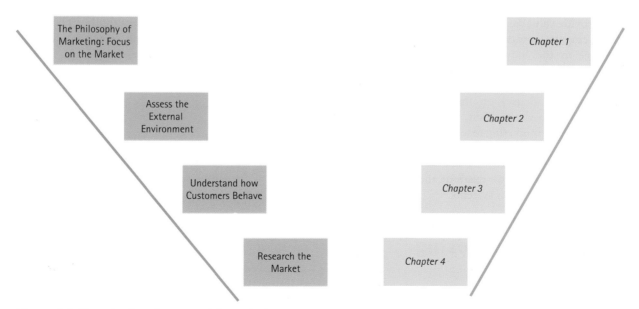

Figure 4.1 The role of market research in marketing

Table 4.1 Global marketing research expenditure 2003

Country	Turnover in US$ million	Spend per capita in US$
UK	1997	33.80
Sweden	273	30.82
France	1580	26.40
USA	6660	22.88
Switzerland	162	22.55
Germany	1805	21.90
Finland	113	21.72
Norway	90	19.94
Denmark	106	19.89
Australia	383	19.60
Netherlands	305	18.97
New Zealand	70	18.11
Belgium	164	15.90
Canada	477	15.26
Ireland	59	15.06
Italy	581	10.11
Singapore	39	9.44
Japan	1164	9.13
Hong Kong	62	8.83
Luxembourg	4	8.33

Source: Esomar (www.esomar.org)

€7058 million in Europe. Table 4.1 provides details of levels of marketing research expenditure throughout the world. Defining the boundaries of marketing research is not easy. Casual discussions with customers at exhibitions or through sales calls can provide valuable informal information about their requirements, competitor activities and future happenings in the industry. More formal approaches include the conduct of marketing research studies or the development of marketing information systems. This chapter focuses on these formal methods of information provision. First, we will describe the different types of marketing research and the approaches used to conduct research studies. Then we will look at the process of marketing research and its uses in more detail. Finally, we examine the development of marketing information systems.

Types of marketing research

In the first instance we need to distinguish between ad hoc and continuous research.

Ad hoc research

Ad hoc research focuses on a specific marketing problem, collecting data at one point in time from one sample of respondents. Examples of ad hoc studies are usage and attitude surveys, product and concept tests, advertising development and evaluation studies, corporate image surveys and customer satisfaction surveys. Ad hoc surveys are either custom-designed or omnibus studies.

Custom-designed studies

This type of study is based on the specific needs of the client. The research design is based on the research brief given to the marketing research agency or internal marketing researcher. Because they are tailor-made, such surveys can be expensive.

Omnibus surveys

An alternative to the custom-designed study is the **omnibus survey** in which space is bought on questionnaires for face-to-face or telephone interviews. An interview may cover many topics, as questionnaire space is bought by a number of clients, who benefit from cost sharing. Usually the type of information sought is relatively simple (e.g. awareness levels and ownership data). Often the survey will be based on demographically balanced samples of 1000–2000 adults. However, more specialist surveys covering the markets for children, young adults, mothers and babies, the 'grey' market and motorists exist.

Continuous research

Continuous research involves the interviewing of the same sample of people repeatedly. The main types of continuous research are consumer panels, retail audits and television viewership panels.

Consumer panels

When large numbers of households are recruited to provide information on their purchases over time, together they make up a **consumer panel**. For example, a grocery panel would record the brands, pack sizes, prices and stores used for a wide range of supermarket brands. By using the same households over a period of time, measures of brand loyalty and switching can be achieved, together with a demographic profile of the type of person who buys particular brands.

Retail audits

Another type of continuous research is the **retail audit**. By gaining the co-operation of retail outlets (e.g.

supermarkets), sales of brands can be measured by means of laser scans of barcodes on packaging, which are read at the checkout. Although brand loyalty and switching cannot be measured, retail audits can provide an accurate assessment of sales achieved by store. A major provider of retail audit data is ACNielsen.

Television viewership panels

A television viewership panel measures audience size on a minute-by-minute basis. Commercial breaks can be allocated ratings points (the proportion of the target audience watching), which are the currency by which television advertising is bought and judged. In the UK, the system is controlled by the Broadcasters' Audience Research Board (BARB) (www.barb.co.uk), and run by AGB and RSMB. AGB handles the measurement process and uses 'people meters' to record whether a set is on/off, which channel is being watched and, by means of a hand console, who is watching. Technological developments continue to revolutionize TV audience measurement. Personal video recorders (PVRs), build up a profile of viewers' likes and dislikes, and record their favourite programmes automatically, but the box also relays every button press on its remote control back to the manufacturer, providing exact details of what programmes people watch on what channels.

Marketing databases

Companies collect data on customers on an ongoing basis. The data are stored on marketing databases, containing each customer's name, address, telephone number, past transactions and, sometimes, demographic and lifestyle data. Information on the types of purchase, frequency of purchase, purchase value and responsiveness to promotional offers may be held (see Chapter 10). For example, retailers are encouraging the collection of such data through introducing loyalty card schemes, which are popular with supermarkets, department stores and petrol retailers. Customers collect points that can be redeemed for cashback or gifts while at the same time the retailer collects valuable information about the customer each time the card is used.

e-Marketing: From hits to web analytics

In the early days of e-commerce, many Internet companies proudly trumpeted the number of hits their websites received. A hit is recorded when a web user clicks on any one element (such as an image, text, etc.) of one web page. Other common metrics include unique users (when a person visits a website) and page views (the number of pages that the visitor looks at). Increasingly, these basic metrics are considered to be woefully inadequate in measuring website effectiveness and are often seriously misleading—for instance, when the use of frames on a web page can significantly increase the number of page views. With Internet marketing becoming more sophisticated, it is now possible to get much better information, not only on who is visiting a website but also what they are doing once they get there. This emerging field is known as web analytics.

Several aspects of how consumers behave while visiting a website are worth monitoring. First, where did they come from—for example, did they come via a search engine or from a link in another site? Second, where do they go once they are on the site? What options are selected, what visuals are viewed, and so on. Did they respond to particular offers, promotions or site design changes? And, if the company is an online retailer, what percentage of consumers proceeded to the checkout and, for those that don't, at what stage in the process did they drop out? Similarly, websites that depend on advertising as a source of revenue need to be able to provide reliable information on visitor numbers as well as information on who these visitors are.

Basic customer behaviour patterns on a website are tracked through technologies such as logfiles, which are a record of all activity on a site, and cookies, which are files located on the visitor's hard drive. For example, click-through or click-stream analysis looks at logfiles to see where users go when they visit a site. Web analytics combines these basic metrics with demographic and subscription information to provide a more detailed analysis of visitor behaviour. In actual fact, the biggest challenge facing website owners is how to deal with the potential masses of customer data the Internet generates. The solution is to clearly identify, in advance, the role of the website in the company's marketing mix and then use this to guide the web research exercise.

Based on: Bowen (2003);[6] Guenther (2003);[7] Phippen, Sheppard and Furnell (2004)[8]

Customer relationship management (CRM) systems

A potential problem with the growth of marketing databases is that separate ones are created in different departments of the company. For example, the sales department may have an account management database containing information on customers, while call centre staff may use a different database created at a different time also containing information on customers. This fragmented approach can lead to problems, when, for example, a customer transaction is recorded on one but not the other database. Issues like this have led to the development of customer relationship management (CRM) systems where a single database is created from customer information to inform all staff who deal with customers. CRM is a term for the methodologies, technologies and e-commerce capabilities used by companies to manage customer relationships[4] (see Chapter 10).

Website analysis

Continuous data can also be provided by analysing consumers' use of websites. Measurements of the areas of the site most frequently visited, which products are purchased and the payment method used can be made. Other measures include how well the site loads on browsers, how well it downloads, whether it ranks within the top three pages on major search engines and the number of sites to which it is linked. Online retailers can get valuable information through website analysis. For example, an online camera store can track sales by time of day, or they can be related to promotional campaigns. The retailer can analyse a customer's behaviour to build a profile of their habits. For example, if a shopper visits a website but does not buy, a promotional voucher discount might be sent to persuade them to try again.[5] The growth of web analytics is discussed in e-Marketing 4.1.

A breakdown of expenditure on the different types of marketing research in the UK is shown in Table 4.2.

Approaches to conducting marketing research

There are two main ways for a company to carry out marketing research, depending on the situation facing it. It might either carry out the work itself or employ the services of a market research agency. The advantage of using an agency is that it will have the specialist skills and experience of conducting studies; these advantages may be offset, however, by the prohibitively high cost of using the agency's services. Where the study is small in scale, such as gathering infor-

Table 4.2 Different types of marketing research, UK

Type of marketing research	Share of overall market (2003)
Face-to-face interviews	26.9
Telephone interviews	22.0
Consumer panels	11.0
Focus groups	10.0
Hall tests	7.8
Mail questionnaires	7.5
Depth interviews	3.3
Mystery shopping	3.2
Internet interviews	0.6

Source: Euromonitor

mation from libraries or interviewing a select number of industrial customers, companies may choose to conduct the work themselves. This is particularly feasible if a company has a marketing department and/or a marketing research executive on its staff. Other companies prefer to design the research themselves and then employ the services of a fieldwork agency to collect the data. Alternatively, where resources permit and the scale of the study is larger, companies may employ the services of a market research agency to conduct the research. The company will brief the agency about its market research requirements and the agency will do the rest. The typical stages involved in completing a market research study are described next; full-service agencies generally conduct all the activities described below.

Stages in the marketing research process

Figure 4.2 provides a description of a typical marketing research process. Each of the stages illustrated will now be discussed.

Initial contact

The process usually starts with the realization that a marketing problem (e.g. a new product development or advertising decision) requires information to aid its solution. Marketing management may contact internal marketing research staff or an outside agency. Let us assume that the research requires the assistance of a marketing research agency. A meeting will be arranged to discuss the nature of the problem and the client's research needs. If the client and its markets are new to the agency, some rudimentary exploratory research (e.g. a quick library search for information about the client and its markets) may be conducted prior to the meeting.

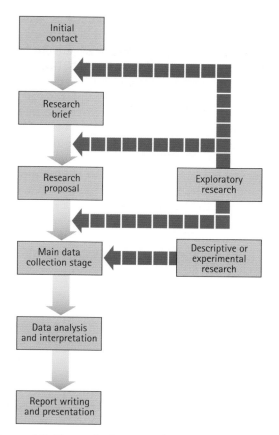

Figure 4.2 The marketing research process

Research brief

At a meeting to decide what form the research will need to take, the client explains the marketing problem and outlines the company's research objectives. The marketing problem might be the need to attract new customers to a product group, and the research objectives to identify groups of customers (market segments) who might have a use for the product and the characteristics of the product that appeal to them most.[9]

Other information that should be provided for the research agency includes the following.[10]

1   *Background information*: the product's history and the competitive situation.
2   *Sources of information*: the client may have a list of industries that might be potential users of the product. This helps the researchers to define the scope of the research.
3   *The scale of the project*: is the client looking for a 'cheap and cheerful' job or a major study? This has implications for the research design and survey costs.
4   *The timetable*: when is the information required?

The client should produce a specific written **research brief**. This may be given to the research agency prior to the meeting and perhaps modified as a result of it but, without fail, should be in the hands of the agency before it produces its **research proposal**. The research brief should state the client's requirements and should be in written form so that misunderstandings are minimized. In the event of a dispute later in the process, the research brief (and proposal) form the benchmarks against which it can be settled. It is typical to brief two or three agencies as the extra time involved is usually rewarded by the benefits of more than one viewpoint on the research problem . . . and a keener quote!

Research proposal

A research proposal lays out what a marketing research agency promises to do for its client, and how much this will cost. Like the research brief, the proposal should be written in a way that avoids misunderstandings. A client should expect the following to be included.

1   *A statement of objectives*: to demonstrate an understanding of the client's marketing and research problems.
2   *What will be done*: an unambiguous description of the research design—including the survey method, the type of sample, the sample size and how the fieldwork will be controlled.
3   *Timetable*: if and when a report will be produced.
4   *Costs*: how much the research will cost and what, specifically, is/is not included in those costs.

When assessing a proposal, a client needs to ensure that it is precise, jargon-free and that it addresses all the issues the client expects.

Exploratory research

Prior to the main qualitative data collection stage, **exploratory research** is employed to carry out the preliminary exploration of a research area. This usually occurs between acceptance of the research proposal and the main data collection stage, but can also take place prior to the client/agency briefing meeting and before submission of the research proposal, as an aid to its construction. Exploratory research techniques allow the researcher to understand the people who are to be interviewed in the main data collection stage, and the market that is being researched. The main survey stage can thus be designed with this knowledge in mind rather than being based on the researcher's ill-informed prejudices and guesswork.

A project may involve all or some of the following exploratory research activities:

- secondary research
- qualitative research (group discussions and depth interviews)
- observation.

Secondary research

Because the data come to the researcher 'second-hand' (i.e. other people have compiled it), this type of study is known as **secondary research**. (When the researcher actively collects new data—for example, by interviewing respondents—this is called primary research.) Secondary research should be carried out before primary research. Without the former, an expensive primary research survey might be commissioned to provide information that is already available from secondary sources. Increasingly a significant amount of market information is available for purchase through companies like Mintel and Euromonitor.

Secondary data can be found via examination of internal records and reports of research previously carried out for a company. External sources include government and European Commission statistics, publishers of reports and directories on markets, countries and industries, trade associations, banks, newspapers, magazines and journals. Given the amount of potential sources of information that are available globally, for many the first port of call is an Internet search engine. The search engine business has grown dramatically in recent years and has led to expressions such as 'to google', after the popular search engine Google (www.google.com), entering the general lexicon. The potential of the Internet as a marketing research medium is demonstrated in e-Marketing 4.2. The range of sources of information available to researchers in the European Union is listed in Appendix 4.1 (at the end of this chapter), which lists some of the major sources classified by research question.

Qualitative research

Group discussions and depth interviews are the main types of **qualitative research**. This kind of research aims to establish customers' attitudes, values, behaviour and beliefs.

Group discussions, sometimes referred to as **focus groups**, involve unstructured or semi-structured dis-

e-Marketing: Predicting fashion trends for the globe

The fashion industry moves at a rapid pace. What's hot one moment is cold the next, so keeping one's finger on the pulse is a constant challenge. The relentless demand for up-to-the-minute information in this industry makes the Internet an ideal medium to distribute data on the latest global fashion trends. Worth Global Style Network (WGSN), now a hugely successful global fashion online service provider, took advantage of this opportunity.

It was the brainchild of two brothers from Nottingham, Julian and Mark Worth. Their textile company, Heatseal, produced badges and transfers for clothing. Up to 90 per cent of the designs were never used so, in 1997, they decided to create a website to sell the unused artwork. It was at this stage that they recognized a much more lucrative opportunity to create a more comprehensive information site for the fashion industry.

Launched in 1998, WGSN now has a team of 100 creative and editorial employees who travel the globe, working with a network of cool hunters, writers, photographers, researchers and analysts, tracking the very latest in what's hot in fashion. This allows the company to produce over 500,000 pages of information on up-to-the-minute fashion news, trend analysis, video transmission of the top fashion shows throughout the world and industry-specialized directories. The wealth of diverse information it offers has gained WGSN many high-profile company subscribers, such as Dolce & Gabbana, Donna Karen, Levi Strauss, Tommy Hilfiger and Diesel.

Its success was recognized in 2003 when it won a Queen's Award for Enterprise, and in 2004 when its founders were named Ernst & Young's London Technology and Communication Entrepreneurs of the year. The ability of this dotcom company to thrive at a time when so many others have failed is proof of the value of having a strong business proposition.

Based on: Bell (1999);[11] Guthrie (2003)[12]

cussions between a moderator or group leader, who is often a psychologist, and a group of consumers. The moderator has a list of areas to cover within the topic, but allows the group considerable freedom to discuss the issues that are important to them. By arranging groups of six to twelve people to discuss their attitudes and behaviour, a good deal of knowledge may be gained about the consumer. This can be helpful when constructing questionnaires, which can be designed to focus on what is important to the respondent (as opposed to the researcher) and worded in language the respondent uses and understands. Sometimes focus groups are used to try to generate new product ideas, as shown in Marketing in Action 4.1.

The traditional focus group takes place face to face, but the rise of the Internet has led to the creation of online focus groups. The Internet offers 'communities of interests', which can take the form of chatrooms or websites dedicated to specific interests or issues. These are useful forums for conducting focus groups or at least for identifying suitable participants. Questions can be posed to participants who are not under time pressure to respond. This can lead to richer insights since respondents can think deeply

about the questions put to them online. Another advantage is that they can comprise people located all over the world at minimal cost. Furthermore, technological developments mean it is possible for clients to communicate secretly online with the moderator while the focus group is in session. The client can ask the moderator certain questions as a result of hearing earlier responses. Clearly, a disadvantage of online focus groups compared with the traditional form is that the body language and interaction between focus group members is missing.[14]

Depth interviews involve the interviewing of individual consumers about a single topic for perhaps one or two hours. The aims are broadly similar to those of the group discussion, but depth interviews are used when the presence of other people could inhibit the expression of honest answers and viewpoints, when the topic requires individual treatment (as when discussing an individual's decision-making process) and where the individual is an expert on a particular topic.

Care has to be taken when interpreting the results of qualitative research because the findings are usually based on small sample sizes, and the more interesting

Marketing in Action: Innovation through focus groups

The 'super group' is a recent development in the area of new product research. Super groups are not like normal focus groups. Rather than discussing and evaluating existing products and ideas, the job of the super group is to originate new concepts and products. Members of the group are chosen carefully and, through brainstorming and looking at a variety of possibilities, they come up with new ideas. The average consumer struggles to visualize how they would benefit from things they have not experienced. Super group consumers are different—they love playing with ideas and making connections between things that seem unrelated to create something new. This is a potentially attractive way for companies to innovate as creative customers often challenge corporations to break new ground. They are not constrained by the conventional thinking in an industry and for them anything is possible.

Becoming a member of a super group is not easy, however. Normally, potential members are first required to write a creative letter. Those who impress are interviewed by phone and in person. At the next stage, they complete a personality inventory and then sit a three-hour test of their verbal and visual creativity. At the end of all this, successful applicants take part in a day-long workshop where they are taught techniques for creative problem solving. In return for this investment, participants receive fees that are substantially higher than those available for normal focus group participation. Once the group is formed, it needs to be managed carefully. Some boundaries need to be put on the group—after all, the object of the exercise is to produce a commercially viable idea. But at the same time it is important not to limit the scope for original thinking. Any ideas developed by the group are first tested on mainstream consumer market segments to assess viability.

Based on: Clegg (2002)[13]

or surprising viewpoints may be disproportionately reported. This is particularly significant when qualitative research is not followed by a quantitative study.

Qualitative research accounts for 10 per cent of all European expenditure on marketing research, of which 60 per cent is spent on group discussions, 30 per cent on in depth interviews and 10 per cent on other qualitative techniques. Because of its ability to provide in-depth understanding, it is of growing importance within the field of consumer research.[15]

Observation

Observation can also help in exploratory research when the product field is unfamiliar, and may be either informal (where marketers take note of shopping patterns, etc.) or formal (where an observation study is designed and conducted). Observation studies can have a number of advantages. First, they do not rely on the respondent's willingness to provide information; second, the potential for the interviewer to bias the study is reduced; and, third, some types of information can be collected only by observation (for example, a traffic count). Observation studies can be conducted either by human or mechanical means, such as video recording, and may be conducted with

or without the customer's knowledge. Video taping consumers going about their daily lives is a rapidly growing segment of the market research industry (see Marketing in Action 4.2). Camera phones are the latest technology to be used for observation studies, with problems arising when they are used covertly. Samsung, the world's leading manufacturer of camera phones, has even banned their use in its factories, fearing industrial espionage.[16] Observation studies are particularly popular in the retail trade where a great deal can be learned by simply watching the behaviour of shoppers in a supermarket or clothing shop.

The objective of exploratory research, then, is not to collect quantitative data and form conclusions but to become better acquainted with the market and its customers. This allows the researcher to base the quantitative survey on informed assumptions rather than guesswork.

The main data collection stage

The design of the main data collection procedures will be done following careful exploratory research. The most usual approach is to undertake survey research to describe customers' beliefs, attitudes,

Marketing in Action: Corporate reality television

4.2

A practice dubbed 'corporate reality television' brings together ethnography—the academic study of humans in their natural environment—and the most advanced video technology. The result is the ability to produce documentary-style video tapes of different types of consumers using products as part of their daily lives. Advertising agency Ogilvy & Mather came upon the idea during the mid-1990s while trying to better understand black South Africans post-apartheid. Focus groups were not deemed to be appropriate to study people living in the poverty-stricken townships. Instead, the agency decided to dispatch camera crews to video tape these consumers. The result was an unexpected demand from clients for similar types of research and O&M now has an entire unit dedicated to this service, which has produced more than 250 documentaries for its various clients.

The demand for this research coincides with the rise in reality television as a form of mass entertainment. It allows marketing executives to know consumers in a more intimate way than other forms of research such as the focus group. More importantly, it provides a mechanism for senior executives to get close to consumer groups they may never come into contact with in their own daily lives because of physical distance and/or social class disparities. But it is a method that is not without its critics. As a form of observation one can see what people are doing but, in the absence of dialogue, it may be difficult to establish why they are doing it. Openness to interpretation can again lead to a distortion of the truth, unintentionally or otherwise. Weaknesses aside, in an age of media-savvy consumers, the video may offer them a more comfortable way to share their true inner feelings and thoughts than being in front of a group of strangers participating in a focus group discussion.

Based on: Nairn (2003);[17] Silverman (2005)[18]

preferences, behaviour, and so on. In general, the research design will be based on the following framework.

- Who and how many people to interview: the sampling process.
- How to interview them: the survey method.
- What questions to ask: questionnaire design.

The sampling process

Figure 4.3 offers an outline of the **sampling process**. This starts with the definition of the population—that is, the group that forms the subject of study in a particular survey. The survey objective will be to provide results that are representative of this group. Sampling planners, for example, must ask questions like 'Do we interview purchasing managers in all software development firms or only those that employ more than 50 people?'

Once the population has been defined, the next step is to search for a sampling frame—that is, a list or other record of the chosen population from which a sample can be selected. Examples include the electoral register and the *Kompass* directory of companies. Researchers then choose between three major sampling methods: simple random sampling (where the sample is drawn at random and each individual has a known and equal chance of being selected); stratified random sampling (where the population is broken into groups and a random sample is drawn from each group); and quota sampling (where interviewers are instructed to ensure that the sample comprises a required number of indi-

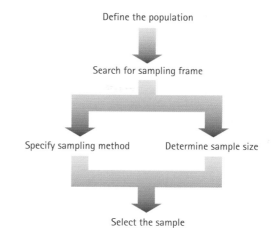

Figure 4.3 The sampling process

viduals meeting pre-set conditions, such as a set percentage of small, medium-sized and large companies).

Finally, the researcher must select an appropriate sample size. The larger the sample size the more likely it is that the sample will represent the population. Statistical theory allows the calculation of sampling error (i.e. the error caused by not interviewing everyone in the population) for various sample sizes. In practice, the number of people interviewed is based on a balance between sampling error and cost considerations. Fortunately, sample sizes of around 1000 (or fewer) can provide measurements that have tolerable error levels when representing populations counted in their millions.

Table 4.3 A comparison of response rates: face-to-face, telephone and mail surveys

	Face to face	**Telephone**	**Mail**	**Internet**
Questionnaire				
Use of open-ended questions	High	Medium	Low	Low
Ability to probe	High	Medium	Low	Low
Use of visual aids	High	Poor	High	High
Sensitive questions	Medium	Low	High	Low
Resources				
Cost	High	Medium	Low	Low
Sampling				
Widely dispersed populations	Low	Medium	High	High
Response rates	High	Medium	Low	Low
Experimental control	High	Medium	Low	Low
Interviewing				
Control of who completes questionnaire	High	High	Low	Low/high
Interviewer bias	Possible	Possible	Low	Low

The survey method

Four options are available to those choosing a survey method: face-to-face interviews, telephone interviews, mail surveys or Internet surveys. Each method has its own strengths and limitations; Table 4.3 gives an overview of these.

A major advantage of face-to-face interviews is that response rates are generally higher than for telephone interviews or mail surveys.[19] It seems that the personal element in the contact makes refusal less likely. Face-to-face interviews are more versatile than telephone and mail surveys. The use of many open-ended questions on a mail survey would lower response rates,[20] and time restrictions for telephone interviews limit their use. Probing for more detail is easier with face-to-face interviews. A certain degree of probing can be achieved with a telephone interview, but time pressure and the less personalized situation will inevitably limit its use.

Face-to-face interviews do, however, have their drawbacks. They are more expensive than telephone and mail questionnaires. Telephone and mail surveys are cheaper because the cost of contacting respondents is much less expensive, unless the population is very concentrated. The presence of an interviewer can cause bias (e.g. socially desirable answers) and lead to the misreporting of sensitive information. For example, O'Dell[21] found that only 17 per cent of respondents admitted borrowing money from a bank

in a face-to-face interview compared to 42 per cent in a comparable mail survey.

In some ways, telephone interviews are a halfway house between face-to-face and mail surveys. They generally have a higher response rate than mail questionnaires but a lower rate than face-to-face interviews; their cost is usually lower than for face-to-face but higher than for mail surveys; and they allow a degree of flexibility when interviewing. However, the use of visual aids is not possible and there are limits to the number of questions that can be asked before respondents either terminate the interview or give quick (invalid) answers in order to speed up the process. The use of computer-aided telephone interviewing (CATI) is growing. Centrally located interviewers read questions from a computer monitor and input answers via the keyboard. Routing through the questionnaire is computer-controlled, thus assisting the process of interviewing.

Given a reasonable response rate, mail survey research is normally a very economical method of conducting research. However, the major problem is the potential for low response rates and the accompanying danger of an unrepresentative sample. Nevertheless, using a systematic approach to the design of a mail survey, such as the Total Design Method (TDM),[22] has been found to have a very positive effect on response rates. The TDM recommends, as ways of improving response rates, both

Marketing in Action: Conducting surveys around the world

Applying a consistent approach to conducting research around the world is important but difficult. The idea of brands, taken for granted in the West, is not readily understood in China. Questions about alcohol have to be left out of surveys in Saudi Arabia. Low literacy levels in some countries means that respondents need more 'hand-holding' by interviewers.

Particular difficulties can be encountered in survey fieldwork. In Argentina, where the long economic crisis has led to a rise in crime, police or fire workers sometimes accompany researchers into the most dangerous neighbourhoods. Face-to-face interviews are necessary, because only about 60 per cent of households have a telephone. Some fieldworkers have been robbed and all are advised not to wear jewellery or expensive clothes, and to carry a small amount of money that they can hand over if threatened. Anywhere that crime is high, researchers will face difficulties entering homes because people are afraid to answer the door.

Because of the difficulties of doorstep surveys, face-to-face research is often conducted in shopping malls. The drawback is that more women than men shop in malls so responses need to be weighted accordingly. The advantage is that shopping malls are seen as neutral, particularly where communities are divided, as in Northern Ireland. In Israel, the security crisis has contributed to a big shift to telephone interviewing, so that now only about 20 per cent of surveys are face to face.

Based on: Maitland (2003)[24]

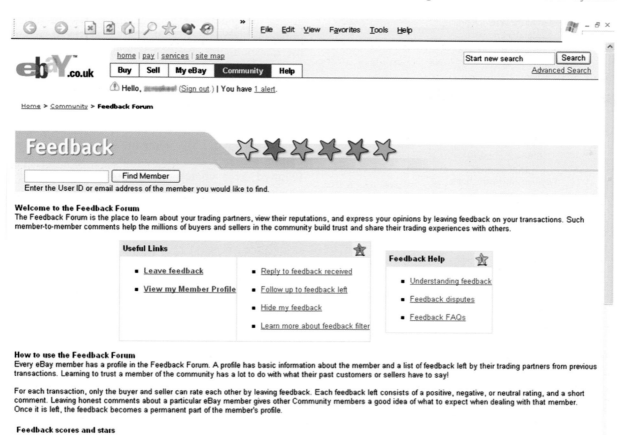

Exhibit 4.2 Web-based research like this at eBay is becoming increasingly popular

the careful design of questionnaires to make them easy to complete, as well as accompanying them with a personalized covering letter emphasizing the importance of the research. Studies using the TDM on commercial populations have generated high response rates.[23]

The Internet is a new medium for conducting survey research. The Internet questionnaire is usually administered by e-mail or signals its presence on a website by registering key words or using banner advertising on search engines to drive people to the questionnaire. The major advantage of the Internet as a marketing research vehicle is its low cost, since printing and postal costs are eliminated, making it even cheaper than mail surveys. In other ways, its characteristics are similar to mail surveys: the use of open-ended questions is limited; control over who completes the questionnaire is low; interviewer bias is low; response rates are likely to be lower than for face-to-face and telephone interviews.

Some issues influencing the choice of survey method around the world are outlined in Marketing in Action 4.3.

When response is by e-mail, the identity of the respondent will automatically be sent to the survey company. This lack of anonymity may restrict the respondent's willingness to answer sensitive questions honestly. A strength of the Internet survey is its ability to cover global populations at low cost, although sampling problems can arise because of the skewed nature of Internet users. These tend to be from the younger and more affluent groups in society. For surveys requiring a cross-sectional sample this can be severely restricting.

Questionnaire design

To obtain a true response to a question, three conditions are necessary. First, respondents must understand the question; second, they must be able to provide the information; and, third, they must be willing to provide it. Figure 4.4 shows the three stages in the development of the questionnaire: planning, design and pilot.

The planning stage involves the types of decision discussed so far in this chapter. It provides a firm foundation for designing a questionnaire, which provides relevant information for the marketing problem that is being addressed.

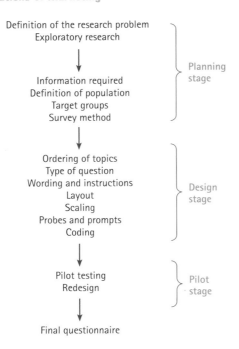

Figure 4.4 Stages in the development of a questionnaire

The design stage deals with the actual construction of the survey instrument and involves a number of important decisions. The first relates to the ordering of topics. It is sensible to start with easy-to-answer questions, in order to relax the respondent, and leave sensitive questions until last. Effective questionnaires are well structured and have a logical flow. Second, the type of question needs to be decided. Generally, three types are used: dichotomous questions (allow two possible answers, such as 'Yes'/'No'), multiple-choice questions, which allow more than two answers, and open questions, where the respondents answer by expressing their opinions.

Great care needs to be taken with both the wording and instructions used in the questionnaire and its layout. Questionnaire designers need to guard against asking ambiguous or leading questions, and using unfamiliar words (see Table 4.4). In terms of layout, the questionnaire should not appear cluttered and, where possible, answers and codes should each form a column so that they are easy to identify.

The use of 'scales' is very common in questionnaire design. For example, respondents are given lists of statements (e.g. 'My company's marketing information system allows me to make better decisions') followed by a choice of five positions on a scale ranging from 'strongly agree' to 'strongly disagree'. 'Probes' are used to explore or clarify what a respondent has said. Following a question about awareness of brand names, the exploratory probe 'Any others?' would seek to identify further names. Sometimes respondents use vague words or phrases like 'I like going on holiday because it is nice.' A clarifying probe such as, 'In what way is it nice?' would seek a more meaningful response. 'Prompts', on the other hand, aid responses to a question. For example, in an aided recall question, a list of brand names would be provided for the respondent. Coding involves the assignment of numbers to specific responses in order to facilitate analysis of the questionnaire later on.

Once the preliminary questionnaire has been designed it should be piloted with a representative sub-sample, to test for faults; this is known as the 'pilot stage'. Piloting tests the questionnaire design and helps to estimate costs. Face-to-face piloting, where respondents are asked to answer questions and comment on any problems concerning a questionnaire read out by an interviewer, is preferable to impersonal piloting where the questionnaire is given to respondents for self-completion and they are asked to write down any problems found.[25] Once the pilot work proves satisfactory, the final questionnaire can be administered to the chosen sample.

Table 4.4 Poorly worded questions

Question	Problem and solution
What type of wine do you prefer?	'Type' is ambiguous: respondents could say 'French', 'red' or 'claret', say, depending on their interpretation. Showing the respondent a list and asking 'from this list ...' would avoid the problem
Do you think that prices are cheaper at Asda than at Aldi?	Leading question favouring Asda; a better question would be 'Do you think that prices at Asda are higher, lower or about the same as at Aldi?' Names should be reversed for half the sample
Which is more powerful and kind to your hands: Ariel or Bold?	Two questions in one: Ariel may be more powerful but Bold may be kinder to the hands. Ask the two questions separately
Do you find it paradoxical that X lasts longer and yet is cheaper than Y?	Unfamiliar word: a study has shown that less than a quarter of the population understand such words as paradoxical, chronological or facility. Test understanding before use

Data analysis and interpretation

Computers are invariably used to carry out the quantitative analysis of questionnaire data. Basic marketing analyses can be carried out using such software analysis packages as SNAP and MARQUIS on a personal computer. More sophisticated analyses can be conducted using packages such as SPSS-PC and NUD.IST.

Basic analysis of questionnaire data may be at the descriptive level (e.g. means, frequency tables and standard deviations) or on a comparative basis (e.g. t-tests and cross-tabulations). More sophisticated analysis may search for relationships (e.g. regression analysis), group respondents (e.g. cluster analysis), or establish cause and effect (e.g. analysis of variance techniques used on experimental data).

When interpreting marketing research results, great care must be taken. One common failing is to infer cause and effect when only association has been established. For example, establishing a relationship that sales rise when advertising levels increase does not necessarily mean that raising advertising expenditure will lead to an increase in sales. Other marketing variables (e.g. salesforce effect) may have increased at the same time as the increase in advertising. A second cautionary note concerns the interpretation of means and percentages. Given that a sample has been taken, any mean or percentage is an estimate subject to 'sampling error'—that is, an error in an estimate due to taking a sample rather than interviewing the entire population. A market research survey which estimates that 50 per cent of males but only 45 per cent of females smoke, does not necessarily suggest that smoking is more prevalent among males. Given the sampling error associated with each estimate, the true conclusion might be that there is no difference between males and females.

Report writing and presentation

Crouch suggests that the key elements in a research report are as follows:[26]

1 title page
2 list of contents
3 preface—outline of agreed brief, statement of objectives, scope and methods of research
4 summary of conclusions and recommendations
5 previous related research—how previous research has had a bearing on this research
6 research method
7 research findings
8 conclusions
9 appendices.

Sections 1–4 provide a concise description of the nature and outcomes of the research for busy man-

Worried about someone looking into your business data?

Exhibit 4.3 This McAfee advertisement highlights the importance of data security, which is a key issue for companies building up an MkIS

agers. Sections 5–9 provide the level of detail necessary if any particular issue (e.g. the basis of a finding, or the analytical technique used) needs checking. The report should be written in language the reader will understand; jargon should be avoided.

Marketing information systems

By carefully following each of the stages described above, researchers can improve the quality of the market information they collect. However, the variety of information that is currently available to companies means that it is sensible to set up a **marketing information system**. A marketing information system has been defined as:

> . . . a system in which marketing information is formally gathered, stored, analysed and distributed to managers in accord with their informational needs on a regular planned basis.[27]

The system is built on an understanding of the information needs of marketing management, and supplies

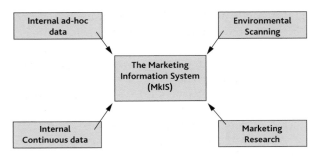

Figure 4.5 The marketing information system (MkIS)

that information when, where and in the form that the manager requires it. Marketing information system (MkIS) design is important since the quality of a marketing information system has been shown to affect the effectiveness of decision-making.[28] The MkIS comprises four elements: internal continuous data, internal ad hoc data, environmental scanning, and marketing research (see Figure 4.5).

Companies possess an enormous amount of marketing and financial data (internal continuous data) that may never be used for marketing decision-making unless organized by means of an MkIS. This includes, for example, information that is available from the company's salesforce, such as number of accounts opened, customer attitudes, etc., as well as financial data such as that regarding sales and profitability.

Company data can also be used for a specific (ad hoc) purpose (this is known as internal ad hoc data). For example, management may look at how sales have reacted to a price increase or a change in advertising copy. Although this could be part of a continuous monitoring programme, specific one-off analyses are inevitably required from time to time. Capturing the data on the MkIS allows specific analyses to be conducted when needed.

The environmental scanning procedures discussed in Chapter 2 also form part of the MkIS. Although often amorphous in nature, environmental analysis—whereby the economic, social, legal, technological and physical forces are monitored—should be considered part of the MkIS. These are the forces that shape the context within which suppliers, the company, distributors and the competition do business. As such, environmental scanning provides an early warning system for the forces that may affect a company's products and markets in the future.[29] In this way, scanning enables an organization to act upon, rather than react to, opportunities and threats.

As discussed in this chapter, marketing research is primarily concerned with the provision of infor-

mation about markets and measuring the reactions of consumers to various marketing actions.[30] As such it is a key part of the MkIS because it makes a major contribution to marketing mix planning.

The use of marketing information systems and marketing research

It is important to understand the factors that affect the use of marketing information systems and marketing research. Systems and marketing research reports that remain unused have no value in decision-making.

Marketing information systems should be designed to provide information on a selective basis (for example, by means of a direct, interactive capability).[31] Senior management should conspicuously support use of the system. These recommendations are in line with Ackoff's view[32] that a prime task of an information system is to eliminate irrelevant information by tailoring information flows to the individual manager's needs. It also supports the prescription of Piercy and Evans that the system should be seen to have top management support,[33] and is consistent with Kohli and Jaworski's view that a market orientation is essentially the organization-wide generation and dissemination of, and responsiveness to, market intelligence.[34]

Marketing research is more likely to be used if researchers appreciate not only the technical aspects of research, but also the need for clarity in report presentation and the political dimension of information provision. It is unlikely that marketing research reports will be used in decision-making if the results threaten the status quo or are likely to have adverse political repercussions. Therefore, perfectly valid and useful information may sometimes be ignored in decision-making for reasons other than difficulties with the way the research was conducted.

Ethical issues in marketing research

It is the aim of marketing research to benefit both the sponsoring company and that company's consumers; the company learns about the needs and buyer behaviour of consumers with the objective of better satisfying their needs. Despite these good intentions, there are four ethical concerns about marketing research. These are: intrusions on privacy, the misuse of marketing research findings, competitive information gathering, and the use of marketing research surveys as a guise for selling.

Many consumers resent the intrusive nature of marketing research, whether this involves questions relating to age and income, being stopped in the street and asked to complete a face-to-face survey or being phoned in their homes at a time that is inconvenient. The right to privacy of the individual is incorporated in the guidelines of many research associations. For example, a code of conduct of the European Society for Opinion and Marketing Research (ESOMAR) (www.esomar.org) recommends that under no circumstances should the information from a survey combined with the address/telephone number of the respondent be supplied to any third party.

Care needs to be taken to ensure that research findings are not misused. For example, individuals in a client organization may have a vested interest in the outcome of the research. In such circumstances, there is the potential for the most favoured outcome to be communicated to the research agency. Where such individuals are influential in the choice of agency, the latter may recognize that giving bad news to the client may sour their relationship and jeopardize future business. While most marketing researchers accept the need for objective studies where there is room for more than one interpretation or study findings, for example, the temptation to present the more favourable representation could be overpowering.

The methods used to gather competitor intelligence can raise ethical questions. Questionable practices include using student projects to gather information without the student revealing the identity of the sponsor of the research, pretending to be a potential supplier who is conducting a telephone survey to understand the market, posing as a potential customer at an exhibition, bribing a competitor's employee to pass on proprietary information, and covert surveillance such as through the use of hidden cameras. Thankfully, competitive information gathering does not exclusively depend on such methods, since much useful information can be gathered by reading trade journals and newspapers, searching the Internet, analysing databases and acquiring financial statements.

The practice of selling in the guise of marketing research, commonly known as 'sugging', is a real danger to the reputation of marketing research. Despite the fact that it is not usually practised by bona fide marketing research agencies but, rather, unscrupulous selling companies who use marketing research as a means of gaining compliance to their requests, it is the marketing research industry that suffers from its aftermath. Usually, the questions begin innocently enough but gradually move towards the real object of the exercise. Often, this is to qualify prospects and ask whether they would be interested in buying a product or have a salesperson call. Marketing research bodies have strict codes of practice about such behaviour.

Summary

This chapter has examined the nature and role of marketing research and marketing information systems. The following key issues were addressed.

1. The importance of marketing research: marketing research is key if an organization is to be truly market-led. It can provide answers to all sorts of marketing questions that the organization may face.

2. The types of marketing research: marketing research can be either ad hoc (to solve specific problems at a point in time) or continuous (to gather information on an ongoing basis).

3. The approaches to conducting research: marketing research can be conducted either by the organization itself or by employing the services of a professional marketing research firm.

4. The stages in the market research process: these include initial contact, the research brief, the research proposal, exploratory research, the main data collection phase, data analysis and report writing/presentation.

5. The nature of marketing information systems: these are systems in which marketing information is formally gathered, stored and distributed on a regular planned basis.

Suggested reading

Carson, D., A. Gilmore and **K. Gronhaug** (2001) *Qualitative Marketing Research*, London: Sage Publications.

Fahy, J. (1998) Improving Response Rates in Cross-Cultural Mail Surveys, *Industrial Marketing Management*, **27**, 459–67.

Grossnickle J. and **O. Raskin** (2001) *The Handbook of Online Marketing Research: Knowing Your Customers Using the Net*, New York: McGraw-Hill.

Lorange, P. (2004) Memo to Marketing, *Sloan Management Review*, **46** (2), 16–20.

McQuarrie, E. (1996) *The Market Research Toolbox, A Concise Guide for Beginners*, London: Sage.

Internet exercises

Sites to visit

1   http://www.statpac.com/research-papers/research-proposal.htm

Exercise

This site describes the elements of a research proposal and report. Critique its content in light of what has been written about the marketing research proposal and marketing research report in this chapter.

2   http://www.mintel.com
http://www.euromonitor.com

Exercise

Select any product or service of your choice. Visit the two websites and evaluate what secondary research is available on it.

3   http://www.census.gov/dmd/www/pdf/d61a.pdf

Exercise

Evaluate the questionnaire suggesting any changes that you feel ought to be made to it.

Study questions

1. What are the differences between secondary and primary data? Explain the roles played by each.
2. Outline the main stages in the marketing research process, identifying particularly the kinds of difficulties that might be faced at each stage.
3. Why are marketing research reports more likely to be used if they conform to the prior beliefs of the client? Does this raise any ethical questions regarding the interpretation and presentation of findings?
4. What are the strengths and limitations of the Internet as a data collection instrument?
5. What is meant by a marketing information system? Discuss, using examples, the main components of such a system.

Key terms

marketing research the gathering of data and information on the market

ad hoc research a research project that focuses on a specific problem, collecting data at one point in time with one sample of respondents

omnibus survey a regular survey, usually operated by a market research specialist company, which asks questions of respondents

continuous research repeated interviewing of the same sample of people

consumer panel household consumers who provide information on their purchases over time

retail audit a type of continuous research

tracking the sales of products through retail outlets

research brief written document stating the client's requirements

research proposal a document defining what the marketing research agency promises to do for its client and how much it will cost

exploratory research the preliminary exploration of a research area prior to the main data collection stage

secondary research data that has already been collected by another researcher for another purpose

qualitative research exploratory research that

aims to understand consumers' attitudes, values, behaviour and beliefs

focus group a group, normally of six to eight consumers, brought together for a discussion focusing on an aspect of a company's marketing

depth interviews the interviewing of consumers individually for perhaps one or two hours with the aim of understanding their attitudes, values, behaviour and/or beliefs

sampling process a term used in research to denote the selection of a subset of the total population in order to interview them

marketing information system a system in which marketing information is formally gathered, stored, analysed and distributed to managers in accordance with their informational needs on a regular, planned basis

References

1. **Grossman, L.** (2003) The Quest for Cool, *Time Canada*, **162** (10), 44; **Langer, J.** (2001) Forecasting Traps can Trip up Trend Spotters, *Advertising Age*, **72** (14), 18; **Terazono, E.** (2003) Squaring the Mainstream Circle, *Financial Times: Creative Business*, 24 June, 2–3; **Wood, D.** (2004) Up on What's Going Down, *Financial Times*, Creative Business, 4 May, 6.

2. **Kohli, A.** and **B. Jaworski** (1990) Market Orientation: The Construct, Research Propositions and Marketing Implications, *Journal of Marketing*, **54**, 1–18; **Narver, J.** and **S. Slater** (1990) The Effect of Market Orientation on Business Profitability, *Journal of Marketing*, **54**, 20–35.

3. **Day, G.** (1994) The Capabilities of Market-driven Organisations, *Journal of Marketing*, **58**, 37–52.

4. **Foss, B.** and **M. Stone** (2001) *Successful Customer Relationship Marketing*, London: Kogan Page.

5. **Pritchard, S.** (2003) Clicking the Habits, *Financial Times*, IT Review, 5 February, 4.

6. **Bowen, D.** (2003) Chasing Customers Through the Internet Maze, *Financial Times*, IT Review, 3 September, 1.

7. **Guenther, K.** (2003) Nothing Measured, Nothing Gained, *Online*, **27** (6), 53–5.

8. **Phippen, A., L. Sheppard** and **S. Furnell** (2004) A Practical Evaluation of Web Analytics, *Internet Research*, **14** (4), 284–93.

9. **Crouch, S.** and **M. Housden** (1999) *Marketing Research for Managers*, Oxford: Butterworth Heinemann, 253.

10. **Crouch, S.** and **M. Housden** (1999) *Marketing Research for Managers*, Oxford: Butterworth Heinemann, 260.

11. **Bell, S.** (1999) Worth Global Style Network, *Database Magazine*, **22** (2), 26–30.

12. **Guthrie, J.** (2003) Brothers Bond with Followers of Fashion, *Financial Times*, 16 December, 16.

13. **Clegg, A.** (2002) Mavericks Help to Break New Ground, *Financial Times*, 15 December, 15.

14. **Gray, R.** (1999) Tracking the Online Audience, *Marketing*, 18 February, 41–3.

15. **Goulding, C.** (1999) Consumer Research: Interpretive Paradigms and Methodological Ambiguities, *European Journal of Marketing*, **33** (9/10), 859–73.

16. **Harper, J.** (2003) Camera Phones Cross Moral, Legal Lines, *Washington Times*, Business, 15 July, 6.

17. **Nairn, A.** (2003) Video Kills the Focus Group, *Financial Times*, Creative Business, 4 November, 6.

18. **Silverman, G.** (2005) Why the Boardroom Believes in Reality TV, *Financial Times*, 1 March, 13.

19. **Yu. J.** and **H. Cooper** (1983) A Quantitative Review of Research Design Effects on Response Rates to Questionnaires, *Journal of Marketing Research*, 20 February, 156–64.

20. **Falthzik. A.** and **S. Carroll** (1971) Rate of Return for Close v Open-ended Questions in a Mail Survey of Industrial Organisations, *Psychological Reports*, **29**, 1121–2.

21. **O'Dell, W.F.** (1962) Personal Interviews or Mail Panels?, *Journal of Marketing*, **26**, 34–9.

22. **Dillman, D.** (1978) *Mail and Telephone Surveys: The Total Design Method*, New York: John Wiley & Sons.

23. See **Fahy, J.** (1998) Improving Response Rates in Cross-cultural Mail Surveys, *Industrial Marketing Management*, 27 (November), 459–67; **Walker, B., W. Kirchmann** and **J. Conant** (1987) A Method to Improve Response Rates in Industrial Mail Surveys, *Industrial Marketing Management*, **16** (November), 305–14.

24. **Maitland, A.** (2003) When the Word on the Street is Danger, *Financial Times*, 5 March, 16.

25. **Reynolds, N.** and **A. Diamantopoulos** (1998) The Effect of Pretest Method on Error Detection Rates: Experimental Evidence, *European Journal of Marketing*, **32** (5/6), 480–98.

26. **Crouch, S.** (1992) *Marketing Research for*

Managers, Oxford: Butterworth Heinemann, 253.

27. **Jobber, D.** and **C. Rainbow** (1977) A Study of the Development and Implementation of Marketing Information Systems in British Industry, *Journal of the Marketing Research Society,* **19** (3), 104–11.

28. **Van Bruggen, A., A. Smidts** and **B. Wierenga** (1996) The Impact of the Quality of a Marketing Decision Support System: An Experimental Study, *International Journal of Research in Marketing,* **13**, 331–43.

29. **Jain, S.C.** (1981) *Marketing Planning and Strategy,* South Western Publishing.

30. **Moutinho, L.** and **M. Evans** (1992) *Applied Marketing Research,* Colorado Springs, CO: Wokingham: Addison-Wesley, 5.

31. **Jobber, D.** and **M. Watts** (1986) Behavioural Aspects of Marketing Information Systems, *Omega,* **14** (1), 69–79; **Wierenga, B.** and **P.A.M. Oude Ophis** (1997) Marketing Decision Support Systems: Adoption, Use and Satisfaction, *International Journal of Research in Marketing,* 14, 275–90.

32. **Ackoff, R.L.** (1967) Management Misinformation Systems, *Management Science,* **14** (4), 147–56.

33. **Piercy, N.** and **M. Evans** (1983) *Managing Marketing Information,* Beckenham: Croom Helm.

34. **Kohli, A.** and **B. Jaworski** (1990) Market Orientation: The Construct, Research Propositions and Marketing Implications, *Journal of Marketing,* **54**, 1–18.

Appendix 4.1

Sources of European marketing information

Is there a survey of the industry?

Euromonitor GMID Database has in-depth analysis and current market information in the key areas of country data, consumer lifestyles, market sizes, forecasts, brand and country information, business information sources and marketing profiles.

Reuters Business Insight Reports are full-text reports available online in the sectors of healthcare, financial services, consumer goods, energy, e-commerce and technology.

KeyNote Reports cover size of market, economic trends, prospects and company performance.

Mintel Premier Reports cover market trends, prospects and company performance.

Snapshots on CD-Rom The 'Snapshots' CD series is a complete library of market research reports, providing coverage of consumer, business-to-business and industrial markets. Containing 2000 market research reports, this series provides incisive data and analysis on over 8000 market segments for the UK, Europe and the United States.

British Library Market Research is a guide to British Library Holdings. It lists titles of reports arranged by industry. Some items are available on inter-library loan; others may be seen at the British Library in London.

International Directory of Published Market Research, published by Marketsearch.

How large is the market?

European Marketing Data and Statistics Now available on the Euromonitor GMID database.
International Marketing Data and Statistics Now available on the Euromonitor GMID database.
CEO Bulletin
A–Z of UK Marketing Data
European Marketing Pocket Book
The Asia Pacific Marketing Pocket Book
The Americas Marketing Pocket Book

Where is the market?

Regional Marketing Pocket Book
Regional Trends gives the main economic and social statistics for UK regions.
Geodemographic Pocket Book

Who are the competitors?

British companies can be identified using any of the following.
Kompass (most European countries have their own edition)
Key British Enterprises
Quarterly Review—KPMG
Sell's Products and Services Directory (Gen Ref E 380.02542 SEL)

For more detailed company information consult the following.
Companies Annual Report Collection
Carol: Company Annual Reports online at www.carol.co.uk
Fame DVD (CD-Rom service)
Business Ratio Reports
Retail Rankings

Overseas companies sources include:
Asia's 7,500 Largest Companies
D&B Europa
Dun's Asia Pacific Key Business Enterprises
Europe's 15,000 Largest Companies
Major Companies of the Arab World
Million Dollar Directory (US)
Principal International Businesses

What are the trends?

Possible sources to consider include the following.
The Book of European Forecasts Now available on the Euromonitor GMID database.
Marketing in Europe
European Trends
Consumer Europe Now available on the Euromonitor GMID database.
Consumer Goods Europe
Family Expenditure Survey
Social Trends
Lifestyle Pocket Book

Drink Trends
Media Pocket Book
Retail Business
Mintel Market Intelligence
OECD (Organization for Economic Cooperation and Development)
EU statistical and information sources

'Eurostat' is a series of publications that provide a detailed picture of the EU; they can be obtained by visiting European Documentation Centres (often in university libraries) in all EU countries; themes include general statistics, economy and finance, and population/social conditions.

Eurostat Yearbook

European Access is a bulletin on issues, policies, activities and events concerning EU member states.

Marketing and Research Today is a journal that examines social, political, economic and business issues relating to Western, Central and Eastern Europe.

European Report is a twice-weekly news publication from Brussels on industrial, economic and political issues.

Abstracts and indexes

Business Periodicals Index
ANBAR Marketing and Distribution Abstracts
ABI Inform
Research Index
Times Index
Elsevier Science Direct
Emerald
Wiley Interscience and Boldideas

Guides to sources

A great variety of published information sources exists; the following source guides may help you in your search.
Marketing Information
Guide to European Marketing Information
Compendium of Marketing Information Sources
Croner's A–Z of Business Information Sources
McCarthy Cards: a card service on which are reproduced extracts from the press covering companies and industries; it also produces a useful guide to its sources: *UK and Europe Market Information: Basic Sources*

Statistics

Guide to Official Statistics
Sources of the Unofficial UK Statistics

Sources: the authors thank the University of Bradford School of Management Library for help in compiling this list

Case 4 The *Südkurier*

The *Südkurier*[1] is a regional daily newspaper in south-western Germany. On average 310,000 people in the area read the newspaper regularly. The great majority of those readers subscribe to its home delivery service, which puts the paper on their doorsteps early in the morning. On the market for the past 35 years, the *Südkurier* contains editorial sections on politics, the economy, sports, local news, entertainment and features, as well as advertising. The newspaper is financially independent and its staff is free of any political affiliation. Management at the *Südkurier* would like to bring the paper into line with the current needs of its readers. For this purpose, the management team is considering the use of market research.

Management would like to have information about the following.

1 What newspapers or other media are the *Südkurier*'s main competitors?
2 Do most readers read the *Südkurier* for the local news, sports and classified ads, and should these sections therefore be expanded at the expense of the sections on politics and the economy?
3 Should the *Südkurier*'s layout be modernized?
4 Do mostly lower levels of society read the *Südkurier*?
5 Into what political category do readers and non-readers put the *Südkurier*?
6 Which suppliers of products and services consider the *Südkurier* especially appropriate for their advertising?
7 What advertising or information do the readers think is missing from the *Südkurier*?

You are an employee of the *Südkurier* who has been instructed to obtain the requested information and to prepare your findings for the decision-makers. You are in the fortunate position of receiving regular reports about people's media use from the Arbeitsgemeinschaft Media-Analyse e.V. Relevant excerpts from the most recent survey are shown here as Tables C4.1 and C4.2.

Table C4.1 Media analysis of readership structure

Range in Circulation Area (1)		Readers per edition of *SÜDKURIER*			National average in %
		Range		Total in %	
		in %	Absolute		
Total		53.5	310,000	100.0	100.0
Gender	Men	55.5	150,000	49.0	47.2
	Women	51.6	160,000	51.0	52.8
Age Groups	14–19 years	51.8	20,000	8.0	7.2
	20–29 years	41.0	50,000	15.0	19.1
	30–39 years	52.1	50,000	16.0	16.4
	40–49 years	61.8	50,000	16.0	15.2
	50–59 years	61.1	60,000	19.0	16.5
	60–69 years	53.6	40,000	13.0	13.5
	70 years and older	57.4	40,000	13.0	12.2
Educational Level	Secondary school without apprenticeship	49.4	60,000	18.0	17.6
	Secondary school with apprenticeship	50.8	100,000	31.0	39.6
	Continuing education without Abitur	60.8	110,000	36.0	27.0
	Abitur, university preparation, university/college	49.7	50,000	15.0	15.8
Occupation	Trainee, pupil, student	44.7	40,000	11.0	11.0
	Full-time employee	54.6	160,000	50.0	51.7

[1] There really is a newspaper called *Südkurier* and the data provided here are real. The case study, however, is completely fictitious.

Table C4.1 continued

	Retiree, pensioner	57.3	70,000	23.0	21.8
	Unemployed	52.4	50,000	16.0	15.5
Occupation of main wage earner	Self-employed, mid- to large businesses/Freelancer	63.8	20,000	5.0	3.1
	Self-employed, small business, /Farmer	59.9	30,000	10.0	7.1
	Managers and civil servants	58.6	30,000	9.0	8.7
	Other employees and civil servants	49.3	120,000	40.0	42.9
	Skilled staff	57.6	100,000	32.0	32.5
	Unskilled staff	38.7	10,000	4.0	5.6
Net Household Income/ month	4500 and more	62.7	100,000	31.0	23.9
	3500–4500	52.7	60,000	19.0	20.8
	2500–3500	54.9	80,000	26.0	25.9
	to 2500	44.1	70,000	23.0	29.3
Number of wage earners	1 earner	45.4	100,000	33.0	40.4
	2 earner	56.5	130,000	41.0	42.6
	3 earner	62.7	80,000	25.0	16.9
Household Size	1 Person	41.8	50,000	14.0	17.9
	2 Persons	55.5	90,000	29.0	31.8
	3 Persons	59.5	70,000	22.0	22.4
	4 Persons and more	54.8	110,000	35.0	27.9
Children in Household	Children less than 2 years of age	52.7	10,000	4.0	3.8
	2 to less than 4 years	38.4	10,000	4.0	5.4
	4 to less than 6 years	45.8	10,000	5.0	5.2
	6 to less than 10 years	43.8	20,000	8.0	8.5
	10 to less than 14 years	54.1	30,000	10.0	9.2
	14 to less than 18 years	57.7	50,000	16.0	13.7
	No children under 14	54.9	250,000	79.0	77.4
	No children under 18	53.6	210,000	67.0	68.1
Driving Licence	yes	55.2	250,000	80.0	73.0
	no	47.3	60,000	20.0	27.0
Private Automobile		55.5	270,000	86.0	80.0
Garden	own garden	60.4	240,000	76.0	57.0
	without garden	39.8	70,000	23.0	43.0
Housing	own house	62.1	180,000	58.0	46.0
	own apartment	45.9	10,000	3.0	3.0
	rent house or apartment	44.7	120,000	38.0	49.0

Table C4.1 continued

Electrical Appliances	Freezer/Deep freeze	59.6	200,000	62.0	51.0
Last Holiday Journey	Within the last 12 months	55.1	190,000	62.0	n.a.
	1–2 years ago	51.0	40,000	14.0	n.a.
	More than two years ago	48.6	50,000	16.0	n.a.
	Never	55.4	30,000	9.0	n.a.
Last Holiday Destination	Germany	57.4	70,000	23.0	n.a.
	Austria, Switzerland, South Tyrol	48.7	60,000	20.0	n.a.
	Elsewhere in Europe	53.4	130,000	42.0	n.a.
	Country outside Europe	51.4	20,000	5.0	n.a.
	Did not travel	56.4	30,000	9.0	n.a.

1) Entire circulation area 310,000 readers per edition

Example:
53.5% of people older than 14 years in the circulation of the *Südkurier* read the *Südkurier* daily.
55.5% of all men older than 14 years and 51.6% of women older than 14 read the *Südkurier* daily; that is 150,000 men and 160,000 women.

Table C4.2 Reader behaviour

What purchasing information is used? Media purchasing information for medium and long-term acquisition (11 product areas; Basis: total population)		Credibility of advertising in the media Advertising in … is generally believable and reliable (Basis: broadest user group in each case)	
Daily newspapers	61%	Regional newspapers (subscription)	49%
Posters on the street	9%	Television	30%
Leaflets	36%	Public radio	20%
Television	24%	Privately-owned radio	14%
Radio	13%	Magazines	15%
Magazines	27%	Free newspapers	23%
Free newspapers	49%		
Advertising in … is most informative (Basis: broadest reading group)		**Time spent reading daily newspaper** (Basis: broadest user group)	
Regional newspapers (subscription)	62%	less than 15 minutes	7%
Television	47%	15–24 minutes	21%
Public radio	29%	25–34 minutes	28%
Privately owned radio	26%	35–65 minutes	34%
Magazines	27%	more than 65 minutes	10%
Free newspapers	36%		
I often consult/depend on advertising in … (Basis: broadest user group in each case)			
Regional newspapers (subscription)	27%		
Television	11%		
Public radio	8%		
Privately owned radio	6%		
Magazines	7%		
Free newspapers	18%		

Source: Regional Press Study, GfK-Medienforschung Contest-Census

Questions

1. Explain how you will methodically go about compiling the requested information covered in the seven questions for management. Include in your explanation an estimate of the expense involved in obtaining the information.
2. Develop a 10-question questionnaire for the purpose of making a survey.

This case was written by Jens-Mogens Holm, professor for marketing at European School of Business, Reutlingen University and president of Europäische Fernhochschule Hamburg. The material was drawn from publicly available sources. The case study, however, is completely fictitious.

CHAPTER 5

MARKET SEGMENTATION, TARGETING AND POSITIONING

Learning Objectives

By the end of this chapter you will understand:

1 the process of market segmentation and why it is important

2 the methods used to segment both consumer and organizational markets

3 the criteria for effective segmentation

4 the process of market targeting and the four target market strategies—undifferentiated, differentiated, focused and customized marketing

5 the concept of positioning and the keys to successful positioning

6 the concept of repositioning and the repositioning options available to the firm.

Marketing Spotlight

Segmentation and Positioning at MTV

MTV is one of world's best-known brand names. The company, which began life broadcasting music videos in the USA in 1981 has grown into a multi-billion-dollar corporation controlling 96 channels around the world. Because of its early lead in the industry, MTV became synonymous with music television and was immortalized in songs by Dire Straits and George Michael. From the outset, it targeted viewers in the 16–25 age group. The business proposition was a compelling one. The content was free in the form of music videos developed by record companies to support their artists, which kept costs low. Revenues came from two sources, namely from fees agreed with the platform operators such as cable companies who carried MTV and from the advertising revenues paid for by companies for whom 16–25 year olds were a key target market.

Having become successful through its firm focus on the youth segment, MTV expanded its business geographically and demographically. It has now developed 38 separate regionalized music channels around the world, including 24 in Europe alone. MTV quickly realized that it needed to localize its content in the individual countries that it went into and to distance itself from its American roots. In India, that means emphasizing Hindi film music, in Brazil, Latino sounds, love songs in China, and in Italy shows feature more food than most. Further expansion was achieved by offering additional music channels such as MTV2, MTV Hits and MTV Dance, all of which appeal to different sub-segments within the company's main market. Other age segments were targeted with the launch of new channels. With the arrival of Nickelodeon (featuring programming for children), and Country Music Television and VH1 Classics, aimed at older music lovers, the company has been described as having an audience from the cradle to the grave. And its viewer base is now male and female, urban and rural, affluent and poor, gay and straight.

However, over the years, competition has become intense. It is estimated that there are 16 different music channels in the UK alone, eight offered by MTV Networks and seven by its major rival Emap Performance. Fees available from platform operators have fallen drastically due to the greater range of choice available. Advertising revenues have also suffered from the fragmentation of the market caused by the growth of digital television and the number of competing music channels seeking business. The challenge facing MTV is how to effectively maintain the position of market leader in the current competitive environment. Its strategy has been to move itself away from being solely a music channel. Instead of simply broadcasting music videos, it now develops much of its own programming, such as *Total Request Live* in the afternoons, and hit shows like *Punk'd* and *The Osbournes*. In doing so, it is in effect positioning itself as competing with channels like E4 and Sky One instead of simply other music channels. It has also invested heavily in events like the MTV awards (of which there are 11 different versions), which are aimed at strengthening the brand. Innovations like texting and gaming have become new sources of revenue. Through a combination of new channels, alternative revenue streams and increased localization, MTV aims to stay ahead of the competition.[1]

In our review of customer behaviour in Chapter 3, we saw that there are a variety of influences on the purchase decisions of customers. Their needs and wants vary and no matter how good a company's product or service is, not all customers will want it or will be willing to pay the same price for it. For example, airlines such as British Airways and SAS recognize that business and pleasure travellers are different in terms of their price sensitivity and the level of service required. In the home furnishings market, the type of person who buys luxury leather suites is very different from the type of person who buys conventional sofas; their reasons for purchase are different (style and prestige versus economy) and the type of furniture they want is different in terms of appearance and materials. Therefore, to implement the marketing concept and satisfy customer needs successfully, different product and service offerings must be made to the diverse customer groups that typically comprise a market.

The technique used by marketers to get to grips with the diverse nature of markets is called **market segmentation**. Market segmentation is defined as 'the identification of individuals or organizations with similar characteristics that have significant implications for the determination of marketing strategy'.

Thus, market segmentation involves the division of a diverse market into a number of smaller sub-markets that have common features. The objective is to identify groups of customers with similar requirements so that they can be served effectively, while being of a sufficient size for the product or service to be supplied efficiently. Usually, particularly in consumer markets, it is not possible to create a marketing mix that satisfies every individual's particular requirements exactly. Market segmentation, by grouping together customers with similar needs, provides a commercially viable method of serving these customers. It is therefore at the heart of strategic marketing, since it forms the basis by which marketers understand their markets and develop strategies for serving their chosen customers better than the competition.

There are a number of reasons why it is sensible for companies to segment their markets. Most notably, it allows companies the opportunity to enhance their profits. Many customers are willing to pay a premium for products or services that match their needs. For example, first-class air travellers regularly pay thousands of pounds for long-haul flights, though the additional costs of catering for these customers is only marginally higher than that of catering for economy-class customers. Similarly, the premium-priced segment of the car market is one of the fastest-growing segments, having risen by 82 per cent in the 10 years to 2004, and is expected to continue to grow. At the same time, profit margins in this segment are three times that of the mainstream segment, meaning that brands like Lexus, BMW and Mercedes will compete aggressively to exploit this opportunity.[2]

Second, through segmenting markets, companies can examine growth opportunities and expand their product lines. For example, in marketing its over-the-counter cough medicines, the Pfizer corporation offers different products for different types of cough under the Benylin brand. In its children's medicines range, it offers separate products for chesty coughs, dry coughs and night coughs, while there are five different cough brands in its adult range. Finally, in many competitive markets, companies are not able to compete across all segments effectively; by segmenting markets, companies can identify which segments they might most effectively compete in and develop strategies suited for that segment. For example, in the audio equipment business, one of the leading brands is Bose, which has built a global reputation as a manufacturer of high-quality sound systems that are only available through select stores and at premium prices. By pursuing this strategy, Bose has successfully differentiated itself from competitors like Sony, Samsung and Pioneer and, despite its premium prices, still has sales revenues of over US$1 billion per annum.

Segmenting consumer markets

Consumer segmentation criteria may be divided into three main groups: behavioural, psychographic and profile variables. Since the purpose of segmentation is to identify differences in behaviour that have implications for marketing decisions, behavioural variables, such as benefits sought from the product and buying patterns, may be considered the ultimate bases for segmentation. **Psychographic segmentation** is used when researchers believe that purchasing behaviour is correlated with the personality or lifestyle of consumers. Having found these differences, the marketer needs to describe the people who exhibit them and this is where **profile segmentation** such as socio-economic group or geographic location is valuable.[3] For example, a marketer may see whether there are groups of people who value low calories in soft drinks and then attempt to profile them in terms of their age, socio-economic groupings, etc. Figure 5.1

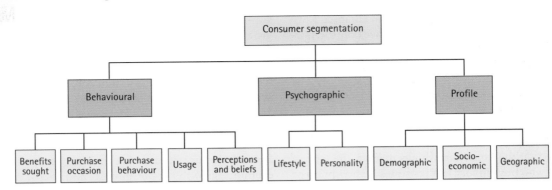

Figure 5.1 Segmenting consumer markets

shows the major segmentation variables used in consumer markets and Table 5.1 describes each of these variables in greater detail.

Consumer segmentation criteria

Table 5.1 shows the variety of criteria that might be considered when segmenting a consumer market. In practice there is no prescribed way of segmenting a market, and different criteria and combinations of criteria may be used. In the following paragraphs we will examine some of the more popular bases for segmentation.

Benefits sought

Benefit segmentation provides an understanding of why people buy in a market, and can aid the identification of opportunities. It is a fundamental method of segmentation because the objective of marketing is to provide customers with benefits that they value. For example, a basic product like toothpaste can confer a variety of benefits, ranging from

Table 5.1 Consumer segmentation methods

Variable	Examples
Behavioural	
Benefits sought	Convenience, status, performance
Purchase occasion	Self-buy, gift
Purchase behaviour	Solus buying, brand switching, innovators
Usage	Heavy, light
Perceptions and beliefs	Favourable, unfavourable
Psychographic	
Lifestyle	Trendsetters, conservatives, sophisticates
Personality	Extroverts, introverts, aggressive, submissive
Profile	
Age	Under 12, 12–18, 19–25, 26–35, 36–49, 50–64, 65
Gender	Female, male
Life cycle	Young single, young couples, young parents, middle-aged empty-nesters, retired
Social class	Upper middle, middle, skilled working, unwaged
Terminal education age 16, 18, 21 years	
Income	Income breakdown according to study objectives and income levels per country
Geographic	North vs south, urban vs rural, country
Geodemographic	Upwardly mobile young families living in larger owner-occupied houses, older people living in small houses, European regions based on language, income, age profile and location

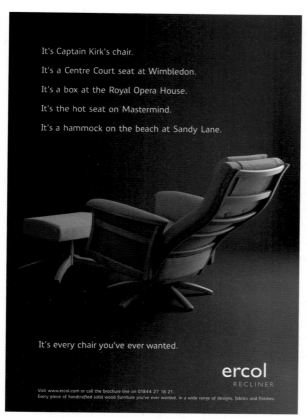

It's Captain Kirk's chair.

It's a Centre Court seat at Wimbledon.

It's a box at the Royal Opera House.

It's the hot seat on Mastermind.

It's a hammock on the beach at Sandy Lane.

It's every chair you've ever wanted.

ercol
RECLINER

Visit www.ercol.com or call the brochure line on 01844 27 18 21.
Every piece of handcrafted solid wood furniture you've ever wanted, in a wide range of designs, fabrics and finishes.

Exhibit 5.1 This advertisement for the Ercol Recliner highlights the benefits of owning the product

decay prevention to great taste to white teeth. Brands like Colgate have developed sub-brands that provide each of these benefits, such as Colgate Maximum Fluoride Protection (decay prevention), Colgate Junior toothpaste (taste) and Colgate Sensation whitening toothpaste (white teeth). Similarly, in the clothing market, one of the most rapidly growing segments is the plus-size market—that is, women's size 14 and up. In the USA, this market is estimated to be worth US$17.2 billion. The challenge for manufacturers is to produce clothing for this market that fits well and is still fashionable.[4] Focusing on benefits helps companies to spot business development opportunities, as demonstrated in Marketing in Action 5.1.

Purchase behaviour

The degree of brand loyalty in a market is a useful basis for segmenting customers. Solus buyers are totally brand loyal, buying only one brand in the product group. For example, a person might invariably buy Ariel Automatic washing powder. Most customers, however, practise brand-switching behaviour. Some may have a tendency to buy Ariel Automatic but also buy two or three other brands;

others might show no loyalty to any individual brand but switch brands on the basis of special offers (e.g. money off) or because they are variety seekers who look to buy a different brand each time. A recent trend in retailing is 'biographics'. This is the linking of actual purchase behaviour to individuals. The growth in loyalty schemes in supermarkets, such as the Tesco Clubcard scheme, has provided the mechanism for gathering this information. Customers are given cards that are swiped through an electronic machine at the checkout so that points can be accumulated towards discounts and vouchers. The more loyal the shopper, the higher the number of points gained. The supermarket also benefits by knowing what a named individual purchases and where. Such biographic data can be used to segment and target customers very precisely. For example, it would be easy to identify a group of customers who were ground coffee purchasers and target them through direct mail. Analysis of the data allows the supermarkets to stock products in each of their stores that are more relevant to their customers' age, lifestyle and expenditure. Japanese convenience stores are extensive users of this kind of customer information and, because of space restrictions there, shelves are restocked up to three times per day.[10]

Usage

Another way of segmenting customers is on the basis of whether they are heavy users, light users or non-users of a selected product category. The profiling of heavy users allows this group to receive the most marketing attention (particularly promotion efforts) on the assumption that creating brand loyalty among these people will pay great dividends. Sometimes the 80:20 rule applies, where about 80 per cent of a product's sales come from 20 per cent of its customers. Beer is a market where this rule often applies.[11] However, attacking the heavy-user segment can have drawbacks if all of the competition are also following this strategy. Analysing the light and non-user categories may provide insights that permit the development of appeals that are not being mimicked by the competition. For example, the successful doughnut chain Krispy Kreme is said to be considering manufacturing a sugar-free doughnut, which would give it access to a market segment of 25 million diabetics in the USA.[12] The identity of heavy, light and non-user categories, and their accompanying profiles for many consumer goods, can be accomplished by using survey information provided by the Target Group Index (TGI) (www.tgisurveys.com). This is a large-scale annual survey of buying and media habits in the UK.

Marketing in Action: Hotels target women travellers

Hotels that have traditionally focused on the male business traveller are increasingly waking up to the opportunities presented by the rapid growth in female visitors. It is estimated that 40 per cent of US business travellers are women, a figure that has doubled since 2002 and though the corresponding figure is just 25 per cent for Europe, it is expected to continue to increase.

The needs of women business travellers are different from those of their male counterparts. The annual Barclaycard Travel in Business Survey found that 69 per cent of women dislike drinking alone in a hotel bar, compared with just 29 per cent of men while 42 per cent of women admit being unhappy dining alone in a hotel, more than double the number of men. As a result many hotels are making adjustments to aspects of design, appearance and customer service. Security is an important issue for female customers, with a resulting emphasis on double locks and spy holes on doors. At reception, staff are trained to be conscious of the concerns of women by being discreet in giving details of room numbers and by not allocating ground-floor rooms to lone female visitors. Furthermore, given that many female guests prefer to stay in their rooms at night, some chains have introduced healthy options to their menus.

Room design, layout and features are also important. The Le Meridien chain has introduced an 'Art + Tech' lifestyle theme to a large number of rooms at some of its London properties. These rooms include spacious bathrooms with luxury toiletries and minimalist bedrooms designed in glass, stainless steel and blond wood with 42-inch plasma TV screens and large comfortable beds. The Hilton Hotel at London's Park Lane has a women-only floor, which has a private check-in, 24-hour security cameras and room service delivered by a female. Attention to detail is the key—many conventional hotel rooms will contain a trouser press but no iron, for example. When Isabel Aguilera Navarro became chief operating officer of NH Hoteles, Europe's third largest business hotel chain, she responded to the changes in the market by ensuring that her hotels offered more skirt hangers.

The Carlton George Hotel in Glasgow has gone a step further by providing a Lady Business Traveller Kit. Presented in a stylish gold vanity case, it includes a professional salon hairdryer, a set of GHD ceramic straightening irons, a recent release from Ottakar's Bookstore and a voucher for a treatment at Rainbow Room International. However, it is not all about pampering. Research in the industry shows that women are fussier than men and many are unwilling to pay the premium prices that often accompany the kinds of extra features described above.

Based on: Anonymous (2004);[5] Framley (2003);[6] Spencer (2003);[7] Sullivan (2002);[8] Swengley (2003)[9]

Lifestyle

Lifestyle segmentation aims to categorize people in terms of their way of life, as reflected in their activities, interests and opinions. As we saw in Chapter 3, lifestyle is an important personal factor driving consumer behaviour, and advertisers have identified several different lifestyle groupings. Lifestyle is also a powerful method of segmentation as particular lifestyle groups have fairly predictable media habits. For example, people who enjoy outdoor activities such as hiking and watersports will be likely to read magazines, watch television programmes and visit websites dealing with these topics. Marketers can then use these media to reach their chosen segments.

Lifestyle segmentation describes the way in which many advertising agencies attempt to relate brands (e.g. Martini) to a particular lifestyle (e.g. aspirational).

Age

Age is a factor that has been used in the segmentation of a host of consumer markets.[13] As we saw in Chapter 3, children have become a very important market and now have their own television programmes, cereals, computer games and confectionery. The sweeter tooth of children is reflected in sugared cereal brands targeted at them (e.g. Kellogg's Coco Pops). One of the biggest chil-

Exhibit 5.2 This Nokia 7270 clearly targets young, outgoing females

Social class

Social class is another important segmentation variable. As we saw in Chapter 3, social class groupings are based primarily on occupation. However, people who hold similar occupations may have very dissimilar lifestyles, values and purchasing patterns. Nevertheless, research has found that social class has proved to be useful in discriminating between owning a dishwasher, having central heating and privatization share ownership, for example, and therefore should not be discounted as a segmentation variable.[17] In addition, social classes tend to vary in their media consumption, meaning that these groups can be targeted effectively by advertisers. For example, tabloid newspapers tend to target working-class people, whereas traditional broadsheets see the middle and upper classes as their primary audience. It is important to monitor how consumer behaviour changes within the social classes. For example, sales of ultra-luxury car brands such as Rolls-Royce and Maybach are struggling as the super-rich shun conspicuous consumption. However, the more discreet sales of mega yachts are growing at a rate of 30% annually.[18]

dren's marketers, Disney, has brought out a new web-based video game called *Virtual Magic Kingdom* in an effort to stay relevant to its market, who are spending an increasing amount of time on the Internet. While playing the game, children can collect 'game points' that can be used at the real theme parks in Orlando, Paris, and so on.[14] Age is also an important segmentation variable in services. The holiday market is heavily age segmented, with offerings targeted at the under-30s and the over-60s segments, for example. This reflects the differing requirements of these age groups when on holiday. As a brand's market segment matures, it faces the challenge of appealing to younger age groups. For example, leading UK newspapers such as *The Times* and the *Guardian* have started including free entertainment listings with the papers as a way of attracting younger customers and boosting sales.[15] Similarly, Coca-Cola has had to regularly revise it marketing campaigns to appeal to younger customers. Its latest campaign, 'Real', includes a new website and updated logo graphics and is fronted by the actress Penelope Cruz.[16] Age distribution changes within the European Union are having a profound effect on the attractiveness of various age segments to marketers (see Chapter 2).

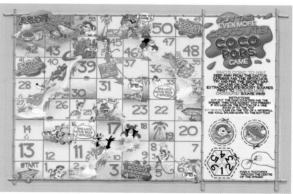

Exhibit 5.3 This Kellogg's advertisement is clearly aimed at the children's segment of the market

Geography

At a very basic level, markets can be segmented on the basis of country, regions within a country or on the basis of city size. More popular in recent years has been the combination of geographic and demographic variables into what are called **geodemographics**. In countries that produce population census data, the potential exists for classifying consumers on the combined basis of location and certain demographic (and socio-economic) information. Households are classified into groups according to a wide range of factors, depending on what is asked on census returns. In the UK, variables such as household size, number of cars, occupation, family size and ethnic background are used to group small geographic areas (known as enumeration districts) into segments that share similar characteristics. Several companies produce analyses of this information—for example, Experian—but the best known is that produced by CACI Market Analysis (www.caci.co.uk) entitled ACORN (from its full title—A Classification Of Residential Neighbourhoods). The main ACORN groupings and their characteristics are shown in Table 5.2.

Geodemographic information, like that in the ACORN groupings, has been used to select recipients of direct mail campaigns, to identify the best locations for stores and to find the best poster sites. This is possible because consumers in each group can be identified by means of their postcodes. Another area where census data are employed is in buying advertising spots on television. Agencies depend on information from viewership panels, which record their viewing habits so that advertisers can get an insight into who watches what. In the UK, census analyses are combined with viewership data via the postcodes of panellists.[19] This means that advertisers who wish to reach a particular geodemographic group can discover the type of programme they prefer to watch and buy television spots accordingly.

A major strength of geodemographics is that it can link buyer behaviour to customer groups. Buying habits can be determined by means of large-scale syndicated surveys—for example, the TGI and MORI Financial Services—or from panel data (for example, the grocery and toiletries markets are covered by AGB's Superpanel). By 'geocoding' respondents, those ACORN groups most likely to purchase a product or brand can be determined. This can be useful for branch location since many service providers use a country-wide branch network and need to match the market segments to which they most appeal to the type of customer in their catchment area. The merchandise mix decisions of retailers can also be affected by customer profile data. Media selections can be made more precise by linking buying habits to geodemographic data.[20]

Table 5.2 The ACORN targeting classification

Categories	% in population	Groups	% in population
A Thriving	20	1 Wealthy achievers, suburban areas 2 Affluent greys, rural communities 3 Prosperous pensioners, retirement areas	15 2 3
B Expanding	12	4 Affluent executives, family areas 5 Well-off workers, family areas	4 8
C Rising	7	6 Affluent urbanites, town and city areas 7 Prosperous professionals, metropolitan areas 8 Better-off executives, inner-city areas	2 3 3
D Settling	24	9 Comfortable middle-agers, mature home-owning areas 10 Skilled workers, home-owning areas	13 11
E Aspiring	14	11 New home owners, mature communities 12 White-collar workers, better-off multi-ethnic areas	10 4
F Striving	23	13 Older people, less prosperous areas 14 Council estate residents, better-off homes 15 Council estate residents, high unemployment 16 Council estate residents, greatest hardship 17 People in multi-ethnic, low-income areas	4 12 3 3 2

Source: © CACI Limited (data source BMRB and OPCS/GRO(S)); © Crown Copyright; all rights reserved; ACORN is a registered trademark of CACI Limited; reproduced with permission
Note: Due to rounding, the percentages total 101

In short, a wide range of variables can be used to segment consumer markets. Flexibility and creativity are the hallmarks of effective segmentation analysis. Often, a combination of variables will be used to identify groups of consumers that respond in the same way to marketing mix strategies.

Segmenting organizational markets

As we noted in Chapter 3, organizational markets, in contrast to consumer markets, tend to be characterized by relatively small numbers of buyers. Nevertheless, there are also many cases where it will be appropriate to segment organizational markets.

Organizational segmentation criteria

Some of the most useful bases for segmenting organizational markets are described below.

Organizational size

Market segmentation in this case may be by size of buying organization. Large organizations differ from medium-sized and small organizations in having greater order potential, more formalized buying and management processes, increased specialization of function, and special needs (e.g. quantity discounts). The result is that they may form important target market segments and require tailored marketing mix strategies. For example, the salesforce may need to be organized on a key account basis where a dedicated sales team is used to service important industrial accounts. List pricing of products and services may need to take into account the inevitable demand for volume discounts from large purchasers, and the salesforce will need to be well versed in the art of negotiation.

Industry

Industry sector—sometimes identified by the Standard Industrial Classification (SIC) codes—is

Marketing in Action: Lily O'Brien's chocolates

Lily O'Brien's is an Irish company that has grown rapidly in the past decade by being responsive to the needs of both the airline industry and grocery retailers. The company was started by Mary-Ann O'Brien and named after her daughter. Initially it was very much a hobby and a cottage business. It wasn't until 1993 and 1994 that the investment was made to build an industrial-scale plant. The company got its first major contract from Superquinn, the Irish grocery retailer. It was so successful in responding to the requirements of Superquinn that within a year it had got the total Superquinn contract and displaced its previous Belgian suppliers. Further contracts with major UK retailers such as Tesco, Sainsbury's and Marks & Spencer followed.

The next target was the airline industry. Again, the initial contract was with an Irish airline, Aer Lingus, and following this the next target was British Airways. BA at the time was being supplied by the legendary Swiss chocolate marker, Lindt. In an effort to displace the incumbent, Lily O'Brien's came up with a range of 'dessert-like' sweets that were carefully designed and packaged. Soon, BA passengers were being served sticky toffee pudding, lemon meringue pie, raspberry mousse and lemon brûlée in sweet form. These products were a hit and Lily O'Brien's displaced Lindt as BA's preferred supplier, a major achievement for a company that had been only five years in operation. Soon, other airline contracts, with Virgin Airlines, Continental Airlines, United Airlines and US Air, were obtained. In 2003, the company sold 8 million pieces of chocolate to the airline industry alone.

Lily O'Brien's now employs 140 people and has an annual turnover in the region of €8 million. Though it is a volume luxury chocolate maker, all of its products are hand-crafted. In the consumer market, it is aimed at the 'self-indulgence' segment of the market, in other words at consumers who want to treat themselves to something better than Cadbury's but not as rarefied or expensive as the top Belgian brands. To increase its brand presence in the consumer market, it is planning to open its first Lily O'Brien's café, selling coffee and, of course, a new range of chocolates.

Based on: O'Brien (2005);[21] Rafferty (2004)[22]

another common segmentation variable. Different industries may have unique requirements from products. For example, software applications suppliers like Oracle and SAP can market their products to various sectors, such as banking, manufacturing, healthcare and education, each of which has unique needs in terms of software programs, servicing price and purchasing practice. Marketing in Action 5.2 shows how Lily O'Brien's chocolate business grew rapidly by focusing on the needs of different sectors. By understanding each industry's needs in depth, a more effective marketing mix can be designed. In some instances, further segmentation may be required. For example, the education sector may be further divided into primary, secondary and further education, as the product and service requirements of these sub-sectors may differ.

Geographic location

The use of geographic location as a basis for differentiating marketing strategies may be suggested by regional variations in purchasing practice and needs. The purchasing practices and expectations of companies in Central and Eastern Europe are likely to differ markedly from those in Western Europe. Their more bureaucratic structures may imply a fundamentally different approach to doing business that needs to be recognized by companies attempting to enter these emerging industrial markets. In Chapter 2, we saw how different cultural factors affect purchasing practices in European countries. These differences, in effect, suggest the need for regional segments since marketing needs to reflect these variations.

Choice criteria

The factor of choice criteria segments the organizational market on the basis of the key criteria used by buyers when they are evaluating supplier offerings. One group of customers may rate price as the key choice criterion, another segment may favour productivity, while a third may be service orientated. These varying preferences mean that marketing and sales strategies need to be adapted to cater for each segment's needs. Three different marketing mixes would be needed to cover the three segments, and salespeople would have to emphasize different benefits when talking to customers in each segment. Variations in key choice criteria can be powerful predictors of buyer behaviour.

Purchasing organization

Another segmentation variable is that of decentralized versus centralized purchasing, because of its influence on the purchase decision.[23] Centralized purchasing is associated with purchasing specialists who become experts in buying a range of products and are particularly popular in sectors like grocery retailing. Specialization means that they become more familiar with cost factors, and the strengths and weaknesses of suppliers than do decentralized generalists. Furthermore, the opportunity for volume buying means that their power base to demand price concessions from suppliers is enhanced. They have also been found to have greater power within the decision-making unit (DMU—see Chapter 3) vis-à-vis technical people like engineers, than decentralized buyers who often lack the specialist expertise and status to challenge the technicians' preferences. For these reasons, purchasing organization provides a good base for distinguishing between buyer behaviour, and can have implications for marketing activities. For example, the centralized purchasing segment could be served by a national account salesforce, whereas the decentralized purchasing segment might be covered by territory representatives.

Criteria for successful segmentation

To determine whether a company has properly segmented its market, five criteria are usually considered.

1. *Effective*: the segments identified should consist of customers whose needs are relatively homogenous within a segment, but significantly different from those in other segments. If buyer needs in different segments are similar, then the segmentation strategy should be revised.
2. *Measurable*: it must be possible to identify customers in the proposed segment, and to understand their characteristics and behaviour patterns. For example, some personality traits, like 'outgoing' or 'conservative', might be difficult to pin down, whereas variables like age or occupation would be more clear-cut.
3. *Accessible*: The company must be able to formulate effective marketing programmes for the segments that it identifies. In other words, it must be clear what kinds of promotional campaign might work best for the segment, how the products might best be distributed to reach the segment, and so on.
4. *Actionable*: The company must have the resources to exploit the opportunities identified through the segmentation scheme. Certain segments—for example, in international markets—might be identified as being very attractive but the company may not have the resources or knowledge necessary to serve them.

5   *Profitable*: Most importantly, segments must be large enough to be profitable to serve. This is what is meant by the clichéd expression 'Is there a market in the gap?' Very small segments may be unprofitable to serve, though advances in production and distribution technologies mean that, increasingly, micro-segments can be profitable (see the section on customized marketing, below). Sometimes large segments may remain untapped. For example, Britain's Asian population has a combined spending power of £14 billion and has been largely ignored by anything other than niche brands. This prompted mobile phone company O^2 to sponsor the UK's six largest *mela*—the summer festivals run each year by Asian communities across the UK—in an effort to build its brand within this lucrative market.[24]

'influentials'. This is why, globally, CNN has focused so much of its distribution effort into gaining access to hotel rooms. Business people know that, wherever they are in the world, they can see international news on CNN in their hotel. Its sports programming is also targeted, with plenty of coverage of upmarket sports such as golf and tennis. Technology can be helpful in targeting particular segments, as demonstrated in e-Marketing 5.1.

The aim of evaluating market segments is for a company to arrive at a choice of one or more segments to enter. Target market selection is the choice of what and how many market segments in which to compete. There are four generic target marketing strategies from which to choose: undifferentiated marketing, differentiated marketing, focused marketing and customized marketing (see Figure 5.2). Each option will now be examined.

Target marketing

Once the market segments have been identified, the next important activity is the selection of target markets. **Target marketing** refers to the choice of specific segments to serve, and is a key element in marketing strategy. An organization needs to evaluate the segments and to decide which ones to serve using the five criteria outlined above. For example, CNN targets its news programmes to what are known as

Undifferentiated marketing

Market analysis will occasionally reveal no pronounced differences in customer characteristics that have implications for a marketing strategy. Alternatively, the cost of developing a separate market mix for different segments may outweigh the potential gains of meeting customer needs more exactly. Under these circumstances a company may decide to develop a single marketing mix for the whole market. This absence of segmentation is called

---

e-Marketing: BMW targets using technology

BMW makes innovative use of technology to market its cars to its target market. Through the website *BMW Films* (www.bmwfilms.com), the company has assembled some of the best action-film directors in the world, including Guy Ritchie, Ang Lee and John Woo. These directors have each developed a short film that can be viewed only through the website, which involves one or two star actors and, of course, a BMW car.

These action movies show some of the best aspects of BMW cars: their speed, handling and solid build, and associate the brand with Hollywood excitement and glamour. Downloading and playing these movies requires a large broadband Internet connection (512 kbits/second and above is preferable). Use of a dial-up connection (56 kbits/second) is at least 10 times as slow and involves a severe degradation of film quality.

Given that broadband Internet connections are still used by only a small minority of the population, does the move to display BMW films only through the website make sense for the company? In a word, yes. BMW figures that the next generation of BMW owners are highly literate in IT and from middle-income families (in many ways they are and can afford to be, early adopters of the latest connections and technologies). In this way, BMW has made a conscious decision to make more sophisticated use of technology, to capture the minds of a small percentage of individuals, rather than using more basic technology with a wider impact. BMW has thus used technology to target a distinct group of consumers.

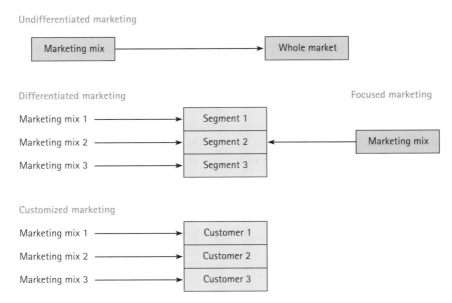

Figure 5.2 Target marketing strategies

undifferentiated marketing. Unfortunately this strategy can occur by default. For example, companies that lack a marketing orientation may practise undifferentiated marketing through lack of customer knowledge. Furthermore, undifferentiated marketing is more convenient for managers since they have to develop only a single product. Finding out that customers have diverse needs, which can be met only by products with different characteristics, means that managers have to go to the trouble and expense of developing new products, designing new promotional campaigns, training the salesforce to sell the new products, and developing new distribution channels. Moving into new segments also means that salespeople have to start prospecting for new customers. This is not such a pleasant activity as calling on existing customers who are well known and liked.

So, the market segmentation process is usually the factor that motivates those companies that practise undifferentiated marketing to embark on one of the three target marketing strategies we will look at below.

Differentiated marketing

Specific marketing mixes can be developed to appeal to all or some of the segments when market segmentation reveals several potential targets. This is called **differentiated marketing**; it is a very popular market targeting strategy that can be found in sectors as diverse as cars, cosmetics and fashion retailing. For example, Arcadia's segmentation of the fashion market revealed distinct customer groups for which specific marketing mixes could be employed. In response the group has a portfolio of shops that are distinctive in terms of shop name, style of clothing, décor and ambience. In all, the company has eight separate brands including, for example, Miss Selfridges (aimed at the 18–24 age group), Dorothy Perkins (aimed at women in their 20s and 30s) and Evans (which stocks women's clothes that are size 16+). Similarly, as part of its turnaround strategy, Marks & Spencer sought to move away from one brand (St Michael) with wide market appeal to a range of sub-brands such as Autograph (an upmarket brand) and Per Una, which is aimed at fashion-conscious women up to the age of 35. A differentiated target marketing strategy exploits the differences between marketing segments by designing a specific marketing mix for each segment. One potential disadvantage of a differentiated compared to a undifferentiated marketing strategy is the loss of cost economies. However, the use of flexible manufacturing systems can minimize such problems. The challenges of pursuing a differentiated marketing strategy are outlined in Marketing in Action 5.3.

Focused marketing

Just because a company has identified several segments in a market does not mean that it should serve them all. Some may be unattractive or out of step with its business strengths. Perhaps the most sensible route would be to serve just one of the market segments. When a company develops a single marketing mix aimed at one target (niche) market it is practising **focused marketing**. This strategy is particularly appropriate for companies with limited resources. Small companies may stretch their resources too far

Marketing in Action: Differentiating Gap Inc.'s brands

Gap Inc. began life as a retailer of Levi's jeans in San Francisco in 1969. Since then its growth has been remarkable. Though primarily retailing basics like khakis, chinos, jeans and T-shirts, Gap Inc. presented itself as a premium brand in the smart casual business and quickly established a strong foothold in the market. The strength of the brand enabled its extension into new segments like GapKids and Baby Gap. Responding to competition in the market, Gap acquired Banana Republic in 1983. Banana Republic was a lifestyle brand targeting customers with a taste for travelling and its stores had an exotic, safari-style theme. Under Gap, the stores were redesigned with a more modern, lifestyle look aimed at stylish, affluent customers such as those looking for 'casuals for Fridays'.

By the early 1990s, overall sales in the Gap corporation were slowing and its brands were under pressure from some new, fashionable competitors like Abercrombie & Fitch. Its response was to bring out a new line of discount clothing aimed at value-conscious family shoppers. Old Navy was launched in 1994, positioned as 'big, loud, fun and cheap'. Over 280 Old Navy stores were opened in the following three years, making a significant contribution to Gap Inc. revenues.

But the positions occupied by each of the brands in the marketplace began to become less clear. The similarities between Gap and Old Navy were starting to become visible, with both stores retailing basics like khakis and jeans at different price points and both using the same style of advertising, featuring celebrities like MTV hosts. When customers saw little difference between the two brands they started opting for the cheaper alternative. To counter this, Gap relaunched its brand, going back to basics and focusing on its core exclusivity. In doing so, it brought the brand closer to Banana Republic in the modern fashion casuals segment. All this confusion in the marketplace was having a significant impact on the bottom line. Net earnings had plunged from US$1.1 billion in 1999 to an US$8 million loss two years later.

Paul Pressler, formerly of Disney theme parks, was appointed chief executive of Gap in September 2002. One of his first tasks was to create a clear distinction between the three brands. For Gap, the strategy was to go back to its classic image of basics; Old Navy was to stay aimed at the value-conscious segment of the market and Banana Republic was re-positioned for the 25–35 age group offering sophisticated casual wear and business casual wear, and given a designer feel. However, many are sceptical that the differentiated strategy is working, citing the decision to use Madonna to front the latest Gap advertising campaign as a further example of the confusion. As of May 2004, there were 1376 Gap outlets in the USA and a further 359 in Europe, Japan and Canada. There were also 436 Banana Republic outlets and 844 Old Navy stores in the USA and Canada. Attention to branding, advertising, store design and merchandising will all be critical to ensuring that the differences between the three brands do not become blurred again.

Based on: Anonymous (2003);[25] Buckley, N. (2004);[26] Collard, J (2004);[27] Gayatri and Madhav (2004);[28] Manning-Schaffel (2002);[29] Walters (2003)[30]

by competing in more than one segment. Focused marketing allows research and development expenditure to be concentrated on meeting the needs of one set of customers, and managerial activities can thus be devoted to understanding and catering for those needs. Large organizations may not be interested in serving the needs of this one segment, or their energies may be so dissipated across the whole market that they pay insufficient attention to their requirements.

An example of a firm pursuing a focused marketing approach is Bang & Olufsen, the Danish audio electronics firm; it targets its stylish music systems at upmarket consumers who value self-development, pleasure and open-mindedness. Anders Kwitsen, the company's chief executive, describes its positioning as 'high quality, but we are not Rolls-Royce—more BMW'. Focused targeting and cost control mean that B&O defies the conventional wisdom that a small manufacturer could not make a profit by marketing consumer electronics in Denmark.[31] It is not uncommon for focused marketers to switch their attention from one segment to another as trends in the market change. For example, Connect Support Services is a London-based computer support company that began life serving the needs of a small number of large corporate clients. But as the negotiation of big contracts became increasingly time-consuming and costly, the company switched its focus to smaller firms with between 5 and 500 PCs, significantly growing its overall number of customers and its turnover.[32]

Some successful focused marketers frequently move on to become differentiated marketers. For example, low-cost airlines like Ryanair and easyJet have successfully targeted the business traveller while continuing to be popular with holiday travellers.

Customized marketing

The requirements of individual customers in some markets are unique, and their purchasing power sufficient to make viable the design of a discrete marketing mix for each customer. Segmentation at this disaggregated level leads to the use of **customized marketing**. Many service providers, such as advertising and marketing research agencies, architects and solicitors, vary their offerings on a customer-by-customer basis. They will discuss face to face with each customer their requirements, and tailor their services accordingly. Customized marketing is also found within organizational markets because of the high value of orders and the special needs of customers. Locomotive manufacturers will design and build products according to specifications given to them by individual rail transport providers. Similarly, in the machine tools industry, the German company Emag is a global leader in making 'multi-tasking' machines that cut metals used in industries like aerospace and vehicles. It practises customized marketing by manufacturing basic products at a cost-effective production site in eastern Germany but then finishing off or customizing these products in factories around the world that are located close to the customer.[33] Customized marketing is often associated with close relationships between suppliers and customers in these circumstances because the value of the order justifies a large marketing and sales effort being focused on each buyer.

One of the most fascinating developments in marketing in recent years has been the introduction of **mass customization** in consumer markets. This practice was initially pioneered by Japanese companies, who exploited their strengths in production systems and logistics to deliver customized products such as men's suits, bicycles and golf clubs to private consumers.[34] So when a Japanese man went to buy a suit he wasn't faced with a rack of ready-made suits, but rather a range of materials and colours from which he could choose. His measurements were then taken and a tailor-made suit was available for him within a week, but at a price that compared favourably with that of mass-produced garments. More and more products are now being customized to the needs of particular individuals. For example, at the Mercedes Sindelfingen plant near Stuttgart, every model passing through the plant has a pre-assigned customer, many of whom configure their cars via the Internet. Furthermore, many customers take delivery of their cars at the plant rather than from a dealer as has traditionally been the case.

Positioning

So far, we have examined two key aspects of the marketing management process, namely market segmentation (where we look at the different needs and preferences that may exist in a market) and market targeting (where we decide which segment or segments of the market we are going to serve). We

Exhibit 5.4 Products like Neville Johnson furniture are customised to the needs of particular users

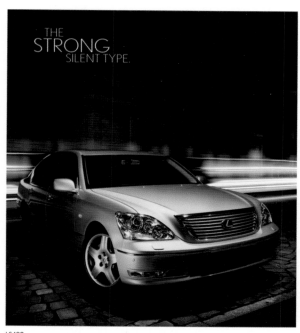

LS430

What you can't hear inside the LS430, you can feel. A pulse quickening 4.3 litre V8 engine with 6-speed automatic transmission producing an exhilarating 278bhp. Sound impressive? Actually it barely makes a sound thanks to advanced sound dampening materials, its air suspension system and a smooth aerodynamic profile. As they say, you have to watch the quiet ones. For more information, call 0845 601 9922 or visit www.lexus.co.uk/silent

Fuel economy figures: extra-urban 8.5 L/100km (33.2 mpg); urban 16.3 L/100km (17.3 mpg), combined 11.4 L/100km (24.8 mpg). CO₂ emissions 270g/km.

Exhibit 5.5 The imagery in this Lexus advertisement conveys a positioning of luxury and quality

now arrive at one of the most important and challenging aspects of marketing: **positioning**. Positioning can be defined as:

> '. . . the act of designing the company's offering so that it occupies a meaningful and distinct position in the target customer's mind.'

This is the challenge that faces all organizations. All firms make products or provide services but, as we saw in Chapter 1, consumers buy benefits. Positioning is essentially that act of linking your product or service to the solutions that consumers seek and ensuring that, when they think about those needs, your brand is one of the first that comes to mind. For example, there is a segment of the car-buying market that values safety as one of its key purchasing criteria. Over the years, Swedish car manufacturer Volvo successfully positioned itself as one of the safest cars in the market through a combination of its design and its advertising messages. When asked which car they thought was the safest, Volvo was consistently mentioned by customers though technical tests showed that it was not significantly safer than other brands in the market. This is the power of effective positioning: ensuring that your brand occupies a meaningful and distinct place in the

target customer's mind. In contrast, see the problems experienced by Sweden's other major car manufacturer, Saab, discussed in Marketing in Action 5.4.

Positioning is both important and difficult. It is important because, today, we live in an over-communicated society.[35] Consumers are constantly exposed to advertising messages, some estimates put the number as high as 1000 messages per day. Add to this the volumes of information available through the print and broadcast media and the Internet, and it is easy to see why consumers could suffer from information overload. To cut through this clutter, a company needs messages that are simple, direct and that resonate with the customer's needs. Failure to gain a position in the customer's mind significantly increases the likelihood of failure in the marketplace.

Developing a positioning strategy

Deciding what position to try to occupy in the market requires consideration of three variables, namely the customers, the competitors and the company itself. In terms of customers we must examine what attributes matter to them—there is little point in seeking a position that is unimportant from the customer's point of view. In many markets, competitors are already well entrenched, so the next challenge is to find some differential advantage that ideally cannot easily be matched. Third, as implied by the resource-based view of the firm, the company should look at building a position based on its unique attributes as this increases the likelihood that advantage can be sustained.[40]

Once the overall positioning strategy is agreed, the next step is to develop a positioning statement. A positioning statement is a memorable, image-enhancing, written summation of the product's

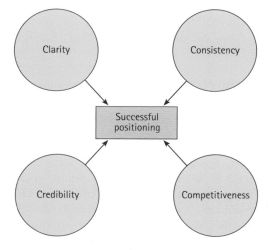

Figure 5.3 Keys to successful positioning

Marketing in Action: Saab's positioning problem

Saab is a venerable Swedish brand that has been making cars since 1947. Over the years, the company has cultivated an idiosyncratic image. Its early cars were VW Beetle-like in their design and its later models in the 1970s and 1980s were described as big and hulking. The cars have novel features such as ignition switches beside the gear stick and cup holders that unfold. Saab promoted its cars as vehicles built by a company that also makes aircraft. Its positioning was high-tech, high performance, something to aspire to. This kind of distinctiveness has resulted in the growth of a loyal customer base. A network of Saab owners clubs have sprung up around the world; they have their own club magazine, entitled *Nines*. In addition, Saab sponsors an annual convention where owners can show off their cars and attend seminars on topics such as restoring old Saab models. Much of its advertising has focused on its distinctiveness. The tag-line 'find your own road', which was used in the 1990s, was replaced with 'welcome to the state of independence' in 2003.

However, while the Saab remains distinctive and Swedish, its positioning in the marketplace has become unclear. It does not have the mass appeal of brands like Audi and, equally, its lacks the exclusivity and price tag of a Porsche. For example, one of its popular brands, the Saab 9-3, which was launched in 1998, is built on the same basic platform as more downmarket brands such as the Opel and Vauxhall Vectra. This problem has not been helped by the fact that General Motors took a 50 per cent stake in Saab in 1989 and full ownership of the company in 2000. Where Saab cars sit in the GM family is not clear and, even worse, its distinctiveness is threatened as GM imposes design changes and manufactures the brand outside of Sweden for efficiency reasons. For example, the 9-2x, a sporty 4x4, was manufactured by Fuji Industries in Japan for sale in the American market. GM own 20 per cent of Fuji Industries, which also manufactures its own 4x4, the Subaru. So close is the 9-2x to the Subaru that it has been nicknamed the Saabaru. Similarly, the Saab SUV is built in Ohio, USA, using the same underlying platform as GM's Buick light truck. And, in a break with Saab tradition, the ignition sits on the steering column rather than beside the gear stick.

Saab's lack of clarity in the marketplace has hit its bottom line hard. Sales of 132,000 units in 2003 were below those achieved by the company in 1987. Since GM's involvement in 1989, Saab has managed to record an annual profit on only two occasions. While Saab is distinctly Swedish and has its core of loyal followers, its inability to attain a distinct position in the consumer's mind remains one of its biggest difficulties. It is hard to see where it can go from here. It doesn't have the volume to be a volume player or the prestige to be a niche player. It has also suffered from a lack of investment by GM and as its parent continues to struggle, the brand could end up being axed entirely. Its troubles emphasize the importance of maintaining a strong brand positioning.

Based on: Anonymous (2005);[36] Cook (2003);[37] George and Mackintosh (2004);[38] Kurylko (2003)[39]

---

desired stature. The statement can be evaluated using the criteria shown in Figure 5.3.

1   *Clarity*: the idea must be perfectly clear, both in terms of target market and differential advantage. Complicated positioning statements are unlikely to be remembered. Simple messages such as 'BMW—The Ultimate Driving Machine', 'Carlsberg—Probably the Best Lager in the World' and 'L'Oréal—Because I'm Worth it' are clear and memorable (see Figures 5.4a and b).

2   *Consistency*: because people are bombarded with messages daily, a consistent message is required to break through this noise. Confusion will arise if this year we position on 'quality of service' and next year change this to 'superior product performance'. Some companies, like McDonald's, have used the same positioning—quality, service, cleanliness and value (Q, S, C + V)—for decades.

3   *Credibility*: the selected differential advantage must be credible in the minds of target customers. An attempt to position roll-your-own

cigarette tobacco as an upmarket exclusive product failed due to lack of credibility. Similarly, the attempt to position Lada as an exciting, sporty car by showing it charging through dirt tracks in Africa failed because of the lack of consonance between image and reality.

4 *Competitiveness*: the chosen differential advantage must possess a competitive edge. It should offer something of value to the customer that the competition is failing to supply. For example, the success of the Apple Macintosh computer in the educational segment was based on the differential advantage of easy-to-use software programs, a benefit that was highly valued in this segment. Because of its different system architecture, IBM was unable to match the Macintosh on this feature.

The perceptual map is a useful tool for determining the position of a brand in the marketplace. It is a visual representation of consumer perceptions of a brand and its competitors, using attributes (dimensions) that are important to consumers. The key steps in producing a perceptual map are as follows.

1 Identify a set of competing brands.
2 Identify—using qualitative research (e.g. group discussions)—the important attributes consumers use when choosing between brands.

Figure 5.4a Adslogans.co.uk's top 10 slogans of all time
Source: www.adslogans.co.uk/ww/prwis14.html

Figure 5.4b As these examples show, the phrase 'It's all about ...' is much overused and therefore unlikely to be effective in creating a clear position in the minds of customers
Source: www.adslogans.co.uk/ww/prwis14.html

3 Conduct quantitative marketing research where consumers score each brand on all key attributes.
4 Plot brands on a two-dimensional map (or maps).

Figure 5.5 shows a perceptual map for seven supermarket chains. The results show that the supermarkets are grouped into two clusters: the high-price, wide product range group; and the low-price, narrow product range group. These are indicative of two market segments and show that supermarkets C and D are close rivals, as measured by consumers' perceptions, and have very distinct perceptual positions in the marketplace compared with E, F and G. Perceptual maps are useful in considering strategic moves. For example, an opportunity may exist to

Figure 5.5 A perceptual map of supermarkets

create a differential advantage based on a combination of wide product range and low prices (as shown by the theoretical position at X). This type of thinking underpinned the opening of a new venue called Club Absinthe in Dublin in 1999. Dublin has an exciting nightlife, ranging from theatre and cinema to pubs and nightclubs. What the founders of Club Absinthe wanted to do was create a venue that was half-theatre and half-pub. It had a café-style design with a relatively muted sound system, but also live performances of music and comedy.[41]

Repositioning

Occasionally, perhaps because of changing customer tastes or poor sales performance, a product or service will need to be repositioned. **Repositioning** involves changing the target markets, the differential advantage or both (see Figure 5.6). The first option is to keep product and target market the same but to change the image of the product. In markets where products act as a form of self-expression, the product may be acceptable in functional terms but fail because it lacks the required image. In the sports shoe market, Nike and Adidas have moved the

	Product	
	Same	**Different**
Target market **Same**	Image repositioning	Product repositioning
Different	Intangible repositioning	Tangible repositioning

Figure 5.6

emphasis from shoe performance to street cred by using advertising that features sports personalities such as Eric Cantona and David Beckham, and by using famous slogans like Nike's 'Just Do It'. Similarly, Levi's is attempting to change the image of its famous 501 jeans from the 1950s retro-American made famous by the Nick Kamen launderette advertisement to something that is more relevant to today's youth culture, by employing ads shot in contemporary Los Angeles.[42] An alternative approach is to keep the same target market but to modify the product. For example, in 1992, Allied Breweries rejigged the formulation and can size of its Castlemaine XXXX lager brand to improve its appeal. The product's alcohol content was raised from 3.7 to 3.9 per cent in pubs and to 4 per cent in supermarkets; its can size was also increased from 440 ml to 500 ml.

Some repositioning strategies involve retaining the product but changing the market segment it is aimed at. Lucozade, a carbonated drink, is a famous example of this kind of so-called 'intangible repositioning'. Manufactured by Beecham's Foods, it was initially targeted at sick children. Marketing research found that mothers were drinking it as a midday pick-me-up and the brand was consequently repositioned to aim at this new segment. Subsequently the energy-giving attributes of Lucozade have been used to appeal to a wider target market—young adults—by means of advertisements featuring British Olympians such as Daley Thompson and Linford Christie. The history of Lucozade shows how a combination of repositioning strategies over time has been necessary for successful brand building. Similarly, to counteract declining global sales, the car manufacturer DaimlerChrysler is trying to reposition the Chrysler brand away from the competitive mass market to be a 'premium' brand,[43] while Jose Cuervo is spending US$65 million on a promotional campaign entitled 'Vive Cuervo' (Live Cuervo) to broaden the appeal of tequila, which has traditionally been associated with student parties.[44]

Exhibit 5.6 Through the use of humour, this advertisement for Cross pens takes it into the mainstream market

When both product and target market are changed, a company is said to be practising 'tangible repositioning'. For example, a company may decide to move up- or downmarket by introducing a new range of products to meet the needs of its new target customers. British Midland found it necessary to use both target and product repositioning in the face of growing competition in the airline business. The company was worried about its local British image and set about transforming itself into a global airline. It joined the Star alliance led by Lufthansa and United Airlines, and commenced a long-haul service to the USA. It also spent £15 million on a corporate rebranding initiative to change its name from British Midland to bmi to create a more international appeal.

The decision to reposition a brand should not be taken lightly as there are risks attached to this strategy. For example, in an effort to counteract stagnant sales in the mature men's magazine segment, titles such as *Esquire* and *Arena* repositioned themselves as 'lad's mags' (a market that had been growing rapidly), interspersing scantily clad models and drinking yarns with profiles of politicians. However, the strategy failed badly with lots of readers departing the magazines and not returning when the titles moved back to their original positioning. Sales of *Esquire* in 2003 were 30,000 units down from its peak of 100,000.[45]

Summary

This chapter has examined the key activities of market segmentation, market targeting and positioning. The following issues were addressed.

1. The process of market segmentation: not all consumers in the market have the same needs and we can serve them better by segmenting the market into groups with homogeneous needs.

2. The variety of bases available for segmenting both consumer and industrial markets, and often a combination of bases, are used to effectively segment markets.

3. The five criteria for successful segmentation: effective, measurable, accessible, actionable and profitable.

4. The four generic target marketing strategies: undifferentiated marketing, differentiated marketing, focused marketing and customized marketing.

5. What is meant by the concept of positioning, why it is important, and the need for clarity, consistency, credibility and competitiveness in a positioning statement.

6. The concept of repositioning and the four repositioning strategies: image repositioning, product repositioning, intangible repositioning and tangible repositioning.

Suggested reading

Bardakci, A. and **J. Whitelock** (2004) How 'Ready' Are Customers for Mass Customisation? An Exploratory Investigation, *European Journal of Marketing*, **38** (11/12), 1396–417.

Dibb, S. and **L. Simkin** (2001) Market Segmentation, *Industrial Marketing Management*, **23** (8), 609–23.

Pine, J.B. and **J.H. Gilmore** (2000) *Markets of One— Creating Customer-unique Value through Mass Customisation*, Boston, MA: Harvard Business School Press.

Ries, A. and **J. Trout** (2001) *Positioning: The Battle for Your Mind*, New York: Warner.

Zeithaml, V., R. Rust and **K. Lemon** (2001) The Customer Pyramid: Creating and Serving Profitable Customers, *California Management Review*, **43** (4), 118–42.

Internet exercises

Sites to visit

1   www.arcadiagroup.co.uk

Exercise

Identify the segments being targeted by each of the eight Arcadia group brands and evaluate its differentiated marketing strategy.

2   www.ups.com
     www.cargo-express.co.uk

Exercise

Compare and contrast the target marketing strategies of these two parcel delivery companies.

Study questions

1. Discuss the advantages of market segmentation.
2. You have been asked by a client company to segment the ice cream market. Use at least three different bases for segmentation and describe the segments that emerge.
3. Many consumer goods companies have recently been experimenting with the possibilities of a customized target marketing strategy. What are the advantages and limitations of such a strategy?
4. A friend of yours wants to launch a new breakfast cereal on the market but is unsure how to position the product. Develop a perceptual map of the breakfast cereal market identifying brands that compete in the same space and also if there are gaps where there are currently no major brands.
5. What is the difference between positioning and repositioning? Choose a brand that has been repositioned in the marketplace and describe both its old positioning and its new positioning. Is its repositioning strategy best described as image, product, intangible or tangible repositioning?

Key terms

market segmentation the process of identifying individuals or organizations with similar characteristics that have significant implications for the determination of marketing strategy

psychographic segmentation the grouping of people according to their lifestyle and personality characteristics

profile segmentation the grouping of people in terms of profile variables such as age and socio-economic group so that marketers can communicate to them

benefit segmentation the grouping of people based on the different benefits they seek from a product

lifestyle segmentation the grouping of people according to their pattern of living as expressed in their activities, interests and opinions

geodemographics the process of grouping households into geographic clusters based on such information as type of accommodation, occupation, number and age of children, and ethnic background

target marketing selecting a segment as the focus for a company's offering or communications

undifferentiated marketing a market coverage strategy where a company decides to ignore market segment differences and to develop a single marketing mix for the whole market

differentiated marketing a market coverage strategy where a company decides to target several market segments and to develop separate marketing mixes for each

focused marketing a market coverage strategy where a company decides to target one market segment with a single marketing mix

customized marketing a market coverage strategy where a company decides to target individual customers and to develop separate marketing mixes for each

mass customization the opposite to mass production, which means that all products produced are customized to the predetermined needs of a specific customer

positioning the choice of target market (*where* the company wishes to compete) and differential advantage (*how* the company wishes to compete)

repositioning changing the target market or differential advantage, or both

References

1. **Burt, T.** (2002) Roedy sets a local tone, *Financial Times*, Creative Business, 26 November, 7; **Larsen, P.T.** and **T. Burt** (2003) To Sell the World on a Song, *Financial Times*, 10 October, 12; **Sanghera, S.** (2002) Pop Goes the Monopoly, *Financial Times*, 26 November, 6–7.

2. **Mackintosh, J.** (2004) A Global Drive for the Affluent: Carmakers Seek New Markets for Their Luxury Brands, *Financial Times*, 3 December, 21.

3. **Van Raaij, W.F.** and **T.M.M. Verhallen** (1994) Domain-specific Market segmentation, *European Journal of Marketing*, **28** (10), 49–66.

4. **Foster, L.** (2004) The Plus-size Market Shapes Up, *Financial Times*, 10 December, 13.

5. **Anonymous** (2004) Lone Hotel Stays are Still a Concern for Women, *Birmingham Post*, 15 April, 21.

6. **Framley, R.** (2003) Business Travel: Why Can't All Hotels be Like This for Women?, *Birmingham Post*, 17 December, 21.

7. **Spencer, K.** (2003) Hotel Breaks London: A Floor Bet for Ladies, *Express*, 29 March, 66.

8. **Sullivan, R.** (2002) A Wake-up Call from Women Guests, *Financial Times*, 26 November, 15.

9. **Swengley, N.** (2003) Hotels Learn to be Female-friendly, *The Times*, 4 February, 3.

10. **Fahy, J.** and **F. Taguchi** (1995) Reassessing the Japanese Distribution System, *Sloan Management Review*, **36** (2), 49–61.

11. **Cook, V.J. Jr** and **W.A. Mindak** (1984) A Search for Constants: The 'Heavy-User' Revisited!, *Journal of Consumer Marketing*, **1** (4), 79–81.

12. **Liu, B.** (2004) Krispy Kreme Looks to its Global Roll-out, *Financial Times*, 15 March, 15.

13. **Tynan, A.C.** and **J. Drayton** (1987) Market Segmentation, *Journal of Marketing Management*, **2** (3), 301–35.

14. **Yee, A.** (2005) Disney Woos Visitors Via the Web, *Financial Times*, 27 January, 30.

15. **Grimshaw, C.** (2003) The Entertainment Bandwagon, *Financial Times*, Creative Business, 22 July, 14.

16. **Liu, B.** (2003) Coca-Cola Attempts Younger Connection, *Financial Times*, 10 January, 25.

17. **O'Brien, S.** and **R. Ford** (1988) Can We at Last Say Goodbye to Social Class?, *Journal of the Market Research Society*, **30** (3), 289–332.

18. **Anonymous** (2005) Conspicuous non-consumption, *The Economist*, 8 January, 55–6.

19. **Garrett, A.** (1992) Stats, Lies and Stereotypes, *Observer*, 13 December, 26.

20. **Mitchell, V.W.** and **P.J. McGoldrick** (1994) The Role of Geodemographics in Segmenting and Targeting Consumer Markets: A Delphi Study, *European Journal of Marketing*, **28** (5), 54–72.

21. **O'Brien, D.** (2005) My Chocolates are all About Selling Sex, *Sunday Times*, Business, 22 May, 7.

22. **Rafferty, E.** (2004) Chocolate Maker Savours its Sweet Desserts, *Financial Times*, 20 April, 13.

23. **Corey, R.** (1978) *The Organisational Context of Industrial Buying Behaviour*, Cambridge, MA: Marketing Science Institute, 6–12.

24. **Carter, M.** (2003) O2's Cultural Pitch for the Ethnic Pound, *Financial Times*, 3 July, 13.

25. **Anonymous** (2003) Outsider Who Plugged the Gap, *The Business*, 24 August, 13.

26. **Buckley, N.** (2004) Numbers Man Bridges the Gap, *Financial Times*, 24 August, 10.

27. **Collard, J.** (2004) How Gap Bounced Back, *Financial Times*, 21 February, 48.

28. **Gayatri, D.** and **T. Phani Madhav** (2004) Gap and Banana Republic: Changing Brand Strategies with Fashion, Case 504-087-1, *European Case Clearing House*.

29. **Manning-Schaffel, V.** (2002) Can Gap Mend its Brand?, *Brandchannel.com*, 1 April.

30. **Walters, J.** (2003) Madonna's Gap Year, *Observer*, 17 August, 3.

31. **Richards, H.** (1996) Discord Amid the High Notes, *The European*, 16–22 May, 23.

32. **Bird, J.** (2003) A Switch to Safety in Numbers, *Financial Times*, 30 January, 11.

33. **Marsh, P.** (2004) Mass-produced for Individual Tastes, *Financial Times*, 22 April, 12.

34. **Westbrook R.** and **P. Williamson** (1993) Mass Customisation: Japan's New Frontier, *European Management Journal*, **11** (1), 38–45.

35. **Ries, A.** and **J. Trout** (2001) *Positioning: The Battle For Your Mind*, New York: Warner.

36. **Anonymous** (2005) Brand MOT—Saab, *Brand Strategy*, February, 10–11.

37. **Cook, B.** (2003) Membership Has its Privileges, *Brandchannel.com*, 26 May.

38. **George, N.** and **J. Mackintosh**, (2004) Saab Tries to Escape a Cul-de-sac, *Financial Times*, 11 March, 14.

39. **Kurylko, D.T.** (2003) Saab Stresses Freedom in New Ad Campaign, *Automotive News*, 5 December, 12.

40. **Fahy, J.** (2001) *The Role of Resources in Global Competition*, London: Routledge.

41. **Boyd, B.** (1999) Absinthe Makes the Heart Grow Fonder, *Irish Times*, 23 February, 9.

42. **Benady, A.** (2005) Levi's Looks to the Bottom Line, *Financial Times*, 15 February, 14.

43. **Grant, J.** (2003) Chief of Unit Faces Twists and Turns on Road to Rebranding, *Financial Times*, 16 June, 28.

44. **Silver, S.** (2003) Tequila Tries to Get Out of the Slammer, *Financial Times*, 22 May, 15.

45. **Grimshaw, C.** (2003) Let's Get Serious, *Financial Times*, Creative Business, 28 January, 12.

Learning Centre

When you have read this chapter log on to the Online Learning Centre for *Foundations of Marketing* at **www.mcgraw-hill.co.uk/textbooks/jobber** where you'll find multiple choice test questions, links and extra online study tools for marketing.

Turn the page for a Case Study on Unilever in Brazil

Case 5 Unilever in Brazil: marketing strategies for low-income customers

After three successful years in the Personal Care division of Unilever in Pakistan, Laercio Cardoso was contemplating an attractive leadership position in China when he received a phone call from Robert Davidson, head of Unilever's Home Care division in Brazil, his home country. Robert was looking for someone to explore growth opportunities in the marketing of detergents to low-income consumers living in the north-east of Brazil and felt that Laercio had the seniority and skills necessary for the project. Though he had not been involved in the traditional Unilever approach to marketing detergents, his experience in Pakistan had made him acutely aware of the threat posed by local detergent brands targeted at low-income consumers.

At the start of the project—dubbed 'Everyman'—Laercio assembled an interdisciplinary team and began by conducting extensive field studies to understand the lifestyle, aspirations and shopping habits of low-income consumers. Increasing detergent use by these consumers was crucial for Unilever given that the company already had 81 per cent of the detergent powder market. But some in the company felt that it should not fight in the lower end of the market where even local companies with lower cost structures struggled to break even. How could Laercio justify diverting money from a best-selling brand like Omo to invest in a lower-margin segment?

Consumer behaviour

The 48 million people living in the north-east (NE) of Brazil lag behind their south-eastern (SE) counterparts on just about every development indicator. In the NE, 53 per cent of the population live on less than two minimum wages versus 21 per cent in the SE. In the NE, only 28 per cent of households own a washing machine versus 67 per cent in the SE. Women in the NE scrub clothes in a washbasin or sink using bars of laundry soap, a process that requires intense and sustained effort. They then add bleach to remove tough stains and only a little detergent powder at the end, primarily to make the clothes smell good. In the SE, the process is similar to European or North American standards. Women mix powder detergent and softener in a washing machine and use laundry soap and bleach only to remove the toughest stains.

The penetration and usage of detergent powder and laundry soap is the same in the NE and the SE (97 per cent). However, north-easterners use a little less detergent (11.4 kg per years versus 12.9 kg) and a lot more soap (20 kg versus 7 kg) than south-easterners. Many women in the NE view washing clothes as one of the pleasurable routine activities of their week. This is because they often do their washing in a public laundry, river or pond where they meet and chat with their friends. In the SE, in contrast, most women wash clothes alone at home. They perceive washing laundry as a chore and are primarily interested in ways to improve the convenience of the process.

People in the NE and SE differ in the symbolic value they attach to cleanliness. Many poor north-easterners are proud of the fact that they keep themselves and their families clean despite their low income. Because it is so labour intensive, many women see the cleanliness of clothes as an indication of the dedication of the mother to her family, and personal and home cleanliness is a main subject of gossip. In the SE, where most women own a washing machine, it has much lower relevance for self-esteem and social status. Along with price, the primarily low-income consumers of the NE evaluate detergents on six key attributes (Figure C5.1 provides importance ratings, the range of consumer expectations, and the perceived positioning of key detergent brands on each attribute).

Competition

In 1996 Unilever was a clear leader in the detergent powder category in Brazil, with an 81 per cent market share, achieved with three brands: Omo (one of Brazil's favourite brands across all categories) Minerva (the only brand to be sold as both detergent powder and laundry soap with a more hedonistic 'care' positioning) and Campeiro (Unilever's cheapest brand). Procter & Gamble, which had recently entered the Brazilian market, had 15 per cent of the market with three brands (Ace, Bold and the low-price brand Pop). Other competitors were smaller local companies (see Figure C5.2).

The Brazilian fabric wash market consists of two categories: detergent powder and laundry soap. In 1996 detergent powder was a US$106 million (42,000 tons) market in the NE. In 1996 the NE market for laundry soap bars was as large as the detergent powder market (US$102 million for 81,250 tons). The NE market for laundry soap is very fragmented because laundry soap is much easier to produce than powdered laundry detergent. Laundry soap is a multi-use product that has many home and personal care uses. Table C5.1 provides key information on all powder and laundry soap brands (packaging, positioning, key historical facts, and financial and market data).

Decisions

Robert Davidson, head of Unilever's Home Care division in Brazil, and Laercio Cardoso, head of the 'Everyman' research project aimed at understanding the low-income consumer segment, must re-examine Unilever's strategy for low-income consumers in the NE region of Brazil and make three important decisions.

1   *Go/no go.* Should Unilever divert money from its premium brands to invest in a lower-margin segment of the market? Does Unilever have the right skills and structure to be profitable in a market in which even small local entrepreneurs struggle to break even? In the long run, what would Unilever gain and what would it risk losing?

2   *Marketing and branding strategy.* Unilever already has three detergent brands with distinct positionings. Does it need to develop a new brand with a new value proposition or can it reposition its existing brands or use a brand extension?

3   *Marketing mix.* What price, product, promotion and distribution strategy would allow Unilever to deliver value to low-income consumers without cannibalizing its own premium brands too heavily? Is it just a matter of price?

Product

Unilever could produce a product comparable to Campeiro, its cheapest product, but would it deliver the benefits that low-income consumers wanted? Alternatively, Unilever could use Minerva's formula but it might be too expensive for low-income consumers. If they could eliminate some ingredients, Unilever's scientists could develop a third formula that would cost about 10 per cent more than Campeiro's formula. The difficulty would be in determining which attributes to elimi-

nate, which to retain and which, if any, would actually need to be improved relative to both existing brands.

Larger packages would reduce the cost per kilo but could price the product out of the weekly budget range of the poorest consumers. Unilever could use a plastic sachet, which would cost 30 per cent of the price of traditional cardboard boxes, but market research data had shown that low-income consumers were attached to boxes and regarded anything else as good for only second-rate products. One solution might be to launch multiple types and sizes.

Price

Priced significantly above Campeiro and Minerva soap, the product would be out of reach for the target segment. Priced too low, it would increase the cost of the inevitable cannibalization of existing Unilever brands. Should Unilever use coupons or other means to reduce the cost of the product for low-income consumers? Or should it change the price of Omo, Minerva and Campeiro?

Promotion

In the low-income segment, lower margins meant that volume had to be reached very quickly for the product to break even. It was therefore crucial to find a radical 'story', one that would immediately put the new brand on the map. What would be the objective of the communication? What should be the key message? Low-income consumers might be reluctant to buy a product advertised 'for low-income people' especially as products with that kind of message are typically of inferior quality. On the other hand, using the classic aspirational communication of most Brazilian brands could confuse consumers and lead to unwanted cannibalization.

In regular detergent markets Unilever had established that the most effective allocation of communication expenditure was 70 per cent above-the-line (media advertising) and 30 per cent below-the-line (trade promotions, events, point-of-purchase marketing). The advantages of using primarily media advertising are its low cost per contact and high reach because almost all Brazilians, irrespective of income, are avid television watchers. One alternative would be to use 70 per cent below-the-line communication. At US$0.05 per kg, this plan would require only one-third of the cost of a traditional Unilever communication plan. On the other hand, it would lower the reach of communication, increase the cost per contact, and make a simultaneous launch in all north-eastern cities more difficult to organize.

Distribution

Unilever did not have the ability to distribute to the approximately 75,000 small outlets spread over the NE, yet access to these stores was key because low-income consumers rarely shopped in large supermarkets like Wal-Mart or Carrefour. Unilever could rely on its existing network of generalist wholesalers who supplied its detergents and a wide variety of products to small stores. These wholesalers had national coverage and economies of scale but did not directly serve the small stores where low-income consumers shopped, necessitating another layer of smaller local wholesalers, which increased their cost to US$0.10 per kg. Alternatively, Unilever could contract with dozens of specialized distributors who would get exclusive rights to sell the new Unilever detergent. These specialized distributors would have a better ability to implement point-of-purchase marketing and would cost less ($0.05 per kg).

Questions

1. Describe the consumer behaviour differences among laundry products' customers in Brazil. What market segments exist?

2. Should Unilever bring out a new brand or use one of its existing brands to target the north-eastern Brazilian market?

3. How should the brand be positioned in the marketplace and within the Unilever family of brands?

4. What marketing mix should be employed to build the brand in the market?

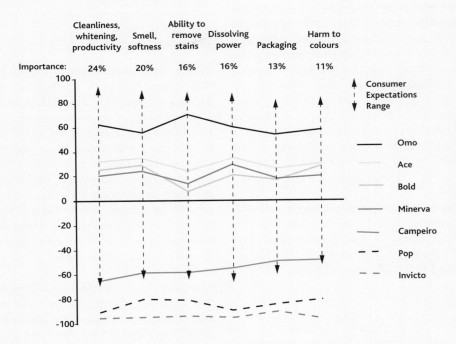

Figure C5.1 Attribute importance, brand positioning and consumer expectations in the north-east

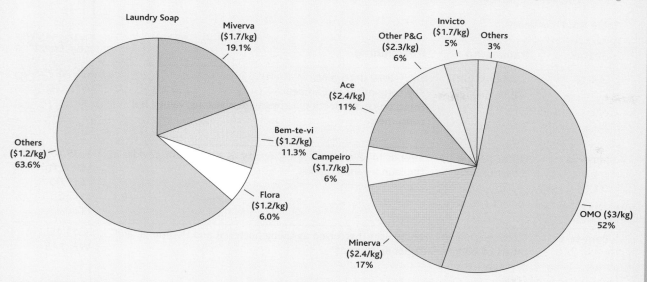

Figure C5.2 Market Share and Wholesale Price of Major Brands in the Laundry Soap and Detergent Powder Categories in the Northeast in 1996

Table C5.1 Key information for detergent powder and laundry soap brands in Brazil

Brand	Packaging	Positioning	Key Data[1]
OMO	Cardboard pack: 1kg & 500g.	Removes stains with low quantity of product when used in washing machines, thus reducing the need for soap or bleach.	S: 55.20 WP: 3.00 FC: 1.65 PKC: 0.35 PC: 0.35
Minerva	Cardboard pack: 1kg & 500g.	Emotional appeal ('care'). Delivers a pleasant perfume and softness to your clothes. 'New perfume: Aphrodite's touch in your clothes'.	S: 17.60 WP: 2.40 FC: 1.40 PKC: 0.35 PC: 0.30
Campeiro	Cardboard pack: 1kg & 500g.	Price brand. Focus on cost reduction across all dimensions valued by consumers.	S: 6.05 WP: 1.70 FC: 0.90 PKC: 0.35 PC: 0.20
Ace	Cardboard pack: 1kg & 500g.	Offers superior whiteness. Removes the dirt and protects the fabrics.	S: 11.80 WP: 2.35
Bold	Cardboard pack: 1kg & 500g.	Key competitor of Minerva with a similar positioning. Focus on softness.	S: 5.35 WP: 2.50
Pop	Cardboard pack: 1kg & 500g.	Price brand with small sales in the Northeast. Focus on cost reduction across all dimensions valued by consumers.	S: 1.40 WP: 1.70

Table C5.1 continued

Brand	Packaging	Positioning	Key Data[1]
Invicto	Cardboard pack: 1kg & 500g.	Entry-level detergent. Key competitor of Campeiro. Focus on cost reduction across all dimensions, valued by consumers.	S: 5.20 WP: 1.70
Minerva	Plastic pack with 5 bars of 200g.	Intends to leverage its brand equity as a detergent powder in the laundry soap market.	S: 19.40 WP: 1.70 FC: 1.00 PKC: 0.15 PC: 0.25
Bem-te-vi	Plastic pack with 5 bars of 200g or single bar of 200g.	Multi-uses (perceived as killing bacteria) and traditional and regional values.	S: 11.45 WP: 1.15

This case was written by Pierre Chandon, Assistant Professor of Marketing at INSEAD. It is a summary of the INSEAD case no. 02/2004-5188, 'Unilever in Brazil: Marketing Strategies for Low-Income Consumers' (written with Pedro Pacheco Guimaraes). The original case won the 2004 Case Writing Competition organized by the European Foundation for Management Development. The original case is available from the European Case Clearing House at www.ecch.cranfield.ac.uk.

---

1   S = Sales ($ million), WP = Wholesale price ($ per kg), i.e., the price at which the retailer buys the product, FC = Formulation costs ($ per kg), PKC = Packaging costs ($ per kg), PC = Promotional costs ($ per kg).

CHAPTER
6

PRODUCT AND BRAND MANAGEMENT

Learning Objectives

By the end of this chapter you will understand:

1 the differences between products and brands
2 the key aspects of building and managing a successful brand
3 how to manage a diverse product or brand portfolio
4 how product performance evolves over time
5 the importance of innovation and the new product development process
6 some of the ethical issues related to product management.

Marketing Spotlight

Human Branding

Of all the brands that are spread throughout the world, some of the most powerful are an elite group of 'human brands' featuring people like David Beckham, Kylie Minogue, Eric Cantona, Elle Macpherson, Jamie Oliver and others. Human brands work in exactly the same way as product or service brands. They communicate values and perceptions—cool, sexy, funny, independent, revolutionary or whatever—that resonate with a particular target market. These values translate into everything that the individual does and the products they produce or endorse. Like product brands, human brands go through a life cycle and need to be managed carefully and, where necessary, re-invented.

One brand that is currently facing some challenges is Madonna's 'Madge' brand. Madonna is a classic branding success story. Ever since her 'launch' on a career that saw her sell 250 million records, Madonna has done what any successful global brand should do—be clear, consistent and simple. That is, clear in what she stood for, consistent in the way she communicated it and simple in the message that she wanted to get through. This was communicated through her music, her appearance and in the products she developed and endorsed. All her expressions had the same look and feel, gave us the same experiences and followed the same Madonna values.

Madonna has also been a master at re-inventing her brand (her latest tour in 2004 was even called the Reinvention Tour). She started out in the early 1980s with a very 'nothing can stop me now' attitude that appealed to girls around the world. By the late 1980s it was about freedom and self-expression ('Vogue' era). In the early 1990s, she shocked the world with sexuality and fantasies ('Erotica' era). By the late 1990s, she was focusing on her spiritual side and making statements about wisdom, vanity and fulfilment (Kabbalah era). All were clear, powerful messages.

Currently the Madge brand is starting to look confused. On the one hand, there was her latest re-invention as a sophisticated mother, who endorsed the first of her children's books, *The English Roses*, wearing floral dresses and teacher-style spectacles, appealing perhaps to quasi-spiritual suburban mothers. At the same time, she has appeared with a rapper in a provocative advertising campaign for Gap, possibly appealing to the African-American market. And she caused a storm by kissing Britney Spears and Christina Aguilera on-stage at the MTV Video Music Awards—an action that may see her appealing to rebellious twentysomethings and gays.

Can she be all things to all people? As with all brands, the answer is no and she will have to make some hard choices regarding which re-invention is most appropriate. Her popularity is waning as record sales and movie receipts fall. On top of that, there is the additional difficult choice as to whether or not she should retire now while still popular and become a legacy brand—like Elvis—that lasts for ever.[1]

Exhibit 6.1 Car manufacturers are consistently trying to augment their products. This Mercedes Benz M Class advertisement lists a range of new extra features

As we saw in Chapter 1, the essence of marketing is the delivery of value to some customer group. Products and brands are often the embodiment of that value proposition. For example, Kodak may well manufacture film but it understands that its business is allowing its customers to collect and retain memories. That's just as well because film technology is rapidly being replaced by digital technology and by consumers collecting and sharing memories via mobile phones or CDs. Old 'technologies' like 35 mm film and paper printing are quickly becoming outdated. Kodak has responded by phasing out its declining film-based business, involving 10,000 job cuts, and shifting its focus to digital photography and mobile phones through Kodak Mobile.[2] But the pace of consumer change has been even faster than Kodak anticipated and it fell to number 53 in the annual *Business Week*/Interbrand 2004 survey of brand values—a fall of 33 per cent between 2003 and 2004 alone.

This chapter will deal with all of these issues. First, we will examine the difference between a product and a brand, which is one of the most important distinctions that students of marketing must grasp. Then we will take a comprehensive look at the different aspects of managing modern brands. Many firms, such as global corporations like Diageo or Colgate, can have an extensive range of brands, so we will also examine how to manage these portfolios of brands or products. As the Kodak and Madonna examples show, the

demand for products can change very rapidly, so we will look too at how to manage products and brands effectively over time. An important element of this is innovation and ensuring a steady supply of new products, which is also discussed. Finally, the chapter closes with a discussion of the ethical issues involved in managing products.

Products versus brands

A product can be anything that has the capacity to satisfy customer needs. In everyday speech we often distinguish between products and services, with products being tangible (e.g. a car) and services mainly intangible (e.g. a medical examination). When we look at what the customer is buying, it is essentially a benefit, whether the means are tangible or intangible. For example, a car provides the benefit of transportation; the medical examination provides the benefit of a health check. Consequently, it is logical to include services within the definition of the product. Hence, there are physical products such as a watch, car or gas turbine, and service products such as medical services, insurance or banking. All of these provide benefits to customers—for example, a gas turbine provides power, and insurance reduces financial risk. The principles discussed in this chapter apply equally to physical and service products. However, because there are special considerations associated with service products (e.g. intangibility) and as service industries (e.g. tourism, consulting) form an important and growing sector, the next chapter is dedicated to services marketing in detail.

Branding is the process by which companies distinguish their product offerings from the competition. The word 'brand' is derived from the old Norse word 'brandr', which means 'to burn' as brands were and still are the means by which livestock owners mark their animals to identify ownership.[3] Building and maintaining a brand is one of the critical tasks of the marketing manager. We now live in a world where the technical differences between products are becoming fewer and fewer. For example, different makes of cars or DVD players or running shoes all have similar and comparable features. In most cases, consumers will not know (and often will not care) where the products are made. What will determine which company's product is purchased will be how consumers feel about the **brand**. Branding permits customers to develop associations (e.g. prestige, status, economy) and eases the purchase decision.[4] The power of brands to affect perceptions is particularly noticeable in blind product testing, where customers often fail to distinguish between competing offerings even though they may have a high level of loyalty to one brand.

For some time now it has been conventional for marketers to think in terms of different levels of product

(see Figure 6.1). At the most basic level, there is the core benefit provided by the product, such as cars that provide transportation or telephones that provide a means of communication. Understanding the core benefits provided by products is important in terms of identifying potential sources of competition. For example, paper diaries manufactured by companies like Filofax are under threat because the same benefit is delivered, arguably more effectively, through hand-held devices like PDAs and the diaries available on personal computers. Similarly, the growing popularity of MP3 players is having a significant effect on the demand for music CDs. Around the basic benefit is the 'actual product' the consumer purchases, which comprises certain features, styling, and so on, which go to make up the brand. For example, a Nokia mobile phone is an actual product, which is a blend of design, style, features and packaging designed to meet the needs of the market. There is also a third level of product, namely the 'augmented product'. This is the additional bundle of benefits that are added to a product, and typically include elements like guarantees, additional services and additional brand values. For example, the new Lexus GS includes extras like a keyless entry system, air-conditioned front seats, Bluetooth connectivity for mobile phones, parking-assist sensors and a rear electric sunshade.

Viewing a product in terms of these three levels is very important in helping to make product

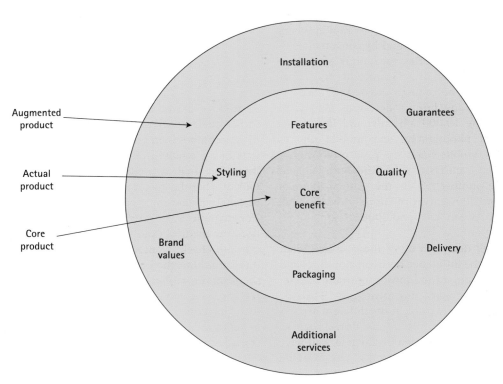

Figure 6.1 The three levels of product

management decisions. In order to differentiate their brands in a crowded and competitive marketplace, companies are always looking for new ways to augment their product and add additional values to it. On the other hand, it is quite interesting that, for example, the low-fares airlines like Ryanair and easyJet have gone in the opposite direction. Instead of looking at ways to augment their product, these companies have stripped away aspects of the actual and augmented product and focused heavily on the core benefit: transportation at a low price. In their view, aspects of the actual and augmented product did not deliver valuable benefits to consumers and there was merit in going back to the core benefit of moving people from A to B. This shift in strategic thinking has revolutionized air travel and low-fares airlines are now growing faster and are significantly more profitable than traditional airlines.

Branding

Developing a brand is difficult, expensive and takes time. We have seen that brands enable companies to differentiate their products from competitive offerings, but we must look at the benefits of brands in more detail.

The benefits of brands

Strong brands deliver the following benefits to companies.

Company value

The financial value of companies can be greatly enhanced by the possession of strong brands. For example, Nestlé paid £2.5 billion (€3.6 billion) for Rowntree, a UK confectionery manufacturer—a sum six times its balance sheet value. However, the acquisition gave Nestlé access to Rowntree's stable of

Marketing in Action: Brand communities

The relationship between consumers and brands is a complex one, but what is increasingly becoming evident is the emergence of brand communities: groups of people tied together by their admiration for certain brands. A brand community has been formally defined as a 'specialized, non-geographically bound community based on a structured set of relationships among admirers of a brand'. Others take a broader view and also include motivated employees, strategic partners and investors who are committed to a brand.

What is interesting is that brand communities take on all the major trappings of social communities. First, there is a shared consciousness, which is the intrinsic connection that members feel to one another, and their collective sense of difference from others not in the community. Second, there are the shared rituals and traditions that perpetuate the community's values. The third indicator of community is a sense of moral responsibility or obligation to the community as a whole and to its individual members.

These traits can be found in the behaviour of people, including customers, of cult or iconic brands such as Harley-Davidson. Harley is a 103-year-old brand that still ranks in the global top 50 brands in terms of value. The Harley Owners Group—initially set up to counter the damage to the company's image caused by an association with Hell's Angels—consists of 866,000 members who organize bike rides, training courses, social events and charity fundraisers. They pore over motorcycle magazines and wear Harley-branded gear to feel like rugged individualists. Over 250,000 attended the brand's centenary, held in Milwaukee in 2003.

Many other brands are rapidly reaching similar iconic status—for example, Absolut, Amazon, Apple, Barbie, eBay, IKEA, Lexus, Singapore Airlines, Tiffany's, and so on. Brand communities are likely to form around any brand, but are most likely where brands have a strong image, a rich and lengthy history, threatening competition and are publicly consumed. The growth of the Internet has helped to foster brand communities by providing a medium where information about the brand can be gathered and where exchanges between community members on a global basis are facilitated. Many leading brands, such as CNN and Disney, host online communities through bulletin boards, forums and chatrooms. Heineken allows individuals to establish their own virtual bars where, as bartender, they can chat to other visitors and meet their friends.

Based on: McWilliam (2000);[8] Muniz and O'Guinn (2001);[9] Upshaw and Taylor (2001)[10]

brands, including KitKat, Quality Street, After Eight and Polo.

Consumer preference and loyalty

Strong brand names can have positive effects on consumer perceptions and preferences. This in turn leads to brand loyalty where satisfied customers continue to purchase a favoured brand. Over time some brands, such as Apple, Harley-Davidson and Virgin, become cult brands: consumers become passionate about the brand and levels of loyalty go beyond reason[5] (see Marketing in Action 6.1). The strength of brand loyalty can be seen when companies try to change brands, such as Coca-Cola's proposed introduction of New Coke, or when the brand is threatened with extinction such as Bewley's Cafés in Dublin.[6]

Barrier to competition

The impact of the strong, positive perceptions held by consumers about top brands means it is difficult for new brands to compete. Even if the new brand performs well on blind taste tests, this may be insufficient to knock the market leader off the top spot. This may be one of the reasons that Virgin Coke failed to dent Coca-Cola's domination of the cola market.

High profits

Strong, market-leading brands are rarely the cheapest. Brands such as, Kellogg's, Coca-Cola, Mercedes, Nokia and Microsoft are all associated with premium prices. This is because their superior brand equity means that consumers receive added value over their less powerful rivals. Strong brands also achieve distribution more readily and are in a better position to resist retailer demands for price discounts. Research into return on investment for US food brands supports the view that strong brands are more profitable. The number one brand's average return was 18 per cent, number two achieved 6 per cent, number three returned 1 per cent, while the number four position was associated with a 6 per cent average return on investment.[7]

Base for brand extensions

A strong brand provides a foundation for leveraging positive perceptions and goodwill from the core brand to brand extensions. Examples include Pepsi Max, Lucozade Sport, Smirnoff Ice and Microsoft Internet Explorer. The new brand benefits from the added value that the brand equity of the core brand bestows on the extension.

Consumers as well as companies benefit from brands. The buying decision is simplified because consumers can select brands that they are familiar with or have a preference for. Much of the time, this comes down to the extent to which the consumer trusts the brand. Some of the most trusted brands in Europe include Nokia, Visa, Nivea and Sony.

Building brands

Building brands involves making decisions about the brand name and how the brand is developed and positioned in the marketplace.

Naming brands

Three brand name strategies can be identified: family, individual and combination.

A **family brand name** is used for all products—for example, Philips, Heinz and Del Monte. The goodwill attached to the family brand name benefits all brands, and the use of the name in advertising helps the promotion of all of the brands carrying the family name. The risk is that if one of the brands receives unfavourable publicity or is unsuccessful the reputation of the whole range of brands can be tarnished. This is also known as 'umbrella branding'. Some companies create umbrella brands for part of their brand portfolios to give coherence to their range of products. For example, Cadbury created the umbrella brand of Cadburyland for its range of children's chocolate confectionery[11] and Sony has created PlayStation for its range of video game consoles.

The **individual brand name** does not identify a brand with a particular company—for example, Procter & Gamble does not use its company name on its brands—Ariel, Fairy Liquid, Daz, Pampers, and so on (we will look at this later, in Table 6.5). This may be necessary when it is believed that each brand requires a separate, unrelated identity. In some instances, the use of a family brand name when moving into a new market segment may harm the image of the new **product line**. One example is the decision to use the Levi's family brand name on a new product line—Levi's Tailored Classics—despite marketing research information which showed that target customers associated the name Levi's with casual clothes, thus making it incompatible with the smart suits the company was launching. This mistake was not repeated by Toyota, which abandoned its family brand name when it launched its upmarket executive car, simply called the Lexus.

In the case of combination brand names, family and individual brand names are combined, this capitalizes on the reputation of the company while allowing the individual brands to be distinguished and identified (e.g. Kellogg's All Bran, Nokia 8910, Microsoft Windows XP).

Much careful thought should be given to the choice of brand name since names convey images. For example, Renault chose the brand name Safrane for one of its executive saloons because research showed that this brand name conveyed an image of luxury, exotica, high technology and style. The brand name Pepsi Max was chosen for the diet cola from Pepsi targeted at men as it conveyed a masculine image in a product category that was associated with women. So one criterion for deciding on a good brand name is that it evokes positive associations.

Brand names are equally important in the context of industrial products. In particular, brands are becoming more important due to increased competition from low-cost countries such as China. Good brands give industrial manufacturers the opportunity to compete on bases other than price. A recent study found that the most valuable industrial brands in the world were 3M (industrial products), Tyco (industrial products), Honeywell (industrial products), Caterpillar (construction machines), United Technologies (lifts, air conditioners), Emerson (motors, control systems) and Ingersoll-Rand (industrial products).[12]

Another important criterion is that the brand name should be memorable and easy to pronounce. Short names such as Esso, Shell, Daz, Ariel, Novon and Mini fall into this category. For example UBS, Europe's third largest bank, has dropped its family names UBS Warburg and UBS PaineWebber in favour of the simple UBS name. There are exceptions to this general rule, as in the case of Häagen-Dazs, which was designed to sound European in the USA where it was first launched. A brand name may suggest product benefits—as in the case of Right Guard (deodorant), Alpine Glade (air and fabric freshener), Head & Shoulders (anti-dandruff shampoo), Compaq (portable computer)—or express what the brand is offering in a distinctive way, such as Toys 'R' Us. Technological products may benefit from numerical brand naming (e.g. BMW 300, Lotus 1–2–3, Porsche

Table 6.1 Brand name considerations

A good brand name should:
1 evoke positive associations
2 be easy to pronounce and remember
3 suggest product benefits
4 be distinctive
5 use numerals when emphasizing technology
6 not infringe an existing registered brand name

Table 6.2 Brand name categories

People:	Cadbury, Mars, Heinz
Places:	National Westminster, Halifax Building Society
Descriptive:	I Can't Believe It's Not Butter, the Body Shop, Going Places
Abstract:	KitKat, Kodak, Prozac
Evocative:	Egg, Orange, Fuse
Brand extensions:	Dove Deodorant, Virgin Direct, Playtex Affinity
Foreign meanings:	Lego (from 'play well' in Danish), Thermos (meaning 'heat' in Greek)

Source: adapted from Miller, R. (1999) Science Joins Art in Brand Naming, *Marketing*, 27 May, 31–2.

911). This also overcomes the need to change brand names when marketing in different countries.

Some specialist companies have been established to act as brand name consultants. Market research is used to test associations, memorability, pronunciation and preferences. It is important to seek legal advice to ensure that a brand name does not infringe an existing brand name. Interesting controversies can arise relating to brand names and trademarks such as Victoria Beckham's efforts to stop Peterborough United Football Club trademarking their decades-old nickname 'Posh'. More controversially, some companies are also trying to obtain the legal rights to

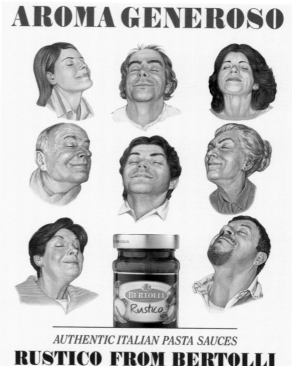

Exhibit 6.2 Brands like Bertolli pasta sauces highlight their authentic Italian heritage in their advertising

slogans – such as Nestlé for the KitKat slogan 'Have a Break'. Table 6.1 summarizes those issues that are important when choosing a brand name, while Table 6.2 shows how brand names can be categorized.

Developing brands

A brand is created by means of the augmentation of a core product to add brand values. The core product offers core benefits (see Figure 6.1 on pp140). Crisps are a satisfying snack, but all crisps can achieve that benefit. Branding allows marketers to create added values that distinguish one brand from another. Crisp producer Walkers, for example, has created a sense of fun around its products, as well as emphasizing product quality through the use of celebrity endorsers like Gary Lineker in its advertising (see Marketing in Action 1.3). Successful brands are those that create a set of brand values that are superior to those of other, rival, brands. So brand building involves a deep understanding of both the functional (e.g. ease of use) and emotional (e.g. confidence) values that customers use when choosing between brands, and the ability to combine them in a unique way to create an augmented product that customers will prefer.

Building successful brands is an extremely challenging marketing task. In fact, of Britain's top 50 brands, only 18 per cent have been developed since 1975.[13] This also implies that when a brand becomes established, it tends to endure for a very long time. Table 6.3 lists the world's leading brands, some of which are over 100 years old, so we can see that brand building is a long-term activity. There are many demands on people's attention; generating awareness, communicating brand values and building customer loyalty usually takes many years, which is why the rapid rise to prominence of brands like Amazon and Google is so admirable. Similarly, the Korean company Samsung has moved from being seen as a company that produced cheap television and microwave ovens to a leading global, premium brand in sectors like mobile phones, memory chips and flat panels. This was achieved through doubling its marketing spend to US$3 billion, advertising that showed the company's prowess in technology, product placement in futuristic films like *Matrix Reloaded* and sponsorship of the Athens Olympics, which increased general awareness of the brand. The value of the Samsung brand is now seen as being close to that of Sony.[14]

Table 6.3 The top 20 must valuable brands worldwide

	Company	2004 brand value (US$ billions)	2003 brand value (US$ billions)	% change
1	Coca-Cola	67.39	70.45	−4 per cent
2	Microsoft	61.37	65.17	−6 per cent
3	IBM	53.79	51.77	4 per cent
4	GE	44.11	41.34	4 per cent
5	Intel	33.50	31.11	8 per cent
6	Disney	27.11	28.04	23 per cent
7	McDonald's	25.00	24.70	1 per cent
8	Nokia	24.04	29.44	−18 per cent
9	Toyota	22.67	20.78	9 per cent
10	Marlboro	22.18	22.18	0 per cent
11	Mercedes	21.33	21.37	0 per cent
12	Hewlett-Packard	20.97	19.86	6 per cent
13	Citibank	19.97	18.57	8 per cent
14	American Express	17.68	16.83	5 per cent
15	Gillette	16.72	15.98	5 per cent
16	Cisco	15.95	15.80	1 per cent
17	BMW	15.88	15.11	5 per cent
18	Honda	14.87	15.62	−5 per cent
19	Ford	14.48	17.06	−15 per cent
20	Sony	12.75	13.15	−3 per cent

Source: Business Week, 9–16 August 2004

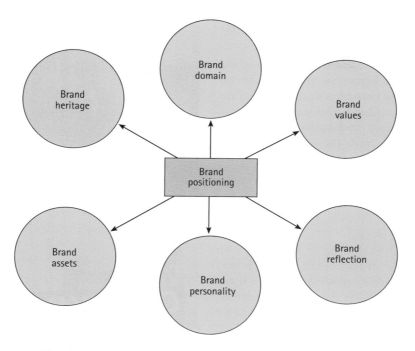

Figure 6.2 The anatomy of brand positioning

Management must be prepared to provide a consistently high level of brand investment to establish and maintain the position of a brand in the marketplace. Unfortunately, it can be tempting to cut back on expenditure in the short term, particularly when there is a downturn in the economy. Such cutbacks need to be resisted in order for the brand to be supported, as it is one of the key drivers of shareholder value.[15]

Figure 6.2 is an analytical framework that can be used to dissect the current position of a brand in the marketplace, and to form the basis of a new brand positioning strategy. The strength of a brand's position in the marketplace is built on six elements: brand domain, brand heritage, brand values, brand assets, brand personality and brand reflection. The first of these, brand domain, corresponds to the choice of target market (where the brand competes); the other five elements provide avenues for creating a clear differential advantage with these target consumers. These elements are expanded on briefly below.

1   *Brand domain*: the brand's target market, i.e. where it competes in the marketplace.
2   *Brand heritage*: the background to the brand and its culture. How it has achieved success (and failure) over its life.
3   *Brand value*: the core values and characteristics of the brand.
4   *Brand assets*: what makes the brand distinctive from other competing brands (symbols, features, images and relationships, etc.).
5   *Brand personality*: the character of the brand described in terms of other entities, such as people, animals or objects. Celebrity endorsement of brands gives them personality. Sales of Kia Kaha, a small New Zealand-based company, were significantly boosted when Michael Campbell won the US Open golf tournament wearing its clothing.[16]
6   *Brand reflection*: how the brand relates to self-identity; how the customer perceives him/herself as a result of buying/using the brand.

Brand managers can form an accurate portrait of how brands are positioned in the marketplace by analysing each of the elements listed above. Brand building is expensive and great care needs to be taken with brand investment decisions. For example, Unilever spent over £7 million on just redesigning its logo to make it more 'open and friendly'. The new logo combines the sun ('the ultimate symbol of vitality'), a bird ('a symbol of freedom') and a shirt ('representing fresh laundry and looking good').[17]

Brand management issues

Finally, firms may face a number of issues with respect to the management of brands. We will turn to these now.

Manufacturer brands versus own-label brands

Manufacturer brands are created by producers and bear their own chosen brand names. The responsibility for marketing the brand lies in the hands of the producer. Examples include Kellogg's Cornflakes, Gillette Sensor razors and Ariel washing powder. The value of the brand lies with the producer and, by building major brands, producers can gain distribution and customer loyalty.

Own-label brands (sometimes called distributor brands) are created and owned by distributors. Sometimes the entire **product mix** of a distributor may be own-label, as was the case for some time with Marks & Spencer's St Michael brand, or only part of the mix may be own-label, as is the case with many supermarket chains. In many developed economies, sales of own-label products are growing at a faster rate than manufacturer brands. Own-label branding, if associated with the tight quality control of suppliers, can provide consistent high value for customers, and be a source of retail power as own-label brands compete effectively with **manufacturer brands**. The power of low-price supermarket **own-label brands** has focused many producers of manufacturer brands on introducing so-called fighter brands (i.e. their own low-price alternatives).

A major decision that producers have to face is whether to agree to supply own-label products for distributors. The danger is that should customers find out about this, they may believe that there is no difference between the manufacturer brand and its cheaper own-label equivalent. For other producers, supplying own-label goods may be a means of filling excess capacity and generating extra income from the high sales volumes contracted with distributors.

Brand extension and stretching

Tangible value is added to a company by the goodwill associated with a respected brand name, and through the higher sales and profits that result. This higher financial value is called brand equity. Brand names with high **brand equity** are candidates to be used on other new brands since their presence has the potential to enhance their attractiveness. A **brand extension** is the use of an established brand name on a new brand within the same broad market. For example, the Anadin brand name has been extended to related brands: Anadin Extra, Maximum Strength, Soluble, Paracetamol and Ibuprofen. Unilever has successfully expanded its Dove soap brand into deodorants, shower gel, liquid soap and bodywash.[18] **Brand stretching** is when an

Exhibit 6.3 The powerful Virgin brand name has been stretched into a range of industries including mobile telephony

established brand name is used for brands in unrelated markets. A popular trend at present is where celebrities extend their brand into a variety of product categories, such as Jennifer Lopez who markets jlo clothes, sunglasses, swimwear, fragrances, accessories and lingerie.

Some companies have been very successful in their employment of brand extensions and stretching; Richard Branson's Virgin company is a classic example. Beginning in 1970 as Virgin Records the company grew through Virgin Music (music publishing), Megastores (music retailing), Radio, Vodka, Cola, Atlantic Airways (long-haul routes), Express (short-haul routes), Rail, Direct (direct marketing of financial services) and One (one-stop banking). Other companies have been less successful, such as the Penguin ice cream bar and Timotei facial care products.

The use of the brand extension is an important marketing tool. A study by ACNielsen showed that brand extensions account for approximately 40 per cent of new grocery launches.[19] Two key advantages of brand extension in releasing new products are that it reduces risk and is less costly than alternative launch strategies.[20] Both distributors and consumers may perceive less risk if the new brand comes with an established brand name. Distributors may be reassured about the saleability of the new brand and therefore be more willing to stock it. Consumers appear to attribute the quality associations they have of the original brand to the new one.[21] Launch costs can also be reduced by using brand extension. Since the established brand name is already well known, the task of building awareness of the new brand is eased. Consequently, advertising, selling and promotional costs are reduced. Furthermore, there is the likelihood of achieving advertising economies of scale since advertisements for the original brand and its extensions reinforce each other.[22]

These arguments can, however, be pushed too far. Brand extensions that offer no functional, psychological or price advantage over rival brands often fail.[23] There is also a danger that marketing management will underfund the launch, believing that the spin-off effects of the original brand name will compensate. This can lead to low awareness and trial. 'Cannibalization', which refers to a situation where the new brand gains sales at the expense of the established brand, can also occur. Anadin Extra, for example, could cannibalize the sales of the original Anadin brand. There is also the danger that bad publicity for one brand can affect the reputation of other brands under the same name. One example was the problem of the sudden, sharp acceleration of the Audi 5000, which affected sales of both the Audi 4000 and the Audi Quattro even though they did not suffer from the problem.[24]

If a brand name is extended too far there can be a loss of credibility, and this is something that management needs to guard against. This is particularly relevant when using brand stretching. Virgin's extension into rail services has been unsuccessful, while the use of the Pierre Cardin name for such disparate products as clothing, toiletries and cosmetics, for example, diluted the brand name's credibility.[25] Brand extensions are likely to be successful if they make sense to the consumer. If the values and aspirations of the new target segment(s) match those of the original segment, and the qualities of the brand name are likewise highly prized then success is likely.

Pan-European and global branding

The expanding economic union in Europe and the growing globalization of business has created an interest in the prospects for pan-European and **global branding** respectively. A pan-European brand is one that has successfully penetrated the European market, while a global brand is one that has achieved global penetration levels. In Europe, the promise of pan-European branding has caused leading manufacturers to seek to extend their market coverage and to build their portfolio of brands. Nestlé has widened its brand portfolio by the acquisition of such companies as Rowntree (confectionery) and Buitoni-Perugina (pasta and chocolate). Mars has replaced its Treets and Bonitos brands with M&M's, and changed the name of its third-largest UK brand, Marathon, to Snickers, the name that is used in the rest of Europe. Many other brands, such as Toyota, Sony, Coca-Cola, BMW and Nokia, are global successes.

Pan-European and global brands have a number of advantages. The most important of these is that they can attain tremendous economies of scale. Gillette's global success with its Sensor razor was based on a highly standardized approach: the product, brand name, the message ('The Best a Man Can Get'), advertising visuals and packaging were all standardized; only the voice-overs in the advertisements were changed to cater for 26 languages across Europe, the USA and Japan. Using the same advertising approach throughout the world saved the company approximately US$20 million.[26] The uniform image of many global brands is reassuring to consumers. For example, McDonald's customers know what to expect irrespective of where in the world they visit a McDonald's. Being globally scaled also means that many companies become the preferred provider. For example, consulting companies like PricewaterhouseCoopers may be attractive to potential clients because of their ability to offer a worldwide service.

However, while many brands seek pan-European or global status, national differences make it difficult to implement a standardized branding strategy across countries. For example, the fact that the French eat four times more yoghurt than the British, and the British buy eight times more chocolate than the Italians reflects the kinds of national differences that will affect the marketing strategies of manufacturers.[27] The question is not whether brands can be built on a global scale (clearly they can), but which parts of the brand can be standardized and which must be varied across countries. For example,

Unilever found that for detergent products, brand image and packaging could be standardized but the brand name, communications execution and brand formulation needed to vary across countries.[28] For its fabric conditioner it used the image of a cuddly teddy bear across countries, but the product was named differently in Germany (Kuschelweich), France (Cajoline), Italy (Coccolini), Spain (Mimosin), the USA (Snuggle) and Japan (Fa-Fa). Brand image and packaging were the same but the name and formulation (fragrance, phosphate levels and additives) differed between countries. Jagermeister, the German schnapps brand, uses a differentiated strategy in its major markets, as shown in Marketing in Action 6.2.

Co-branding

A popular strategy for some companies today is co-branding where two brands are combined. This may take the form of **product-based co-branding** or **communications-based co-branding**. Product-based co-branding involves the linking of two or more existing brands from different companies to form a product in which both brand names are visible to the consumer. There are two variants of this approach. **Parallel co-branding** occurs when two independent brands join forces to form a combined brand such as HP and Apple iPod to form the HP iPod. **Ingredient co-branding** is where one supplier explicitly chooses to position its brand as an ingredient of a product, such as when U2 launched the album *How to Dismantle an Atomic Bomb* pre-installed on an Apple iPod. Intel is one of the best-known ingredient brands through its popular slogan 'Intel inside', seen on PCs worldwide.

There are a number of advantages to product-based co-branding. First, the co-branding alliance can capture multiple sources of brand equity and therefore add value and provide a point of differentiation. Combining Häagen-Dazs ice cream and Bailey's liqueur creates a brand that adds value through distinctive flavouring that is different from competitive offerings. Second, a co-brand can position a product for a particular target market. This was the reason that Ford formed an alliance with *Elle* magazine to create the Ford Focus Elle, targeting women. The *Elle*-branded Focus has features such as heated

Marketing in Action: Jagermeister: traditional schnapps and trendy college drink

Jagermeister is a 127-year-old German liqueur brand that is manufactured in the town of Wolfenbuttel. It is made to a closely guarded recipe using 56 herbs and spices, and has a brown colour and tangy herbal taste that is said to resemble a mixture of root beer, black liquorice and the cough mixture Vicks Formula 44. It is packaged in a chunky green bottle emblazoned with a stag's head. Over half of the brand's annual sales of €250 million now come from outside Germany.

But what is particularly interesting about this brand is that it has a very different image in some of its major markets. For example, in Germany, Jagermeister is still seen as a traditional schnapps, though with a cool image resulting from a recent advertising campaign featuring two talking wall-mounted stags. In Italy, its second biggest export market, it is seen as an upmarket version of local after-dinner drinks such as Ramazzotti. But in contrast, in the USA, it is the stuff of wild college parties. The core of its promotion in the USA is the Jagerettes, over 1000 young women employed by the company to dispense ice-cold Jagermeister shots in bars and clubs along with T-shirts, hats, frisbees and other merchandise. In this market its major competitors are Jack Daniels and Jose Cuervo.

Unlike in Germany, the company does no media advertising in the USA but concentrates all of its budget on product promotions and sponsorship. For example, the Jagermeister Music Tour, featuring US metal bands like Slayer, has been running successfully for four years. With sales of over 1 million cases a year, it is now the third biggest-selling imported liquor in the USA. But, as with all global brands, successful innovations in one market are transferred to others. For example, the Jagerettes now operate in Germany as well, but focus less on universities and music sponsorship. And the 'tap machine' that sits on bar tops and dispenses ice-cold shots in the USA has been introduced in Germany as a way of increasing the brand's visibility.

Based on: Todd (2003);[29] Waddell (2003);[30] Wassener (2003)[31]

Table 6.4 Co-branding: some examples

Parallel co-brands
Häagen-Dazs and Bailey's Cream Liqueur form
Häagen-Dazs with Baileys flavour ice cream
Ford Focus and Elle women's magazine form Ford
Focus Elle car
Nike and Lego Bionicle form Bionicle by Nike trainers

Ingredient co-brands
Intel as a component in Hewlett-Packard computers
Nutrasweet as an ingredient in Diet Coke
Scotchgard as stain protector in fabrics

Communications-based co-brands
Ariel and Whirlpool: joint advertising campaign
McDonald's and Disney: joint store promotions
Shell and Ferrari: sponsorship

leather seats, metallic livery and special wheels that appeal to women who choose cars on the basis of look and style.[32] Finally, co-branding can reduce the cost of product introduction since two well-known brands are combined, accelerating awareness, acceptance and adoption.[33]

Communications-based co-branding involves the linking of two or more existing brands from different companies or business units for the purposes of joint communications. For example, one brand can recommend another, such as Whirlpool's endorsement of Ariel washing powder.[34] Also the alliance can be used to stimulate interest or provide promotional opportunities, such as the deal between McDonald's and Disney, which gives the former exclusive global rights to display and promote material relating to new Disney movies in its outlets. Communications alliances are very popular in sponsorship deals, such as Shell's brand name appearing on Ferrari cars. Table 6.4 lists some examples of co-branding.

Managing brand and product portfolios

Some companies have a large portfolio of brands (see Table 6.5). They normally fall within a company's product line and mix. A product line is a group of brands that are closely related in terms of their functions and the benefits they provide (e.g. Dell's range of personal computers or Philips Consumer Electronics' line of television sets). The *depth* of the product line refers to the number of variants offered within the product line. A 'product mix' is the total set of brands marketed in a company. It is the sum of the product lines offered. Thus, the *width* of the product mix can be gauged by the number of product lines an organization offers. Philips, for example, offers a wide product mix comprising the brands found within its product lines of television, audio equipment, video recorders, camcorders, and so on. Other companies have a much narrower product mix comprising just one product line, such as TVR, which produces high-performance cars.

The process of managing groups of brands and product lines is called **portfolio planning**. This can be a very complex and important task. Some product lines will be strong, others weak. Some will require investment to finance their growth, others will generate more cash than they need. Somehow companies must decide how to distribute their limited resources among the competing needs of products so as to achieve the best performance for the company as a whole. Specifically, management need to decide which brands to invest in, hold or withdraw support from.

The Boston Consulting Group's (BCG's) growth-share matrix is a technique borrowed from strategic management that has proved useful in helping companies to make product mix and/or product line

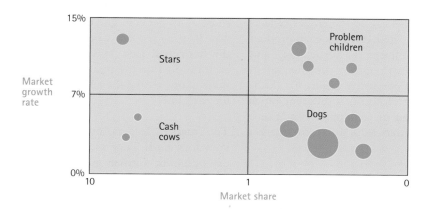

Figure 6.3 The Boston Consulting Group growth-share matrix

Table 6.5 Sample brand portfolios of leading companies

Johnson & Johnson	Procter & Gamble	Nestlé	Unilever	L'Oréal	Diageo
BandAid	Ariel	Nescafé	Persil	Vichy	Guinness
Neutrogena	Bounce	Perrier	Surf Comfort Domestos	Garnier	Baileys
RoC	Daz Fairy Pampers	Vittel KitKat Quality Street	Cif	La Roche-Posay Maybelline	Smirnoff J&B Johnnie Walker
Johnson's	Tampax	Polo	Dove	Lancôme	Captain Morgan
Baby	Crest	Rolo	Timotei	Ralph Lauren perfumes	Moët & Chandon
Clean & Clear	Vicks	After Eight	Organics	Helena Rubinstein	Jose Cuervo
Aveeno	Head & Shoulders	Carnation	Flora	Giorgio Armani perfumes	Tanqueray
Acuvue	Vidal Sassoon	Lean Cuisine		Cacherel	Malibu
Pepcid	Camay	Buitoni	Lipton	Biotherm	Gordon's Gin
Tylenol	Hugo Boss	Nesquik	Ragu		Archers
Imodium	Cover Girl	Libby's	Oxo		Bells
Stayfree	Old Spice	Chef	HP Ice Cream		Piat d'Or
Piz Buin	Pringles Sunny Delight	Purina Friskies	Hellmann's		
Benecol			Knorr Ben & Jerry's SlimFast Lynx Impulse Calvin Klein cosmetics		
Reach toothbrushes					

decisions (see Figure 6.3). The matrix allows portfolios of products to be depicted in a 2×2 box, the axes of which are based on market growth rate and relative market share. The size of the circles reflects the proportion of revenue generated by each product line. Market growth rate forms the vertical axis and indicates the annual growth rate of the market in which each product line operates; in Figure 6.3 this is shown as 0–15 per cent although a different range could be used depending on economic conditions. Market growth rate is used as a proxy for market attractiveness.

Relative market share refers to the market share of each product relative to its largest competitor, and is shown on the horizontal axis. This acts as a proxy for competitive strength. The division between high and

low market share is 1. Above this figure a product line has a market share greater than its main competitor. For example, if our product had a market share of 40 per cent and our main competitor's share was 30 per cent this would be indicated as 1.33 on the horizontal axis. Having plotted the position of each product on the matrix, a company can begin to think about setting the appropriate strategic objective for each line.

The market leaders in high-growth markets are known as *stars*. They are already successful and the prospects for further growth are good. Resources should be invested to maintain/increase the leadership position. Competitive challenges should be repelled. These are the cash cows of the future (see below) and need to be protected.

Problem children are cash drains because they have low profitability and require investment to enable them to keep up with market growth. They are so called because management has to consider whether it is sensible to continue the required investment. The company faces a fundamental choice: to increase investment (build) to attempt to turn the problem child into a star, or to withdraw support, either by harvesting (raising the price while lowering marketing expenditure) or divesting (dropping or selling it). In a few cases a third option may be viable: to find a small market segment (niche) where dominance can be achieved. Unilever, for example, identified its speciality chemicals business as a problem child. It realized that it had to invest heavily or exit. Its decision was to sell and invest the billions raised in predicted future winners such as personal care, dental products and fragrances products.[35]

The high profitability and low investment associated with high market share in low-growth markets mean that *cash cows* should be defended. Consequently, the appropriate strategic objective is to hold sales and market share. The excess cash that is generated should be used to fund stars, problem children that are being built, and research and development for new products.

Dogs are weak products that compete in low-growth markets. They are the also-rans that have failed to achieve market dominance during the growth phase and are floundering in maturity. For those products that achieve second or third position in the marketplace (*cash dogs*) a small positive cash flow may result and, for a few others, it may be possible to reposition the product into a defendable niche. For the bulk of dogs, however, the appropriate strategic objective is to *harvest*—that is, to generate a positive cash flow for a time—or to *divest*, which allows resources and managerial time to be focused elsewhere.

The strength of the BCG's growth-share matrix is its simplicity. Once all of the company's products have been plotted it is easy to see how many stars, problem children, cash cows and dogs there are in the portfolio. Cash can be allocated as necessary to the different product lines to ensure that a balanced portfolio is maintained. However, the tool has also attracted a litany of criticism.[36] Some of the key problems with using the technique are as follows.

1 The matrix was based on cash flow but perhaps profitability (e.g. return on investment) is a better criterion for allocating resources.

2 Since the position of a product on the matrix depends on market share, this can lead to an unhealthy preoccupation with market share gain. In addition, market definition (which determines market share) can be very difficult.

3 The matrix ignores interdependences between products. For example, a dog may need to be marketed because it complements a star or a cash cow (it may be a spare part or an accessory, for example). Alternatively, customers and distributors may value dealing with a company that supplies a full product line. For these reasons dropping products because they fall into a particular box may be naive.

4 Treating market growth rate as a proxy for market attractiveness, and market share as an indicator of competitive strength is to oversimplify matters.

There are many other factors that have to be taken into account when measuring market attractiveness (e.g. market size, the strengths and weaknesses of competitors) and competitive strengths (e.g. exploitable marketing assets, potential cost advantages) besides market growth rates and market share. This led to the introduction of more complex portfolio matrices such as the McKinsey/GE market attractiveness–competitive position matrix, which used a variety of measures of market attractiveness and competitive strength. However, in recent years, major global companies have sought to manage complexity by focusing on building major power brands or superbrands. This involves offloading marginal brands and reinvesting the money in leading brands in growing markets. For example, in 2000, P&G owned 10 brands with annual sales of over US$1 billion. By 2004 this number had risen to 16 and the recent purchase of Gillette adds a further five superbrands to the group.[37]

The main contribution of the portfolio matrices generally has been to demonstrate that *different products should have different roles* in the product portfolio. For example, to ask for a 20 per cent return on investment (ROI) for a star may result in under-investment in an attempt to meet the profit requirement. On the other hand, 20 per cent ROI for a cash cow or a harvested product may be too low. However, the models should be used only as an aid to managerial judgement, and other factors that are not adequately covered by the models should be considered when making product mix decisions.

Managing brands and product lines over time: the product life cycle

Both individual brands and product lines need to be managed over time. A useful tool for conceptualizing the changes that may take place during the time that a product is on the market is called the **product life cycle**. The classic product life cycle (PLC) has four stages (see Figure 6.4): introduction, growth, maturity and decline.

The PLC emphasizes the fact that nothing lasts for ever (see Marketing in Action 6.3). There is a danger that management may fall in love with certain products, as in the case of a company that was founded on the success of a particular product. The PLC underlines the fact that companies have to accept that products need to be terminated and new products developed to replace them. Without this sequence a company may find itself with a group of products all in the decline stage of their PLC. A nicely balanced product array would see the company marketing some products in the mature stage of the PLC, a number at the growth stage and the prospect of new product introductions in the near future.

The PLC emphasizes the need to review marketing objectives and strategies as products pass through the various stages. Changes in market and competitive conditions between the PLC stages suggest that marketing strategies should be adapted to meet them. Table 6.6 shows a set of stylized marketing responses to each stage. Note that these are broad generalizations rather than exact prescriptions, but they do serve to emphasize the need to review marketing objectives and strategies in the light of environmental change.

Marketing in Action: The decline of hi-fi

Once the staple of the sitting room or bedroom, sales of home audio units are starting to fall dramatically. For example, in the USA, sales of stand-alone compact disc players and stereo amplifiers were down by 30 per cent in the first half of 2003. Sales of complete audio systems, known as 'minis' and 'micros', were down by 20 per cent. The stereo hi-fi (high-fidelity) grew in popularity in the post-war years. Despite several technological changes, such as the move from vacuum tubes to transistors and from LPs to CDs, the business prospered. However, from a high of over 2 million units in the USA in 1985, sales of audio components were down to fewer than 100,000 in 2003. The hi-fi is in decline.

What has caused the dramatic reversal in the fortunes of this product? Two technological changes are driving its fall. The rise of DVDs, which store both sound and images, means that DVD players play audio as well as video. But a bigger force is digitization, which has really caused the established industry boundaries in consumer electronics to crumble. Mobile phones take photographs, Personal organizers play music and computers make phone calls over the Internet. In a world where video, voice and data are converging, stand-alone units do not make sense.

But the decline has also been hastened by social changes. It is not that people are listening to less music, they are probably listening to more. But it is usually as an accompaniment to other activities such as jogging, commuting or working on a computer. For many in the past, it was not unusual to sit down and listen to a 60-minute pre-packaged album. But today's music equipment buyers (people in their late teens and 20s) have grown up with digital media including personal computers, video games and mobile phones, and they like their media to be portable, interactive and customizable.

These developments present real challenges for the makers of hi-fi products such as Sony, Philips, Pioneer and Matsushita who make Panasonic. Their response has been to launch new 'music-only' products such as music servers that store thousands of songs in digital form on a computer hard disk, and networked hi-fi components that download music from the Internet. Whether these will be successful, only time will tell.

Based on: Hegarty (2004);[38] London (2003)[39]

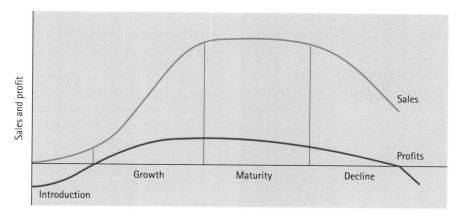

Figure 6.4 The product life cycle

Table 6.6 Marketing objectives and strategies over the product life cycle

	Introduction	**Growth**	**Maturity**	**Decline**
Strategic marketing objective	Build	Build	Hold	Harvest/manage for cash
Strategic focus	Expand market	Penetration	Protect share	Productivity
Brand objective	Product awareness/ trial	Brand preference	Brand loyalty	Brand exploitation
Products	Basic	Differentiated	Differentiated	Rationalized
Promotion	Creating awareness/trial	Creating awareness/trial repeat purchase	Maintaining awareness/repeat purchase	Cut/eliminated
Price	High	Lower	Lowest	Rising
Distribution	Patchy	Wider	Intensive	Selective

Introduction

When a product is first introduced on to the market its sales growth is typically low and losses are incurred as a result of heavy development and initial promotional costs. Companies will be monitoring the speed of product adoption and, if it is disappointing, may terminate the product at this stage.

The strategic marketing objective is to build sales by expanding the market for the product. The brand objective will be to create product (as well as brand) awareness so that customers will become familiar with generic product benefits. The product is likely to be fairly basic, with an emphasis on reliability and functionality rather than special features to appeal to different customer groups. Promotion will support the brand objectives by gaining awareness for the brand and product type, and stimulating trial. Advertising has been found to be more effective at the start of the life of a product than in later stages.[40] Typically, price will be high because of the heavy development costs and the low level of competition. Distribution will be patchy as some dealers will be

wary of stocking the new product until it has proved successful in the marketplace.

Growth

This second stage is marked by a period of faster sales and profit growth. Sales growth is fuelled by rapid market acceptance and, for many products, repeat purchasing. Profits may begin to decline towards the latter stages of growth as new rivals enter the market attracted by the twin magnets of fast sales growth and high profit potential. For example, the MP3 market and the Internet search engine business are two that have been growing rapidly and delivering very high profits for some incumbent firms. The end of the growth period is often associated with 'competitive shake-out', whereby weaker suppliers cease production.

The strategic marketing objective during the growth phase is to build sales and market share. The strategic focus will be to penetrate the market by building brand preference. To accomplish this task the product will be redesigned to create differentiation,

Exhibit 6.4 Companies like Green & Black are prospering in the growing market for environmentally-friendly products

and promotion will stress the functional and/or psychological benefits that accrue from the differentiation. Awareness and trial are still important, but promotion will begin to focus on repeat purchasers. As development costs are defrayed and competition increases, prices will fall. Rising consumer demand and increased salesforce effort will widen distribution.

Maturity

Sales will eventually peak and stabilize as saturation occurs, hastening competitive shake-out. Mobile phone adoption rates, for example, are well over 90 per cent in Western European countries. The survivors now battle for market share by introducing product improvements, using advertising and sales promotional offers, dealer discounting and price cutting; the result is strain on profit margins, particularly for follower brands. The need for effective brand building is felt most acutely during maturity as brand leaders are in the strongest position to resist pressure on profit margins.[41]

Decline

During the decline stages—when new technology or changes in consumer tastes work to reduce demand for the product—sales and profits fall. Suppliers may decide to cease production completely or reduce product depth. Promotional and product development budgets may be slashed, and marginal distributors dropped as suppliers seek to maintain (or increase) profit margins. Products like black-and-white televisions, and audio and video tapes have all declined in the face of new and superior technologies. Ricard, manufactured by the French spirits group Pernod-Ricard is France's best-selling spirit but sales of the drink are declining steadily and it is likely to be overtaken by whisky.[42] Specialist business news channels were popular during the late 1990s at the height of many global stock markets but some networks, like CNNfn, have already been taken off air.[43]

Like the BCG's growth-share matrix, the PLC theory has been the subject of a significant amount of criticism. First, not all products follow the classic S-shaped curve. The sales of some products 'rise like a rocket then fall like the stick'. This is normal for fad products such as Rubik's cubes, which in the 1980s saw phenomenal sales growth followed by a rapid sales collapse as the youth market moved on to another craze. Similarly, many see (and some hope) that reality television will be a similar kind of fad that will fade out quickly. Second, the duration of the PLC stages is unpredictable. The PLC outlines the four stages a product passes through without defining their duration. For example, e-books have languished in the introduction stage of the product life cycle for longer than anticipated, as shown in e-Marketing 6.1. Clearly this limits its use as a forecasting tool since it is not possible to predict when maturity or decline will begin. Finally, and perhaps most worryingly, it has been argued that the PLC is the *result* of marketing activities, not the cause. Clearly, sales of a product may flatten out or fall simply because it has not received enough marketing attention, or because there has been insufficient product redesign or promotional support. Using the PLC, argue its critics, may lead to inappropriate action (e.g. harvesting or dropping the product) when the correct response should be increased marketing support (e.g. product replacement, positioning reinforcement or repositioning). Like many marketing tools, the PLC should not be viewed as a panacea to marketing thinking and decision-making, but as an aid to managerial judgement.

Nevertheless, the dynamic nature of brands and product lines focuses attention on the key marketing challenge of developing new products and services. It is to this issue that we turn next.

e-Marketing: e-books fail to become bestsellers

Any product that can be digitized lends itself very well to an online business. That's why industries like music, video and computer software were among the first to experience significant change due to the efforts of companies like Napster and RealNetworks. For many, electronic book, or e-books, also represented a field full of promising possibilities. Ever since computers had been invented, written matter had been stored on them, but technological advances increased the likelihood that the e-book business would grow. Hardware developments like small lightweight laptops, PDAs and dedicated readers like the Rocket e-book and the Everybook Dedicated Reader provided plenty of options for storing and reading books.

On the back of predictions that e-books would gain about 10 per cent of all sales by 2005, significant investments were made in the industry. Publishers like Random House and Time Warner both set up digital imprints, while the retailer Barnes & Noble invested US$20 million in MightyWords, a site where authors can sell directly to readers. But, by 2004, many of these investments were being reversed.

Though e-books are still selling, their take-up has not been nearly as quick as anticipated. There are several reasons for this. First, there are the technological difficulties. Many e-book readers are still in relatively early stages of development, giving an inadequate user experience while, for some consumers, the need to purchase additional electronic equipment has proved unappealing. Second, publishers have pursued a skimming strategy, selling e-books at a relatively high price, which is also turning some consumers away. Third, there is no centralized Internet database for finding a digitized book, so searching for them is difficult. Finally, it is apparent that many consumers still love conventional books. They collect them, scribble on them, fill shelves with them, and borrow and lend them.

The latter factor is probably the most difficult hurdle that e-books will have to overcome. Recent data shows that sales continue to rise, reaching a level of US$3.3 million in 2004, up 28 per cent on the previous year. The e-bestsellers include Dan Brown's *The Da Vinci Code* and Kevin Ryan's *Van Helsing*, but only time will tell if the printed book is going to go the way of 33-inch vinyl disc or the analogue tape.

Based on: Chu (2003);[44] Hearne (2001);[45] Rao (2001);[46] Taylor (2004)[47]

New product development

The introduction of new products to the marketplace is the life blood of corporate success. Changing customer tastes, technological advances and competitive pressures mean that companies cannot afford to rely on past product successes.

Instead they have to work on new product development programmes and nurture an innovative climate in order to lay the foundations for new product success. The 3M company, for example, relies heavily on new product introductions. Each of its divisions is expected to achieve a quarter of its revenue from products that have been on the market for under six years. The reality of new product development is that it is a risky activity and most new products fail. However, failure has to be tolerated; it is endemic in the whole process of developing new products.

Some new products reshape markets and competition by virtue of the fact that they are so fundamentally different from products that already exist. However, a shampoo that is different from existing products only by means of its brand name, fragrance, packaging and colour is also a new product. In fact four brand categories of new product exist.[48]

1 *Product replacements*: these account for about 45 per cent of all new product launches, and include revisions and improvements to existing products (e.g. the Ford Mondeo replacing the Sierra), repositioning (existing products such as Lucozade being targeted at new market segments) and cost reductions (existing products being reformulated or redesigned so that they cost less to produce).

2 *Additions to existing lines*: these account for about 25 per cent of new product launches and take

Exhibit 6.5 Niche brands like Havana Cuban Rum are growing their global appeal

the full benefits of the product until it is on the market and they get the chance to experience them. Furthermore, it may take time for products to be accepted. For example, the Sony Walkman was initially rejected by marketing research since the concept of being seen in a public place wearing headphones was alien to most people. After launch, however, this behaviour was gradually accepted by younger age groups. At the other extreme, adding a brand variation to an existing product line lacks significant risk but is also unlikely to proffer significant returns.

Managing the new product development process

New product development is expensive, risky and time consuming—these are three inescapable facts. Gillette, for example, spent in excess of £100 million over more than 10 years developing its Sensor razor brand. The new product concept was to develop a non-disposable shaver that would use new technology to produce a razor that would follow the contours of a man's face, giving an excellent shave (due to two spring-mounted platinum-hardened chromium blades) with fewer cuts. This made commercial sense given that shaving systems are more profitable than disposable razors and allow more opportunity for creating a differential advantage. Had the brand failed,

the form of new products that add to a company's existing product lines. This produces greater product depth. An example is the launch by Weetabix of a brand extension, Fruitibix, to compete with the numerous nut/fruit/cereal product combinations that have been gaining market share.

3   *New product lines*: these total around 20 per cent of new product launches and represent a move into a new market. For example, in Europe, Mars has launched a number of ice cream brands, which make up a new product line for this company. This strategy widens a company's product mix.

4   *New-to-the-world products*: these total around 10 per cent of new product launches, and create entirely new markets. For example, the video games console, the video recorder and the camcorder have created new markets because of the highly valued customer benefits they provide.

Of course, the degree of risk and reward involved will vary according to the new product category. New-to-the-world products normally carry the highest risk since it is often difficult to predict consumer reaction. Often, market research will be unreliable in predicting demand as people do not really understand

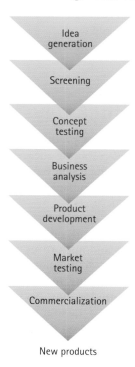

Figure 6.5 The seven-stage new product development process

Gillette's position in the shaving market could have been irreparably damaged.

A seven-step new product development process is shown in Figure 6.5; this consists of idea generation, screening, concept testing, business analysis, product development, market testing and commercialization. Although the reality of new product development may resemble organizational chaos, the discipline imposed by the activities carried out at each stage leads to a greater likelihood of developing a product that not only works, but also confers customer benefits. We should note, however, that new products pass through each stage at varying speeds: some may dwell at a stage for a long period while others may pass through very quickly.[49]

Idea generation

The sources of new product ideas can be internal to the company: scientists, engineers, marketers, salespeople and designers, for example. Some companies use the **brainstorming** technique to stimulate the creation of ideas, and use financial incentives to persuade people to put forward ideas they have had. 3M's Post-it adhesive-backed notepaper was a successful product that was thought of by an employee who initially saw the product as a means of preventing paper falling from his hymn book as he marked the hymns that were being sung. Because of the innovative culture within 3M, he bothered to think of commercial applications and acted as a product champion within the company to see the project through to commercialization and global success.

Sources of new product ideas can also be external to the company. Examining competitors' products may provide clues to product improvements. Distributors can also be a source of new product ideas directly, since they deal with customers and have an interest in selling improved products. A major source of good ideas is the customers themselves. Their needs may not be satisfied with existing products and they may be genuinely interested in providing ideas that lead to product improvement (see Marketing in Action 4.1). For example, the Dutch electronics group, Philips employs anthropologists and cognitive psychologists to gather insights into the desires and needs of people around the world to enable it to compete more effectively with Asian rivals such as Sony who are more renowned for their design capabilities.[50] In organizational markets, keeping in close contact with customers who are innovators and market leaders in their own marketplaces is likely to be a fruitful source of new product ideas.[51] These

'lead customers' are likely to recognize required improvements ahead of other customers as they have advanced needs and are likely to face problems before other product users. Some recent innovations such as GE's Light Speed VCT, which provides a three-dimensional image of a beating heart, and Staples' Wordlock, a padlock that uses words instead of numbers, have been developed in co-operation with lead customers. In recent years, the growth of online communities and easy-to-use design tools has enabled firms to involve their customers more in product innovation.[52]

Screening

Once new product ideas have been developed they need to be screened in order to evaluate their commercial value. Some companies use formal checklists to help them judge whether the product idea should be rejected or accepted for further evaluation. This ensures that no important criterion is overlooked. Criteria may be used that measure the attractiveness of the market for the proposed product, the fit between the product and company objectives, and the capability of the company to produce and market the product. Other companies may use a less systematic approach, preferring more flexible open discussion among members of the new product development committee to gauge likely success.

Concept testing

Once a product idea has been deemed worthy of further investigation, it can be framed into a specific concept for testing with potential customers. The concept may be described verbally or pictorially so that the major features are understood. In many instances the basic product idea will be expanded into several product concepts, each of which can be compared by testing with target customers. For example, a study into the acceptability of a new service—a proposed audit of software development procedures that would lead to the award of a quality assurance certificate—was expressed in eight service concepts depending on which parts of the development procedure would be audited (e.g. understanding customer needs, documentation, benchmarking). Each concept was evaluated by potential buyers of the software to gauge which were the most important aspects of software development that should be audited.[53] **Concept testing** thus allows the views of customers to enter the new product development process at an early stage. The buying intentions of potential customers are a key factor in judging whether any of the concepts are worth pursuing further.

Business analysis

Estimates of sales, costs and profits will be made, based on the results of the concept test, as well as on considerable managerial judgement. This is known as the **business analysis** stage. In order to produce sensible figures a marketing analysis will need to be undertaken. This will identify the target market, its size and projected product acceptance over a number of years. Consideration will be given to various prices and the implications for sales revenue (and profits) discussed. By setting a tentative price this analysis will provide sales revenue estimates. Costs will also need to be estimated. If the new product is similar to existing products (e.g. a brand extension) is should be fairly easy to produce accurate cost estimates. For radical product concepts, costings may be nothing more than informal guesstimates.

When the quantity needed to be sold to cover costs is calculated, *break-even analysis* may be used to establish whether the project is financially feasible. *Sensitivity analysis*, in which variations from given assumptions about price, cost and customer acceptance, for example, are checked to see how they impact on sales revenue and profits, can also prove useful at this stage. 'Optimistic', 'most likely' and 'pessimistic' scenarios can be drawn up to estimate the degree of risk attached to a project. If the product concept appears commercially feasible this process will result in marketing and product development budgets being established based on what appears to be necessary to gain customer awareness and trial, and the work required to turn the concept into a marketable product.

Product development

This stage involves the development of the actual product. It is usually necessary to integrate the skills of designers, engineers, production, finance and marketing specialists so that product development is quicker, less costly and results in a high-quality product that delights customers. For example, the practice of 'simultaneous engineering' means that designers and production engineers work together rather than passing the project from one department to another once the first department's work is finished. Costs are controlled by a method called target costing. Target costs are worked out on the basis of target prices in the marketplace, and given as engineering/design and production targets.

A key marketing factor in many industries is the ability to cut time to market by reducing the length of the product development stage. There are two reasons why product development is being acceler-

ated. First, markets such as those for personal computers, video cameras and cars change so fast that to be slow means running the risk of being out of date before the product is launched. Second, cutting time to market can lead to competitive advantage. This may be short-lived but is still valuable while it lasts. For example, Rolls-Royce gained an 18-month window of opportunity by cutting lead times on its successful Trent 800 aero-engine.[54] Marketing has an important role to play in the product development stage. R&D and engineering may focus on the functional aspects of the product, whereas seemingly trivial factors may have an important bearing on customer choice.

Product testing concentrates on the functional aspects of a product, as well as on consumer acceptance. Functional tests are carried out in the laboratory and in the field to check such aspects as safety, performance and shelf-life. Products also need to be tested with consumers to check their acceptability in use. Care at this stage can avoid expensive product recalls later, such as that faced by Mitsubishi Motors, which had to recall more than 80,000 vehicles because of faulty wheels, and Boots, which had to recall its range of 'Delicious' Christmas truffles after the fillings were found to be mouldy.[55] For consumer goods this often takes the form of in-house product placement. 'Paired companion tests' are used when the new product is used alongside a rival so that respondents have a benchmark against which to judge the new offerings. Alternatively, two (or more) new product variants may be tested alongside one another. A questionnaire is administered at the end of the test, which gathers overall preference information as well as comparisons on specific attributes. For example, two soups might be compared on taste, colour, smell and richness.

Market testing

Up to this point in the development process, although potential customers have been asked if they intend to buy the product, they have not been placed in the position of having to pay for it. **Market testing** takes measurement of customer acceptance one crucial step further than product testing, by forcing consumers to put their money where their mouth is, so to speak. The basic idea is to launch the new product in a limited way so that consumer response in the marketplace can be assessed. There are two major methods: the simulated market test and **test marketing**.

Simulated market tests take a number of forms, but the main idea behind them is to set up a realistic market situation in which a sample of consumers choose to buy goods from a range provided by the organizing company (usually a market research organization). For example, a sample of consumers may be recruited to buy their groceries from a mobile supermarket that visits them once a week. They are provided with a magazine in which advertisements and sales promotions for the new product can appear. This method allows the measurement of key success indicators such as penetration (the proportion of consumers who buy the new product at least once) and repeat purchase (the rate at which purchasers buy again) to be made. If penetration is high but repeat purchase low, buyers can be asked why they rejected the product after trial. Simulated market tests are therefore useful as a preliminary to test marketing by spotting problems, such as in packaging and product formulation, that can be rectified before test market launch. They can also be useful in eliminating new products that perform so badly compared to the competition in the marketplace that test marketing is not justified.

When the new product is launched in one, or a few, geographical areas chosen to be representative of its intended market, this is known as test marketing. Towns or television areas are chosen in which the new product is sold into distribution outlets so that performance can be gauged face to face with rival products. Test marketing is the acid test of new product development since the product is being promoted as it would be in a national launch, and consumers are being asked to choose it against competitor products as they would if the new product went national. It is a more realistic test than the simulated market test and therefore gives more accurate sales penetration and repeat purchasing estimates. By projecting test marketing results to the full market an assessment of the new product's likely success can be gauged. However, test marketing does have a number of potential problems. Test towns and areas may not be representative of the national market, and thus sales projections may be inaccurate. Competitors may invalidate the test market by giving distributors incentives to stock their product, thereby denying the new product shelf space. Also, test markets need to run for long enough to enable the measurement of repeat purchase rates for a product since this is a crucial indicator of success for many products (e.g. groceries and toiletries). Finally, test marketing is open to manipulation, as shown in Marketing in Action 6.4. One of the main advantages of test marketing is that the information it provides facilitates the 'go/no go' national launch decision.

Marketing in Action: Coca-Cola accused of manipulating test results

2003 was a difficult year for the world's best known brand, Coca-Cola. Sales volumes had been slowing and the company shed 1000 jobs. On top of that there were problems with some of its products such as Dasani, its brand of bottled water, and Frozen Coke.

Frozen Coke was a new 'slushy' drink product that was being launched as part of a deal with Burger King. As part of its side of the bargain, Burger King spent US$30 million on the equipment to produce Frozen Coke and required its franchisees to sell the product. So it wanted proof that children would actually like it. To ensure that the market test results were positive and to force a national roll-out, a Coca-Cola executive signed off plans to falsify the results of a marketing test in Richmond, Virginia. A local man was paid €10,000 to bring hundreds of children to Burger King restaurants and purchase value meals. Frozen Cokes came with the value meals.

The revelations came to light in a lawsuit filed by a former Coca-Cola employee, whose allegations are now the subject of an SEC inquiry. Coca-Cola was forced to apologize to Burger King, who in July 2003 announced plans to phase out Frozen Coke, citing poor sales results. The biggest problem in the long run is likely to be the damage to its relationship with Burger King, which is still Coke's second largest fast-food chain customer in North America after McDonald's, accounting for 7–8 per cent of Coke's sales there.

Based on: Anonymous (2003);[56] Liu (2003);[57] Silkos (2004)[58]

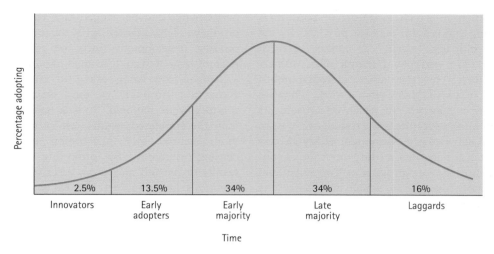

Figure 6.6 Diffusion of an innovation

Commercialization

An effective commercialization strategy relies on marketing management making clear choices regarding the target market (*where* it wishes to compete), and the development of a marketing strategy that provides a differential advantage (*how* it wishes to compete). These two factors define the new product positioning strategy, as discussed in Chapter 5.

An understanding of the **diffusion of innovation process** is a useful starting point for choosing a target market.[59] This explains how a new product spreads throughout a market over time. Particularly important is the notion that not all people or organizations who comprise a market will be in the same state of readiness to buy a new product when it is launched. In other words, different actors in the market will have varying degrees of 'innovativeness'—that is, their willingness to try something new. For example, some consumers will be much quicker to adopt a new technology like the Blackberry wireless handheld device than others. Figure 6.6 shows the diffusion of innovation curve that categorizes people or organizations according to how soon they are willing to adopt an innovation.

The curve in Figure 6.6 shows that those actors (innovators and early adopters) who are willing to buy a new product soon after launch are likely to form a minor part of the total number of actors who will eventually be willing to buy it. As the new product is accepted and approved by these customers, and the decision to buy the new product therefore becomes less risky, so the bulk of the market comprising the early and late majority begin to try the product themselves. Finally, after the product has

gained full market acceptance, a group suitably described as the laggards adopts the product. By the time laggards have begun buying the product, innovators and early adopters have probably moved on to something new.

These diffusion of innovation categories play a crucial role in the choice of target market. The key is to understand the characteristics of the innovator and early adopter categories, and to target them at launch. For example, innovators are often adventurous and like to be different; they are willing to take a chance with an untried product.[60] In consumer markets they tend to be younger, better educated, more confident and more financially affluent, and consequently can afford to take a chance on buying something new. In organizational markets, they tend to be larger and more profitable companies if the innovation is costly, and have more progressive, better-educated management. They may themselves have a good track record in bringing out new products, and may have been the first to adopt innovations in the past. As such they may be easy to identify.

As far as the commercialization strategy goes, the second key decision is with regard to the choice of a marketing strategy that will establish a differential advantage. The more added benefits a product offers a customer, the more customers will be willing to buy it.

In summary, bringing out new products and services is the key to long-term corporate success. It is a risky activity, but a systematic approach is likely to improve the chances of success.

Ethical issues concerning products

There are three major ethical issues connected with products: product safety, planned obsolescence and deceptive packaging. We will now look at each of these in turn.

Product safety

Recently, one of the major concerns about product safety has been that of the safety of genetically modified (GM) products. Vociferous pressure groups such as Greenpeace have spoken out about the dangers of genetic modification. Such concerns, and the attendant publicity, have led one of the pioneers of genetic modification, Monsanto, to back away from further development of GM foods, and supermarket chains to ban such produce from their shelves. Supporters state that many new products are introduced with a certain degree of risk being acceptable. For example, a new pharmaceutical product may harm a tiny percentage of users but the utilitarianist principle of 'the greatest good for the greatest number' would support its launch. It is the reality of modern-day business that new products such as cars, pharmaceuticals and foods undergo extensive safety testing before launch. Anything less would violate the consumer's 'right to safety'.

Planned obsolescence

Many of the products on the market have not been designed to last for a long time. From the producers' point of view this is sensible as it creates a repeat-purchase situation. Hence, cars rust, computer software is quickly outdated and fashion items are replaced by the latest styles. Consumers accept that nothing lasts for ever, but the main thrust of this issue concerns what is an acceptable length of time before replacement is necessary. One driving force is competition. To quell the Japanese invasion, car manufacturers such as Ford and Volkswagen have made the body shells of their cars much more rust-resistant than they were before. Furthermore, it has to be recognized that many consumers welcome the chance to buy new clothes, new appliances with the latest features, and the latest model of car. Critics argue that planned obsolescence reduces consumers' 'right to choose' since some consumers may be quite content to drive an old car so long as its body shell is free from rust and the car functions well. As we have noted, the forces of competition may act to deter the excesses of planned obsolescence.

Deceptive packaging

This is something that can happen when, say, a product is presented in an oversized package, giving the impression that the consumer is getting more than is actually the case. This is known as 'slack' packaging[61] and has the potential to deceive when the packaging is opaque. Products such as soap powders and breakfast cereals have the potential to suffer from 'slack' packaging. A second area where packaging may be deceptive is through misleading labelling. This may take the form of the 'sin of omission'—for example, the failure of a package to state that a product contains GM soya. This relates to the consumer's 'right to be informed', and can include the stating of ingredients (including flavouring and colourants), nutritional contents and country of origin on labels. Nevertheless, labelling can still be misleading. For example, in the UK, the 'country of origin' is only the last country where the product was 'significantly changed'. So oil pressed from Greek olives in France can be labelled 'French' and foreign imports that are packed in the UK can be labelled 'produce of the UK'. Consumers should be wary of loose terminology. For example, Bachelors Sugar Free Baked Beans actually contain 1.7 grammes of sugar per 100 grammes, Kerry's Low Low Spread, which is marketed as low in fat, contains 38 g of fat per 100 g, and Walkers Lite crisps are a hefty 22 per cent fat. Similarly EU legislation aims to outlaw vague claims such as 'vitalize your body and mind' (Red Bull) or 'cleanse and refresh your body and soul' (Kombucha).[62] At the same time, the rise in food allergies related to products like peanuts, shellfish, eggs, milk and wheat are forcing manufacturers to take more care with product labelling.[63]

Summary

In this chapter we have explored a number of issues involved in the marketing of products and brands. The following key issues were addressed.

1. The important distinction between products and brands. A product is anything that is capable of satisfying customer needs. Brands are the means by which companies differentiate their offerings from those of their competitors.

2. The key aspects involved in building brands, including decisions regarding the brand name, and developing and positioning brands.

3. The key issues involved in brand management, including the challenges presented by the growth of own-label brands, brand extension decisions, pan-European and global branding decisions and co-branding decisions.

4. The challenge of managing a diverse group of products and brands, and the role of portfolio planning in assisting with this process.

5. The challenge of managing products and brands over time and the role of the product life cycle concept in assisting with this process.

6. The importance of new product development and the process by which products are taken from the idea stage through to commercialization.

Suggested reading

Court, D.C. *et al.* (1997) If Nike Can 'Just Do It', Why Can't We?, *McKinsey Quarterly*, **3**, 24–34.

Gladwell, M. (2000) *The Tipping Point: How Little Things Can Make a Big Difference*, London: Abacus.

Glemet, F. and **R. Mira** (1993) Solving the Brand Leader's Dilemma, *McKinsey Quarterly*, **4**, 87–98.

Hill, S., R. Ettenson and **D. Tyson** (2005) Achieving the Ideal Brand Portfolio, *Sloan Management Review*, **46** (2), 85–91.

Holman, R., H. Kaas and **D. Keeling** (2003) The Future of Product Development, *McKinsey Quarterly*, **3**, 28–40.

Joachimsthaler, E. and **D.A. Aaker** (1997) Building Brands Without Mass Media, *Harvard Business Review*, January/February, 38–51.

Moon, Y. (2005) Break Free From the Product Life Cycle, *Harvard Business Review*, **83** (5), 86–95.

Roberts, K. (2004) *The Future Beyond Brands: Lovemarks*, Powerhouse Books: New York, NY.

Internet exercises

Sites to visit

1   www.brandchannel.com

Exercise

Participate in a brand debate and view past debates from the *brandchannel.com* debate archive.

2   www.shopjlo.com
    www.fetishbyeve.com

Exercise

Compare and contrast the brand values being delivered by these two female singers turned brand building machines.

3   www.jnj.com

Johnson & Johnson is a global conglomerate with a variety of member companies. Examine the companies that make up the group, and the breadth and depth of their product lines.

Study questions

1. Explain the difference between a product and a brand.

2. Think of five brand names. To what extent do they

meet the criteria of good brand naming as laid out in Table 6.1? Do any of the names legitimately break these guidelines?

3. What are the advantages and disadvantages of co-branding? Suggest two co-branding alliances that you think might be successful, explaining why.

4. The product life cycle is more likely to mislead marketing management than provide useful insights. Discuss.

5. Many companies comprise a complex group of business units, which in turn often have wide product lines. Discuss the techniques available to the marketer for managing this complexity.

6. Outline the main stages in the new product development process, identifying the potential sources of failure at each stage.

Key terms

brand values the core values and characteristics of a brand

brand a distinctive product offering created by the use of a name, symbol, design, packaging, or some combination of these, intended to differentiate it from its competitors

family brand name a brand name used for all products in a range

individual brand name a brand name that does not identify a brand with a particular company

product line a group of brands that are closely related in terms of the functions and benefits they provide

product mix the total set of products marketed by a company

manufacturer brands brands that are created by producers and bear their chosen brand name

own-label brands brands created and owned by distributors or retailers

brand equity the goodwill associated with a brand name, which adds tangible value to a company through the resulting higher sales and profits

brand extension the use of an established brand name on a new brand within the same broad market

brand stretching the use of an established brand name for brands in unrelated markets

global branding achievement of brand penetration worldwide

product-based co-branding the linking of two or more existing brands from different companies or business units to form a product in which the brand names are visible to the consumer

communications-based co-branding the linking of two or more existing brands from different companies or business units for the purposes of joint communication

parallel co-branding the joining of two or more independent brands to produce a combined brand

ingredient co-branding the explicit positioning of a supplier's brand as an ingredient of a product

portfolio planning managing groups of brands and product lines

product life cycle a four-stage cycle in the life of a product, illustrated as a curve representing the demand; the four stages being introduction, growth, maturity and decline

brainstorming the technique whereby a group of people generate ideas without initial evaluation; only when the list of ideas is complete is each one then evaluated

concept testing testing new product ideas with potential customers

business analysis a review of the projected sales, costs and profits for a new product to establish whether these factors satisfy company objectives

market testing the limited launch of a new product to test sales potential

test marketing the launch of a new product in one or a few geographic areas chosen to be representative of the intended market

diffusion of innovation process the process by which a new product spreads throughout a market over time

References

1. **Kavounis, Y.** (2003) What Went Wrong with the Madge Brand?, *Financial Times*, Creative Business, 4 November; **Sacks, D.** (2003) Who's That Girl?, *Fast Company*, 76, 32; **Duerden, N.** (2004) Queen of the Comeback: Icon, Lover, Mother, Mogul, *Independent*, 24 May, 2, 3.

2. **Yee, A.** (2005) Kodak Job Cuts Rise by 10,000 As Film Sales Slide, *Financial Times*, 21 July, 24; **Yee, A.** (2003) Kodak's Focus Shifts to Phones, *Financial Times*, 12 November, 32.

3. **Keller, K.** (2003) *Strategic Brand Management*, New Jersey: Pearson.

4. **Chernatony, L. de** (1991) Formulating Brand Strategy, *European Management Journal*, 9 (2), 194–200.

5. **Roberts, K.** (2004) *The Future Beyond Brands: Lovemarks*, New York: Powerhouse Books.

6. **Healy, A.** (2004) Campaigners Appeal for Cafes to be Rescued, *Irish Times*, 25 November, 6.

7. **Reyner, M.** (1996) Is Advertising the Answer?, *Admap*, September, 23–6.

8. **McWilliam, G.** (2000) Building Stronger Brands Through Online Communities, *Sloan Management Review*, Spring, 43–54.

9. **Muniz, A.** and **T. O'Guinn** (2001) Brand Community, *Journal of Consumer Research*, 27 (4), 412–33.

10. **Upshaw, L.** and **E. Taylor** (2001) Building Business by Building a Masterbrand, *Brand Management*, 8 (6), 417–26.

11. **Wilkinson, A.** (1999) Trebor Slims Down for Leaner Branding, *Marketing Week*, 26 August, 20.

12. **Marsh, P.** (2005) Industry Plays the Name Game, *Financial Times*, 8 February, 12.

13. **Brady, J.** and **I. Davis** (1993) Marketing's Mid-life Crisis, *McKinsey Quarterly*, 2, 17–28.

14. **Anonymous** (2005) As Good As It Gets, *Economist*, 15 January, 60–2.

15. **Doyle, P.** (2000) *Value-based Marketing*, Chichester: John Wiley & Sons.

16. **Richards, H.** (2005) A Clothing Hit—on the Back of a Golfing Hero, *Financial Times*, 13 July, 16.

17. **Jones, A.** (2004) Unilever's Friendly Facelift Costs £7m, *Financial Times*, 13 May, 1.

18. **Pandya, N.** (1999) Soft Selling Soap Brings Hard Profit, *Guardian*, 2 October, 28.

19. **Sullivan, M.W.** (1990) Measuring Image Spillovers in Umbrella-branded Products, *Journal of Business*, July, 309–29.

20. **Sharp, B.M.** (1990) The Marketing Value of Brand Extension, *Marketing Intelligence and Planning*, 9 (7), 9–13.

21. **Aaker, D.A.** and **K.L. Keller** (1990) Consumer Evaluation of Brand Extensions, *Journal of Marketing*, 54 (January), 27–41.

22. **Roberts, C.J.** and **G.M. McDonald** (1989) Alternative Naming Strategies: Family versus Individual Brand Names, *Management Decision*, 27, (6), 31–7.

23. **Saunders, J.** (1990) Brands and Valuations, *International Journal of Advertising*, 9, 95–110.

24. **Sharp, B.M.** (1990) The Marketing Value of Brand Extension, *Marketing Intelligence and Planning*, 9 (7), 9–13.

25. **Aaker, D.A.** (1990) Brand Extensions: The Good, the Bad and the Ugly, *Sloan Management Review*, Summer, 47–56.

26. **Reisenbeck, H.** and **A. Freeling** (1991) How Global are Global Brands?, *McKinsey Quarterly*, 4, 3–18.

27. **Barwise, P.** and **T. Robertson** (1992) Brand Portfolios, *European Management Journal*, 10 (3), 277–85.

28. **Halliburton, C.** and **R. Hünerberg** (1993) Pan-European Marketing—Myth or Reality, Proceedings of the European Marketing Academy Conference, Barcelona, May, 490–518.

29. **Todd, H.** (2003) Let's Do Some Shots, *Beverage World*, 15 November, 10.

30. **Waddell, R.** (2003) Jagermeister Rocks Hard, *Billboard*, 13 September, 10.

31. **Wassaner, B.** (2003) Schnapps Goes to College, *Financial Times*, 4 September, 15.

32. **Brech, P.** (2002) Ford Focus Targets Women with *Elle* Tie, *Marketing*, 8 August, 7.

33. **Keller, K.** (2003) *Strategic Brand Management*, New Jersey: Pearson.

34. **Kapferer, J.** (1997) *Strategic Brand Management*, London: Kogan Page.

35. **Brierley, D.** (1997) Spring-cleaning a Statistical Wonderland, *European*, 20–26 February, 28.

36. See, e.g., **Day, G.S.** and **R. Wensley** (1983) Marketing Theory with a Strategic Orientation, *Journal of Marketing*, Fall, 79–89; **Haspslagh, P.** (1982) Portfolio Planning: Uses and Limits, *Harvard Business Review*, January/February, 58–73; **Wensley, R.** (1981) Strategic Marketing: Betas, Boxes and Basics, *Journal of Marketing*, Summer, 173–83.

37. **Anonymous** (2005) The Rise of the Superbrands, *Economist*, 5 February, 60–2.

38. **Hegarty, S.** (2004) DVDs Killed the Video Star, *Irish Times*, Weekend Review, 27 November, 2.

39. **London, S.** (2003) The Sound of Stereo Fades into History, *Financial Times*, 18 November, 14.

40. **Vakratsas, D.** and **T. Ambler** (1999) How Advertising Works: What Do We Really Know?, *Journal of Marketing*, 63, January, 26–43.

41. **Doyle, P.** (1989) Building Successful Brands: The Strategic Options, *Journal of Marketing Management*, 5 (1), 77–95.

42. **Jones, A.** (2005) Pernod Bottles Up Concerns

Over French Drinking Habits, *Financial Times*, 30 June, 20.

43. **Anonymous** (2004) Bad Business, *Economist*, 6 November, 66–7.

44. **Chu, H.** (2003) Electronic Books: Viewpoints from Users and Potential Users, *Library Hi Tech*, **21** (3), 340–6.

45. **Hearne, J.** (2001) A New Way to Browse a Book, *Irish Times*, 28 May, 8.

46. **Rao, S.** (2001) Familiarisation of Electronic Books, *Electronic Library*, **19** (4), 247–56.

47. **Taylor, P.** (2004) Rising Sales Hint at New Chapter for e-Books, *Financial Times*, 22 September, 15.

48. **Booz, Allen** and **Hamilton** (1982) *New Product Management for the 1980s*, New York: Booz, Allen & Hamilton, Inc.

49. **Cooper, R.G.** and **E.J. Kleinschmidt** (1986) An Investigation into the New Product Process: Steps, Deficiencies and Impact, *Journal of Product Innovation Management*, June, 71–85.

50. **Tomkins, R.** (2005) Products That Aim Straight For Your Heart, *Financial Times*, 29 April, 13.

51. **Parkinson, S.T.** (1982) The Role of the User in Successful New Product Development, *R&D Management*, **12**, 123–31.

52. **Anonymous** (2005) The Rise of the Creative Customer, *Economist*, 12 March, 61–2.

53. **Jobber, D., J. Saunders, G. Hooley, B.**

Gilding and **J. Hatton-Smooker** (1989) Assessing the Value of a Quality Assurance Certificate for Software: An Exploratory Investigation, *MIS Quarterly*, March, 19–31.

54. **Pullin, J.** (1997) Time is Money on the Way to Market, *Guardian*, 5 April, 99.

55. **Grande, C.** (2005) Lingering Cost of Goods That Empty Shelves, *Financial Times*, 21 March, 3.

56. **Anonymous** (2003) A Bit of a Fizz, *Economist*, 19 July, 54.

57. **Liu, B.** (2003) Coke Chief Dunn Resigns Beverages, *Financial Times*, 19 December, 35.

58. **Silkos, R.** (2004) Coke Takes Bitter Gulp of the 'Reality Thing', *Sunday Telegraph*, Money & Pensions, 28 March, 5.

59. **Rogers, E.M.** (1983) *Diffusion of Innovations*, New York: Free Press.

60. **Rogers, E.M.** (1983) *Diffusion of Innovations*, New York: Free Press.

61. **Smith, N.C.** (1995) Marketing Strategies for the Ethics Era, *Sloan Management Review*, Summer, 85–97. See also **T.W. Dunfee, N.C. Smith** and **W.T. Ross Jr** (1999) Social Contracts and Marketing Ethics, *Journal of Marketing*, **63** (July), 14–32.

62. **Hegarty, S.** (2003) You Are What You Think You Eat, *Irish Times*, Weekend Review, 19 July, 1.

63. **McNulty, S.** (2003), A Matter of Life and Death, *Financial Times*, 10 September, 14.

Online **LearningCentre** with POWERWEB

When you have read this chapter log on to the Online Learning Centre for *Foundations of Marketing* at **www.mcgraw-hill.co.uk/textbooks/jobber** where you'll find multiple choice test questions, links and extra online study tools for marketing.

Turn the page for a Case Study on Nivea

Case 6 Nivea: managing an umbrella brand

'In many countries, consumers are convinced that Nivea is a local brand, a mistake which Beiersdorf, the German makers, take as a compliment.'

(Quoted on leading brand consultancy Wolff-Olins' website, www.wolff-olins.com)

An ode to Nivea's success

In May 2003, a survey of 'Global Mega Brand Franchises' revealed that the Nivea cosmetics brand had a presence in the maximum number of product categories and countries. The survey, conducted by US-based ACNielsen, aimed at identifying those brands that had 'successfully evolved beyond their original product categories'. A key parameter was the presence of these brands in multiple product categories as well as countries.[1]

Nivea's performance in this study prompted a yahoo.com news article to name it the 'Queen of Mega Brands'. This title was appropriate since the brand was present in over 14 product categories and was available in more than 150 countries. Nivea was the market leader in skin creams and lotions in 28 countries, in facial cleansing in 23 countries, in facial skin care in 18 countries, and in suntan products in 15 countries. In many of these countries, it was reportedly believed to be a brand of local origin—having been present in them for many decades. This fact went a long way in helping the brand attain lead-ership status in many categories and countries (see Table C6.1).

In its home country Germany, too, many of Nivea's products were the market leaders in their segments. This market leadership status translated into superior financial performance. Between 1991 and 2001, Nivea posted double-digit growth rates every year. For 2001, the brand generated revenues of €2.5 billion, amounting to 55 per cent of the parent company's (Beiersdorf) total revenue for the year. The 120-year-old, Hamburg-based Beiersdorf has often been credited with meticulously building the Nivea brand into the world's number one personal care brand. According to a survey conducted by ACNielsen in the late 1990s, the brand had a 15 per cent share in the global skin care products market. While Nivea had always been the company's star performer, the 1990s were a period of phenomenal growth for the brand. By successfully extending what was essentially a 'one-product wonder' into many different product categories, Beiersdorf had silenced many critics of its umbrella branding decisions.

The marketing game plan for Nivea

Millions of customers across the world have been familiar with the Nivea brand since their childhood. The visual (colour and packaging) and physical attributes (feel, smell) of the product stayed on in their

Table C6.1 Nivea: market positions

CATEGORY COUNTRY	Skin care	Face care	Baby care	Sun protection	Men's care
Austria	1	1	2	1	1
Belgium	1	1	3	1	1
UK	1	3	–	2	1
Germany	1	1	3	1	1
France	1	1	1	2	3
Italy	1	1	5	1	1
Netherlands	1	1	5	1	1
Spain	1	4	–	2	1
Switzerland	1	1	4	1	1

Source: www.germandata.com

[1] The study covered 200 consumer packaged goods brands from over 50 global manufacturers. The brands had to be available in at least 15 of the countries studied; the same brand name had to be used in at least three product categories and meet brand franchise criteria in at least three of the five geographical regions.

minds. According to analysts, this led to the formation of a complex emotional bond between customers and the brand, a bond that had strong positive undertones. According to a *superbrands.com.my* article, Nivea's blue colour denoted sympathy, harmony, friendship and loyalty. The white colour suggested external cleanliness as well as inner purity. Together, these colours gave Nivea the aura of an honest brand.

The key brand values of Nivea (namely mildness, reliability, gentleness, protection, high quality and value for money) ensured that generations of customers kept using it. Commenting on the reasons behind the brand's popularity, Uwe Wolfer, a Beiersdorf board member, said, 'Outstanding quality products to meet consumer needs at the right time and constant updating of the advertising approach—these are the essential factors in Nivea's success, keeping the brand young, attractive, sympathetic and familiar.'

To customers, Nivea was more than a skin care product. They associated Nivea with good health, graceful ageing and better living. The company's association of Nivea with many sporting events, fashion events and other lifestyle-related events gave the brand a long-lasting appeal. In 2000, Franziska Schmiedebach, Beiersdorf's Corporate Vice President (Face Care and Cosmetics), commented that Nivea's success over the decades was built on the following pillars: innovation, brand extension and globalization (see Table C6.2 for the brand's sales growth from 1995–2002).

Innovations and brand extensions

Innovations and brand extensions went hand in hand for Nivea. Extensions had been made back in the 1930s and had continued in the 1960s when the face care range Nivea Visage was launched. However, the first major initiative to extend the brand to other products came in the 1970s. Naturally, the idea was to cash in on Nivea's strong brand equity. The first major extension was the launch of 'Nivea For Men' aftershave in the 1970s. Unlike the other aftershaves

available in the market, which caused the skin to burn on application, Nivea For Men soothed the skin. As a result, the product became a runaway success.

The positive experience with the aftershave extension inspired the company to further explore the possibilities of brand extensions. Moreover, Beiersdorf felt that Nivea's unique identity, the values it represented (trustworthiness, simplicity, consistency, caring) could easily be used to make the transition to being an umbrella brand. The decision to diversify its product range was also believed to have been influenced by intensifying competitive pressures. L'Oréal's Plenitude range, Procter & Gamble's Oil of Olay range, Unilever's Pond's range, and Johnson & Johnson's Neutrogena range posed stiff competition to Nivea.

Though Nivea was the undisputed market leader in the mass-market face cream segment worldwide, its share was below Oil of Olay's, Pond's and Plenitude's in the US market. While most of the competing brands had a wide product portfolio, the Nivea range was rather limited. To position Nivea as a competitor in a larger number of segments, the decision to offer a wider range was inevitable.

Beiersdorf's research centre—employing over 150 dermatological and cosmetics researchers, pharmacists and chemists—supported its thrust on innovations and brand extensions. During the 1990s, Beiersdorf launched many extensions, including men's care products, deodorants (1991), Nivea Body (1995) and Nivea Soft (1997). Most of these brand extension decisions could be credited to Rolf Kunisch, who became Beiersdorf's CEO in the early 1990s. Rolf Kunisch firmly believed in the company's 'twin strategy' of extension and globalization.

By the beginning of the twenty-first century, the Nivea umbrella brand offered over 300 products in 14 separate segments of the health and beauty market (see Table C6.3 and Figure C6.1 for information on Nivea's brand extensions). Commenting on Beiersdorf's belief in umbrella branding, Schmiedebach said, 'Focusing your energy and investments on one umbrella brand has strong

Table C6.2 Nivea: worldwide sales growth (%)

Sales Growth	1995	1996	1997	1998	1999	2000	2001	2002
In Million €	1040	1166	1340	1542	1812	2101	2458	2628
In per cent	9.8	12.1	14.9	15.1	17.5	16.0	17.0	6.9

Source: www.beiersdorf.com.

synergetic effects and helps build leading market positions across categories.' A noteworthy aspect of the brand extension strategy was the company's ability to successfully translate the 'skin care' attributes of the original Nivea cream to the entire gamut of products.

The company ensured that each of its products addressed a specific need of consumers. Products in all the 14 categories were developed after being evaluated on two parameters with respect to the Nivea mother brand. First, the new product had to be based on the qualities that the mother brand stood for and, second, it had to offer benefits that were consistent with those that the mother brand offered. Once a new product cleared the above test, it was evaluated for its ability to meet consumer needs and its scope for proving itself to be a leader in the future. For instance, a Nivea shampoo not only had to clean hair, it also had to be milder and gentler than other shampoos in the same range.

Beiersdorf developed a 'Nivea Universe' framework for streamlining and executing its brand extension efforts. This framework consisted of a central point, an inner circle of brands and an outer circle of brands (see Figure C6.1).

The centre of the model housed the 'mother brand', which represented the core values of trustworthiness, honesty and reliability. While the brands in the inner circle were closely related to the core values of the Nivea brand, the brands in the outer circle were seen as extensions of these core values. The inner-circle brands strengthened the existing beliefs and values associated with the Nivea brand. The outer circle brands, however, sought to add new dimensions to the brand's personality, thereby opening up avenues for future growth.

The 'global–local' strategy

The Nivea brand retained its strong German heritage and was not treated as a global brand for many decades. In the early days, local managers believed that the needs of customers from their countries were significantly different from those of customers in other countries. As a result, Beiersdorf was forced to offer different product formulations and packaging, and different types of advertising support. Consequently, it incurred high costs.

It was only in the 1980s that Beiersdorf took a conscious decision to globalize the appeal of Nivea. The

Table C6.3 Nivea: brand portfolio

Category	Products*
Nivea Bath Care	Shower gels, shower specialists, bath foams, bath specialists, soaps, kids' products, intimate care
Nivea Sun (sun care)	Sun protection lotion, anti-ageing sun cream, sensitive sun lotion, sun-spray, children's sun protection, deep tan, after tan, self-tan, Nivea baby sun protection
Nivea Beauté (colour cosmetics)	Face, eyes, lips, nails
Nivea For Men (men's care)	Shaving, after shaving, face care, face cleansing
Nivea Baby (baby care)	Bottom cleansing, nappy rash protection, general cleansing, moisturizing, sun protection
Nivea Body (body care)	Essential line, performance line, pleasure line
Nivea Creme	Nivea creme
Nivea Deodorants	Roll-ons, sprays, pump sprays, sticks, creams, wipes, compact
Nivea Hand (hand care)	Hand care lotions and creams
Nivea Lip Care	Basic care, special care, cosmetic care, extra protection care
Nivea Visage (face care)	Daily cleansing, deep cleansing, facial masks (cleansing/care), make-up remover, active moisture care, advanced repair care, special care
Nivea Vital (mature skin care)	Basic face care, specific face care, face cleansing products, body care
Nivea Soft	Nivea soft moisturizing cream
Nivea Hair Care	Hair care (shampoos, rinse, treatment, sun); hair styling (hairspray and lacquer, styling foams and specials, gels and specials)

* Within these broad line of products, many different brands and formulations were made available.
Source: www.nivea.com

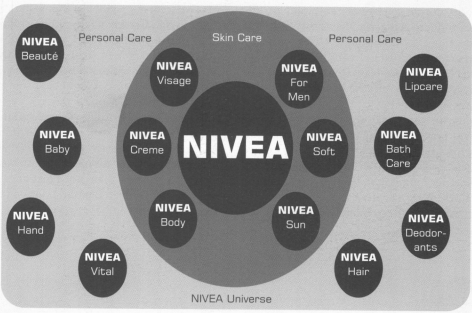

Figure C6.1 The Nivea Universe

aim was to achieve a common platform for the brand on a global scale and offer customers from different parts of the world a wider variety of product choices. This was a radical departure from its earlier approach, in which product development and marketing efforts were largely focused on the German market. The new decision was not only expected to solve the problem of high costs, it was also expected to further build the core values of the brand.

To globalize the brand, the company formulated strategies with the help of a team of 'international' experts with 'local expertise'. This team developed new products for all the markets. Their responsibilities included, among others, deciding about the way in which international advertising campaigns should be adapted at the local level. The idea was to leave the execution of strategic decisions to local partners. However, Beiersdorf monitored the execution to ensure that it remained in line with the global strategic plan.

This way, Beiersdorf ensured that the nuances of consumer behaviour at the local level were understood and that their needs were addressed. Company sources claimed that by following the above approach, it was easy to transfer know-how between headquarters and the local offices. In addition, the motivation level of the local partners also remained on the higher side.

The company established a set of guidelines that regulated how the marketing mix of a new product/brand was to be developed. These guidelines stipulated norms with respect to product, pricing,

promotion, packaging and other related issues. For instance, a guideline regarding advertising read, 'Nivea advertising is about skin care. It should be present visually and verbally. Nivea advertising is simple, it is unpretentious and human.'

Thus all advertisements for any Nivea product depicted images related to 'skin care' and 'unpretentious human life' in one way or the other. The company consciously decided not to use supermodels to promote its products. The predominant colours in all campaigns remained blue and white. However, local issues were also kept in mind. For instance, in the Middle East, Nivea relied more on outdoor media as it worked out to be much more cost-effective. And since showing skin in the advertisements went against the region's culture, the company devised ways of advertising skin care without showing skin.

Many brand management experts have spoken of the perils of umbrella management, such as brand dilution and the lack of 'change' for consumers. However, the umbrella branding strategy worked for Beiersdorf. In fact, the company's growth was the most dynamic since its inception during the 1990s—the decade when the brand extension move picked up momentum. The strong yearly growth during the 1990s and the quadrupling of sales were attributed by company sources to the thrust on brand extension.

Questions

1. Discuss the reasons for the success of the Nivea range of products across the world. Why did

Beiersdorf decide to extend the brand to different product categories? In the light of Beiersdorf's brand extension of Nivea, critically comment on the pros and cons of adopting an umbrella branding strategy. Compare the use of such a strategy with the use of an independent branding strategy.

2. According to you, what are the core values of the Nivea brand? What type of brand extension framework did Beiersdorf develop to ensure that these core values did not get diluted? Do you think the company was able to protect these core values? Why/why not?

3. What were the essential components of Beiersdorf's global expansion strategy for Nivea? Under what circumstances would a 'global strategy–local execution' approach be beneficial for a company? When and why should this approach be avoided?

This case was written, using various published sources, by A. Mukund, ICFAI Center for Management Research (ICMR). © 2004 ICFAI. It is intended to be used as a basis for class discussion rather than to illustrate either effective or ineffective handling of a management situation.

SERVICES MARKETING MANAGEMENT

Learning Objectives

By the end of this chapter you will understand:

1 the nature and special characteristics of services
2 the differences between products and services
3 the composition of the services marketing mix
4 the key issues in managing services enterprises
5 the special importance of relationship marketing in
   services businesses.

The Demise of Bewleys

When Bewley's Campbell Group announced in late 2004 its intention to close the Bewley's Oriental Café division it came as a great shock to Ireland's coffee-drinking public and tourists alike. In operation for over a century, Bewley's was almost as much a part of Dublin as James Joyce and Molly Malone, and was described by the poet Brendan Kennelly as the 'heart and the hearth of Dublin'.

The company began as a tea and coffee importation business as far back as 1835. It opened its first coffee shop in 1984, which was followed by a second outlet in 1900. It then opened its landmark branch located in Grafton Street, Dublin's busiest pedestrian street, in 1927, complete with its much-loved stained-glass windows. Over time, 10 other outlets were opened throughout Dublin city and its suburbs. The cafés were frequented by writers like Joyce and Patrick Kavanagh, actors like Cyril Cusack, and associated with many of Dublin's historical events such as the founding of the Irishwomen's Liberation Movement. Complete with their marble tables, coal fires and uniformed staff, many of whom worked their entire careers with the company, the cafés were renowned for their atmosphere.

However, as profits fell and some branches closed, Bewley's was taken over by the Campbell Catering Group in 1986. Ten years later, it invested €12 million in modernizing its facilities but still the cafés failed to become profitable. There are a variety of opinions regarding why the cafés failed despite some excellent locations around the city. The most common view is that they had become increasingly out of step with the modern tastes and changing lifestyles that accompanied Ireland's rapid growth during its 'Celtic tiger' years. Paradoxically, the coffee market in Ireland was booming at the same time as Bewley's was failing. A variety of new chains emerged, including O'Brien's Sandwich Bars, Insomnia, Café Sol, Perk and West Coast Coffee, all of which are profitable. Insomnia, which was founded in 1998, is predicting that it will double its turnover in two years and it is also expected that leading US coffee house Starbucks will enter the Irish market.

When Bewley's closed its Grafton Street branch in November 2004 for the last time, long queues formed as customers sought the visit the café for the last time. Even this enviable level of brand loyalty couldn't, it seems, save this service company when it had lost touch with the market and its business costs rose to levels where ensuing losses were unsustainable.[1]

For a number of decades now, it has been recognized that the marketing of **services** enterprises presents some additional challenges for the marketing manager. In the main, these challenges stem from the unique characteristics of services. For example, in many instances, services are produced and consumed at the same time, unlike traditional goods businesses where products are made in a factory, stored and then delivered, sometimes through a long distribution channel, to the market. This means that running a services business creates some unique issues. It does not imply, however, that the principles of marketing covered in earlier chapters of this book do not apply to services, they do, but some additional considerations need to be borne in mind as well.

The services sector continues to become increasingly important. Throughout much of the developed world, its growth has been very rapid and accounts for up to 60 to 70 per cent of the gross national product of some countries, thus far outweighing that of manufacturing and agriculture.

The unique characteristics of services

There are four key distinguishing characteristics of services, namely intangibility, inseparability, variability and perishability (see Figure 7.1).

Intangibility

Pure services cannot be seen, tasted, touched or smelled before they are bought—that is, they are intangible. Rather a service is a deed, performance or effort, not an object, device or thing.[2] **Intangibility** may mean that a customer may find difficulty in evaluating a service before purchase. For example, it is virtually impossible to judge how enjoyable a holiday will be before taking it because the holiday cannot be shown to a customer before consumption.

For some services, their intangible nature leads to difficulty in evaluation after consumption. For example, it is not easy to judge how thorough a car service has been immediately afterwards—there is no way of telling if everything that should have been checked has been checked.

The challenge for the service provider is to use tangible cues to service quality. For example, a holiday firm may show pictures of the holiday destination, display testimonials from satisfied holidaymakers and provide details in a brochure of the kind of entertainment available. The staff of US-based computer

Exhibit 7.1 As many services cannot be evaluated in advance, advertising like this from the AA aims to reassure customers through featuring real people in its advertising

services company the Geek Squad are clearly distinguishable through their short-sleeved white shirts, black ties and badges, and their colourful 'Geek Mobiles' in which they drive to house calls.[3] The important role played by tangible cues in the airline business is illustrated in Marketing in Action 7.1

The task is to provide evidence of service quality. McDonald's does this by controlling the physical settings of its restaurants and by using the golden arches as a branding cue. By having a consistent offering, the company has effectively dealt with the difficulties that consumers have in evaluating the quality of a service. Standard menus and ordering procedures have also ensured uniform and easy access for customers, while allowing quality control.[5]

Intangibility also means that the customer cannot own a service. Payment is for use or performance. For example, a car may be hired or a medical operation performed. Service organizations sometimes stress the benefits of non-ownership such as lower capital costs and the spreading of payment charges.

Inseparability

Unlike physical goods, services have **inseparability**—that is, they have simultaneous production and consumption. For example, a haircut, a medical operation, psychoanalysis, a holiday and a pop concert are produced and consumed at the same time. This contrasts with a physical good that is produced, stored and distributed through intermediaries before being bought and consumed. This illustrates the importance of the service provider, who is an integral part of the satisfaction gained by the consumer. How service providers conduct themselves may have a crucial bearing on repeat business over and above the technical efficiency of the service task. For example, how courteous and friendly the service provider is may play a large part in the customer's

Marketing in Action: Not all airlines are low frills

In recent years, low-cost airlines like Ryanair and easyJet have been getting most of the attention as they drive down the cost of air travel with a business model that has proven to be very successful (see Chapter 8). But as any good marketer knows, there are different ways to compete. Many of Europe's major airlines—such as BA, Lufthansa and Scandinavian Airlines (SAS)—continue to compete on the strength of their brands and the quality reputations they have built up over the years. And for service businesses like airlines, tangibles are an important element of this overall proposition. So while the low-cost carriers are trimming away all the extras and frills, some of more traditional carriers are going in the opposite direction.

Take Air France, for example. It has recently invested €20 million in the design and development of new uniforms for its 36,000 staff. In keeping with its tradition of commissioning famous designers to work on its uniforms, on this occasion it employed the services of Christian Lacroix. The challenge for the designer was to combine the carrier's identity with classic elegance and functional practicality. The two-year project resulted in a uniform in traditional shades of inky blue and grey with red accents, and consisted of 100 different items from which staff could pick their preferences. Once selections were made, the formidable logistics demanded the measurement of staff worldwide, using 60 tailors, to ensure exact fit.

Staff uniforms are an important aspect of the tangibles of an airline. As Air France's chairman, Jean Cyril Spinnetti commented, 'an airline uniform represents first and foremost the image of the company, its history, value and culture'.

Based on: McQuillan (2005)[4]

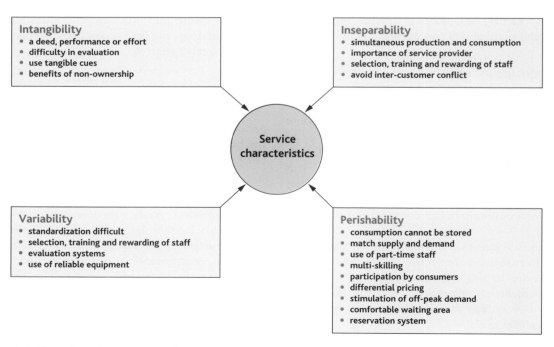

Figure 7.1 The unique characteristics of services

perception of the service experience. The service must be provided not only at the right time and in the right place but also in the right way.[6]

Often, in the customer's eyes, the photocopier service engineer or the insurance representative *is* the company. Consequently, the selection, training and rewarding of staff who are the frontline service people is of fundamental importance in the achievement of high standards of service quality. This notion of the inseparability of production and consumption gave rise to the idea of relationship marketing in services, as we shall see later. In such circumstances, managing buyer–seller interaction is central to effective marketing and can be fulfilled only in a relationship with the customer.[7]

Furthermore, the consumption of the service may take place in the presence of other consumers. This is apparent with restaurant meals, air, rail or coach travel, and many forms of entertainment, for example. Consequently, enjoyment of the service is dependent not only on the service provided, but also on other consumers. Therefore service providers need to identify possible sources of nuisance (e.g. noise, smoke, queue jumping) and make adequate provision to avoid inter-customer conflict. For example, a restaurant layout should provide reasonable space between tables and non-smoking areas so that the potential for conflict is minimized.

Marketing managers should not underestimate the role played by customers in aiding other customers in their decision-making. A study into service interactions in IKEA stores found that almost all customer–employee exchanges related to customer concerns about 'place' (e.g. 'Can you direct me to the pick-up point?') and 'function' (e.g. 'How does this chair work?'). However, interactions between customers took the form of opinions on the quality of materials used in products, advice on bed sizes and how to move around the in-store restaurant. Many customers appeared to display a degree of product knowledge or expertise bordering on that of contact personnel.[8]

Variability

Service quality may be subject to considerable **variability**, which makes standardization difficult. Two restaurants within the same chain may have variable service owing to the capabilities of their respective managers and staff. Two marketing courses at the same university may vary considerably in terms of quality, depending on the lecturer. Quality variations among physical products may be subject to tighter controls through centralized production, automation and quality checking before dispatch. Services, however, are often conducted at multiple locations, by people who may vary in their attitudes (and tiredness), and are subject to simultaneous production and consumption. The last characteristic means that a service fault (e.g. rudeness) cannot be quality checked and corrected between production and consumption, unlike a physical product such as misaligned car windscreen wipers.

The potential for variability in service quality emphasizes the need for rigorous selection, training and rewarding of staff in service organizations. Training should emphasize the standards expected of personnel when dealing with customers. *Evaluation systems* should be developed that allow customers to report on their experiences with staff. Some service organizations, notably the British Airports Authority, tie reward systems to customer satisfaction surveys, which are based, in part, on the service quality provided by their staff.

Service standardization is a related method of tackling the variability problem. For example, a university department could agree to use the same software package when developing overhead transparencies for use in lectures. The use of reliable equipment rather than people can also help in standardization—for example, the supply of drinks via vending machines or cash through bank machines. However, great care needs to be taken regarding equipment reliability and efficiency. For example, bank cash machines have been heavily criticized for being unreliable and running out of money at weekends.

Perishability

The fourth characteristic of services is their **perishability** in the sense that consumption cannot be stored for the future. A hotel room or an airline seat that is not occupied today represents lost income that cannot be gained tomorrow. If a physical good is not sold, it can be stored for sale later. Therefore it is important to match supply and demand for services. For example, if a hotel has high weekday occupancy but is virtually empty at weekends, a key marketing task is to provide incentives for weekend use. This might involve offering weekend discounts, or linking hotel use with leisure activities such as golf, fishing or hiking.

Service providers also have the problem of catering for peak demand when supply may be insufficient. A physical goods provider may build up inventory in slack periods for sale during peak demand. Service

Nowhere else makes you feel this good

www.champneys.com
08703 300 300

Exhibit 7.2 Because services are perishable, companies like Champneys will often use differential pricing to manage demand

theatre seats for afternoon performances). Stimulation of off-peak demand can be achieved by special events (e.g. golf or history weekends for hotels). If delay is unavoidable then another option is to make it more acceptable, for example, by providing a comfortable waiting area with seating and free refreshments. Finally, a reservation system as commonly used in restaurants, hair salons, and theatres can be used to control peak demand and assist time substitution.

In summary, intangibility, inseparability, variability and perishability combine to distinguish services from products. But it is important to remember that they are not completely distinct and in most instances it is a matter of degree. For example, a marketing research study would provide a report (physical good) that represents the outcome of a number of service activities (discussions with client, designing the research strategy, interviewing respondents and analysing the results). Figure 7.2 shows a physical goods–service continuum with the position of each offering dependent upon its ratio of the tangible/intangible elements. At the pure goods end of the scale is clothing, as the purchase of a skirt or socks is not normally accompanied by a service. Machinery purchase may involve more service elements in the form of installation and maintenance. Software design is positioned on the service side of the continuum since the value of the product is dependent on design expertise rather than the cost of the physical product (disk). Finally, psychotherapy may be regarded as a pure service since the client receives nothing tangible from the transaction. Opportunities for competitive advantage often lie in the service components. For example, cinemas are once again suffering falling audiences as films are quickly released on DVD and watched at home by viewers.[9] Improving the service component represents one of the few avenues for cinemas to wrest back patrons.

providers do not have this option. Consequently alternative methods need to be considered. For example, supply flexibility can be varied through the use of part-time staff doing peak periods. Multiskilling means that employees may be trained in many tasks. Supermarket staff can be trained to fill shelves, and work at the checkout at peak periods. Participation by consumers may be encouraged in production (e.g. self-service breakfasts in hotels). Demand may be smoothed through differential pricing to encourage customers to visit during off-peak periods (for example, lower-priced cinema and

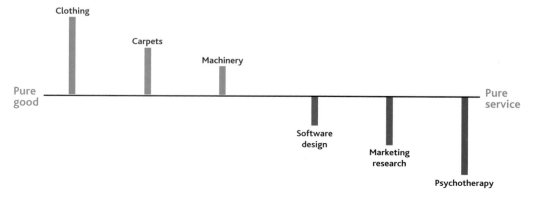

Figure 7.2 The physical goods–service continuum

The services marketing mix

The **services marketing mix** is an extension of the 4-Ps framework introduced in Chapter 1. The essential elements of product, promotion, price and place remain but three additional variables—people, physical evidence and process—are included to produce a 7-Ps mix.[10] The need for the extension is due to the high degree of direct contact between the firm and the customer, the highly visible nature of the service assembly process, and the simultaneity of production and consumption. While it is possible to discuss people, physical evidence and process within the original 4-Ps framework (for example, people could be considered part of the product offering) the extension allows a more thorough analysis of the marketing ingredients necessary for successful services marketing. As we shall see, the management of each element of the marketing mix is influenced by the unique characteristics of services discussed above.

Product

Physical products can be inspected and tried before buying, but pure services are intangible; you cannot go to a showroom to see a marketing research report or medical operation that you are considering. This means that service customers suffer higher perceived risk in their decision-making and that the three elements of the extended marketing mix—people, physical evidence and process—are crucial in influencing the customer's perception of service quality. These will be discussed later.

The brand name of a service can also influence the perception of that service. Four characteristics of successful brand names are as follows.[11]

1 *Distinctiveness*: it immediately identifies the services provider and differentiates it from the competition.
2 *Relevance*: it communicates the nature of the service and the service benefit.
3 *Memorability*: it is easily understood and remembered.
4 *Flexibility*: it not only expresses the service organization's current business but also is broad enough to cover foreseeable new ventures.

Credit cards provide examples of effective brand names: Visa suggests internationality and MasterCard emphasizes top quality. Obviously the success of the brand name is heavily dependent on the service organization's ability to deliver on the promise it implies. The key role played by the brand

A BANK THAT'S HERE TO HELP BUSINESSES GROW

We don't do average. So we're not like your average bank. We're here to help businesses grow.

We're commercial and effective, and we think this makes us easy to work with. Not average at all.

Factor in one of the sharpest teams in the business and you'll see why we're convinced it works well.

But don't take our word for it.

Hear it from our customers at: www.bankofscotland.co.uk/the-truth

LOOK AT THINGS DIFFERENTLY

0845 605 7092 ✳ BANK OF SCOTLAND
CORPORATE

Part of the HBOS Group

Exhibit 7.3 This advertisement for Bank of Scotland Corporate highlights the benefits that it provides to its business customers

name in a services context is demonstrated by the case of UBS, as shown in Marketing in Action 7.2.

Promotion

The intangible element of a service may be difficult to communicate. For example, it may be difficult to represent courtesy, hard work and customer care in an advertisement. Once again the answer is to use tangible cues that will help customers understand and judge the service. A hotel, for example, can show the buildings, swimming pool, friendly staff and happy customers; an investment company can provide tangible evidence of past performance; testimonials from satisfied customers can also be used to communicate services benefits. Netto, the Danish-based supermarket chain, used testimonials from six customers in its UK advertising to explain the advantages of shopping there.

Advertising can be used to communicate and reinforce the image of a service. For example, store image

Marketing in Action: Rebranding at UBS

UBS was formed in 1998 through the merger of two venerable Swiss banks: Union Bank of Switzerland and Swiss Bank Corporation. Since then it has built itself into a global firm mainly through acquisitions of leading financial services firms in the USA and the UK such as SG Warburg, Philips & Drew and Dillion Read. In late 2000, the company purchased PaineWebber, then the fifth largest retail broker in the USA. Its business is spread across a range of sectors including investment banking, asset management and wealth management/private banking as well as having a retail presence in Switzerland.

But this rapid growth through acquisition presented real problems for the company in trying to present a consistent image of itself around the world. Different brands sold similar products and services to the same clients in the same regions. In many cases different marketing departments competed with each other as much as worked together. In many of the company's businesses, the notion of branding was seen as much less important than the individual investment banker or private banker working in them. And UBS was also faced with the challenge of trying to present a coherent image to a market that ranged from individuals in Switzerland to wealthy Far Eastern investors to the CEOs of US multinationals.

In response to these issues, it decided to adopt the single UBS name everywhere in June 2003. It was a decision that involved a significant amount of work. The process started with extensive market research in which over 3500 clients and potential clients and 300 staff were interviewed in 14 countries. Subsequent qualitative research then tested the potential appeal of specific benefit statements for each of the company's different client segments. What the research showed was that all financial clients had a common desire for confidence in the financial decisions they were making irrespective of the amount of money involved. This emotional quality is captured in UBS's advertising slogan, 'you and us'.

Moving to a single global brand was also an expensive exercise. For example, the company had to write off US$1 billion on its 2002 balance sheet when it dropped the name PaineWebber in the USA because of the loss of assumed brand value. But it has helped the firm to overcome some of the problems that it had with the lack of a consistent image and appeal. And the effort appears to be paying off. In 2004, the annual league table of the top 100 global brands compiled by *BusinessWeek*, ranked UBS as a new entry, straight in at number 45.

Based on: Simonian (2005);[12] Thirkell-White (2004)[13]

---

can enhance customer satisfaction and build store loyalty.[14] The new media can also be used to promote services. For example, some online retailers use targeted e-mails to encourage customers to visit their sites. The travel and leisure retailer Lastminute.com sends more than two million e-mails to customers every week with the content tailored to fit the recipient's age and lifestyle.[15]

Word of mouth is critical to success for services because of their experiential nature. For example, talking to people who have visited a resort or hotel is more convincing than reading holiday brochures. Promotion, therefore, must acknowledge the dominant role of personal influence in the choice process and stimulate word-of-mouth communication. Cowell suggests four approaches:[16]

1. persuading satisfied customers to inform others of their satisfaction (e.g. American Express rewards customers who introduce others to its service)
2. developing materials that customers can pass on to others
3. targeting opinion leaders in advertising campaigns
4. encouraging potential customers to talk to current customers (e.g. open days at universities).

Communication should also be targeted at employees because of their importance in creating and maintaining service quality. Internal communications can define management expectations of staff, reinforce the need to delight the customer and explain the rewards that follow from giving excellent service. External communications that depict service quality can also influence internal staff if they include employees and show how they take exceptional care of their customers.

Care should be taken not to exaggerate promises in promotional material since this may build up unachievable expectations. For example, Delta Airlines used the advertising slogan 'Delta is ready when you are'. This caused problems because it built up customers' expectations that the airline would always be ready—an impossible task. This led Delta to change its slogan to the more realistic 'We love to fly and it shows'.[17]

Price

Price is a key marketing tool for three reasons. First, as it is often difficult to evaluate a service before purchase, price may act as an indicator of perceived quality. For example, in a travel brochure the price charged by hotels may be used to indicate their quality. Some companies expect a management consultant to charge high fees, otherwise they cannot be particularly good. Second, price is an important tool in controlling demand: matching demand and supply is critical in services because they cannot be stored. Creative use of pricing can help to smooth demand. Third, a key segmentation variable with services is price sensitivity. Some customers may be willing to pay a much higher price than others. Time is often used to segment price-sensitive and price-insensitive customers. For example, the price of international air travel is often dependent on the length of stay. Travellers from Europe to the USA will pay a lot less if they stay a minimum of six nights (including Saturday). Airlines know that customers who stay for less than that are likely to be businesspeople who are willing and able to pay a higher price.

Place

Distribution channels for services are usually more direct than for many physical goods. Because services are intangible, the services marketer is less concerned with storage, the production and consumption is often simultaneous, and the personal nature of services means that direct contact with the service provider (or at best its agent) is desirable. Agents are used when the individual service provider cannot provide a sufficiently wide selection for customers. Consequently agents are often used for the marketing of travel, insurance and entertainment. However, the advent of the Internet means that direct dealings with the service provider are becoming more frequent.

Growth for many service companies means opening new facilities in new locations. Whereas producers of physical goods can expand production at one site to serve the needs of a geographically spread market, the simultaneous production and consumption of hotel, banking, catering, retailing and accounting services, for example, means that expansion often means following a multi-site strategy. The evaluation of store locations is therefore a critical skill for services marketers. Much of the success of top European supermarket chains has been their ability to choose profitable new sites for their retailing operations.

People

Because of the simultaneity of production and consumption in services, the firm's personnel occupy a key position in influencing customer perceptions of product quality.[18] In fact, service quality is inseparable from the quality of the service provider. John Carlzon, head of the airline SAS, called this interaction 'moments of truth'. He explained that SAS faced 65,000 moments of truth per day and that the outcomes determined the success of SAS. Research on customer loyalty in the service industry showed that only 14 per cent of customers who stopped patronizing service businesses did so because they were dissatisfied with the quality of what they had bought. More than two-thirds stopped buying because they found service staff indifferent or unhelpful.[19]

In order for service employees to be in the frame of mind to treat customers well, they need to feel that their company is treating them well. An important marketing task, then, is to set standards to improve the quality of service provided by employees and monitor their performance. Without training and control, employees tend to be variable in their performance, leading to variable service quality.

The selection of suitable people is the starting point of the process as the nature of the job requires appropriate personality characteristics. Once selected, training is required to familiarize recruits to the job requirements and the culture of the organization. Socialization then allows recruits to experience the culture and tasks of the organization. Service quality may also be affected by the degree to which staff are empowered or given the authority to satisfy customers and deal with their problems. For example, each member of staff of Marriott Hotels is allowed to spend up to £1000 on their own initiative to solve customer problems.[20] Maintaining a motivated workforce in the face of irate customers, faulty support systems and the boredom that accompanies some service jobs is a demanding task. Some service companies (e.g. Holiday Inn) give employee-of-the-month awards in recognition of outstanding service. Reward and remuneration is also important. For example, the US retailer Costco competes against Wal-Mart in the discount warehouse sector. But its pay and conditions are far superior to its main rival and it has a staff turnover rate of 17 per cent annually compared with 70 per cent for the sector.[21]

Physical evidence

This is the environment in which the service is delivered and any tangible goods that facilitate the performance and communication of the service. Customers look for clues to the likely quality of a service by inspecting the tangible evidence. For example, prospective customers may gaze through a restaurant window to check the appearance of the waiters, the décor and furnishings. The ambience of a retail store is highly dependent on décor, and colour can play an important role in establishing mood because colour has meaning. For example, black signifies strength and power, whereas green suggests mildness. The interior of jet aircraft is pastel-coloured to promote a feeling of calm, whereas many night-clubs are brightly coloured with flashing lights, to give a sense of excitement.

The layout of a service operation can be a compromise between the operation's need for efficiency, and marketing's desire for effectively serving the customer. For example, the temptation to squeeze in an extra table in a restaurant or seating in an aircraft may be at the expense of customer comfort.

Process

This is the procedures, mechanisms and flow of activities by which a service is acquired. Process decisions radically affect how a service is delivered to customers. For example, a self-service cafeteria is very different from a restaurant. Marketing managers need to know if self-service is acceptable (or indeed desirable). Queuing may provide an opportunity to create a **differential advantage** by reduction/elimination, or making the time spent waiting more enjoyable. Certainly waiting for service is a common experience for customers and is a strong determinant of overall satisfaction with the service and customer loyalty. Research has shown that an attractive waiting environment can prevent customers becoming irritated or bored very quickly, even though they may have to wait a long time. Both appraisal of the wait and satisfaction with the service improved when the attractiveness of the waiting environment (measured by atmosphere, cleanliness, spaciousness and climate) was rated higher.[22] Providing a more effective service (shorter queues) may be at odds with

operations as the remedy may be to employ more staff.

Reducing delivery time—for example, the time between ordering a meal and receiving it—can also improve service quality. This need not necessarily cost more if customers can be persuaded to become involved in the production process, as reflected in the successful growth of self-service breakfast bars in hotels.

Managing services enterprises

Successfully implementing the services marketing mix and coping with the unique challenges of services enterprises places a number of demands on managers. First, the variability and inseparability of services presents some unique challenges in managing service productivity. Second, all the company's activities must be geared towards delivering a given level of service quality, which can be key in differentiating the offerings of one provider from those of another. Finally, a focus on quality and service excellence creates the opportunity for building long-term relationships with clients that can be very beneficial to the company.

Managing service productivity

Productivity is a measure of the relationship between an input and an output. For example, if more people can be served (output) using the same number of staff (input), productivity per employee has risen. Clearly there can be conflict between improving service productivity (efficiency) and raising service quality (effectiveness). For example, a doctor who reduces consultation time per patient, or a university that increases tutorial group size, raise productivity at the risk of lowering service quality.

Clearly, a balance must be struck between productivity and service quality. There are ways of improving productivity without compromising quality. Technology, obtaining customer involvement in production of the service, and balancing supply and demand are three methods of achieving this.

Technology

Technology can be used to improve productivity and service quality. For example, airport X-ray surveil-

e-Marketing: **Travel goes online**

The arrival of the Internet was forecast to revolutionize many industries. While so far this has failed to come to pass, one sector that has felt the winds of change has been the travel industry. Whether it is for business or pleasure, significant shares of these markets have migrated online, with dramatic consequences for the players involved.

Traditionally, the travel agent was one of the key players in the business, distributing package holidays put together by tour operators, booking flights on scheduled airlines and dispensing advice to customers on the best travel options available to them. Many built successful businesses by developing strong relationships with a local client base over a period of time. But these relationships have proved to be no match for the Internet. Scheduled airlines, particularly the low-cost carriers, began cutting the 10 per cent commissions paid to travel agents and encouraging their customers to book online. For example, the reception area in easyJet's headquarters at Luton airport is dominated by a poster stating that the airline is a 'travel agent-free zone'. Most major scheduled carriers now allow online booking, meaning that much of this lucrative business is lost to the travel agent. British Airways sells five times as many tickets via ba.com as it does over the phone.

As consumers have become more comfortable with the Internet, many are now making their own travel plans. This is particularly the case in the leisure travel sector, where tourists are putting together their own itineraries combining travel, car hire and accommodation, which have all been sourced and booked via the web. One UK survey revealed that 50 per cent of people were likely to use the Internet to book a holiday in the next two years. For tour operators like Thomas Cook or First Choice, who have built businesses selling one- and two-week package holidays, this is a worrying trend. The total turnover of EU tour operators is estimated to be at least €60 billion, so it is big business.

The Internet has also spawned a new generation of travel companies such as Lastminute.com, eBookers, Expedia and Travelocity, who moved from the 'commission model' to a 'merchant model'. In other words, they buy travel products such as hotel rooms and airline seats at wholesale prices and then retail them via the web, often at margins of up to 25 per cent. In addition, these websites have software that enables customers to put together their own itineraries in what has become known in the industry as 'dynamic packaging'.

Ironically, one of the problems with online travel is that there are now so many sites offering products that it is often hard to find the best deal. A new generation of 'metasearch' websites promise to have the answer. They apply sophisticated search engine technology to the travel sector, giving users a wider range of deals and greater price transparency than before. Travelsupermarket.com, one of the largest travel price-comparison websites, allows holiday-makers to submit their holiday requirements and then search through the results from all the operators on the web. Metasearch companies generate revenue by collecting a small commission when they drive traffic to websites. Everyone, it seems, wants to get a piece of an industry that is predicted to be worth US$91 billion in the USA alone by 2009.

Based on: Bray (2004);[24] Done and Garrahan (2005);[25] Garrahan (2005);[26] Yee (2005)[27]

lance equipment raises the throughput of passengers (productivity) and speeds the process of checking in (service quality). Automatic cash dispensers in banks increase the number of transactions per period (productivity) while reducing customer waiting time (service quality). Automatic vending machines increase the number of drinks sold per establishment (productivity) while improving accessibility for cus-

tomers (service quality). Computerization can also raise productivity and service quality. For example, Direct Line, owned by the Royal Bank of Scotland, uses computer software that produces a motor insurance quote instantaneously. Callers are asked for a few details (such as how old they are, where they live, what car they drive, and years since last claim) and this is keyed into the computer, which automatically produces a quotation.[23] Advances in technology have had a significant impact on some services industries, as shown in e-Marketing 7.1.

Customer involvement in production

The inseparability between production and consumption provides an opportunity to raise both productivity and service quality. For example, self-service breakfast bars and petrol stations improve productivity per employee and reduce customer waiting time (service quality). The effectiveness of this tactic relies heavily on customer expectations, and on managing transition periods. It should be used when there is a clear advantage to customers in their involvement in production. The significant amount of customer involvement in production such as reading electricity meters, self-service at filling stations, and online booking of hotel rooms and airline seats is likely to create some customer dissatisfaction and create opportunities for high service providers.

Balancing supply and demand

Because services cannot be stored, balancing supply and demand is a key determinant of productivity. Hotels or aircraft that are less than half full incur low productivity. If in the next period, the hotel or airline

is faced with excess demand, the unused space in the previous period cannot be used to meet it. The combined result is low productivity and customer dissatisfaction (low service quality). By smoothing demand or increasing the flexibility of supply, both productivity and service quality can be achieved.

Smoothing demand can be achieved through differential pricing and stimulating off-peak demand (e.g. weekend breaks). Increasing supply flexibility may be increased by using part-time employees, multi-skilling and encouraging customers to serve themselves.

Managing service quality

Intuitively, it makes sense to suggest that improving service quality will increase customer satisfaction, leading to higher sales and profits.

Indeed, it has been shown that companies that are rated higher on service quality perform better in terms of market share growth and profitability.[28] Yet for many companies high standards of service quality remain elusive. There are four causes of poor perceived quality (see Figure 7.3). These are the barriers that separate the perception of service quality from what customers expect.[29]

Exhibit 7.4 This advertisement for ABN-AMRO positions it as delivering a high-quality service

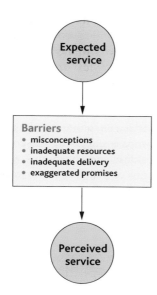

Figure 7.3 Barriers to the matching of expected and perceived service levels

Barriers to the matching of expected and perceived service levels

Misconceptions barrier: this arises from management's misunderstanding of what the customer expects. Lack of marketing research may lead managers to misconceive the important service attributes that customers use when evaluating a service, and the way in which customers use attributes in evaluation.

Inadequate resources barrier: managers may understand customer expectations but be unwilling to provide the resources necessary to meet them. This may arise because of a cost reduction or productivity focus, or simply because of the inconvenience it may cause.

Inadequate delivery barrier: managers may understand customer expectations and supply adequate

resources but fail to select, train and reward staff adequately, resulting in poor or inconsistent service. This may manifest itself in poor communication skills, inappropriate dress, and unwillingness to solve customer problems.

Exaggerated promises barrier: even when customer understanding, resources, and staff management are in place, a gap between customer expectations and perceptions can still arise through exaggerated promises. Advertising and selling messages that build expectations to a pitch that cannot be fulfilled may leave customers disappointed even when receiving a good service.

Meeting customer expectations

A key to providing service quality is the understanding and meeting of customer expectations. To do so requires a clear picture of the criteria used to form these expectations, recognizing that consumers of services value not only the outcome of the service encounter but also the experience of taking part in it. For example, an evaluation of a haircut depends not only on the quality of the cut but also the experience of having a haircut. Clearly, a hairdresser needs not only technical skills but also the ability to communicate in an interesting and polite manner. The following 10 criteria may be used when evaluating the outcome and experience of a service encounter.[30]

1 *Access*: is the service provided at convenient locations and times with little waiting?
2 *Reliability*: is the service consistent and dependable?
3 *Credibility*: can customers trust the service company and its staff?
4 *Security*: can the service be used without risk?
5 *Understanding the customer*: does it appear that the service provider understands customer expectations?

Exhibit 7.5 This advertisement for Royal Mail is capitalising on the importance of customer relationships for businesses

6 *Responsiveness*: how quickly do service staff respond to customer problems, requests and questions?

7 *Courtesy*: do service staff act in a friendly and polite manner?

8 *Competence*: do service staff have the required skills and knowledge?

9 *Communication*: is the service described clearly and accurately?

10 *Tangibles*: how well managed is the tangible evidence of the service (e.g. staff appearance, décor, layout)?

These criteria form a useful checklist for service providers wishing to understand how their customers judge them. A self-analysis may show areas that need improvement but the most reliable approach is to check that customers use these criteria and conduct marketing research to compare performance against competition. Where service quality is dependent on a succession of service encounters (for example, a hotel stay may encompass check-in, the room itself, the restaurant, breakfast and check-out) each should be measured in terms of their impact on total satisfaction so that corrective action can be taken if necessary.[31]

Marketing in Action: Customer service excellence at Singapore Airlines

Singapore Airlines (SIA) has an outstanding reputation for the quality of its customer service and is a frequent winner of awards in this area. For example, in 2003 it was awarded 'Airline of the Year' and 'Best Trans-Pacific Airline' by OAG in the UK, and received the 'World's Best Service Award' from US magazine *Travel & Leisure*. In previous years it has won awards in categories such as 'Best Long-Haul Airline', 'Best First Class', 'Best Economy Class', 'Best Foreign Airline' and 'Best Crisis Management'.

So what makes this company so good? In short, it has had a focus on delighting its customers since its formation and, over the years, has built up a reputation for consistently good service. In terms of in-flight service, SIA emphasizes the quality of its food (designed by an international culinary panel of chefs), seats are designed to be comfortable, the in-flight entertainment system (Krisworld) provides individual video screens for each passenger, and so on. But what separates SIA from other airlines that offer similar tangibles is the empathy and responsiveness shown by cabin crew in responding to the needs of particular customers. This quality service is captured by the 'Singapore girl', which is the iconic image standing for Asian charm and hospitality that appears in all the company's marketing.

Like all service leaders, there is a commitment to customer service that runs all the way down from the senior management and throughout the organization. For example, as a former CEO of SIA commented, 'our passengers are our raison d'être'. If SIA is successful, it is because we have never allowed ourselves to forget that important fact.' Systems have been put into place that allow the quality of service to flourish. For example, SIA has a service development department that hones and tests any change before it is introduced. It also employs an innovation approach it calls 40-30-30, where it focuses 40 per cent of resources on training, 30 per cent on review of process and procedures, and 30 per cent on creating new products and services. Training is key and new stewardesses undergo training for four months, longer than any other airline. It also has one attendant for every 22 seats, which is higher than all of its competitors.

Successful service is all about an eye for detail. For example, from next year SIA plans to offer live television on its flights. Similarly, when things go wrong it keeps the customer in mind in its responses. When an SIA flight crashed in 2000, the company offered US$400,000 to families of the deceased, over five times the amount it was liable to pay.

The results of this strategy speak for themselves. Even though SIA fares are often more expensive than those of other airlines, the company has been consistently profitable since the beginning in an industry renowned for its cyclicality and difficult years.

Based on: Heracleous, Wirtz and Johnston (2004);[34] Kingi (2003)[35]

Developing and managing customer relationships

Delivering excellent service quality creates the opportunity to build an ongoing relationship with customers (see Marketing in Action 7.3). The idea of **relationship marketing** can be applied to many industries. It is particularly important in services since there is often direct contact between service provider and consumer—for example, doctor and patient, hotel staff and guests. The quality of the relationship that develops will often determine its length. Not all service encounters have the potential for a long-term relationship, however. For example, a passenger at an international airport who needs road transportation will probably never meet the taxi driver again, and the choice of taxi supplier will be dependent on the passenger's position in the queue rather than free choice. In this case the exchange—cash for journey—is a pure transaction: the driver knows that it is unlikely that there will ever be a repeat purchase.[32] Organizations, therefore, need to decide when the practice of relationship marketing is most applicable. The following conditions suggest the use of relationship marketing activities.[33]

- There is an ongoing or periodic desire for the service by the customer, e.g. insurance or theatre service versus funeral service.
- The customer controls the selection of a service provider, e.g. selecting a hotel versus entering the first taxi in an airport waiting line.
- The customer has alternatives from which to choose, e.g. selecting a restaurant versus buying water from the only utility company service in a community.

The existence of strong customer relationships brings benefits both for organizations and customers. There are six benefits to service organizations in developing and maintaining strong customer relationships.[36] The first is *increased purchases*. Customers tend to spend more because, as the relationship develops, trust grows between the partners. Second is *lower costs*. The start-up costs associated with attracting new customers are likely to be far higher than the cost of retaining existing customers. Third, loyal customers generate a significant *lifetime value*. If a customer spends £80 in a supermarket per week, resulting in £8 profit, and uses the supermarket 45 times a year over 30 years, the lifetime value of that customer is almost £11,000. Fourth, the intangible aspects of a relationship are not easily copied by the competition,

generating a *sustainable competitive advantage* (again, see Marketing in Action 7.3). Fifth, satisfied customers generate additional business due to the importance of *word-of-mouth* promotion in services industries. Finally, satisfied, loyal customers raise *employee's job satisfaction* and lower job turnover.

The net result of these six benefits of developing customer relationships is high profits. A study has shown across a variety of service industries that profits climb steeply when a firm lowers its customer defection rate.[37] Firms could improve profits from 25 to 85 per cent (depending on industry) by reducing customer defections by just 5 per cent. The reasons are that loyal customers generate more revenue for more years and the costs of maintaining existing customers are lower than the costs of acquiring new ones.

Entering into a long-term relationship can also reap benefits for the customer. First, since the intangible nature of services makes them difficult to evaluate before purchase relationships can help to reduce the risk and stress involved in making choices. Second, strong relationships allow the service provider to provide a higher-quality service, which can be customized to particular needs. Maintaining a relationship reduces the customer's switching costs and, finally, customers can reap social and status benefits from the relationship, such as when restaurant managers get to know them personally.

Two key aspects of building relationships are bonding and service recovery. We will turn to these next.

Bonding

Retention strategies vary in the degree to which they bond the parties together. One framework that illustrates this idea distinguishes between three levels of retention strategy based on the types of bond used to cement the relationship.[38]

1. *Level 1*: at this level the bond is primarily through financial incentives—for example, higher discounts on prices for larger-volume purchases, or frequent flyer or loyalty points resulting in lower future prices. The problem is that the potential for a sustainable competitive advantage is low because price incentives are easy for competitors to copy even if they take the guise of frequent flyer or loyalty points.

2. *Level 2*: this higher level of bonding relies on more than just price incentives and consequently raises the potential for a sustainable competitive advantage. Level 2 retention strategies build long-term relationships through

social as well as financial bonds, capitalizing on the fact that many service encounters are also social encounters. Customers become clients, the relationship becomes personalized and the service customized. Characteristics of this type of relationship include frequent communication with customers, providing personal treatment like sending cards, and enhancing the core service with educational or entertainment activities such as seminars or visits to sporting events. Some hotels keep records of their guests' personal preferences such as their favourite newspaper and alcoholic drink.

3   *Level 3*: this top level of bonding is formed by financial, social and structural bonds. Structural bonds tie service providers to their customers through providing solutions to customers' problems that are designed into the service delivery system. For example, logistics companies often supply their clients with equipment that ties them into their systems.

Service recovery

Service recovery strategies should be designed to solve the problem and restore the customer's trust in the firm, as well improve the service system so that the problem does not recur in the future.[39] They are crucial because an inability to recover service failures and mistakes lose customers directly as well as through their tendency to tell other actual and potential customers about their negative experiences.

The first ingredient in a service recovery strategy is to set up a tracking system to identify system failures. Customers should be encouraged to report service problems since it is those customers that do not complain that are least likely to purchase again. Second, staff should be trained and empowered to respond to service complaints. This is important because research has shown that the successful resolution of a complaint can cause customers to feel more positive about the firm than before the service failure. For example, when P&O had to cancel a round-the-world cruise because of problems with its ship, the *Aurora*, it reportedly offered passengers their money back plus a discount on their next booking. Many passengers said they planned to travel on a P&O cruise in the future.[40]

Finally, a service recovery strategy should encourage learning so that service recovery problems are identified and corrected. Service staff should be motivated to report problems and solutions so that recurrent failures are identified and fixed. In this way, an effective service recovery system can lead to improved customer service, satisfaction and higher customer retention levels.

Summary

In this chapter, we examined the particular issues that arise when marketing services businesses. The following key issues were addressed.

1.   There are four unique characteristics of services, namely intangibility, inseparability, variability and perishability, that have implications for how services are marketed.

2.   The services marketing mix is broader than the marketing mix that is used for products in that attention needs to be paid to the issues of people, physical evidence and process.

3.   Frontline employees are critical to the success of a service organization and great attention needs to be paid to their selection, training and motivation. Employee empowerment is a key element of service quality and service recovery.

4.   Because of service variability and inseparability, good productivity can be difficult to achieve. Technology, customer involvement in production, and the balancing of supply and demand can influence productivity levels.

5.   Service quality is a crucial element of services marketing. Essentially, it involves measuring how service perceptions match up against the expectations that customers have of the service provider.

6.   Service businesses have the opportunity to build strong relationships with customers. Two key aspects of relationship building are bonding and service recovery.

Suggested reading

Ahmed, P.K. and **R. Mohammed** (2003) Internal Marketing: Issues and Challenges, *European Journal of Marketing*, **37** (9), 1177–87.

Berry, L.L. and **A. Parasuraman** (1991) *Marketing Services*, New York: The Free Press.

Lovelock, C.H., S. Vandermerwe and **B. Lewis** (1999) *Services Marketing—A European Perspective*, New York: Prentice-Hall.

Roberts, K., S. Varki and **R. Brodie** (2003) Measuring the Quality of Relationships in Consumer Services: An Empirical Study, *European Journal of Marketing*, **37** (1/2), 169–97.

Shugan, S.M. and **X. Jinhong** (2004) Advance Selling for Services, *California Management Review*, **46** (3), 37–55.

Internet exercises

Sites to visit

1   www.costa.co.uk
www.caffenero.com
www.starbucks.com

Exercise

Discuss the positioning strategies of these major coffee chains and the types of marketing mixes used to implement these strategies.

Sites to visit

2   www.mckinsey.com
www.bostonconsulting.com

Exercise

Compare and contrast the services provided by the these two major global consulting firms.

Study questions

1   The marketing of services is no different to the marketing of physical goods. Discuss.

2   What are the barriers that can separate expected from perceived service? What must service providers do to eliminate these barriers?

3   Discuss the role of service staff in the creation of a quality service. Can you give examples from your own experiences of good and bad service encounters?

4   Discuss the benefits to organizations and customers of developing and maintaining strong customer relationships.

5   One of the biggest difficulties with services is that they cannot be stored. Discuss the strategies open to marketers to balance supply and demand for services.

Key terms

service any deed, performance or effort carried out for the customer

intangibility a characteristic of services, namely that they cannot be touched, seen, tasted or smelled

inseparability a characteristic of services, namely that their production cannot be separated from their consumption

variability a characteristic of services, namely that being delivered by people the standard of their performance is open to variation

perishability a characteristic of services, namely that the capacity of a service business, such as a hotel room, cannot be stored—if it is not occupied, there is lost income that cannot be recovered

services marketing mix product, place, price, promotion, people, process and physical evidence

differential advantage a clear performance differential over competition on factors that are important to target customers

misconceptions barrier a failure by marketers to understand what customers really value about their service

inadequate resources barrier a barrier to the matching of expected and perceived service levels caused by the unwillingness of service providers to provide the necessary resources

inadequate delivery barrier a barrier to the matching of expected and perceived service levels caused by the failure of the service provider to select, train and reward staff adequately, resulting in poor or inconsistent delivery of service

exaggerated promises barrier a barrier to the matching of expected and perceived service levels caused by the unwarranted building up of expectations by exaggerated promises

relationship marketing the process of creating, maintaining and enhancing strong relationships with customers and other stakeholders

References

1. **Creaton, S.** (2004) Café Market is Expanding Worldwide, *Irish Times*, 30 October, 3; Humphreys, J. (2004) Bewley's to Close its Landmark Cafes, *Irish Times*, 29 October, 10; Oram, H. (2004) No More the Nostalgic Aroma of Coffee or the Touch of Sticky Buns, *Irish Times*, 30 October, 3.

2. **Berry, L.L.** (1980) Services Marketing is Different, *Business Horizons*, May–June, 24–9.

3. **Foster, L.** (2004) The March of the Geek Squad, *Financial Times*, 24 November, 13.

4. **McQuillan, D.** (2005) High Flyers in Fashion, *Irish Times*, Weekend, 9 April, 4.

5. **Edgett, S.** and **S. Parkinson** (1993) Marketing for Services Industries: A Review, *Service Industries Journal*, 13 (3), 19–39.

6. **Berry, L.L.** (1980) Services Marketing is Different, *Business Horizons*, May–June, 24–9.

7. **Aijo, T.S.** (1996) The Theoretical and Philosophical Underpinnings of Relationship Marketing, *European Journal of Marketing*, 30 (2), 8–18; Grönoos, C. (1990) *Services Management and Marketing: Managing the Moments of Truth in Service Competition*, Lexington, MA: Lexington Books.

8. **Baron, S., K. Harris** and **B.J. Davies** (1996) Oral Participation in Retail Service Delivery: A Comparison of the Roles of Contact Personnel and Customers, *European Journal of Marketing*, 30 (9), 75–90.

9. **Parkes, C.** (2005) Cinemas Feel the Pinch as Viewers Stay on the Sofa, *Financial Times*, 26 June, 25.

10. **Booms, B.H.** and **M.J. Bitner** (1981) Marketing Strategies and Organisation Structures For Service Firms, in **Donnelly J.H.** and **W.R. George** (eds) *Marketing of Services*, Chicago: American Marketing Association, 47–51.

11. **Berry, L.L., E. E. Lefkowith** and **T. Clark** (1980) In Services: What's in a Name?, *Harvard Business Review*, Sept–Oct, 28–30.

12. **Simonian, H.** (2005) Three Letters Gain a Personality, *Financial Times*, 18 April, 12.

13. **Thirkell-White, J.** (2004) UBS: Brand Building in a Global Market, *Admap*, July/August, 22–4.

14. **Bloemer, J.** and **K. de Ruyter** (1998) On the Relationship Between Store Image, Store Satisfaction and Store Loyalty, *European Journal of Marketing*, 32 (5/6), 499–513.

15. **Cole, G.** (2003) Window Shopping, *Financial Times*, IT Review, 5 February, 4.

16. **Cowell, D.** (1995) *The Marketing of Services*, London: Heinemann, 35.

17. **Sellers, P.** (1988) How to Handle Customer Gripes, *Fortune*, 118 (October), 100.

18. **Rafiq, M.** and **P.K. Ahmed** (1992) The Marketing Mix Reconsidered, *Proceedings of the Annual Conference of the Marketing Education Group*, Salford, 439–51.

19. **Schlesinger, L.A.** and **J.L. Heskett** (1991) The Service-driven Service Company, *Harvard Business Review*, Sept–Oct, 71–81.

20. **Bowen, D.E.** and **L.L. Lawler** (1992) Empowerment: Why, What, How and When, *Sloan Management Review*, Spring, 31–9.

21. **Birchall, J.** (2005) Pile High, Sell Cheap and Pay Well, *Financial Times*, 11 July, 12.

22. **Pruyn, A.** and **A. Smidts** (1998) Effects of Waiting on the Satisfaction With the Service: Beyond Objective Time Measures, *International Journal of Research in Marketing*, 15, 321–34.

23. **Mudie, P.** and **A. Cottam** (1997) *The Management and Marketing of Services*, Oxford: Butterworth-Heinemann, 211.

24. **Bray, R.** (2004) Tour Operators Feel the Pinch from DIY, *Financial Times*, 9 November, 13.

25. **Done, K.** and **M. Garrahan** (2005) Revolution Takes Wing in Leisure Industry, *Financial Times*, 8 March, 4.

26. **Garrahan, M.** (2005) Holidaymakers are Footloose and Fancy-Free, *Financial Times*, IT Review, 13 July, 1.

27. **Yee, A.** (2005) How Surfers are Creating a Tide of Advantage, *Financial Times*, 9 February, 11.

28. **Buzzell, R.D.** and **B.T. Gale** (1987) *The PIMS Principles: Linking Strategy to Performance*, New York: Free Press, 103–34.

29. **Parasuraman, A., V.A. Zeithaml** and **L.L. Berry** (1985) A Conceptual Model of Service Quality and its Implications for Future Research, *Journal of Marketing*, Fall, 41–50.

30. **Parasuraman, A., V.A. Zeithaml** and **L.L. Berry** (1985) A Conceptual Model of Service Quality and its Implications for Future Research, *Journal of Marketing*, Fall, 41–50.

31. **Danaher, P.J.** and **J. Mattsson** (1994) Customer Satisfaction During the Service Delivery

Process, *European Journal of Marketing*, **28** (5), 5–16.

32. **Egan, C.** (1997) Relationship Management, in **Jobber, D.** (ed.) *The CIM Handbook of Selling and Sales Strategy*, Oxford: Butterworth-Heinemann, 55–88.

33. **Berry, L.L.** (1995) Relationship Marketing, in **Payne, A., M. Christopher, M. Clark** and **H. Peck** (eds) *Relationship Marketing for Competitive Advantage*, Oxford: Butterworth-Heinemann, 65–74.

34. **Heracleous, L., J. Wirtz** and **R. Johnston** (2004) Cost-effective Service Lessons from Singapore Airlines, *Business Strategy Review*, **15** (1), 33–8.

35. **Kingi, S.** (2003) Customer Service at Singapore Airlines, *European Case Clearing House*, 503-114-1.

36. **Zeithaml, V.A.** and **M.J. Bitner** (2002) *Services Marketing*, New York: McGraw-Hill, 174–8.

37. **Reichheld F.F.** and **W.E. Sasser Jr** (1990) Zero Defections: Quality Comes To Services, *Harvard Business Review*, Sept–Oct, 105–11.

38. **Berry, L.L.** and **A. Parasuraman** (1991) *Managing Services*, New York: Free Press, 136–42.

39. **Kasper, H., P. van Helsdingen** and **W. de Vries Jr** (1999) *Services Marketing Management*, Chichester: Wiley, 528.

40. **Witzel, M.** (2005) Keep your Relationship With Clients Afloat, *Financial Times*, 31 January, 13.

LearningCentre

When you have read this chapter log on to the Online Learning Centre for *Foundations of Marketing* at **www.mcgraw-hill.co.uk/textbooks/jobber** where you'll find multiple choice test questions, links and extra online study tools for marketing.

Turn the page for a Case Study on Pret a Manger

Case 7 Pret a Manger: passionate about food

Introduction

Pret a Manger (French for 'ready to eat') is a chain of coffee shops that sells a range of upmarket, healthy sandwiches and desserts as well as a variety of coffees to an increasingly discerning set of lunchtime customers. Started in London, England, in 1986 by two university graduates, Pret a Manger has more than 120 stores across the UK. In 2002 it sold 25 million sandwiches and 14 million cups of coffee, and had a turnover of over £100 million. Buckingham Palace reportedly orders more than £1000 worth of sandwiches a week and British Prime Minister Tony Blair has had Pret sandwiches delivered to number 10 Downing Street for working lunches. The company also has ambitious plans to expand further—it already has stores in New York, Hong Kong and Tokyo, and has set its sights on further international growth.

Background and company history

In 1986, Pret a Manger was founded with one shop, in central London, and a £17,000 loan, by two property law graduates, Julian Metcalf and Sinclair Beecham, who had been students together at the University of Westminster in the early 1980s. At that time the choice of lunchtime eating in London and other British cities was more limited than it is today. Traditionally, some ate in restaurants while many favoured that well-known British institution, the pub, as a choice for lunchtime eating and drinking. There was, however, a growing awareness among many people of the benefits of healthy eating and a healthy lifestyle, and lunchtime habits were changing. There was a general trend towards taking shorter lunch breaks and, among office workers, to take lunch at their desks. For those who wanted food to take away, the choice in fast food was dominated by the large chains such as McDonald's, Burger King and Kentucky Fried Chicken (now KFC) while other types of carry-out food, such as pizzas, were also available.

Sandwiches also played an important part in British lunchtime eating. Named after its eighteenth-century inventor, the Earl of Sandwich, the humble sandwich had long been a popular British lunch choice, especially for those with little time to spare.

Prior to Pret's arrival on the scene, sandwiches were sold mainly either pre-packed in supermarkets and high-street variety chain stores such as Marks and Spencer and Boots, or in the many small sandwich bars that were to be found in the business districts of large cities like London. Sandwich bars were usually small, independently owned or family run shops that made sandwiches to order for customers who waited in a queue, often out on to the pavement outside.

Dissatisfied with the quality of both the food and service from traditional sandwich bars, Metcalf and Beecham decided that Pret a Manger should offer something different. They wanted Pret's food to be high quality and healthy, and preservative and additive free. In the beginning, they shopped for the food themselves at local markets and returned to the store where they made the sandwiches each morning. Pret's offering was based around premium-quality sandwiches and other health-orientated lunches including salads, sushi and a range of desserts, priced higher than at traditional sandwich bars, and sold pre-packed in attractive and convenient packaging ready to go. There was also a choice of different coffees, as well as some healthy alternatives. Service aimed to be fast and friendly to give customers a minimum of queuing time.

Pret a Manger: 'Passionate about What We Do'

Pret a Manger strongly emphasizes the quality of its products. Its promotional material and website claims that it is:

> 'passionate about food, rejecting the use of obscure chemicals, additives and preservatives common in so much of the prepared and fast food on the market today ... if there's a secret to our success so far we like to think its determination to focus continually on quality—not just our food, but in every aspect of what we do'.

Great importance is also placed on freshness. Unlike those sold in high-street shops or supermarkets, Pret's sandwiches are still all hand-made by staff in each shop starting at 6.30 every morning, rather than being prepared and delivered by a supplier or from a central location. Beecham and Metcalf believe this gives their sandwiches a freshness and distinctiveness. All food that hasn't been sold in the shops by the end of the day is given away free to local charities.

Careful sourcing of supplies for quality has also always been important. Genetically modified ingredients are banned and the tuna Pret buys, for example, must be 'dolphin friendly'. There is also a drive for constant product improvement and innovation—the company claims that its chocolate brownie dessert has been improved 33 times over the last few years—and, on average, a new product is tried out in the stores every four days. Aware that some of its customers are increasingly health conscious, Pret's website menu carefully lists not only what is available, but also the ingredients and nutritional values in terms of energy, protein, fats and dietary fibre for each item.

The level and quality of service from staff in the shops is a critical factor. The stores are self-service, with customers helping themselves to sandwiches and other products from supermarket-style refrigerated cabinets. Staff at the counter at the back of the store then serve customers coffee and take payment. Service is friendly, smiling and efficient, in contrast to many retail and restaurant outlets in Britain where, historically, service quality has not always been high. Pret puts an emphasis on human resource management issues such as effective recruitment and training so as to have frontline staff who can show the necessary enthusiasm and also remain fast and courteous under the pressure of a busy lunchtime sales period. These staff are usually young and enthusiastic, some are students, many are international. The pay they receive is above the fast-food industry average and staff turnover is 98 per cent a year, which sounds high—however, this is against an industry norm of around 150 per cent. In 2001, Pret had 55,000 applications for 1500 advertised vacancies.

Recently, *Fortune* magazine voted Pret one of the top 10 companies to work for in Europe. According to its own promotional recruitment material, Pret is an attractive and fun place to work: 'We don't work nights, we wear jeans, we party!' Service quality is checked regularly by the use of mystery shoppers: if a shop receives a good report, then the staff there receive a 75p an hour bonus in the week of the visit. Head office managers also visit stores on a regular basis and every three or four months every one of these managers works as a 'buddy', where they spend a day making sandwiches and working on the floor in one of the shops to help them keep in touch with what is going on. Store employees work in teams and are briefed daily, often on the basis of customer responses that come in from in-store reply cards, telephone calls and the company website. The website, which lists the names and phone numbers of its senior executives, actively invites customers to comment or complain about their experience with Pret, and encourages them to contact the company. Great importance is placed on this customer feedback, both positive and negative, which is discussed at weekly management meetings.

The design of the stores is also distinctive. Prominently featuring the company logo, they are fitted out in a high-tech style with metal cladding and interiors in Pret's own corporate dark red colour. Each store plays music, helping to create a stylish and lively atmosphere. Although the shops mainly sell carry out food and coffee in the morning and through the lunchtime period, many also have tables and seating where customers can drink coffee and eat inside the store or, weather permitting, on the pavement outside.

Growth and competition

Three years after the first Pret shop was launched another was opened and, after that, the chain began to grow so that, by 1998, there were 65 throughout London. In the late 1990s stores were also opened in other British cities such as Bristol, Cambridge and Manchester. Although growth in the UK has been rapid—between 2000 and 2002 the company opened over 40 new outlets and there are now over 120 throughout Britain—Pret's policy has always been to own and manage all its own stores and not to franchise to other operators. In 2002, £1 million was spent on launching an Internet service that enables customers to order sandwiches online.

Plans for international growth have been more cautious. In 2000 the company made its first move overseas when it opened a shop near Wall Street in New York. However, there were problems on several fronts in moving into the USA. Metcalf is quoted as saying, 'As a private company its very difficult to set up abroad. We didn't know where to begin in New York—we ended up having all the equipment for the shop made here and shipped over.' There were also staffing and service quality difficulties—Pret reportedly found it difficult to recruit people in New York who had the required friendliness to serve in the stores and had to import British staff. Despite these problems, several other shops in New York have followed and, in 2001, Pret opened its first outlet in Hong Kong.

During the 1990s, coffee shops boomed as the British developed a growing taste for drinking coffee in pavement cafés, and competition for Pret grew as other chains entered the fray. Rivals like Coffee Republic, Caffè Nero, Costa Coffee (now owned by leisure group Whitbread) Aroma (owned by McDonald's) and American worldwide operator Starbucks all came into the market, as well as a number of smaller independents. All these chains offer a wide range of coffees but with varying product offerings in terms of food, pricing and style (Starbucks, for example, offers comfortable armchairs around tables, which encourage people to linger or work on a laptop in the store). In a London shopping street it is not uncommon to see three or four rival outlets next door to or within a few yards of each other. However, it quickly became clear that the sector was overcrowded and, apart from Starbucks, some of the other chains reportedly struggled to make a profit. In 2002 Coffee Republic was taken over by Caffè Nero, which also eventually acquired the ailing Aroma chain from McDonald's. Costa Coffee was the largest chain overall with over 300 shops throughout Britain, while Starbucks was expanding aggressively and aimed to have an eventual 4000 stores worldwide.

The future

As work and lifestyles get busier, the demand for convenience and fast foods continues to grow. In 2000, some estimates put the total value of the fast-food market in Britain, excluding sandwiches, at over £6 billion and growing at about £200–£300 million a year. While the growth in sales of some types of fast food, like burgers, was showing signs of slowing down, sandwiches continued to increase in popularity so that by 2002 sales were an estimated £3 billion. Customers are also getting more health conscious and choosy about what they eat and, increasingly, want nutritional information about food from labelling and packaging.

In January 2001, in a surprise move, Pret's two founders sold a 33 per cent stake in the company to fast-food giant McDonald's for an estimated £25 million. They claim that McDonald's will not have any influence over what Pret does or the products it sells, but that the investment by McDonald's will help their plans for future development. According to Metcalf:

> 'We'll still be in charge—we'll have the majority of shares. Pret will continue what it does and McDonald's will continue as it does ... The deal wasn't about money—we could have sold the shares for much more to other buyers but they wouldn't have provided the support we need.'

After a long run of success, Pret has ambitious plans for the future. It hopes to open at least 20 new stores a year in the UK. In late 2002 it opened its first store in Tokyo, Japan, in partnership with McDonald's. The menu there is described as being 75 per cent 'classic Pret' with the remaining 25 per cent designed more to please local tastes. In other international markets, the plan is to move cautiously—Pret's first move will be to open more stores in New York and Hong Kong, where it has already been successful.

Questions

1. How has Pret a Manger positioned its brand?
2. Explain how the different elements of the services marketing mix support and contribute to the positioning of Pret a Manger.

This case was written by Clive Helm, Westminster Business School, University of Westminster, London, from various published sources. © Clive Helm 2005.

CHAPTER 8

PRICING STRATEGY

Learning Objectives

By the end of this chapter you will understand:

1 the three basic approaches to setting prices
2 the importance of adopting an integrated approach to price setting
3 the key factors that influence price setting decisions
4 some of the ethical issues involved in pricing
5 the major issues involved in managing pricing decisions over time.

EasyGroup Expands the Low Price Proposition

How easy is the low price model? That's probably the question many commentators are asking as they watch the growth of the easyGroup (www.easy.com). Stelios Haji-Ioannou, who describes himself as a serial entrepreneur, first came to prominence in 1995 when he founded low-fares airline easyJet. By maintaining a high public profile and using characteristically catchy advertising such as 'Fly to Scotland for the price of a pair of jeans', Stelios quickly grew this no-frills air travel business. By 1999, easyJet had been voted 'Best Low Cost Airline' by readers of *Business Traveller* magazine, but already Stelios was examining whether this approach would work elsewhere. In July of the same year, the easyInternetcafe chain was launched with its first outlet in London.

Once the business is up and running successfully, Stelios brings in a professional management team and moves on to the next venture. The basic criterion in moving into a new industry is that there must be an opportunity to significantly reduce costs. This is done by taking a simple no-frills approach to the business, ensuring that product quality is good and reducing marketing costs through online ordering. For example, when easyCar was launched in 2000, many car rental frills such as renting with a full petrol tank (which incurs costs of checking and refuelling) and car cleaning were eliminated or charged for. Initially, only the Mercedes A Class was available to rent, in keeping with the notion of quality hardware, while the Internet was the main marketing medium used to deal with customers.

Low costs provide the opportunity to charge low prices but extensive use of yield management ensures that high prices are also charged in periods of high demand, an approach that is sometimes called dynamic pricing. For example, in easyInternetcafes, prices on busy summer shopping days are higher than on quieter days, and each store also has a yield manager whose job it is to monitor store occupancy levels on a daily basis adjusting prices by a small amount depending on demand.

The only question that seems to remain is whether there are limits to this business model, which has since been extended into areas like easyHotels, easyCruises, easyJobs and easyMoney. For example, in 2003, easyGroup launched easyCinema and easyPizza. But, to many, these are impulse purchases unlike air travel or car hire. In other words, consumers are not going to be booking a trip to the cinema a month in advance. Only time will tell if dynamic pricing over the course of a day or a week will boost cinema occupancy levels or pizza consumption. Similarly, the group's latest venture in 2005, easyMobile, is the ultimate in no-frills as it is a mobile phone product without a phone. Users simply buy an easyMobile SIM card over the Internet and make calls over the T-Mobile network. This contrasts with the strategy of other mobile operators, who have been adding additional services such as multimedia messaging and 3G technology, at a time when research shows that some users are increasingly unhappy about the cost of using their mobiles. This suggests that a low-cost operation may prove successful in this sector as well.[1]

Exhibit 8.1 This advertisement for Magnet demonstrates how people are drawn to sales and the importance that they place on price

Because price is the revenue earner, it is the 'odd one out' of the marketing mix. The price of a product is what the company gets back in return for all the effort that is put in to manufacturing and marketing the product. The other elements of the marketing mix—product, promotion, place, physical evidence, and so on—are costs. Therefore, no matter how good the product, how creative the promotion or how efficient the distribution, unless price covers costs, the company will make a loss. It is therefore essential that managers understand how to set prices, because both undercharging (lost margins) and overcharging (lost sales) can have a dramatic effect on profitability (see Marketing in Action 8.1).

The importance of price is illustrated by the launch of the Mercedes A Class model in Germany. Initially, the company had chosen a price tag of DM29,500, based on the belief that the DM30,000 mark was psychologically important. However, after further market research that examined the value offered to customers in comparison to competitor brands such as the BMW 3 series and the VW Golf, the price was set at DM31,000. Mercedes still hit its sales target of 200,000, but the higher price increased its income by DM300 million a year.[2]

One of the key factors that marketing managers need to remember is that price is just one element of the marketing mix: it should not be set in isolation, but should be blended with product, promotion and place to form a coherent mix that provides superior customer value. The sales of many products, particularly those that are a form of self-expression, such as drinks, cars, perfume and clothing, could suffer from prices that are too low. As we shall see, price is an important part of positioning strategy since it often sends quality cues to customers.

Understanding how to set prices is an important aspect of marketing decision-making, not least because of changes in the competitive arena. Greater price competition is becoming a fact of life, with the use of technology helping to drive down costs, greater levels of globalization and retail competition helping to depress price levels, and developments like the Internet and the introduction of the euro giving rise to greater levels of price transparency. Price setting and price management are therefore key activities that influence the profitability of the firm.

Basic methods of setting prices

Shapiro and Jackson[6] identified three methods used by managers to set prices (see Figure 8.1). The first of these—cost-based pricing—reflects a strong internal orientation and, as its name suggests, is based on costs. The second is competitor-orientated pricing, where the major emphasis is on the price levels set by competitors and how our prices compare with those. The final approach is market-led pricing, so called because it focuses on the value that customers place on a product in the marketplace and the nature of the marketing strategy used to support the product. In this section we will examine each of these approaches, and draw out their strengths and limitations.

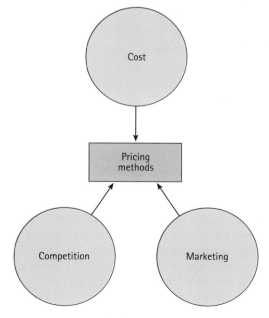

Figure 8.1 Pricing methods

Marketing in Action: The *Harry Potter* series: high sales, low profits

J.K. Rowling's *Harry Potter* series is one of the best known and most successful book series of all time. To date, there have been six books—*Harry Potter and the Philosopher's Stone*, *Harry Potter and the Chamber of Secrets*, *Harry Potter and the Prisoner of Azkaban*, *Harry Potter and the Goblet of Fire*, *Harry Potter and the Order of the Phoenix* and *Harry Potter and the Half-blood Prince*—each more successful than the last. *Order of the Phoenix* broke many records when it was published. Amazon.com, in what it described as the largest event in 'e-commerce history' received 1.3 million pre-orders worldwide. Borders, the US retailer, sold more than 650,000 copies on the first day of sales—double the number it sold of the *Goblet of Fire* in the same time period.

But while sales continue to reach dizzy heights, profitability levels for retailers have been eroded by intense price competition. For example, in the case of *Order of the Phoenix*, the recommended retail price was £16.99. However, Tesco, given its immense size, was able to order 750,000 copies and offer them at £9.97. Customers voted with their wallets and Tesco sold 317,400 editions of the book in the first 24 hours. Similarly Asda, which is owned by Wal-Mart, sold 120,000 copies in the first 24 hours at one of the lowest prices—£8.96—and had a specialist team running a 'sweeping system', moving books from stores that had not sold out to those that had. Also Amazon.com's price was £8.49—half the recommended retail price.

The pattern was repeated for *Harry Potter and the Half-blood Prince* in 2005. With a recommended retail price again of £16.99, the average price was £9.40. KwikSave grabbed most attention by offering a limited number of volumes at £4.99, well below cost price. The book sold over 3 million copies in seven days but specialist book retailers like Ottakars sold just 65,000 copies in the first day, giving it a market share of 3.5 per cent as against its usual launch share of 8 per cent.

This level of price competition means that there is very little margin available to the retailer. Discounters like the supermarkets and online shops will use such a book to drive traffic to their stores/sites in the hope that other products will be sold as well. Some people question whether such a halo effect exists, given the hype surrounding the book, which is likely to result in people taking it home to start reading immediately. Independent book sellers who sell at the recommended retail price will have to content themselves with a smaller share of sales. Paradoxically, some reported that the retail price being charged for *Order of the Phoenix* in the supermarkets was less than the wholesale price they had paid, implying that it would have been better for them to order the book from Tesco or Asda than the publishers. It is no wonder that it has been suggested that the next in the series should be called *Harry Potter and the Price Cutters Gloom*.

Based on: Graff and McLaren (2003);[3] Voyle (2003);[4] Wilson and Woodhouse (2005)[5]

Cost-based pricing

Cost-based pricing is a useful approach to price setting in that it can give an indication of the minimum price that needs to be charged in order to break even. Cost-based pricing can best be explained by using a simple example (see Table 8.1). Imagine that you are given the task of pricing a new product and the cost figures given in Table 8.1 apply. Direct costs such as labour and materials work out at £2 per unit. As output increases, more people and materials will be needed and so total costs increase. Fixed costs (or overheads) per year are calculated at £200,000. These costs (such as office and manufacturing facili-

ties) do not change as output increases. They have to be paid whether 1 or 200,000 units are produced.

Once we have calculated the relevant costs, it is necessary to estimate how many units we are likely to sell. We believe that we produce a good-quality product and therefore sales should be 100,000 in the first year. Therefore total (full) cost per unit is £4 and using the company's traditional 10 per cent mark-up a price of £4.40 is set.

So that we may understand the problems associated with using **full cost pricing**, we should assume that

Table 8.1 Cost-based pricing

Year 1	
Direct costs (per unit)	=£2
Fixed costs	=£200,000
Expected sales	=100,000
Cost per unit	
Direct costs	=£2
Fixed costs (200,000 ÷ 100,000)	=£2
Full costs	=£4
Mark-up (10 per cent)	=£0.40
Price (cost plus mark-up)	=£4.40

Year 2	
Expected sales	=50,000
Cost per unit	
Direct costs	=£2
Fixed costs (200,000 ÷ 50,000)	=£4
Full costs	=£6
Mark-up (10 per cent)	=£0.60
Price (cost plus mark-up)	=£6.60

below full costs (known as direct cost pricing or **marginal cost pricing**). As we saw in the previous chapter this is a popular strategy for services companies. For example, where seats on an aircraft or rooms in hotels are unused at any time, that revenue is lost. In such situations, pricing to cover direct costs plus a contribution to overheads is sensible to reduce the impact of excess capacity, though this approach is not sustainable in the long term.

Competitor-orientated pricing

Competitor-orientated pricing may take any one of three forms:

1 where firms follow the prices charged by leading competitors
2 where producers take the going-rate price
3 where contracts are awarded through a **competitive bidding** process.

Some firms are happy simply to benchmark themselves against their major competitors, setting their prices at levels either above, the same as or below them. This is very popular in the financial services area where, for example, the price of a loan (that is, the interest rate) is often very similar across a wide range of competitors. It can be a risky approach to take, particularly if the firm's cost position is not as good as that of its competitors (see 'Cost-based pricing', above). It is also important to have a broad view of who potential competitors are, as shown in e-Marketing 8.1.

In other circumstances, all competitors receive the same price because it is the going rate for the product. **Going-rate prices** are most typically found in the case of undifferentiated commodities such as coffee beans or cattle meat. The challenge for the marketer in this situation is to find some creative ways of differentiating the product in order to charge a different price.

In addition, many contracts are won or lost on the basis of competitive bidding. The most usual process is the drawing up of detailed specifications for a product and putting the contract out to tender. Potential suppliers quote a price, which is known only to themselves and the buyer (known as a 'sealed bid'), or the bidding may take place in a public auction where all competitors see what prices are being bid. All other things being equal, the buyer will select the supplier that quotes the lowest price. A major focus for suppliers, therefore, is the likely bid price of competitors. Increasing price pressures, European competition legislation and the growing use of technology has resulted in more and more

the sales estimate of 100,000 is not reached by the end of the year. Because of poor economic conditions or as a result of setting the price too high, only 50,000 units are sold. The company believes that this level of sales is likely to be achieved next year. What happens to price? Table 8.1 gives the answer: it is raised because cost per unit goes up. This is because fixed costs (£200,000) are divided by a smaller expected sales volume (50,000). The result is a price rise in response to poor sales figures. This is clearly nonsense and yet can happen if full cost pricing is followed blindly. A major UK engineering company priced one of its main product lines in this way and suffered a downward spiral of sales as prices were raised each year, with disastrous consequences.

So, the first problem with cost-based pricing is that it leads to an increase in the price as sales fall. Second, the procedure is illogical because a sales estimate is made *before* a price is set. Third, it focuses on internal costs rather than customers' willingness to pay. Finally, there may be a technical problem in allocating overheads in multi-product firms.[7]

Although this method forces managers to calculate costs, it also gives an indication of the minimum price necessary to make a profit. Once direct and fixed costs have been measured, 'break-even analysis' can be used to estimate the sales volume needed to balance revenue and costs at different price levels. Therefore, the procedure of calculating full costs is useful when other pricing methods are used since full costs may act as a constraint. If they cannot be covered then it may not be worthwhile launching the product. In practice, some companies will set prices

e-Marketing: Buying drugs online

The Internet has increased price transparency, but in many cases it has increased price competition as well. Take, for example, the purchasing of prescription drugs in the USA. Canada is a regulated market and often the prices of common medications are up to 50 per cent cheaper in Canada than in the USA, though the level of the difference is influenced by exchange rates between the two countries. In cities close to the border, this situation has for years given rise to a 'walk-in' trade, where US consumers cross the border to fill their prescriptions, while some enterprising businesspeople organize bus trips to take consumers across the border. But it is the growing use of the Internet, even by elderly patients, that has given rise to a booming business in the cross-border sale of drugs.

Canada's Internet pharmacy business more than doubled in 2003, with sales of £251 million at wholesale prices. It is estimated that, in the same year, American customers bought in the region of US$1.1 billion in drugs from Canada. Consumers seem to be happy to order the drugs online, even though they cannot always be sure of their source. Some of the Internet sites operating in Canada have no connection with the country other than having a maple leaf on their homepage. The growing business has also created significant supply shortages in the cases of some drugs, such is their level of demand from the USA. Others argue, though, that the supply shortages are being artificially created by leading drugs manufacturers, who are reluctant to supply the Internet companies as this reduces their sales and profitability levels in the USA.

Based on: Anonymous (2004);[8] Goldberg (2004);[9] Warn (2004)[10]

supply contracts being subject to competitive bidding. For example, traditionally, many hospital supply companies sold directly to doctors and nurses in hospitals, which meant that suppliers invested in developing selling skills and building relationships with these customers. Now, the norm is that supply contracts are put out to tender, with the winning bidder often securing the contract for a period of three to five years. Thus supply firms have had to develop skills in different areas such as tender preparation and pricing. Online auctions present a whole new set of demands (see Chapter 3).

The main advantage of the competitor-orientated pricing approach is that it is simple and easy to use,

except in the case of competitive bidding, where it may be difficult to guess what prices competitive bids will come in at. Increased price transparency in Europe, brought about by the introduction of the euro and the growing use of the Internet as a tool for comparing prices, will perhaps increase the level of attention being given to competitor-orientated pricing. It also suffers, however, from two significant flaws. First, it does not take account of any differential advantages the firm may have, which may justify its charging a higher price than the competition. As we have seen, the creation of a differential advantage is a fundamental marketing activity, and firms should seek to reap the rewards of this investment. This re-affirms the importance of blending pricing with the other

Exhibit 8.2 This TK Maxx advertisement demonstrates the power of a price proposition

elements of the marketing mix rather than viewing it as an isolated decision. Second, as noted above, competitor-orientated pricing is risky where a firm's cost position is weaker than that of its competitors.

Market-led pricing

A key marketing consideration when setting prices is estimating a product's value to the customer. In brief, the more value a product gives compared to the competition, the higher the price that can be charged. Simply because one product costs less to make than another does not imply that its price should be less. The logic of this position is borne out by Glaxo's approach when it launched Zantac, an ulcer treatment drug. It set the price for the drug at 50 per cent more than that of SmithKline Beecham's Tagamet, which was then the world's best-selling drug. Thanks to its fewer side-effects, Zantac overtook Tagamet and the resulting superior revenues transformed Glaxo from a mid-sized UK company to a global powerhouse.[11]

In this section we shall explore a number of ways of estimating value to the customer. Marketers have at their disposal, three useful techniques for uncovering customers' value perceptions: trade-off analysis, experimentation and **economic value to the customer (EVC)** analysis.

Trade-off analysis

Measurement of the trade-off between price and other product features—known as trade-off analysis or conjoint analysis—enables their effects on product preference to be established.[12] Respondents are not asked direct questions about price, instead product profiles consisting of product features and price are described, and respondents are asked to name their preferred profile. From their answers the effect of price and other product features can be measured using a computer model. For example, respondents are shown different combinations of features such as speed, petrol consumption, brand and price in the case of a car and asked which combinations they prefer. This exercise enables one to measure the impact on preferences of increasing or reducing the price. Companies like 3M, who are renowned for their product innovation, use trade-off analysis at the test marketing stage for new products. Different combinations of variables such as the brand, packaging, product features and price are tested to establish the price level customers are prepared to pay.[13]

Experimentation

A limitation of trade-off analysis is that respondents are not asked to back up their preferences with cash expenditure. Consequently there can be some doubt whether what they say they prefer would be reflected in an actual purchase when they are asked to part with money. 'Experimental pricing research' attempts to overcome this drawback by placing a product on sale at different locations with varying prices. Test marketing (see Chapter 6) is often used to compare the effectiveness of varying prices. For example, the same product could be sold in two areas using an identical promotional campaign, but with different prices between areas. Obviously, the areas would need to be matched (or differences allowed for) in terms of target customer profile so that the result would be comparable. The test needs to be long enough so that trial and repeat purchase at each price can be measured. This is likely to be between 6 and 12 months for products whose purchase cycle lasts more than a few weeks.

EVC analysis

Experimentation is more usual when pricing consumer products. However, industrial markets have a powerful tool at their disposal when setting the price of their products: economic value to the customer (EVC) analysis. Many organizational purchases are motivated by economic value considerations since reducing costs and increasing revenue are prime objectives for many companies. If a company can produce an offering that has a high EVC, it can set a high price and yet still offer superior value compared to the competition. A high EVC may be because the product generates more revenue for the buyer than competition or because its operating costs (such as maintenance, operation or start-up costs) are lower over its lifetime. EVC analysis is usually particularly revealing when applied to products whose purchase price represents a small proportion of the lifetime costs to the customer.[14]

For example, assume a manufacturer is buying a robot to use on its production line. The robot costs €100,000 but this represents only one-third of the customer's total life cycle costs. An additional €50,000 is required for start-up costs such as installation and operator training, while a further €150,000 needs to be budgeted for in post-purchase costs such as maintenance, power, etc. Assume also that a new product comes on the market that due to technological advances reduces start-up costs by €20,000 and post-purchase costs by €50,000. Total costs then have been reduced by €70,000 and the EVC that the new product offers is €170,000 (€300,000−€130,000). Thus the EVC figure is the total amount that the customer would have to pay to make the total life cycle costs of the new and existing robot the same. If the new robot was priced at €170,000 this would be the case—any price below that level would create an economic incentive for the buyer to purchase the new robot.

The main advantage of market-led pricing is that it keeps customer perceptions and needs at the forefront of the pricing decision. However, in practice it is sensible for a company to adopt an integrated approach to pricing, paying attention not only to customer needs but also to cost levels (cost-based pricing) and competitor prices (competitor-orientated pricing).

Key factors influencing price-setting decisions

Aside from the basic dimensions of cost, competitive prices and customer value, various aspects of the firm's marketing strategy will also affect price-setting decisions. In particular, marketing decisions such as positioning strategies, new product launch strategies, product-line strategies, competitive marketing strategies, distribution channel strategies and international marketing strategies will have an impact on price levels.

Positioning strategy

As we saw in Chapter 5, a key decision that marketing managers face is positioning strategy, which involves the choice of target market and the creation of a differential advantage. Each of these factors can have an enormous impact on price. Price can be used to convey a differential advantage and to appeal to a certain market segment (see Marketing in Action 8.2). Leading European retail chains such as Aldi and Lidl target cost-conscious grocery shoppers through a policy of lowest prices on a range of frequently purchased household goods. At the other end of the spectrum, many firms will charge very high prices in order to appeal to individuals with a high net worth. Products such as yachts, luxury cars, golf club memberships, luxury holidays, and so on, are sold in this way. Price is a powerful positioning tool because, for many people, it is an indicator of quality. This is particularly the case for products where objective measurement of quality is not possible, such as drinks and perfume, and for services where quality cannot be assessed before consumption.

Because price perceptions are so important to customers, many companies engage in what is called **psychological pricing**—that is, the careful manipulation of the reference prices that consumers carry in their heads. Consequently, the price of most grocery products end in '.99' because the psychological dif-

Exhibit 8.3 This Boots advertisement positions the company as being competitive on price

ference between £2.99 and £3.00 is much greater than the actual difference. Similarly, during the euro changeover in Ireland, many firms still preferred to prominently display the 'old' Irish punt price for a product because it was a lower number than the euro equivalent.

New product launch strategy

When launching new products, price should be carefully aligned with promotional strategy. Figure 8.2 shows four marketing strategies based on combinations of price and promotion. Similar matrices could also be developed for product and distribution, but for illustrative purposes promotion will be used here. A combination of high price and high promotion expenditure is called a 'rapid skimming strategy'. The high price provides high-margin returns on investment and the heavy promotion creates high levels of product awareness and knowledge. The launches of Microsoft's Xbox and Apple's iPod are examples of a rapid skimming strategy. A 'slow skimming strategy'

Marketing in Action: Fopp's simple pricing strategy

At a time when much of music retailing is moving from the record store to the Internet, Fopp is fast becoming one of the UK's offline success stories. The company was founded in 1981 by Gordon Montgomery as a market stall in the West End of Glasgow selling records he had picked up cheaply as overstock or deleted tracks. The company, which takes its name from a track by 1970s dance band The Ohio Players, has since grown to a chain of 14 stores throughout the UK, with offices in Glasgow, Edinburgh and Bristol.

Straightforward pricing is a key element of Fopp's positioning strategy. For example, CDs are sold for £10, £7, £5 and £3, with the company not using psychological pricing or offering multi-product deals. Fopp targets the serious music fan who is an obsessive collector and buyer, through its stock of an unusually wide range of music—it aims to have at least 20,000 titles at any one time. By offering low prices, customers will typically purchase several items and this is central to the company's strategy. Fopp describes its customers as loyal, well informed and as having a higher level of consumption than many other entertainment customers. Its 'suck it and see' no-quibble returns policy has also helped to increase its levels of customer loyalty. The company has also expanded into selling books and DVDs, which now account for 25 per cent of its annual sales of approximately £30 million.

Offering such low prices means that Fopp has to be very efficient and keep costs low. Montgomery is still the company's main record buyer and he has continued a policy of buying overstocks and overproduction as well as buying in bulk, saving on procurement costs. Fopp also chooses its store sites carefully, placing them in locations where rents are low but also in vibrant, affluent university cities where it is likely to find a receptive customer base. It spends very little on advertising, relying instead on word of mouth, often generated through in-store performances by cutting-edge bands.

In recognition of its success as a business, it has received several awards, including Medium Sized Business of the Year at the National Business Awards of Scotland in 2000 and UK Breakthrough Company of the Year from *Music Week* in 2003.

Based on: Anonymous (2003);[15] Dow (2004);[16] Fopp.co.uk; Sexton (2004)[17]

combines high price with low levels of promotional expenditure. High prices mean big profit margins, but high levels of promotion are believed to be unnecessary, perhaps because word of mouth is more important and the product is already well known (Rolls-Royce, say) or because heavy promotion is thought to be incompatible with product image, as with cult products. One company that uses a skimming pricing policy effectively is German car components supplier Bosch. It has applied an extremely profitable skimming strategy, supported by patents, to its launch of fuel injection and anti-lock brake systems.[18] Companies that combine low prices with heavy promotional expenditure are practising a 'rapid penetration strategy'. The aim is to gain market share rapidly, perhaps at the expense of a rapid skimmer. For example, low-fares airlines like easyJet and Ryanair have successfully attacked incumbents like British Airways and Lufthansa using this strategy as has Direct Line in the sale of general insurance products. Finally, a 'slow penetration strategy' combines low price with low promotional expenditure. Own-label brands use this strategy: promotion is not necessary to gain distribution and low promotional expenditure helps to maintain high profit margins for these brands. This price/promotion framework is useful when thinking about marketing strategies at launch.

The importance of picking the right strategy is illustrated by the failure of TiVo in the UK. TiVo make

		Promotion	
		High	Low
Price	High	Rapid skimming	Slow skimming
	Low	Rapid penetration	Slow penetration

Figure 8.2 New product launch strategies

personal video recorders (PVRs), which are high-technology recorders capable of storing up to 40 hours of television and with features such as the facility to rewind live television programmes and memorize selections so that favourite programmes are automatically recorded. But the product has failed to take off and TiVo has withdrawn from the UK market. Part of the reason for the failure is that consumers did not seem to fully understand what PVRs can do and therefore couldn't justify spending in the region of £300 plus a monthly subscription fee for a recorder. Some analysts estimate that the product would have to be priced in the region of £100 for the product to take off, suggesting that a penetration rather than a skimming strategy would have been more appropriate.[19]

High price (skimming) strategies and low price (penetration) strategies may be appropriate in different situations. A skimming strategy is most suitable in situations where customers are less price sensitive, such as where the product provides high value, where customers have a high ability to pay and where there are under high pressure to buy. However, setting the price too high can lead to problems generating sales. For example, when Nissan launched its 350Z sports car, it was priced at levels similar to top sports cars like the Porsche Boxster and BMW Z4. However, poor sales levels forced it to cut its retail price by €10,000, a move that brought it closer to the next level of sports cars like the Mazda RX-8. Penetration pricing strategies are more likely to be driven by company circumstances where the company is seeking to dominate the market, where it is comfortable to establish a position in the market initially and make money later, and/or where it seeks to create a barrier to entry for competitors. An example of using price to gain market presence is that of the Proton car, which in the UK achieved a 2 per cent market share within five years of launch by drastically undercutting the competition on price. In 1992, in a depressed market, sales rose by 40 per cent.

Marketing in Action: Levi's introduces a cut-price range

Through its superior marketing and branding, Levi's has traditionally been able to charge a premium price for its products, up to approximately 40 per cent more than competing brands. It has also resisted bringing out a cheaper version of its jeans and it took Tesco to court for selling its jeans at bargain prices. Tesco had been importing Levi's jeans from outside the EU and selling them in its stores, but Levi's claimed that this infringed its trademark and damaged its reputation when a pair of Levi's could be bought beside products like baked beans. The European Court of Justice ruled in favour of Levi's.

But markets change and marketing strategies need to change as well. By the end of the last century, the jeans business had suffered another downturn. At the top end of the market, Levi's was facing significant competition from the products being offered by the likes of Calvin Klein, Tommy Hilfiger and Armani, while sales of casual clothing by mass-market retailers also continued to grow. Levi's recognized that the two fastest-growing segments were super-premium and discount. It had a choice of remaining in just one or choosing to straddle both, and has taken the latter route. At the top end of its range, Levi's jeans still sell for £175 a pair. But it has also introduced a new discount range called Signature, which is a complete assortment of T-shirts, jackets and jeans for both men and women. Signature jeans sell for about 40 per cent less than the classic 501 range, retailing at around £25, and do not have the distinctive red Levi's tab, pocket stitching and waistband patch. They are designed specifically for sale in supermarkets and discount stores, ironically meaning that Levi's has had to begin dealing with Tesco again.

The Signature range was first launched in Wal-Mart stores in the USA in March 2003 and later that summer the product became available in Europe. In April 2004, Tesco began selling the Signature range. There are serious risks for the manufacturer in bringing out a discount version of a designer product. But so far the results appear to be good for Levi's. First-quarter sales for 2004 were up almost 10 per cent, much of this credited to the success of the Signature range.

Based on: Anonymous (2003);[20] Brandchannel.com (2001);[21] Buckley (2004);[22] Butler (2003);[23] Hughes (2003)[24]

Product-line strategy

Marketing-orientated companies also need to take account of where the price of a new product fits into its existing product line. Where multiple segments appear attractive, modified versions of the product should be designed, and priced differently, not according to differences in costs, but in line with the respective values that each target market places on a product. All the major car manufacturing companies have products priced at levels that are attractive to different market segments, namely economy cars, family saloons, executive cars, and so on.

Some companies prefer to extend their product lines rather than reduce the price of existing brands in the face of price competition. They launch cut-price 'fighter brands' (see Chapter 6) to compete with the low-price rivals. This has the advantage of maintaining the image and profit margins of existing brands. For example, Apple has introduced the iPod Shuffle, retailing at US$99, to compete with low-price MP3 players, and has also introduced the Mac Mini computer to compete against cheaper PCs coming on to the market from companies like Lenovo in China. By producing a range of brands at different price points, companies can cover the varying price sensitivities of customers and encourage them to trade up to the more expensive, higher-margin brands (see Marking in Action 8.3).

Competitive marketing strategy

The pricing of products should also be set within the context of the firm's competitive strategy. Four strategic objectives are relevant to pricing: build, hold, harvest and reposition.

Build objective

For price-sensitive markets, a build objective for a product implies a price lower than that of the competition. If the competition raise their prices we would be slow to match them. For price-insensitive markets, the best pricing strategy becomes less clear-cut. Price in these circumstances will be dependent on the overall positioning strategy thought appropriate for the product.

Hold objective

Where the strategic objective is to hold sales and/or market share, the appropriate pricing strategy is to maintain or match the price relative to the competition. This has implications for price changes: if the competition reduces prices then our prices would match this price fall.

Harvest objective

A harvest objective implies the maintenance or raising of profit margins, even though sales and/or market share are falling. The implication for pricing strategy would be to set premium prices. For products that are being harvested, there would be much greater reluctance to match price cuts than for products that were being built or held. On the other hand, price increases would swiftly be matched.

Reposition objective

Changing market circumstances and product fortunes may necessitate the repositioning of an existing product. This may involve a price change, the direction and magnitude of which will be dependent on the new positioning strategy for the product.

The above examples show how developing clear strategic objectives helps the setting of price and clarifies the appropriate reaction to competitive price changes. Price setting, then, is much more sophisticated than simply asking 'How much can I get for this product?' The process starts by asking more fundamental questions like 'How is this product going to be positioned in the marketplace?' and 'What is the appropriate strategic objective for this product?' Answering these questions is an essential aspect of effective price management.

Channel management strategy

When products are sold through intermediaries such as distributors or retailers, the list price to the customer must reflect the margins required by them. Some products, such as holidays, carry margins of typically less than 10 per cent for middlemen (in this case travel agents) and many are being sold direct to the consumer. Other products, such as jewellery, may carry a margin of several hundred per cent. When Müller yoghurt was first launched in the UK, a major factor in gaining distribution in a mature market was the fact that its high price allowed attractive profit margins for the supermarket chains. Conversely, the implementation of a penetration pricing strategy may be hampered if distributors refuse to stock a product because the profit per unit is less than that available on competitive products.

The implication is that pricing strategy is dependent on understanding not only the ultimate customer but also the needs of distributors and retailers who form the link between them and the manufacturer. If their needs cannot be accommodated, product launch may not be viable or a different distribution system (such as direct selling) might be required.

International marketing strategy

The firm's international marketing strategy will also have a significant impact on its pricing decisions. The first challenge that managers have to deal with is that of **price escalation**. This means that a number of factors can combine to put pressure on the firm to increase the prices it charges in other countries. These include the additional costs of shipping and transporting costs to a foreign market, margins paid to local distributors, customs duties or tariffs that may be charged on imported products, differing rates of sales taxes and changes to the price that may be driven by exchange rates and differing inflation rates. All of these combine to mean that the price charged in a foreign market is often very different to that charged on the home market. Sometimes it is higher, but it can also be lower if circumstances dictate that low prices are necessary to gain sales, as would be the case in countries where levels of disposable income are low. In such instances it is important for firms to guard against **parallel importing**—this is when products destined for an international market are re-imported back into the home market and sold through unauthorized channels at levels lower than the company wishes to charge (see, for example, e-Marketing 8.1 and Marketing in Action 8.3).

While most firms seek to standardize as many elements of the marketing mix as possible when operating internationally, pricing is one of the most difficult to standardize for the reasons outlined above. Sometimes the price differences are driven by cost variations, but sometimes they are also due to the absence of competitors or different customer value perceptions, which can lead to accusations of ripping off customers. Now that international prices are much easier to compare through, for example, the introduction of the euro, price differences across markets have become much more controversial (see Table 8.2, where some big differences in the pre-tax prices of new cars can be observed throughout Europe).

Managing price changes

So far, our discussion has concentrated on those factors that affect pricing strategy; but in a highly competitive world, pricing is dynamic—managers need to know when and how to raise or lower prices, and whether or not to react to competitors' price moves. The extent to which price is used as a major marketing tool is illustrated in Marketing in Action 8.4. First, we shall discuss initiating price changes before analysing how to react to competitors' price changes.

Three key issues associated with initiating price changes are: the circumstances that may lead a company to raise or lower prices, the tactics that can be used, and estimating competitor reaction. Table 8.3 illustrates the major points relevant to each of these considerations.

Circumstances

Marketing research (for example, **trade-off analysis** or experimentation) which reveals that customers place a higher value on the product than is reflected in its price could mean that a price increase is justified. Rising costs, and hence reduced profit margins, may also stimulate price rises. Another factor that leads to price increases is excess demand. This regularly happens, for example, in the residential property market where the demand for houses can often grow at a faster pace than houses can be built by construction companies, resulting in house price inflation. A company that cannot supply the demand created by its customers may choose to raise prices in an effort

Table 8.2 EU car price comparison

Pre-tax prices: all prices in euros				
Country	Audi A4	Renault Laguna	Toyota Corolla	VW Golf
Germany	22,926	17,211	12,802	12,559
Spain	21,959	15,146	11,171	11,846
France	22,431	15,761	11,865	11,481
Ireland	21,702	13,570	13,061	10,543
UK	23,313	17,416	13,492	11,978
Greece	20,771	14,453	11,392	9,799
Denmark	18,467	12,861	9,596	9,732
Sweden	20,141	15,288	11,422	11,581

Source: European Commission

Table 8.3 Initiating price changes

	Increases	**Cuts**
Circumstances	Value greater than price Rising costs Excess demand Harvest objective	Value less than price Excess supply Build objective Price war unlikely Pre-empt competitive entry
Tactics	Price jump Staged price increases Escalator clauses Price unbundling Lower discounts	Price fall Staged price reductions Fighter brands Price bundling Higher discounts
Estimating competitor	Strategic objectives Self-interest Competitive situation Past experience	

Marketing in Action: Battling it out in a price war

While all aspects of the marketing mix are important, it is interesting to observe the frequency with which price is being used as a major marketing weapon in a variety of industries. The strategy of many companies is to assume a price leadership position and to maintain it through an ongoing strategy of discounting and price reduction. For example, in the UK grocery retailing sector, Tesco and Asda have pursued a strategy of price reduction and share building. In 2005, both companies announced plans to spend in the region of £250 million lowering prices. Tesco claims its price cuts across 500 products will save customers £2.82 on a basket of 25 everyday products. Tesco commands 29 per cent of supermarket spending in the UK, while Asda, which has 17 per cent, is backed by Wal-Mart. The third and fourth chains, Sainsbury's and Morrisons have been significantly weakened by their inability to match the aggressive pricing of the market leaders.

Price has become a significant issue for the personal computer industry too. The fastest growing segment of the market is the sub-US$1000 segment, where consumers want a basic machine that will provide the most commonly used services such as access to the Internet, word processing and basic multimedia. Over the last five years, Dell, IBM and Hewlett-Packard have been battling it out in this segment with the major loser during that period being Compaq Computer Corp, which was taken over by HP. New entrants to the sector, such as the Apple iMac, and Internet start-ups like eMachines, who were first to retail a US$399 PC, have been very successful. The price war has extended up the chain to the memory chip market where Intel and AMD in particular have been competing aggressively. Intel is the dominant market leader with a share of over 80 per cent, but it responded to AMD's inroads in the market with aggressive price discounting. For example, in 2002, Intel cut the price of its top-performing Pentium 4 chip by 57 per cent in just six weeks in a move that affected the profit margins of both companies. The same pattern has been repeated in 2005 in the flash memory sector (a technology that is used by mobile phone manufacturers) with price cutting by Intel leading to AMD's share of the market falling from 28 per cent to 20 per cent in just six months.

So from groceries to PCs and from tabloids to airfares, price wars are commonplace. When to cut a price and when to follow such a price cut have become very important decisions.

Based on: Anonymous (1999);[25] Barnes (2005);[26] Nuttall (2005);[27] Popovich (2002);[28] Rigby (2005)[29]

to balance demand and supply. This can be an attractive option as profit margins are automatically widened. The final circumstance when companies may decide to raise prices is when embarking on a harvest objective. Prices are raised to increase margins even though sales may fall.

In the same way, price cuts may be provoked by the discovery that a price is high compared to the value that customers place on a product, by falling costs and by excess supply leading to excess capacity. A further circumstance that may lead to price falls is the adoption of a build objective. When customers are thought to be price sensitive, price cutting may be used to build sales and market share. A damper on this tactic would be when a price war might be provoked, as happened when Reemtsma Cigarettenfabriken cut the price of its West brand from DM3.80 to DM3.30 in West Germany.[30] This was the first price-cutting move of this severity since the 1940s and led to competitor retaliation, which saw the collapse of cigarette prices and margins.

Tactics

There are many ways in which price increases and cuts may be implemented. The most direct is the

Exhibit 8.4 This Dell advertisement is an example of price unbundling, where the cost of accessories are shown separately

'price jump', or fall, which increases or decreases the price by the full amount at one go. A price jump avoids prolonging the pain of a price increase over a long period, but may raise the visibility of the price increase to customers. This happened in India, where Hindustan Lever, the local subsidiary of Unilever, used its market power to raise the prices of its key brands at a time when raw materials were getting cheaper. As a result operating margins grew from 13 per cent in 1999 to 21 per cent in 2003. Subsequently, though, sales fell sharply due to competition from P&G and Nirma, a local brand, as well as consumer disaffection.[31] Using staged price increases might make the price rise more palatable but may elicit accusations of 'always raising your prices'. A one-stage price fall can have a high-impact, dramatic effect that can be heavily promoted but also has an immediate impact on profit margins. Staged price reductions have a less dramatic effect but may be used when a price cut is believed to be necessary although the amount necessary to stimulate sales is unclear. Small cuts may be initiated as a learning process that proceeds until the desired effect on sales is achieved.

'Escalator clauses' can also be used to raise prices. The contracts for some organizational purchases are drawn up before the product is made. Constructing the product—for example, a new defence system or motorway—may take a number of years. An escalator clause in the contract allows the supplier to stipulate price increases in line with a specified index (for example, increases in industry wage rates or the cost of living).

Another tactic that effectively raises prices is **price unbundling**. Many product offerings actually consist of a set of products to which an overall price is set (for example, computer hardware and software). Price unbundling allows each element in the offering to be priced separately in such a way that the total price is raised. A variant on this process is charging for services that were previously included in the product's price. For example, manufacturers of mainframe computers have the option of unbundling installation and training services, and charging for them separately.

Yet another approach is to maintain the list price but lower discounts to customers. In periods of heavy demand for new cars, dealers lower the cash discount given to customers, for example. Similarly if demand is slack, customers can be given greater discounts as an incentive to buy. However, there are risks if this strategy is pursued for too long a period of time. For example, due to poor sales of its car models, GM pursued a four-year price discounting strategy in the US market, with disastrous effects. The latest iteration of the scheme, which is known as 'Employee Discounts for Everyone', offers buyers a discount averaging US$400–US$500 off the price of a new car. This takes the total in incentives available to the buyer to over US$7000, or over 20 per cent off the suggested retail price of the car.[32] The resulting price war with Ford and Chrysler, who have followed with similar schemes, has hurt profits. But, more worryingly, the effect of the campaign seems to be that GM customers simply bring forward purchases that they were going to make anyway to avail themselves of the discounts, and customer attention has switched to price rather than the value offered by the product.[33]

Quantity discounts can also be manipulated to raise the transaction price to customers. The percentage discount per quantity can be lowered, or the quantity that qualifies for a particular percentage discount can be raised.

Those companies contemplating a price cut have three choices in addition to a direct price fall.

1   A company defending a premium-priced brand that is under attack from a cut-price competitor may choose to maintain its price while introducing a fighter brand. The established brand keeps its premium-price position while the fighter brand competes with the rival for price-sensitive customers.

2   Where a number of products and services that tend to be bought together are priced separately, price bundling can be used to effectively lower price. For example, televisions can be offered with 'free three-year repair warranties' or cars offered with 'free service for two years'.

3   Finally, discount terms can be made more attractive by increasing the percentage or lowering the qualifying levels.

Estimating competitor reaction

The extent of competitor reaction is a key factor in the price change decision. A price rise that no competitor follows may turn customers away, while a price cut that is met by the competition may reduce industry profitability. Four factors affect the extent of competitor reaction: their strategic objectives, what is in their self-interest, the competitive situation at the time of the price change, and past experience.

Firms should attempt to gauge their competitors' strategic objectives for their products. By observing pricing and promotional behaviour, talking to distributors and even hiring their personnel, estimates of whether competitor products are being built, held or harvested can be made. This is crucial information—their response to our price increase or cut will depend upon it. They are more likely to follow our price increase if their strategic objective is to hold or harvest. If they are intent on building market share, they are more likely to resist following our price increase. Conversely, they are more likely to follow our price cuts if they are building or holding, and more likely to ignore our price cuts if they are harvesting.

When estimating competitor reactions, self-interest is also important. Managers initiating price changes should try to place themselves in the position of their competitors. What reaction is in their best interests? This may depend on the circumstances of the price change. For example, if price is raised in response to cost inflation, the competitor firms are more likely to follow than if price is raised because of the implementation of a harvest objective. Price may also depend on the competitive situation. For example, if competition has excess capacity a price cut is more likely to be matched than if this is not the case. Similarly, a price rise is more likely to be followed if competition is faced with excess demand.

Looking at their reactions to previous price changes can also help one to judge competitor reaction. While past experience is not always a reliable guide it may provide an insight into the way in which competitor firms view price changes and the likely actions they might take.

Reacting to competitors' price changes

Companies need to analyse their appropriate reactions when their competitors initiate price changes. Three issues are relevant here: when to follow, what to ignore and the tactics to use if the price change is to be followed. Table 8.4 summarizes the main considerations.

When to follow

When competitive price increases are due to general rising cost levels or industry-wide excess demand, they are more likely to be followed. In these circumstances the initial pressure to raise prices is the same on all parties. Following a price rise is also more likely

Table 8.4 Reacting to competitors' price changes

	Increases	Cuts
When to follow	Rising costs Excess demand Price-insensitive customers Price rise compatible with brand image Harvest or hold objective	Falling costs Excess supply Price-sensitive customers Price fall compatible with brand image Build or hold objective
When to ignore	Stable or falling costs Excess supply Price-sensitive customers Price rise incompatible with brand image Build objective	Rising costs Excess demand Price-insensitive customers Price fall incompatible with brand image Harvest objective

Tactics
  Quick response
  Slow response
	Margin improvement urgent
	Gains to be made by being customer's friend
		Offset competitive threat
		High customer loyalty

when customers are relatively price insensitive, which means that the follower will not gain much advantage by resisting the price increase. Where brand image is consistent with high prices, a company is more likely to follow a competitor's price rise as to do so would be consistent with the brand's positioning strategy. Finally, a price rise is more likely to be followed when a company is pursuing a harvest or hold objective because, in both cases, the emphasis is more on profit margin than sales/market share gain.

When they are stimulated by general falling costs or excess supply, price cuts are likely to be followed. Falling costs allow all companies to cut prices while maintaining margins, and excess supply means that a company is unlikely to allow a rival to make sales gains at its expense. Price cuts will also be followed in price-sensitive markets since allowing one company to cut price without retaliation would mean large sales gains for the price cutter. This has happened in the UK toiletries market where Boots has failed to follow Tesco in aggressive price cutting on products like shampoo and skin cream. Boots' profits and share price have been falling while Tesco's continue to grow.[34] The image of the company can also affect reaction to price cuts. Some companies position themselves as low-price manufacturers or retail outlets. In such circumstances they would be less likely to allow a price reduction by a competitor to go unchallenged for to do so would be incompatible with their brand image. Finally, price cuts are likely to be followed when the company has a build or hold strategic objective. In such circumstances an aggressive price move by a competitor would be followed to prevent sales/market share loss. In the case of a build objective, the response may be more dramatic, with a price fall exceeding the initial competitive move.

When to ignore

In most cases, the circumstances associated with companies not reacting to a competitive price move are simply the opposite of the above. Price increases are likely to be ignored when costs are stable or falling, which means that there are no cost pressures forcing a general price rise. In the situation of excess supply, companies may view a price rise as making the initiator less competitive and therefore allow the rise to take place unchallenged, particularly when customers are price sensitive. Companies occupying low-price positions may regard a price rise in response to a price increase from a rival to be incompatible with their brand image. Finally, companies pursuing a build objective may allow a competitor's price rise to go unmatched in order to gain sales and market share.

Price cuts are likely to be ignored in conditions of rising costs, excess demand and when servicing price-insensitive customers. Premium-price positioners may be reluctant to follow competitors' price cuts for to do so would be incompatible with their brand image. For example, some luxury brands, such as Lacoste, have suffered heavily because of pursuing a strategy of discounting when faced with excess capacity while competitors chose not to follow.[35] Lastly, price cuts may be resisted by companies using a harvest objective.

Tactics

If a company decides to follow a price change, it can do this quickly or slowly. A quick price reaction is likely when there is an urgent need to improve profit margins. Here, the competitor's price increase will be welcomed as an opportunity to achieve this objective.

In contrast, a slow reaction may be the best approach when a company is pursuing the image of customers' friend. The first company to announce a price increase is often seen as the high-price supplier. Some companies have mastered the art of playing low-cost supplier by never initiating price increases and following competitors' increases slowly.[36] The key to this tactic is timing the response: too quick and customers do not notice; too long and profit is foregone. The optimum period can be found only by experience but, during it, salespeople should be told to stress to customers that the company is doing everything it can to hold prices for as long as possible.

If a firm wishes to ward off a competitive threat, a quick response to a competitor's price fall is called for. In the face of undesirable sales/market share erosion, fast action is needed to nullify potential competitor gains. However, reaction will be slow when a company has a loyal customer base willing to accept higher prices for a period so long as they can rely on price parity over the longer term.

Ethical issues in pricing strategy

Some key ethical issues relating to pricing include price fixing, predatory pricing, deceptive pricing, price discrimination and product dumping.

Price fixing

Competition is one of the driving forces towards lower prices. Therefore, it can be in the interests of producers to agree among themselves not to compete on price. This is known as the 'act of collusion' and is banned in many countries and regions, including the EU. Article 83 of the Treaty of Rome is designed to ban practices preventing, restricting or distorting competition, except where these contribute to efficiency without inhibiting consumers' fair share of the benefit. Groups of companies that collude are said to be acting as a cartel, and these are by no means easy to uncover. One of the European Commission's most famous success stories is the uncovering of an illicit cartel among 23 of Europe's top chemical companies from the UK, France, Germany, Belgium, Italy, Spain, the Netherlands, Finland, Norway and Austria. Through collusion they were able to sustain levels of profitability for low-density polyethylene and PVC in the face of severe overcapacity. Quotas were set to limit companies' attempts to gain market share through price competition, and prices were fixed to harmonize the differences between countries in order to discourage

customers from shopping around for the cheapest deals.[37] Opponents of price fixing claim that it is unethical because it restrains the consumer's freedom of choice and interferes with each firm's interest in offering high-quality products at the best price. Its proponents argue that, under harsh economic conditions, price fixing is necessary to ensure a fair profit for the industry and to avoid price wars that might lead to bankruptcies and unemployment (see also Marketing in Action 8.5).

Predatory pricing

Predatory pricing refers to a situation that occurs when a firm reduces its prices with the aim of driving out the competition. The firm is content to incur losses with the intent that high profits will be generated through higher prices once the competition has been eliminated. Budget airline easyJet accused British Airways of predatory pricing through its no-frills subsidiary Go; easyJet claimed that the low prices charged by Go were being subsidized by the profits made by BA's other operations. Similarly, Microsoft has been accused of predatory activities by bundling new software such as its Internet browser with its best-selling operating system Windows. This meant that this new software was effectively available to customers free of charge and it resulted in the then leading Internet browser company in the field, Netscape, being eliminated from the business.

Deceptive pricing

Deceptive pricing occurs when consumers are misled by the price deals offered by companies. Two examples are misleading price comparisons and 'bait and switch'. Misleading price comparisons occur when a store sets artificially high prices for a short time so that much lower 'sale' prices can be claimed later. The purpose is to deceive the customer into believing they are being offered a bargain. Some countries, such as the UK and Germany, have laws that state the minimum period over which the regular price should have been charged before it can be used as a reference price in a sale. Bait and switch is the practice of advertising a very low price on a product (the bait) to attract customers to a retail outlet. Once in the store the salesperson persuades the customer to buy a higher-priced product (the switch). The customer may be told that the lower-priced product is no longer in stock or that it is of inferior quality.

Price discrimination

Price discrimination occurs when a supplier offers a better price for the same product to a buyer, resulting in that buyer gaining an unfair competitive

Marketing in Action: Price fixing in the toy industry

Because of the inherent seasonality of toy sales, price cutting is frequent as manufacturers and retailers seek to cash in on the popularity of particular toys during short selling seasons such as Christmas. It was perhaps for this reason that Hasbro, one of the world's leading toy makers, and two British retailers, Argos and Littlewoods, got together to fix the price of certain toys in a move that was to result in record fines being handed out by the Office of Fair Trading (OFT). Hasbro makes games such as Monopoly and Scrabble, as well as Action Man and Harry Potter merchandise, and has 18 per cent of the UK toy market. In November 2002, it was found guilty by the OFT of preventing 10 of its distributors from selling its toys below list prices, and fined £9 million, which was later reduced to £4.95 million. Subsequently, Hasbro co-operated with further investigations by the OFT, which resulted in Argos and Littlewoods being found guilty of agreeing not to sell Hasbro toys below set prices. The anti-competitive agreement with the toy maker lasted from about spring 1999 until May 2001. Argos was fined £17.28 million and Littlewoods ordered to pay £5.37 million, which combined were a record fine for price fixing. The fines could have been more severe as the law allows the OFT to penalize firms up to 10 per cent of their UK turnover for a maximum of three years.

Argos and Littlewoods appealed the decision of the OFT but it was upheld by the Competition Appeals Tribunal in 2005. The chairman of the OFT, John Vickers, said the prosecution of the two retailers was responsible for a significant fall in the price of some toys with, for example, the price of the Monopoly board game having fallen by more than £4 since the OFT investigation began in 2001. However, the GUS group, which owns Argos as well as Homebase, Burberry and others, plans to take the case to the Court of Appeal.

Under the new powers given to the OFT by the Competition Act 2000, it has become more aggressive in pursuing price fixing allegations. Its strategy is a clever one as price fixing by definition involves a number of parties. However, if one party 'co-operates' with the investigations, it can get discounts of up to 100 per cent by being the first to reveal the wrongdoing. Hasbro could have potentially faced a fine of £15.59 million but chose instead to blow the whistle on Argos and Littlewoods. Aside from levying fines, the OFT will also have the power to offer directors immunity from prosecution, as price fixing has become a criminal offence under the Enterprise Act 2003.

Based on: Dixon (2005);[38] Power (2005);[39] Sherwood (2003)[40]

advantage. Price discrimination can be justified when the costs of supplying different customers varies, where the price differences reflect differences in the level of competition, and where different volumes are purchased.

Product dumping
Product dumping involves products being exported at a much lower price than that charged in the domestic market, sometimes below the cost of production. Products are 'dumped' for a variety of reasons. First, unsold stocks may be exported at a low price rather than risk lowering prices in the home market. Second, products may be manufactured for sale overseas at low prices to fill otherwise unused production capacity. Finally, products that are regarded as unsafe at home may be dumped in countries that do not have such stringent safety rules. For example, the US Consumer Product Safety Commission ruled that three-wheeled cycles were dangerous. Many companies responded by selling their inventories at low prices in other countries.[41]

Summary

Price is a major element in developing an effective marketing strategy because it is the only component of the marketing mix that directly generates revenue—all the others are costs. In this chapter the following key issues were addressed.

1. There are three bases upon which prices are set, namely cost, competition and market value. We noted that all three should be taken into account when setting prices.

2. That the pricing levels set may also be influenced by a number of other marketing strategy variables, namely, positioning strategy, new-product launch strategy, product-line strategy, competitive strategy, channel management strategy and international marketing strategy.

3. That prices are dynamic, therefore marketers are faced with decisions relating to initiating price changes or responding to the price changes made by competitors. Whether prices are rising or falling, various factors need to be taken into account and these are important decisions as they affect the overall profitability of the firm.

4. That there are five main ethical issues with respect to pricing, namely price fixing, predatory pricing, deceptive pricing, price discrimination and product dumping.

Suggested reading

Davis, G. and E. Brito (2004) Price and Quality Competition between Brands and Own Brands: A Value Systems Perspective, *European Journal of Marketing*, **38** (1/2), 30–56.

Florissen, A., B. Maurer, B. Schmidt and T. Vahlenkamp (2001) The Race to the Bottom, *McKinsey Quarterly*, **3**, 98–108.

Jobber, D. and D. Shipley (1998) Marketing-orientated Pricing Strategies, *Journal of General Management*, **23** (4), 19–34.

Marn, M., Roegner, E. and C. Zawada (2003) Pricing New Products, *McKinsey Quarterly*, **3**, 40–50.

Pitt, L., P. Berthon, R. Watson and M. Ewing (2001) Pricing Strategy and the Net, *Business Horizons*, **44** (2), 45–55.

Internet exercises

Sites to visit

1   www.ticketmaster.com
www.just4tickets.net
www.centralticketbureau.com

Exercise

Visit each of these websites and compare the prices charged for tickets for four artists or events of your choice. How would you explain any price differences that you find?

Sites to visit

2   www.vodafone.co.uk
www.o2.co.uk
www.orange.co.uk
www.easymobile.co.uk

Exercise

Visit each of these websites and compare the prices that they charge for their products. How difficult is it to make an accurate comparison of the cost of a mobile phone package? Why do you think this is so?

Study questions

1. Accountants are always interested in profit margins; sales managers want low prices to help push sales; and marketing managers are interested in high prices to establish premium positions in the marketplace. To what extent do you agree with this statement in relation to the setting of prices?

2. Why is value to the customer a more logical approach to setting prices than cost of production? What role can costs play in the setting of prices?

3. How would you justify the price differences for a cup of coffee that you might encounter if you purchase it in a local coffee shop versus a top-class hotel?

4. Discuss how a company pursuing a build strategy is likely to react to both price rises and price cuts by competitors.

5. Discuss the specific issues that arise when pricing products for international markets.

Key terms

dynamic pricing an outcome of yield management where prices are frequently adjusted depending on demand for the product or service

full cost pricing pricing so as to include all costs, and based on certain sales volume assumptions

marginal cost pricing the calculation of only those costs that are likely to rise as output increases

competitive bidding drawing up detailed specifications for a product and putting the contract out to tender

going-rate prices prices at the rate generally applicable in the market, focusing on competitors' offerings rather than on company costs

economic value to the customer (EVC) the amount a customer would have to pay to make the total life cycle costs of a new and a reference product the same

psychological pricing taking into consideration the psychological impact of the price level that is being set

price escalation the additional costs incurred in taking products to an international market, including transportation costs, distribution costs, taxes and tariffs, exchange rates and inflation rates

parallel importing when importers buy products from distributors in one country and sell them in another to distributors who are not part of the manufacturer's normal distribution; caused by significant price differences for the same product between different countries

trade-off analysis a measure of the trade-off customers make between price and other product features, so that their effects on product preference can be established

price unbundling pricing each element in the offering so that the price of the total product package is raised

References

1. **Doz, Y.** and **A. Balchandani** (2003) Extending the 'easy' Business Model: What Should the easyGroup do Next?, Case 303-093-1, *European Case Clearing House*; **Lester, R.** (2005) No Resting Easy in the Stelios Empire, *Marketing Week*, 3 March, 22–3; **Lewis, E.** (2002) Easing Towards a Philosophy, *Brand Strategy*, October, 23; **Malkani, G.** (2003) Cut-price Gladiator Goes to the Cinema, *Financial Times*, 15 May, 15.

2. **Lester, T.** (2002) How To Ensure That the Price is Exactly Right, *Financial Times*, 30 January, 15.

3. **Graff, V.** and **G. McLaren** (2003) Harry Potter Price Cut Sparks War of Bookstores, *Independent*, 20 June, 5.

4. **Voyle, S.** (2003) Harry and a Fierce Scramble for the Elusive Potter Gold, *Financial Times*, 20 June, 22.

5. **Wilson, B.** and **C. Woodhouse** (2005) Potter Price War, *Evening Standard*, 1 April, 28.

6. **Shapiro, B.P.** and **B.B. Jackson** (1978) Industrial Pricing to Meet Customer Needs, *Harvard Business Review*, Nov/Dec, 119–27.

7. **Christopher, M.** (1982) Value-in-use Pricing, *European Journal of Marketing*, **16** (5), 35–46.

8. **Anonymous** (2004) Drug Firm's Lives Depend on 'Unfair' Pricing, *Sunday Telegraph*, 7 September, 34.

9. **Goldberg** (2004) Drug Wars: Perils of Importing Drugs From Canada, *Ripon Forum*, Summer, 14.

10. **Warn** (2004) Internet Drug Trade Proves a Bitter Pill for Canada, *Financial Times*, 21 April, 8.

11. **London, S.** (2003) The Real Value in Setting the Right Price, *Financial Times*, 11 September, 15.

12. **Kucher, E.** and **H. Simon** (1987) Durchbruch bei der Preisentscheidung: Conjoint-Measurement, eine neue Technik zur Gewinnoptimierung, *Harvard Manager*, **3**, 36–60.

13. **Lester, T.** (2002) How To Ensure That the Price is Exactly Right, *Financial Times*, 30 January, 15.

14. **Forbis, J.L.** and **N.T. Mehta** (1979) Economic Value to the Customer, McKinsey Staff Paper, Chicago: McKinsey and Co. Inc., February, 1–10.

15. **Anonymous** (2003) Keeping it Simple is the Key for Expanding Fopp Chain, *Music Week*, 6 September, 8–9.

16. **Dow, J.** (2004) Fopp Founder has his Finger Firmly on Public's Musical Pulse, *Scotsman*, 9 January, 29.

17. **Sexton, P.** (2004) Sound Profits From an Offbeat Philosophy, *Financial Times*, 27 January, 13.

18. **Simon, H.** (1992) Pricing Opportunities—And How to Exploit Them, *Sloan Management Review*, Winter, 55–65.

19. **Cane, A.** (2003) TiVo, Barely Used . . ., *Financial Times*, Creative Business, 25 February, 12.

20. **Anonymous** (2003) Levi to Sell Jeans in Supermarkets After All, *Daily Mail*, 25 April, 15.

21. *Brandchannel.com* (2001) It Ain't Easy Being Blue, 26 February.

22. **Buckley, N.** (2004) Levi Sees Discount Gamble Pay Off, *Financial Times*, 14 April, 23.

23. **Butler, S.** (2003) Levi's Launch to Target Discount Stores, *The Times*, 24 April, 27.

24. **Hughes, D.** (2003) Levi-Strauss, *The Business*, 1 June, 14.

25. **Anonymous** (1999) Price Wars, *Fortune*, **139** (10), 33–8.

26. **Barnes, R.** (2005) Asda to Battle Tesco With Price Campaign, *Marketing*, 1 December, 16.

27. **Nuttall, C.** (2005) AMD Warns as Price War with Intel Takes Toll, *Financial Times*, 12 January, 24.

28. **Popovich, K.** (2002) Intel to Cut Chip Pricing by 57 per cent, *eWeek*, 4 January, 16.

29. **Rigby, E.** (2005) Price Cuts Fuel Supermarket War, *Financial Times*, 4 April, 21.

30. **Simon, H.** (1992) Pricing Opportunities—And How to Exploit Them, *Sloan Management Review*, Winter, 55–65.

31. **Anonymous** (2004) Slow Moving: Can Unilever's Indian Arm Recover From Some Self Inflicted Wounds, *Economist*, 6 November, 67–8.

32. **Simon, B.** (2005) GM's Price Cuts Drive Record Sales, *Financial Times*, 5 July, 28.

33. **Simon, B.** (2005) Detroit Giants Count Cost of Four-year Price War, *Financial Times*, 19 March, 29.

34. **Buckley, C.** (2005) Boots Bears Brunt of Slump, *Sunday Business Post*, Money & Markets, 3 April, 2.

35. **Dowdy, C.** (2003) Wealth, Taste and Cachet at Bargain Prices, *Financial Times*, 9 October, 17.

36. **Ross, E.B.** (1984) Making Money with Proactive Pricing, *Harvard Business Review*, Nov/Dec, 145–55.

37. **Welford, R.** and **K. Prescott** (1996) *European Business*, London: Pitman Publishing.

38. **Dixon, G.** (2005) GUS Falls as Appeal Against Argos Price-fixing Fine Rejected, *Scotland on Sunday*, 1 May, 10.

39. **Power, H.** (2005) Top Silks Fail to Help Argos and Littlewoods, *The Lawyer*, 10 January, 8.

40. **Sherwood, B.** (2003) Argos and Littlewoods Receive Record Fine for Price Fixing, *Financial Times*, 20 February, 1.

41. **Mitchell, A.** (2000) Why Car Trade is Stalling Over New Pricing Policy, *Marketing Week*, 17 February, 40–1.

Online **LearningCentre** with POWERWEB

When you have read this chapter log on to the Online Learning Centre for *Foundations of Marketing* at **www.mcgraw-hill.co.uk/textbooks/jobber** where you'll find multiple choice test questions, links and extra online study tools for marketing.

Turn the page for a Case Study on Ryanair

Case 8 Ryanair: the low fares airline

The year 2004 did not begin well for Ryanair. On 28 January, the airline issued its first profits warning and ended a run of 26 quarters of rising profits. On that day, when the markets opened, the company was worth €5 billion. By close of business, its value had shrunk to €3.6 billion, as its share price plunged from €6.75 to €4.86. Investors were dismayed by the airline's admission that it was facing 'an enormous and sudden reduction of 25 to 30 per cent in yields' (i.e. average fare levels) in the first quarter of 2004 (the last fiscal quarter of 2004).[1] This was on top of an earlier fall of 10 to 15 per cent in the first nine months.[2]

In April 2004, Chief Executive Michael O'Leary forecast a 'bloodbath', an 'awful' 2004/2005 winter for European airlines, amid continuing fare wars, with a shakeout among the many budget airlines. 'We will be helping to make it awful,' warned Mr O'Leary, as he announced an 800,000 free seats giveaway. The most difficult markets were predicted to be Germany and the UK regions where many new carriers, which were 'losing money on an heroic scale', had entered the arena.[3] O'Leary anticipated that the company's 2004 profits would decline by 10 per cent, while 2005 profits would increase by up to 20 per cent with a 5 per cent drop in yields. However, if yields were to fall by as much as 20 per cent, the 2005 outcome would be break-even, at best.

Yet, by 31 May 2005, on Ryanair's 20th birthday, the carrier was able to announce record results for the year ended 31 March 2005. Both passenger volumes and net profits grew year-on-year by 19 per cent to 27.6 million from 23.1 million, and to €268.9 from €226.6 million respectively. The all-important passenger yield figure (revenue per passenger) grew by 2 per cent, partially offsetting the 14 per cent yield decline in 2003/2004. Ancillary revenues were 40 per cent higher, rising faster than passenger volumes, which resulted in total revenues rising by 24 per cent to €1.337 billion. Operating costs rose 25 per cent, fractionally more than revenue growth, due principally to higher fuel costs. The 2005 results announcement was followed by a 3.4 per cent jump in the company's share price, to close at €6.46 on the day.

Ryanair's adjusted after-tax margin for the full year at 20 per cent compared very favourably to figures for Aer Lingus, British Airways, easyJet, Lufthansa, Southwest and Virgin, with margins of 8, 1, 3, minus 5, 7 and .1 per cent respectively (2003/2004 results). Despite the dire warnings and the temporary dip in fiscal 2004, Ryanair had arguably come through its crisis with flying colours. How did it manage this?

Overview of Ryanair

Ryanair, Europe's first budget airline, with 229 routes across 20 countries as of May 2005, is one of the world's most profitable, fastest-growing carriers. Founded in 1985 by the Ryan family as an alternative to the then state monopoly carrier Aer Lingus, Ryanair started out as a full-service airline. After accumulating severe financial losses, finally, in 1990/91, the company came up with a survival plan, spearheaded by Michael O'Leary and the Ryans, to transform itself into a low-fares no-frills carrier, based on the model pioneered by Southwest Airlines, the Texas-based operator. Ryanair, first floated on the Dublin Stock Exchange in 1997, is quoted on the Dublin and London Stock exchanges and on NASDAQ, where it was admitted to the NASDAQ-100 in 2002. In June 2005, Ryanair's market capitalization stood at €5 billion, the second highest carrier in the world, next to Southwest Airlines, and ahead of airlines with vastly greater turnover—but significantly lower profitability—such as Lufthansa with capitalization at €4.7 billion, British Airways at €4.3 billion and Air France/KLM at €3.5 billion. Its market capitalization was nearly four times that of easyJet, its UK-based budget airline rival. This was despite easyJet's higher turnover, similar passenger volumes and a slightly larger fleet.

Ryanair's fares strategy

Ryanair's core strategy entails offering the lowest fares, and the airline claims that it generally makes its lowest fares widely available by allocating a majority of seat inventory to its two lowest fare categories. In fact, was Ryanair, originally styled as the 'low-fares airline', actually becoming a 'no-fares airline'? Half of Ryanair's passengers will be flying for free by 2009, pledged Michael O'Leary in an interview with a German newspaper. He said that ticket prices would fall by an average 5 per cent a year over the next five years, as passenger numbers grew by five million annually. One analyst speculated that Ryanair's pronouncement on free seats 'is designed to put the wind up potential competitors in the hotly contested German market'.[4] Of course, a balance must be struck between low fares to attract customers and a sufficient yield to ensure viability.

An integral part of the low fares strategy is revenue enhancement through ancillary activities, increasingly used to subsidize airfares in order to improve Ryanair's margins to compensate for falls in fare yields. These include on-board sales, charter flights, travel reservations and insurance, car rentals, in-flight television advertising, and advertising outside its aircraft, whereby a corporate sponsor pays to paint an aircraft with its logo. Advertising on Ryanair's popular website also provides ancillary income. Despite the abolition of duty-free sales on intra-EU travel in 1999, Ryanair's revenue from duty-paid sales and ancillary services has continued to rise. In 2005, ancillary revenues comprised 18.3 per cent of total operating revenue, up from 16.1 per cent the year before, and the ambition is to grow at twice the rate of increase in its passenger traffic. The company has outlined plans to continue raising ancillary revenues through further penetration of existing products and the introduction of new ones, especially on-board entertainment and gaming products/services. Ryanair is also considering entering the highly competitive mobile phone market and has been in talks with various UK operators with a view to forming a joint venture.

Its low fares policy notwithstanding, Ryanair was able to realize a 2 per cent growth in yields in fiscal 2005. This is attributable to a number of favourable factors in the competitive landscape. Underlying passenger growth volumes returned in the industry as a whole, reducing the intensity of competition. Mainstream European operators like British Airways, Lufthansa and Air France/KLM were increasingly abandoning the short-haul sector, preferring to concentrate their growth on more lucrative long-haul routes. Moreover, these airlines reacted to the massive price rise in the cost of aviation fuel by introducing a fuel surcharge on their fares. For example, the surcharge levied by British Airways equated to 22 per cent of an average Ryanair fare.

Another favourable factor was the failure of the threat of new entrants to materialize. Michael O'Leary's prophecy of a 2004/2005 winter bloodbath in the European airline industry had been based on the forecast of many new entrants into the budget airlines sector, thus intensifying overcapacity. While new rivals continued to enter the fray, at any one time large numbers were also dying off. Autumn 2004 saw the demise of a number of budget airlines—for example, Volare, an Italian low-fare and charter operator, and V-Bird, a Dutch-owned carrier. Yet, new entrants were still launching. However, it was agreed that the industry could not sustain the some 47 low-fares airlines operating as of the end of November 2004. Michael O'Leary predicted that the anticipated shake-out would be accelerated by rising oil prices. 'Many of our competitor airlines who were losing money heroically when fuel was US$25 a barrel are doomed the longer it stays at US$50. We anticipate there will be further airline casualties as the perfect storm of declining fares and record high oil prices force loss-making carriers out of the industry.'[5]

Low fares require cost savings

To quote Michael O'Leary, 'Any fool can sell low air fares and lose money. The difficult bit is to sell the lowest air fares and make profits. If you don't make profits, you can't lower your air fares or reward your people or invest in new aircraft or take on the really big airlines like BA and Lufthansa.'

According to the company, its no-frills service allows it to prioritize features important to its clientele, such as frequent departures, advance reservations, baggage handling and consistent on-time services. Simultaneously, it eliminates non-essential extras that interfere with the reliable, low-cost delivery of its basic flights. The eliminated extras include advance seat assignments, in-flight meals, multi-class seating, access to a frequent-flyer programme, complimentary drinks and other amenities. In 1997, Ryanair dropped its cargo services, at an estimated annual cost of IR£400,000 in revenue. Without the need to load and unload cargo, the turnaround time of an aircraft was reduced from 30 to 25 minutes, according to the company. It claims that business travellers, attracted by frequency and punctuality, comprise 40 per cent of its passengers, despite often less conveniently located airports and the absence of pampering.

In conjunction with the elimination of non-essential extras, the organization of its operations enables the airline to minimize costs, based on five main sources.

1   *Fleet commonality* (Boeing 737s, like Southwest Airlines): this results in lower maintenance and staff training costs. In 2005, the company negotiated a new Boeing deal that takes down its per-seat costs for all post-January 2005 deliveries to rock-bottom levels. This deal not only establishes a platform for growth; a younger fleet also enables further cost reductions through lower fuel utilization and maintenance costs.

2   *Contracting out* of aircraft cleaning, ticketing, baggage handling and other services, other than at Dublin Airport; this is more economical and flexible, while it entails less aggravation in terms of employee relations.

3   *Airport charges and point-to-point route policy*: Ryanair uses secondary airports that are less congested, motivated to offer better deals and have fewer delays, resulting in increased punctuality and shorter turnaround times.

4   *Staff costs and productivity*: productivity-based pay schemes and non-unionized staff.

5   *Marketing costs*: Ryanair was the first airline to reduce and finally eliminate travel agents' fees. In January 2000, Ryanair launched its www.ryanair.com website. This has had the effect of saving money on staff costs, agents' commissions and computer reservation charges, while significantly contributing to growth. In 2005, Internet sales accounted for 97 per cent of all bookings. Ryanair supplements its advertising with the use of free publicity to highlight its position as the low fares champion, by attacking various constituencies that threaten its cost structure. These include EU regulators, airport authorities, politicians and trades unions. Its per passenger marketing costs of 60c are considered to be the lowest across the European airline sector.[6]

The year 2005 saw enormous volatility in the price of oil, and the global airline industry faced losses of US$6 billion. Ryanair, which had been unhedged with respect to oil prices since September 2004, announced on 1 June that it was hedging 75 per cent of its fuel needs for the October 2005 to March 2006 period, at a price of US$47 a barrel. At times, in previous weeks, the price had stood at US$53-plus per barrel. At the end of June, the price had hit US$60 and analysts were predicting it would rise to US$70-plus in the coming months.

Low costs contribute to a low break-even load factor of 62 per cent, so the airline can make money even if it fills fewer seats than other budget competitors with higher costs and higher break-even load factors. For example, easyJet's break-even load factor is 73 per cent, while that of Virgin Express is 83 per cent. Table C8.1 shows Ryanair's operating cost structure.

Customer service

The airline's claims of attention to customer service are encompassed in its Passenger Charter, which embraces a number of doctrines:

Table C8.1 Ryanair consolidated profit and loss accounts

		Year ended 31 March 2005 €000		Year ended 31 March 2004 €000
Operating revenues				
Scheduled revenues		1,128,116		924,566
Ancillary revenues		208,470		149,658
Total operating revenues—continuing				
operations	1,336,586		1,074,224	
Operating expenses				
Staff costs		140,997		123,624
Depreciation and amortization		98,703		98,130
Other operating expenses				
Fuel and oil		265,276		174,991
Maintenance, materials and repairs	37,934		43,420	
Marketing and distribution costs	19,622		16,141	
Aircraft rentals		33,471		11,541
Route charges		135,672		110,271
Airport and handling charges		178,384		147,221
Other		97,038		78,034
Total operating expenses	1,007,097		803,373	
Operating profit before exceptional costs, and goodwill		329,489		270,851
Profit for the year		266,741		206,611

- sell the lowest fares at all times on all routes and match competitors' special offers
- allow flight and name changes with requisite fee
- strive to deliver on-time performance
- provide information to passengers regarding commercial and operational conditions
- provide complaint response within seven days
- provide prompt refunds
- eliminate overbooking and involuntary denial of boarding
- publish monthly service statistics
- eliminate lost or delayed luggage
- Ryanair will not provide refreshments or meals or accommodation to passengers facing delays; any

passengers who wish to avail themselves of such services will be asked to pay for them directly to the service provider

- Ryanair facilitates wheelchair passengers travelling in their own wheelchairs; where passengers require a wheelchair, Ryanair directs those passengers to a third-party wheelchair supplier at the passenger's own expense; Ryanair is lobbying the handful of airports that do not provide a free wheelchair service to do so.

The company has confirmed that it would introduce a number of cost-cutting new features on its flights. For instance, the Ryanair fleet would heretofore be

Table C8.2 Punctuality statistics, departures and arrivals (September 2003)

Reporting airport/airline	Origin/ destination	% early to No. of 15 minutes		Average delay Planned flights	
		flights	late	(minutes)	unmatched
Birmingham—Ryanair	Dublin	180	88	6	0
Birmingham—Aer Lingus	Dublin	299	89	7	2
Birmingham—MyTravel	Dublin	4	50	20	0
Heathrow—Aer Lingus	Dublin	785	71	16	2
Heathrow—bmi British Midland	Dublin	432	71	14	0
Stansted—Ryanair	Dublin	727	79	11	1
Gatwick—British Airways	Dublin	180	82	9	0
Gatwick—Ryanair	Dublin	298	87	8	2
Heathrow—bmi British Midland	Brussels	354	73	13	1
Heathrow—British Airways	Brussels	452	84	9	2
Heathrow—bmi British Midland	Palermo	8	25	37	0
Heathrow—Alitalia	Milan (Linate)	174	63	15	0
Heathrow—British Airways	Milan (Linate)	178	80	10	0
Heathrow—bmi British Midland	Milan (Linate)	172	68	13	0
Heathrow—Alitalia	Milan (Malpensa)	298	48	24	0
Heathrow—British Airways	Milan (Malpensa)	180	80	10	0
Stansted—Ryanair	Bergamo	172	76	10	0
Stansted—easyJet	Bologna	60	70	14	0
Stansted—easyJet	Milan (Linate)	60	42	39	0
Stansted—easyJet	Rome (Ciampio)	120	76	12	0
Stansted—Ryanair	Rome (Ciampio)	356	79	9	0
Stansted—easyJet	Edinburgh	327	60	20	0
Stansted—easyJet	Nice	120	70	24	0
Stansted—Virgin Express	Nice	1	0	184	0
Stansted—Ryanair	Montpellier	59	76	14	2
Stansted—Ryanair	Prestwick	562	87	6	4
Stansted—easyJet	Glasgow	276	87	8	0
Glasgow—Aer Lingus	Dublin	176	80	9	4
Glasgow—bmi British Midland	Dublin	2	100	0	0

Table C8.3 *Which?* magazine holiday survey

Ratings	–	?	☺	☺	●
	Best				Worst
		1 = Sample size too small			

	Cabin Crew	Catering	Check-in Staff	Cleanliness of Interior	Entertainment	Legroom	Seat allocation	Seat Comfort	Toilets	Value for Money
Go	☺	☺	☺	☺	[1]	●	?	☺	☺	–
Virgin Atlantic	?	?	?	?	?	?	?	?	?	?
Buzz	☺	☺	☺	☺	[1]	●	☺	☺	☺	☺
easyJet	☺	☺	☺	☺	[1]	●	☺	☺	☺	–
bmiBaby	?	●	☺	☺	[1]	☺	☺	☺	☺	–
bmi British Midland	☺	☺	☺	☺	[1]	☺	☺	☺	☺	☺
Ryanair	☺	●	☺	●	[1]	●	●	●	●	–
British Airways	☺	☺	☺	☺	[1]	☺	☺	☺	☺	–
Flybe British European	☺	☺	?	☺	[1]	☺	?	?	☺	☺
Aer Lingus	☺	☺	☺	☺	[1]	☺	☺	☺	☺	☺
Lufthansa	☺	☺	☺	?	☺	☺	☺	☺	☺	☺
MyTravel Airways	☺	☺	☺	☺	●	●	☺	●	☺	☺

devoid of reclining seats, window blinds, headrests, seat pockets and other 'non-essentials'. Leather seats instead of cloth ones would allow faster turnaround times since leather is quicker and easier to clean. More controversially, Michael O'Leary hoped eventually to wean passengers off checked-in luggage, eliminating the need for baggage handling, suitcase holding areas and lost property. In 2004, Ryanair had one of the lowest baggage allowances of any major airline, at 15 kg a person, and charged up to €7 for every additional kilo, one of the highest surcharges in European aviation.

Successive Annual Reports cite on-time performance (defined as up to 15 minutes after scheduled time in UK Civil Aviation Authority statistics) and baggage handling as of key importance to customers. On punctuality, Ryanair claims to be the most punctual airline between Dublin and London. On baggage handling, Ryanair claims less than one bag lost per 1000 carried, better than even the best US airline, Alaska Airlines, with 3.48 bags per 1000 lost, and considerably better than its role model Southwest Airlines with 5.00 per 1000 lost.

Tables C8.2 and C8.3, and Figure C8.1 provide some independent comparisons of Ryanair with other airlines on punctuality and customer perceptions.

On punctuality, it must be borne in mind that one is not necessarily comparing like with like when contrasting figures for congested Heathrow with Stansted or Luton, even if all serve London. Also not counted in the statistics were cancelled flights. Ryanair has been known to 'consolidate' passengers by transferring them from their original flight to later or alternative routing without any notice, if passengers were unfortunate enough to have originally been booked on a low seat occupancy flight. Ryanair has announced that it would ignore European Commission proposals stipulating that passengers whose flight has been cancelled and who have to wait for an alternative flight should be provided with care while waiting, stating 'we do not, and never will offer refreshments'.[7]

Clouds on the horizon?

Despite its winning performance in its 2005 results, a number of issues faced Ryanair.

* While the competitive threat of new budget carriers had not emerged, some of the mainstream carriers were becoming quasi-budget airlines on short-haul routes. An important instance of this was Aer Lingus, the national state-owned airline of Ireland, operating domestic and international services, with a fleet of 30 aircraft. The events of 11 September 2001 were particularly traumatic for Aer Lingus, as the airline teetered on the verge of bankruptcy. In late 2001, the choice was to change, or to be taken over or liquidated. Led by a determined and focused chief executive and senior management team, the company set about cutting costs. By the end of 2002, Aer Lingus had turned a 2001 €125 million loss into a €33 million profit, and it improved still further in 2003 with a net profit of €69.2 million. In essence, Aer Lingus claimed that it had transformed itself into a low-fares airline, and that it matched Ryanair fares on most routes, or that it was only very slightly higher. The airline's chief operating officer said that 'Aer Lingus no longer

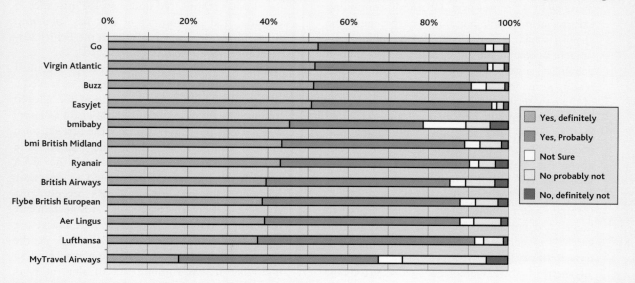

Figure C8.1 Would you recommend the airline to a friend?

offers a gold-plated service to customers, but offers a more practical and appropriate service . . . it clearly differentiates itself from no-frills carriers. We fly to main airports and not 50 miles away. We assign seats for passengers, we beat low fares competitors on punctuality, even though we fly to more congested airports, and we always fulfil our commitment to customers—unlike no frills carriers.'[8] While Aer Lingus had been an early adopter, other mainstream airlines like British Airways and Air France/KLM were also converting short-haul intra-European routes to the value model offered by Aer Lingus.

Further sources of pressure came from the EU. A decision from the EU Commission in February 2004 ruled that Ryanair had been receiving illegal state subsidies for its base airport at publicly owned Charleroi Airport (styled 'Brussels South' by Ryanair). Of course, it was not only the Charleroi decision but also the precedent it could set that was of concern. Other deals with public airports would come under scrutiny, although the vast majority of the airline's slots were at private airports. Also, it was estimated that Ryanair would have to repay between €2.5 million and €7 million to Charleroi's regional government. Ryanair appealed the decision, but also threatened to initiate state aid cases and complaints against every other airline flying into any state airports offering concessions and discounts. Airport fees comprised 19 per cent of Ryanair's operating costs and were deemed to be an inherent part of the airline's low-cost model. Thus, Ryanair warned that there was no mid-cost alternative model. Nevertheless, two months after the Charleroi verdict, Ryanair confirmed that it had agreed a new deal there. It would keep flying all its 11 routes from Charleroi, continuing existing airport and handling charges until the airport, which accommodated 1.8 million passengers a year at the time, reached two million passengers a year. The EU Commission was not readily convinced and initiated an investigation of the new settlement.

On another regulatory matter, the EU had devised fresh rules to cover overbooking that results in boarding denials to passengers by airlines. Air travellers bumped off overbooked flights by EU airlines would receive automatic compensation of between €250 and €600. Compensation might also be claimed when flights are cancelled for reasons that are the carrier's responsibility, provided the passengers have not been given two weeks' notice or offered alternative flights. Ryanair declared that the new rules would not impact its operations, as it did not overbook its flights, and had the fewest number of cancellations and the best punctuality record in Europe. It suggested that, if the EU is serious, it should just outlaw the practice of overbooking entirely.

A few days prior to the EU decision on Charleroi, on 30 January 2004, at the Central London County Court, a disabled man won a landmark case against Ryanair after it charged him £18 (€25) for a wheelchair he needed at Stansted to get from the check-in desk to the aircraft. The passenger was awarded £1336 (€2400) in compensation from Ryanair, as the UK-based Disability Commission said it may launch a class action against the airline on behalf of 35 other passengers. Ryanair's immediate reaction was to levy 70c a flight on all customers using the affected airports. In December 2004, the decision against Ryanair was upheld on appeal, although it was somewhat mitigated when the Court of Appeal decided that Stansted Airport was also answerable and had to pay half of Ryanair's liability for damages, with interest. In response, Ryanair's lawyer suggested that the 50:50 split in liability was unclear and unexplained, and 'could well have been delivered by King Solomon'.[9]

Also in 2004, a disgruntled Ryanair passenger set up a website inviting complaints about the airline. Ryanair moved to have the website shut down in early 2005, on the grounds that it contained material that is 'untrue, unfounded, malicious and deeply damaging to the good name and trading reputation of Ryanair', and that the name and appearance of the site, which resembled that of Ryanair's home website, could be construed as 'abusive registration'.[10] However, the site has reappeared under an ISP provider in Canada, and its number of hits has increased since the incident was reported in the British satirical magazine *Private Eye*.

- On another front, Ryanair was in dispute against the British Airports Authority (BAA), as it filed a writ at the High Court in London for alleged 'monopoly abuse' at Stansted. Michael O'Leary warned that the action was only the first skirmish in what would become 'the mother and father of a war'.[11] The Chief Executive of the BAA announced that he did not intend to negotiate further reductions to Ryanair's deeply discounted deal on landing charges at Stansted, due to finish in March 2007. The average charge per passenger would rise from £3 to £5 at the airport, whose capacity utilization was now so high that it was running out of slots at peak times. Meanwhile, Michael O'Leary was scathing about 'grandiose plans' to build a second runway at Stansted at a cost of £4 billion, 'when the cost of a runway and even a second terminal should run to no more than £400 million.[12]

- As if these issues were not enough, a number of Dublin-based Ryanair pilots were planning to establish their own association, the Ryanair European Pilots Association with links to the British Airline Pilots Association (BALPA), the Irish Airline Pilots Association (IALPA) and the European Cockpit Association. In November 2004, these pilots, supported by IALPA, took a complaint about victimization against Ryanair to the Irish Labour Court. Ryanair could potentially face a compensation bill of €44 million if 170 victimization claims brought by its Dublin-based pilots were to be upheld. The company had outlined various consequences to pilots if they joined a trades union: possible redundancy when the existing 737-200 fleet was phased out, no share options or pay increases, no promotions and no payment for future recurrent training. The airline declared its determination to keep out trades unions and to take a case to the High Court to prove that legislation attempting to force companies to negotiate with unions was unconstitutional. A ruling favourable to the pilots in February 2005 by the Irish Labour Relations Commission, ordering that Ryanair had to attend a hearing dealing with the pilots' complaints, was dismissed by Michael O'Leary: 'It is no surprise that the brothers have found in favour of the brothers. We will fight them on the beaches, in the fields, and in the valleys,' he said.[13] Meanwhile, the airline is also fighting a number of legal challenges, including proceedings against IALPA, accusing it of conducting an organized campaign of harassment and intimidation of Ryanair pilots through a website, warning them off flying the airline's new aircraft. Indeed, the carrier claims that specific threats issued on the website are being investigated by the Irish police.
- In April 2005, Ryanair abandoned an experiment in paid-for in-flight entertainment, after passengers were reluctant to rent the consoles at the £5 required to receive the service. Apparently, market research discovered passengers are unwilling to invest on such short flights, with the ideal being six-hour flights to longer-haul holiday destinations. When the experiment was launched in November 2004, Michael O'Leary hailed the move as 'the next revolution of the low-fares industry ... we expect to make enormous sums of money'.[14]

Questions

1. How does Ryanair's pricing strategy account for its successful performance to date? Would you suggest any changes to Ryanair's pricing approach? Why/why not?
2. Is the 'no-fares' strategy a useful approach for Ryanair in the short term? In the long term?
3. Do the issues facing Ryanair threaten its low-fares model?

References

This case was written by Dr Eleanor O'Higgins, University College, Dublin as a basis for class discussion.

1. **Done, K.** (2004) Ryanair's dream comes to an end, *Financial Times*, 29 January.
2. Ryanair's year-end is 31 March.
3. **Done, K.** (2004) O'Leary forecasts an 'awful' winter for European airlines, *Financial Times*, 21 April.
4. **McCaffrey, U.** (2003) Ryanair says 50% of seats will be free by 2009, *Irish Times*, 19 August.
5. **Done, K.** and **A. Michaels** (2004) Sharks smell a short-haul shake-up, *Financial Times*, November 24, 30.
6. Goodbody Stockbrokers Report, April 2005.
7. *Irish Times*, 10 January 2002.
8. **Creaton, S.** (2003) Aer Lingus's new model airline takes off, *Irish Times*, 8 August.
9. **Tait, N.** (2004) Disabled man wins wheelchair charging appeal, *Financial Times*, December 22, 4.
10. **Frawley, M.** (2005) Ryanair moves to gag complaining customers, *Sunday Tribune*, January 30, 8.
11. **Done, K.** (2004) O'Leary locks horns with BAA in fight to end, *Financial Times*, July 23, 24.
12. **Done, K.** (2005) O'Leary attacks BAA over Stansted plans, *Financial Times*, 1 June.
13. **Creaton, S.** (2005) LRC to hear Ryanair pilots' case, *Irish Times*, 5 February.
14. **Done, K.** (2005) Ryanair drops paid-for service, *Financial Times*.

CHAPTER 9

INTEGRATED MARKETING COMMUNICATIONS 1: MASS COMMUNICATIONS TECHNIQUES

Learning Objectives

By the end of this chapter you will understand:

1 the concept of integrated marketing communications
2 the key characteristics of the seven major promotional tools
3 how to develop an integrated communications campaign—target audience analysis, objective setting, budgeting, message and media decisions, and campaign evaluation
4 the nature and importance of advertising in the promotional mix
5 the role of sales promotion, public relations/publicity and sponsorship in the promotional mix.

Adidas Advertising Strategy

Sportswear is an intensely competitive business with several leading brands, such as Nike, Adidas, Reebok and Puma, battling it out for the hearts, minds and wallets of the consumer. These brands spent millions each year promoting themselves around the world. A wide variety of techniques are employed, with advertising and sponsorship being the most popular. Ever since Nike's famous relationship with US basketball star, Michael Jordan, the leading sportswear companies seek to outdo each other in signing up the latest sporting sensation to endorse their products. For example, a basketball endorsement is critical to building sales in the US athletic shoe market, which is the largest in the world. That's why Nike was particularly pleased to sign LeBron James in a US$90 million deal when it looked as though only Adidas and Reebok were in the running for his signature. Outside the USA, Adidas has been more successful by capturing both David Beckham and Jonny Wilkinson, leading players in soccer and rugby respectively, to endorse its products.

It is also commonplace for sports stars to then appear in the company's advertising campaigns, as Beckham and Wilkinson did for Adidas in the run-up to the Rugby World Cup 2003 or as a number of soccer stars such as Roberto Carlos and Edgar Davids did for Nike during the soccer World Cup of 2002. But during the Athens Olympics in 2004, Adidas went a step further with its 'impossible is nothing' campaign. In it, Adidas pitted the stars of today against the stars of yesteryear as a creative expression of its long athletics tradition. Adidas first came to fame at the 1936 games in Germany when Jesse Owens won four gold medals with shoes made by the company's founder Adi Dassler. In an advertisement labelled 'Jesse', old and new film footage is merged to show Owens running against current sprint champion Kim Collins, who wins and breaks the 10-second barrier for the 100 metres. This positioning is taken further by the fact that when Collins competes in current events, he wears a retro Adidas outfit.

Other creative treatments featured Muhammad Ali in the ring against his daughter Laila, the famous Romanian gymnast Nadia Comaneci taking on the young Russian Nastia Liukin as they aim to score a perfect 10, and the leading Ethiopian distance runner Haile Gebrselassie running against eight other Hailes. The campaign was varied around the world, with its Australian version, for example, featuring two of that country's leading athletes, swimmer Ian Thorpe and sprinter Jana Pittman.

The focus on athletics is a risky strategy for Adidas given the controversies surrounding the use of drugs in the sport by many of its leading stars. However, it can also be argued that the Adidas campaign harks back to a time when the sport was honest and pure, and not tarnished by big money and drugs. The campaign opened up additional public relations opportunities through the 'Vertical Sprint'. In this event, which was held in Hong Kong and Osaka, competitors had to 'sprint' 100 metres by hauling themselves up the sides of buildings on which an eight-lane tartan track had been laid. The popularity of this competition may well see it becoming an extreme sport.[1]

As the above example shows, promoting products and services is a key marketing activity but, unfortunately, some people think that promotion is all there is to marketing. Readers of this book will by now, however, recognize that there is much more to marketing than just promotion. Promotional activities can be broad—that is, aimed at the market as a whole. These are known as mass communication techniques and will be the focus of this chapter. However, recent years have seen a significant increase in promotion that is targeted at individuals. This is known as direct communication and we will examine these developments in the next chapter. The overall range of techniques available to the marketer is usually known as the 'promotional mix' and comprises seven main elements.

1   *Advertising*: any paid form of non-personal communication of ideas or products in the prime media (television, press, posters, cinema and radio).
2   *Sales promotion*: incentives to consumers or the trade that are designed to stimulate purchase.
3   *Publicity*: the communication of a product or business by placing information about it in the media without paying for the time or space directly.
4   *Sponsorship*: the association of the company or its products with an individual, event or organization.
5   *Direct marketing*: the distribution of products, information and promotional benefits to target consumers through interactive communication in a way that allows response to be measured.
6   *Internet marketing*: the distribution of products, information and promotional benefits to consumers and businesses through Internet technologies.
7   *Personal selling*: oral communication with prospective purchasers with the intention of making a sale.

In addition to these key promotional tools, the marketer can also use other techniques, such as exhibitions and product placement in movies or TV shows, which have been growing in popularity in recent years. Before proceeding any further, however, it is important to stress that promotional mix decisions should not be made in isolation. As we saw with pricing, all aspects of the marketing mix need to be blended together carefully. The promotional mix used must be aligned with the decisions made with regard to product, pricing and distribution, in order to communicate benefits to a target market.

Integrated marketing communications (IMC)

Given the variety of techniques available to marketers, a key marketing decision is the choice of the promotional blend needed to communicate to the **target audience**. Each of the seven major promotional tools has its own strengths and limitations; these are summarized in Table 9.1. Marketers will carefully weigh these factors against promotional objectives to decide the amount of resources they should channel into each tool. For example in 2002, the consumer foods giant Unilever, spent €7.3 billion on marketing, with just over half of this, €4 billion, being spent on advertising.[2]

Usually, the following five considerations will have a major impact on the choice of the promotional mix.

1   *Resource availability and the cost of promotional tools*: to conduct a national advertising campaign may require several million pounds. If resources are not available, cheaper tools such as sales promotions or publicity may have to be used.
2   *Market size and concentration*: if a market is small and concentrated then personal selling may be feasible, but for mass markets that are geographically dispersed, selling to the ultimate customer would not be cost-effective. In such circumstances advertising or direct marketing may be the correct choice.
3   *Customer information needs*: if a complex technical argument is required, personal selling may be preferred. If all that is required is the appropriate brand image, advertising may be more sensible.
4   *Product characteristics*: because of the above arguments, industrial goods companies tend to spend more on personal selling than advertising, whereas consumer goods companies tend to do the reverse.
5   *Push versus pull strategies*: a **distribution push** strategy involves an attempt to sell into channel intermediaries (e.g. retailers) and is dependent on personal selling and trade promotions. A **consumer pull** strategy bypasses intermediaries to communicate to consumers directly. The resultant consumer demand persuades intermediaries to stock the product. Advertising and consumer promotions are more likely to be used.

Table 9.1 Key characteristics of seven key promotional mix tools

Advertising
- Good for awareness building because it can reach a wide audience quickly
- Repetition means that a brand positioning concept can be effectively communicated; TV is particularly strong
- Can be used to aid the sales effort: legitimize a company and its products
- Impersonal: lacks flexibility and questions cannot be answered
- Limited capability to close the sale

Personal selling
- Interactive: questions can be answered and objectives overcome
- Adaptable: presentations can be changed depending on customer needs
- Complex arguments can be developed
- Relationships can be built because of its personal nature
- Provides the opportunity to close the sale
- Sales calls are costly

Direct marketing
- Individual targeting of consumers most likely to respond to an appeal
- Communication can be personalized
- Short-term effectiveness can easily be measured
- A continuous relationship through periodic contact can be built
- Activities are less visible to competitors
- Response rates are often low
- Poorly targeted direct marketing activities cause consumer annoyance

Internet promotion
- Global reach at relatively low cost
- The number of site visits can be measured
- A dialogue between companies, and their customers and suppliers can be established
- Catalogues and prices can be changed quickly and cheaply
- Convenient form of searching for and buying products
- Avoids the necessity of negotiating and arguing with salespeople

Sales promotion
- Incentives provide a quick boost to sales
- Effects may be only short term
- Excessive use of some incentives (e.g. money off) may worsen brand image

Publicity
- Highly credible as message comes from a third party
- Higher readership than advertisements in trade and technical publications
- Lose control: a press release may or may not be used and its content distorted

Sponsorship
- Very useful for brand building and generating publicity
- Provides an opportunity to entertain business partners
- Can be used to demonstrate the company's goodwill to its local community or society in general
- Becoming increasingly popular due to the fragmentation of traditional media

As the range of promotional techniques expands, there is an increasing need to co-ordinate the messages and their execution. This problem is often exacerbated by the fact that, for example, advertising is controlled by the advertising department, whereas personal selling strategies are controlled by the sales department, leading to a lack of co-ordination. This has led to the adoption of **integrated marketing communications** by an increasing number of companies. Integrated marketing communications is the system by which companies co-ordinate their marketing communications tools to deliver a clear, consistent, credible and competitive message about the organization and its products. For example, it means that website visuals are consistent with the images portrayed in **advertising** and that the messages conveyed in a direct marketing campaign are in line with those developed by the public relations department.

The application of this concept of integrated marketing communications can lead to improved consistency and clearer positioning of companies and their brands in the minds of consumers. One company that benefited from this approach was American Express, which found that the messages, images and styles of presentation between its advertising and direct marketing vehicles were inconsistent. Using an integrated marketing communications approach, the team worked to produce the consistency required to achieve a clear position among its target audience.

A simple model of the communication process is shown in Figure 9.1. The source (or communicator) encodes a message by translating the idea to be communicated into a symbol consisting of words or pictures, such as an advertisement. The message is transmitted through media, such as television or posters, which are selected for their ability to reach the desired target audience in the desired way. 'Noise'—distractions and distortions during the communication process—may prevent transmission to some of the target audience. The vast amount of promotional messages a consumer receives daily makes it a challenge for marketers to cut through this noise. When a receiver sees or hears the message it is decoded. This is the process by which the receiver interprets the symbols transmitted by the source. Communicators need to understand their targets before encoding messages so that they are credible. Otherwise the response may be disbelief and rejection. In a **personal selling** situation, feedback from buyer to salesperson may be immediate as when objections are raised or a sale is concluded. For other types of promotion, such as advertising

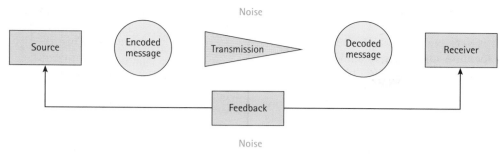

Noise

Figure 9.1 The communication process

and sales promotion, feedback may rely on marketing research to estimate reactions to commercials, and increases in sales due to incentives.

Stages in developing an integrated communications campaign

For many small and medium-sized firms, marketing communications planning involves little more than assessing how much the firm can afford to spend, allocating it across some media and, in due course, looking at whether sales levels have increased or not. It is clear that to avoid wasting valuable organizational resources, marketing communications should be planned and evaluated carefully. The various stages involved in doing this are outlined in Figure 9.2.

The process begins by looking at the firm's overall marketing strategy, its positioning strategy and its intended target audience. What is the firm trying to achieve in the marketplace and what role can marketing communications play? If, for example, the firm is trying to reposition a brand then advertising is likely to play an important role in this, but it must be integrated with the other marketing mix elements. Objectives need to be set for the IMC campaign and they should be quantifiable. For example, the objective is to increase sales by a given amount or to increase awareness among the youth market by a given percentage. Only after these stages are complete should the company begin thinking about what it is going to say (the message decisions) and where and how it is going to say it (the promotional mix decisions). These are complex decisions, which are discussed in detail in this and the next chapter. A budget for the campaign needs to be agreed, usually at board level in the company. Then after the campaign has been run, it is imperative that it is fully evaluated to assess its effectiveness. We will now examine some of the key mass communications techniques in more detail.

Exhibit 9.1 The target audience of this Eurostar advertisement is its Premium and Business-First customers

Advertising

Advertising is very big business. In 2001, over £17 billion was spent on advertising in the UK. There has long been considerable debate about how advertising works. The consensus is that there can be no single all-embracing theory that explains how all advertising works because it has varied tasks. For example, advertising that attempts to make an instant sale by incorporating a return coupon that can be used to order a product is very different from corporate image advertising that is designed to reinforce attitudes. One view of advertising sees it as being powerful enough to encourage consumers to buy by moving them through the stages of awareness, interest, desire and action (known by the acronym AIDA). An alternative approach—the awareness, trial, reinforcement (ATR) model—sees a key role of advertising as being to defend brands, by reinforcing beliefs so that existing customers may be retained. Advertising is likely to have different roles depending on the nature of the product and the degree of involvement of the customer.

Developing advertising strategy

Each of the steps identified in Figure 9.2 is appropriate irrespective of whether the firm is conducting an advertising campaign, a **direct marketing** or **sales promotion** campaign, all that changes is the detail involved. Here we examine some specific advertising issues.

Defining advertising objectives

Although, ultimately, advertising is a means of stimulating sales and increasing profits, a clear understanding of its communication objectives is of more operational value. Advertising can have a number of communications objectives. First, it can be used to create awareness of a brand or a solution to a company's problem. Awareness creation is critical when a new product is being launched or when the firm is entering a new market. Second, advertising can be used to stimulate trial, such as car advertising encouraging motorists to take a test drive. Third, and as we saw in Chapter 5, advertising is used to help position products in the minds of consumers, such as BMW's repeated use of the slogan 'The Ultimate Driving Machine' or Ronseal's 'Does Exactly What it Says on the Tin'. Other objectives of advertising include the correction of misconceptions about a product or service, reminding customers of

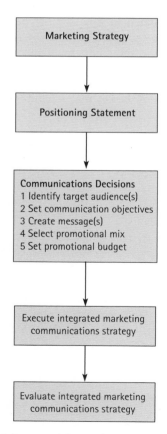

Figure 9.2 A framework for implementing integrated marketing conditions

Exhibit 9.2 The objective of this Orange advertisement is to generate customer trial

sales or special offers, and providing support for the company's salesforce.

Setting the advertising budget

The amount that is spent on advertising governs the achievement of communication objectives. There are four methods of setting advertising budgets. A simple method is the 'percentage of sales' method, whereby the amount allocated to advertising is based on current or expected revenue. However, this method is weak because it encourages a decline in advertising expenditure when sales decline, a move that may encourage a further downward spiral of sales. Furthermore, it ignores market opportunities, which may suggest the need to spend more (not less) on advertising.

Alternatively, companies may set their advertising budgets based upon matching competitors' expenditures, or using a similar percentage of sales figure as their major competitor. Again this method is weak because it assumes that the competition has arrived at the optimum level of expenditure, and ignores market opportunities and communication objectives. Sometimes firms make a decision on the basis of what they think they can afford. While affordability needs to be taken into account when considering any corporate expenditure, its use as the sole criterion for budget setting neglects the communication objectives that are relevant for a company's products, and the market opportunities that may exist, to grow sales and profits.

The most effective method of setting advertising budgets is the 'objective and task' method. This has the virtue of being logical since the advertising budget depends upon communication objectives and the costs of the tasks required to achieve them. It forces management to think about objectives, media exposure levels and the resulting costs. In practice, the advertising budgeting decision is a highly political process.[3] Finance may argue for monetary caution, whereas marketing personnel, who view advertising as a method of long-term brand building, are more likely to support higher advertising spend. During times of economic slowdown, advertising budgets are among the first to be cut, though this can be the time when advertising expenditure is most effective.

Message decisions

An **advertising message** translates a company's basic selling proposition or **advertising platform** into words, symbols and illustrations that are attractive and meaningful to the target audience. In the 1980s, IBM realized that many customers bought its

Exhibit 9.3 This Hovis advertisement combines humour with a slightly risqué visual to get attention

computers because of the reassurance they felt when dealing with a well-known supplier. The company used this knowledge to develop an advertising campaign based on the advertising platform of reassurance/low risk. This platform was translated into the advertising message 'No one ever got the sack for buying IBM'.

Most of those who look at a press advertisement read the headline but not the body copy. Because of this, some advertisers suggest that the company or brand name should appear in the headline otherwise the reader may not know the source of the advertisement. For example, the headlines 'Good food costs less at Sainsbury's' and 'United colors of Benetton' score highly because in one phrase or sentence they link a customer benefit or attribute with the name of the company. Even if no more copy is read, the advertiser has got one message across by means of a strong headline.

Messages broadcast via television also need to be built on a strong advertising platform (see Marketing in Action 9.1). Because TV commercials are usually of a duration of 30 seconds or less, most communicate only one major selling appeal—sometimes called the 'single-minded proposition'—which is the single most motivating and differentiating thing that can be said about the brand.[4] A variety of creative treatments can be used from lifestyle, to humour to shock advertising. Cosmetic brands like Estée Lauder have traditionally favoured the lifestyle approach to advertising though many have now moved to using top models and celebrities in their advertising. Until recently sex was used very frequently as a shock or attention-getting tactic in advertising, though recent research suggests that its ability to do so is waning.[5]

Television advertising is often used to build a brand personality. The brand personality is the message the advertisement seeks to convey. Lannon suggests that people use brand personalities in different ways,[6] such as acting as a form of self-expression, reassurance, a communicator of the brand's function and an indicator of trustworthiness. The value of the brand

Marketing in Action: 'Fun, anyone?': PlayStation 2

The games console business has seen more than its share of successes and failures over the years. The pioneer in the business, Atari, is now nowhere to be seen. Sega, one of the early industry leaders, tried to keep its position in the industry with the launch of the Sega Dreamcast in 1999. A huge marketing budget was set aside for the launch, including sponsorship of the Arsenal football team, but the product flopped dramatically. And with the battle for industry leadership now being fought out between giants like Sony, Microsoft and Nintendo, promotion decisions are critical to maintaining popularity in this rapidly changing market.

With the launch of PlayStation 1 (PS1) in 1995, Sony's focus was on getting people to try the product out. This was done by showing people the delights of computer game play through advertising that adopted a high-quality film production style using the expertise of top Hollywood directors like David Lynch. The campaign was highly successful, with over 7 million units of the game sold in the UK alone, and when Microsoft launched its Xbox in 2002 it copied the PlayStation-type advertising.

However, with the launch of PlayStation 2 (PS2), Sony adopted a more subtle positioning strategy. The new emphasis was not on getting people to try the brand but rather to remove the obstacles that stop those not already into gaming from having a try. The intention was to show that gaming is not elitist but rather something that anyone can enjoy, hence the tag-line 'Fun, anyone?' The high-quality TV ads were replaced by a more back-to-basics style that featured rough animation and more irreverent content. For example, the UK ads poked fun at Britain's inability to succeed at sporting events. In 'Restaurant', a man holds a pizza aloft as though it was some kind of trophy, while in 'Runner' a man is seen breaking through a police cordon on a street as though he was racing through the finish line. In 'Supermarket' a man celebrates his 'win' at the checkout by spraying a bottle everywhere. The headline on all the ads reads, 'Britain needs champions this summer. Fun, anyone?'

The TV and print campaign was backed by a broader brand identity effort called Freedom. This involved live events such as the four-day PlayStation Experience event held in London, which enabled 40,000 visitors to sample PlayStation games before they were released and enjoy a range of entertainment from sporting and music personalities associated with their games. Broadening the appeal of PlayStation is a clever strategy as the hardware on which games are played is likely to become more mainstream. For example, in 2005, Sony launched its first mobile gaming device, the PSP, which takes it into the portable gaming devices market currently dominated by Nintendo. Again, it sought to bring mobile gaming to the 18–34 age group through a more sophisticated and varied range of games than Nintendo, while its handheld can also double as a music and video player. Similarly, PlayStation 3, which is being launched in 2006, will be backwards-compatible with PS1 and PS2 games, will have wireless and Internet capability and can also be plugged into high-definition TVs to give panoramic views and extended game play.

Based on: Anonymous (2004);[7] Carter (2003);[8] Gardner (2004);[9] Waters (2004)[10]

personality to consumers will differ by product category and this will depend on for what purpose they use brand imagery. In 'self-expressive' product categories, such as perfumes, cigarettes, alcoholic drinks and clothing, brands act as 'badges' for making public an aspect of personality ('I choose this brand [e.g. Holsten Pils bottled lager] to say this about myself').

Media decision

Choice of media class (for example, television versus press) and media vehicle (e.g. a particular newspaper or magazine) are two key media decisions. Both of these will be examined next.

Table 9.2 lists the major media class options (the media mix). The media planner faces the choice of using television, press, cinema, posters, radio or a combination of media classes. Creative factors have a major bearing on the choice of media class. For example, if the objective is to position the brand as having a high-status, aspirational personality, television would be better than posters. However, if the communication objective is to remind the target audience of a brand's existence, a poster campaign may suffice.

Each medium possesses its own set of creative qualities and limitations. Television can be used to demonstrate the product in action, or to use colour and sound to build an atmosphere around the product, thus enhancing its image. Although TV was traditionally one of the most powerful advertising mediums, concerns about fragmentation of the TV audience have led many leading advertisers to move away from it (see e-Marketing 9.1). Furthermore, recent research has again questioned whether viewers actually watch ads when they are on, finding that consumers may spend as little as 23 per cent of the time the ads are on watching them, with the remainder spent talking, reading, surfing between channels or doing tasks such as cleaning, ironing or office work.[11] Despite these developments, television is still the largest advertising medium (see Figure 9.3).

Press advertising is useful for providing factual information and offers an opportunity for consumers to re-examine the advertisement at a later stage. Advertisers are increasingly using colour print ads to ensure that their brands stand out. Leaders in this field include the likes of Orange and easyJet, as well as retail chains like Marks & Spencer. Colour advertising in newspapers has risen by 53 per cent as against an 8 per cent growth in mono advertising.[12] Posters are a very good support medium, as their message has to be short and succinct because consumers such as motorists will normally only have time to glance at the content. Lavazza, the Italian coffee brand, is an exten-

Share of Medium, 2004 (%)

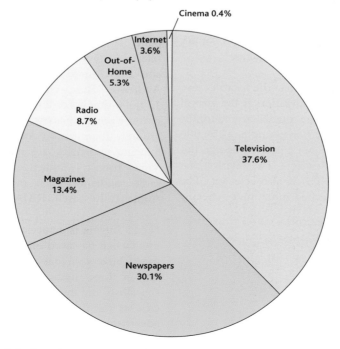

Figure 9.3 Global shares of display advertising revenue
Source: ZenithOptimedia

The principle behind our latest contact lenses

Specsavers' latest contact lenses are made from special materials that allow more oxygen through to your eye. That means you can wear them more comfortably, for longer. You don't even need to bother with cleaning solutions, if you choose Daily Disposable or Continuous

Wear lenses. So even if you have tried contact lenses before and found you couldn't get on with them, we're confident you will now. That's why we're offering you a free trial. Just call freephone 0800 0680 241 to find your nearest Specsavers Opticians.

Specsavers Opticians®

Exhibit 9.4 This advertisement for Specsavers is a classic print advertisement with a strong visual, headline, body copy and company logo

sive user of poster sites in airports and metropolitan areas where its glamorous, fashion magazine-style adverts are used to build awareness and image of the brand. Radio is limited to the use of sound and is therefore more likely to be useful in communicating factual information rather than building image, while cinema benefits from colour, movement and sound, as well as the presence of a captive audience.

A number of other factors also affect the **media class decision**. An important consideration is the size of the advertising budget. Some media are naturally more expensive than others. For example, £250,000 may be sufficient for a national poster campaign but woefully inadequate for television. The relative cost per opportunity to see (OTS) is also relevant. The target audience may be reached much more cheaply

Table 9.2 Media class options

1 Television
2 Press
National newspapers
Regional newspapers
Trade and technical
Magazines
3 Posters
4 Cinema
5 Radio

using one medium rather than another. However, the calculation of OTS differs according to media class, making comparisons difficult. For example, in the UK, an OTS for the press is defined as 'read or looked at any issue of the publication for at least two minutes', whereas for posters it is 'traffic past site'. A further consideration is competitive activity. A company may decide to compete in the same medium as a competitor or seek to dominate an alternative medium. For example, if a major competitor is using television, a firm may choose posters, where it could dominate, thus achieving a greater impact. Finally, for many consumer goods producers, the views of the retail trade (for example, supermarket buyers) may influence the choice of media class. Advertising expenditure is often used by salespeople to convince the retail trade to increase the shelf space allocated to existing brands, and to stock new brands. For example, if it is known that supermarkets favour television advertising in a certain product market, the selling impact on the trade of £1 million spent on television may be viewed as greater than the equivalent spend of 50:50 between television and the press.

The choice of a particular newspaper, magazine, television spot, poster site, etc., is called the **media vehicle decision**. Although creative considerations still play a part, cost per thousand calculations are the dominant influence. This requires readership and viewership figures. In the UK, readership figures are produced by the National Readership Survey, based on 28,000 interviews per year. Viewership is measured by the Broadcasters' Audience Research Board (BARB), which produces weekly reports based on a panel of 5000 households equipped with metered television sets (people meters). Traffic past poster sites is measured by Outdoor Site Classification and Audience Research (OSCAR), which classifies 130,000 sites according to visibility, competition (one or more posters per site), angle of vision, height above ground, illumination and weekly traffic past site. Cinema audiences are monitored by Cinema and Video Industry Audience Research (CAVIAR) and radio audiences are measured by Radio Joint Audience Research (RAJAR).

Media buying is a specialist area and a great deal of money can be saved on rate card prices by powerful media buyers. Media buying is accomplished through one of three methods: full service agencies, media specialists and media buying clubs. Full service agencies, as the name suggests, provide a full range of advertising services for their clients including media buying. Independent media specialists grew in the early 1990s as clients favoured their focused expertise and negotiating muscle. Media buying clubs were

e-Marketing: From the 'Real Thing' to mycokemusic.com

Coca-Cola is renowned for its television advertising, and it has been an extensive user of television globally as it built its brand over the decades. Some of its famous campaigns, such as 'I'd like to buy the world a Coke' in the 1970s and 'always Coca-Cola' in the 1990s, were television friendly and globally appealing. But mass marketing of this kind is getting more difficult as media like television become increasingly fragmented. Digital television has created hundreds of channels; technologies like digital video recorders make it easy to skip ads and the Internet in particular is competing for audience attention.

Thus even venerable companies like Coca-Cola have had to change their ways. In 2001, Coke spent US$268.1 million on television advertising but, by 2003, this was down to less than US$200 million. Coke has found that it has to take new routes to stay in touch with and remain relevant to, the youth market. In 2001, Coke made its advertisements available on 10 websites with a pop-up windows prompting surfers to click on the play button and view the full advertisement. In 2002, it developed a new programme called 'My Vision' to launch the Coca-Cola Youth Partnership initiative, which is designed to showcase the talent of young artists in the fields of the arts, achievements and athletics. Aimed primarily at high-school students, winners receive savings bonds from Coke and have their work displayed on local tours. This has evolved into a broader experiential marketing concept built around Coke's 'Red Lounges'—spaces where young people can hang out, watch videos, listen to music and, of course, drink Coke.

In 2004, Coke launched its own music site called mycokemusic.com, which is an online music seller with about 250,000 songs. The site has proved a hit, selling 50,000 tracks in its first week. On the back of this success, Coke launched a new global marketing initiative called iCoke in 2005, aimed at reconnecting with its market via a mix of digital music, mobile and branded entertainment. On-pack promotions are used to drive customers to the site, which also has draws for giveaways such as ringtones and downloads.

But Coca-Cola is far from finished with television advertising. It is still spending millions via the medium, though what has changed is that the ads are now produced locally for local markets rather than the global approach to advertising that had traditionally been favoured. This is illustrated by the 'Real Band' campaign in the UK, where a specially formed band is seen serenading football fans by telling them they are the best thing in football. The song is, of course, available at mycokemusic.com and has an associated ringtone.

Based on: Anonymous (2005);[13] Barnes (2004);[14] Buckley and Liu (2004);[15] Kumar (2004)[16]

---

formed by full service agencies joining forces to pool buying power. However, the current trend is back to full service agencies, but with one major difference: today the buying is done by separate profit-making subsidiaries. With very few exceptions, all the world's top media-buying operations are now owned by global advertising companies such as WPP and Publicis.

Executing the campaign

When an advertisement has been produced and the media selected, it is sent to the chosen media vehicle for publication or transmission. A key organizational issue is to ensure that the right advertisements reach the right media at the right time. Each media vehicle has its own deadlines after which publication or transmission may not be possible.

Evaluating advertising effectiveness

Measurement can take place before, during and after campaign execution. Pre-testing takes place before the campaign is run and is part of the creative process. In television advertising, rough advertisements are created and tested with target consumers. This is usually done with a focus group, which is shown perhaps three alternative commercials and the group members are asked to discuss their likes, dislikes and understanding of each one. Stills from the proposed commercial are shown on a television screen with a voice-over. This provides an inexpensive but realistic portrayal of what the commercial will be like if it is shot. The results provide important input from the target consumers themselves rather than relying solely on **advertising agency** views.

Such research is not without its critics, however. They suggest that the impact of a commercial that is repeated many times cannot be captured in a two hour group discussion. They point to the highly successful Heineken campaign—'Refreshes the parts other beers cannot reach'—which was rejected by target consumers in the pre-test.[17]

Post-testing can be used to assess a campaign's effectiveness once it has run. Sometimes formal post-testing is ignored through laziness, fear or lack of funds. However, checking how well an advertising campaign has performed can provide the information necessary to plan future campaigns. The top three measures used in post-test television advertising research are image/attitude change, actual sales and usage, though other financial measures such as cash flow, shareholder value and return on investment are increasingly being used. Image/attitude change is believed to be a sensitive measure, which is a good predictor of behavioural change. Those favouring the actual sales measure argue that, despite difficulties in establishing cause and effect, sales change is the ultimate objective of advertising and therefore the only meaningful measure. Testing recall of adverts is also popular. Despite the evidence suggesting that recall may not be a valid measure of advertising effectiveness, those favouring recall believe that because the advertising is seen and remembered it is effective.

Organizing for campaign development

There are four options open to an advertiser when organizing for campaign development. First, small companies may develop the advertising in co-operation with people from the media. For example, advertising copy may be written by someone from the company, but the artwork and final layout of the advertisement may be done by the newspaper or magazine. Second, the advertising function may be conducted in-house by creating an advertising department staffed with copy-writers, media buyers and production personnel. This form of organization locates total control of the advertising function within the company, but since media buying is on behalf of only one company, buying power is low. Cost-conscious companies such as Ryanair do most of their advertising work in-house. Third, because of the specialist skills that are required for developing an advertising campaign, many advertisers opt to work with an advertising agency. Larger agencies offer a full service, comprising creative, media planning and buying, planning and strategy development, market research and production. Because agencies work for many clients, they have a wide range of experience and can provide an objective outsider's view of what is required and how problems can be solved (see e-

Marketing 9.2). Four large global conglomerates—Omnicom, WPP Group, Interpublic and Publicis—with combined sales revenues of US$28 billion, dominate the industry. These corporations have grown in response to major multinational companies like Samsung and Nestlé, who want their global advertising handled by one firm.[18] A fourth alternative is to use in-house staff (or their full service agency) for some advertising functions, but to use specialist agencies for others. The attraction of the specialist stems, in part, from the large volume of business that each controls. This means that they have enormous buying power when negotiating media prices. Alternatively, an advertiser could employ the services of a 'creative hot-shop' to supplement its own or its full service agency's skills. Saatchi & Saatchi began life as a creative hot-shop before developing into a full service agency.

The traditional system of agency payment was by commission from the media owners. This was because advertising agencies were originally set up on behalf of media owners who wished to provide advertising services to enhance the likelihood of selling advertising space. Hence, it was natural that payment should be from them. Under the commission system, media owners traditionally offered a 15 per cent discount on the rate card (list) price to agencies. For example, a £1 million television advertising campaign would result in a charge to the agency of £1 million minus 15 per cent (£850,000). The agency invoiced the client at the full rate card price (£1 million). The agency commission therefore totalled £150,000.

Large advertisers have the power to demand some of this 15 per cent in the form of a rebate. For example, Unilever announced that it was allowing its advertising agencies 13 per cent commission.[19] Given its worldwide advertising expenditure of €4 billion it could probably have demanded a lower figure (possibly 11 per cent) but the company chose not to exercise all of its muscle since it believed that low commission rates ultimately made for poor-quality advertising. The second method of paying agencies is by fee. For smaller clients, commission alone may not be sufficient to cover agency costs. Also, some larger clients are advocating fees rather than commission, on the basis that this removes a possible source of agency bias towards media that pay commission rather than a medium like direct mail for which no commission is payable.

Payment by results is the third method of remuneration. This involves measuring the effectiveness of the advertising campaign using marketing research, and basing payment on how well communication objec-

e-Marketing: Beam.TV: changing the way ad agencies work

Many of the largest advertising agencies are global operators with hundreds of offices scattered across the globe (for example, Omnicom, the world's biggest agency, has 1500 subsidiaries). At the same time, they are likely to have thousands of tapes and storyboards for campaigns spread throughout these offices. The movement of copies of 30-second adverts or tapes in need of post-production work has traditionally been done via courier, which is both slow and expensive. Beam.TV has come up with a simple solution to this problem, which is to store production work in a digital format that then can be downloaded anywhere in the world via the Internet.

The company provides two main services. The first is an archiving and asset-management service for clients. Ad agencies can store all their tapes and artwork centrally on Beam.TV's servers rather than having them scattered throughout their offices. Beam.TV effectively becomes a central repository for all the agency's production work, which can then be accessed and shared more effectively. In this way, an agency's global creative director becomes much more informed about all the material that is potentially available within the organization. In addition, access to the material is instant from anywhere in the world. Customers can either view the material online through a password-protected web page or on television through a 'Beam Box', which downloads, stores and plays back the material. The Beam Box is a hard disk-based video recorder in the mould of other TV set-top boxes such as TiVo or Sky Plus. The benefit of this feature is that everyone involved in the production of an ad can view it at every stage, such as auditioning for actors or approving storyboards, even though they may not be in the same building or even in the same country. This contrasts with the traditional approach, which saw each additional UMatic tape of an ad that had to be made costing £100 while courier costs could be anything in the region of £20–£50 a time.

The system can also be used to play out ads to broadcast direct from an archive, safe in the knowledge that the correct ad will go out. Industry sources predict that Beam.TV will change the way the business operates. It has already signed up Saatchi & Saatchi and TBWA, and the company had revenues in the region of £2 million in 2003. One customer estimated that it saved £126,000 on one account alone through using the services provided by Beam.TV.

Based on: Burgoyne (2003);[20] Cane (2003);[21] Goldrich (2004)[22]

tives have been met. For example, payment might be based on how awareness levels have increased, brand image improved or intentions-to-buy risen. Another area where payment by results has been used is media buying. For example, if the normal cost per thousand to reach men in the age range 30–40 is £4.50, and the agency achieves a 10 per cent saving, this might be split 8 per cent to the client and 2 per cent to the agency.[23] Procter & Gamble uses the payment by results method to pay its advertising agencies, which include Saatchi & Saatchi, Leo Burnett, Grey and D'Arcy Masius Benton & Bowles. Remuneration is tied to global brand sales, so aligning their income more closely with the success (or otherwise) of their advertising.[24]

Ethical issues in advertising

Because it is so visible most people have a view on advertising. Certainly it has its critics as well as its supporters. Some of the key ethical issues include misleading advertising, advertising's influence on society's values and advertising to children.

Misleading advertising can take the form of exaggerated claims and concealed facts. For example, the Food and Drug Administration (FDA) in the USA has warned Pfizer about making misleading claims regarding the safety and efficacy of one of its drugs, Celebrex. A Celebrex print ad had claimed that the drug was more effective than competing brands for the treatment of osteoarthritis when there was no clinical evidence to support these claims. Nevertheless, most countries accept a certain amount of puffery, recognizing that consumers are intelligent and interpret the claims in such a way that they are not deceptive. In the UK, the advertising slogan 'Carlsberg—Probably the Best Lager in the World' is acceptable for this reason. Advertising can also deceive by omitting important facts from its message. Such concealed facts may give a misleading impression to the audience. Many industrialized countries have their own codes of practice that protect the consumer from deceptive advertising. For example, in the UK the Advertising Standards Authority (www.asa.org.uk) administers the British Code of Advertising Practice, which insists that advertising should be 'legal, decent, honest and truthful'. Shock advertising, such as that pursued in the past by companies like Benetton and FCUK, is often the subject of many complaints to the ASA.

Critics argue that advertising images have a profound effect on society. They claim that advertising promotes materialism and takes advantage of human frailties. Advertising is accused of stressing the importance of material possessions, such as the ownership of a car or the latest in consumer electronics. Critics argue that this promotes the wrong values in society. A related criticism is that advertising takes advantage of human frailties such as the need to belong or the desire for status. For example, a UK Government white paper has proposed a ban on junk food advertising at certain times in the same way as cigarette and alcohol advertising is restricted. Supporters of advertising counter that these ads do not prey on human frailties but basic psychological characteristics that would be served even if advertising did not exist.

One particularly controversial area is that of advertising to children. Critics argue that children are especially susceptible to persuasion and that they therefore need special protection from advertising. Others counter by claiming that the children of today are remarkably 'streetwise' and can look after themselves. They are also protected by parents who can, to some extent, counteract advertising influence. Many European countries have regulations that control advertising to children. For example, in Germany, the advertising of specific types of toy is banned, and in the UK alcohol advertising is controlled. The Broadcasting Commission of Ireland (BCI) has introduced a new code for children's advertising that bans 'Christmas-themed' advertising before 1 November each year, and also bans celebrities and sports stars from advertising food and soft drinks aimed at children. However, the difficulties involved in regulating advertising in this way are illustrated by the advertising industry's response to such restrictions, which was to suggest companies would simply move this kind of advertising to non-Irish TV channels such as Sky, UTV and MTV that also broadcast in Ireland.[25]

Sales promotion

As we have already seen, sales promotions are incentives to consumers or the trade that are designed to stimulate purchase. Examples include money off and free gifts (consumer promotions), and discounts and salesforce competitions (trade promotions). A vast amount of money is spent on sales promotion and many companies are engaging in joint promotions. Peattie and Peattie explain the growth in sales promotion as follows.[26]

- *Increased impulse purchasing*: the retail response to greater consumer impulse purchasing is to demand more sales promotions from manufacturers.
- *Sales promotions are becoming respectable*: through the use of promotions by market leaders and the increasing professionalism of the sales promotion agencies.
- *The rising cost of advertising and advertising clutter*: these factors erode advertising's cost-effectiveness.
- *Shortening time horizons*: the attraction of the fast sales boost of a sales promotion is raised by greater rivalry and shortening product life cycles.
- *Competitor activities*: in some markets, sales promotions are used so often that all competitors are forced to follow suit.

Exhibit 9.5 This Boots promotion is an example of a bonus pack

- *Measurability*: measuring the sales impact of sales promotions is easier than for advertising since its effect is more direct and, usually, short term. The growing use of electronic point-of-sale (EPOS) scanner information makes measurement easier.

If sales require a 'short, sharp shock', sales promotion is often used to achieve this. In this sense it may be regarded as a short-term tactical device. The long-term sales effect of the promotion could be positive, neutral or negative. If the promotion has attracted new buyers who find that they like the brand, repeat purchases from them may give rise to a positive long-term effect.[27] Alternatively, if the promotion (e.g. money off) has devalued the brand in the eyes of consumers, the effect may be negative.[28] Where the promotion has caused consumers to buy the brand only because of its incentive value with no effect on underlying preferences, the long-term effect may be neutral.[29] An international study of leading grocery brands has shown that the most likely long-term

effect of a price promotion for an existing brand is neutral. Such promotions tend to attract existing buyers of the brand during the promotional period rather than new buyers.[30]

Sales promotion strategy

As with advertising, a systematic approach should be taken to the management of sales promotions involving the specification of objectives for the promotion, decisions on which techniques are most suitable and an evaluation of the effectiveness of the promotion.

Sales promotions can have a number of objectives. The most usual goal is to boost sales over the short term. Short-term sales increases may be required for a number of reasons, including the need to reduce inventories or meet budgets prior to the end of the financial year, moving stocks of an old model prior to a replacement, and to increase stock-holding by consumers and distributors in advance of the launch of a

Marketing in Action: Building demand for Krispy Kreme doughnuts

Krispy Kreme was founded in North Carolina way back in 1937 and for many years was a cult brand and a must-have in the southern states of the USA. But in the past few years it has expanded rapidly. The company went public in 2000 and since then has doubled its number of stores around the world to 360 through an aggressive international expansion path, which has seen it move into the UK, Australia, Mexico and Asia, although it is still much smaller than its main rival, Dunkin' Donuts, which has some 3600 stores. In 2003 alone, Krispy Kreme added 99 new outlets and generated total sales of US$185 million. The company has achieved this impressive growth despite doing very little traditional advertising.

Instead it relies heavily on sales promotion and word-of-mouth advertising to build awareness of its products. The opening of a new store is designed to generate as much publicity as possible. In the months leading up to an opening, the company gives away 250,000 doughnuts to news media, charities and sporting events to encourage trial and secure media coverage. Long queues have accompanied many of the store openings around the world as people wait in line, often overnight, to be first to taste the hot, glazed doughnuts. Inside, Krispy Kreme stores are, in effect, mini-factories, where the doughnuts are cooked on the premises from a pre-prepared mix. Customers can then watch the machines carry the fried confections through a waterfall of snowy white glaze, in what is described as a 'doughnut theater'. Krispy Kreme has also been a strong supporter of local causes and when nine miners became trapped in a Pennsylvania mine in 2002, rescue workers were kept awake on a diet of doughnuts and coffee.

The company has also benefited greatly from enthusiastic endorsements from the likes of Homer Simpson, Madonna, US presidents and the *Sex and the City* girls. Recently, however, it has begun to look like the party is coming to an end. In May 2004, Krispy Kreme suffered its first quarterly profit fall since going public. Its stock price fell sharply, too, on investor fears that it had expanded too quickly and that negative commentary about the health effects of eating high-calorie doughnuts would impact on future sales and profits.

Based on: Foster (2004);[31] Hollins (2003);[32] Liu (2004);[33] Mesure (2004);[34] Rushe (2003)[35]

competitor's product. A highly successful method of sales promotion involves encouraging trial (see Marketing in Action 9.2). Home sampling and home couponing are particularly effective methods of inducing trial. Certain promotions, by their nature, encourage repeat purchasing of a brand over a period of time. Any promotion that requires the collection of packet tops or labels (e.g. free mail-ins and promotions such as bingo games) attempts to increase the frequency of repeat purchasing during the promotional period. Some promotions are designed to encourage customers to purchase larger pack sizes. Finally, trade promotions are usually designed to gain distribution and shelf space. Discounts, free gifts and joint promotions are methods used to encourage distributors to stock brands.

Selecting the type of sales promotion to use

There is a very wide variety of promotional techniques that a marketer can consider using (see Figure 9.4). Major consumer sales promotion types are money off, bonus packs, premiums, free samples, coupons, prize promotions and loyalty cards. A sizeable proportion of sales promotions are directed at the trade, including price discounts, free goods, competitions and allowances.

Consumer promotion techniques

Money-off promotions provide direct value to the customer and therefore an unambiguous incentive to purchase. They have a proven track record of stimulating short-term sales increases. However, price reductions can easily be matched by competitors and if used frequently can devalue brand image. **Bonus packs** give added value by giving consumers extra quantity at no additional cost and are often used in the drinks, confectionery and detergent markets. The promotion might be along the lines of 'Buy 10 and get 2 extra free'. Because the price is not lowered, this form of promotion runs less risk of devaluing the brand image. When two or more items are banded together the promotion is called a multibuy. These are frequently used to protect market share by encouraging consumers to stock up on a particular brand when two or more items of the same brand are banded together, such as a shampoo and conditioner. Multibuys can also generate range trial when, for example, a jar of coffee is banded with samples of other coffee varieties such as lattes and mochas. **Premiums** are any merchandise offered free or at low cost as an incentive to purchase a brand; they can come in three forms: free in- or on-pack gifts, free in-the-mail offers and self-liquidating offers, where consumers are asked to pay a sum of money to cover the costs of the merchandise. The main role of premiums is in encouraging bulk purchasing and maintaining share. For example, Sunday newspapers have been giving away free CDs to encourage switching and maintain market share.

Free samples of a brand may be delivered to the home or given out in a store and are used to encourage trial. For new brands or brand extensions this is an effective, if sometimes expensive, way of generating trial. Coupons can be delivered to the home, appear in magazines or newspapers, or appear

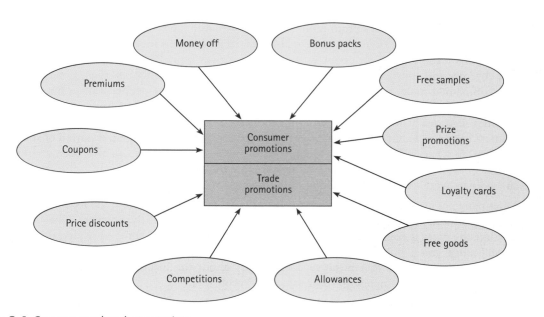

Figure 9.4 Consumer and trade promotions

on packs, and are used to encourage trial or repeat purchase. They are a popular form of sales promotion, although they are usually less effective in raising initial sales than money-off promotions because there is no immediate saving and the appeal is almost exclusively to existing consumers.[36] There are three main types of prize promotion: competitions, draws and games. These are often used to attract attention or stimulate interest in a brand. Competitions require participants to exercise a certain degree of skill and judgement and entry is usually dependent on purchase at least. Draws make no demand on skill and judgement, the result simply depends on chance.

Finally, a major development in retailing is the offering of loyalty cards to customers. Points are gained every time money is spent at an outlet, which can be used against purchases at the store in future. The intention is to attract customers back to the store but, as we shall see in the next chapter, loyalty cards are an excellent source of customer information, which can be used in direct marketing campaigns. Loyalty cards are very popular in the UK, with over 90 per cent of people holding at least one card and 78 per cent having two or more. Card schemes can be specific to one company such as the Tesco Clubcard (see Case 10.1 at the end of the next chapter) or a joint venture between several companies such as the Nectar card, which involves companies like Debenhams, Sainsbury's, BP, Barclaycard and Vodafone, and boasts over 11 million customers. Similarly, online retailers use schemes like MyPoints, which reward shoppers for reading e-mails, visiting sites and making purchases.

The role of loyalty cards in retaining customers has been the focus of much attention as it is known that keeping customers has a direct impact on profitability. A study conducted by PricewaterhouseCoopers showed that a 2 per cent increase in customer retention has the same profit impact as a 10 per cent reduction in overhead costs.[37] Customer retention programmes are aimed at maximizing a customer's lifetime value to the company. For example, airlines can identify their best customers (often business travellers) by analysis of their database and reward them for their loyalty. By collecting and analysing data the airlines identify and profile their frequent flyers, learn how best to develop a relationship with them, and attempt to acquire new customers with similar profiles.

Despite their growth, loyalty schemes have attracted their critics. Such schemes may simply raise the cost of doing business and, if competitors respond with me-too offerings, the final outcome may be no more than a minor tactical advantage.[38] Shell, for example, reportedly spent £20 million on hardware and software alone to launch its Smart Card, which allows drivers to collect points when purchasing petrol.[39] A second criticism is that the proliferation of loyalty schemes is teaching consumers promiscuity. Evidence from a MORI (www.mori.co.uk) poll found that 25 per cent of loyalty card holders are ready to switch to a rival scheme if it has better benefits.[40] Far from seeing a loyalty scheme as a reason to stay with a retailer, consumers may be using such schemes as criteria for switching.

The national laws governing sales promotions throughout Europe vary tremendously (see Table 9.3).

Trade promotion techniques

The trade may be offered (or may demand) discounts in return for purchase, which may be part of a joint promotion whereby the retailer agrees to devote extra shelf space, buy larger quantities, engage in a joint competition and/or allow in-store demonstrations. An alternative to a price discount is to offer more merchandise at the same price (free goods). For example, the 'baker's dozen' technique involves offering 13 items (or cases) for the price of 12. Manufacturers may use competitions, such as providing prizes for a distributor's salesforce, in return for achieving sales targets for their products. Finally, a manufacturer may offer an allowance (a sum of money) in return for retailers providing promotional facilities in store (display allowance). For example, allowances would be needed to persuade a supermarket to display cards on its shelves indicating that a brand was being sold at a special low price.

The pharmaceutical industry is one of the biggest users of trade promotion. For example, in 2004, pharmaceutical companies in the USA spent US$14.7 billion on marketing to healthcare professionals as against US$3.6 billion on direct-to-consumer advertising activities. Trade promotions involve gifts, samples and industry-sponsored training courses. It is a highly competitive business with roughly 102,000 pharmaceutical 'detailers' or salespeople all trying to meet with the top prescribers among America's 870,000 physicians.[41]

The final stage in a sales promotion campaign involves testing the promotion. As with advertising, both pre-testing and post-testing approaches are available. The major pre-testing techniques include **group discussions** (testing ideas on groups of potential targets), **hall tests** (bringing a sample of

Table 9.3 Guidelines on sales promotion regulations in Europe

	UK	Ireland	Spain	Germany	France	Denmark	Belgium	The Netherlands	Portugal	Italy	Greece	Luxembourg	Austria	Finland	Norway	Sweden	Switzerland	Russia	Hungary	Czech Republic
On-pack price reductions	Y	Y	Y	Y	Y	Y	Y	Y	Y	Y	Y	Y	Y	Y	Y	Y	Y	Y	Y	Y
Banded offers	Y	Y	Y	Y	Y	C	C	Y	Y	Y	Y	N	C	C	C	C	N	Y	Y	Y
In-pack premiums	Y	Y	Y	C	C	C	C	C	Y	Y	Y	N	C	Y	C	C	N	Y	Y	Y
Multiple-purchase offers	Y	Y	Y	C	Y	C	C	Y	Y	Y	Y	N	C	C	C	C	N	C	Y	Y
Extra product	Y	Y	Y	C	Y	Y	C	C	Y	Y	Y	Y	C	Y	Y	C	C	Y	Y	Y
Free product	Y	Y	Y	C	Y	Y	C	Y	Y	Y	Y	Y	Y	Y	Y	Y	Y	Y	Y	Y
Reusable/alternative use pack	Y	Y	Y	Y	Y	Y	Y	Y	Y	Y	Y	Y	C	Y	Y	Y	Y	Y	Y	Y
Free mail-ins	Y	Y	Y	N	Y	C	C	Y	Y	Y	Y	C	N	Y	C	N	N	Y	Y	Y
With-purchase premiums	Y	Y	Y	C	Y	C	C	C	Y	Y	Y	N	C	C	C	C	N	Y	Y	Y
Cross-product offers	Y	Y	Y	N	C	C	N	C	Y	Y	Y	N	C	C	C	C	N	Y	Y	Y
Collector devices	Y	Y	Y	N	C	C	C	C	Y	Y	Y	N	N	C	N	N	N	Y	Y	Y
Competitions	Y	Y	Y	C	C	C	C	C	Y	Y	Y	C	Y	C	Y	Y	Y	Y	Y	Y
Self-liquidating premiums	Y	Y	Y	Y	Y	Y	Y	C	Y	Y	Y	C	C	Y	Y	Y	N	Y	Y	Y
Free draws	Y	Y	Y	N	Y	N	N	N	N	Y	Y	N	N	Y	N	Y	N	Y	C	Y
Share-outs	C	Y	Y	N	C	N	N	N	N	Y	Y	N	N	N	N	N	N	Y	Y	Y
Sweepstake/lottery	C	C	C	C	C	N	C	C	C	C	C	C	C	C	C	N	N	Y	C	C
Money-off vouchers	Y	Y	Y	N	Y	C	Y	Y	Y	C	Y	C	C	Y	C	C	Y	Y	Y	C
Money off next purchase	Y	Y	Y	N	Y	N	Y	Y	Y	C	Y	N	N	C	N	N	N	Y	Y	Y
Cash backs	Y	Y	Y	C	Y	Y	Y	Y	Y	N	N	N	Y	C	C	C	N	Y	Y	Y
In-store demos	Y	Y	Y	Y	Y	Y	Y	Y	Y	Y	Y	Y	Y	Y	Y	Y	Y	Y	C	Y

Y = Permitted

N = Not permitted

C = May be permitted with certain conditions

Note: this guide should be used only as a first indication of promotional opportunities; local legal advice should be taken before implementing any activities

Source: IMP Europe, London (reproduced with permission)

customers to a room where alternative promotions are tested) and **experimentation** (where, for example, two groups of stores are selected and alternative promotions run in each). After the sales promotion has been implemented the effects must be monitored carefully. Care should be taken to check sales both during and after the promotion so that post-promotional sales dips can be taken into account (a lagged effect). In certain situations a sales fall can precede a promotion (a lead effect). If consumers believe a promotion to be imminent they may hold back purchases until it takes place. Alternatively, if a retail sales promotion of consumer durables (e.g. gas fires, refrigerators, televisions) is accompanied by higher commission rates for salespeople, they may delay sales until the promotional period.[42] If a lead effect is possible, sales prior to the promotion should also be monitored.

Ethical issues in sales promotion

Ethical concerns regarding sales promotion include the use of trade inducements and the malredemption of coupons. To encourage their salespeople to push the manufacturer's products, retailers sometimes accept inducements from manufacturers. These often take the form of bonus payments to salespeople. The result is that there is an incentive for salespeople, when talking to customers, to pay special attention to those product lines that are linked to such bonuses. Customers may, therefore, be subjected to pressure to buy products that do not best meet their needs.

The malredemption of coupons is the attempt by customers in supermarkets to redeem reduced-price coupons without buying the associated product. When faced with a large shopping trolley full of goods it is easy for supermarket checkout attendants to accept coupons without verification. The key to stopping this practice is thorough training of supermarket employees so that they always check coupons against goods purchased. In the future it is likely that coupons will be distributed via loyalty cards, thus reducing this risk.

Public relations and publicity

If it wishes to succeed, a company must be dependent on many groups. The marketing concept focuses on customers and distributors, but the needs and interests of other groups (such as employees, shareholders, the local community, the media, government and pressure groups) are also important (see Figure 9.5). **Public relations** is concerned with all of these groups, and public relations activities include **publicity**, corporate advertising, seminars, publications, lobbying and charitable donations. PR can accomplish many objectives:[43] it can foster prestige and reputation, which can help companies to sell products, attract and keep good employees, and promote favourable community and government relations; it can promote products by creating the desire to buy a product through unobtrusive material that people read or see in the press, or on radio and television; awareness and interest in products and companies can be generated; it can be used to deal with issues or opportunities, or to overcome misconceptions about a company that may have been generated by bad publicity; and it can have a key role to play in fostering goodwill among customers, employees, suppliers, distributors and the government (see Marketing in Action 9.3). For example, Vodafone used a carefully orchestrated public relations strategy in its legal battle with Eddie Jordan over the sponsorship of Jordan's Formula 1 team. Vodafone, which easily won the case, was concerned that it would be seen as a Goliath beating up Jordan's David. It hired a communications expert and at the end of each day of the trial, the media were given a summary of the trial plus a clear analysis of Vodafone's legal position.

A study by Kitchen and Proctor showed that public relations is a growth area in the UK.[44] The three major reasons for this were recognition by marketing teams of the power and value of public relations, increased advertising costs leading to an exploration of more cost effective communication routes, and improved understanding of the role of public relations.

Publicity is a major element of public relations. It can be defined as the communication about a product or organization by the placing of news about it in the media without paying for the time or space directly. The three key tasks of a publicity department are responding to requests for information from the media, supplying the media with information on important events in the organization and stimulating the media to carry the information and viewpoint of the organization.[49] Information dissemination may be through news releases, news conferences, interviews, feature articles, photocalls and public speaking (at conferences and seminars, for example). No matter which of these means is used to carry the information, publicity has three important characteristics.

1   *The message has high credibility*: the message has greater credibility than advertising because it appears to the reader to have been written inde-

Marketing in Action: Dyson: good and bad publicity

Dyson Appliances Ltd has had something of a rollercoaster ride in the British press. The company was founded by James Dyson in 1993 and at first it was revered as a template for British manufacturing. Dyson had revolutionized the vacuum cleaning business with his invention of the bagless cyclone vacuum cleaner—a 'high suction' machine that dispensed of the need for bags. The success of the innovation catapulted Dyson to market share leadership in the £530 million industry, which is served by large multinational players like Electrolux. James Dyson's personal profile also soared. He was acclaimed as a living example of the great British inventor and he became one of a select group of businesspeople picked by Tony Blair to be part of his innovation review group.

But, in 2002, Dyson announced that it was moving its production of vacuum cleaners from the small town of Malmesbury in Wiltshire to Malaysia with the loss of 800 jobs. While Dyson is far from alone in shifting manufacturing to lower-cost locations, what seemed to really cause problems was how the move was handled. Dyson justified the move as a way of keeping the company in good financial shape, but this sounded hollow to staff who knew they were working in a very profitable company. Others speculated that the reasons for the move related to specific local issues such as opposition to a planned expansion at the plant. So from being the great inventor, Dyson had, in the eyes of some, become the pursuer of cheap labour. This was exacerbated in 2003 when it was announced that all Dyson production in the UK, including that of its best-selling washing machines, was to move to Malaysia. Commenting on the move, a union official remarked that 'Dyson is no longer a UK product'.

This negative publicity was also damaging Dyson's position in the market. Its market share in vacuum cleaners in 2003 was 15 per cent in volume terms down from 20 per cent in 2002. Because of its premium pricing, this 15 per cent in volume translated into 38 per cent by value but that too was down from 44 per cent a year earlier. Furthermore, low-cost rivals such as Samsung and LG from South Korea, who sell products at less than 50 per cent of the price of the Dyson brand, began to make inroads in the market. And perhaps of most concern to the company was the finding of some research, which indicated that only 35 per cent of owners of a Dyson vacuum cleaner would buy another. However, on the positive side, the strengths of its product design have seen it grow steadily in the large US market where its share grew from 4.5 per cent in 2003 to over 20 per cent in 2005. The USA now accounts for over 40 per cent of Dyson turnover.

Similarly, the P&G soft drink Sunny Delight has had its ups and downs in the UK media. At first everything looked rosy when in August 1999, a headline in the *Sun* proclaimed that Sunny Delight was bigger than Coke as its sales reached £160 million. But as the story moved on, health lobby groups began to comment on the sugar content and additives contained in the drink, leading to headlines such as the *Daily Mail*'s 'Health row as sugary water sales reach £160m'. Sales plummeted and the brand is now worth an estimated £35.6 million.

Based on: Collins (20030);[45] Marsh (2003);[46] Moorish (2002);[47] Murphy (2003)[48]

pendently (by a media person) rather than by an advertiser. Because of this enhanced credibility it can be argued that it is more persuasive than a similar message used in an advertisement.

2 *No direct media costs*: since space or time in the media does not have to be bought there is no direct media cost. However, this is not to say that it is cost free. Someone has to write the

news release, take part in the interview or organize the news conference. This may be organized internally by a press officer or publicity department, or externally by a public relations agency.

3 *No control over publication*: unlike advertising, there is no guarantee that the news item will be published. This decision is taken out of the

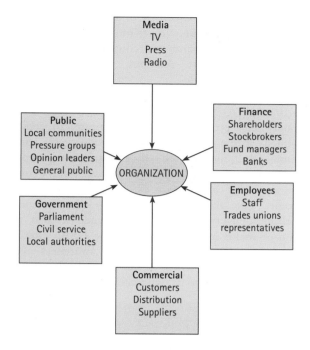

Figure 9.5 An organization and its publics

Ethical issues in PR

One of the ethical issues relating to public relations is the use of third-party endorsements to publicize a product, where the person gives a written, verbal or visual recommendation of the product. A well-known, well-respected person is usually chosen but, given that payment often accompanies the endorsement, the question arises as to its credibility. Supporters of endorsements argue that consumers know that endorsers are usually paid and are capable of making their own judgements regarding their credence.

Sponsorship

Sponsorship has been defined by Sleight as:[50]

> 'a business relationship between a provider of funds, resources or services and an individual, event or organisation which offers in return some rights and association that may be used for commercial advantage'.

control of the organization and into the hands of an editor. A key factor in this decision is whether the item is judged to be newsworthy. Newsworthy items include where a company does something first, such as a new product or research breakthrough, new employees or company expansions, sponsorships, etc. A list of potentially newsworthy topics is provided in Table 9.4. Equally there is no guarantee that the content of the news release will be published in the way that the news supplier had intended or that the publicity will occur when the company wants it to.

Potential sponsors have a wide range of entities and activities from which to choose, including sports, arts, community activities, teams, tournaments, individual personalities or events, competitions, fairs and shows. Sport sponsorship is by far the most popular sponsorship medium as it offers high visibility through extensive television coverage, the ability to attract a broad cross-section of the community and to service specific niches, and the capacity to break down cultural barriers. For example, the Olympics, the biggest global sporting event, attracted over US$1.4 billion in sponsorship for the 2004 Athens Games, which represented one-third of the revenue generated by the Games. Such is the scramble for sponsorship oppor-

Table 9.4 Potentially newsworthy topics

Being or doing something first	**Financial issues**
Marketing issues	Financial statements
New products	Acquisitions
Research breakthroughs: future new products	Sales/profit achievements
Large orders/contracts	
Sponsorships	**Personal issues**
Price changes	Training awards
Service changes	Winners of company contests
New logos	Promotions/new appointments
Export success	Success stories
	Visits by famous people
Production issues	Reports of interviews
Productivity achievements	
Employment changes	**General issues**
Capital investments	Conferences/seminars/exhibitions
	Anniversaries of significant events

tunities that even a soccer team's pre-season tour can be sponsored; this was the case with a tour of China by Spanish club Real Madrid, which was sponsored by local cigarette company Hong Ta Shan (see Marketing in Action 9.4).

Vodafone is very active in sports sponsorship, with a portfolio that includes Manchester United, the Australian rugby team and Ferrari. These links help to build the image of Vodafone as being a global force. For example, when Manchester United tours Asia with its stars, Vodafone laps up coverage in the region, and the Ferrari sponsorship gives it television coverage in over 200 countries. It has formed a sponsorship strategy team in Germany, which interacts in local teams in key markets. The aim is to ensure that all of its markets are exploiting sponsorship opportunities to the maximum extent.[53]

The five principal objectives of sponsorship are to gain publicity, create entertainment opportunities, foster favourable brand and company associations, improve community relations, and create promotional opportunities.

Gaining publicity

Sponsorship provides ample opportunity to create publicity in the news media. Worldwide events such as major golf, football and tennis tournaments supply the platform for global media coverage. Such **event sponsorship** can provide exposure to millions of people. For example DHL, the German-owned package delivery company, has signed a deal to sponsor major league baseball in the USA. This is part of a strategy by DHL to raise its awareness level in the US market where it has a small share and which is also home to its two major global rivals, UPS

Marketing in Action: From sponsor to event creator

Sponsorship has evolved dramatically from a time when all the sponsor did was provide some money and have its name displayed prominently at the event it was funding. As the sponsor's concern for how the event reflects on its branding and positioning grows, marketers are getting increasingly involved in the actual events themselves. Sometimes the involvement is subtle, sometimes not. For example, one of the most popular shows on Dutch late-night television is *6Pack*—an offbeat programme where the show's hosts get up to various pranks. One episode, for example, involved a presenter bluffing his way into the French Open tennis tournament so that he could meet his idol, John McEnroe.

The series is the outcome of a brainstorming session between the Dutch production company CCCP and the Dutch brewer Heineken. Having expected to get no more than 40,000 viewers, the show is regularly attracting audiences of over 100,000. However, Heineken maintains a low profile in the show, restricting itself to the credits and, if beer is to be consumed on air, it must be Heineken.

However, an emerging trend is one where sponsors eschew certain events in favour of creating new events themselves. For example, while Guinness was sponsoring the annual St Patrick's Day parade, its rival Stella Artois launched the Stella Screen Outdoor Tour in 1997. The tour shows films in appropriate locations such as *Braveheart* in Stirling Castle, while the Stella brand is the main refreshment available. These tours now sell 3 million barrels of beer to 12 million drinkers. Similarly, Reebok created the Reebok Sofa Games, a five-a-side tournament that toured Dublin, Brighton, Glasgow and Manchester. The games increased Reebok sales in partner stores by 10–15 per cent during the promotional period.

These initiatives build on the pioneering approaches of the likes of MTV and Red Bull. MTV's music awards show, which was launched in 1993, has become a successful brand franchise in its own right and MTV has extended this approach into other events such as the dance festival, the Isle of MTV. Red Bull has its own in-house event management team running competitions like the Red Bull Soap Box Races. Companies that create their own events feel that they represent better value than traditional forms of sponsorship, but many critics see it as yet another example of marketing's remorseless advance into all spheres of people's lives through its commercialization of leisure activities.

Based on: Bickerton (2003);[51] Lewis (2003)[52]

and FedEx.[54] Similarly, Red Bull's entry into Formula 1 motor racing through its sponsorship of the Jaguar team is seen as part of a strategy of broadening its market appeal. The publicity opportunities of sponsorship can provide major awareness shifts. For example, Canon's sponsorship of football in the UK raised awareness of the brand name from 40 per cent to 85 per cent among males. Similarly Texaco's prompted recall improved from 18 per cent to 60 per cent because of motor racing sponsorship.[55]

Creating entertainment opportunities

A major objective of much sponsorship is to create entertainment opportunities for customers and the trade. Sponsorship of music, the arts and sports events can be particularly effective. For example, Barclays Capital sponsored a fashion show at London's Natural History Museum for 450 of its clients that were attending a global borrowers and investors forum. Often, key personalities are invited to join the sponsor's guests to add further attractiveness to the event. Similarly, sponsors of the Global Challenge yacht race, such as Norwich Union, BP and BT, used the event to entertain their best clients on board sponsored boats in desirable locations like Boston and Cape Town.[56]

Fostering favourable brand and company associations

A third objective of sponsorship is to create favourable associations for the brand and company. For example, sponsorship of athletics by SmithKline Beecham for its Lucozade Sport brand reinforces its market position and its energy associations. Similarly, Procter & Gamble spent the entire marketing budget for its shampoo Wash & Go, totalling €8.4 million, on sponsoring football's English Premier League. The intention was to position it as a sports brand with the tag-line 'A simply great supporter of football'.[57] Both the sponsor and the sponsored activity become involved in a relationship with a transfer of values from activity to sponsor. The audience, finding the sponsor's name, logo and other symbols threaded through the event, learns to associate sponsor and activity with one another. Figure 9.6 shows some broad values conferred on the sponsor from five sponsorship categories.

Improving community relations

Sponsorship of schools—for example, by providing low-cost personal computers as Tesco has done—and supporting community programmes can foster a socially responsible, caring reputation for a company. Many multinational companies get involved in com-

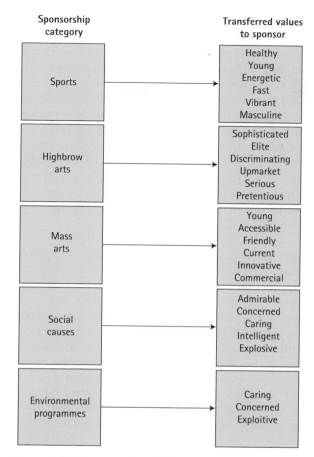

Figure 9.6 Values transferred from sponsorship categories

munity initiatives in local markets. For example, Nortel Networks, the Canadian telecommunications company, has had a very successful association with the Galway Arts Festival, one of the leading festivals in the Republic of Ireland.

Creating promotional opportunities

Sponsorship events provide an ideal opportunity to promote company brands. Sweatshirts, bags, pens, and so on, carrying the company logo and name of the event can be sold to a captive audience. When the brand is consumed during the event, such as Stella Artois at a tennis tournament, this provides an opportunity for customers to sample the brand, perhaps for the first time.

New developments in sponsorship

Sponsorship has experienced a major growth in the past 15 years. Some of the factors driving the rise in sponsorship expenditure include, the escalating costs of media advertising, restrictive government policies on tobacco and alcohol advertising, the fragmentation of traditional mass media, the proven record of sponsorship and greater media coverage of sponsored events.[58] Accompanying the growth of event sponsorship has been the phenomenon of **ambush marketing.** Originally, the term referred to the activities of companies that tried to associate themselves with an event without paying any fee to the event owner. Nike has been a particularly successful ambush marketer at various Olympic Games and indeed emerged as the name Asian viewers most closely associated with the Athens Games even though it was not one of the event's official sponsors.[59] The activity is legal so long as no attempt is made to use an event symbol, logo or mascot. More recently, ambush marketing activities have become more subtle with, for example, companies sponsoring the television coverage of an event rather than the event itself.

The selection of an event or individual to sponsor requires that consideration is given to a number of key questions. These include the firm's communication objectives, its target market, the risks associated with the sponsorship, the promotional opportunities presented and the costs involved. As with all communications initiatives, the sponsorship should be carefully evaluated against the initial objectives to assess whether it was successful or not. For example, Volvo's £2 million sponsorship of tennis resulted in 1.4 billion impressions (number of mentions or sightings, audience size), which it calculated was worth £12 million in media advertising.[60] Similarly, BT estimated that media coverage of its sponsorship of the Global Challenge yacht race covered costs by a multiple of three and the official website attracted more than 30 million hits per race.

Other promotional tools

Because of the fragmentation of traditional audiences such as press and television, a variety of other promotional techniques are becoming more commonplace. Two popular mass communications tools include exhibitions and product placement, which are examined below. In addition, other companies use their brands to create entertainment opportunities. For example, Guinness opened the Guinness Storehouse in Dublin in 2000. By 2002, it had seen its one millionth visitor and it has become the number one fee-paying tourist attraction in Ireland.[61]

Exhibitions

Exhibitions are unique in that, of all the promotional tools available, they are the only one that brings buyers, sellers and competitors together in a commercial setting. In Europe, the Cologne trade exhibitions bring together 28,000 exhibitors from 100 countries with 1.8 million buyers from 150 countries.[62] Exhibitions are a particularly important part of the industrial promotional mix. One study into the relative importance of promotional media placed exhibitions as a source of information on the industrial buying process second only to personal selling, and ahead of direct mail and print advertising.[63]

Exhibitions are growing in their number and variety. Aside from the major industry exhibitions such as motor shows and property shows, more specialized lifestyle exhibitions are emerging in niche markets. For example, the Cosmo show, featuring cosmetics targets young women, attracts over 55,000 visitors. The 1999 event was the launch pad for Olay Colour (formerly Oil of Ulay) to reveal its new identity and for the launch of Cussons' new moisturizer, Aqua Source.

Exhibitions can have a variety of objectives, including identifying prospects and determining their needs, building relationships, providing product demonstrations, making sales, gathering competitive intelligence and fostering the image of the company. They require careful planning and management to ensure that they run smoothly. And a post-show evaluation needs to take place to determine its effectiveness. Fortunately, there are a variety of variables that can easily be quantified, which can be used to measure success. These include number of visitors to the stand, number of leads generated, number of orders received and their value, and so on. Following up the trade show through contact with prospects and customers is also important.

Product placement

Product placement is the deliberate placing of products and/or their logos in movies and television, usually in return for money. The appearance of these brands in the media is unlikely to be by accident—vast sums of money are often paid to secure exposure. For example, Steven Spielberg's sci-fi film *Minority Report* featured more than 15 major brands, including Gap, Nokia, Pepsi, Guinness, Lexus and Amex, with their logos appearing on video billboards throughout the film. These product placements earned Dreamworks and 20th Century Fox US$25 million, which went some way towards reducing the US$102 million production costs of the film.[64] Similarly, when the hip-hop artist Busta Rhymes had a smash hit with 'Pass the Courvoisier', US sales of the cognac rose by 14 per cent in volume and 11 per cent in value. Allied Domecq, the brand's owner, claims it did not pay for the plug, but McDonald's is more upfront, offering hip-hop artists US$5 each time they mention Big Mac in a song.[65] The value of product placement deals in the USA grew from £174 million in 1974 to £3.5 billion in 2004, and is forecast to grow to US$7 billion by 2009.[66]

Product placement has grown significantly in recent years for the following reasons: media fragmentation means it is increasingly hard to reach mass markets; the brand can benefit from the positive associations it gains from being in a film or TV show; many consumers do not realize that the brand has been product-placed; repetition of the movie or TV show means that the brand is seen again and again; careful choice of movie or TV show means that certain segments can be targeted; and promotional and merchandising opportunities can be generated on the shows' websites. For example, the clothes and accessories worn by actresses in popular TV shows like *Sex and the City* and *Desperate Housewives* have been in great demand from viewers and some have quickly sold out. Show producers are increasingly looking at the merchandising opportunities that their shows can present. Technological developments in the online gaming sector allow for different products to be placed in games at different times of the day or in different geographic locations, expanding the marketing possibilities available to companies.[67]

Though product placement is becoming very popular, it is important to remember that there are risks involved. If the movie or TV show fails to take off it can tarnish the image of the brand and reduce its potential exposure. Audiences can become annoyed by blatant product placement, also damaging the image, and brand owners may not have complete control over how their brand is portrayed. Also the popularity of product placement is fast giving rise to claims that it constitutes deceptive advertising. Lobby groups in the USA claim that one of the difficulties with product placement is that it can't be controlled by the consumer in the way the traditional advertising breaks can through zapping, and want it restricted.

Product placement is subject to the same kinds of analysis as all the other promotional techniques described in this chapter. For example, in the James Bond movie *Die Another Day*, the Ford Motor Company had three of its car brands 'starring' in the film: an Aston Martin Vanquish, a Thunderbird and a Jaguar XKR. Movie-goers were interviewed both before and after seeing the film to see if their opinions of the brands had changed. In addition, the product placement was part of an integrated campaign including public relations and advertising, which

ensured that even people who had not seen the film were aware of Ford's association with it. During the film's peak viewing periods in the USA and UK, Ford's research found that the number of times its name appeared in the media increased by 34 per cent and that Ford corporate messages appeared in 29 per cent of the Bond-related coverage.[68]

Exhibit 9.6 Advertising like this for milk chocolate vodka shots is likely to be controversial for both its content and its creative treatment

Summary

This chapter has provided an overview of the promotional mix and examined some important mass communications techniques. The following key issues were addressed. (overleaf)

1. The promotional mix is broad, comprising seven elements, namely advertising, sales promotion, publicity, sponsorship, direct marketing, Internet and online marketing, and personal selling.

2. Because of the breadth of promotional techniques available, it is important to adopt an integrated approach to marketing communications. This means that companies carefully blend the promotional mix elements to deliver a clear, consistent, credible and competitive message in the marketplace.

3. It is important to take a systematic approach to communications planning. The various steps involved include consideration of the company's marketing and positioning strategy, identifying the target audience, setting communications objectives, creating the message, selecting the promotional mix, setting the promotional budget, executing the strategy and evaluating the strategy.

4. Advertising is a highly visible component of marketing, but it is only one element of the promotional mix. Advertising strategy involves an analysis of the target audience, setting objectives, budgeting decisions, message and media decisions, and evaluating advertising effectiveness.

5. Sales promotions are a powerful technique for giving a short-term boost to sales or for encouraging trial.

6. Publicity plays a very important role in the promotional mix because of its high credibility.

7. Sponsorship is a rapidly growing and important element of the promotional mix.

Suggested reading

Eagle, L. and **P. Kitchen** (2000) IMC, Brand Communications and Corporate Cultures, *European Journal of Marketing*, **34** (5/6), 667–87.

Fahy, J., F. Farrelly and **P. Quester** (2004) Competitive Advantage Through Sponsorship: A Conceptual Model and Research Propositions, *European Journal of Marketing*, **38** (8), 1013–31.

Fitzgerald, M. and **D. Arnott**, (2000) *Marketing Communications Classics*, London: International Thomson Publishing.

Raghubir, P., J. Inman and **H. Grande** (2004) The Three Faces of Consumer Promotions, *California Management Review*, **46** (4), 23–43.

Silvera, D. and **B. Austed** (2004), Factors predicting the effectiveness of celebrity endorsement advertisements, *European Journal of Marketing*, **38** (11/12), 1509–27.

Internet exercises

Sites to visit
1   www.barb.co.uk
    www.oaa.org.uk
    www.pearlanddean.com
    www.rajar.co.uk

Exercise

Review and evaluate the information provided by these sites about the relative attractiveness of television, outdoor, cinema and radio as advertising media.

Sites to visit
2   www.americanbrandstand.com
    www.commercialalert.org

Exercise

Visit americanbrandstand.com and discuss the extent to which brands appear in song lyrics. Visit commercialalalert.org and examine attitudes to product placement on this site.

Study questions

1. What is meant by integrated marketing communications? Explain the advantages of taking an integrated approach to marketing communications.

2. Select three recent advertising campaigns with which you are familiar. Discuss the target audience, objectives and message executions adopted in each case.

3. It is frequently argued that much promotional expenditure is wasteful. Discuss the ways in which the effectiveness of the various promotional techniques described in this chapter can be measured.

4. Discuss the role of sponsorship in the promotional mix.

5. There is no such thing as bad publicity. Discuss.

Key terms

target audience the group of people at which an advertisement or message is aimed

distribution push the targeting of channel intermediaries with communications (e.g. promotions) to *push* the product into the distribution chain

consumer pull the targeting of consumers with communications (e.g. promotions) designed to create demand that will *pull* the product into the distribution chain

integrated marketing communications the concept that companies co-ordinate their marketing communications tools to deliver a clear, consistent, credible and competitive message about the organization and its products

advertising any paid form of non-personal communication of ideas or products in the prime media (i.e. television, the press, posters, cinema and radio, the Internet and direct marketing)

personal selling oral communication with prospective purchasers with the intention of making a sale

direct marketing (1) acquiring and retaining customers without the use of an intermediary; (2) the distribution of products, information and promotional benefits to target consumers through interactive communication in a way that allows response to be measured

sales promotion incentives to customers or the trade that are designed to stimulate purchase

advertising message the use of words, symbols and illustrations to communicate to a target audience using prime media

advertising platform the aspect of the seller's product that is most persuasive and relevant to the target consumer

media class decision the choice of prime media (i.e. the press, cinema, television, posters, radio) or some combination of these

media vehicle decision the choice of the particular newspaper, magazine, television spot, poster site, etc.

advertising agency an organization that specializes in providing services such as media selection, creative work, production and campaign planning to clients

money-off promotions sales promotions that discount the normal price

bonus pack pack giving the customer extra quantity at no additional cost

premiums any merchandise offered free or at low cost as an incentive to purchase

group discussion a group, usually of six to eight consumers, brought together for a discussion focusing on an aspect of a company's marketing strategy

hall tests bringing a sample of target consumers to a room that has been hired so that alternative marketing ideas (e.g. promotions) can be tested

experimentation the application of stimuli (e.g. two price levels) to different matched groups under controlled conditions for the purpose of measuring their effect on a variable (e.g. sales)

public relations the management of communications and relationships to establish goodwill and mutual understanding between an organization and its public

publicity the communication of a product or business by placing information about it in the media without paying for time or space directly

sponsorship a business relationship between a provider of funds, resources or services and an individual, event or organization that offers in return some rights and association that may be used for commercial advantage

event sponsorship sponsorship of a sporting or other event

ambush marketing any activity where a company tries to associate itself or its products with an event without paying any fee to the event owner

exhibition an event that brings buyers and sellers together in a commercial setting

product placement the deliberate placing of products and/or their logos in movies and television programmes, usually in return for money

References

1. **Gapper, J.** (2003) The Big Bucks That Keep Nike in the Big League, *Financial Times*, 4 November, 19; **Gardner, R.** (2004) Athletes Face Legends in Global Adidas Spots, *Campaign*, 23 July, 9; **Parpis, E.** (2004) TBWA Put Olympic Spin on Adidas 'Impossible is Nothing', *Adweek*, 19 July, 12; **Plaskett, S.** (2004) Adidas Makes the Most of Olympic Hopefuls, *B&T*, 9 July, 3; **Shaw, S.D.** (2004) 'Impossible Sprint' Delivers Global PR Bang for Adidas, *Media Asia*, 27 August, 19.

2. **Benady, A.** (2003) Hundreds of Brands, Billions to Spend, *Financial Times*, Creative Business, 25 February, 2–3.

3. **Piercy, N.** (1987) The Marketing Budgeting Process: Marketing Management Implications, *Journal of Marketing*, **51** (4), 45–59.

4. **Saatchi & Saatchi Compton** (1985) *Preparing the Advertising Brief*, 9.

5. **Anonymous** (2004) Sex Doesn't Sell, *Economist*, 30 October, 46–7.

6. **Lannon, J.** (1991) Developing Brand Strategies across Borders, *Marketing and Research Today*, August, 160–7.

7. **Anonymous** (2004) Hand-to-Hand Combat, *Economist*, 18 December, 118.

8. **Carter, M.** (2003) Staying Ahead of the Game, *Financial Times*, 24 July, 14.

9. **Gardner, R.** (2004) PS2 Work Celebrates 'Sporting Champions', *Campaign*, 7 February, 5.

10. **Waters, R.** (2004) Rivals in Contest to Take Gaming to the Next Level, *Financial Times*, 5 May, 13.

11. **Ritson, M.** (2003) It's the Ad Break ... and the Viewers are Talking, Reading and Snogging, *Financial Times Creative Business*, 4 February, 8–9; **Silverman, G.** (2005) Advertisers are Starting to Find Television a Turn-off, *Financial Times*, 26 July, 20.

12. **Grimshaw, C.** (2003) Standing Out in the Crowd, *Financial Times, Creative Business*, 6 May, 7.

13. **Anonymous** (2005) Mr Bongo Pushes The Real Thing with Coca Cola TV ad theme, *Musicweek*, 28 May, 44.

14. **Barnes, R.** (2004) Retailers Take on Digital Music, *Marketing*, 25 March, 15.

15. **Buckley, N.** and **B. Liu** (2004) Coca-Cola Search For New Boss, *Financial Times*, 10 March, 17.

16. **Kumar, G.S.** (2004) Coke's Promotional Themes, *European Case Clearing House*, 504-055-1.

17. **Bell, E.** (1992) Lies, Damned Lies and Research, *Observer*, 28 June, 46.

18. **Anonymous** (2005) Consumer Republic, *Economist*, 19 March, 63, 66.

19. **Mead, G.** (1992) Why the Customer is Always Right, *Financial Times*, 8 October, 17.

20. **Burgoyne, P.** (2003) Beam Me Up, *Creative Review*, March, 39.

21. **Cane, A.** (2003) Ads Go Down The Line, *Financial Times, Creative Business*, 22 April, 12–13.

22. **Goldrich, R.** (2004) TBWA Fills DAM With Beam.TV, *Shoot*, 4 September, 1–2.

23. **Smith, P.R.** (1993) *Marketing Communications: An Integrated Approach*, London: Kogan Page, 116.

24. See **Tomkins, R.** (1999) Getting a Bigger Bang for the Advertising Buck, *Financial Times*, 24 September, 17; and **Waters, R.** (1999) P&G Ties Advertising Agency Fees to Sales, *Marketing Week*, 16 September, 1.

25. **Oliver, E.** (2004) Advertisers Uneasy Over Regulator Code for Children, *Irish Times*, 27 March, 16.

26. **Peattie, K.** and **S. Peattie** (1993) Sales Promotion: Playing to Win?, *Journal of Marketing Management*, **9**, 255–69.

27. **Rothschild, M.L.** and **W.C. Gaidis** (1981) Behavioural Learning Theory: Its Relevance to Marketing and Promotions, *Journal of Marketing*, **45** (Spring), 70–8.

28. **Tuck, R.T.J.** and **W.G.B. Harvey** (1972) Do Promotions Undermine the Brand?, *Admap*, January, 30–3.

29. **Brown, R.G.** (1974) Sales Response to Promotions and Advertising, *Journal of Advertising Research*, **14** (4), 33–9.

30. **Ehrenberg, A.S.C., K. Hammond** and **G.J. Goodhardt** (1994) The After-effects of Price-related Consumer Promotions, *Journal of Advertising Research*, **34** (4), 1–10.

31. **Foster, L.** (2004) Krispy Kreme Defies Healthy Eating Trend, *Financial Times*, 11 March, 20.

32. **Hollins, J.** (2003) The Shape of Things To Come, *Birmingham Evening Mail*, 30 September, 8.

33. **Lin, B.** (2004) Krispy Kreme Looks to its Global Roll-out, *Financial Times*, 15 March, 15.

34. **Mesure, S.** (2004) Krispy Kreme Profits Plummet 40%, *Independent*, Business, 37 August 38.

35. **Rushe, D.** (2003) Hole in One for Cult Doughnut, *Sunday Times*, Business, 21 September, 6.

36. **Davidson, J.H.** (1998) *Offensive Marketing*, Harmondsworth: Penguin, 249–71.

37. **Murphy, J.** (1997) The Art of Satisfaction, *Financial Times*, 23 April, 14.

38. **Dowling, G.R.** and **M. Uncles** (1997) Do

Loyalty Programs Really Work?, *Sloan Management Review*, **38** (4), 71–82.

39. **Burnside, A.** (1995) A Never Ending Search for the New, *Marketing*, 25 May, 31–5.

40. **Murphy, C.** (1999) Addressing the Data Issue, *Marketing*, 28 January, 31.

41. **Anonymous** (2005) An Overdose of Bad News, *Economist*, 19 March, 69–71.

42. **Doyle, P.** and **J. Saunders** (1985) The Lead Effect of Marketing Decisions, *Journal of Marketing Research*, **22** (1), 54–65.

43. **Lesly, P.** (1991) *The Handbook of Public Relations and Communications*, Maidenhead: McGraw-Hill, 13–19.

44. **Kitchen, P.J.** and **T. Proctor** (1991) The Increasing Importance of Public Relations in Fast Moving Consumer Goods Firms, *Journal of Marketing Management*, **7** (4), 357–70.

45. **Collins, N.** (2003) Dyson's Not Making Suckers of Anyone, *Daily Telegraph*, 25 August, 18.

46. **Marsh, P.** (2003) Dust is Settling on the Dyson Market Clean-up, *Financial Times*, 12 December, 12.

47. **Moorish, J.** (2002) In Malmesbury, There are Few Tears for Mr Dyson and his Miracle Cleaner, *Independent on Sunday*, 10 February, 14.

48. **Murphy, C.** (2003) Sunny Delight Tries to Find a New Dawn, *Financial Times*, 27 June, 12.

49. **Lesly, P.** (1991) *The Handbook of Public Relations and Communications*, Maidenhead: McGraw-Hill, 13–19.

50. **Sleight, S.** (1989) *Sponsorship: What it is and How to Use it*, Maidenhead, McGraw-Hill, 4.

51. **Bickerton, I.** (2003) 6Pack's Muscle Helps Push up Heineken Sales, *Financial Times*, 26 June, 13.

52. **Lewis, E.** (2003) A Tactical Withdrawal, *Financial Times, Creative Business*, 13 May, 4-5.

53. **Fry, A.** (2001) How to Profit from Sport Sponsorship, *Marketing*, 16 August, 25.

54. **Ward, A.** (2005) DHL Goes For Home Run in Rival's Back Yard, *Financial Times*, 6 April, 31.

55. **Mintel** (1991) *Sponsorship: Special Report*, London: Mintel International Group Ltd.

56. **Friedman, V.** (2003) Banks Step on to the Catwalk, *Financial Times*, 3 July, 12.

57. **McKelvey, C.** (1999) Washout, *Marketing Week*, 2 December, 27–9.

58. **Miles, L.** (1995) Sporting Chancers, *Marketing Director International*, **6** (2), 50–2.

59. **Bowman, J.** (2004) Swoosh Rules Over Official Olympic Brands, *Media Asia*, 10 September, 22.

60. **Smith, P.R.** (1993) *Marketing Communications: An Integrated Approach*, London: Kogan Page, 116.

61. **Parmar, A.** (2003) Guinness Intoxicates, *MarketingNews*, 10 November, 4, 6.

62. **O'Hara, B., F. Palumbo** and **P. Herbig** (1993) Industrial Trade Shows Abroad, *Industrial Marketing Management*, **22**, 233–7.

63. **Parasuraman, A.** (1981) The Relative Importance of Industrial Promotional Tools, *Industrial Marketing Management*, **10**, 277–81.

64. **Anonymous** (2002) The Top Ten Product Placements in Features, *Campaign*, 17 December, 36.

65. **Tomkins, R.** (2003) The Hidden Message: Life's a Pitch, and Then You Die, *Financial Times*, 24 October, 14; **Armstrong, S.** (2005) How To Put Some Bling into Your Brand, *Irish Times, Weekend*, 30 July, 7.

66. **Silverman, G.** (2005) After the Break: The 'Wild West' Quest to Bring the Consumers to the Advertising, *Financial Times*, 18 May, 17.

67. **Nuttall, C.** (2005) There's a New Game in Town For Television Advertisers, *Financial Times*, 17 May, 14.

68. **Dowdy, C.** (2003) Thunderbirds Are Go, *Financial Times, Creative Business*, 24 June, 10.

Turn the page for a Case Study on Absolute Vodka

Case 9 Absolut Vodka: creating advertising history

Figure C9.1 Absolut vodka

Table C9.1 A brief list of awards won by Absolut advertisements

Year	Award(s)
1989	The Kelly Grand Prize for the ad 'Absolut LA'
1990	Grand EFFIE Award for Absolut advertising campaign
1991	The Kelly Grand Prize for the ad 'Absolut Glasnost'
1992	'Award of Excellence' for animation on the Internet by the Communication Arts magazine
1993	Absolut Advertising Campaign introduced in the 'Hall of Fame' by the American Marketing Association
2000	Four Cresta Awards for International Advertising for the ads 'Absolut Accessory', 'Absolut Auckland', 'Absolut Voyeur' and 'Absolut Space' from Creative Standards International and the International Advertising Association
2002	Insight Award for Best online advertising
2003	EFFIE Gold Award for sustained success of the Absolut advertising campaign

Source: compiled from various sources

'Absolut advertising is celebrated not just for its longevity but also for its ingenuity. Readers tear out the advertisements and hang them on their walls. Librarians have to guard their magazines from being de-Absoluted. College students actually collect and trade ads. A SoHo antique shop hawks copies of Absolut Wonderland, while a Madison Avenue newsstand carefully razors the Absolut pages from its stock and sells them for a few dollars apiece.'

(From the article, 'A Visual Analysis of the Absolut Vodka Advertising Campaign', written by a student at www.southwestern.edu, 2002)

The Absolut advertising campaign was often regarded by advertising experts as one of the most brilliant, innovative, successful and long-running campaigns ever. The several prestigious awards that the campaign has won since its first ad was launched stand as testimony to this fact (see Table C9.1 for details of some of the awards).

'Absolut adventure': the making of a legend

In early 1979, Absolut vodka was launched in the USA at the liquor trade convention held at Fairmont Hotel in New Orleans. Initially, the company concentrated its marketing efforts in and around New York, Los Angeles, San Francisco and Boston because these were the places where new trends were created, media attention was intense and the bar culture prevailed.

V&S had sold around 25,000 cases of Absolut vodka when the advertising agency TBWA took over its ad account in late 1979. Two admen at TBWA, Graham Turner and Geoff Hayes, were assigned the job of creating the ads for the 'still not so popular Swedish vodka'. The duo began by getting familiar with the product's taste and conducting extensive research on different liquor ads of the previous 10 years. They found that most ads were pretentious and pompous, featuring people dressed in expensive attire and living lavish lifestyles with a small liquor bottle tucked in some corner. Moreover, none of the ads was targeted at people below 40.

After extensive research and effort, the admen came up with three different advertisement samples. The first featured a Russian soldier looking through a pair of binoculars with each lens reflecting the Absolut vodka bottle, accompanied by a slogan that read 'Here's something that Russians would really love to put behind bars.' This ad was aimed at challenging the Russian vodka brand Stolichnaya. The second ad featured some of the favourite pastimes of Swedes, with a picture of the bottle; the slogan read 'There's nothing the Swedes enjoy more when it's cold.' The third ad featured only the Absolut vodka bottle with a halo over it, with a two-word slogan: 'Absolut Perfection' (a modified version of one of the ads created at NW Ayer). This ad was designed with the intention of humorously portraying Absolut as pure and natural.

The admen had come up with a dozen designs, which depicted the bottle in different ways accompanied by a two-word slogan. It was one of the simplest themes anyone associated with Absolut had created up until then. The ads featured the Absolut bottle, a description of the product and the two-word slogan with one word describing the theme and the other the brand name itself. In early 1980, V&S launched the first advertisement, 'Absolut Perfection', along these lines. Since then, the bottle has been retained as the centrepiece for every advertisement of Absolut vodka accompanied by a two-word slogan.

All Absolut ads were published in popular American newspapers and magazines like *Newsweek*, *Time*, *New York*, *Los Angeles*, *New Yorker*, *New York Times*, *Interview* and *GQ*. Carillon decided to continue using the same ad concept with a variety of themes. Experts felt that by using the same concept to depict various events, people or things, Absolut ads always gave people something to think about. Soon the ads had become a topic of interest among liquor consumers.

People began drinking Absolut not only because it was a new premium brand available on the market, but also to experience the image that its advertisement had created—that of simplicity and purity. Analysts credited the popularity of Absolut to its advertisements as they involved viewers in a creative process. Within three years, Absolut vodka was being exported to 16 different markets worldwide as well as its home country, Sweden. In 1984, V&S exported six million litres of Absolut vodka. In the USA, sales were doubling every year (see Table C9.2).

In 1985, Michel Roux, President of Carillon and in charge of US distribution, came up with the idea of getting the Absolut bottle painted and using it as an ad. Initially, there was opposition to this idea as it was a departure from the campaign's central idea of having the bottle photographed. However, Roux went ahead and commissioned celebrated artist Andy Warhol to paint the bottle, marking the beginning of Absolut's association with art. The painting attracted a lot of accolades and the celebrity association gave the brand a great deal of mileage.

Thereafter, several artists painted their own interpretations of the Absolut bottle. Analysts observed that painting an Absolut bottle had apparently become an issue of pride for many leading artists. Big names

Table C9.2 V&S: income statements, 1997–2002 (SEK million)

Particulars/year	1997	1998	1999	2000	2001	2002
Net sales	3223.6	3,446.9	4028.6	5711.5	6725.1	9092.8
Other operating revenues	(10.3)	32.3	43.2	104.3	175.3	149.6
Operating expenses	(2449.8)	(2626.8)	(2924.9)	(4177.4)	(4741.2)	(6686.6)
Depreciation, amortization and write-downs	(105.7)	(130.7)	(85.6)	(235.0)	(394.9)	(519.2)
Non-recurring items	(17.0)	287.3	(143.3)	46.1	–	–
Operating profit	640.8	1009.0	918.0	1449.5	1764.3	2036.6
Financial items, net	31.5	50.6	46.0	(16.2)	(292.6)	(167.6)
Profit before taxes	672.3	1059.6	964.0	1433.3	1471.7	1869.0
Taxes	(175.0)	(197.3)	(273.5)	(437.2)	(462.0)	(598.5)
Minority share	(0.4)	(0.8)	(0.3)	(61.9)	(0.5)	(5.7)
Net profit for the period	496.9	861.5	690.2	934.2	1009.2	1264.8

Source: www.vinspirit.se

such as Keith Haring, Kenny Scharf, Stephen Sprouse, Edward Ruscha, Arman and Britto made their own interpretations of the Absolut bottle (see Table C9.3 for details). The above exercise was not only in the form of painting, but also in sculpture, glasswork, photography, folk art, wood work, computer/digital art and many other media. As Absolut's association with the world of art gave the brand a lot of media attention and publicity, the company began regularly publishing these art ads along with the regular ads. Analysts noted that what began as an advertising campaign to promote an unknown

Swedish vodka brand had become a part of American culture.

Roux now began toying with the idea of making ads that were 'stylish, hip and audacious'. With this began Absolut's association with the world of fashion. In 1988, Roux commissioned the famous American fashion designer David Cameron to design an advertisement for the bottle. Instead of featuring the Absolut bottle, Cameron designed a dress (with the Absolut Vodka name and the text printed on it) that was modelled by a famous model of the day, Rachel

Table C9.3 Absolut's association with art and fashion

Year	Name	Description
ABSOLUT ART		
1990	Absolut Glasnost	This art collection featured paintings contributed by 26 Russian artists including Alexander Kosolapov, Evgeny Mitta and Leonid Lamm.
1993	Absolut Latino	This collection featured artwork contributed by 16 artists from South and Central America. This collection showcased the artist's interpretations of the absolute bottle in traditional and contemporary Latino themes depicting the relationship between reality and illusion. Some of the artists who contributed to this collection were, Alberto Icaza, Vik Muniz and Monica Castillo.
1997	Absolut Expressions	This collection featured art work contributed by 14 African and American artists. The artists (including Anita Philyaw, Maliaka Favorite and Frank Bowling among others) presented their interpretations of the bottle in traditional African art, early American folk art and in abstract imagery through mediums like canvas, quilts and sculptures.
1998–99	Absolut Originals	This included paintings contributed by 16 European artists including Damien Hirst, Maurizio Cattelan and Francesco Clemente.
2000	Absolut Ego (Paris) Absolut Exhibition (New York) Absolut Art (Stockholm)	Collections featured paintings contributed by famous artists like Damien Hirst and Nam June Paik.
ABSOLUT FASHION		
1995	Absolut Newton	This campaign featured designer wear created by famous fashion designers John Galliano, Helmut Lang, Anna Molinari and Martine Sitbon. It was first featured as an eight-page insert in *Vogue*, a popular fashion magazine.
1997	Absolut Versace	This eight-page insert in *Vogue* featured designer wear created by Gianni Versace, the famous Italian fashion designer. Gianni's creations were modelled by famous models like Naomi Campbell, Kate Moss, Mark Findley and Marcus Schenkenberg, and photographed by famous fashion photographer Herb Ritts.
1999	Absolut Tom Ford/ Absolut Gucci	This campaign included designer collections created by Tom Ford (of Gucci) a famous American fashion designer. The campaign was shot at a discotheque in Paris and was included as an eight-page insert in *Vogue*.
2002	Absolut Gaultier	This campaign featured designs by Jean Paul Gaultier, inspired by Absolut and other Swedish legends. It was included as an eight-page insert in *Vogue* and other popular European fashion magazines.

Source: The Absolut Spirits Company

Williams (she 'represented' the bottle). This print ad, named 'Absolut Cameron', was launched in February 1988 and gained tremendous publicity. On the day of its publication, 5000 women reportedly called TBWA wanting to buy the dress shown in the ad.

This led to the next phase of Absolut's advertising strategy, wherein the bottle began to be represented in new, innovative ways. By the mid-1990s TBWA ran several ads linked to fashion, like Absolut Fashion (eight pages of coverage in *Vogue*), Absolut Style and Absolut Menswear, in popular fashion magazines like *Vogue*, *Elle* and *GQ* (see Table C9.3 for details).

As the themes for the advertisements became more complicated, the cost of producing them went up substantially. For instance, some of the Absolut Christmas ads cost more than US$1 million to produce. Thus, over the years, V&S continually increased its advertising budget. TBWA spent approximately US$25 million on Absolut ads in 1990, an increase from US$750,000 in 1981. In 1997, Absolut also became associated with The Ice Hotel (an entire hotel made from ice) in Jukkasjarvi, Sweden. An 'Absolut Ice Bar' was added to the Ice Hotel, where different kinds of drinks made from various Absolut brands were served in glasses also made of ice.

By the end of the 1990s, Absolut ads began targeting not only the sophisticated, upper-class consumers but also sports fans, professionals, artists, intellectuals and even those who could not comprehend subjects like art or literature. Clearly, V&S was now aiming at a broader set of customers as the ads were featured in almost all kinds of magazines: sports, entertainment, art and fashion, business, and so on. By now the company had launched more than 1000 Absolut ads all over the world.

'Absolut continuity': the brand marches strongly ahead

By 2000, Absolut advertisements were recognized the world over for their stylish, humorous and innovative attributes. As people began collecting the ads, analysts observed that the brand had become an advertising phenomenon. More importantly, sales of Absolut were increasing rapidly over the years. Apart from the USA, Absolut was now exported to Russia and many Asian and Latin America countries. The brand generated most of its sales in the USA, Canada, Sweden, Greece, Spain, Germany and Mexico. In 2002, total sales stood at 7.5 million

cases, making it the world's second largest premium spirits brands.

In 2002, Absolut was presented with the international advertising industry's most prestigious awards for its online advertising on its website, www.absolut.com, and the Absolut fashion campaign. Advertising experts regarded the website as 'a premier online brand and lifestyle destination'.

Commenting on the creativity that Absolut ads stood for, Richard W. Lewis, author of *Absolut book: The Absolut Vodka Advertising Story*, says, 'Readers enjoy a relationship with this advertising that they have with few other advertising campaigns, especially in the print media. They are challenged, entertained, tickled, inspired, and maybe even befuddled as they try to figure out what is happening inside an Absolut ad.'

In January 2003, the company launched Absolut Vanilia. Unlike the previous variants, Absolut Vanilia was launched in a white bottle. The launch of the new flavour was not only supported by print advertisements, but also with radio and outdoor ad campaigns. These ads were launched in a phased manner, beginning with teaser ads in different magazines in April 2003 followed by interactive online ads. The online ads were featured on websites like Maxim.com, EntertainmentWeekly.com, style.com and Wired.com. These ads were created specifically to suit the product tag-line 'a different kind of vanilla'.

In October 2003, in line with its penchant for creativity/innovation, Absolut ventured into the world of music with the launch of the Absolut Three Tracks project. This campaign featured music created by different artists according to their interpretations of the Absolut bottle. Analysts felt that with the Absolut Three Tracks project, Absolut had opened an entirely new chapter in brand communications, as it enabled users to 'listen' to the Absolut brand. Commenting on this, Michael Persson, Director, Market Communications, ASC, said, 'For years, our consumers have seen interpretations of the brand by some of the world's most prominent artists and designers. With this new project they will also be able to listen to the brand: this is the voice of Absolut.'

Advertising experts felt that even 25 years after its launch, the Absolut advertising campaign was still going strong, innovatively, without changing the central theme. Even while creating music for Absolut Three Tracks, the bottle was used as the central theme. Aril Brikha, one of the artists who created a music track for Absolut Three Tracks said, 'I had scanned the shape into a computer program that turns a picture into a tone—a futuristic way of including a picture without letting the listener know. I find it quite similar to previous Absolut projects where the bottle has been hidden in a picture.' Industry observers as well as customers agreed on one issue: whatever the mode of expression—be it art, photography, technology, fashion or music—Absolut had until now stood for 'brilliance in advertising'. Said an analyst, 'We are surprised each year by the creativity and innovation of the brand. It is successful because it is contemporary. There is no end to the campaign.'

Questions

1. Discuss the role advertising plays in increasing brand awareness and brand loyalty among consumers, especially for products that have very subtle differentiable attributes. In the above context, examine the impact Absolut advertisements had on its target audience. Do you think the advertisements fulfilled their purpose?

2. 'The Absolut advertising campaign is successful because it is contemporary.' How did TBWA maintain the 'freshness' of the Absolut campaign? Discuss with respect to the brand's association with different media: art, fashion, technology and music.

3. Even though Absolut ads have been depicted in different media, the central theme of the campaign has remained unchanged (the bottle and the two-word slogan) over the years. In light of the above statement, do you think that the campaign will manage to hold sway or lose its impact in the near future? Give reasons to support your arguments.

This case was written by V. Sarvani, under the direction of A. Mukund, ICFAI Center for Management Research (ICMR). It is intended to be used as a basis for class discussion rather than to illustrate either effective or ineffective handling of a management situation.

The case was compiled from published sources.

CHAPTER 10

INTEGRATED MARKETING COMMUNICATIONS 2: DIRECT COMMUNICATIONS TECHNIQUES

Learning Objectives

By the end of this chapter you will understand:

1 the importance of database management as the foundation for direct marketing activities
2 the reasons for the growth in customer relationship management (CRM)
3 the meaning of direct marketing and how to manage a direct marketing campaign
4 what is meant by e-commerce and Internet marketing
5 the marketing opportunities presented by the developments in Internet technologies, and the role of the Internet as a direct marketing medium
6 the role of personal selling in the promotional mix, and the key issues involved in selling and sales management.

United Reaches Out to Its Fans

The relationship between football clubs and their supporters is a unique one. Unlike companies and brands that can quickly lose their customers if they fail to perform, a unique feature of many football supporters is their very high levels of loyalty to their team even though its performances on the field may be poor for years. Football clubs are now increasingly recognizing the value that can be had from interacting with these supporters, and direct marketing techniques are becoming a popular way to do so. For big clubs like Manchester United, which has a support base of over 50 million fans scattered all over the world, direct marketing is a very effective way of connecting with them.

Manchester United has come from humble origins. The club was formed by workers at the Lancashire and Yorkshire Railway Company in 1878 but, today, is one of the biggest and most recognized sports brands in the world. It is a powerful brand standing for flair, passion, camaraderie and working together, and these brand values are reflected by the players and the way they play each week. Sponsors have been quick to recognize the value of this association and Manchester United has agreed sponsorship deals with leading companies such as Nike, Vodafone, Pepsi, Ladbrokes and Anheuser-Busch. The success of its marketing and brand-building efforts has led to United becoming one of the biggest and most profitable clubs in the world, with a turnover in excess of £173 million and profits of £39 million in 2003. Over three-quarters of its revenues now come from its merchandising and commercial activities.

Driving this growth has been its retailing and direct marketing activities. Merchandise sales are a key source of income, and products like replica shirts and other items are retailed through its megastore at Old Trafford and a chain of Manchester United shops in leading cities around the world. A newer retailing venture is the Reds Café restaurants in the Asia Pacific region. The first cafés were opened on a franchise basis in Beijing and Singapore in 2002 and there are plans to develop up to 90 in the region by 2012. Manchester United Television (MUTV) was launched in 1998. It operates five channels and offers subscribers the opportunity to watch all Premiership matches, archive footage, interviews and highlights of games. Similarly, its website allows fans access to merchandise, information, news and updates, and a recent link-up with Viatel means fans can have a Manchester United e-mail address. Its relationship with Vodafone has also enabled it to explore the possibilities provided by mobile marketing. For example, fans will be able to get access to information and action from games via their mobile phones. Overall revenues from MU Interactive were worth £1.5 million in 2003.

The power of direct marketing can be seen in the 'One United' approach. Though Old Trafford can hold only 68,000 fans, the objective of 'One United' is to convert all its other armchair fans into paying customers for merchandise, television, updates and other products, thus generating greater revenues for the club. For example, MU Finance already has 57,000 subscribers availing themselves of everything from mortgages to credit cards, and generating sales of £1.2 million for the club.

The next stage of development for the club will be expanding its customer relationship management (CRM) capabilities. Its fan base can be segmented in a variety of ways: by age, sex, region, ethnic background, level of loyalty, etc. Data mining will enable the company to analyse its customers and tailor offerings based on specific preferences. It currently has 1 million fans on its database, including 100,000 supporters from China who have registered since it launched a Chinese version of its website in 2002. It particularly wants to target children as team allegiance is usually decided very young and remains unswerving throughout adult life.[1]

For many decades, mass communications techniques were favoured by marketers, and the promotional mix was heavily weighted towards tools like advertising and sales promotion. But in recent times, direct communications techniques have started to become very popular. There are a number of reasons for this. As we saw in the previous chapter, both the audience and the media have begun to fragment significantly, making it very difficult for companies to reach the mass market through the classic 30-second television advertisement, for example. In its place, the emergence of some new technologically based solutions, such as customer relationship management (CRM) and online marketing, promise a much more direct

Marketing in Action: Putting a buzz into business

The view has long been held that positive 'word of mouth' is probably the best form of promotion a company can have because it is seen as more credible and authoritative than communications through the media. Currently, word-of-mouth is enjoying something of a renaissance under the label of 'buzz marketing', which is when firms seek to deliberately orchestrate a word-of-mouth campaign. Its revival can be explained by advances in technology that enable the rapid spread of news, such as e-mail, websites and mobile telephones, and by the difficulty encountered by advertisers in getting their messages across through traditional channels.

Buzz marketing involves getting trendsetters in any community to carry the brand's message, creating interest with no overt advertising or promotion. The Austrian energy drink Red Bull was an early user of this strategy. One of its first marketing techniques was to hire student brand managers in university campuses, giving each one a case of Red Bull and encouraging them to throw a party. It hired hip locals to drive around in cars emblazoned with its logo and equipped with a four-foot model of the trademark silver-and-blue can. The cars carried fridges stocked with more than 250 cans of Red Bull to be distributed to 'those in need of energy' — shift workers, truck drivers, students, athletes, clubbers and executives.

The tactic has also been used by some of Britain's biggest boy bands, such as Busted and McFly. Their record company, Universal, recruits a 'school chairman' who is given the task of spreading the word about a particular band in their school. This involves giving out flyers, putting up posters on school noticeboards and then sending back evidence that this has been done. In return, the 'chairman'—who is typically a 12–15-year-old schoolgirl—is rewarded with free merchandise and a chance to meet the members of her favourite band.

Running a buzz marketing campaign involves first targeting the 'alphas'—the trendsetters that adopt new ideas and technologies early on—and the 'bees', who are the early adopters. Brand awareness then trickles down to 'ordinary' customers, who seek to emulate the trendsetters. Sometimes this process is accelerated by publicity stunts and promotional extravaganzas that make the brand a talking point. The message may be spread physically (people are seen with the brand), verbally (it can crop up in conversation) or virtually (via e-mail and mobile phone).

However, buzz marketing is not restricted to products aimed solely at the youth market such as Pokémon, Harry Potter, *The Blair Witch Project* and Beanie Babies. Two of the biggest spenders on buzz marketing are Proctor & Gamble and Unilever. When P&G launched Crest Whitestrips (a tooth-whitening product) in 2000, event marketing backed by carefully selected press, poster and radio advertising generated enough interest to secure US$40 million in Internet sales before the product was in the shops. Other well-known brands like FCUK, Calvin Klein, Ben & Jerry's and Viagra are extensive users of buzz marketing.

Buzz marketing is also sometimes referred to as stealth marketing or guerrilla marketing, and can incorporate a variety of techniques including brand pushers, celebrity marketing, viral marketing, bait-and-tease marketing, and marketing in video games and pop music. It would appear that word-of-mouth promotion is finally creating quite a buzz.

Based on: Dye (2000);[2] Kumar and Linguri (2003);[3] Pidd (2004);[4] Salzman (2003)[5]

and interactive relationship with the customer base. An ultimate form of **direct marketing** is where customers help to promote your product for you (see Marketing in Action 10.1). Also, one of the perennial challenges for marketers has been to justify promotional budgets, and demonstrate the impact of expenditure on awareness and sales. Direct communication techniques such as direct response advertising allow for a more tangible assessment of impact.

This chapter will examine the growing area of direct marketing communications. Many direct marketing communications techniques rely on the availability of a database of customers, which is the foundation upon which campaigns can be built. We shall first examine database marketing, which has evolved into one of the biggest growth areas in marketing, namely customer relationship management (CRM). We shall then go on to look at the field of direct marketing itself, which has grown out of the old mail order business. Then we will examine Internet marketing. At the turn of the century, the Internet promised to revolutionize marketing and there were some spectacular successes as well as many failures. However, despite this shaky start, e-commerce continues to grow and become a mainstream means of doing business. Finally, we shall examine one of the core elements of marketing namely, personal selling and sales management.

Database marketing

A marketing database is an 'electronic filing cabinet' containing a list of names, addresses, telephone numbers, and lifestyle and transactional data on customers and potential customers. Information such as types of purchase, frequency of purchase, purchase value and responsiveness to promotional offers may be held.

Database marketing is defined as:[6] an interactive approach to marketing that uses individually addressable marketing media and channels (such as mail, telephone and the salesforce) to:

- provide information to a target audience
- stimulate demand, and
- stay close to customers by recording and storing an electronic database memory of customers, prospects and all communication and transactional data.

Database marketing has some key characteristics. The first of these is that it allows direct communi-

cation with customers through a variety of media including **direct mail**, **telemarketing** and **direct response advertising**. Second, it usually requires the customer to respond in a way that allows the company to take action (such as contact by telephone, sending out literature or arranging sales visits). Third, it must be possible to trace the response back to the original communication. The potential of database marketing is enormous. For example, one supermarket analysed its sales and found that it was making a loss on a certain brand of cheese. Before cutting the line altogether, it correlated information about the people who were buying the product and found that they bought other high-ticket items and spent more on average on luxury goods. The supermarket concluded that it would make sense to continue selling the cheese in order to please these high-value customers.[7]

Computer technology provides the capability of storing and analysing large quantities of data from diverse sources, and presenting information in a convenient, accessible and useful format. The creation of a database relies on the collection of information on customers, which can be sourced from:

- company records
- responses to sales promotions
- warranty and guarantee cards
- offering samples that require the consumer to give name, address, telephone number, etc.
- enquiries
- exchanging data with other customers
- salesforce records
- application forms (e.g. to join a credit or loyalty scheme)
- complaints
- responses to previous direct marketing activities
- organized events (e.g. wine tastings).

However a key challenge for companies now is how to handle information overload due to the size and complexity of the data available. Winter Corporation's survey of databases found that over 90 per cent of those that it studied contained over 1 terabyte (1000 gigabytes) of data compared with just 25 per cent in 2001. Kmart had 12.6 terabytes of data covering stocks, sales, customers and suppliers, but this was not enough to save it from bankruptcy.[8]

Collecting information is easiest for companies that have direct contact with customers, such as those in financial services or retailing. However, even for those where the sales contact is indirect, building a database is often possible. For example, Seagram, the drinks company, built up a European database through telephone and written enquiries from customers, sales promotional returns, tastings in store, visits to company premises, exhibitions and promotions that encouraged consumers to name like-minded friends and colleagues.[9]

Figure 10.1 shows the sort of information that is recorded on a database. Customer and prospect information typically includes names, addresses, telephone numbers, names of key decision-makers within DMUs and general behavioural information. Transactional information refers to past transactions that contacts have had with the company. Transactional data must be sufficiently detailed to allow FRAC (frequency, recency, amount and category) information to be extracted for each customer. Frequency refers to how often a customer buys. Recency measures when the customer last bought; if customers are waiting longer before they rebuy (i.e. recency is decreasing) the reasons for this (e.g. less attractive offers or service problems) need to be explored. Amount measures how much a customer has bought and is usually recorded in value terms. Finally, category defines the type of product being bought.

Promotional information covers what promotion campaigns have been run, who has responded to them, and what the overall results were in terms of contacts, sales and profits. Product information would include which products have been promoted, who responded, when and from where. Finally, geodemographics includes information about the geographic location of customers and prospects, and the social, lifestyle and business category to which

they belong. Cross-tabulating these details with transactional information can reveal the customer profile most likely to buy a particular product.

The main applications of database marketing are as follows.

- *Direct mail*: a database can be used to select customers for mailings.
- *Telemarketing*: a database can store telephone numbers so that customers and prospects can be contacted.
- *Distributor management systems*: a database can be the foundation on which information is provided to distributors and their performance monitored.
- *Loyalty marketing*: loyal customers can be selected from the database for special treatment as a reward for their loyalty.
- *Target marketing*: groups of individuals or businesses can be targeted as a result of analysing the database.

Databases can also be used to try to build or strengthen relationships with customers. For example, Highland Distillers switched all of its promotional budget for its Macallan whisky brand from advertising to direct marketing. It built a database of 100,000 of its most frequent drinkers (those who consume at least five bottles a year), mailing them every few months with interesting facts about the brand, whisky memorabilia and offers.[10] It is these kinds of efforts to improve customer relationships that have caused the evolution of database marketing into what is now known as customer relationship management (CRM).

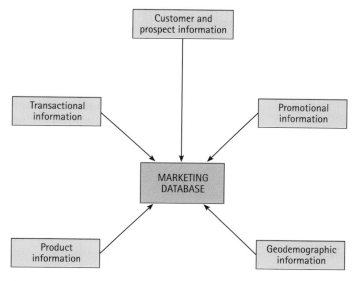

Figure 10.1 A marketing database

Exhibit 10.1 Companies like Mothercare are extensive users of loyalty programmes

Customer relationship management

Customer relationship management (CRM) is a term for the methodologies, technologies and e-commerce capabilities used by firms to manage customer relationships.[11] In particular, CRM software packages aid the interaction between the customer and the company, enabling the company to co-ordinate all of the communications effort so that the customer is presented with a unified message and image. CRM companies offer a range of information technology-based services, such as call centres, data analysis and website management. The basic principle behind CRM is that company staff have a single-customer point of view for each client. Customers are now using multiple channels more frequently. They may buy one product from a salesperson but another from the company website. Interactions between the customer and the company may take place in a variety of

ways—through the salesforce, call centres, e-mail, distributors, websites, and so on (see Figure 10.2).

Therefore, it is crucial that, no matter how a customer contacts a company, frontline staff have instant access to the same, up-to-date data about the customer, such as his/her details and past purchases. This usually means the consolidation of many databases held by individual departments in a company into one centralized database that can be accessed by all relevant staff on a computer screen. However, CRM is much more than the technology. A thorough examination of the CRM process is provided by the QCi customer management model (see Figure 10.3). This model can be used by companies to understand how well they are managing their CRM effort.[12] Each of the elements of the model will now be discussed.

Analysis and planning

Effective CRM begins by understanding the value, attitudes and behaviour of various customers and prospects. Once this has been achieved customers and prospects should be segmented so that planning activity can be as effective as possible. The planning will focus on such areas as the cost-effective retention and acquisition of customers.

Proposition

Once segments of customers are identified and understood, the proposition to each segment needs to be defined, and appropriate value-based offers planned. The proposition must then be communicated to both customers and the people responsible for delivering it.

Information and technology

These provide the foundations for the whole model. Data needs to be collected, stored, analysed and used in a way that provides information that is consistent with the CRM strategy, the way people work and the way that customers want to access the company. Technology enables an organization to acquire, analyse and use the vast amounts of data involved in managing customers. It needs to deliver the right information to relevant people at the right time so that they can achieve their role in the managing of customers.

People and organization

An organization's frontline staff need to be recruited, trained, developed and motivated to deliver high standards of customer relations. Key elements are an organizational structure that supports effective customer management, role identification, training

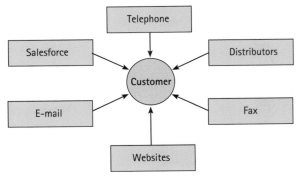

Figure 10.2 Customer company contact points

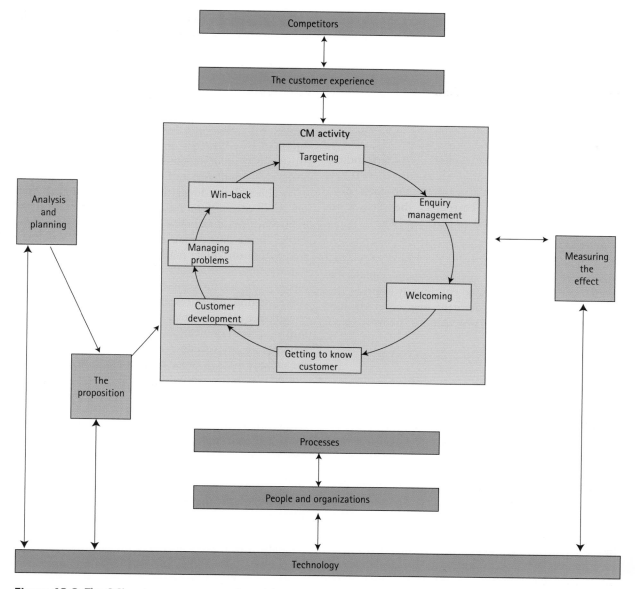

Figure 10.3 The QCi customer management model

requirements and resources, and employee satisfaction. The reason for the failure of many CRM initiatives has been inadequate attention to the people issues involved.

Process management

In an environment where customer contact can take place at several different points, processes can be difficult to implement and manage. Nevertheless, clear and consistent processes for managing customer relations need to be developed and reviewed in the light of changing customer requirements.

Customer management activity

This concerns the implementation of the plans and processes to deliver the propositions to the target segments, and involves:

- targeting customer and prospect groups with clearly defined propositions
- enquiry management—this starts as soon as an individual expresses an interest and continues through qualification, lead handling and outcome reporting
- welcoming—this covers new customers and those upgrading their relationship; it covers simple 'thank you' messages to sophisticated contact strategies
- getting to know—customers need to be persuaded to give information about themselves; this information needs to be stored, updated and used; useful information includes attitude and satisfaction information and relationship 'healthchecks'
- customer development—decisions need to be

made regarding which customers to develop through higher levels of relationship management activity, and which to maintain or drop

- managing problems—this involves early problem identification, complaint handling and 'root cause' analysis to spot general issues that have the potential to cause problems for many customers
- win-back—activities include understanding reasons for loss, deciding which customers to try to win back, and developing win-back programmes that offer customers the chance to come back and a good reason to do so.

Measuring the effect

Measuring performance against a plan enables the refinement of future plans to continually improve the CRM programme; measurement may cover people, processes, campaigns, proposition delivery and channel performance.

Customer experience

External measurement of customer experiences needs to take place and includes satisfaction tracking, loyalty analysis and mystery shopping.

Competitors

Their strengths and weaknesses need to be monitored and the company's performance on the above issues evaluated in light of the competition.

To date, CRM initiatives have had a very mixed success rate. Some of the factors that have been associated with success are:[13]

- having a customer orientation and organizing the CRM system around customers
- taking a single view of the customer across departments, and designing an integrated system so that all customer-facing staff can draw information from a common database
- having the ability to manage cultural change issues that arise as a result of system development and implementation
- involving users in the CRM design process
- designing the system in such a way that it can readily be changed to meet future requirements
- having a board-level champion of the CRM project, and commitment within each of the affected departments to the benefits of taking a single view of the customer

- creating 'quick wins' to provide positive feedback on the project programmes.

Direct marketing

Direct marketing attempts to acquire and retain customers by contacting them without the use of an intermediary. Whereas mass advertising reaches a broad spectrum of people, some of whom may not be in the target audience and may only buy at some later unspecified date, direct marketing uses media that can more precisely target consumers and request an immediate direct response. The origins of direct marketing lie in direct mail and mail-order catalogues and, as a result, direct marketing is sometimes seen as synonymous with 'junk mail'. However, today's direct marketers use a wide range of media, such as telemarketing, direct response advertising and e-mail to interact with people. Also, unlike many other forms of communication, direct marketing usually requires an immediate response, which means that the effectiveness of most direct marketing campaigns can be assessed quantitatively.

A definition of direct marketing is: 'the distribution of products, information and promotional benefits to target consumers through interactive communication in a way that allows response to be measured'.

A direct marketing campaign is not necessarily a short-term response-driven activity. More and more companies are using direct marketing to develop ongoing direct relationships with customers. Some estimates consider that the cost of attracting a new customer is five times that of retaining existing customers. Direct marketing activity can be one tool in the armoury of marketers in their attempt to keep current customers satisfied and spending money. Once a customer has been acquired, there is the opportunity to sell that customer other products marketed by the company. Direct Line, a UK insurance company, became market leader in motor insurance by bypassing the insurance broker to reach the consumer directly through direct response television advertisements using a freefone number and financial appeals to encourage car drivers to contact them. Once they have sold customers motor insurance, trained telesales people offer substantial discounts on other insurance products including buildings and contents insurance. In this way, Direct Line has built a major business through using a combination of direct marketing methods.

Direct marketing covers a wide array of methods, including:

- direct mail
- telemarketing (both in-bound and out-bound)
- direct response advertising (coupon response or 'phone now')
- catalogue marketing
- electronic media (Internet, e-mail, interactive cable TV)
- inserts (leaflets in magazines)
- door-to-door leafleting.

A survey of large consumer goods companies across Europe by the International Direct Marketing Network measured the use of these techniques (excluding catalogue marketing and online channels).[14] It found that 84 per cent of companies used some form of direct marketing, but there was a wide variation between countries. For example, 40 per cent used outbound telemarketing in Germany whereas none did in France. Overall, direct mail was the most commonly used technique (52 per cent) followed by coupon advertisements in the press (41 per cent). Telemarketing was not widely employed, although its use is more often associated with business-to-business marketing. In the UK, the proportion of the promotional budget being devoted to direct marketing has been increasing steadily, with one study finding companies planning to increase their spend on it by over 20 per cent.[15] The potential for growth in the area is reflected by the fact that per capita spend on direct marketing in the UK is US$71 compared with US$152 in the Netherlands and US$428 in the United States.[16]

The significant growth in direct marketing activity over the past ten years has been explained by five factors. The first is the growing fragmentation of media and markets. The growth of specialist magazines and television channels means that traditional mass advertising is less effective. Similarly, mass markets are disappearing as more and more companies seek to customize their offerings to target groups (see Chapter 5). Second, developments in technology, such as databases, and software that generates personalized letters, have eased the task for direct marketers. Third, there is a significantly increased supply of mailing lists available. List brokers act as an intermediary in the supply of lists from list owners (often either companies that have built lists through transactions with their customers, or organizations that have compiled lists specifically for the purpose of renting them). List brokers thus aid the process of finding a suitable list for targeting purposes. Fourth, more sophisticated analytical techniques such as geodemographic analysis (see Chapter 5) can be used to pinpoint targets for mailing purposes. Finally, the high costs of other techniques, such as **personal selling**, have led an increasing number of companies to take advantage of direct marketing techniques, such as direct response advertising and telemarketing, to make salesforces more cost-effective.

Direct marketing activity, including direct mail, telemarketing and telephone banking, is regulated by a European Commission Directive that came into force at the end of 1994. Its main provisions are that:

- suppliers cannot insist on pre-payments
- customers must be told the identity of the supplier, the price and quality of the product and any transport changes, the payment and delivery methods, and the period over which the solicitation remains valid
- orders must be met within 30 days unless otherwise indicated
- a cooling-off period of 30 days is mandatory and cold calling by telephone, fax or electronic mail is restricted unless the receiver has given prior consent.

Managing a direct marketing campaign

Direct marketing as with all promotional campaigns, should be fully integrated with all marketing mix elements to provide a coherent marketing strategy. Direct marketers need to understand how the product is being positioned in the marketplace as it is crucial that messages, sent out as part of a direct marketing campaign, do not conflict with those communicated by other channels such as advertising or the salesforce.

The stages involved in conducting a direct mail campaign are similar to those for mass communications techniques described in the previous chapter (see Figure 10.4). The first step is the identification of the target audience, and one of the advantages of direct mail is that audience targeting can be very precise. For example, it may be possible to target only existing customers or lapsed customers provided that mailing lists of these groups are available.

The objectives of direct marketing campaigns can be the same as those of other forms of promotion: to improve sales and profits, to acquire or retain customers or to create awareness. However, one of the benefits of direct marketing is that it usually has clearly defined short-term objectives against which performance can be measured, which makes the evaluation of effectiveness relatively easy. For

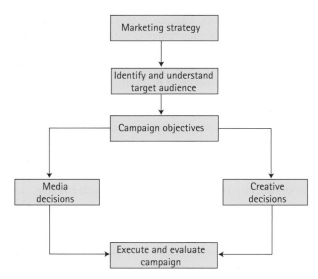

Figure 10.4 Managing a direct marketing campaign

example, objectives can be set in terms of response rate (proportion of contacts responding), total sales, number of enquiries, and so on.

The next major decision involves the media to be used for conducting the direct marketing campaign. Each of the major alternatives available to the marketer is discussed below. Once the media have been selected, the creative decisions must be made. The creative brief usually contains details of the communications objectives, the product benefits, the target market analysis, the offer being made, the communication of the message and the action plan (i.e. how the campaign will be run). As direct marketing is more orientated to immediate action than advertising, recipients will need to see a clear benefit before

responding. For example, Direct Line's success in the motor insurance business was built on a clear consumer benefit, namely substantial cost savings. Its positioning as a direct motor insurer was achieved through a visual featuring a red telephone on wheels.

Finally, the campaign needs to be executed and evaluated. Execution can be in-house or through the use of a specialist agency. As we noted earlier, direct marketing does lend itself to quantitative measurement. Some of the most frequently used measures are response rate (the proportion of contacts responding), total sales, sales rate (percentage of contacts purchasing), enquiry rate, cost per contact or enquiry or sale, and repeat purchase rate.

Direct mail

Material sent through the postal service to the recipient's home or business address, with the purpose of promoting a product and/or maintaining an ongoing relationship, is known as direct mail. Direct mail at its best allows close targeting of individuals in a way not possible using mass advertising media. For example, Heinz employs direct mail to target its customers and prospects. By creating a database based on responses to promotions, lifestyle questionnaires and rented lists, Heinz has built a file of 4.6 million households. Each one now receives a quarterly 'At Home' mailpack, which has been further segmented to reflect loyalty and frequency of purchase. Product and nutritional information is combined with coupons to achieve product trial.[17] A major advantage of direct mail is its cost. For example, in business-to-business marketing, it might cost £50 to visit potential cus-

Exhibit 10.2 Direct Mail is becoming an increasingly popular promotional tool for insurance companies like Axa

tomers, £5 to telephone them but less than £1 to send out a mailing.[18]

A key factor in the effectiveness of a direct mail campaign is the quality of the mailing list. Mailing lists are variable in quality. For example, in one year in the UK, 100 million items were sent back marked 'return to sender'. So the effectiveness of direct mail relies heavily on the quality of the list being used to target potential customers. Poor lists raise costs and can contribute to the growing negative perception of 'junk mail' since recipients are not interested in the contents of the mailing. As a result, it is often preferable to rent lists from list houses rather than purchase them.

Direct mail facilitates specific targeting to named individuals. For example, by hiring lists of subscribers to gardening catalogues, a manufacturer of gardening equipment could target a specific group of people who would be more likely to be interested in a promotional offer than the public in general. Elaborate personalization is possible and the results directly measurable. Since the objective of direct mail is immediate—usually a sale or an enquiry—success can be measured easily. Some organizations, such as *Reader's Digest*, spend money researching alternative creative approaches before embarking on a large-scale mailing. Factors such as type of promotional offer, headlines, visuals and copy can be varied in a systematic manner and, by using code numbers on reply coupons, response can be tied to the associated creative approach.

Telemarketing

When trained specialists use telecommunications and information technologies to conduct marketing and sales activities, this marketing communications system is known as telemarketing. Telemarketing can be a most cost-efficient, flexible and accountable medium.[19] The telephone permits two-way dialogue that is instantaneous, personal and flexible, albeit not face to face.

Technological advances have significantly assisted the growth of telemarketing. For example, integrated telephony systems allow for callers to be identified even before the agent has answered the call. The caller's telephone number is relayed into the computer database and his/her details and account information appear on the screen even before the call is picked up. Technology has also greatly improved the effectiveness and efficiency of outbound telemarketing. For example, predictive dialling enables multiple outbound calls to be made from a call centre. Calls are only delivered to agents when the customer answers, cutting out wasted calls to answering machines, engaged signals, fax machines and unanswered calls. In addition, scripts can be created and stored on the computer so that operators have ready and convenient access to them on-screen.

It can be used in a number of roles, and this versatility has also assisted the growth of telemarketing activities in recent years. Telemarketing can be used for direct selling when the sales potential of a customer does not justify a face-to-face call or, alternatively, an incoming telephone call may be the means of placing an order in response to a direct mail or television advertising campaign. Second, it can be used to support the field salesforce, for example, in situations where customers may find contacting the salesforce difficult given the nature of their job. Third, telemarketing can be used to generate leads through establishing contact with prospective customers and arranging a sales visit. Finally, an additional role of telemarketing is to maintain and update the firm's marketing database.

Telemarketing has a number of advantages. First, it has lower costs per contact than a face-to-face salesperson visit. Second, it is less time consuming than personal visits. Third, the growth in telephone ownership has increased access to households, and the use of toll-free lines (800 or 0800 numbers) has reduced the cost of responding by telephone. Next, the increasing sophistication of new telecommunications technology has encouraged companies to employ telemarketing techniques. For example, digital networks allow the seamless transfer of calls between organizations. The software company Microsoft and its telemarketing agency can smoothly transfer calls between their respective offices. If the caller then asks for complex technical information, this can be transferred back to the relevant Microsoft department.[20] Finally, despite the reduced costs, compared to a personal visit, the telephone retains the advantage of two-way communication. On the other hand, telephone selling is often considered intrusive, leading to consumers objecting to receiving unsolicited telephone calls. For example, legislation introduced in the UK in 2004 bans marketing companies from cold calling businesses, with fines of up to £5000 for violations of the law, although this applies only to call centres located in Britain. Also, although cost per contact is cheaper than a personal sales call, it is more expensive than direct mail or media advertising.

Mobile marketing

Mobile marketing, which is the sending of short text messages direct to mobile phones, is becoming extremely popular with the rapid penetration of mobile phones in society. Every month in the UK over a billion chargeable text messages are sent. Marketers have been quick to spot the opportunities of this medium to communicate, particularly to a youth audience. Marketers now send out messages to potential customers via their mobile phones to promote such products as fast food, movies, banks, alcoholic drinks, magazines and books. The acronym SMS (short messaging service) has appeared to describe this medium, while MMS (multimedia messaging service) is used to describe the sending of messages incorporating features like music, video, graphic, and so on.

Mobile marketing has several advantages. First, it is very cost effective. The cost per message is between 15p and 25p, compared with 50p to 75p per direct mail shot, including print production and postage. Second, it can be targeted and personalized. SMS use among 15–25 year olds is 86 per cent, and 87 per cent among 25–34 year olds; mobile marketing has high potential as a youth targeting tool. Third, it is interactive: the receiver can respond to the text message, setting up the opportunity for two-way dialogue and relationship development. Fourth, it is a time-flexible medium. Text messages can be sent at any time, giving greater flexibility when trying to reach the recipient. Finally, like other direct marketing techniques, it is immediate and measurable, and can assist in database development.

Mobile marketing does have certain limitations, however. First, the number of words in a text message is limited to 160 characters, though technological advances are likely to remove this restriction. Second, text messages are visually unexciting, though again advances in multimedia messaging are likely to overcome this. Third, there is the possibility of wear-off: mobile marketing is still novel and sceptics argue that once the novelty has worn off and consumers receive more and more messages, its effectiveness will wane. Finally, as with other aspects of direct mail, poor targeting, giving rise to 'junk mail', leads to customer annoyance and poor response rates.

However, at present, mobile marketing is very popular. Research by the Mobile Marketing Association showed that 68 per cent of consumers would be likely to recommend the service to their friends, and 43 per cent said that they would respond to messages positively, perhaps by visiting a website or viewing an advertisement.[21]

Direct response advertising

Although direct response advertising appears in prime media, such as television, newspapers and magazines, it differs from standard advertising in that it is designed to elicit a direct response such as an order, enquiry or a request for a visit. Often, a freefone telephone number is included in the advertisement or, for the print media, a coupon response mechanism is used. This combines the ability of broadcast media to reach large sections of the population with direct marketing techniques that allow a swift response on behalf of both prospect and company. The acceptability and accessibility of a freefone number was proven during the launch of Daewoo cars in the UK. All Daewoo advertising and literature contained its freefone number when its cars were launched in April 1995. Daewoo hoped that the campaign would attract about 3500 enquiries in the first month following launch. The actual response was over 43,000, rising to over 190,000 four months after launch for a previously unknown product. Direct response advertising had played its part in the successful introduction of a car brand in a new overseas market.[22]

Direct response television (or interactive television, as it is sometimes called) has experienced fast growth (see e-Marketing 10.1). It is an industry worth £3 billion globally and comes in many formats. The most basic is the standard advertisement with telephone number; 60-, 90- or 120-second advertisements are sometimes used to provide the necessary information to persuade viewers to use the freefone number for ordering. Other variants are the 25-minute product demonstration (these are generally referred to as 'infomercials') and live home shopping programmes broadcast by companies such as QVC. Home shopping has a very loyal customer base. For example, Shoppingtelly.com, a website that offers home shoppers news and information on home shopping products, receives between 20,000 and 35,000 hits per day and some of the leading home shopping presenters, such as Paul Lavers and Julia Roberts, have their own very popular websites.[23] A popular misconception regarding direct response television (DRTV) is that it is suitable only for products such as music compilations and cut-price jewellery. In Europe, a wide range of products (such as leisure and fitness products, motoring and household goods, books and beauty care products) are marketed in this way through pan-European channels such as Eurosport, Super Channel and NBC.

Catalogue marketing

The sale of products through catalogues distributed to agents and customers, usually by mail or at stores if the catalogue marketer is a store owner, is known as **catalogue marketing**. This method is popular in

e-Marketing: The television leaves the sitting room

As we saw in the previous chapter, television advertising is under increasing pressure as consumers use the available technologies to skip advertising breaks, and an increasing proportion of the consumer's time is spent with other media such as the Internet and electronic music players. But if the customer doesn't come to the television, one response is to bring the television to the customer. Whether it's the supermarket, the shopping centre, the post office or on the train, there is an increasing number of dedicated, out-of-home television networks.

The thinking behind this move is to try to place television screens where captive audiences exist. For example, i-vu has launched a network of 500 televisions in hair and beauty salons throughout the UK. Consumers that traditionally flicked through a magazine while they were having their hair done, now have the option of watching a television designed for their individual use should they choose to do so. The content is a selection of lifestyle, fashion and news items mixed with salon-specific material. Since clients spend on average £100 per visit to a top salon and stay for approximately an hour, they represent an attractive audience for advertisers. Total spending in hair salons is about £4.1 billion per year, further demonstrating the appeal of the market to i-vu clients like L'Oréal, BMG and Audi.

Advertisers have also long recognized that the point of purchase is a critical time to influence a consumer, so retail television promises to be a major growth area. Tesco has successfully experimented with the medium by launching Tesco TV in 100 of its largest stores. If the service is fully rolled out, it is expected to reach about 10 million shoppers per week, which shows its potential given that a leading ITV show in 2004, *I'm a Celebrity . . . Get Me Out of Here!* reached a similar figure each night. At a time when the number of television channels is growing, the number of retail chains is falling, making the supermarket aisle a potential medium for advertisers to reach consumers. And they also capitalize on the fact that consumers are in shopping mode. Recency theory suggests that the sooner you see an ad before making a purchase the better. Spar, which has also trialled in-store TV, reported that on-screen brand messages achieved average weighted sales increases of 10 per cent, while price promotions secured an average weighted increase of 24–25 per cent.

One of the key attractions of this kind of television is its interactive possibilities; i-vu screens have on-screen buttons for more information on certain items, as well as prizes, competitions and special offers. And it is these interactive response rates that appeal to advertisers. Supporters of the technology claim that it has response rates of over 8 per cent compared with less than half of 1 per cent for interactive TV at home. It is also possible to add an e-commerce facility to interactive television so that consumers can not only find out all they want to know about a particular product but they can order it too.

Based on: Harvey (2003);[24] Ray (2004);[25] Rowan (2004);[26] Wilkinson (2004)[27]

Europe with such organizations as Germany's Otto-Versand, the Next Directory in the UK, La Redoute in France and IKEA in Sweden (see Marketing in Action 10.2). Many of these companies operate in a number of countries; La Redoute, for instance, has operations in France, Belgium, Norway, Spain and Portugal. Catalogue marketing is popular in Austria because legislation restricts retail opening hours.[28] A common form of catalogue marketing is mail order, where catalogues are distributed and, traditionally, orders received by mail. Some enterprising companies, notably Next, saw catalogue marketing as

an opportunity to reach a new target market: busy, affluent, middle-class people who valued the convenience of choosing products at home.

Used effectively, catalogue marketing to consumers offers a convenient way of selecting products at home that allows discussion between family members in a relaxed atmosphere away from crowded shops and the high street. Often, credit facilities are available too. For remote rural locations this method provides a valuable service, obviating the need to travel long distances to town shopping centres. For catalogue

Marketing in Action: The IKEA catalogue

In this era of electronic communications, some companies still rely on good old-fashioned printed matter as the centrepiece of their promotional activity. The IKEA catalogue is a core element of that company's promotional mix, accounting for approximately 50 per cent of its total spend. It is distributed in 46 versions in 36 countries and in 28 languages. In the UK 14 million catalogues are distributed, while in the USA, 11 million are sent out. In Sweden, every house-hold gets a copy unless their letterbox specifically says 'no advertising'. The European and North American version runs to 360 pages and weighs just over 1 lb.

Every market that the catalogue is distributed to brings its challenges. In Greece, many apartments do not have letterboxes so it has to be hung in a plastic bag on the door. In China where the company has two stores, letterboxes are too small, while in Malaysia, catalogues have to be specially wrapped because of the humidity. Typically, the catalogue contains about 4000 items, which is one-third of IKEA's product offering. Featured items typically sell two to three times better than non-featured items.

Production takes about 18 months from the start of planning to distribution. In keeping with IKEA's low cost strategy, the photography avoids expensive and glamorous locations and the company's own employees are used instead of models. About 90 per cent of the material is common to the European and North American versions, saving on printing costs. The width of the paper used is not a fraction of a millimetre bigger than necessary. The catalogue is presented as a lifestyle magazine and other companies with similar brand values are allowed to advertise on its pages, further defraying the cost of production.

Based on: Anonymous (2002);[29] Brown-Humes (2003)[30]

Exhibit 10.3 French company La Redoute is one of the world's biggest catalogue marketers

marketers, the expense of high-street locations is removed and there is an opportunity to display a wider range of products than could feasibly be achieved in a shop. Distribution can be centralized, lowering costs. Nevertheless, catalogues are expensive to produce (hence the need for some retailers to charge for them) and they require regular updating, particularly when selling fashion items. They do not allow goods to be tried (e.g. a vacuum cleaner) or tried on (e.g. clothing) before purchase. Although products can be seen in a catalogue, variations in colour printing can mean that the curtains or suite that are delivered do not have exactly the same colour tones as those appearing on the printed page.

Internet marketing

The impact of the **Internet** on society has been described as being as significant as some of the greatest technological innovations in history, such as the telephone and the motor car. The Internet is a global web of over 50,000 computer networks containing millions of web pages, which users can access once they connect to a server. The commercial possibilities created by these developments were obvious and the early stages of e-commerce were likened to the Californian gold rush of 1849. Entrepreneurs raced to register domain names and create **websites** in the hope of making big returns. A significant level of hype was generated, with predictions that the Internet would revolutionize the way business could be done, and this led to a boom in the valuation of Internet-based companies. Thousands of start-ups came and went quickly, but many others, such as eBay, Yahoo! and Amazon survived the shake-out and went on to become large, global companies and household names.

Electronic commerce or **e-commerce** has been defined as 'a wide range of technologies used to streamline business interactions such as the Internet, **electronic data interchange** (EDI), e-mail, electronic payment systems, advanced telephone systems, hand-held digital devices, interactive television, self-service kiosks and smart cards'.

Therefore, e-commerce—or e-business, as it is also described—is a broad term and represents an evolution in the process of using the currently available technology to improve business processes or the delivery of service to customers. For example, prior to the advent of the Internet, many companies had EDI systems (and some still do), which linked computers in and between organizations to enable the rapid exchange of information, such as that between suppliers and customers.

Internet marketing has been defined as, 'the achievement of marketing objectives through the utilization of the Internet and web-based technologies'.

Though sometimes the terms are used interchangeably, e-marketing is broader than Internet marketing in that it refers to the achievement of marketing objectives via a wider range of communications technologies such as mobile phones and digital television. The first step in Internet marketing is the registration of a **domain name**, which is the address that Internet sites have and which performs the role of being a 'telephone number' for individuals wishing to reach them. Next, companies develop a website that contains web pages, which are **World Wide Web** files that contain text, pictures and/or sound. Websites then become the public face of the company in the same way that brochures traditionally did; many early websites were simply no more than brochures presented online. But as we shall see below, effective Internet marketing involves much more than simply putting up a website.

The growth of e-commerce

The prospects for e-commerce continue to provoke quite a bit of debate. Much of the reason for this stems from the hype that surrounded the initial wave of e-businesses beginning in 1995. A generation of online companies were formed and the publicity surrounding them suggested that these companies were going to radically alter the way that business was done. Billions were invested in these start-ups and much of that money was lost when the boom turned into a bust in 2000. There have been some successful ventures, such as Amazon (even though its losses reached US\$1.4 billion in 2000), eBay, Yahoo! and Google, though the stock market valuations of most Internet companies have never reached the heights achieved in the late 1990s.

While business-to-business e-commerce has always claimed the dominant share of e-business, the indicators suggest that business-to-consumer e-commerce may gradually achieve some of the levels predicted by early commentators. Central to this is the growth of broadband connections, which permit high-speed access to the Internet, thus making the experience more user-friendly. Over 23 per cent of American consumers have a broadband connection, and research shows that these users spend twice as much time online as narrowband users and are more likely to shop and bank online.[31] It is estimated that over 40 per cent of UK homes will have broadband by 2008. In general, consumers are spending more time online (see Table 10.1). Figures from Europe show that over 60 per cent of UK and German consumers go online at least once a month while the comparable figure is over 45 per cent for consumers in Italy and France.[32]

With greater numbers spending time online, the prospects for Internet businesses improve. Estimates are that online spending will grow by 35 per cent in the UK in 2005, taking total spending to £19.6 million.[33] Over 35 per cent of people aged between 25 and 44 reported having shopped online in the past month in the UK while over 30 per cent of 16–24 year olds did so.[34] The sectors forecast to see the biggest growth in Europe are leisure travel, computer hardware and software, event tickets, books, music/DVDs/videos and consumer electronics. But, in a change from the first wave of e-commerce, the biggest share of sales is not being accounted for by start-up Internet companies but rather traditional retailers and mail order companies that have developed an online presence and are adopting a 'multi-channel' strategy that sees sales through a website, shops and mail order catalogues.

Table 10.1 Consumption and expenditure on US media

Medium	% US ad spending on medium	% Time US households spend on medium
TV	38	32
Newspapers	36	9
Radio	14	19
Magazines	8	6
Internet	5	33

Source: Forrester Research

Another indicator of the growth in the sector is the increase in online advertising expenditure. UK Internet advertising expenditure is expected to reach £615 million in 2005, which is a 14-fold increase from the 1999 level.[35] Banner ads and pop-up ads, which were the most popular format in the early days of the Internet, have been replaced by search advertising (see e-Marketing 10.3). Globally, Internet advertising is predicted to reach US$20 billion by 2007 and an indication of its size is that the combined advertising revenues of Google and Yahoo! are predicted to equal that of the three major US advertising networks, ABC, NBC and CBS by 2006.[36]

Internet marketing opportunities

Once a company has decided to adopt e-commerce as a way to exploit new, entrepreneurial opportunities, one immediate outcome is that the organization's knowledge platform becomes much more closely linked with other knowledge sources, such as suppliers and customers, elsewhere within the market system. The reason for this is that once buyers and sellers become electronically linked, volumes of data interchange increase dramatically as trading activities begin to occur in real time. The outcome is the emergence of very dynamic, rapid responses by both customer and supplier to changing circumstances within their market systems. For example, when a customer places an order with Dell, this order also automatically goes to Dell's suppliers so that product components can immediately begin their journey to a Dell assembly plant.

The extent of e-commerce is borne out by the fact that all possible combinations of exchange between consumers and business organizations take place (see Figure 10.5). Business-to-business exchanges take place through the use of EDI interchanges: companies such as Cisco Systems have transferred nearly all of their purchases to the Internet. This is the largest form of e-commerce at present. The most apparent form of e-commerce is that from business to consumer (B2C), with established retailers such as

Tesco setting up home-shopping facilities, and a variety of Internet-based companies like Amazon dominating their markets.

E-commerce from consumer to business (C2B) is less common, but demonstrates the versatility of the Internet. An example is the facility provided by Priceline.com whereby would-be passengers bid for airline tickets, leaving the airlines to decide whether or not to accept these offers. The Internet also permits consumers to trade with other consumers via auctions: consumer to consumer (C2C). Would-be sellers can offer products through such sites as eBay or QXL to potential customers.

It was the growth in consumer-to-consumer interactions that also revolutionized the music industry. File sharing between music fans grew in popularity due to the existence of a variety of websites like Napster. Consequently, music industry sales decreased and the industry had to embrace the new distribution medium (see Chapter 2). Many of the Internet's marketing possibilities arise from communications and interactions between consumers on the Internet (see e-Marketing 10.2). Of particular interest to marketers has been the growth of virtual communities, which are groups of people with similar interests that visit websites for online chats and the exchange of information. These groups represent potentially valuable sources of market information and feedback on marketing initiatives, as well as potential sales.

	From business	From consumer
To business	B2B Cisco	C2B Priceline
To consumer	B2C Amazon	C2C eBay

Figure 10.5 Forms of e-commerce

e-Marketing: Looking for love and playing games online

As a global communications network, the Internet has the power to bring people together. Two of the biggest growth areas are online dating and online gaming. Revenues from the leading European dating websites are expected to more than double in the next five years from US$200 million to over US$450 million. Meetic.com is the biggest dating website in Europe, with sites in 11 countries: France, Italy, Spain, Austria, Germany, Belgium, Denmark, the Netherlands, Sweden, Switzerland and the UK. It has 10 million members and sales in the region of US$55 million. In France, one adult in 15 is a Meetic member. Online dating is also big business in the USA, with a number of leading websites, such as Match.com, True.com and eHarmony.com. There are also special interest websites such as SeniorsCircle.com for the over-50s, VeggieDate.com for vegetarians and JDate.com for Jewish singles. The sites publicize themselves through organizing parties for members and supplying 'volunteers' to appear on television chat shows such as *Oprah*.

On most dating websites, members can join free of charge. They then post their profile and can browse those of other members. Premium services such as personality matchmaker software, which cross-references members' preferences, usually cost in the region of US$18 per month. The sites are also vetted. Each profile is checked by a moderator and another software system weeds out users who post rude or offensive messages during chat sessions, who can then be blacklisted from the site. A further potential growth area is mobile phone dating services. Meetic has paired up with Vodafone to enable members to contact each other via SMS or MMS. Though mobile revenues account for only 3 per cent of sales at present, this is expected to grow significantly. The growth of online dating is creating new challenges for newspapers and magazines that carry classified personal ads.

Traditionally, playing computer games was quite a solitary activity where gamers often spent quiet hours racking up ever higher scores. The arrival of games consoles became the catalyst for multiplayer games, when up to four people plug in together in front of the television. But when Microsoft, the world's biggest computer company, entered the games business in 2002 with its Xbox, the potential for playing games online was quickly explored. Online play means no longer having to wait for your friends to have a free evening—a permanent supply of willing gamers is available throughout the world.

One of the chief attractions of online gaming is voice communication, which is standard on most games for the Xbox live service. Players can chat or taunt each other while racing motor bikes or teaming up as commandos. Despite early scepticism, online play has quickly taken off. By June 2003, Microsoft was claiming that it had 500,000 online players while Sony's response—the PS2 online service—claimed 600,000 players. And from being a solitary activity, leading gamers are now becoming major celebrities. The World Cyber Games in Seoul in 2002 attracted more than 100,000 spectators. Top Korean and Japanese gamers are millionaires, earning vast sums from prize money and sponsorship contracts. Their prowess is watched by television audiences of millions with action replays and expert analysis.

Based on: Cole (2003);[37] Kirchgaessner (2003);[38] Poole (2003);[39] van Winkle (2004)[40]

Furthermore, the Internet helps to create business opportunities through the inherent benefits it offers to customers. The first of these is convenience. Access to a website is available 24 hours a day, seven days a week, and is significantly more convenient than offline distribution channels, which may involve driving, queuing, etc. Second, the Internet is a global medium. Consumers can get easier access to prod-ucts/information from different parts of the world than is possible through other channels. Third, it can provide excellent value. Price comparison technologies allow consumers to search for the cheapest brands and to do immediate, real-time comparisons of the prices being charged by different vendors. For example, the Internet brought price transparency to the car rental market with the result that Avis, one of the market leaders and a premium-priced competitor, was forced to reduce its prices and saw its profits fall from £111 million in 1999 to around £20 million in 2005.[41] Finally, as the Internet is an information resource, it assists with the buying decision process by enabling consumers to evaluate alternative brands or service providers.

From a business point of view, the Internet provides many benefits, but it also has some limitations. These are summarized in Table 10.2. The benefits have been exploited by Internet start-ups to gain advantages over their offline rivals in four ways, as described below.

Lower costs and prices

Communicating with customers online is significantly cheaper than serving them via telephone or person to person. Therefore, organizations like banks are encouraging their customers to carry out basic financial transactions such as account enquiries and bill payments online rather than at bank branches. Online banks typically offer better interest rates on savings and cheaper loans than their offline counter-

parts. The Internet also permits suppliers to make contact with customers without using an intermediary, further reducing their costs. The savings generated by the removal of the intermediary from the transaction can be passed on to the customer in the form of lower prices. An example of this form of competitive advantage is provided by low-fares airlines such as easyJet and Ryanair. The advent of the Internet allowed these companies to create automated, online flight enquiry and booking services, and ticket assurance systems. The process of bypassing traditional intermediaries such as travel agents is known as 'disintermediation'. Similarly, consumers are now able to book holidays directly and often can do so at prices lower than those advertised by tour operators (see e-Marketing 7.1).

Improved service quality

It is almost impossible—in most service markets—to offer a product proposition that is very different from that of the competition. As a result one of the few ways of gaining a competitive advantage is through being able to deliver a superior level of customer service. A key influencer of service quality is

Table 10.2 Potential benefits and limitations of Internet technologies to consumers

Benefits	Limitations
Convenience in terms of being able to provide access 24 hours a day, 365 days a year. Furthermore, the customer can permit avoidance of driving to a store, searching for products or queuing at the checkout.	*Delivery times* are not quite so flexible. The logistical complexities of getting physical goods the last mile to the customer's home can mean that the customer must stay in and wait until the goods arrive.
As an *information resource*, the Internet enables the end user to acquire detailed information about products, pricing and availability without leaving their home or the office.	*Information overload*: the amount of information that can be accessed via the Internet by an end user can be overwhelming.
Multimedia: through exploitation of the latest technology, customers can gain a better understanding of their needs by, for example, examining 3D displays of car interiors or hotel accommodation	*Access to technology*: the greater the capacity to incorporate multimedia content into e-commerce operations, the higher the required specifications of the computer to download such content. Many consumers in and around the globe do not have access to even the most basic means of accessing the Internet.
New products and services can be purchased in areas such as online financial services, and there is the ability to mix together audio, music and visual materials to customize the entertainment goods being purchased.	*Security*: many consumers are concerned about using credit and/or debit cards to purchase goods online for fear that their details will be captured by 'crackers'.
Lower prices: it is possible to search for the lowest price available for brands. Specific sites (e.g. Kelkoo and Froogle) allows consumers to surf the Internet to find the best available price.	*Cost implications*: the consumer has to make an initial investment in suitable equipment, pay for consumables like printer ink and fund the cost of downloading company information.

the speed of information interchange between the supplier and the customer. Clearly, therefore, the information interchange capability of the Internet offers some interesting opportunities to be perceived as superior to other firms in the same market. For many years, Federal Express has been a global leader in the application of IT, providing a superior level of customized delivery services to customers. The firm has enhanced its original customer-service software system, COSMOS, by providing major clients with terminals and software that use the Internet to take them into the Federal logistics management system. In effect, Federal Express now offers customers the ability to create a state-of-the-art distribution system without having to make any investment in self-development of shipping expertise inside their own firms.

Greater product variety

In terms of the amount of space available to display goods, the average high-street retail shop is physically restricted. Hence its customers, who may already have faced the inconvenience of having to travel to the retailer's location, may encounter the frustration of finding that the shop does not carry the item they wish to purchase. Online retailers do not face the same space restrictions their 'bricks and mortar' competitors do. As a result, they can use their website to offer a much greater variety of goods to potential customers. Possibly one of the best-known examples of a firm that has exploited this source of competitive advantage is online bookseller Amazon.com. This phenomenon is sometimes described as the 'long tail of e-commerce'. About one-third of Amazon's sales come from outside its 130,000 top-selling book titles, while Rhapsody, a streaming music service, streams more tracks from outside than inside its top 10,000 tunes.[42]

Product customization

Many manufacturers have come to realize, over the past 20 years, that adoption of just-in-time (JIT) production can offer the potential to customize products to meet the needs of individual customers. Dell Computer Corporation's extensive experience of computer direct marketing permitted it to be a 'first mover' in exploiting the Internet as part of its strategy to offer customized products. Customers who visit the Dell website are offered assistance in selecting the type of technology most suited to their needs. These data provide the inputs to an online help system, which guides the customer through the process of evolving the most appropriate specification from a range of choices. Once a final selection has been made, the customer receives an instant quote on both the price of their purchase and the date on which it will be delivered. Several online marketers are attempting to gain competitive advantage through this idea of mass customizing products and services to customers (see Chapter 5). In commenting on this approach, Jeffrey Bezos, founder of Amazon.com, has used the analogy of the e-commerce retailer behaving like the small-town shopkeeper of yesteryear, as large firms can now also develop a deep understanding of everybody who comes into the online store through software that is able to track their online behaviour. Armed with such in-depth knowledge—like the shopkeeper in the village store—the large retailer can personalize its service to suit the specific needs of every individual customer across a widely dispersed geographic domain.

Having reviewed the benefits and limitations in Table 10.2, the organization is then at the stage where it can begin to determine an entry point into e-commerce. Most organizations realize that the Internet is a technological tool, the use of which will evolve and change as the organization gains experience of trading in cyberspace. Hart et al. discovered that UK retailers had different approaches to Internet adoption.[43] Initially, Internet technologies were found to be used to provide a range of information about a company on a website. The next stage was to incorporate various forms of interactive marketing into the website—for example, surveys and e-mail questionnaires to encourage direct, two-way communication with customers. The final stage involved permitting customers to use an online marketing platform to place orders and make payments via the Internet.

The Internet as a direct marketing medium

Because of the benefits and the advantages it confers, as described above, the Internet is a powerful marketing medium. It presents novel ways of configuring the marketing mix, as shown in Figure 10.6.

Product

There are several ways that the Internet offers an opportunity for product enhancement:

- *individual*—personal specifications can lead to highly individual products being created
- *customized*—Tesco's online shopping website captures details of shopper's regular purchase choices and then provides a customized list of favourites; the main benefit for the customer is speedier online shopping
- *digital*—emergence of the Internet has facilitated the growth and distribution of bit-based

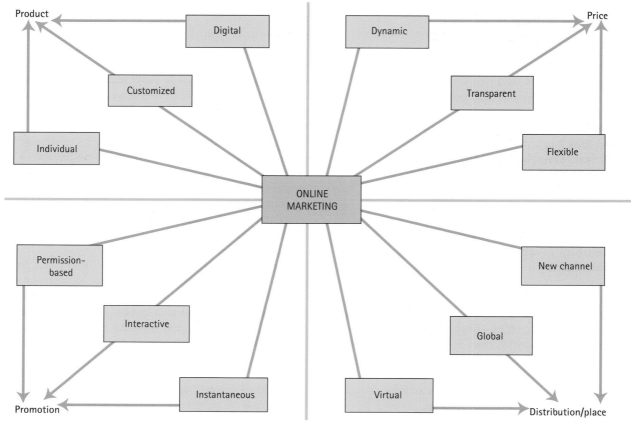

Figure 10.6 Online marketing and the marketing mix

products; bit-based products are digital goods and services that can be delivered via the Internet straight to an online customer's desktop—for example, information, software upgrades, computer games, flight bookings and hotel reservations; once the customer makes a payment, they can download the product regardless of the physical location of the supplier or the buyer; information in the form of market analysts' and consultants' reports is another form of bit-based product and the market for such goods has grown significantly since the commercialization of the Internet.

Price

A major impact of Internet technologies on economics is that they potentially reduce the search costs that buyers incur when looking for information about new products and services. The net effect is a reduction in suppliers' power to control and therefore charge higher prices as pricing strategies become more transparent. Additionally prices become more dynamic, as shown by the popularity of the auction site eBay. Priceline.com demonstrates how collective buying can change the price paid by the consumer, creating an opportunity for flexible pricing strategies.

Promotion

The Internet is becoming increasingly important as a marketing communications tool. Research has discovered that the web is being used extensively by consumers in the USA as a research tool.[44] When using the Internet as part of a marketing communications strategy, a company can send permission-based e-mailings, regular bulletins containing information about, say, the latest product features and any promotional offers that the customer has agreed to accept.

This kind of agreement can enable a company to begin to build a longer-term online relationship with the customer. Furthermore, the Internet enables the customer to respond by interacting with communications message, unlike traditional broadcast and print media where a two-way dialogue is not possible on a large scale. Interactive features can be incorporated into online promotions in a number of different forms, such as surveys, competitions, banner advertisements (static, animated or interactive) and interstitials (adverts that pop up when Internet users visit particular websites and/or pages).

Another innovative characteristic of communications via the Internet is that they can be instantaneous, as

Exhibit 10.4 Ads like Hamlet's 'typical male', which was an email attachment, are an example of viral marketing

'Giving something for nothing' is another effective means of increasing the viral effect. Hotmail (www.hotmail.com) became the number-one, web-based e-mail supplier, with over 14 million users worldwide, most from a message sent to a handful of paid e-mail users. The prospect of free e-mail was hard to resist and it was impossible not to tell others. The same strategy has been employed by Skype, whose software for making free telephone calls over the Internet has been downloaded 130 million times since the company was founded in 2003.[45] Companies like 5pm.co.uk (www.5pm.co.uk) now send e-mails promoting specific off-peak restaurant deals, only redeemable through unique links noted on the e-mail, with the intention that these will be passed on to 'new' customers.[46]

E-mail has also been found to be an effective medium. A study by the Direct Marketing Association (DMA) in the USA has found that return on investment from business-to-consumer e-mail marketing is about twice that of direct mail. But the biggest problem faced by e-mail is that of 'spam'— that is, unsolicited e-mail messages—which is estimated to account for over two-thirds of all e-mail messages sent.

Finally, a key consideration for companies is getting their websites identified by search engines. This requires marketing their websites to the search engines so that they can easily be found by web users (see e-Marketing 10.3). A second consideration is trying to improve the placing of a website on search engine page rankings. The higher the placing, the more likely the web user will visit the website. The Internet also promises to revolutionize the field of public relations (see e-Marketing 10.4).

Distribution

The Internet has created opportunities for companies to utilize a new channel to market. It has distinct advantages over traditional channels in reducing barriers to entry. The location issue, considered to be a key determinant of retail patronage in the physical sense, is reduced, along with the enormous capital investment in stores. Trading exchanges take place in a virtual market space, and these networks are global.

The commonest distribution model in the majority of offline consumer goods markets is to delegate both transaction and logistics processes (e.g. major brands such as Coca-Cola being marketed via supermarket chains). This can be contrasted with the online world where absolute delegation of all processes is a somewhat rarer event. The reason for this situation is that many firms, having decided that e-commerce offers

data is transmitted through fibre-optic cables and via satellite links at the speed of light, providing opportunities for immediate responses to enquiring customers. A particular example of this is what has become known as **viral marketing**. Most commonly associated with e-mail, viral marketing is essentially electronic word-of-mouth promotion where jokes are shared among friends, or calls for action such as those in support of the Live8 concerts for poverty relief are publicized. Companies attempt to harness this viral effect by building messages that are suitably engaging and promote an aspect of their company with content that customers want to read and send on. This requires some creativity and a good understanding of the customer base. Humour is one way of creating a strong viral effect. Pepsi famously e-mailed a series of streaming video adverts prior to the 2002 World Cup, stealing a march on its largest competitor.

e-Marketing: Sponsoring key words on Internet searches

The first port of call for most Internet users is the search engine or portal, where leading companies like Google, Yahoo! and MSN help browsers to find the sites that they are looking for. One of the fastest-growing sources of revenue for these companies is word sponsorship. This is the practice whereby the search engine sells key words such as 'holiday' or 'hotel' to the highest-bidding advertiser in an online auction. The buyer then 'owns' the key word, so that when an Internet user searches for that subject, the advertiser's site appears at the top of the list of websites turned up by the search. On sites like Google, sponsored search results are clearly distinguished from general search results, though this is not always the case on other search websites.

'Paid search' advertising was pioneered by Overture, one of the early search engine entrants, which was bought by Yahoo! in 2003 and still commands a significant share of the market. It is big business. In 2002, the market was worth over US$1.26 billion and is expected to grow to over US$6 billion by 2007 according to Jupiter Research. Sponsoring key words represents an attractive option for websites seeking to promote their business. People using search engines are usually looking for something specific and click-through rates are much higher on sponsored searches than on ordinary banner ads. Google reports that its clients experience on average a 2 per cent response rate, which is about 10 times higher than that for banner ads. It is also a relatively efficient form of promotion as advertisers pay on the basis of 'price per click'. Every time the user clicks through on a sponsored search link, the advertiser pays a small sum, which can be a few pence, although it can rise depending on the value of the product being sold.

However, a raft of legal challenges may threaten the development of the paid search industry. In July 2002, American Blind asked Google to stop selling key words such as 'American blind' and 'American wallpaper' as these infringed its trademarks. Similarly, leading companies like Dell, eBay and Hewlett-Packard have requested that it stop selling key words against their names. In France, Louis Vuitton is suing Google for trademark infringement and Playboy Enterprises is suing Netscape and AOL for using terms like 'playboy' and 'playmate' in banner advertising. If more and more key words and phrases are linked to trademarks, it will significantly constrain the scope of search engines to provide useful search results.

Based on: Anonymous (2003);[47] Harvey (2003);[48] Thompson (2004);[49] Waters (2004)[50]

an opportunity for revising distribution management practices, perceive cyberspace as offering a way to regain control over transactions by cutting out intermediaries and selling direct to their end-user customers. This process, in which traditional intermediaries may be squeezed out of channels is, as we have already seen, usually referred to as disintermediation. Hence, for those firms engaged in assessing the e-commerce distribution aspects of their marketing mix, there is a need to recognize that the technology has the following implications.

- Distance ceases to be a cost influencer because online delivery of information is substantially the same no matter what the destination of the delivery.
- Business location becomes an irrelevance because the e-commerce corporation can be based anywhere in the world.

- The technology permits continuous trading, 24 hours a day, 365 days a year.

Finally, a characteristic of offline distribution channels is the difficulty that smaller firms face in persuading intermediaries (e.g. supermarket chains) to stock their goods (see e-Marketing 10.5). This scenario is less applicable in the world of e-commerce. Firms of any size face a relatively easy task in establishing an online presence. Market coverage can then be extended by developing trading alliances based on offering to pay commission to other online traders who attract customers to the company's website. This ease of entry reduces the occurrence of firms' marketing efforts being frustrated because they are unable to gain the support of intermediaries in traditional distribution channels. Eventually e-commerce may lead to a major increase in the total number of firms offering goods and services across world markets.

e-Marketing: Blogging: public relations goes direct

They may be new terms but weblogs, or blogs for short, are something we are likely to hear a great deal more about. Blogs are easily published online diaries that provide comment, opinion and unfiltered, uncensored information on topics from gadgets to politics to fashion. They facilitate conversations because they enable people to post comment and link to other blogs. A new blog is created every 2.2 seconds, which means that around 38,000 blogs are created daily. There are about 10 million US blogs and some 34 million worldwide. *Time* magazine declared 2004 the 'year of the blog'.

So who are all these bloggers? Microsoft alone has 800 corporate bloggers, who provide information and opinions on developments in the computer industry. Their leading blogger, Robert Scoble (http://radio.weblogs.com/0001011/) has a huge following of information technology enthusiasts who regularly read his commentaries in which he has often been critical of Microsoft's products. Similarly, Sun Microsystems has about 1000 employee blogs. Its chief executive, Jonathan Schwartz, has his own blog (http://blogs.sun.com/jonathan) where he can air his thoughts and reflections; it has 30,000 readers. Weblogs like these allow corporate executives to speak directly and simultaneously to a variety of constituencies such as employees, investors, customers, suppliers, and so on.

Weblogs have several advantages. They allow corporate leaders to explain and disseminate strategy to relevant parties. They give writers an opportunity to answer critics or deal with questions in a controlled forum. Compared with conferences or printed memos to all staff, they are highly cost effective. And in an era of negative corporate sentiment, they can help to provide a human face to a corporation, as Microsoft's bloggers have done. But they also have a number of disadvantages. Chief executives, particularly of public companies, are very restricted in terms of what they can say as regulations require that market-sensitive information be released to all investors at the same time. There is also the danger that sensitive company information might be released. For example, Apple sued one of its employees for releasing details of Apple products on his weblog before they were launched. Second, blogs must come across as genuine and interesting to read. Those that try to hype up the company or its brands are likely to be ridiculed, as has happened Mazda and Raging Cow (a flavoured milk drink). Finally, there is the danger that an ill-judged comment will be seized upon by a disgruntled investor or the media.

To date, research in the USA by Forrester has shown that almost 50 per cent of the population have never heard of blogs and only 5 per cent regularly read one. But their growth once again indicates how consumers are changing the way in which they consume information. They are moving from traditional mass channels to more individual and interactive media. Blogs help to increase the power of the consumer as they enable product research and the exchange of information between interested individuals. And this power should not be underestimated. For example, two-thirds of the websites devoted to France's referendum on the European Constitution favoured the 'No' campaign and played an important role in swinging public opinion against the treaty. But they also represent a useful way for companies to get feedback from customers on products and services.

Based on: Anonymous (2005);[51] Gapper (2005);[52] Lewis (2005);[53] Thornhill (2005)[54]

Personal selling

The final major element of the promotional mix is personal selling. This involves face-to-face contact with a customer and, unlike advertising, promotion and other forms of non-personal communication, personal selling permits a direct interaction between buyer and seller. This two way communication means that the seller can identify the specific needs and problems of the buyer and tailor the sales presentation in the light of this knowledge. The particular concerns of the buyer can also be dealt with on a one-to-one basis.

e-Marketing: **Riverford goes direct**

One of the biggest challenges that small food firms face is gaining shelf space in the major supermarkets, where they must compete against the financial muscle of the major manufacturers as well as the retailers' own brands. The Internet provides these small firms with the opportunity to bypass the middleman and go direct to the customer. Riverford, a small, UK-based organic vegetable company, has pursued just such a strategy.

Guy Weston began farming at Riverford in 1985 and after his farm was fully converted to organic status in 1987, he began delivering his vegetables to local shops. With this in place, home delivery was the next step and a network of local distributors was set up to operate the home delivery box scheme, with all the vegetables being packed at Riverford farm. Production was expanded through the South Devon Organic Producer group, which is a network of 13 family-run farms that share machinery, labour and knowledge of growing organic vegetables. Approximately 85 different varieties of vegetables are harvested so that vegetable boxes can be kept interesting all year around. A suite of different box sizes are sold, ranging from a mini box costing £7 to a large box costing £12.50 and a fruit and vegetable combination box selling at £12.

The company's award-winning website, Riverford.co.uk, is a critical element of its marketing strategy. It entertains customers with recipes and information about its products, as well as allowing them to place and pay for orders. But it is also an essential infrastructure for managing the supply chain. Orders are delivered by a network of franchisees. There are currently 26 franchisees operating in the south and south-west of the UK with plans to expand into London and the Midlands. Boxes are collected from a chilled hub, meaning that Riverford customers will always have vegetables that are packed one day at the farm and delivered the next. Customers have access to their orders and can make changes up to 36 hours before delivery; they can also track their order history. The company currently delivers over 11,000 boxes per week.

Based on: Anonymous (2004);[55] Anonymous (2005)[56]

Such flexibility comes at a price, however. The cost of a car, travel expenses and sales office overheads can mean that the total annual bill for a field salesperson is often twice the level of a salary. In industrial marketing, over 70 per cent of the marketing budget is usually spent on the salesforce. This is because of the technical nature of the products being sold, and the need to maintain close personal relationships between the selling and buying organizations.

The make-up of the personal selling function is changing, however. Organizations are reducing the size of their salesforces in the face of greater buyer concentration, moves towards centralized buying, and recognition of the high costs of maintaining a field sales team. For example, Pfizer is cutting its 38,000-strong global sales force due to falling margins and greater competition from generic drugs. The concentration of buying power into fewer hands has also fuelled the move towards relationship management, often through key account selling. This involves the use of a small number of dedicated sales teams, which service the accounts of major buyers as opposed to having a large number of salespeople. Instead of sending salespeople out on the road, many companies now collect a large proportion of their sales through direct marketing techniques such as the telephone or computer.

The three main types of salespeople are order-takers, order-creators and order-getters. Order-takers respond to already committed customers such as a sales assistant in a convenience store or a delivery salesperson. Order-creators have traditionally been found in industries like healthcare, where the sales task is not to close the sale but to persuade the medical representative to prescribe or specify the seller's products. Order-getters are those in selling jobs where the major objective is to persuade the customer to make a direct purchase. They include consumer salespeople such as those selling double glazing or insurance, through to organizational salespeople, who often work in teams where products may be highly technical and negotiations complex.

Exhibit 10.5 This advertisement for the FBD Insurance Company is designed to help its sales force by offering customer calling

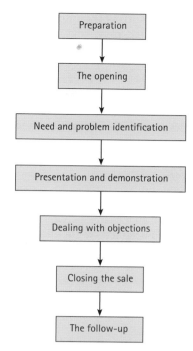

Figure 10.7 The selling process

Personal selling skills

While the primary responsibility of a salesperson is to increase sales, there are a number of additional enabling activities carried out by many salespeople, including **prospecting**, maintaining customer records, providing service, handling complaints, relationship management and self-management. Prospecting involves searching for and calling on potential customers. Prospects can be identified from several sources including talking to existing customers, and searching trade directories and the business press. Customer record-keeping is an important activity for all repeat-call salespeople because customer information is one of the keys to improving service and generating loyalty. Salespeople should be encouraged and rewarded for sending customer and market information back to head office. Providing service to customers—including, for example, advice on ways of improving productivity and handling customer complaints—can also be a key salesforce activity. This is particularly true in cases where the selling situation is not a one-off activity. In general, there has been a rise in the number of salespeople involved in relationship management roles

with large organizational customers. Trust is an important part of relationship development and is achieved through a high frequency of contact, ensuring promises are kept, and reacting quickly and effectively to problems. Finally, given the flexibility of the salesperson's job, many are required to practise self-management, including decisions on call frequencies and journey routing, for example.

Many people's perception of a salesperson is of a slick, fast-talking confidence trickster devoted to forcing unwanted products on gullible customers. In reality, success in selling comes from implementing the marketing concept when face to face with customers, not denying it at the very point when the seller and buyer come into contact. The sales interview offers an unparalleled opportunity to identify individual customer needs and match behaviour to the specific customer that is encountered.[57] In order to develop personal selling skills it is useful to distinguish six phases of the selling process (see Figure 10.7). We will now discuss each of these in turn.

Preparation

The preparation carried out prior to a sales visit can reap dividends by enhancing confidence and performance when the salesperson is face to face with the customer. Some situations cannot be prepared for: the unexpected question or unusual objection, for example. But many customers face similar situations, and certain questions and objections will be raised repeatedly. Preparation can help the salesperson respond to these recurring situations. Salespeople will benefit from gaining knowledge of their own and competitors' products, by understanding buyer behaviour, by having clear sales call objectives and by having planned their sales presentation. This is because the success of the sales interview is customer-dependent. The aim is to convince the customer; what the salesperson does is simply a means to that end.

The opening

It is important for salespeople to consider how to create a favourable initial impression with customers as this can often affect later perceptions. Good first impressions can be gained by adopting a businesslike approach, being friendly but not overly familiar, being attentive to detail, observing common courtesies like waiting to be asked to sit down and by showing the customer appreciation for having taken the time to see you.

Need and problem identification

Consumers will buy a product because they have a 'problem' that gives rise to a 'need'. Therefore the first task is to identify the needs and problems of each customer. Only by doing this can a salesperson connect with each customer's situation. Effective need and problem identification requires the development of questioning and listening skills. The hallmark of inexperienced salespeople is that they do all the talking; successful salespeople know how to get the *customer* to do most of the talking.

Presentation and demonstration

It is the presentation and demonstration that offers the opportunity for the salesperson to convince customers that they can supply the solution to their problem. It should focus on **customer benefits** rather than **product features**. The salesperson should continue to ask questions during the presentation to ensure that the customer has understood what he or she has said, and to check that what the salesperson has talked about really is of importance to the customer. This can be achieved by asking questions like 'Is that the kind of thing you are looking for?'

Dealing with objections

Salespeople rarely close a sale without first having to overcome customer objections. Although objections can cause problems, they should not be regarded negatively since they highlight issues that are important to the buyer. The secret of dealing with objections is to handle both the substantive and emotional aspects. The substantive part is to do with the objection itself. If the customer objects to the

product's price the salesperson needs to use convincing arguments to show that the price is not too high. But it is a fact of human personality that the argument that is supported by the greater weight of evidence does not always win since people resent being proven wrong. Therefore, salespeople need to recognize the emotional aspects of objection handling. Under no circumstances should the buyer be caused to lose face or be antagonized during this process. Two ways of minimizing this risk are to listen to the objection without interruption and to employ the 'agree and counter' technique, where the salesperson agrees with the buyer but then puts forward an alternative point of view.

Closing the sale

The inexperienced salesperson will sometimes imagine that an effective presentation followed by the convincing handling of any objections should guarantee that the buyer will ask for the product without the seller needing to work to close the sale. This does occasionally happen but, more often, it is necessary for the salesperson to take the initiative. This is because many buyers still have doubts in their minds that may cause them to wish to delay the decision to purchase. Closing techniques include simply asking for the order, summarizing the key points and asking for the order, or offering a special deal to close the sale (the concession close).

The follow-up

Once an order has been placed there may be a temptation for the salesperson to move on to other customers, neglecting the follow-up visit. However, this can be a great mistake since most companies rely on repeat business. If problems arise, customers have every right to believe that the salesperson was interested only in the order, and not their complete satisfaction. By checking that there are no problems with delivery, installation, product use and training (where applicable), the follow-up can show that the salesperson really does care about the customer.

Sales management

Because of the unique nature of the selling job, sales management is a challenging activity. For example, many salespeople spend a great deal of their time in the field, separated from their managers, while others may suffer repeated rejections in trying to close sales, causing them to lose confidence. Therefore, the two main aspects of the sales manager's job are designing the salesforce and managing the salesforce.

Designing the salesforce

The critical design decisions are determining salesforce size and organizing the salesforce. The most practical method for deciding the number of salespeople required is called the 'workload approach'. It is based on the calculation of the total annual calls required per year divided by the average calls per year that can be expected from one salesperson.[58]

There are three alternative approaches to organizing the salesforce. A *geographic* structure is where the sales area is broken down into territories based on workload and potential, and a salesperson is assigned to each one to sell all of the product range. This provides a simple, unambiguous definition of each salesperson's sales territory, and the proximity to customers encourages the development of personal relationships. A *product* structure might be effective where a company has a diverse product range selling to different customers (or at least different people within a given organization). A *customer-based* structure is where salesforces are organized on the basis of market segments, account sizes or new versus existing account lines. This structure enables salespeople to acquire in-depth knowledge of particular customer groups.

A growing form of customer-based salesforce organization is **key account management**, which reflects the increasing concentration of buying power into fewer but larger customers. These are serviced by a key account salesforce comprising senior salespeople who develop close personal relationships with customers, can handle sophisticated sales arguments and are skilled in the art of negotiation. A number of advantages are claimed for a key account structure, including that it enables close working relationships with customers, improved communication and coordination, better follow-up on sales and service, more in-depth penetration of the DMU, higher sales and the provision of an opportunity for advancement for career salespeople.

Managing the salesforce

The following elements are involved in salesforce management: setting specific salesperson objectives; recruitment and selection; training; **salesforce motivation** and compensation; and **salesforce evaluation**. These activities have been shown to improve salesperson performance, indicating the key role that sales managers play as facilitators, helping salespeople to perform better. Sales objectives are usually set in sales terms (sales quotas) but, increasingly, profit targets are being used, reflecting the need to guard against sales being bought cheaply by

excessive discounting. The importance of recruiting high-calibre salespeople cannot be overestimated. A study into salesforce practice asked sales managers the following question: 'If you were to put your most successful salesperson into the territory of one of your average salespeople and made no other changes, what increase in sales would you expect after, say, two years?'[59] The most commonly stated increase was 16–20 per cent, and one-fifth of all sales managers said they would expect an increase of over 30 per cent. Based on extensive research, Mayer and Greenberg reduced the number of qualities believed to be important for effective selling to empathy and ego drive.[60] These are the kinds of qualities that need to be looked for in new salespeople.

It is believed by many sales managers that their salespeople can best train themselves by just doing the job. This approach ignores the benefits of a training programme, which can provide a frame of reference in which learning takes place. Training should include not only product knowledge, but also skills development. Success at selling comes when the skills are performed automatically, without consciously thinking about them, just as a tennis player or footballer succeeds.

A deep understanding of salespeople as individuals, their personalities and value systems, is the basis for effective motivation. Managers can motivate their sales staff by getting to know what each salesperson values and what they are striving for, increasing the responsibility given to salespeople in mundane jobs, providing targets that are attainable and challenging, and recognizing that rewards can be both financial and non-financial (e.g. praise). In terms of financial rewards, sales staff can be paid either a fixed salary, commission only, or on a salary-plus commission basis. Salaries provide security while commissions are an incentive to sell more as they are directly tied to sales levels. Great care must be taken in designing commission and bonus structures. For example, a Chrysler car dealership in the USA found that monthly sales for April were significantly down because salespeople who knew that they would not hit their targets for that month were encouraging customers to delay sales until May in hope of getting the May bonus.[61]

Salesforce evaluation gathers the information required to check whether targets are being achieved and provides raw information that will help guide training and motivation. By identifying the strengths and weakness of individual salespeople, training can be focused on the areas in need of development, and incentives can be aimed at weak spots such as poor prospecting performance. Often, performance will be measured on the basis of quantitative criteria such as sales revenues, profits generated or number of calls. However, it is also important to use qualitative criteria such as sales skills acquired, customer relationships, product knowledge and self-management.

Ethical issues in direct communications techniques

A number of ethical questions arise with respect to direct communications techniques. These are discussed below.

Intrusions on privacy

Direct marketing has been criticized for being intrusive and for invading people's privacy. Receiving unsolicited calls from telemarketing companies can be annoying, while many consumers fear that every time they subscribe to a club, society or magazine their names, addresses and other information will be entered on a database and that this will guarantee a flood of mail from the supplier. Many consumers are registering with suppression files indicating that they do not want to be recipients of direct marketing activities.

Similarly, some of those people using the Internet are extremely wary of online shopping because of the use of cookies and the information they store and provide about consumers. Cookies are tiny computer files that a marketer can download on to the computer of online shoppers who visit a company's website so that details of these visits may be recorded. Cookies serve many useful functions: they remember users' passwords so they do not have to log on each time they revisit a site; they remember users' preferences so they can be provided with the right pages or data; and they remember the contents of consumers' shopping baskets from one visit to the next. However, because they can provide a record of users' movements around the web, cookies can also give a very detailed picture of people's interests and circumstances. For example, cookies contain information provided by visitors such as product preferences, personal data and financial information, including credit card details.[62] From a marketer's point of view, cookies allow customized and personalized content for online shoppers. However, most Internet users probably do not know this information is being collected and would object if they knew. (Incidentally, online users

can check if their drive contains cookies by opening any file named 'cookies'.) Some people fear that companies will use this information to build psychographic profiles that will enable them to influence customer behaviour; others simply object to information about them being held without their express permission. Although users are identified by a code number rather than a name and address (and this, therefore, does not violate EU data protection regulations), the fear is that direct marketing databases will be combined with information on online shopping behaviour to create a major new way of peering into people's private lives.

Another form of invasion of privacy is the sending of unsolicited e-mails (spam), as mentioned above. Recipients find spam intrusive and annoying. One remedy is for Internet service providers to install protection against spam on behalf of their customers. The EU's Electronic Data Protection Directive states that marketers must not send e-mails to consumers who have not expressly stated their wish to receive them.

Social exclusion

Another ethical consideration is the fear that the growing use of the Internet will exclude the poorest members of society from partaking of the benefits of online shopping since they can afford neither a computer nor the associated charges. For example, Prudential, the financial services company, has faced strong criticism for the way Egg, its high-interest savings bank, cut itself off from mainstream customers by offering Internet-only access, thereby creating a system which ensures that it attracts only the wealthiest customers. In addition, some utility companies may be discriminating against low income groups by offering cut-price energy only over the Internet.[63] However, many other public and private organizations throughout the European Union are committed to finding ways to support sectors of the community that are currently excluded from the growing knowledge economy. Abbey National, working in conjunction with the charity Age Concern, has invested in free computer and Internet taster sessions for the over-50s as part of the UK's initiative to encourage use of the Internet. Similarly, the rights of disabled users to use company websites are covered by the Disability Discrimination Act 1995.

The quantity of poorly targeted mail

Poorly targeted mail, usually called junk mail, also irritates many people and leads to the view that much marketing expenditure is wasteful and contributes only to the increasing prices of products. The direct marketing industry is responding to these concerns and is becoming increasingly sophisticated in how it targets prospects.

Deception by salespeople

A dilemma that, sooner or later, is likely to face most salespeople is the choice of telling the customer the whole truth and risk losing a sale, or misleading the customer in order to clinch a sale. Such deception may take the form of exaggeration, lying or withholding important information that significantly reduces the appeal of a product. Such actions can be avoided by influencing the behaviour of salespeople through training, by sales management that encourages ethical behaviour, which is demonstrated through salespeople's own actions and words, and by establishing codes of conduct for salespeople. Nevertheless, from time to time evidence of malpractice in selling reaches the media. For example, in the UK it was alleged that some financial services salespeople mis-sold pensions by exaggerating the expected returns. This scandal cost the companies involved millions of pounds in compensation.[64]

The hard sell

The use of high-pressure sales tactics to close a sale is another criticism levelled at personal selling. Some car dealerships have been deemed unethical due to their use of hard-sell tactics to pressurize customers into making a fast decision on a complicated purchase that may involve expensive credit facilities. Such tactics encouraged Daewoo to approach the task of selling cars in a fundamentally different way by replacing salespeople with computer stations where consumers could gather product and price information.

Bribery

Bribery is the act of giving payment, gifts or other inducements in order to secure a sale. Bribes are considered unethical because they violate the principle of fairness in commercial negotiations. A major problem is that, in some countries, bribes are an accepted part of business life: bribes are an essential part of competing. When an organization succumbs, it is usually castigated in its home country if the bribe becomes public knowledge. Yet, without the bribe, it may have been operating at a major commercial disadvantage. Companies need to decide whether they are going to market in those countries where bribes are commonplace. Taking an ethical stance may cause difficulties in the short term but in the long run the positive publicity that can follow may be of greater benefit.

Summary

This chapter has provided an overview of the direct communications techniques available to the marketer. In particular, the following issues were addressed.

1. The marketing database is the foundation upon which direct marketing campaigns are built. Technological developments have greatly assisted with database development.

2. Customer relationship management (CRM) is an outgrowth of database marketing and describes the use of technologies to build and foster relationships with customers.

3. Direct marketing is a growing area where consumers are precisely targeted through a variety of different techniques including direct mail, telemarketing, mobile marketing, direct response advertising and catalogue marketing.

4. The growth of the Internet has facilitated the growth of novel business possibilities such as C2C enterprises. Internet-based businesses have four potential advantages over their offline rivals, namely lower costs and prices, superior customer service, greater product variety, and product customization.

5. Internet technologies allow for some very innovative ways of adapting the marketing mix to business problems.

6. Personal selling plays an important role in the promotional mix and salespeople are required to develop a range of selling skills including preparing for the sale, opening the sale, identifying customer needs and problems, presenting and demonstrating, dealing with objections, closing the sale and following up. Sales management involves designing and managing a sales team.

Suggested reading

Economist (2005) Crowned At Last: A Survey of Consumer Power, 2 April, 3–16.

Jobber, D. and **G. Lancaster** (2006) *Selling and Sales Management*, 7th edn, Harlow: Pearson Education.

Kaikati, A.M. and **J.G. Kaikati** (2004) Stealth Marketing: How to Reach Customers Surreptitiously, *California Management Review*, **46** (4), 6–23

Rigby, D.K. and **D. Ledingham** (2004) CRM Done Right, *Harvard Business Review*, **82** (11), 118–28.

Sargeant, A. and **D. West** (2001) *Direct and Interactive Marketing*, Oxford: Oxford University Press.

Internet exercises

Sites to visit

1   www.globalfreeloaders.com
     www.ratemyteachers.com

Exercise

Review these websites and comment on the impact of the Internet on people's everyday lives

Sites to visit

2   www.netflix.com

Exercise

Review this website and comment on the advantages that online video and DVD rental services have over their offline counterparts. What impact will this innovation have on traditional video rental outlets.

Study questions

1. Customer relationship management (CRM) is currently one of the 'hot topics' in marketing. Say what is meant by CRM and discuss the role that it plays in the organization.
2. Companies now have a variety of direct marketing media that they can consider when planning a direct marketing campaign. Compare and contrast any two direct marketing media. In your answer, give examples of the kinds of markets in which the media you have chosen might be useful.
3. Discuss the kinds of advantages an Internet-based business might have over one that does not have an online presence.
4. Discuss the impact of the Internet on each aspect of the marketing mix.
5. Salespeople are born, not made. Discuss.

Key terms

direct marketing (1) acquiring and retaining customers without the use of an intermediary; (2) the distribution of products, information and promotional benefits to target consumers through interactive communication in a way that allows response to be measured

database marketing an interactive approach to marketing, which uses individually addressable marketing media and channels to provide information to a target audience, stimulate demand and stay close to customers

direct mail material sent through the postal service to the recipient's house or business address, promoting a product and/or maintaining an ongoing relationship

telemarketing a marketing communications system whereby trained specialists use telecommunications and information technologies to conduct marketing and sales activities

direct response advertising the use of the prime advertising media, such as television, newspapers and magazines, to elicit an order, enquiry or a request for a visit

customer relationship management (CRM) the methodologies, technologies and e-commerce capabilities used by firms to manage customer relationships

personal selling oral communication with prospective purchasers with the intention of making a sale

mobile marketing the sending of text messages to mobile phones to promote products and build relationships with customers

catalogue marketing the sale of products through catalogues distributed to agents and customers, usually by mail or at stores

Internet a vast global computer network that permits instant communication, such as the gathering and sharing of information, and that offers the facility for users to communicate with one another

website a collection of various files including text, graphics, video and audio content created by organizations and individuals

e-commerce the use of technologies such as the Internet, electronic data interchange (EDI), e-mail and electronic payment systems to streamline business transactions

electronic data interchange (EDI) a pre-Internet technology, which was developed to permit organizations to use linked computers for the rapid exchange of information

Internet marketing the achievement of marketing objectives through the utilization of the Internet and web-based technologies

domain names global system of unique names for addressing web servers; the Domain Name System (DNS) is the method of administering such names. Each level in the system is given a name and is called a domain: gTDL refers to global top-level domain names (e.g. .com, .edu .org); ccTDL refers to country code top-level domain names of which there are about 250 (e.g. .uk, .fr); domain names are maintained by the Internet Corporation for Assigned Names (ICANN) (www.icann.org)

World Wide Web a collection of computer files that can be accessed via the Internet, allowing documents containing text, images, sound and/or video to be used

viral marketing electronic word of mouth, where promotional messages are spread using e-mail from person to person

prospecting searching for and calling upon potential customers

customer benefits those things that a customer values in a product; customer benefits derive from product features (see separate entry)

product features the characteristics of a product that may or may not convey a customer benefit

key account management an approach to selling that focuses resources on major customers and uses a team selling approach

salesforce motivation the motivation of salespeople by a process that involves needs, which set encouraging drives in motion to accomplish goals

salesforce evaluation the measurement of salesperson performance so that strengths and weaknesses can be identified

References

1. **Anonymous** (2004) Manchester United Aims to Expand New Media Use, *New Media Age*, 30 September, 4; **McCosker, P.** (2004) Manchester United: The Transformation of a Football Club into a Global Brand, European Case Clearing House, 304-178-1; **Mortimer, R.** (2003) Footie we Play, United we Brand, *Brand Strategy*, January, 18–20.

2. **Dye, R.** (2000) The Buzz on Buzz, *Harvard Business Review*, November–December, 138–47.

3. **Kumar, N.** and **S. Linguri** (2003) Buzz, Chat and Branding Give Red Bull Wings, *Financial Times*, 8 August, 13.

4. **Pidd, H.** (2004) Lessons in Hard Sell, *Guardian*, 20 December, 14.

5. **Salzman, M.** (2003) Getting a Buzz Out of Marketing to Consumers, *Brand Strategy*, June, 6.

6. **Stone, M., D. Davies** and **A. Bond** (1995) *Direct Hit: Direct Marketing with a Winning Edge*, London: Pitman.

7. **Harvey, F.** (2003) They Know What You Like, *Financial Times*, Creative Business, 6 May, 4.

8. **London, S.** (2004) Choked by a Data Surfeit, *Financial Times*, 29 January, 17.

9. **Nancarrow, C., L.T. Wright** and **J. Page** (1997) Seagram Europe and Africa: The Development of a Consumer Database Marketing Capability, *Proceedings of the Academy of Marketing*, July, Manchester, 1119–30.

10. **Murphy, C.** (2002) Catching up with its Glitzier Cousin, *Financial Times*, 24 July, 13.

11. **Foss, B.** and **M. Stone** (2001) *Successful Customer Relationship Marketing*, London: Kogan Page.

12. See **Foss, B.** and **Stone, M.** (2001), op. cit. **Woodcock, N., M. Starkey, J. Stone, P. Weston** and **J. Ozimek** (2001) *State of the Nation II: 2002, An Ongoing Global Study of how*

Companies Manage Their Customer, QCi Assessment Ltd., West Byfleet.

13. See **Ryals, L., S. Knox,** and **S. Maklan** (2002) *Customer Relationship Management: Building the Business Case,* London: FT Prentice-Hall; **H. Wilson, E. Daniel** and **M. McDonald** (2002) Factors for Success in Customer Relationship Management Systems, *Journal of Marketing Management,* **18** (1/2), 193–200.

14. **North, B.** (1995) Consumer Companies Take Direct Stance, *Marketing,* 20 May, 24–5.

15. **Curtis, J.** (2003) Down, But a Bit Up, *Financial Times,* Creative Business, 15 April, 4–5.

16. **Elgie, D.** (2003) A is for Ad Agency Angst …, *Financial Times,* Creative Business, 6 May, 11.

17. **Clegg, A.** (2000) Hit or Miss, *Marketing Week,* 13 January, 45–9.

18. **Benady, D.** (2001) If Undelivered, *Marketing Week,* 20 December, 31–3.

19. **McHatton, N.R.** (1988) *Total Telemarketing,* New York: Wiley, 269.

20. **Stevens, M.** (1993) A Telephony Revolution, *Marketing,* 16 September, 38.

21. **Blythe, J.** (2003) in **Jobber, D.** and **G. Lancaster,** *Selling & Sales Management,* Harlow: FT Pearson.

22. **Starkey, M.** (1997) Telemarketing, in D. Jobber (ed.) *The CIM Handbook of Selling and Sales Strategy,* Oxford: Butterworth-Heinemann, 130.

23. **McCann, G.** (2003) Just Like Members of the Family, *Financial Times,* 15 January, 13.

24. **Harvey, F.** (2003) Telly, Telly on the Wall, *Financial Times,* Creative Business, 22 July, 6.

25. **Ray, A.** (2004) Ensuring Funds for a Captive Audience, *Financial Times,* Creative Business, 28 September, 12.

26. **Rowan, D.** (2004) The Next Big Thing—Supermarket TV, *The Times Magazine,* 9 October, 12.

27. **Wilkinson, A.** (2004) Box on Shelf on Box on …, *Marketing Week,* 26 February, 24–7.

28. **Mühlbacher, H., M. Botshen** and **W. Beutelmeyer** (1997) The Changing Consumer in Austria, *International Journal of Research in Marketing,* 14, 309–19.

29. **Anonymous** (2002) IKEA Catalogue, *Marketing,* 31 October, 10.

30. **Brown-Humes, C.** (2003) IKEA Creates a Challenge for Postmen of the World, *Financial Times,* 14 August, 18.

31. **Reitsma, R.** (2005) Broadband Surges Ahead, *Financial Times,* Information Technology, 20 April, 6.

32. **Reitsma, R.** (2005) op. cit.

33. **Rigby, E.** (2005) Online Shopping Expected to Grow by 35% This Year, *Financial Times,* 6 April, 7.

34. **Anonymous** (2004) Here Come the Home Truths, *Financial Times,* Creative Business, 21 December, 15.

35. **Silverman, G.** (2004) Spending on Internet Advertising Set to Soar, *Financial Times,* 29 November, 3.

36. **Anonymous** (2005) The Online Ad Attack, *Economist,* 30 April, 53–4.

37. **Cole, G.** (2003) Generation Gap Electronics Groups are Developing A New Range of Broadband Products, *Financial Times,* Creative Business, 10 June, 2.

38. **Kirchgaessner, S.** (2003) The Minute You Clicked on the Site, *Financial Times,* 27 January, 13.

39. **Poole, S.** (2003) Global Gaming Goes Live, *Sunday Times,* Culture, 9 March, 51.

40. **Van Winkle, W.** (2004) Alternative Dating, *PC Magazine,* 19 October, 157.

41. **Davoudi, S.** (2005) From Brand Leader to Struggler in Eight Years, *Financial Times,* 17 June, 24.

42. **Anonymous,** (2005) Profiting from Obscurity, *Economist,* 7 May, 73.

43. **Hart, C., N. Doherty** and **F. Ellis-Chadwick** (2002) Retailer Adoption of the Internet—Implications for Retail Marketing, *European Journal of Marketing,* **34** (8), 954–74.

44. **Anonymous** (2005) Motoring Online, *Economist,* 2 April, 11–12.

45. **Gapper, J.** (2005) How to Make a Million Connections, *Financial Times,* 8 July, 12.

46. **Anonymous** (2003) EU Rules to Outlaw Spam, *Marketing Business,* May, 2003.

47. **Anonymous** (2003) How Good is Google, *Economist,* 11 January, 57–8.

48. **Harvey, F.** (2003) Paid Searches Find the Route to Online Riches, *Financial Times,* 1 July, 14.

49. **Thompson, C.** (2004) Search Engines Invite New Problems, *Marketing Management,* **13** (2), 52–3.

50. **Waters, R.** (2004) Billboards on the Superhighway, *Financial Times,* 3 December, 17.

51. **Anonymous** (2005) Chief Humanising Officer, *Economist,* 12 February, 58.

52. **Gapper, J.** (2005) A Blog Reveals the Mind of Sun, *Financial Times,* 22 April, 13.

53. **Lewis, E.** (2005) To Blog or Not to Blog?, *Brand Strategy,* May, 24–7.

54. **Thornhill, J.** (2005) Internet Study Warns Politicians on Power of the Blog, *Financial Times,* 13 July, 8.

55. **Anonymous** (2004) Online Award for Growth, *Business Franchise,* November, 10.

56. **Anonymous** (2005) Warfare in the Aisles, *Economist,* 2 April, 6–7.

57. **Weitz, B.A.** (1981) Effectiveness in Sales

Interactions: A Contingency Framework, *Journal of Marketing*, 45, 85–103.

58. **Talley, W.J.** (1961) How to Design Sales Territories, *Journal of Marketing*, **25** (3), 16–28.

59. **PA Consultants** (1979) *Sales Force Practice Today: A Basis for Improving Performance*, Cookham: Institute of Marketing.

60. **Mayer, M.** and **G. Greenberg** (1964) What Makes a Good Salesman, *Harvard Business Review*, **42** (July/August), 119–25.

61. **Griffith, V.** (2001) Targets that Distort a Company's Aim, *Financial Times*, 21 November, 18.

62. **Berkowitz, E.N., R.A. Kerin, S.W. Hartley** and **W. Rudelius** (2000) *Marketing*, Boston, MA: McGraw-Hill.

63. **Benady, D.** (2000) Class War, *Marketing Week*, 27 January, 28–31.

64. **Mackintosh, J.** (1999) Pensions Mis-selling Cost May Rise by £1bn, *Financial Times*, 18/19.

Online **LearningCentre** with POWERWEB

When you have read this chapter log on to the Online Learning Centre for *Foundations of Marketing* at **www.mcgraw-hill.co.uk/textbooks/jobber** where you'll find multiple choice test questions, links and extra online study tools for marketing.

Turn the page for a Case Study on Tesco

Case 10 Tesco: the customer relationship management champion

'They [Tesco] know more than any firm I have ever dealt with how their customers actually think, what will impress and upset them, and how they feel about grocery shopping.'

(*Jim Barnes, Executive Vice President of Bristol Group, a Canada-based marketing communications and information firm, and a CRM expert*)

Every three months, millions of people in the UK receive a magazine from the country's number one retailing company, Tesco. Nothing exceptional about the concept—almost all leading retailing companies across the world send out mailers/magazines to their customers. These initiatives promote the store's products, introduce promotional schemes and contain discount coupons. However, what sets Tesco apart from such run-of-the-mill initiatives is the fact that it has mass-customized these magazines.

Every magazine had a unique combination of articles, advertisements related to Tesco's offerings and third-party advertisements. Tesco ensured that all its customers received magazines that contained material suited to their lifestyles. The company had worked out a mechanism for determining the advertisements and promotional coupons that would go in each of the over 150,000 variants of the magazine. This had been made possible by its world-renowned customer relationship management (CRM) strategy framework.

According to Tesco sources, the company's CRM initiative was not limited to the loyalty card scheme; it was more of a company-wide philosophy. Industry observers felt that Tesco's CRM initiatives enabled it to develop highly focused marketing strategies. Thanks to its CRM initiatives, the company became UK's number one retailer in 1995, having struggled at number two behind arch-rival Sainsbury's for decades. In 2003, the company's market share was 26.7 per cent, while Sainsbury's market share was just 16.8 per cent.

CRM the Tesco way

Tesco's efforts towards offering better services to its customers and meeting their needs can be traced back to the days when it positioned itself as a company that offered good-quality products at extremely competitive prices. Even its decision to offer premium-end merchandise and services in the

Table C10.1 Tesco: core purpose and values

CORE PURPOSE
Creating value for customers, to earn their lifetime loyalty
VALUES
1. No one tries harder for customers: understand customers better than anyone be energetic, be innovative and be first for customers use our strengths to deliver unbeatable value to our customers look after our people so they can look after our customers
2. Treat people how we like to be treated: all retailers, there's one team—the Tesco Team trust and respect each other strive to do our very best give support to each other and praise more than criticize ask more than tell and share knowledge so that it can be used enjoy work, celebrate success and learn from experience

Source: www.tesco.com

1970s was prompted by growing customer demand for the same (see Table C10.1 for the company's 'core purpose' and 'values', which highlight the importance placed on customer service).

The biggest customer service initiative (and the first focused CRM drive) came in the form of the loyalty card scheme that was launched in 1995. This initiative was partly inspired by the growing popularity of such schemes in other parts of the world and partly by Tesco's belief that it would be able to serve its customers in a much better (and more profitable) manner by using such a scheme. Tesco knew that, at any of its outlets, the top 100 customers were worth as much as the bottom 4000 (in terms of sales). While the top 5 per cent of customers accounted for 20 per cent of sales, the bottom 25 per cent accounted for only 2 per cent. The company realized that by giving extra attention to the top customers (measured by the frequency of purchases and the amount spent) it stood to gain a great deal.

To ensure the programme's success, it was essential that all Tesco employees understood the rationale for it as well as its importance. So, the company distributed over 140,000 educational videos about the programme to its staff at various stores. These videos

Table C10.2 Tesco: classifying customers

EXPENDITURE	SHOPPING FREQUENCY					
	Daily	Twice weekly	Weekly	Stop start	Now and then	Hardly ever
High Spend	PREMIUM		STANDARD		POTENTIAL	
Medium Spend	STANDARD		POTENTIAL		UNCOMMITTED	
Low Spend	POTENTIAL		UNCOMMITTED			
	FREQUENT		INFREQUENT		RARE	

Source: www.ecrnet.org

explained why the initiative was being undertaken, what the company expected to gain from it, and why it was important for employees to participate whole-heartedly in it.

Impressed with the programme's results over six months, the company had introduced the scheme in all its stores by February 1995. The stores captured every one of the over 8 million transactions made per week at Tesco stores in a database. All the transactions were linked to individual customer profiles and generated over 50 gigabytes of data every week. Dunnhumby used state-of-the-art data-mining techniques to manage and analyse the database. Initially, it took a few weeks to analyse the vast amount of data generated. To overcome this problem, Dunnhumby put in place new software that reduced this time to just a few days. As a result, it became possible to come up with useful and timely insights into customer behaviour in a much faster way.

The analysis of the data collected enabled Tesco to accurately pinpoint the time when purchases were made, the amount the customer spent, and the kinds of products purchased. Based on the amount spent and the frequency of shopping, customers were classified into four broad categories: Premium, Standard, Potential and Uncommitted (see Table C10.2). Further, profiles were created for all the customers on the basis of the types of products they purchased. Customers were categorized along dimensions such as Value, Convenience, Frozen, Healthy Eating, Fresh and Kids.

Tesco also identified over 5000 need segments based on the purchasing habits and behaviour patterns of its customers. Each of these segments could be targeted specifically with tailor-made campaigns and advertisements. The company also identified eight 'primary life stage' need segments based on the profiles of its customers. These segments included 'single

Table C10.3 How Tesco used the information generated by its Clubcards

Pricing	Discounts were offered on goods that were bought by highly price-conscious customers. While the company kept prices low on often-bought goods/staples, for less familiar lines it adopted a premium pricing policy.
Merchandising	The product portfolio was devised based on customer profiles and purchasing behaviour records. Depending on the loyalty shown by customers towards a particular product, the substitutes available for the same, and the seasonality, the product ranges were modified.
Promotion	Promotions were aimed at giving special (and more) rewards to loyal customers. Few promotions were targeted at the other customers.
Customer service	Extra attention was given to stocking those products that were bought by loyal customers.
Media effectiveness	The effectiveness of media campaigns could be evaluated easily by noticing changes in the buying patterns of those customers whom the said campaign was targeted at.
Customer acquisition	The launch of new ventures (such as TPF and Tesco.com) went smoothly since Tesco targeted the 'right' kinds of customers.
Market research	While conducting marketing research, Tesco was able to tap those customers that fitted accurately into the overall research plan.
Customer communication	It was possible to mass customize communication campaigns based on individual customer preferences and characteristics. Tesco began holding 'customer evenings' for interacting with customers, gathering more information, and gaining new customers through referrals.

Source: adapted from an article on www.clarityblue.com

adults', 'pensioners' and 'urban professionals', among others.

Using the information regarding customer classification, Tesco's marketing department devised customized strategies for each category. Pricing, promotion and product-related decisions were taken after considering the preferences of customers. Also, customers received communications that were tailored to their buying patterns. The data collected through its Clubcard loyalty card scheme allowed Tesco to modify its strategies on various fronts such as pricing, inventory management, shopping analysis, customer acquisition, new product launches, store management, online customer behaviour and media effectiveness (see Table C10.3).

Tesco began giving many special privileges, such as valet parking and personal attention from the store manager, to its high-value customers. Special cards were created for students and mothers, discounts were offered on select merchandise, and the financial services venture was included in the card scheme. The data generated were used innovatively (e.g. special attention given to expectant mothers in the form of personal shopping assistants, priority parking and various other facilities). The company also tied up with airline companies and began offering Frequent Flyer Miles to customers in return for the points on their Clubcards.

Reaping the benefits

Commenting on the way the data generated were used, sources at Dunnhumby said that the data allowed Tesco to target individual customers (the rifle-shot approach) instead of targeting them as a group (the carpet-bombing approach). Since the customers received coupons that matched their buying patterns, over 20 per cent of Tesco's coupons were redeemed—as against the industry average of 0.5 per cent. The number of loyal customers has increased manifold since the loyalty card scheme was launched (see Figure C10.1).

The quarterly magazine Tesco sent to its customers was customized based on the segments identified. Customers falling into different categories received magazines that were compiled specifically for them— the articles covered issues that interested them, and the advertisements and discount coupons were about those products/services that they were most likely to purchase. This customization attracted third-party advertisers, since it assured them that their products/services would be noticed by those very cus-

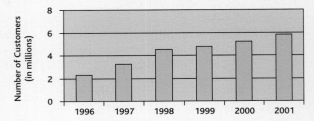

Figure C10.1 Tesco: increasing number of loyal customers
Source: www.clarityblue.com

tomers they planned to target. Naturally, Tesco recovered a large part of its investment in this exercise through revenues generated by outside advertisements.

The data collected through the cards helped the company enter the financial services business as well. The company carried out targeted research on the demographic data and zeroed in on those customers who were the most likely to opt for financial services. Due to the captive customer base and the cross-selling opportunity, the cost of acquiring customers for its financial services was 50 per cent less than it would be for a bank or financial services company.

Reportedly, the data generated by the Clubcard initiative played a major role in the way the online grocery retailing business was run. The data helped the company identify the areas in which customers were positively inclined towards online shopping. Accordingly, the areas in which online shopping was to be introduced were decided upon. Since the prospective customers were already favourably disposed, Tesco.com took off to a good start and soon emerged as one of the few profitable dotcom ventures worldwide. By 2003, the website was accessible to 95 per cent of the UK population and generated business of £15 million per week.

By sharing the data generated with manufacturers, Tesco was able to offer better services to its customers. It gave purchasing pattern information to manufacturers, but withheld the personal information provided by customers (such as names and addresses). The manufacturers used this information to modify their own product mixes and promotional strategies. In return for this information, they gave Tesco customers subsidies and incentives in the form of discount coupons.

The Clubcards also helped Tesco compete with other retailers. When Tesco found out that around 25 per cent of its customers who belonged to the high-income bracket were defecting to rival Marks & Spencer, it developed a totally new product range, 'Tesco Finest', to lure them back. This range was then promoted to affluent customers through personalized promotions. As planned, the defection of customers from this segment slowed down considerably.

In February 2003, Tesco launched a new initiative targeted at its female customers. Named 'Me Time', the new loyalty scheme offered ladies free sessions at leading health spas, luxury gyms and beauty saloons, and discounts on designer clothes, perfumes and cosmetics. This scheme was rather innovative since it allowed Tesco customers to redeem the points accumulated through their Clubcards at a large number of third-party outlets. Company official Crawford Davidson remarked, 'Up until now, our customers have used Tesco Clubcard vouchers primarily to buy more shopping for the home. However, from now on, "Me Time" will give customers the option of spending the rewards on themselves.'

As a result of the above strategies, Tesco was able to increase returns even as it reduced promotions. Dunnhumby prepared a profit and loss statement for the activities of the marketing department to help assess the performance of the Clubcard initiative. Dunnhumby claimed that Tesco saved around £300 million every year through reduction in expenditure on promotions. The money saved thus was ploughed back into the business to offer more discounts to customers.

By the end of the 1990s, over 10 million households in the UK owned around 14 million Tesco Clubcards. This explained why as high as 80 per cent of the company's in-store transactions and 85 per cent of its revenues were accounted for by the cards. Thanks largely to this initiative, Tesco's turnover went up by 52 per cent between 1995 and 2000, while floor space during the same period increased by only 15 per cent.

An invincible company? Not exactly . . .

Tesco's customer base and the frequency with which each customer visited its stores had increased significantly over the years. However, according to reports, the average purchase per visit had not gone up as much as Tesco would have liked. Analysts said that this was not a very positive sign. They also said that, while it was true that Tesco was the market leader by

a wide margin, it was also true that Asda and Morrisons were growing rapidly.

Tesco's growth was based largely on its loyalty card scheme. But in recent years, the very concept of loyalty cards has been criticized on various grounds. Some analysts claimed that the popularity of loyalty cards would decline in the future as all retailing companies would begin offering more or less similar schemes. Critics also commented that the name 'loyalty card' was a misnomer since customers were primarily interested in getting the best price for the goods and services they wanted to buy.

Research conducted by Black Sun, a company specializing in loyalty solutions, revealed that though over 50 per cent of UK's adult population used loyalty cards, over 80 per cent of them said that they were bothered only about making cheaper purchases. Given the fact that many companies in the UK, such as HSBC, Egg and Barclaycard had withdrawn their loyalty cards, industry observers were sceptical of Tesco's ability to continue reaping the benefits of its Clubcard scheme. Black Sun's Director (Business Development) David Christopherson, said, 'Most loyalty companies have a direct marketing background, which is results-driven, and focuses on the short term. This has led to a "points for prizes" loyalty model, which does not necessarily build the long-term foundations for a beneficial relationship with customers.'

Commenting on the philosophy behind Tesco's CRM efforts, Edwina Dunn said, 'Companies should be loyal to their customers—not the other way round.' Taking into consideration the company's strong performance since these efforts were undertaken, there would perhaps not be many who would disagree with Edwina.

Questions

1. Analyse Tesco's Clubcard scheme in depth and comment on the various customer segmentation models the company developed after studying the data gathered.

2. How did Tesco use the information collected to modify its marketing strategies? What sort of benefits was the company able to derive as a result of such modifications?

3. What measures did Tesco adopt to support the CRM initiatives on the operational and strategic front? Is it enough for a company to implement loyalty card schemes (and CRM tools in general) in isolation? Why?

CHAPTER 11

DISTRIBUTION MANAGEMENT

Learning Objectives

By the end of this chapter you will understand:

1 the different types of distribution channel for consumer goods, industrial products and services
2 the three components of channel strategy—channel selection, intensity and integration
3 the five key channel management issues—member selection, motivation, training, evaluation and conflict management
4 the key retailing management decisions
5 the components of a physical distribution system—customer service, order processing, inventory control, warehousing, transportation and materials handling
6 the ethical issues involved in distribution.

Agent Provocateur: Building an Exclusive Image

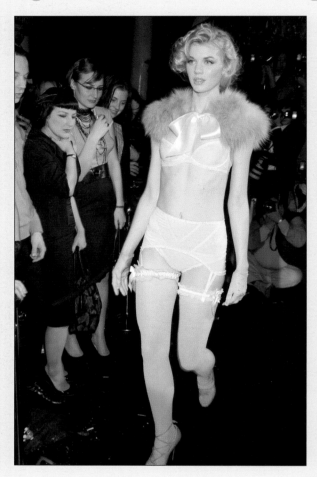

The lingerie business is one of the fastest growing segments of the fashion industry. Total sales of lingerie in the UK in 2002 were about £1.16 billion and this figure is expected to rise to £1.42 billion by 2007. Agent Provocateur (AP), the French-sounding company with British origins is one of the fastest-growing lingerie retailers in the UK. Founded in 1994, the company's sales had reached £8 million by 2004. AP has four outlets in the UK and two shops in the USA, with further plans to open outlets in major capitals such as Moscow and Dubai. Its success has been put down to its careful branding and retail positioning.

Positioning a lingerie retail concept is a tricky business as there is a thin line between sexy and smutty, and between provocative and pornographic. Thus AP was careful to position its shops in a way that differentiated them from sex shop chains like Ann Summers. The company positioned itself as an upmarket outlet, fitting out its shops with an opulent décor and low lighting to create a sense of quality and intimacy. Staff were trained to make customers of both sexes feel at ease, with men getting special attention. In addition, the company has been very selective in where it has opened new outlets, restricting itself to a limited number of stores in major cities to create an image of exclusivity.

However, the company also uses two other distribution channels. In 1999, it signed a deal with Marks & Spencer, by far the biggest-selling retailer of lingerie in the UK. But the AP products were sold under the name 'Salon Rose', which enabled it to reach a national customer base without damaging its premium positioning. Its website, also launched in 1999, now accounts for 10–15 per cent of its sales direct to its customer base.

Agent Provocateur has grown despite the fact that it spends very little on advertising. It relies largely on publicity and world-of-mouth promotion. One of its most successful publicity initiatives was a cinema advertisement it created in 2001 using Kylie Minogue. The ad, entitled 'Cheeky Valentine', which featured Minogue wearing AP lingerie while riding a pink-velvet quilted rodeo simulator, rapidly migrated to the Internet where it became one of the most successful examples of viral marketing ever.[1]

Necessary, but not sufficient, conditions for customer satisfaction are: producing products that customers want, pricing them correctly and developing well-designed promotional plans. The final part of the jigsaw is distribution, the 'place' element of the marketing mix. Products need to be available in adequate quantities, in convenient locations and at times when customers want to buy them. In this chapter we will examine the functions and types of distribution channel, the key decisions that determine channel strategy, how to manage channels, the nature of retailing and issues relating to the physical flow of goods through distribution channels (physical distribution management).

Producers need to consider the requirements of **channel intermediaries**—those organizations that facilitate the distribution of products to customers—as well as the needs of their ultimate customers. For example, success for Müller yoghurt in the UK was dependent on convincing a powerful retail group (Tesco) to stock the brand. The high margins that the brand supported were a key influence in Tesco's decision. Without retailer support, Müller would have found it uneconomic to supply consumers with its brand. Clearly, establishing a supply chain that is efficient and meets customers' needs is vital to marketing success. This supply chain is termed a **channel of distribution**, and is the means by which products are moved from the producer to the ultimate customer. Gaining access to distribution outlets is not necessarily easy. For example, in the consumer food products sector, many brands vie with each other for prime positions on supermarket shelves.

An important aspect of marketing strategy is choosing the most effective channel of distribution. The development of supermarkets effectively shortened the distribution channel between producer and consumer by eliminating the wholesaler. Prior to their introduction, the typical distribution channel for products like food, drink, tobacco and toiletries was producer to wholesaler to retailer. The wholesaler would buy in bulk from the producer and sell smaller quantities to the retailer (typically a small grocery shop). By building up buying power, supermarkets could shorten this chain by buying direct from producers. This meant lower costs to the supermarket chain and lower prices to the consumer. The competitive effect of this was to drastically reduce the numbers of small grocers and wholesalers in this market. By being more efficient and better meeting customers' needs, supermarkets had created a competitive advantage for themselves. In the same way, the more recent success of online music distribution companies is presenting a major challenge to leading retail chains like Tower Records and HMV.

We will now explore the different types of channel that manufacturers use to supply their products to customers, and the types of function provided by these channel intermediaries.

Types of distribution channel

Whether they be consumer goods, business-to-business goods or services, all products require a channel of distribution. Industrial channels tend to be shorter than consumer channels because of the small number of ultimate customers, the greater geographic concentration of industrial customers and the greater complexity of the products that require close producer/customer liaison. Service channels also tend to be short because of the inseparability of the production and consumption of many services.

Consumer channels

Figure 11.1 shows four alternative consumer channels. We will now look briefly at each one in turn.

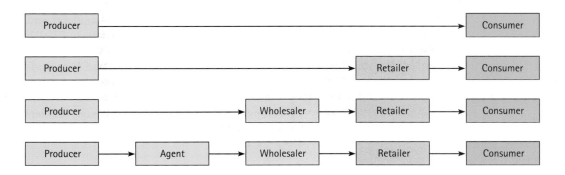

Figure 11.1 Distribution channels for consumer goods

Producer direct to consumer

This option may be attractive to producers because it cuts out distributors' profit margins. Direct selling between producer and consumer has been a feature of the marketing of many products, ranging from the sale of fruit in local markets to the sale of Avon Cosmetics and Tupperware plastic containers. For example, Avon is a 119-year-old company that had sales of $6 billion in 2003, marketing everything from beauty products to dietary supplements through its legendary army of 'Avon ladies' — its direct sales force.[2] Avon UK now plans to add a financial services division to its operations, selling products like life insurance, motor insurance and credit cards.[3] As discussed in the previous chapter, direct marketing is growing in importance in Europe, and the Internet is also a direct distribution channel for digital products such as music, books and computer software.

Exhibit 11.1 This advertisement for William Morrison demonstrates the convenience provided by the modern supermarket

Producer to retailer to consumer

It has become economic for producers to supply retailers direct, rather than through wholesalers, thanks to the growth in retailer size. As a result, consumers have the convenience of viewing and/or testing a product at the retail outlet. Retailers provide the basic service of enabling consumers to view a wide assortment of products under one roof, while manufacturers continue to gain economies of scale from the bulk production of a limited number of items. Supermarket chains exercise considerable power over manufacturers because of their enormous buying capabilities and they have been expanding into other areas of retailing, as shown in Marketing in Action 11.1.

Producer to wholesaler to retailer to consumer

The use of wholesalers makes economic sense for small retailers (e.g. small grocery or furniture shops) with limited order quantities. Wholesalers can buy in bulk from producers, and sell smaller quantities to numerous retailers (this is known as 'breaking bulk'). The danger is that large retailers in the same market have the power to buy directly from producers and thus cut out the wholesaler. In certain cases, the buying power of large retailers has meant that they can sell products to their customers more cheaply than a small retailer can buy from the wholesaler. Longer channels like this tend to occur where retail oligopolies do not dominate the distribution system. In Europe, long channels involving wholesalers are common in France and Italy. In France, for example, the distribution of vehicle spare parts is dominated by small, independent wholesalers.[7]

Producer to agent to wholesaler to retailer to consumer

This is a long channel, sometimes used by companies entering foreign markets, which may delegate the task of selling the product to an agent (who does not take title to the goods). The agent contacts local wholesalers (or retailers) and receives a commission on sales. Overseas sales of books are sometimes generated in this way. Some countries, like Japan, have traditionally had long and complex distribution channels, often involving three or more intermediaries, though this situation is changing rapidly as manufacturers and large retailers look to improve efficiency.[8]

Marketing in Action: Supermarkets expand into convenience

11.1

The evolution over the years of the convenience store format and the supermarket has been an interesting one. The growth of the supermarket, with its greater scale, buying power and branding capability, has sounded the death knell for many convenience stores as consumers have responded to the superior value proposition of the supermarket. However, it would now appear that the convenience store is undergoing something of a revival. As the average household size decreases, due to people choosing not to have families and high divorce rates, the need to do a large weekly shop decreases. Also as we saw in Chapter 3, lots of people are cash-rich and time-poor, and are thus willing to pay a bit more to do their shopping on their doorstep. 'Value for time' appears to be more important than 'value for money' when shopping at convenience stores. Sales through this channel accounted for about 20 per cent of the £115 billion grocery market in the UK in 2003 and this is expected to rise to 26 per cent or £30 billion by 2008, making it the fastest-growing sector of the grocery market.

Not surprisingly, the main supermarkets recognize this trend and are rapidly expanding into the convenience sector. In 2004, Sainsbury's acquired both the Bells chain of 54 convenience stores and the Jacksons chain of 115 stores for a combined total of over £120 million. This follows earlier moves by Tesco, who in 2002 acquired the 1200 outlets of the T&S store chain and in 2004 an additional 45 outlets of the Adminstore chain in the London area, which traded under names such as Cullens, Europa and Harts. Somerfield bought Aberness, the Scotland-based 170-store chain, while Musgraves, the Irish wholesaler distributor which also owns Budgens, bought Londis for £60 million in 2004. In total, there are approximately 55,000 convenience stores in the UK, of which 28,000 are independent, meaning that there is likely to be a great deal more consolidation in this sector.

The supermarkets have brought their marketing and merchandising expertise to the convenience sector. The Tesco chain of convenience stores is branded Tesco Express and Tesco Metro, while Sainsbury's has become Sainsbury Local. Store design and displays are modern and slicker than many traditional cornershops. As in supermarkets an everyday low price strategy is employed. Research has shown that consumers spend 30 per cent more time and 20 per cent more money in these shops than they did in the traditional convenience store.

Based on: Barnes (2005);[4] Gregory (2004);[5] Rigby (2004)[6]

Business-to-business channels

Common business-to-business distribution channels are illustrated in Figure 11.2. A maximum of one channel intermediary is used under normal circumstances.

Producer to industrial customer

Supplying business customers direct is common practice for expensive business-to-business products such as gas turbines, diesel locomotives, and aero-engines. There needs to be close liaison between supplier and customer to solve technical problems, and the size of

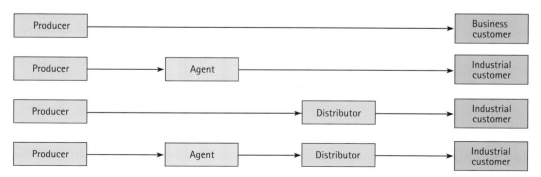

Figure 11.2 Distribution channels for industrial goods

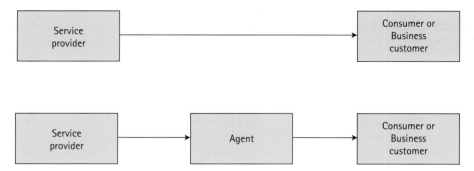

Figure 11.3 Distribution channels for services

the order makes direct selling and distribution economic.

Producer to agent to business customer

Instead of selling to business customers using their own salesforce, a business-to-business goods company could employ the services of an agent who may sell a range of goods from several suppliers (on a commission basis). This spreads selling costs and may be attractive to those companies that lack the reserves to set up their own sales operations. The disadvantage is that there is little control over the agent, who is unlikely to devote the same amount of time selling these products as a dedicated sales team.

Producer to distributor to business customer

For less expensive, more frequently bought business-to-business products, distributors are used; these may have both internal and field sales staff.[9] Internal staff deal with customer-generated enquiries and order placing, order follow-up (often using the telephone) and checking inventory levels. Outside sales staff are more proactive; their practical responsibilities are to find new customers, get products specified, distribute catalogues and gather market information. The advantage to customers of using distributors is that they can buy small quantities locally.

Producer to agent to distributor to business customer

Where business customers prefer to call upon distributors, the agent's job will require selling into these intermediaries. The reason why a producer may employ an agent rather than a dedicated salesforce is usually cost-based (as previously discussed).

Services channels

Distribution channels for services are usually short, either direct or via an agent (see Figure 11.3). Since stocks are not held, the role of the wholesaler, retailer or industrial distributor does not apply.

Service provider to consumer or business customer

The close personal relationships between service providers and customers often means that service supply is direct. Examples include healthcare, office cleaning, accountancy, marketing research and law.

Service provider to agent to consumer or business customer

A channel intermediary for a service company usually takes the form of an agent. Agents are used when the service provider is geographically distant from customers, and where it is not economical for the provider to establish their own local sales team. Examples include insurance, travel, secretarial and theatrical agents.

Channel strategy and management

The design of the distribution channel is an important strategic decision that needs to be integrated with other marketing mix decisions. For example, products that are being positioned as upmarket, premium items are usually only available in a select number of stores. **Channel strategy** decisions involve the selection of the most effective distribution channel, the most appropriate level of distribution intensity and the degree of channel integration. Once the key channel strategy decisions have been made, effective implementation is required. Channel management decisions involve the selection, motivation, training and evaluation of channel members, and managing conflict between producers and channel members.

Channel selection

Ask yourself why Procter & Gamble sells its brands through supermarkets rather than selling direct. Why does General Motors sell its locomotives direct to train operating companies rather than use a distributor? The answers are to be found by examining the following factors that influence channel selection. These influences can be grouped under the headings of market, producer, product and competitive factors.

Market factors

Buyer behaviour is an important market factor; buyer expectations may dictate that a product be sold in a certain way. Buyers may prefer to buy locally and in a particular type of shop. Failure to match these expectations can have catastrophic consequences, as when Levi Strauss attempted to sell a new range of clothing (suits) in department stores, even though marketing research had shown that its target customers preferred to buy suits from independent outlets. The result was that the new range (called Tailored Classics) was withdrawn from the marketplace.

The geographical concentration and location of customers also affects channel selection. The more local and clustered the customer base, the more likely it is that direct distribution will be feasible. Direct distribution is also more prevalent when buyers are few in number and buy large quantities such as in many industrial markets. A large number of small customers may mean that using channel intermediaries is the only economical way of reaching them (hence supermarkets). Buyers' needs regarding product information, installation and technical assistance also have to be considered. For example, products that require facilities for local servicing, such as cars, often use intermediaries to carry out the task.

Producer factors

When a producer lacks adequate resources to perform the functions of the channel, this places a constraint on the channel decision. Producers may lack the financial and managerial resources to take on channel operations. Lack of financial resources may mean that a salesforce cannot be recruited and sales agents and/or distributors are used instead. Producers may feel that they do not possess the customer-based skills to distribute their products, and prefer to rely on intermediaries instead.

The desired degree of control of channel operations also influences the selection of channel members. The use of independent channel intermediaries reduces producer control. For example, by distributing their products through supermarkets, manufacturers lose total control of the price charged to consumers. Furthermore, there is no guarantee that new products will be stocked. Direct distribution gives producers control over such issues.

Product factors

Large and/or complex products are often supplied direct to the customer. The need for close personal contact between producer and customer, and the high prices charged, mean that direct distribution and selling is both necessary and feasible. Perishable products, such as frozen food, meat and bread, require relatively short channels to supply the customer with fresh stock. Finally, bulky or difficult to handle products may require direct distribution because distributors may refuse to carry them if storage or display problems arise.[10]

Competitive factors

An innovative approach to distribution may be required if competitors control traditional channels of distribution—for example, through franchise or exclusive dealing arrangements. Two available alternatives are to recruit a salesforce to sell direct or to set up a producer-owned distribution network (see the information about administered vertical marketing systems, a topic discussed later in this chapter under the heading 'Conventional marketing channels'). Producers should not accept that the channels of distribution used by competitors are the only ways to reach target customers. Direct marketing provides opportunities to supply products in new ways, as many online companies have shown. Increasingly, traditional channels of distribution for personal computers through high-street retailers are being circumvented by direct marketers such as Dell, which use direct response advertising to reach buyers. The emergence of the more computer-aware and experienced buyer, and the higher reliability of these products as the market reaches maturity has meant that a local source of supply (and advice) is less important.

Distribution intensity

The choice of distribution intensity is the second channel strategy decision. The three broad options are intensive, selective and exclusive distribution. We will look at each of these now.

Intensive distribution

By using all available outlets, **intensive distribution** aims to provide saturation coverage of the market. With many mass-market products, such as cigarettes, foods, toiletries, beer and newspapers, sales are a direct function of the number of outlets penetrated. This is because consumers have a range of acceptable brands from which they choose and, very often, the decision to purchase is made on impulse. If a brand is not available in an outlet, an alternative is bought. The convenience aspect of purchase is paramount. New outlets may be sought that hitherto had not stocked the products, such as the sale of confectionery and grocery items at petrol stations.

Selective distribution

Selective distribution also enables market coverage to be achieved. In this case, a producer uses a limited number of outlets in a geographical area to sell its products. The advantages to the producer are: the opportunity to select only the best outlets to focus its efforts to build close working relationships, to train distributor staff on fewer outlets than with intensive distribution, and, if selling and distribution is direct, to reduce costs. Upmarket aspirational brands like Hugo Boss are often sold in carefully selected outlets. Retail outlets and industrial distributors like this arrangement since it reduces competition. Selective distribution is more likely to be used when buyers are willing to shop around when choosing products. This means that it is not necessary for a company to have its products available in all outlets. Products such as audio and video equipment, cameras, clothing and cosmetics may be sold in this way.

Problems can arise when a retailer demands distribution rights but is refused by producers. This happened in the case of Superdrug, a UK discount store chain that requested the right to sell expensive perfume but was denied by manufacturers, which claimed that its stores did not have the right ambience for the sale of luxury products. Superdrug maintained that its application was refused solely because it wanted to sell perfumes for less than their recommended prices. A Monopolies and Mergers Commission investigation supported current practice. European rules allow perfume companies to confine distribution to retailers who measure up in terms of décor and staff training. Manufacturers are not permitted to refuse distribution rights on the grounds that the retailer will sell for less than the list price.[11]

Exclusive distribution

Exclusive distribution is an extreme form of selective distribution in which only one wholesaler, retailer or business-to-business distributor is used in a particular geographic area. Cars are often sold on this basis, with only one dealer operating in each town or city. This reduces a purchaser's power to negotiate prices for the same model between dealers, since to buy in a neighbouring town may be inconvenient when servicing or repairs are required. It also allows very close co-operation between producer and retailer over servicing, pricing and promotion. The right to **exclusive distribution** may be demanded by distributors as a condition for stocking a manufacturer's product line. Similarly, producers may wish for exclusive dealing where the distributor agrees not to stock competing lines.

Exclusive distribution arrangements can restrict competition in a way that may be detrimental to consumer interests. The European Court of Justice rejected an appeal by Unilever over the issue of exclusive outlets in Germany. By supplying freezer cabinets, Unilever maintained exclusivity by refusing to allow competing ice creams into its cabinets. The Court's ruling may affect ice cream distribution in other European countries, including the UK.[12] However, the European Court rejected an appeal by the French Leclerc supermarket group over the issue of the selective distribution system used by Yves Saint Laurent perfumes. The judges found that the use of selective distribution for luxury cosmetic products increased competition and that it was in the consumer's and manufacturer's interests to preserve the image of such luxury products.

Channel integration

Channel integration can range from conventional marketing channels—comprising an independent producer and channel intermediaries—through a franchise operation to channel ownership by a producer. Producers need to consider the strengths and weaknesses of each system when selecting a channel strategy.

Conventional marketing channels

The producer has little or no control over channel intermediaries because of their independence. Arrangements such as exclusive dealing may provide a degree of control, but separation of ownership means that each party will look after its own interests. Conventional marketing channels are characterized by hard bargaining and, occasionally, conflict. For example, a retailer may believe that cutting the price of a brand is necessary to move stock, even though the producer objects because of brand image considerations.

Exhibit 11.2 Irish company O'Brien's Sandwich Bars is a rapidly growing service franchise

A manufacturer that, through its size and strong brands, dominates a market may exercise considerable power over intermediaries even though they are independent. This power may result in an **administered vertical marketing system** where the manufacturer can command considerable co-operation from wholesalers and retailers. For example, the big Hollywood studios carefully manage the distribution of movies through a sequence of cinema, video/DVD sale, video/DVD rental to pay-per-view television and finally free television to maximize their returns.[13] Retailers, too, can control an administered vertical marketing system. For example, when the retail entrepreneur Philip Green bought the Arcadia group in 2002, he wrote to all suppliers setting out new terms and conditions, imposing a retrospective 1.25 per cent discount and lengthening the number of days taken to pay suppliers from 28 to 30. He then consolidated the number of suppliers completely, delisting some and increasing the work given to others.[14]

Franchising

A legal contract in which a producer and channel intermediaries agree each member's rights and obligations is called a **franchise**. Usually, the intermediary receives marketing, managerial, technical and financial services in return for a fee. Franchise organizations such as McDonald's, Benetton, Hertz, the Body Shop and Starbucks combine the strengths of a large sophisticated marketing-orientated organization with the energy and motivation of a locally owned outlet, and hence have been highly successful in building global businesses. Although a franchise operation gives a degree of producer control, there are still areas of potential conflict. For example, the producer may be dissatisfied with the standards of service provided by the outlet, or the franchisee may believe that the franchising organization provides inadequate promotional support. Goal conflict can also arise. For example, some McDonald's and Starbucks' franchisees are displeased with the company's rapid expansion programme, which has meant that new restaurants have opened within a mile of existing outlets. This has led to complaints about lower profits and falling franchise resale values.[15] A franchise agreement provides a **contractual vertical marketing system** through the formal co-ordination and integration of marketing and distribution activities.

Three economic explanations have been proposed to explain why a producer might choose franchising as a means of distribution.[16] Franchising may be a means of overcoming resource constraints whereby the cost of distribution is shared with the franchisee. It may also be an efficient system for overcoming producer/distributor management problems, because producers may value the notion of the owner-manager who has a vested interest in the success of the business. Finally, franchising may be a way for a producer to access the local knowledge of the franchisee. Franchising may therefore be attractive when a producer is expanding into new international markets.

Franchising can occur at four levels of the distribution chain.

1. *Manufacturer and retailer*: the car industry is dominated by this arrangement. The manufacturer gains retail outlets for its cars and repair facilities without the capital outlay required with ownership.

2. *Manufacturer and wholesaler*: this is commonly used in the soft drinks industry. Manufacturers such as Schweppes, Coca-Cola and Pepsi grant wholesalers the right to make up and bottle their concentrate in line with their instructions, and to distribute the products within a defined geographic area.

3. *Wholesaler and retailer*: this is not as common as other franchising arrangements, but is found with car products and hardware stores. It allows wholesalers to secure distribution of their product to consumers.

4. *Retailer and retailer*: an often used method that frequently has its roots in a successful retailing operation seeking to expand geographically by means of a franchise operation, often with great success. Examples include McDonald's, Benetton, Pizza Hut and Kentucky Fried Chicken.

Channel ownership

Channel ownership brings with it total control over distributor activities. This establishes a **corporate vertical marketing system**. By purchasing retail outlets, producers control their purchasing, produc-

Table 11.1 Franchising arrangements in selected industries

Sector	Sample Franchisors	Number of Franchises
Automotive Repair	Midas International Corp.	2,600
Chicken Restaurants	Kentucky-Fried Chicken	10,040
Children's Tutoring	Kumon Math & Reading Centres	27,630
Commercial Cleaning	Jani-King	10,932
Convenience Stores	7-Eleven	23,350
Executive Search	MRI Worldwide	1,338
Fitness	Curves	8,009
Haircare	Supercuts	973
Hardware	Snap-on Tools	4,664
Hotels	InterContinental Hotel Group	2,975
Mexican Fast Food	Taco Bell Corp.	4,850
Pizza	Domino's Pizza	6,953
Real Estate	RE/Max International Corp.	5,045
Sandwiches	Subway	22,481
Technical Training	New Horizons Computer Learning Centres Inc.	233
Windscreen Repair	Novus Auto Glass	2,366
Vitamins/Health Products	GNC Franchising Inc.	2,023

Source: www.entrepreneur.com/franchise500

tion and marketing activities. In particular, control over purchasing means a captive outlet for the manufacturer's products. For example, the purchase of Pizza Hut and Kentucky Fried Chicken by Pepsi has tied these outlets to the company's soft drinks brands.

The benefits of control have to be balanced against the high price of acquisition and the danger that the move into retailing will spread managerial activities too widely. Nevertheless, corporate vertical marketing systems have operated successfully for many years in the oil industry where companies such as Shell, Texaco and Statoil own not only considerable numbers of petrol stations but also the means of production.

Channel management

Channels need to be managed on an ongoing basis once the key channel strategy decisions have been made. This involves the selection, motivation, training and evaluation of channel members, and the resolution of any channel conflict that arises.

Selection

The selection of channel members involves two main activities: first, the identification of potential channel members and, second, development of selection criteria. A variety of potential sources can be used to identify candidates, including trade sources such as trade associations and participation at exhibitions, talking to existing customers and/or to the field salesforce, and taking enquiries from interested resellers.[17] Common selection criteria include market, product and customer knowledge, market coverage, quality and size of salesforce (if applicable), reputation among customers, financial standing, the extent to which competitive and complementary products are carried, managerial competence and hunger for success, and the degree of enthusiasm for handling the producer's lines. In practice, selection may be complex because large, well-established distributors may carry many competing lines and lack enthusiasm for more. Smaller distributors, on the other hand, may be less financially secure and have a smaller salesforce, but be more enthusiastic and hungry for success.

Motivation

Once they have been chosen, channel members need to be motivated to agree to act as a distributor, and allocate adequate commitment and resources to the producer's lines. The key to effective motivation is to understand the needs and problems of distributors, since needs and motivators are linked. For example, a distributor who values financial incentives may respond more readily to high commission than one who is more concerned with having an exclusive territory. Possible motivators include financial rewards, territorial exclusivity, providing resource support (e.g. sales training, field sales assistance, provision of marketing research information, advertising and promotion support, financial assistance and management training) and developing strong work relationships (e.g. joint planning, assurance of long-term commitment, appreciation of effort and success, frequent interchange of views and arranging distributor conferences). In short, management of independent distributors is best conducted in the context of informal partnerships.[18]

Training

Channel members' training requirements obviously depend on their internal competences. Large supermarket chains, for example, may regard an invitation by a manufacturer to provide marketing training as an insult. However, many smaller distributors have been found to be weak on sales management, marketing, financial management, stock control and personnel management, and may welcome producer initiatives on training.[19] From the producer's perspective, training can provide the necessary technical knowledge about a supplier company and its products, and help to build a spirit of partnership and commitment.

Evaluation

Channel member evaluation has an important impact on distributor retention, training and motivation decisions. Evaluation provides the information necessary to decide which channel members to retain and which to drop. Shortfalls in distributor skills and competences may be identified through evaluation, and appropriate training programmes organized by producers. Where a lack of motivation is recognized as a problem, producers can implement plans designed to deal with the root causes of demotivation (e.g. financial incentives and/or fostering a partnership approach to business).[20] It needs to be understood, however, that the scope and frequency of evaluation may be limited where power lies with the channel member. If producers have relatively little power because they are more dependent on channel members for distribution, then in-depth evaluation and remedial action will be restricted. Where manufacturer power is high through having strong brands, and many distributors from which to choose, evaluation may be more frequent and wider in scope. Evaluation criteria include sales volume and value, profitability, level of stocks, quality and position of display, new accounts opened, selling and marketing capabilities, quality of service provided to customers, market information feedback, ability and willingness to keep commitments, attitudes and personal capability.

Managing conflict

Finally, given that producers and channel members are independent, conflict will inevitably occur from time to time. First, such discord may arise because of differences in goals—for example, an increase in the proportion of profits allocated to retailers means a reduction in the amount going to manufacturers (see Marketing in Action 11.2). For example, when the Irish tour operator, Budget Travel cut the commissions its pays to travel agents for selling its holidays from 10 to 5 per cent, its subsequent research found that many agents were omitting Budget from the list of choices being presented to customers. Its response was to reach out directly to the end consumer through a $1 million multimedia campaign urging consumers to consider Budget as one of their potential travel choices.[21] Second, in seeking to expand their businesses many resellers add additional product lines. For example, UK retailer WHSmith originally specialized in books, magazines and newspapers but has grown by adding new product lines such as computer disks, video tapes and software supplies. This can cause resentment among its primary suppliers who perceive the reseller as devoting too much effort to selling secondary lines. Third in trying to grow their business, producers can use multiple distribution channels, such as selling directly to key accounts or other distributors, which may irritate existing dealers. Direct distribution has become a major issue in the video games business where digital downloading services are expected to grow significantly in the years ahead. Digital distribution is much cheaper than having the produce and ship hard copies to retailers and video gamers are also the kind of people who are comfortable with the new approach as they tend to download music and movies on demand.[22] Similarly, Alanis Morissette's record company, Maverick Records created a significant amount of channel conflict in North America when it gave exclusive rights for the sale of her *Jagged Little Pill* album to Starbucks, which was allowed to sell the record for six weeks in its 4,800 stores before it became available elsewhere. HMV reacted by removing all the artist's music from the shelves of its Canadian stores.[23] Finally, an obvious source of conflict is when parties in the supply chain do not perform to expectations.

There are several ways of managing conflict. Developing a partnership approach calls for frequent interaction between producer and resellers to develop a spirit of mutual understanding and co-operation. First, sales targets can be mutually agreed, and training and promotional support provided. Second, staff may need some training in conflict handling to ensure that situations are handled calmly and that possibilities for win/win outcomes are identified. Third, where the conflict arises from multiple distribution channels, producers can try to partition markets. For example, Hallmark sells its premium greetings cards under its Hallmark brand name to upmarket department stores, and its standard cards under the Ambassador name to discount retailers.[24]

Fourth, where poor performance is the problem, the most effective solution is to improve performance so that the source of conflict disappears. Finally, in some cases, the conflict might be eliminated through the purchase of the other party or through coercion, where one party gains compliance through the use of force such as where a large retailer threatens to delist a manufacturer. The recent merger between Proctor & Gamble and Gillette was seen by many as a move

Marketing in Action: Manufacturers versus retailers: from conflict to co-operation?

The relationship between branded goods manufacturers and the major supermarket chains has evolved significantly over the years. Two to three decades ago, the power resided with the manufacturers. They used their marketing muscle to build strong brands, which were then distributed through a fragmented distribution channel comprising a variety of supermarket chains with relatively low overall market shares. Then, through aggressive growth, branding and the use of information technology, the channel became concentrated and the balance of power shifted to the retailer. In the UK, for example, almost 70 per cent of all food spending is accounted for by four chains: Tesco, Asda, Sainsbury's and Morrisons.

The growth of the supermarkets gave rise to a period of significant conflict as they battled for supremacy in the supply chain. In the early 1990s, supermarkets began bringing out own-label products to compete with those made by manufacturers, and made significant inroads in many categories, such as baked beans, kitchen towels and nappies. Several litigation cases ensued as manufacturers claimed the retail versions bore too close a resemblance to their brands and infringed their trademarks. The retailers moved on unperturbed, increasing the space devoted to private label goods, extracting greater concessions from manufacturers and delisting brands that were underperforming. Manufacturers were faced with increased listing fees, fees for shelf space, and demands for trade promotion and co-operative advertising, which often meant that they were spending much more promoting their brands in the channel than they were in promoting to the end customer.

However, now the whisper coming from both camps is of the need to be co-operative again and to build 'strategic partnerships'. This process began with the move to 'category management', where retailers selected particular manufacturers to be 'category captains' who were expected to make merchandising, stocking and pricing recommendations to the retailer for the category. Some of these category captains are now becoming 'preferred partners', which involves both the manufacturer and the retailer working together to grow the category. Customer data is shared, joint promotions are organized and, often, personnel from both parties work together on projects. For example, when P&G launched its Physique haircare brand in the UK, it was distributed exclusively through Tesco channels, using Tesco publications and based on the combined customer data of both companies. Similarly, because most Safeway (now owned by Morrisons) stores are less than 20,000 square feet, it has to be very careful about its product selection and merchandising. It worked jointly with Coca-Cola to develop chiller cabinets, paid for by Safeway, that displayed cans and 500 ml bottles of Coke adjacent to checkouts. Coca-Cola also started attaching merchandising material to cardboard palettes of drinks so that they could be unloaded straight from the truck to the shop floor, often in front of the entrance. When Vanilla Coke was launched in 2003, Safeway was able to get the drink into its stores three days before its competitors, increasing its market share while Coca-Cola benefited from an early commitment to orders from Safeway and a chance to send sampling teams into its stores.

Based on: Dawar (2004);[25] Harrison (2003);[26] Murphy (2003)[27]

to put these two manufacturers on an equal footing with giant retailers like Wal-Mart.

Retailing

Most retailing is conducted in stores such as supermarkets, catalogue shops and departmental stores, but non-store retailing, such as online, mail order and automatic vending, also accounts for a large proportion of sales. Many large retailers exert enormous power in the distribution chain because of the vast quantities of goods they buy from manufacturers. This power is reflected in their ability to extract 'guarantee of margins' from manufacturers. This is a clause inserted in a contract that ensures a certain profit margin for the retailer, irrespective of the retail price being charged to the customer. One manufacturer is played against another, and own-label brands are used to extract more profit.[28]

Major store and non-store types

Supermarkets

Supermarkets are large self-service stores, which traditionally sell food, drinks and toiletries, but the broadening of their ranges by some supermarket chains means that such items as non-prescription pharmaceuticals, cosmetics and clothing are also being sold. While one attraction of supermarkets is their lower prices compared with small independent grocery shops, the extent to which price is a key competitive weapon depends on the supermarket's positioning strategy. For example, in the UK, Sainsbury's, Waitrose and Tesco are less reliant on price than KwikSave, Aldi or Netto. In the UK, Tesco is now the undisputed leader in this space having opened more stores than Sainsbury's, Asda and Morrisons combined in the 2001–04 period. It is estimated that 60 per cent of the British public now enters a Tesco store at least once a month. Its brand range stretches from its Value range to the Tesco Finest range to Organics and Healthy Eating, and means that it appeals to all segments.[29]

Department stores

Department stores are titled thus because related product lines are sold in separate departments, such as men's and women's clothing, jewellery, cosmetics, toys and home furnishings. In recent years such stores have been under increasing pressure from discount houses, speciality stores and the move to out-of-town shopping. Nevertheless, many continue to perform well in this competitive arena through a strategy of becoming one-stop shops for a variety of leading manufacturer brands, which are allocated significant store space.

Speciality shops

As their name suggests, these outlets specialize in a narrow product line. Many town centres, for example, have shops selling confectionery, cigarettes and newspapers in the same outlet. Many speciality outlets, such as Tie Rack and Sock Shop, sell only one product line. Specialization allows a deep product line to be sold in restricted shop space. Some speciality shops, such as butchers and greengrocers, focus on quality and personal service. Speciality shops can, however, be vulnerable when tastes change or competition increases. For example, speciality sports retailers such as JJB Sports and John David Group have been reporting disappointing results as the blending of sportswear and fashion, driven by cultural icons such as David Beckham, has opened up the market to a host of other retailers such as fashion shops and supermarkets.[30]

Discount houses

Discount houses sell products at low prices by accepting low margins, selling high volumes and bulk buying. Low prices, sometimes promoted as sale prices, are offered throughout the year. As an executive of Dixons, a UK discounter of electrical goods, commented, 'We only have two sales, each lasting six months.' Many discounters operate from out-of-town retail warehouses with the capacity to stock a wide range of merchandise. One of the fastest-growing

Exhibit 11.3 La Senza is a rapidly growing chain of lingerie shops in the UK and Ireland

Marketing in Action: £1 buys success

Traditionally, pound shops have had a poor image, being seen as places that sell poor-quality, end-of-line stock to people on very low incomes. But the globalization of business and intense competition in the retail sector is changing all that. Many pound shops are now stocked primarily with good-quality, branded products as well as novelty items.

Leading players in this business are developing sophisticated buying skills, enabling them to extract good deals from manufacturers who may wish to capitalize on opportunities like sell-offs of Christmas stock in January. Products are also sourced from 'grey markets'—that is, branded products bought on foreign markets at lower prices than those at home, or from new emerging centres of production like China and Vietnam.

The retail proposition is very strong: everything sells for £1. Pound shops typically sell products like toiletries, kitchen and gardening equipment, tools, stationery, toys, ornaments, snack foods, fashion accessories and gadgets of all types. Rapid turnover is essential and shops occasionally stock bizarre items in order to generate excitement and attract customers. Increasingly, they are attracting shoppers from all walks of life through a promotional approach which stresses that they have something for everyone.

Despite operating on very tight margins, sometimes as low as 2–3 per cent, some of the sector's leading players are very profitable. The Poundland chain, which has 126 stores and markets itself as providing 'the irresistible shopping experience', had a turnover of £240 million in 2005, with pre-tax profits in excess of £10 million. Similarly, the Quids In chain of 62 shops based in Scotland and northern England had sales of £13 million in 2004 and has been profitable from day one. The business is still dominated by independently owned shops and rapid consolidation of the sector is expected as leading players seek to gain economies of scale.

Based on: **Guthrie** (2004);[31] **Tighe** (2005)[32]

sectors is the ultimate discount house: the pound shop (see Marketing in Action 11.3).

Category killers

These retail outlets have a narrow product focus, but an unusually wide width and depth to that product range. Category killers emerged in the USA in the early 1980s as a challenge to discount houses. They are distinct from speciality shops in that they are bigger, and carry a wider and deeper range of products within their chosen product category; they are distinct from discount houses in their focus on only one product category. Two examples of the category killer are Toys 'R' Us and Nevada Bob's Discount Golf Warehouses.[33]

Convenience stores

Convenience stores, true to their name, offer customers the convenience of a close location and long opening hours every day of the week. Because they are small they pay higher prices for their merchandise than supermarkets, and therefore have to charge higher prices to their customers. Some of these stores—such as Spar—join buying groups to gain some purchasing power and lower prices. The main

customer need they fulfil is that for top-up buying—for example, when a customer is short of a carton of milk or loaf of bread, say. Although average purchase value is low, convenience stores prosper because of their higher prices and low staff costs: many are family businesses. As we saw in Marketing in Action 11.1, convenience stores have become a popular takeover target for the major supermarket chains.

Catalogue stores

This type of retail outlet promotes its products through catalogues, which are either mailed to customers or available in-store for customers to view on-site or take home (see Chapter 10). Purchase is in city-centre outlets where customers fill in order forms, pay for the goods and then collect them from a designated place in the store. In the UK, Argos is a successful catalogue retailer selling a wide range of discounted products such as electrical goods, jewellery, gardening tools, furniture, toys, car accessories, sports goods, luggage and cutlery.

Mail order

This non-store form of retailing may also employ catalogues as a promotional vehicle, but the purchase transaction is conducted via the mail. Alternatively, outward communication may be by direct mail, television, magazine or newspaper advertising. Increasingly, orders are being placed by telephone or over the Internet, a process that is facilitated by the use of credit cards as a means of payment. Goods are then sent by mail. Otto-Versand (the German mail-order company) owns Grattan, a UK mail-order retailer, and has leading positions in Austria, Belgium, Italy, the Netherlands and Spain. Its French rival, La Redoute, has expanded into Belgium, Italy and Portugal. Mail order offers the prospect of pan-European catalogues, central warehousing and processing of cross-border orders.

Automatic vending

Offering such products as drinks, confectionery, soup and newspapers in convenient locations, 24 hours a day, vending machines are particularly popular in some countries, such as Japan. No sales staff are required although restocking, servicing and repair costs can be high. Cash dispensers at banks have improved customer service by permitting round-the-clock financial services. However, machine breakdowns and out-of-stock situations can annoy customers.

Online retailing

After a slow start, the prospects for online retailing continue to improve. Between 1997 and 2002, the number of online shopping households in the USA grew from 5 million to 36.5 million and online sales rose from $2.4 billion to more than $72 billion. Forrester Research estimates that by 2007, 63 million people or nearly two thirds of all US households will shop online[34]. Online retailing can take any of three major forms. First, in pure online retailing scenario, the product is ordered, paid for and received online in a completely electronic transaction. Any product that can be digitized such as a piece of music, computer software or a book can be retailed in this way. Second, products can be ordered online and then distributed either through the postal system or through the use of local distribution companies in the case of groceries or wine for example. Finally, most leading retailers have an online presence. For example, Wal-Mart's website, www.walmart.com had 350 million visits in 2004. It carries about 200,000 products as opposed to approximately 100,000 in a typical store and consumers have the option, for example, of ordering one-hour photo processing online and picking them up later in a local store[35].

Key retail marketing decisions

A retail outlet needs to be thought of as a brand involving the same set of decisions we discussed when we looked at branding in Chapter 6. Retailers need to anticipate and adapt to changing environmental circumstances, such as the growing role of information technology and changing customer tastes. However,

Exhibit 11.4 Sainsbury's move into banking shows the extent to which many retailers are engaged in scrambled merchandizing

there are a number of specific issues that relate to retailing, and are worthy of separate discussion. These are **retail positioning**, store location, product assortment and services, price and store atmosphere.

Retail positioning

Retail positioning—as with all marketing decisions—involves the choice of target market and differential advantage. Targeting allows retailers to tailor their marketing mix (which includes product assortment, service levels, store location, prices and promotion) to the needs of their chosen customer segment. Differentiation provides a reason to shop at one store rather than another. A useful framework for creating a differential advantage has been proposed by Davies, who suggests that innovation in retailing can come only from novelty in the process offered to the shopper, or from novelty in the product or product assortment offered to the shopper.[36] The catalogue shop Argos in the UK has offered innovation in the process of shopping, whereas Next achieved success through product innovation (stylish clothes at afford-

able prices). Similarly, Target is one of the fastest-growing chains in the USA, generating sales of over US$41 billion across 1200 stores by effectively positioning itself through its product mix as appealing to both upmarket and downmarket buyers at the same time. It carries more apparel than its major competitor, Wal-Mart and an usually high 80 per cent of its clothing is private-label, which is sold at discounted prices. Yet the typical Target shopper has an annual income of US$50,000 compared with US$30,000 for a Wal-Mart shopper. Toys 'R' Us is an example of both product and process innovation through providing the widest range of toys at one location (product innovation) and thereby offering convenient, one-stop shopping (process innovation).

Store location

Conventional wisdom has it that the three factors critical to the success of a retailer are location, location and location. Convenience is an important issue for many shoppers, and so store location can

e-Marketing: Divorce on special offer at Tesco.com

As supermarkets look to expand their product assortments, one of their major constraints is store size: there are only so many products that can be displayed in a given retail space. But, with online shopping, there are no such restrictions. Tesco has been one of the first supermarkets to aggressively exploit this opportunity through its website, Tesco.com. Shoppers can choose both from products available at its grocery stores as well as from a range of products delivered from Tesco warehouses, which has enabled it to extend into a variety of other businesses such as books, CDs, games and DVDs, electronic equipment and home furnishings.

But it is perhaps its move into areas like personal finance, and particularly the provision of legal services, that has generated most controversy. Tesco opened its legal store on its website in 2004 offering, for example, a DIY separation and divorce kit 'on special offer' at £7.49 and triple Clubcard points with its £9.99 last will and testament kit, in a move that came as a shock to many in the traditional and relatively closed legal profession. In addition, the site offers a 'jargon buster' designed to demystify the legal issues, as well as a pocket guide to your rights. Even before the store had opened, Tesco had received a great deal of free publicity when Lord Falconer, the Lord Chancellor, coined the term 'Tesco law' in support of proposals to deregulate the legal profession in the UK.

However, there are significant risks for Tesco in its move into the legal arena. Critics argue that it needs to assess the impact offering legal services is likely to have on its brand values as legal actions are often time consuming, expensive and with no guaranteed outcome, which is not the kind of proposition normally offered by a leading marketer. For example, 'getting a divorce at Tesco' is hardly a positive message for the supermarket chain. Concerns have also been raised about the potential conflict of interest that arises from the legal profession's requirements for integrity and impartiality, and the corporation's goal of profit maximization. Nevertheless, the legal market is a very lucrative one and these issues are unlikely to deter leading companies from offering basic legal services as a way of testing the potential of the market.

Based on: Benady (2004);[38] Rowley (2003);[39] Sherwood (2004);[40] Shrimsley (2004)[41]

have a major bearing on sales performance. Retailers have to decide on regional coverage, the towns and cities to target within regions, and the precise location to select within a given town or city. The choice of town or city will depend on such factors as correspondence with the retailer's chosen target market, the level of disposable income in the catchment area, the availability of suitable sites and the level of competition (see Marketing in Action 8.2, which discusses Fopp's choice of store sites). The choice of a particular site may depend on the level of existing traffic (pedestrian and/or vehicular) passing the site, parking provision, access to the outlet for delivery vehicles, the presence of competition, planning restrictions and whether there is an opportunity to form new retailing centres with other outlets. For example, an agreement between two or more non-competing retailers (e.g. Sainsbury's and Boots) to locate outlets together out of town results in greater pulling power than each could achieve individually. Having made that decision, the partners will look for suitable sites near their chosen town or city.

Product assortment

Retailers have to make a decision on the breadth and depth of their product assortment. A supermarket, for example, may decide to widen its product assortment from food, drink and toiletries to include clothes and toys: this is called 'scrambled merchandizing'. The rapid extent to which some supermarkets

Marketing in Action: Building the atmosphere at Louis Vuitton

Louis Vuitton is a manufacturer of high-quality, crafted luggage and expensive leather accessories; it is one of the best-known luxury brands in the world. The company was founded in Paris in 1854 as a manufacturer of trunks before moving on to become renowned for its custom-made luggage. Many of its early customers were the aristocracy of Europe, something that has underpinned its premium positioning ever since. In 1987, the company merged with Moët Hennessy, the premium champagne and cognac producer to become the world's largest luxury goods company, which was named LVMH.

The positioning of Louis Vuitton is unashamedly exclusive. One of its most successful marketing tactics is to bring out limited-edition LV products every year. For example, in 2004 it launched the Theda bag, which was priced at US$5500 and initially only available in the USA at LV's Fifth Avenue store in New York. Within a few weeks of its launch, there was a waiting list for the product running into months.

Celebrities like Jennifer Lopez front its advertising, and manufacturing is carefully restricted to locations in France, Spain and the USA. Louis Vuitton began opening its first retail stores in 1977 and now has a portfolio of over 300 stores around the world. But, again, all of these stores are wholly owned by the company, which does not have any distributor or franchise agreements.

Therefore, the challenge in opening each new store is to keep redefining the meaning of luxury. One of its most recently opened stores, in Tokyo, places a high emphasis on atmosphere and has been described as a mixture of museum, theatre and shop. The outlet is located in Roppongi, one of the city's centres of nightlife, and is designed to reflect this. Customers enter a spacious atrium known as the 'Dancefloor' where they can browse through the collections. The centrepiece of the outlet is an operatically grand limestone staircase, flanked by a network of hundreds of fibre-optic cables that twinkle and glow with a series of abstract and semi-abstract images. The nightclub theme continues upstairs, where there is the 'Bag Bar', the 'Shoe Salon' and the 'Luggage Lounge'. MP3 jukeboxes have even been installed on the first and second floors, where customers can download selected songs from a DJ mix that is playing in the store.

However, it is the exterior of the building that has received the most attention. It has no window in the traditional sense but rather comprises a 12.5-metre high by 36-metre long wall built from 40,000 glass tubes, which resembles the chequerboard pattern of LV's Damier brand. The architects explain that the idea was to create a 'mirage', something that would be mysterious, shimmering and would seem to dance as visitors viewed it from different angles. Who'd have thought a shop front could be capable of so much!

Based on: Heathcote (2003);[43] Pearson (2004);[44] Sisodia and Chaudhuri (2004)[45]

are diversifying their product portfolio is illustrated in e-Marketing 11.1. Within each product line, it can choose to stock a deep or shallow product range. Some retailers, like Tie Rack, Sock Shop and Toys 'Я' Us stock one deep product line. Department stores, however, offer a much broader range of products including toys, cosmetics, jewellery, clothes, electrical goods and household accessories. Some retailers begin with one product line and gradually broaden their product assortment to maximize revenue per customer. For example, petrol stations broadened their product range to include motor accessories and, more recently, confectionery, drinks, flowers and newspapers. A by-product of this may be to reduce customers' price sensitivity since selection of petrol station may be based on the availability of other products there rather than the fact that it offers the lowest price.

Own-label branding gives rise to another product decision. Major retailers may decide to sell a range of own-label products to complement national brands. Often the purchasing power of these large retail chains means that prices can be lower and yet profit margins higher than for competing national brands. This makes the activity an attractive proposition for many retailers. Supermarkets have moved into this area, as have UK electrical giants such as Dixons, which uses the Chinon brand name for cameras and Saisho for brown goods such as hi-fi and televisions, and Currys , which has adopted the Matsui brand name. In both cases the use of a Japanese-sounding name (even though some of the products were sourced in Europe) was believed to enhance their customer appeal.

Price

Price is a key factor in store choice for some market segments. Consequently some retailers major on price as their differential advantage. This requires vigilant cost control and massive buying power. A recent trend is towards the 'everyday low prices' favoured by retailers, rather than the higher prices supplemented by promotions that are supported by manufacturers. Retailers such as B&Q the do-it-your-self discounter, maintain that customers prefer predictable low prices rather than occasional money-off deals, three-for-the-price-of-two offers and free gifts. Supermarket chains are also pressurizing suppliers to provide consistently low prices rather than temporary promotions. This action is consistent with the desire to position themselves on a low price platform. The importance of price competitiveness is reflected in the alliance of European food retailers called Associated Marketing Services. Retailers such as Argyll (UK), Ahold (the Netherlands), ICA (a federation of Swedish food retailers), Casino (France),

Superquinn (Ireland) and others have joined forces to foster co-operation in the areas of purchasing and marketing of brands. Their range of activities includes own branding, joint buying, the development of joint brands and services, and the exchange of information and skills. A key aim is to reduce cost price since this accounts for 75 per cent of the sales price to customers.[42]

Store atmosphere

Atmosphere is created by a combination of the design, colour and layout of a store (see Marketing in Action 11.4). Both exterior and interior design affect atmosphere. External factors include architectural design, signs, window displays and use of colour, which create an identity for a retailer and attract customers. The Body Shop, for example, projects its environmentally caring image through the green exterior of its shops, and through window displays that focus on environmental issues. Interior design also has a major impact on atmosphere. Store lighting, fixtures and fittings, and layout are important considerations. Colour, sound and smell can affect mood. Department stores often place perfume counters near the entrance, and supermarkets may use the smell of baking bread to attract customers, and upmarket shirt companies like Thomas Pink even pump the smell of freshly laundered linen around their stores. In addition, supermarkets often use music to create a relaxed atmosphere, whereas some boutiques use pop music to draw in their target customers.

Physical distribution

Earlier in this chapter we examined channel strategy and management decisions, which concern the choice of the correct outlets to provide product availability to customers in a cost-effective manner. Physical distribution decisions focus on the efficient movement of goods from producer to intermediaries and the consumer. Clearly, channel and physical distribution decisions are interrelated, although channel decisions tend to be made earlier. Physical distribution is defined as a set of activities concerned with the physical flows of materials, components and finished goods from producer to channel intermediaries and consumers. It is a business that has become increasingly complex as customers such as Wal-Mart, Tesco and others extend their global reach. This has given rise to mergers between logistics companies such as that involving Exel and Tibbet & Britten, as companies seek to provide integrated solutions for their clients ranging from warehouse management to home delivery.[46]

Distribution aims to provide intermediaries and customers with the right products, in the right quantities, in the right locations, at the right time. Physical distribution activities have been the subject of managerial attention for some time because of the potential for cost savings and improving customer service levels. Cost savings can be achieved by reducing inventory levels, using cheaper forms of transport and shipping in bulk rather than small quantities. For example, Benetton's blueprint for reviving its fortunes has been predicated on getting clothes from the factory to the shop rail faster to enable it to compete with fast fashion retailers like Zara and H&M.[47] Customer service levels can be improved by fast and reliable delivery, including just-in-time (JIT) delivery, holding high inventory levels so that customers have a wide choice and the chances of stock-outs are reduced, fast order processing, and ensuring that products arrive in the right quantities and quality. Physical distribution management concerns the balance between cost reduction and meeting customer service requirements. Trade-offs are often necessary. For example, low inventory and slow, cheaper transportation methods reduce costs but lower customer service levels and satisfaction.

As well as the trade-offs between physical distribution costs and customer service levels, there is the potential for conflict between elements of the physical distribution system itself. For example, low-cost containers may lower packaging costs but raise the cost of goods damaged in transit. This fact, and the need to co-ordinate order processing, inventory and transportation decisions, means that physical distribution needs to be managed as a system, with a manager overseeing the whole process. It can be a very challenging task as demonstrated by the problems suffered by Sainsbury's, the leading British supermarket. It invested £3 billion in its supply chain focused around four regional distribution centres. But the changeover led to several problems. Suppliers were not packing orders to suit the new centres, deliveries were arriving at the wrong time, labour was often in the wrong place and stocks were frequently in the store room or delivery yard rather than on the shelves. The system was designed to generate savings of £600 million per year, but in 2004, Sainsbury's chief executive, Justin King admitted that it had been a failure.[48] The key elements of the physical distribution system are customer service, order processing, inventory control, warehousing, transportation and materials handling.

Customer service

It is essential to set customer service standards. For example, a customer service standard might be that 90 per cent of orders are delivered within 48 hours of receipt and 100 per cent are delivered within 72 hours. Higher customer service standards normally mean higher costs as inventory levels need to be higher. In some cases, customers value consistency in delivery time rather than speed. For example, a customer service standard of guaranteed delivery within five working days may be valued more than 60 per cent within two and 100 per cent within seven days. Customer service standards should be given considerable attention for they may be the differentiating factor between suppliers: they may be used as a key customer choice criterion. Methods of improving customer service standards include improving product availability, improving order cycle time, raising information levels and improving flexibility. An example of raising information levels is the kind of service now being provided online by courier companies like Federal Express and UPS, which offer their customers a facility whereby they can log on and get immediate updates on delivery status.

Order processing

This relates to the question of how orders are handled. Reducing time between a customer placing an order and receiving the goods may be achieved through careful analysis of the components that make up order processing time. A computer link between the salesperson and the order department may be effective. Electronic data interchange can also speed order processing time by checking the customer's credit rating, and whether the goods are in stock, issuing an order to the warehouse, invoicing the customer and updating the inventory records.

Inventory control

Inventory control deals with the question of how much inventory should be held. A balance has to be found between the need to have products in stock to meet customer demand and the costs incurred in holding large inventories. Having in stock every conceivable item a customer might order would normally be prohibitively expensive for companies marketing many items. Decisions also need to be taken about when to order new stocks. These order points are normally before stock levels reach zero because of the lead time between ordering and receiving inventory. The JIT inventory system is designed to reduce lead times so that the order point (the stock level at which re-ordering takes place), and overall inventory levels for production items, are low. The more variable the lead time between ordering and receiving stocks, and the greater the fluctuation in customer demand, the higher the order point.

e-Marketing: How RFID technology will impact on the supply chain

Radio frequency identification (RFID) technology has been in use for about 10 years, most commonly in the easy-pass systems that allow drivers to speed through toll booths on highways around the world. But the technology now looks set to also revolutionize the movement of goods through the supply chain. Containers, palettes or even products are fitted with a tiny silicon chip and antenna, about the size of a pinhead, which contains a unique serial number and extensive information about each item. These chips are read by a 'reader' that sends out a high-frequency radio signal that beams back the information and points to a web page containing detailed specifications for the product. But, in a big advance on traditional barcodes, the tag reader can scan dozens of items simultaneously and does not need a direct line of sight. Tags can be read from a distance of up to 20 yards and even through walls, and are read automatically once they come within range of the receiver.

RFID technology promises to improve the efficiency of warehouse operations by lowering error rates and requiring less time and labour. For example, the contents of palettes can be read without being opened and fewer staff members will be needed to track and reconcile shipments and inventory. Estimates are that total labour warehouse costs could be cut by 3 per cent. The technology has already been used at marine terminals in California where cargos are transferred from international to domestic containers for delivery to regional distribution centres. By switching from manual operations to RFID tags, NYK Logistics reduced trucker turnaround times by more 50 per cent to an average of 14 minutes, and was able to increase the number of trucks it could handle at its facility from 70,000 to 120,000 without any increase in space. Similarly, speedier information on inventory levels will enable manufacturers to reduce stock-out costs in the channel. Another potential application is the removal of the long queue at checkouts as traditional scanners are replaced with an RFID-type system.

A variety of major corporations around the world are experimenting with the technology. For example, Wal-Mart has required that its top 100 suppliers begin using it. In 2004, Delta Airlines announced that it would invest US$25 million to deploy disposable radio tags to track and locate lost luggage, which costs the airline US$100 million annually. IBM has suggested that banks should issue their best customers with cards containing the tags, allowing them to get special treatment, and Gillette ordered 500 million tags in 2003 in its first large-scale test of the technology.

However, there are also significant privacy fears over these developments. One of its attractions is that individual products can be tagged, which would significantly help with problems like shoplifting, though at the moment this is not possible as the cost of each tag (roughly 30 cents) is prohibitive. However, if costs fall, tags could be sewn into clothing or embedded in shoes, which would make it possible to track consumers as they enter and leave stores. Some schools in the USA and Japan are tagging students as a way of monitoring attendance and tracking their movements. These kinds of application mean that we haven't heard the last of RFID.

Based on: Anonymous (2004);[49] Ferguson (2002);[50] Gilligan (2004);[51] Kelly (2003);[52] Leach (2004);[53] London (2003);[54] Mongelluzzo (2004);[55] Niemeyer, Pat and Ramaswamy (2003)[56]

This is because of the uncertainty caused by the variability leading to the need for **safety (buffer) stocks** in case lead times are unpredictably long or customer demand unusually high. How much to order depends on the cost of holding stock and order-processing costs. Orders can be small and frequent, or large and infrequent. Small, frequent orders raise order-processing costs but reduce inventory carrying costs; large, infrequent orders raise inventory costs but lower order-processing expenditure.

Warehousing

This part of the distribution chain involves all the activities required in the storing of goods between the time they are produced and the time they are transported to the customer. These activities include breaking bulk, making up product assortments for delivery to customers, storage and loading. Storage warehouses hold goods for moderate or long time periods, whereas distribution centres operate as central locations for the fast movement of goods.

Retailing organizations use regional distribution centres where suppliers deliver products in bulk. These shipments are broken down into loads that are then quickly transported to retail outlets. Distribution centres are usually highly automated, with computer-controlled machinery facilitating the movement of goods. A computer reads orders and controls the fork-lift trucks that gather goods and move them to loading bays. Further technological advances are likely to have a significant impact on warehousing and the movement of goods through the supply chain (see e-Marketing 11.2). Warehousing strategy involves the determination of the location and the number of warehouses to be used. As with most physical distribution decisions, the optimum number and location of warehouses is a balance between customer service and cost considerations. Usually, the more locally based warehouses a company uses, the better the customer service, but the higher the cost.

Transportation

This refers to the subject of how products will be transported; the five major modes are rail, road, air, water and pipeline. Railways are efficient at transporting large, bulky freight on land over long distances and are often used to transport coal, chemicals, oil, aggregates and nuclear flasks. Rail is more environmentally friendly than road, but the major problem with it is lack of flexibility. Motorized transport by road has the advantage of flexibility because of direct access to companies and warehouses. This means that lorries can transport goods from supplier to receiver without unloading en route. However, the growth of road transport in Europe, and particularly the UK, has received considerable criticism because of increased traffic congestion and the damage done to roads by heavy juggernauts. The key advantages of air freight are its speed and long distance capabilities. Its speed means that it is often used to transport perishable goods and emergency deliveries. Its major disadvantages are high cost, and the need to transport goods by road to and from air terminals. Water transportation is slow but inexpensive. Inland transportation is usually associated with bulky, low-value, non-perishable goods such as coal, ore, grain, steel and petroleum. Ocean-going ships carry a wider range of products. When the cost benefits of international sea transportation outweigh the speed advantage of air freight, water shipments may be chosen. Finally, pipelines are a dependable and low-maintenance form of transportation for liquids and gases such as crude petroleum, water and natural gas.

Materials handling

Materials handling involves the activities related to the moving of products in the producer's plant, warehouses and transportation depots. Modern storage facilities tend to be of just one storey, allowing a high level of automation. In some cases robots are used to conduct materials-handling tasks. Lowering the human element in locating inventory and assembling orders has reduced error and increased the speed of these operations. Two key developments in materials handling are unit handling and containerization. Unit handling achieves efficiency by combining multiple packages on pallets that can be moved by fork-lift trucks. Containerization involves the combination of large quantities of goods (e.g. car components) in a single large container. Once sealed, such containers can easily be transferred from one form of transport to another.

Ethical issues in distribution

Five key ethical issues in distribution are the use of slotting allowances, grey markets, exclusive dealing, restrictions on supply and fair dealing.

Slotting allowances

In the packaged consumer goods industry, the power shift from manufacturers to retailers has meant that slotting allowances are often demanded before products are taken. A slotting allowance is a fee paid to a retailer in exchange for an agreement to place a product on the retailer's shelves. Critics argue that these represent an abuse of power and work against small manufacturers who cannot afford to pay such fees. Retailers argue that they are simply charging rent for a valuable scarce commodity: shelf space.[57]

Grey markets

Nothing to do with the age-related 'grey market' (i.e. the burgeoning number of older people that make up the consumer population), this type of grey market occurs when a product is sold through an unauthorized distribution channel. When this occurs in international marketing the practice is called 'parallel importing' (see Chapter 8). Usually a distributor buys goods in one country (where prices are low) and sells them in another (where prices are high) at below the going market price (see Marketing in Action 11.3). This causes anger among members of the authorized distribution channel who see their prices being undercut. Furthermore, the products may well be sold in downmarket outlets that discredit the image of the product, which has been built up by high advertising expenditures which was the central issue in the case taken against Tesco by Levi's.

Exclusive dealing

This restrictive arrangement involves a manufacturer prohibiting the distributors that market its products from selling the products of competing suppliers. This action may restrict competition and hamper the entry of new competitors and products into a market. It may be found where a large supplier can exercise power over weaker distributors. The supplier may be genuinely concerned that anything less than an exclusive agreement will mean that insufficient effort will be made to sell its products by a distributor and that, unless such an agreement is reached, it may be uneconomic to supply the distributor.

Restrictions in supply

A particular concern of small suppliers is that the power of large manufacturers and retailers will lead to their being squeezed out of the supply chain altogether. In the UK, farmers and small grocery suppliers have joined forces to demand better treatment from large supermarket chains, which are forging exclusive deals with major manufacturers. They claim the problem is made worse by the growth of category management, where retailers appoint 'category captains' from their suppliers who act to improve the standing of the whole product category, such as breakfast cereals or confectionery. The small suppliers believe this forces them out of the category altogether as category captains look after their own interests. They would like to see a system similar to that used in France where about 10 per cent of shelf space is given to small suppliers by law.[58]

Fair trading

One problem that arises from free market forces is that, when small commodity producers are faced with large powerful buyers, the result can be very low prices. This can bring severe economic hardship to the producers who may be situated in developing countries. As we saw in Chapter 2, the Fairtrade mark was established to highlight this issue and to promote a better deal for weaker members of the supply chain.

Summary

In this chapter we have examined the final key element of the marketing mix, namely that of delivering products and services to customers. In particular, the following issues were addressed.

1. There are important differences in the structure of consumer, industrial and service channels.

2. Channel strategy involves three key decisions, namely channel selection, distribution intensity and channel integration.

3. The key channel management issues are the selection and motivation of middlemen, providing them with training, evaluating their performance and resolving any channel conflict issues that may arise.

4. There is a diverse range of retail types, including supermarkets, department stores, speciality shops, discount houses, category killers, convenience stores, catalogue stores, mail order, vending machines and online retailing.

5. The key retail marketing decisions include retail positioning, store location, product assortment, price and store atmosphere.

6. Physical distribution concerns decisions relating to customer service, order processing, inventory control, warehousing, transportation and materials handling, which impact on the efficiency and effectiveness of the supply chain.

7. There are a number of ethical issues in distribution, including slotting allowances, grey markets, exclusive dealing, restrictions in supply and fair trading.

Suggested reading

Corstjens, J. and **M. Corstjens** (1995) *Store Wars: The Battle for Mindspace and Shelfspace*, New York: John Wiley & Sons.

Ferdows, K., M.A. Lewis and **J. Machuca** (2004) Rapid-fire Fulfillment, *Harvard Business Review*, **82** (11), 104–11.

Moore, C.M., G. Birtwistle and **S. Burt** (2004) Channel Power, Conflict and Conflict Resolution in International Fashion Retailing, *European Journal of Marketing*, **38** (7), 749–70.

Myers, J.B., A.D. Pickersgill and **E.S. Van Metre** (2004) Steering Customers to the Right Channels, *McKinsey Quarterly*, **4**, 36–48.

Underhill, P. (2004) *The Call of the Mall: How We Shop*, New York: Profile Books.

Internet exercises

Sites to visit

1   www.tesco.com
www.walmart.com

Exercise

Discuss the extent to which the internet has allowed these retailers to expand their product assortments

Sites to visit

2   Entrepreneur.com/franchise500
Exercise

Evaluate the range of industries and businesses in which franchising has become a popular distribution structure.

Study questions

1. A tour operator has just established a business in the UK selling short-break package holidays throughout Europe. Advise the founder on her options for distributing the company's products.
2. Distribution intensity decisions should be integrated with all other marketing mix decisions. Discuss.
3. Describe situations that can lead to conflict between channel members. What can be done to avoid and resolve conflict?
4. Describe the different retail types that exist in the marketplace. Which ones are most vulnerable to the growing popularity of online shopping and why?
5. Why is there usually a trade-off between customer service and physical distribution costs? What can be done to improve customer service standards in physical distribution?

Key terms

channel intermediaries organizations that facilitate the distribution of products to customers

channel of distribution the means by which products are moved from the producer to the ultimate consumer

channel strategy the selection of the most effective distribution channel, the most appropriate level of distribution intensity and the degree of channel integration

intensive distribution the aim of intensive distribution is to provide saturation coverage of the market by using all available outlets

selective distribution the use of a limited number of outlets in a geographical area to sell the products of a particular supplier

exclusive distribution an extreme form of selective distribution where only one wholesaler, retailer or industrial distributor is used in a geographical area to sell the products of a particular supplier

channel integration the way in which the players in the channel are linked

administered vertical marketing system a channel situation where a manufacturer that dominates a market through its size and strong brands may exercise considerable power over intermediaries even though they are independent

franchise a legal contract in which a producer and channel intermediaries agree each other's rights and obligations; the intermediary usually receives marketing, managerial, technical and financial services in return for a fee

contractual vertical marketing system a franchise arrangement (e.g. a franchise) tying producers and resellers together

corporate vertical marketing system a channel situation where an organization gains control of distribution through ownership

retail positioning the choice of target market and differential advantage for a retail outlet

safety (buffer) stocks stocks or inventory held to cover against uncertainty about resupply lead times

References

1. **Anonymous** (2004), Lingerie Brand to Follow Kylie Work with Digital Blitz, *Marketing*, 22 January, 4; **Tyrell, P.** (2004), A Naughty But Nice Little Earner, *Financial Times*, 27 April, 13.
2. **Foster, L.** (2003), Mistress of the Turnaround Answers Avon's Calling, *Financial Times*, 6 November, 14.
3. **Guthrie, J.** (2005), Avon to Recruit 20,000 More Ladies for New Expansion into Financial Services, *Financial Times*, 16 February, 1.
4. **Barnes, R.** (2005), Sainsbury's At Fills Top Role, *Marketing*, 5 January, 8.
5. **Gregory, H.** (2004), The Price of Convenience, *Marketing*, 22 September, 32.
6. **Rigby, E.** (2004), Sainsbury Continues Big Retail's March into the Neighbourhood, *Financial Times*, 17 August, 23.
7. **Dudley, J.W.** (1990), 1992 *Strategies for the Single Market*, London: Kogan Page, 327.
8. **Fahy, J.** and **F. Taguchi** (1995), Reassessing the Japanese Distribution System, S*loan Management Review*, Winter.
9. **Narus, J.A.** and **J.C. Anderson** (1986), Industrial Distributor Selling: The Roles of Outside and Inside Sales, *Industrial Marketing Management*, 15, 55–62.
10. **Rosenbloom, B.** (1987), *Marketing Channels: A Management View*, Hinsdale, Ill: Dryden, 160.
11. **Laurance, B.** (1993), MMC in Bad Odour Over Superdrug Ruling, *Guardian*, 12 November, 18.
12. **Anonymous** (1993), EC Rejects Unilever Appeal on Cabinets, *Marketing*, 25 February, 6.
13. **Horsman, M.** (2003), Rights Issues, *Financial Times, Creative Business*, 20 May, 4–5.
14. **Voyle, S.** (2003), Supply Chain Feels Fresh Pressure, *Financial Times*, 28 April, 23.
15. **Helmore, E.** (1997), Restaurant Kings or Just Silly Burgers, *Observer*, 8 June, 5.
16. **Hopkinson, G.C.** and **S. Hogarth Scott** (1999), Franchise Relationship Quality: Microeconomic Explanations, *European Journal of Marketing*, 33 (9/10), 827–43.
17. **Rosenbloom** (1987), op. cit.
18. **Shipley, D.D., D. Cook** and **E. Barnett** (1989), Recruitment, Motivation, Training and Evaluation of Overseas Distributors, *European Journal of Marketing*, 23 (2), 79–93.
19. See **Shipley, D.D.** and **S. Prinja** (1988), The Services and Supplier Choice Influences of Industrial Distributors, *Service Industries Journal*, 8 (2), 176–87; **Webster, F.E.** (1976), The Role of the Industrial Distributor in Marketing Strategy, *Journal of Marketing*, 40, 10–16.
20. See **Pegram, R.** (1965), *Selecting and Evaluating Distributors*, New York: National Industrial Conference Board, 109–25; **Shipley, Cook** and **Barnett** (1989) op. cit.
21. **Coyle, D.** (2004), Budget Travel Accuses Agents of Blacklisting, *Irish Times*, 16 November, 16; **Coyle, D.** (2005), Challenges Circle Overhead For Tour Operator, *Irish Times Business*, 7 January, 22.
22. **High, K.** (2005), A Digital Distribution Revolution Gathers Pace, *Financial Times*, 21 June, 14.
23. **Sexton, P.** (2005) A Music Sales Storm is Brewing in a Coffee Shop, *Financial Times*, 21 June, 14.
24. **Hardy, K.G.** and **A.J. Magrath** (1988), Ten Ways for Manufacturers to Improve Distribution Management, *Business Horizons*, Nov–Dec, 68.
25. **Dawar, N.** (2004), What are Brands Good For?, *Sloan Management Review*, 46 (1), 31–37.
26. **Harrison, A.** (2003), Let's Innovate for Chocolate, *Financial Times Creative Business*, 17 June, 9.
27. **Murphy, C.** (2003), Grocers Cook up a Recipe for Growth, *Financial Times*, 13 November, 17,
28. **Krishnan, T.V.** and **H. Soni** (1997), Guaranteed Profit Margins: A Demonstration of Retailer Power, *International Journal of Research in Marketing*, 14, 35–56.
29. **Tricks, H.** and **E. Rigby** (2005), Tesco's Juggernaut Shows no Sign of Stalling, *Financial Times*, 2 June, 22.
30. **Rigby, E.** (2004), Sports Specialists Lose Their Way in Quest to be Followers of Fashion, *Financial Times*, 20 August, 21.

31. **Guthrie, J.** (2004), Store Piles up Profit One Pound at a Time, *Financial Times*, 25 May, 11.

32. **Tighe, C.** (2005), From Haven for the Hard-up to Retail Success Story, *Financial Times*, 2 June, 4.

33. **Davies, G.** and **N. Sanghavi** (1993), Is the Category Killer a Significant Innovation? ESRC Seminar: Strategic Issues in Retailing, Manchester Business School, 1–23.

34. **Nairn, G.** (2003), Virtual Customers Become a Reality at Web Shopping Malls, *Financial Times IT Review*, 5 February, 2.

35. **Birchall, J.** (2005), Walmart.com Integrates its Clicks and Bricks, *Financial Times*, 7 June, 11.

36. **Davies, G.** (1992), Innovation in Retailing, *Creativity and Innovation Management*, **1** (4), 230.

37. **Anonymous** (2004), On Target, *Economist*, 16 October, 60–61.

38. **Benady, D.** (2004), Divorce One, Sue One Free, *Marketing Week*, 18 March, 26–27.

39. **Rowley, J.E.** (2003), Beds, Insurance and Coffee—A Complete Retail Experience From Tesco Online, *British Food Journal*, **105** (4/5), 274–278.

40. **Sherwood, B.** (2004), Tesco Law Goes Online With the Groceries, *Financial Times*, 22 June, 1.

41. **Shrimsley, R.** (2004), One Law For Tesco, *Financial Times*, 22 June, 20.

42. **Elg, U.** and **U. Johansson** (1996), Networking When National Boundaries Dissolve: The Swedish Food Sector, *European Journal of Marketing*, **30** (2), 62–74.

43. **Heathcote, E.** (2003), The Theatrical Art of High Consumerism, *Financial Times*, 16 September, 19.

44. **Pearson, C.A.** (2004), An International Trio of Architects Collaborates to Give Louis Vuitton a New High-Tech Face in Tokyo, *Architectural Record*, **192** (2), 10–11.

45. **Sisodia, D.** and **S.K. Chaudhuri** (2004), Louis Vuitton: The Making of a Star Brand, *European Case Clearing House*, 304–548–1.

46. **Felsted, A.** and **S. Goff** (2004), Going Global is Crucial To Deliver Goods, *Financial Times*, 17 June, 27.

47. **Anonymous** (2003), Benetton Starts 'Dring' Drive, *Financial Times*, 10 December, 33.

48. **Rigby, E.** (2005), The Tricky Task of Moving From the Warehouse to the Shelves, *Financial Times*, 5 May, 21.

49. **Anonymous** (2004), Tagging Toothpaste and Toddlers, *The Information Management Journal*, September–October, 22.

50. **Ferguson, G.T.** (2002), Have Your Objects Call My Objects, *Harvard Business Review*, June, 2–7.

51. **Gilligan, E.** (2004), How RFID Will Affect Warehousing, *The Journal of Commerce*, 3–9 May, 31.

52. **Kelly, S.** (2003), Mini-Revolution for Supply Chains, *Treasury & Risk Management*, July–August, 15.

53. **Leach, P.T.** (2004), Ready for RFID, *The Journal of Commerce*, 16 October, 12–14.

54. **London, S.** (2003), An Eye on the Shopping Trolley Spy, *Financial Times*, 1 October, 13.

55. **Mongelluzzo, B.** (2004), A Glimpse of the Future, *The Journal of Commerce*, 7–13 June, 35.

56. **Niemeyer, A., M.H. Pak** and **S. Ramaswamy**, (2003), Smart Tags for Your Supply Chain, *McKinsey Quarterly*, 4, 22–23.

57. **Schlegelmilch, B.** (1998), *Marketing Ethics: An International Perspective*, London: International Thomson Business Press.

58. **McCawley, I.** (2000), Small Suppliers Seek Broader Shelf Access, *Marketing Week*, 17 February, 20.

When you have read this chapter log on to the Online Learning Centre for *Foundations of Marketing* at **www.mcgraw-hill.co.uk/textbooks/jobber** where you'll find multiple choice test questions, links and extra online study tools for marketing.

Turn the page for a Case Study on 'Fast Fashion'

Case 11 'Fast Fashion': exploring how retailers get affordable fashion on to the high street

Figure C11.1

The term 'fast fashion' has become very much de rigueur within the fashion retailing industry. Retailers have to react quickly to changes in the market, possess lean manufacturing operations, and utilize responsive supply chains in order to get the latest fashions to the mass market. Stores such as H&M, Zara, Mango, Top Shop and Benetton have been tremendously successful in being responsive to the fashion needs of the market. Excellent logistical and marketing information systems are seen as key to the implementation of the 'fast fashion' concept. 'Fast fashion' is the emphasis of putting fashionable and affordable design concepts, which match consumer demand, on to the high street as quickly as possible. These retailers get sought-after fashions into stores in a matter of weeks, rather than the previous industry norm, which relied on production lead times ranging from six months to a year. The concept of 'fast fashion' relies on a number of central components: excellent marketing information systems, flexible production and logistics operations, excellent communications within the supply chain, and leveraging advanced IT systems. These components allow stores to track consumer demand, and deliver a rapid response to changes in the marketplace. The results are invigorating for fashion retailers, with 'fast fashion' retailers' sales growing by 11 per cent, compared with the industry norm of 2 per cent.

Within the fashion industry a number of different levels exist, the exclusive haute couture ranges (made to measure), the designer ready-to-wear collections, and then copycat designs by mass-market retailers. Fashion has now gone to the high street, becoming more democratic for the mass market. The traditional fashion-retailing model was seasonal, whereby retailers would typically launch two seasons: spring and autumn collections. Fashion retailers would buy for these collections from their supplier network a year in advance, and allow for between 20–30 per cent of their purchasing budgets open to specific fashion changes in the market. Typically, retailers would have perennial offerings that rarely change as well as catering to the whims of fashion, such as basic T-shirts and jeans.

Now, through the 'fast fashion' philosophy, new items are being stocked in stores more frequently. These newer product ranges stimulate shoppers into frequenting these stores on a more regular basis, in some cases weekly to see new fashion items. Savvy brand-loyal shoppers know when new stock is being delivered to their favourite store. Through increased stock replenishment of new, fashionable items, consumers are increasing their footfall to these stores, and furthermore these stores are developing brand images as cutting edge, trendy, and fashionable. This increased footfall, where shoppers regularly visit a store, eliminates the need for major expenditure on advertising and promotion. Also the concept of 'fast fashion' is helping to improve sales conversion ratios within these stores. Due to the limited supply of designs available, this creates an aura of exclusivity for these garments, further enhancing the brands of these 'fast fashion retailers' as leading fashion brands.

Famous for ABBA, Volvos and IKEA, now Sweden has another international success story: H&M. The basic business premise behind H&M is 'fashion and quality at the best price'. The company now has over 1068 stores in 21 countries. H&M sources 50 per cent of its goods in Europe and the remainder in low-cost Asian countries. Sourcing decisions are dependent on cost, quality, lead times and export regulations. The lead times for items can vary from a minuscule two weeks to six months, dependent on the item itself. H&M believes that having very short lead times can be beneficial in terms of stock control, however it is not the most important criteria for all items. Basic clothing garments can have lead times running into months, due to consistent demand. However, items that are more trend- and fashion-conscious require very short lead times, to match demand. H&M is now also in the process of teaming

Table C11.1 Some of the key players in apparel industry

H&M	Next	Benetton
Originated in Sweden	Originated in the UK	Originated in Italy
Chain has 1069 stores in 21 countries	Has 380 stores in the UK and Ireland and has 80 franchise stores overseas	Has a presence in 120 countries and uses a retail network of 5000 stores
Originally called Hennes & Mauritz, renamed globally as H&M. Sells women's and men's apparel. Doesn't own any manufacturing resources. Motto—'Fashion and quality at the best price'.	Sells women's wear, men's wear and homeware. The firm has a very successful catalogue business. Targets the top end of the mass market, focusing on fashionable moderately priced clothing.	Sells under brand names such as Benetton, Playlife, Sisley and Killer Loop. Uses a network of franchises/partner stores. Established huge brand awareness through its infamous ad campaigns.
Zara	**Mango**	**Arcadia**
Originated in Spain	Originated in Spain	Originated in the UK
Chain has 729 Zara stores	Chain has 770 stores in 70 countries	Chain has over 2000 stores
Zara is the main part of the Spanish Inditex group and is valued at nearly €14 billion. Operates under the mantra of affordable fashion, and adopts the principle of market-driven supply.	Operates a successful franchise operation (more than half are franchises). The company specializes exclusively in targeting the young female mid-market.	Operates several different fascia, targeting different types of customer, with stores such as Burton, Dorothy Perkins, Evans, Wallis, Top Shop, Top Man, Miss Selfridge and Outfit. Owner Philip Green also owns BHS stores and Etam UK.

up with prestigious designers like Karl Lagerfeld to create affordable fashion ranges.

The firm utilizes close relationships with its network of production offices and 700 suppliers. Unlike some other clothing retailers, H&M outsources all of its production to independent suppliers. The dyeing of garments is postponed until as late as possible in the production process to allow greater flexibility and adaptation to the whims of the fashion buyer. Items from around the world are shipped to a centralized transit warehouse in Hamburg, Germany, where quality checks are undertaken, and the items are allocated to individual stores or placed in centralized storage. Items that are placed in this 'call-off warehouse' are allocated to stores where there is more demand for the particular item. For example, if pairs of a particular style of jeans are selling well in London, more jeans are shipped from Hamburg to H&M's London stores.

Sourcing low-cost garments with quick response times is a vital element of the concept. Many of the 'fast fashion' retailers utilize a vast network of suppliers, so that their stores are replenished with the latest designs. Some firms are entirely vertically integrated, where the retailer owns and controls the entire supply chain. For example, Zara buys its fabric from a company owned by its parent, Inditex, and buys dyes from another company also within the group. Retailers source their goods from countries such as China, North Africa, Turkey and low-cost Eastern European countries. If cost were the sole basis for supplier selection, then the vast majority of products would be sourced from the Far East. However, the lead times for delivery of goods are quite substantial in comparison to sourcing garments in Eastern Europe (e.g. shipping goods from China can take six weeks, whereas from Hungary takes two days). As a result of this, retailers are using a hybrid approach, sourcing basics (e.g. T-shirts) from the Far East, and sourcing closer to markets for more fashion-orientated lines. The drive towards reduced lead times is allowing companies to be more responsive to fashion changes. The benefits of such a quick response to market changes are reduced costs, lean inventories, faster merchandise flow and closer collaborative supply chain relationships.

The concept of 'postponement' is a key strategy used within the fashion retailing industry. It is the delayed configuration of a garment's final design until the final market destination and/or customer requirement is known and, once this is known, the garment is assembled or customized. The material and styles are kept generic for as long as possible, before final customization. A classic illustration of the concept of postponement is its usage by Benetton. Colours can come in and out of fashion. Benetton delays when its garments are finally product differentiated, so that this matches what is selling. For example, a Benetton sweater would be stitched and assembled from its original grey yarn and then, based on feedback from Benetton's distribution network as to what colours were selling, the sweater would be dyed at the very final stage of production. The concept of postponement allows greater inventory cost saving, and increased flexibility in matching actual demand.

The production and logistics facilities for these 'fast fashion' retailers are colossal in that each design may have several colour variants, and the retailer needs to produce an array of garments in a number of different sizes. The number of stock keeping units (SKUs) is therefore staggering. As a result, companies require a very reliable and sophisticated information system— for example, Zara has to deal with over 300,000 new SKUs every year. Benetton has a fully automated sorting and shipping system, managing over 110 million items a year, with a staff of only 24 employees in its centralized distribution centres. Mango, another successful Spanish fashion chain, also utilizes a high-tech distribution system, which can sort and pack 12,000 folded items an hour and 7000 hanging garments an hour.

Many in the industry see Zara as the classic illustration of the concept of 'fast fashion' in operation. The company can get a garment from design, through production and ultimately on to the shelf in a mere 15 days. The norm for the industry has typically run to several months. The group's basic business philosophy is to seduce customers with the latest fashion at attractive prices. It has grown rapidly as a fashion retail powerhouse by adopting four central strategies: creativity and innovation; having an international presence; utilizing a multi-format strategy; and through vertically integrating its entire supply chain. For the 'fast fashion' concept to be successful, it requires close relationships between suppliers and retailers, information sharing and the utilization of technology. Information is utilized along the entire supply chain, according to what is in demand. It controls design, production and the logistics elements of the business. Real-time demand feeds the production systems.

Zara is part of the Inditex group of fashion retail brands. This group adopts a multi-format strategy with different store brands targeting different types of customer. Zara is its key fashion-retailing brand. Zara opened its first store in 1975 in Spain and has now become a fashion powerhouse, operating in four continents, with 729 stores, located in over 54 countries. It has become very hip all over the world, for its value for money and stylish designs. The chain is building large numbers of brand devotees because of its fashionable designs, which are in tune with the very latest trends, and a very convincing price-quality offering. Each of the different store brands (outlined in Table C11.2) needs to be strongly differentiated in order for the strategy to work effectively.

Zara does not undertake any conventional advertising, except as a vehicle for announcing a new store opening, the start of sales or the start of seasons. The company uses the stores themselves as its main promotional strategy, to convey its image. Zara tries to locate its stores in prime commercial areas. Deep inside the lairs of its corporate headquarters, 25 full-scale store windows are set up, whereby Zara window designers can experiment with design layouts and lighting. The approved design layouts are shipped out to all of Zara's stores, so that a Zara shop front in London will be the same as in Lisbon and throughout the entire chain. The store itself is the company's main promotional vehicle.

One of Zara's key philosophies was the realization that fashion, much like food, has a 'best before' date: that fashion trends change rapidly. What style consumers want this month may not be the same in two months' time. Fashion retailers have to adapt to what the marketplace wants for the here and now. The company is guilty of under-stocking garments, as it does not want to be left with obsolete or out-of-fashion items. The key driving force behind its success is to minimize inventory levels, getting product out on to the retail floor space, and by being responsive to the needs of the market. Zara uses its stores to find out what consumers really want, what designs are selling, what colours are in demand, which items are hot sellers and which are complete flops. It uses a sophisticated marketing information

Table C11.2 Number of Inditex stores by fascia

Zara	729
Pull and Bear	373
Massimo Dutti	330
Bershka	305
Stradivarius	228
Oysho	106
Zara Home	63
Kiddy's Class	131
TOTAL	2265

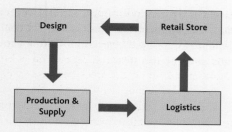

Figure C11.2 Zara's market-led supply

system to provide feedback to headquarters and allow it to respond to what the marketplace wants. Similarly, Mango uses a computerized logistical system that allows the matching of clothes designs to particular stores based on personality traits and even climate variances (i.e. 'Is this garment suitable for the Mediterranean summer?'). This sophisticated IT infrastructure allows for more responsive market-led retailing, matching suitable clothing lines to compatible stores.

At the end of each day, Zara sales assistants report to the store manager using wireless headsets, to communicate inventory levels. The stores then report back to Zara's design and distribution departments on what consumers are buying, asking for or avoiding. Both hard sales data and soft data (i.e. customer feedback on the latest designs) are communicated directly back to the company's headquarters, through open channels of communication. Zara's 250 designers use market feedback for their next creations. Designers work hand in hand with market analysts, in cross-functional teams, to pick up on the latest trends. Garments are produced in comparatively small production runs, so as not to be over-exposed if a particular item is a very poor seller. If a product is a poor seller, it is removed after as little as two weeks. Roughly 10 per cent of stock falls into this unsold category, in direct contrast to industry norms of between 17 and 20 per cent. Zara produces nearly 11,000 designs a year. Stock items are seen as assets that are extremely perishable and, if they are sitting on shelves or racks in a warehouse, they are simply not making money for the organization.

In the course of one year alone, Zara has been able to launch 24 different collections into its network of stores. After designs have been approved, fabrics are dyed and cut by highly automated production lines. These pre-cut pieces are then sent out to nearly 350 workshops in northern Spain and Portugal. These workshops employ nearly 11,000 'grey economy' workers, mainly women, who may want to supplement their income. Seamstresses stitch the pre-cut pieces into garments using easy-to-follow instructions

supplied by Zara. The typical seamstress's wage in Zara's workshop network is extremely competitive when compared with those in 'third world' countries where other fashion retailers mainly outsource their production. Furthermore, the proximity of these workshops allows for greater flexibility and control. Zara achieves greater control over its supply chain through having a high degree of integration within the supply chain. By owning suppliers, Zara has greater control over production capacities, quality and scheduling. This is in stark contrast to Benetton, which is close to being a virtual organization, outsourcing production to third-party suppliers and directly owning only a handful of its stores, the majority being franchises or partner stores.

The finished garments are then sent back to Zara's colossal state-of-the-art logistics centre. Here they are electronically tagged, quality control double-checks them, and then they are sorted into distribution lots, ensuring the items arrive at their ultimate destinations. Each item is tagged with pricing information. There is no pan-European pricing for Zara's products: prices are different in each national market. Zara believes that each national market has its own particular nuances, such as higher salaries or higher taxation, therefore it has to adjust the price of each garment to make it suitable in each country and to reflect these differences. Shipments leave La Coruña bound for every one of the Zara stores in over 54 countries twice a week, every week. The company's average turnaround time from designing to delivery of a new garment takes on average 10 to 15 days, and delivery of goods takes a maximum of 21 days, which is unparalleled in an industry where lead times are usually months, not days. Zara's business model tries to fulfil real-time fashion retailing and not second-guessing what consumers' needs are for next season, which may be six months away. As a result of Zara utilizing this ultra-responsive supply chain, 85 per cent of its entire product range obtains full ticket price, whereas the industry norm is between 60 and 70 per cent.

The successful adoption of the 'fast fashion' concept by these international retailers has drastically altered the competitive landscape in apparel retailing. Consumers' expectations are also rising with these improved retail offerings. Clothes shoppers are seeking out the latest fashions at value-for-money prices in enticing store environments. Now other well-established high-street fashion retailers have to adapt to these challenges, by being more responsive, cost efficient, speedy and flexible in their operations. The rag trade is churning out the latest value-for-money fashions at breakneck speed. 'Fast fashion' is what the marketplace is demanding.

Questions

1. Discuss how supply chain management can contribute to the marketing success of these retailers.

2. Discuss the central components necessary for the fast fashion concept to work effectively.

3. Critically evaluate the concept of 'market-driven supply', discussing the merits and pitfalls of its implementation in fashion retailing.

4. In what other industries could the concept of 'postponement' be used? Explain why?

This case was written by Conor Carroll, University of Limerick. Copyright © Conor Carroll (2005). The material in the case has been drawn from a variety of published sources and research reports.

MARKETING PLANNING AND STRATEGY

Learning Objectives

By the end of this chapter you will understand:

1 the role of marketing planning within businesses
2 the process of marketing planning
3 the rewards and problems associated with marketing
   planning
4 the roles of industry analysis and internal analysis in
   planning and strategy
5 the different competitive strategies, and the sources of
   competitive advantage.

New Challenges for Nokia

The need to have a carefully developed and well-executed marketing strategy is regularly borne out by the trials and tribulations of some of the world's biggest global companies. A few short years ago, companies such as Sony, Volkswagen and Marks & Spencer were being held up as exemplars of business excellence, praised for their high-quality global products and services, and for the innovativeness of their marketing activities. Now all three are struggling to varying degrees to recapture this kind of success. It is a challenge that waits around the corner for all companies. Witness, for example, the difficulties currently being encountered by Nokia.

The Finnish company is the world's leading maker of mobile phones. Its annual revenues exceed €29 billion and it sells over 200 million phones each year, giving it a market share of about 35 per cent. Its enormous size is one of its competitive strengths, enabling it to take advantage of economies of scale. But, like all industries, the mobile phone business is changing and these changes brought an abrupt halt to Nokia's growth in 2004 with its market share falling to a five-year low of 28.9 per cent.

First, Nokia was one of the earliest companies to recognize that mobile phones were fashion items and that the heavy emphasis it placed on product design had helped propel it to market leadership. But when consumer tastes changed, Nokia found it had backed the wrong horse. It continued to favour the 'monobloc' or 'candy bar' phone that did not fold, despite the increasing popularity of flip-phones or 'clamshell' handsets. When it eventually brought out a flip-phone in 2004 it was to mixed reviews. Thus Nokia lost out as consumers upgraded to handsets with cameras and colour screens, leaving it to occupy the low end of the market.

Second, mobile operators began to exert an increasing influence on the brand of mobile phone purchased by the consumer. Leading operators like Vodafone began to brand their own phones, which are manufactured by 'original design manufacturers' (ODMs) like HTC in Taiwan and other smaller handset makers. Own-branded phones are usually locked to prevent them being used on another operator's network, which is attractive to operators as it locks in customers. Leading branded manufacturers like Nokia are the big losers in

this development as they have not been inclined to do deals with the operators and have thus had to concede this growing segment of the market.

Third, the competition from its rivals has been intense. Samsung and Motorola have been locked in a fierce battle for the industry's number two position, with Motorola's highly successful launch of the RAZR V3 phone giving it a market share boost. Another Korean competitor, LG, has also been growing its share of the market, while Siemens—which had been the number four player—is rumoured to have been looking to divest from the industry having shown quarterly losses of €143 million at the end of 2004.

In response to these challenges, Nokia has made a number of strategic changes. First, it killed off some of its product lines and launched some new ones, including several with clamshell designs. In all, the company planned to bring out 40 new handsets in 2005 in response to product lifetimes that are as short as six months. It also cut prices on selected handsets in order to recover market share. A major internal restructuring has taken place, creating separate units for mass-market, business and multimedia phones. And despite its initial reservations, the company has begun to enter the operator-specific segment of the market, with its first custom handset for China Mobile, and to outsource some manufacturing. The medicine seems to be working as its share of the market recovered to 34 per cent at the end of 2004, twice that of Motorola in second place, though profitability has been hurt by tight margins.[1]

In Chapter 1 we introduced the notion of marketing planning. Then, throughout the book, we have examined the nature of customers and markets, and the environmental context within which organizations operate. We have also examined the variety of decisions that need to be taken by marketers. Given the challenging competitive environment in which firms operate, it is important that these decisions are not taken in an *ad hoc* way but rather in a systematic and rational manner. The process by which businesses analyse the environment and their capabilities, decide upon courses of marketing action and implement those decisions is called **marketing planning**, and it is this that will be the focus of this chapter. Equally, it is important to remember that there must be a strategic element to marketing plans—that is, they must map out a direction for the company over the medium to long term. In this chapter we will also examine some of the popular frameworks used by companies to help them answer key strategic questions, such as where and how to compete, and how to grow. Answers to these questions will be central aspects of any marketing plan.

Marketing planning forms part of the broader concept known as 'strategic planning'; this involves not only marketing but also the fit between production, finance and personnel strategies, and the environment. The aim of strategic planning is to shape and reshape a company so that its business and products continue to meet corporate objectives (e.g. profit or sales growth). Because marketing management is charged with the responsibility of managing the interface between the company and its environment, it has a key role to play in strategic planning.

The achievement of an understanding of the role of marketing planning in strategy development is hampered somewhat by the nature of companies. At the simplest level a company may market only one product in one market. The role of marketing planning would be to ensure that the marketing mix for the product matches (changing) customer needs, as well as seeking opportunities to use the companies' strengths to market other products in new markets. Many companies, however, market a range of products in numerous markets. The contribution that marketing planning can make in this situation is similar to that in the first case; however, there is an additional function: that of the determination of the allocation of resources to each product (see Chapter 6). Inasmuch as resource allocation should be dependent, in part, on the attractiveness of the market for each product, marketing is inevitably involved in this decision.

A firm may be composed of a number of businesses (often equating to divisions), each of which serves distinct groups of customers and has a distinct set of competitors. Each business may be strategically autonomous and thus form a **strategic business unit** (SBU). A major component of a corporate plan will be the allocation of resources to each SBU. Strategic decisions at the corporate level are normally concerned with acquisition, divestment and diversification. Here, too, marketing can play a role through the identification of opportunities and threats in the environment as they relate to current and prospective businesses.

Despite these complications, the following essential questions need to be asked in each situation.

- Where are we now?
- How did we get there?
- Where are we heading?
- Where would we like to be?
- How do we get there?
- Are we on course?

While these may seem relatively simple questions, they can be difficult to answer in practice. Businesses are comprised of individuals who may have very different views on the answers to these questions. Furthermore, the outcome of the planning process may have fundamental implications for their jobs. Planning is, therefore, a political activity, and those with a vested interest may view it from a narrow departmental, rather than business-wide, perspective. A key issue in getting planning systems to work is tackling such behavioural problems.[2] However, at this point in this chapter it is important to understand the process of marketing planning. A common approach to the analysis of the marketing planning process is at the business unit level (see, for example, Day)[3] and this is the level adopted here.

The process of marketing planning

The process of marketing planning is outlined in Figure 12.1. The process provides a well-defined path from generating a **business mission** to implementing and controlling the resultant plans. It provides a framework that shows how all the key elements of marketing discussed so far relate to each other. In real life, planning is rarely so straightforward and logical. Different people may be involved at various stages of the planning process, and the degrees to which they accept, and are influenced by the outcomes of earlier planning stages are variable.

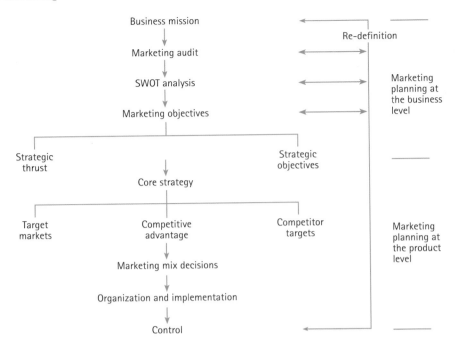

Figure 12.1 The marketing planning process

Business mission

Ackoff defined the business mission as:

> ... a broadly defined, enduring statement of purpose that distinguishes a business from others of its type.[4]

This definition captures two essential ingredients in mission statements: they are enduring and specific to the individual organization.[5] Two fundamental questions that need to be addressed are: 'What business are we in?' and 'What business do we want to be in?' The answers define the scope and activities of the company, and will be determined by an assessment of the needs of the market, the competences of the firm and background of the company plus the personalities of its senior management.

Including the market and needs factors ensures that the business definition is market-focused rather than product-based. Thus the purpose of a company such as Nokia is not to manufacture telephones but to allow people to communicate with each other as is exemplified by its slogan 'connecting people'. The reason for ensuring that a business definition is market-focused is that products are transient, but basic needs such as transportation, entertainment and eating are lasting. Thus, Levitt argued that a business should be viewed as a customer-satisfying process not a goods-producing process.[6] By adopting a customer perspective, new opportunities are more likely to be seen.

Management must be wary of a definition that is too wide, although this advice has merit in advocating the avoidance of a narrow business definition. Levitt suggested that railroad companies would have survived had they defined their business as transportation and moved into the airline business. However, this ignores the limits of business competence of the railroads. Did they possess the necessary skills and resources to run an airline? Clearly a key constraint on a business definition can be the competences (both actual and potential) of management, and the resources at their disposal. Conversely, competences can act as the motivator for widening a business mission. Asda (Associated Dairies) redefined its business mission as a producer and distributor of milk to a retailer of fast-moving consumer goods (fmcg) partly on the basis of its distribution skills, which it rightly believed could be extended to products beyond milk.

The background of the company and the personalities of its senior management are the final determinants of the business mission. Businesses that have established themselves in the marketplace over many years and have a clear position in the minds of the customer may ignore opportunities that are at variance with that position. The personalities and beliefs of the people who run businesses also shape the business mission. This last factor emphasizes the judgemental nature of business definition. There is no right or wrong business mission in abstract. The mission should be based on the vision that top management and their subordinates have of the future of

Table 12.1 External marketing audit checklist

Macroenvironment (see Chapter 2)
Economic: inflation, interest rates, unemployment
Social/cultural: age distribution, lifestyle changes, values, attitudes
Technological: new product and process technologies, materials
Political/legal: monopoly control, new laws, regulations
Ecological: conservation, pollution, energy

The market
Market size, growth rates, trends and developments
Customers: who are they, their choice criteria, how, when, where do they buy, how do they rate us vis-à-vis competition on product, promotion, price, distribution
Market segmentation: how do customers group, what benefits does each group seek
Distribution: power changes, channel attractiveness, growth potential, physical distribution methods, decision-makers and influencers
Suppliers: who and where they are, their competences and shortcomings, trends affecting them, future outlook

Competition
Who are the major competitors: actual and potential
What are their objectives and strategies
What are their strengths (distinctive competences) and weaknesses (vulnerability analysis)
Market shares and size of competitors
Profitability analysis
Entry barriers

the business. This vision is a coherent and powerful statement of what the business should aim to become.[7] The business mission will serve as an over-riding influence on the nature of the marketing plan and should also serve to motivate all staff to attain the targets set out in the plan.

Marketing audit

A **marketing audit** is a systematic examination of a firm's marketing environment, objectives, strategies and activities, which aims to identify key strategic issues, problem areas and opportunities. The marketing audit is, therefore, the basis on which a plan of action to improve marketing performance can be built. The marketing audit provides answers to the following questions.

- Where are we now?
- How did we get there?
- Where are we heading?

The answers to these questions depend on an analysis of the internal and external environments of a business. This analysis benefits from a clear mission statement since the latter defines the boundaries of the environmental scan and aids decisions regarding which strategic issues and opportunities are important.

An internal audit concentrates on those areas that are under the control of marketing management, whereas

Table 12.2 Internal marketing audit checklist

Operating results (by product, customer, geographic region)
Sales
Market share
Profit margins
Costs

Strategic issues analysis
Marketing objectives
Market segmentation
Competitive advantage
Core competences
Positioning
Portfolio analysis

Marketing mix effectiveness
Product
Price
Promotion
Distribution

Marketing structures
Marketing organization
Marketing training
Intra- and interdepartmental communication

Marketing systems
Marketing information systems
Marketing planning system
Marketing control system

an external audit focuses on those forces over which management has no control. The results of the marketing audit are a key determinant of the future direction of the business and may give rise to a rede-

Exhibit 12.1 This Dyson advertisement shows the superiority of its products to competing machines

fined business mission statement. Alongside the marketing audit, a business may conduct audits of other functional areas such as production, finance and personnel. The co-ordination and integration of these audits produces a composite business plan in which marketing issues play a central role since they concern decisions about which products to manufacture for which markets. These decisions clearly have production, financial and personnel implications, and successful implementation depends on each functional area acting in concert. A checklist of those areas that are likely to be examined in a marketing audit is given in Tables 12.1 and 12.2.

External analysis

External analysis covers the macroenvironment, the market and competition. The macroenvironment consists of broad environmental issues that may impinge on the business. These include the economy, social/cultural issues, technological changes, political/legal factors and ecological concerns (as we saw in Chapter 2).

The market consists of statistical analyses of market size, growth rates and trends, and **customer analysis** (including who they are, what choice criteria they use, how they rate competitive offerings and market segmentation bases); next, **distribution analysis** covers significant movements in power bases, channel attractiveness studies, an identification of physical

distribution methods, and understanding the role and interests of decision-makers, and influences within distributors.

Competitor analysis examines the nature of actual and potential competitors, and their objectives and strategies. It would also seek to identify their strengths (distinctive competences), weaknesses (vulnerability analysis), market shares and size. Profitability analysis examines **industry** profitability and the comparative performance of competitors. Finally, entry barrier analysis identifies the key financial and non-financial barriers that protect the industry from competitor attack.

A very popular external analysis framework is Porter's 'five forces' model. Porter was interested in why some industries appeared to be inherently more profitable than others, and concluded that industry attractiveness was a function of five forces: the threat of entry of new competitors; the threat of substitutes; the bargaining power of suppliers; the bargaining power of buyers; and the rivalry between existing competitors. Each of these five forces is, in turn, comprised of a number of elements that combine to determine the strength of each force, as shown in Figure 12.2. So, for example, industries that have high barriers to entry but relatively low levels of buyer/supplier power, low threat of substitutes and relatively benign competition will be more

Marketing in Action: Airbus vs Boeing

Few industries are as concentrated as the aircraft manufacturing business. Here two titans, one in Europe (Airbus) and the other in the United States (Boeing), slug it out for dominance of a business worth over US$40 billion annually. So why are there only two competitors in such a big industry?

First, it is a sector with significant barriers to entry. The manufacture of an aeroplane involves huge technical risks, particularly in terms of safety. So a new-model aircraft requires an upfront R&D spending in the region of US$10 billion even before its first test flight. (By way of comparison, for example, the Channel Tunnel between Britain and France cost US$11 billion.) Once production starts, the learning curve is steep and difficult. Each doubling of production generally yields a cut of one-fifth the unit cost per plane. Consequently it takes production of about 500–600 aircraft before a model starts to earn a profit. This typically amounts to around 10 years of production as industry demand varies between 700 and 800 planes covering all segments such as short-haul, single-aisle, long-range and jumbo aircraft. Both major airlines receive significant state subsidies and access to such financial support represents another significant barrier to entry.

Modern planes sell for between US$50 million and US$250 million, depending on whether they are 120 seaters or jumbos. In general, the bargaining power of buyers is relatively limited as the industry is more concentrated than the buyers, volumes are small, switching costs are high and there is little threat of backward integration. Occasionally, in times of slack demand in the industry generally, buyers are able to extract good deals from the manufacturers. Similarly, the bargaining power of suppliers is relatively limited and the threat of substitutes is not an issue in this business.

Despite these relatively benign industry conditions, the rivalry between the two big players is intense. For a long time, Boeing dominated the industry with a two-thirds share of the market. But in recent years Airbus has steadily gained ground with its share rising from just 32 per cent in 1999 to over 53 per cent in 2004. This has led to accusations by Boeing that Airbus is using state subsidies to discount orders, in a dispute that threatened to develop into a fully fledged trade row between Europe and the USA.

The core of the battle, however, lies in product development. Airbus's fortunes have been revived since it announced development of the A380 in 2000, a product that will take it into the super-jumbo category dominated by Boeing for 35 years. The new plane was rolled out in France in January 2005 complete with orchestra and dancing, a laser light show and plenty of champagne. By that stage 149 confirmed orders had been received and Singapore Airlines will be the first airline to fly the planes, which are expected to cut the cost of carrying one passenger one mile by between 15 and 20 per cent. It will easily be the biggest commercial aeroplane, capable of carrying 555 passengers, 30 per cent more than the Boeing 747 with 50 per cent more floor space.

But like everything in this business it is also a huge gamble. Boeing, in contrast, believes that the market for super-jumbos is limited. Its response has been to plan an upgrade of the 747 to carry 450 passengers. As development costs of the upgrade are lower, this new plane will be more competitively priced than the A380, possibly affecting demand for the latter. Whatever the outcome, it is already too late to turn back.

Based on: Anonymous (2005);[8] Done (2005);[9] Marlowe (2005)[10]

attractive than industries with the opposite set of forces. For an example of the forces affecting profitability in an industry see Marketing in Action 12.1[8, 9, 10]. We shall now look briefly at each of the forces in turn, and see how this framework can assist firms in answering the first three key planning questions identified earlier:

- Where are we now?
- How did we get there?
- Where are we heading?

The threat of new entrants

Because new entrants can raise the level of competition in an industry, they have the potential to reduce its attractiveness. For example, in Denmark the largest banks, Den Danske Bank and Unibank have been hit by new foreign entrants such as Sweden's SE-Banken and Norway's Finax.[11] The threat of new entrants depends on the barriers to entry. High entry barriers exist in some industries (e.g. pharmaceuticals), whereas other industries are much easier to enter (e.g. restaurants). Key entry barriers include:

- economies of scale
- capital requirements
- switching costs
- access to distribution
- expected retaliation.

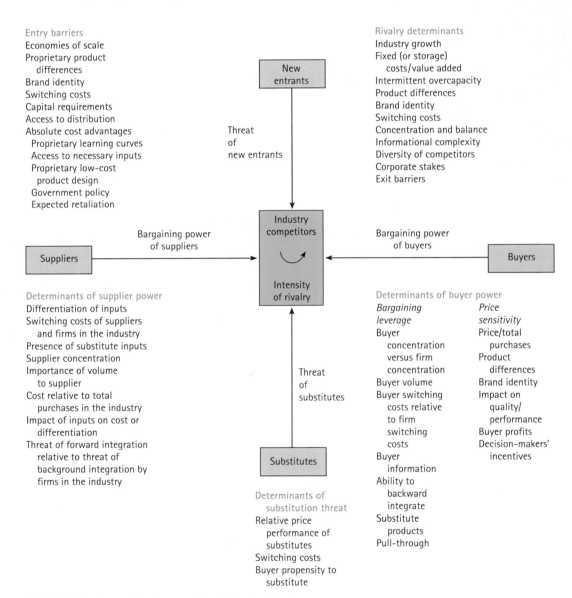

Figure 12.2 The Porter model of competitive industry structure
Source: adapted from Porter, M.E. (1980) *Competitive Strategy*, New York: Free Press, 4. Reprinted with permission of the Free Press, an imprint of Simon and Schuster. Copyright © 1980 by Free Press.

If you enjoy flying first class with our competitors may we recommend our business class cabin?

FIRST
BRITISH AIRWAYS

Exhibit 12.2 This British Airways advertisement makes comparisons with its competitors' offerings. To ensure that the advert stood out from others, it appeared as a bound insert printed on specially imported Italian paper. The premium look and feel was further established through the stylish, minimalist art direction featuring silver embossed text

The bargaining power of suppliers

The cost of raw materials and components can have a major bearing on a firm's profitability. The higher the bargaining power of suppliers, the higher these costs. The bargaining power of suppliers will be high when:

- there are many buyers and few dominant suppliers
- there are differentiated, highly valued products
- suppliers threaten to integrate forward into the industry
- buyers do not threaten to integrate backward into supply
- the industry is not a key customer group to the suppliers.

A firm can reduce the bargaining power of suppliers by seeking new sources of supply, threatening to integrate backward into supply and designing stan-dardized components so that many suppliers are able to produce them.

The bargaining power of buyers

As we saw in Chapter 11, the concentration of European retailing has raised buyers' bargaining power relative to that of manufacturers. Benetton's use of many suppliers has increased its bargaining power. The bargaining power of buyers is greater when:

- there are few dominant buyers and many sellers
- products are standardized
- buyers threaten to integrate backward into the industry
- suppliers do not threaten to integrate forward into the buyer's industry
- the industry is not a key supplying group for buyers.

The threat of substitutes

The presence of substitute products can lower industry attractiveness and profitability because they put a constraint on price levels. For example, tea and coffee are fairly close substitutes in most European countries. Raising the price of coffee, therefore, would make tea more attractive. The threat of substitute products depends on:

- buyers' willingness to substitute
- the relative price and performance of substitutes
- the costs of switching to substitutes.

The threat of substitute products can be lowered by building up switching costs, which may be psychological—for example, by creating strong distinctive brand personalities and maintaining a price differential commensurate with perceived customer values.

Industry competitors

The intensity of rivalry between competitors in an industry depends on the following factors.

- *Structure of competition*: there is more intense rivalry when there are a large number of small competitors or a few equally balanced competitors; there is less rivalry when a clear leader (at least 50 per cent larger than the second) exists with a large cost advantage.
- *Structure of costs*: high fixed costs encourage price cutting to fill capacity.
- *Degree of differentiation*: commodity products encourage rivalry, while highly differentiated products that are hard to copy are associated with less intense rivalry.

- *Switching costs*: when switching costs are high because a product is specialized, the customer has invested a lot of resources in learning how to use a product or has made tailor-made investments that are worthless with other products and suppliers, rivalry is reduced.
- *Strategic objectives*: when competitors are pursuing build strategies, competition is likely to be more intense than when playing hold or harvest strategies.
- *Exit barriers*: when barriers to leaving an industry are high due to such factors as lack of opportunities elsewhere, high vertical integration, emotional barriers or the high cost of closing down plant, rivalry will be more intense than when exit barriers are low.

Internal analysis

An internal audit permits the performance and activities of a business to be assessed in the light of environmental developments. Operating results form the basis of assessment through analysis of sales, market share, profit margins and costs. **Strategic issues analysis** examines the suitability of marketing objectives and segmentation bases in the light of changes in the marketplace. Competitive advantages and the core competences on which they are based would be reassessed and the positioning of products in the market critically reviewed. Finally, product portfolios should be analysed to determine future strategic objectives.

Each aspect of the marketing mix is reviewed in the light of changing customer requirements and competitor activity. The marketing structures on which marketing activities are based should be analysed. Marketing structure consists of the marketing organization, training, and the intra- and interdepartmental communication that takes place within an organization. Marketing organization is reviewed to determine fit with strategy and the market, and marketing training requirements are examined. Finally, communications and relationships within the marketing, department, and between marketing and other functions (e.g. R&D, engineering, production) need to be appraised.

Marketing systems are audited to check their effectiveness. This covers the marketing information, planning and **control** systems that support marketing activities. Shortfalls in information provision are analysed; the marketing planning system is critically appraised for cost effectiveness, and the marketing control system is assessed in the light of accuracy, timeliness (whether it provides evaluations when

managers require them) and coverage (whether the system evaluates the key variables affecting company performance).

The checklists in Tables 12.1 and 12.2 provide the basis for deciding on the topics to be included in the marketing audit. However, to give the same amount of attention and detailed analysis to every item would cause the audit to grind to a halt under the weight of data and issues. In practice, the judgement of those conducting the audit is critical in deciding the key items to focus upon. Those factors that are considered of crucial importance to the company's performance will merit most attention. One by-product of the marketing audit may be a realization that information about key environmental issues is lacking.

All assumptions should be made explicit as an ongoing part of the marketing audit. For example, key assumptions might be:

- inflation will average 5 per cent during the planning period
- VAT levels will not be changed
- worldwide overcapacity will remain at 150 per cent
- no new entrants into the market will emerge.

The marketing audit should not be a desperate attempt to turn around an ailing business, but an ongoing activity. Some companies conduct an annual audit as part of their annual planning system; others, operating in less turbulent environments, may consider two or three years an adequate period between audits. Some companies may feel that the use of an outside consultant to co-ordinate activities and provide an objective, outside view is beneficial while others may believe that their own managers are best equipped to conduct such analyses. Clearly there is no set formula for deciding when and by whom the audit is conducted. The decision ultimately rests on the preferences and situation facing the management team.

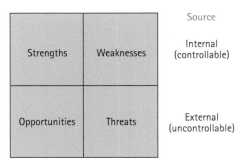

Figure 12.3 Strengths, weaknesses, opportunities and threats (SWOT) analysis

SWOT analysis

A structured approach to evaluating the strategic position of a business by identifying its strengths, weaknesses, opportunities and threats is known as a **SWOT analysis**. It provides a simple method of synthesizing the results of the marketing audit. Internal strengths and weaknesses are summarized as they relate to external opportunities and threats (see Figure 12.3).

For a SWOT analysis to be useful a number of guidelines must be followed. First, not only absolute, but also relative strengths and weakness should be identified. Relative strengths focus on strengths and weaknesses as compared to the competition. Thus, if everyone produces quality products this is not identified as a relative strength. Two lists should be drawn up based on absolute and relative strengths and weaknesses. Strengths that can be exploited can be both absolute and relative, but how they are exploited and the degree to which they can be used depends on whether the competition also possesses them. Relative strengths provide the distinctive competences of a business. But strengths need to be looked at objectively as they can sometimes turn into weaknesses. A case in point is Sony, one of whose

e-Marketing: eBay: the world's largest flea market

During the dotcom boom of the late 1990s, thousands of online businesses were started as entrepreneurs sought to grab the opportunities provided by the growth of the Internet. It almost didn't seem to matter what it was, if it existed there was a website looking to sell it, from fashion to chilli sauces, from pets to financial advice. For most, the opportunity turned out to be a mirage as the business never got off the ground, failed or limped to profitability many years later.

But, from out of this flurry of innovation and investment, one company has emerged that has defied the odds and exceeded all expectations. eBay is the world's largest online auction business. It has over 100 million registered members on its 22 auction sites around the world who use eBay to sell various products and services worth over US$32 billion every year. Unlike so many of its dotcom contemporaries, its revenues, profitability and share price have marched inexorably onward and upward.

So how did it all begin? eBay's founder, Pierre Omidyar, was a 31-year-old software development engineer when he felt that an online auction site could create a highly efficient market. The idea, it appears, arose from the difficulty that his fiancée faced while trying to collect Pez confectionery dispensers in the San Francisco area. He launched the site in September 1995 to enable people to trade with each other, with a mission to help 'practically anyone to trade practically anything on earth'. Initially eBay was a free site and it quickly attracted interest and traffic with its focus on novelties and collectors' items.

What separated eBay from its cash-burning contemporaries was that from the outset it was an idea that had a number of clear revenue-generating streams. A nominal sum could be charged to have an item listed for sale, which varied from 30 cents for an item with an minimum bid under US$10 to over US$3 for an item valued at US$200 or over. By paying additional incremental placement fees, sellers could have items highlighted in certain ways. eBay could also take a small proportion of the final selling price. When this was combined with the inherent network effects of the Internet, the possibilities were limitless. As more people began to use the site, they began to increase the range of products offered for sale on it. As the range of products available increased, this attracted more visitors to the site ... and on it goes, in a virtuous cycle. And as the number of listings and transactions on the site increase so too do eBay's revenues and profits.

From its humble beginnings, eBay is now a global business. For example, in late 2004, less than 10 years after its foundation, the number of listings on eBay's non-US sites began to surpass those in the USA. It has got to this point on the back of a well-conceived idea that exploited an opportunity presented by the emergence of the Internet and through maintaining a strong customer orientation ever since.

Based on: Dutta (2004);[14] Madapati (2005);[15] Waters (2004)[16]

strengths has been its product innovation capabilities. Such was the success of its products, like the Walkman, that it seems to have taken its eye off the market and technological trends. For example, the Walkman has been supplanted by the Apple iPod in the portable audio business and similarly its dominance of cathode ray tube TV technology has caused it to miss the trend towards flat-screen televisions.[12]

An absolute weakness that competitors also possess should be identified because it can clearly become a source of relative strength if overcome. If all businesses in an industry are poor at after-sales service, this should be noted as a weakness, as it provides the potential for gaining competitive advantage. Relative weaknesses should also be listed because these may be the sources of competitive disadvantage to which managerial attention should be focused.

Second, only those resources or capabilities that would be valued by the customer should be included when evaluating strengths and weaknesses.[13] Thus, strengths such as 'We are an old established firm', 'We are a large supplier', and 'We are technologically advanced' should be questioned for their impact on customer satisfaction. It is conceivable that such bland generalizations confer as many weaknesses as strengths.

Third, opportunities and threats should be listed as anticipated events or trends *outside* the business that have implications for performance. They should not be couched in terms of strategies. For example, 'To enter market segment X' is not an opportunity but a strategic objective that may result from a perceived opportunity arising from the emergence of market segment X as attractive because of its growth potential and lack of competition. The ability to spot and exploit an opportunity can lead to success that dramatically exceeds expectations, as the case of eBay demonstrates (see e-Marketing 12.1).

EMI is an example of a company that sought to match its strengths with the opportunities and threats being brought about by changes in the environment when it became the first big music company to sell off its CD manufacturing and distribution operations in the USA and Europe. In a world that has seen music increasingly being downloaded from the Internet, EMI considered that making and distributing CDs is no longer its core business and that it would focus instead on developing and exploiting music.

Exhibit 12.3 This Knorr advertisement is an example of market penetration, seeking to increase sales in its existing markets

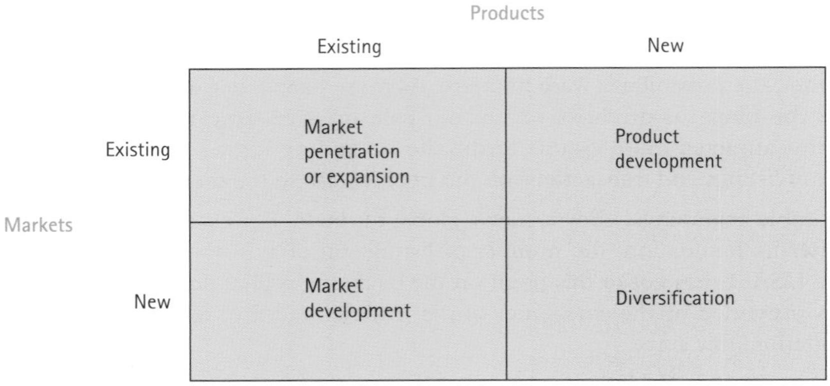

Products

	Existing	New
Existing	Market penetration or expansion	Product development
New	Market development	Diversification

Markets

Figure 12.4 Product growth strategies: the Ansoff Matrix

Marketing objectives

The definition of **marketing objectives** may be derived from the results of the marketing audit and the SWOT analysis. Two types of objective need to be considered: strategic thrust and strategic objectives.

Strategic thrust

Objectives should be set in terms of which products to sell in which markets.[17] This describes the **strategic thrust** of the business. The strategic thrust defines the future direction of the business, and the basic alternatives are summarized in the Ansoff Growth Matrix, as shown in Figure 12.4. These are:

- existing products in existing markets (market penetration or expansion)
- new products for existing markets (product development)
- existing products in new markets (market development)
- new products for new markets (diversification).

We will now look at each of these in turn.

- *Market penetration*: this strategy involves taking the existing product in the existing market and attempting to increase penetration. Existing customers may become more brand loyal (i.e. brand switch less often) and/or new customers in the same market may begin to buy the brand. Other tactics to increase penetration include getting existing customers to use the brand more often (e.g. wash their hair more frequently) and to use a greater quantity when they use it (e.g. two teaspoons of tea instead of one). The latter tactic would also have the effect of expanding the market. Market penetration is usually achieved by more effective use of promotion or distribution, or by cutting prices.
- *Product development*: this strategy involves increasing sales by improving current products or developing new products for current markets. The Ford Mondeo, which replaced the Sierra, is an example of a product development strategy. By improving style, performance and comfort, the aim is to gain higher sales and market share among its present market (especially fleet buyers).
- *Market development*: this strategy is used when current products are sold in new markets. This may involve moving into new international markets or moving into new market segments, as Apple did when it expanded its market (high

penetration of the educational sector) first to desktop publishing and then onto portable audio devices.

- *Diversification*: this strategy occurs when new products are developed for new markets. This is the most risky strategy but may be necessary when a company's current products and markets offer few prospects of future growth. When there is synergy between the existing and new products this strategy is more likely to work. For example, by developing an online library, Google is aiming to become a content provider rather than just a search engine. It has signed deals with a number of leading libraries around the world, where it will scan thousands of volumes and make them available online.[18]

Strategic objectives

Alongside objectives for product/market direction, **strategic objectives** for each product also need to be agreed. This begins the process of planning at the product level. There are four alternatives:

1. build
2. hold
3. harvest
4. divest.

For new products, the strategic objective will inevitably be to build sales and market share. For existing products the appropriate strategic objective will depend on the particular situation associated with the product. This will be determined in the market audit, SWOT analysis and evaluation of the strategic options outlined earlier. In particular, product portfolio planning tools such as the Boston Consulting Group's Growth-Share Matrix (as outlined in Chapter 6) may be used to aid this analysis.

The important point to remember at this stage is that *building* sales and market share is not the only sensible strategic objective for a product. As we shall see, *holding* sales and market share may make commercial sense under certain conditions; *harvesting*, where sales and market share are allowed to fall but profit margins are maximized, may also be preferable to building; finally, *divestment*, where the product is dropped or sold, can be the logical outcome of the situation analysis (see, for example, Marketing in Action 12.2).

Together, strategic thrust and strategic objectives define where the business and its products intend to go in the future.

Marketing in Action: Lenovo buys IBM's PC business

When a little-known Chinese company, Lenovo, comes along and buys IBM's personal computer business it is a clear signal that the world of global business is changing. No longer are the old orders guaranteed. Competition can come from anywhere in the world and new market opportunities are opening up all the time. At present, China is one of the fastest-growing economies in the world and many of its major companies are aggressively expanding overseas. So Lenovo is a name that may soon become as familiar as IBM or Dell or HP.

Lenovo (formerly known as the Legend Group) was one of four major computer hardware manufacturers to emerge from government support for a fledgling PC business. It started off as a distributor for IBM and Hewlett-Packard (HP) printers and peripherals in the mid-1980s. It then began to design and manufacture its own line of PCs for China's big corporate houses and the government. By 1998, Legend had become the largest PC manufacturer in China, making 770,000 computers. But, by April 2003, falling PC prices had begun to put pressure on its profit margins and it started to look outside China for growth opportunities. As part of this strategy, it changed its name to Lenovo.

But it was its purchase of IBM's PC division that really catapulted it into the headlines. In global terms, it was a relatively small company, with US$3 billion in annual revenues. In contrast, IBM's PC business turned over US$9 billion. But, by buying the subsidiary for a price of US$1.75 billion, Lenovo jumped to third place in the industry behind Dell and HP. The deal marked IBM's exit from a market that it created with the first IBM PC in 1981 and in which it had had a dominant position for many years through leading brands like the IBM ThinkPad laptops.

But, for Lenovo, there are now many challenges ahead. First, a major concern is the impact of the deal on IBM staff and customers. Though Lenovo has bought the rights to the IBM brand name for five years there are fears that many customers may decide to buy their PCs elsewhere due to concerns about product quality. Second, as IBM's division was barely profitable, there are questions over what efficiencies Lenovo can bring to it, as IBM already manufactured its PCs in China and other low-wage countries. Then there is the big cultural gap that exists between America and China that will impact on how the business is run. This is particularly true as Lenovo tries to absorb a company three times its size with almost 20,000 staff. Only time will tell if Lenovo can overcome these challenges and build on this deal to become the global leader in personal computers.

Based on: Anonymous (2004);[19] Dickie and Lau (2004);[20] Umaskankar (2005)[21]

Core strategy

When objectives have been set, a way to achieve them must be decided upon. **Core strategy** focuses on how objectives can be accomplished, and consists of three key elements: target markets, competitor targets and establishing a competitive advantage. We shall now examine each of these elements in turn and discuss the relationship between them.

Target markets

The choice of **target market**(s) is a central plank of core strategy. As we saw in Chapter 5, marketing is not about chasing any customer at any price. A decision has to be made regarding those groups of customers (segments) that are attractive to the business, and that match its supply capabilities. To varying degrees, the choice of target market to serve will be considered during SWOT analysis and the setting of marketing objectives. For example, when considering the strategic thrust of the business, decisions regarding which markets to serve must be made. However, this may be defined in broad terms—for example, 'Enter the business personal computer market'. Within that market there will be a number of segments (customer groups) of varying attractiveness and a choice has to be made regarding which segments to serve.

In Chapter 5, we identified a variety of bases for segmenting markets. Information regarding size, growth potential, level of competitor activity, customer requirements and key factors for success is needed to facilitate the assessment of the attractiveness of each segment. This may have been compiled during the marketing audit and should be considered in light of the capabilities of the business to compete effectively in each specific target market. The marketing audit and SWOT analysis will provide the basis for judging the business's capabilities.

Competitor targets

In tandem with decisions regarding markets are judgements about **competitor targets**. These are the organizations against which a company chooses to compete directly, and sometimes the competition is head-on. Weak competitors may be viewed as easy prey and resources channelled to attack them. For example, major airlines are accused from time to time of aggressively targeting the routes used by their smaller competitors, either through heavy promotion or price discounting.

Competitive advantage

The key to superior performance is to gain and hold a competitive advantage. Firms can gain a competitive advantage through differentiation of their product offering, which provides superior customer value, or by managing for lowest delivered cost. Evidence for this proposition was provided by Hall, who examined[22] the competitive strategies pursued by the two leading firms (in terms of return on investment) in eight mature industries characterized by slow growth and intense competition. In each industry, the two leading firms offered either high product differentiation or the lowest delivered cost. In most cases, an industry's return-on-investment leader opted for one of the strategies, while the second-place firm pursued the other.

Competitive strategies

When combined with the competitive scope of activities (broad vs narrow) these two means of competitive advantage result in four generic strategies: differentiation, cost leadership, differentiation focus and cost focus. The differentiation and cost leadership strategies seek competitive advantage in a broad range of market or industry segments, whereas

Exhibit 12.4 Through its renowned advertising such as this ad, Absolut vodka has built a significant differential advantage for itself in the marketplace

differentiation focus and cost focus strategies are confined to a narrow segment.

Differentiation

Differentiation strategy involves the choice of one or more choice criteria that are used by many buyers in an industry. A firm then uniquely positions itself to meet these criteria. For example, firms might seek to be better (i.e. have superior quality), be faster (i.e. respond more quickly) or be closer (i.e. build better relationships with customers).[23] The aim is to differentiate in a way that leads to a price premium in excess of the cost of differentiating. Differentiation gives customers a reason to prefer one product over another and thus is central to strategic marketing thinking. But it can also be a risky strategy, as demonstrated by the case of Volkswagen. In an effort to develop high-quality cars, it has the highest capital spending of any car manufacturer at 8.2 per cent of sales.[24] This level of investment has not resulted in differentiated brands in the marketplace.

Cost leadership

The cost leadership approach involves the achievement of the lowest cost position in an industry.

Many segments in an industry are served and great importance is placed on minimizing costs on all fronts. So long as the price achievable for its products is around the industry average, cost leadership should result in superior performance. Thus, cost leaders often market standard products that are believed to be acceptable to customers. Heinz and United Biscuits are believed to be cost leaders in their industries. They market acceptable products at reasonable prices, which means that their low costs result in above-average profits. Some cost leaders need to discount prices in order to achieve high sales levels. The aim here is to achieve superior performance by ensuring that the cost advantage over the competition is not offset by the price discount. No-frills supermarket discounters like Costco, KwikSave and Aldi fall into this category.

Differentiation focus

By taking a differentiation focus approach, a firm aims to differentiate within one or a small number of target market segments. The special needs of the segment mean that there is an opportunity to differentiate the product offering from competitors who may be targeting a broader group of customers. For example, some small speciality chemical companies thrive on taking orders that are too small or specialized to be of interest to their larger competitors. Similarly, Domino's Pizza has built the world's biggest home-delivery pizza company on the back of a strategy of fast service and consistent quality. The company now delivers a million pizzas a night from 7300 outlets in 50 countries.[25] Those firms adopting a differentiation focus must be clear that the needs of their target group differ from those of the broader market (otherwise there will be no basis for differentiation) and that existing competitors are underperforming.

Cost focus

By adopting a cost focus strategy, a firm seeks a cost advantage with one or a small number of target market segments. By dedicating itself to a segment, the cost focuser can seek economies that may be ignored or missed by broadly targeted competitors. In some instances, competition, by trying to achieve wide market acceptance, may be overperforming (for example, by providing unwanted services) to one segment of customers. By providing a basic product offering, a cost advantage will be gained that may exceed the price discount necessary to sell it. For example, Kiwibank is a low-cost domestic bank that was set up by the New Zealand Government as an alternative to the foreign-owned

banks dominating the market. It has proven particularly attractive to low-income customers because of its low fee structure.[26]

Choosing a competitive strategy

So it seems that the essence of corporate success is to choose a generic strategy and pursue it enthusiastically. Below-average performance is associated with failure to achieve any of these generic strategies. The result is no competitive advantage: a stuck-in-the-middle position that results in lower performance than that of the cost leaders, differentiators or focusers in any market segment (see Marketing in Action 12.3). An example of a company that made the mistake of moving to a stuck-in-the-middle position was General Motors with its Oldsmobile car. The original car (the Oldsmobile Rocket V8) was highly differentiated with a 6-litre V8 engine, which was virtually indestructible, very fast and highly reliable. In order to cut costs this engine was replaced with the same engine that went into the 5-litre Chevrolet V8. This had less power and was less reliable. The result was catastrophic: sales plummeted.

Firms need to understand the generic basis for their success and resist the temptation to blur strategy by making inconsistent moves. For example, a no-frills cost leader or focuser should beware of the pitfalls of moving to a higher cost base (perhaps by adding on expensive services). A focus strategy involves limiting sales volume. Once domination of the target segment has been achieved there may be a temptation to move into other segments in order to achieve growth with the same competitive advantage. This can be a mistake if the new segments do not value the firm's competitive advantage in the same way.

Differentiation and cost leadership strategies are incompatible in most situations: differentiation is achieved through higher costs. However, there are circumstances when both can be achieved simultaneously. For example, a differentiation strategy may lead to market share domination that lowers costs through economies of scale and learning effects. Or a highly differentiated firm pioneers a major process innovation that significantly reduces manufacturing costs leading to a cost leadership position. When differentiation and cost leadership coincide, performance is exceptional since a premium price can be charged for a low-cost product.

Marketing in Action: Hewlett-Packard: 'stuck in the middle'

Hewlett-Packard (HP) is one of the best-known information technology companies in the world. Founded in 1939 in California by Bill Hewlett and David Packard, the company became renowned for the 'HP Way', its caring and respectful attitude to its employees, which it maintained as it grew into a global corporation. Its business is spread across a number of sectors, including printing and imaging, personal computers, data storage systems and servers, and IT services. After struggling for a number of years, it recently fired its chief executive, Carly Fiorina, and is frequently criticized for not having a clear strategy.

It all promised to be so different when Fiorina took the reins of the company in 1999. At that stage HP was performing well in its imaging and printing business, but struggling in the computer side of its operations. Fiorina's big play was to lead the acquisition of the Compaq Computer Corporation to give it a stronger presence, particularly in the PC business. The deal was eventually closed in May 2002 but it has failed to deliver the hoped-for upturn. The acquisition alone did not obviate the need for a well-chosen and well-executed business and marketing strategy.

HP's difficulties are particularly evident in the PC business. Here the market leader is Dell, which aggressively pursues a cost leadership strategy. It outsources manufacturing, sells direct to customers rather than through a channel, does little R&D and keeps overheads at less than 10 per cent of sales. So competitive is this sector, that many firms have chosen to exit it altogether as did IBM (see Marketing in Action 12.2). By buying Compaq, HP chose to take on Dell but it did so by playing to Dell's rules rather than inventing its own. It tried to compete with Dell on price but its cost base never allowed it to do so. It has an annual R&D budget of US$3.5 billion, it continues to employ an expensive salesforce to sell through a distribution channel, its supply chain is not as efficient as Dell's and its overheads are at 18 per cent of sales. As a result, Dell has an operating margin of 8.5 per cent, while HP's is at 1.5 per cent. HP is unable to compete with Dell on cost nor are its PCs clearly differentiated or seen as superior, leaving it 'stuck in the middle' and struggling in this sector.

It is suffering in other parts of its business too. It has difficulties competing with focused rivals such as EMC in the data storage sector. And in the information technology services sector it lags far behind differentiated competitors like IBM, Accenture and EDS. Its inability to compete effectively across the different businesses in which it operates has been reflected in a falling share price. In fact, HP's market capitalization is roughly equal to the value of its imaging and printing business, indicating that investors place little value in the computer side of the company. And, to make matters worse, Dell is now taking its same cost leadership strategy to attack the printer market!

Based on: Anonymous (2005);[27] Morrison (2005);[28] Waters and London (2005)[29]

Sources of competitive advantage

In order to create a differentiated or lowest cost position, a firm needs to understand the nature and location of the potential sources of competitive advantage. The nature of these sources are the superior skills and resources of a firm. Management benefit by analysing the superior skills and resources that offer, or could contribute to, competitive advantage (i.e. differentiation or lowest cost position).

Their identification can be aided by **value chain** analysis (see Figure 12.5). A value chain comprises the discrete activities a firm carries out in order to perform its business.

Superior skills

These are the distinctive capabilities of key personnel, which set them apart from the personnel of competing firms. The benefit of superior skills is the resulting ability to perform functions more effectively than other firms. For example, superior selling skills

GE Healthcare

Heart attacks should be treated early. Say, 50 years before they happen.

Introducing GE Healthcare.
We've combined our medical systems
business with Amersham plc, a leader
in molecular technologies and
biomolecular manufacturing systems.
Together, we're creating revolutionary
new ways to predict medical
conditions like heart disease years
in advance. After all, the best time
to solve a problem is before it even
becomes one.

imagination at work

© 2005 General Electric Company.
GE Medical Systems, a General Electric company, going to market as GE Healthcare.

Exhibit 12.5 This General Electric advertisement highlights the company's technical capabilities

may result in closer relationships with customers than competing firms can achieve. Superior quality assurance skills can result in improved and more consistent product quality.

Superior resources

The tangible requirements for advantage that enable a firm to exercise its skills are known as superior resources. Superior resources include:

- the number of salespeople in a market
- expenditure on advertising and sales promotion

- distribution coverage (the number of retailers who stock the product)
- expenditure on R&D
- scale of and type of production facilities
- financial resources
- brand equity
- knowledge.

Value chain

The value chain provides a useful method for locating superior skills and resources. All firms consist of a set of activities that are conducted to design, manufacture, market, distribute and service its products. The value chain categorizes these into primary and support activities (see Figure 12.5). This enables the sources of costs and differentiation to be understood and located.

- *Primary activities* include in-bound physical distribution (e.g. materials handling, warehousing, inventory control), operations (e.g. manufacturing, packaging), out-bound physical distribution (e.g. delivery, order processing), marketing (e.g. advertising, selling, channel management) and service (e.g. installation, repair, customer training).
- *Support activities* are found within all of these primary activities and consist of purchased inputs, technology, human resource management and the firm's infrastructure. These are not defined within a given primary activity because they can be found in all of them. Purchasing can take place within each primary activity, not just in the purchasing department; technology is relevant to all primary activities, as is human resource management; and the firm's infrastructure—which consists of general management, planning, finance, accounting and quality management—supports the entire value chain.

Primary activities

In-bound logistics	Operations	Out-bound logistics	Marketing and sales	Service	Margin through value
Procurement					
Technology development					
Human resource management					
Firm infrastructure					

Support activities

Figure 12.5 The value chain
Source: Porter M.E. (1985) *Competitive Advantage*, New York: Free Press, 37. Reprinted with the permission of the Free Press, an imprint of Simon and Schuster. Copyright © 1985 by Michael E. Porter.

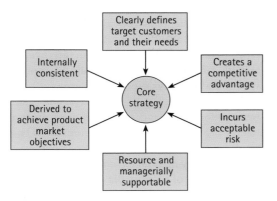

Figure 12.6 Testing core strategy

If management examines each value-creating activity, it can pinpoint the skills and resources that may form the basis of low cost or differentiated positions. To the extent that skills and resources exceed or could be developed to exceed the competition, they form the key sources of competitive advantage. Not only should the skills and resources within value-creating activities be examined but the *linkages* between them should also be examined. For example, greater co-ordination between operations and in-bound physical distribution may give rise to reduced costs through lower inventory levels.

Tests of an effective core strategy

The six tests of an effective core strategy are detailed in Figure 12.6. First, the strategy must be based upon a clear definition of target customers and their needs. Second, an understanding of competitors is required so that the core strategy can be based on a competitive advantage. Third, the strategy must incur acceptable risk. Challenging a strong competitor with a weak competitive advantage and a low resource base would not incur acceptable risk. Fourth, the strategy should be resource and managerially supportable. The strategy should match the resource capabilities and managerial competences of the business. Fifth, core strategy should be derived from the product and marketing objectives established as part of the planning process. A strategy (e.g. heavy promotion), which makes commercial logic following a build objective may make no sense when a harvesting objective has been decided. Finally, the strategy should be internally consistent. The elements should blend to form a coherent whole.

Marketing mix decisions

Decisions regarding each of the elements of the marketing mix make up the next stage of the planning process. As we have seen, these decisions consist of judgements about price levels, the blend of pro-motional techniques to employ, the distribution channels and service levels to use, and the types of products to manufacture. Where promotional, distribution and product standards surpass those of the competition, a competitive advantage may be gained. Alternatively, a judgement may be made only to match or even undershoot the competition on some elements of the marketing mix. To outgun the competition on everything is not normally feasible. Choices have to be made about how the marketing mix can be manipulated to provide a superior offering to the customer at reasonable cost.

Organization and implementation

It is said that no marketing plan will succeed unless it 'degenerates into work'.[30] Consequently, the business must design an organization that has the capabilities necessary to implement the plan. Indeed, organiz-ational weaknesses discovered as part of the SWOT analysis may restrict the feasible range of strategic options. Reorganization could mean the establish-ment of a marketing organization or department in the business. A study of manufacturing organizations by Piercy[31] found that 55 per cent did not have a mar-keting department. In some cases, marketing was carried out by the chief executive, in others the sales department dealt with customers and no need for other marketing inputs was perceived. In other situ-ations, environmental change may cause strategy change, and this may imply reorganization of mar-keting and sales. The growth of large corporate customers with enormous buying power has resulted in businesses focusing their resources more firmly on meeting their needs (strategy change), which has led in turn to dedicated marketing and sales teams being organized to service these accounts (reorganization).

Control

Control is the final stage in the marketing planning process. The aim of control systems is to evaluate the results of the marketing plan so that corrective action can be taken if performance does not match objec-tives. Short-term control systems can plot results against objectives on a weekly, monthly, quarterly and/or annual basis. Measures include sales profits, costs and cash flow. Strategic control systems are more long term. Managers need to stand back from week-by-week and month-by-month results to criti-cally reassess whether their plans are in line with their capabilities and the environment.

Table 12.3 Key questions and the process of marketing planning

Key questions	Stages in marketing planning
Where are we now and how did we get there?	Business mission Marketing audit SWOT analysis
Where are we heading?	Marketing audit SWOT analysis
Where would we like to be?	Marketing objectives
How do we get there?	Core strategy Marketing mix decisions Organization Implementation
Are we on course?	Control

Where this kind of long-term control perspective is lacking this may result in the pursuit of plans that have lost strategic credibility. New competition, changes in technology and moving customer requirements may have rendered old plans obsolete. This, of course, returns the planning process to the beginning since this kind of fundamental review is conducted in the marketing audit. It is the activity of assessing internal capabilities and external opportunities and threats that results in a SWOT analysis. This outcome may mean a redefinition of the business mission, and, as we have seen, changes in marketing objectives and strategies to realign the business with its environment.

How, though, do the stages in marketing planning we have looked at relate to the fundamental planning questions stated earlier in this chapter? Table 12.3 shows this relationship. The questions 'Where are we now?' and 'How did we get there?' are answered by the business mission definition, the marketing audit and SWOT analysis. 'Where are we heading?' is forecast by reference to the marketing audit and SWOT analysis. 'Where would we like to be?' is determined by the setting of marketing objectives. 'How do we get there?' refers to core strategy, marketing mix decisions, organization and implementation. Finally 'Are we on course?' is answered by the establishment of a control system.

The rewards of marketing planning

Various authors[32,33,34] have attributed the following benefits to marketing planning.

- *Consistency*: the plan provides a focal point for decisions and actions. By reference to a common plan, decisions by the same manager over time, and by different managers, should be more consistent and actions co-ordinated more effectively.
- *Encourages the monitoring of change*: the planning process forces managers to step away from day-to-day problems and review the impact of change on the business from a strategic perspective.
- *Encourages organizational adaptation*: the underlying premise of planning is that the organization should adapt to match its environment. Marketing planning, therefore, promotes the necessity to accept the inevitability of change. This is an important consideration since adaptive capability has been shown to be linked to superior performance.[35]
- *Stimulates achievement*: the planning process focuses on objectives, strategies and results. It encourages people to ask 'What can we achieve given our capabilities?' As such, it motivates people, who otherwise might be content to accept much lower standards of performance, to set new horizons for objectives.
- *Resource allocation*: the planning process asks fundamental questions about resource allocation. For example, which products should receive high investment (build), which should be maintained (hold), which should have resources withdrawn slowly (harvest), and which should have resources withdrawn immediately (divest).
- *Competitive advantage*: planning promotes the search for sources of competitive advantage.

However, it should be borne in mind that this logical planning process, sometimes referred to as synoptic, may be at variance with the culture of the business, which may plan effectively using an *incremental* approach.[36] The style of planning must match business culture.[37] Saker and Speed argue that the considerable demands on managers in terms of time and effort implied by the synoptic marketing planning process may mean that alternative planning schemes are more appropriate, particularly for small companies.[38]

An incremental planning approach is more focused on problems, in that the process begins with the realization of a problem (for example, a fall-off in orders) and continues with an attempt to identify a solution. As solutions to problems form, so strategy emerges. However, little attempt is made to integrate consciously the individual decisions that could possibly affect one another. Strategy is viewed as a loosely linked group of decisions that are handled individually. Nevertheless, its effect may be to attune the business to its environment through its problem solving nature. Its drawback is that the lack of a broad situation analysis and strategy option generation renders the incremental approach less comprehensive. For some companies, however, its inherent practicality, rather than its rationality, may support its use.[39]

Problems in making planning work

Research into the marketing planning approaches of commercial firms has discovered that most companies did not practise the kinds of systematic planning procedure described in this chapter and, of those that did, many did not enjoy the rewards described above.[40] However, others have shown that there is a relationship between planning and commercial success (e.g. Armstrong and McDonald).[41,42] The problem is that the 'contextual difficulties' associated with the process of marketing planning are substantial and need to be understood. Inasmuch as forewarned is forearmed, the following paragraphs offer a checklist of potential problems that have to be faced by those charged with making marketing planning work.

Political

Marketing planning is a process of resource allocation. The outcome of the process is an allocation of more funds to some products and departments, and the same or less to others. Since power bases, career opportunities and salaries are often tied to whether an area is fast or slow growing, it is not surprising that managers view planning as a highly political activity. An example is a European bank, whose planning process resulted in the decision to insist that its retail branch managers divert certain types of loan application to the industrial/merchant banking arm of the group where the return was greater. This was required because the plan was designed to optimize the return to the group as a whole. However, the consequence of this was considerable friction between the divisions concerned because the decision lowered the performance of the retail branch.

Opportunity cost

Some busy managers take the view that marketing planning is a time-wasting process that interferes with the need to deal with day-to-day problems. They view the opportunity cost of spending two or three days away at a hotel thrashing out long-term plans as too high. This difficulty may be compounded by the fact that people who are attracted to the hectic pace of managerial life may be the type who prefer to live that way. Hence, they may be ill at ease with the thought of a long period of sedate contemplation.

Reward systems

In business, reward systems are increasingly being geared to the short term. More and more incentives and bonuses are linked, not just to annual but to quarterly results. Managers may thus overemphasize short-term issues and underemphasize medium- and long-term concerns if there is a conflict of time. Marketing planning, then, may be viewed as of secondary importance.

Information

A systematic marketing planning system needs informational inputs in order to function effectively. Market share, size and growth rates are basic inputs into the marketing audit, but may be unavailable. More perversely, information may wilfully be withheld by those with vested interests who, recognizing that knowledge is power, distort the true situation to protect their position in the planning process.

Culture

Efforts to establish a systematic marketing planning process may be at odds with the culture of an organization. As we have already seen, businesses may 'plan' by making incremental decisions. Hence, the strategic planning system may challenge the status quo and be seen as a threat. In other cases, the values and beliefs of some managers may be altogether hostile to a planning system.

How to handle marketing planning problems

Various authors[43,44] have proposed the following recommendations for minimizing the impact of these problems.

- *Senior management support*: top management must be committed to planning and be seen by middle management to give it total support. This should be ongoing support, not a short term fad.
- *Match the planning system to the culture of the business*: how the marketing planning process is managed should be consistent with the culture of the organization. For example, in some organizations the top-down/bottom-up balance will move towards top-down; in other less directive cultures the balance will move towards a more bottom-up planning style.

- *The reward system*: this should reward the achievement of longer-term objectives rather than focus exclusively on short-term results.
- *Depoliticize outcomes*: less emphasis should be placed on rewarding managers associated with build (growth) strategies. Recognition of the skills involved in defending share and harvesting products should be made. At General Electric managers are classified as growers, caretakers and undertakers, and matched to products that are being built, defended or harvested in recognition of the fact that the skills involved differ according to the strategic objective. No stigma is attached to caretaking or undertaking; each is acknowledged as contributing to the success of the organization.
- *Clear communication*: plans should be communicated to those charged with implementation.
- *Training*: marketing personnel should be trained in the necessary marketing knowledge and skills to perform the planning job. Ideally, the management team should attend the same training course so that they each share a common understanding of the concepts and tools involved, and can communicate using the same terminology.

Summary

In this chapter we have examined the important issues of marketing planning and marketing strategy. The following key issues were addressed.

1. The role of marketing planning is to give direction to the organization's marketing effort and to co-ordinate its activities.

2. The various stages of the marketing planning process include developing or adjusting the business mission, conducting a marketing audit, conducting a SWOT analysis, setting marketing objectives, deciding the core strategy, making marketing mix decisions, and organizing, implementing and controlling the marketing effort.

3. There are a number of rewards to be gained for pursuing careful planning, including consistency, encouraging the monitoring of change, encouraging organizational adaptation, stimulating achievement, resource allocation and competitive advantage.

4. Making planning work is difficult because of office politics, perceived opportunity costs, pressures for short-term results, availability of the necessary information and cultural issues.

5. There are four generic competitive strategies open to firms, namely cost leadership, differentiation, cost focus and differentiation focus.

6. Key resources within the organization need to be identified, developed and exploited in order to attain a competitive advantage in the marketplace.

Suggested reading

Day, G.S. (1999) *Market Driven Strategy: Processes for Creating Value*, New York: Free Press.

Gulati, R. and **J. B. Oldroyd** (2005) The Quest For Customer Focus, *Harvard Business Review*, **83** (4), 92–102

McDonald, M.H.B. (2005) *Marketing Plans*, 4th edn, Oxford: Heinemann.

Porter, M.E. (1980) *Competitive Strategy: Techniques for Analysing Industries and Competitors*, New York: Free Press.

Sidhu, J. (2003), Mission Statements: Is it Time To Shelve Them?, *European Management Journal*, **21** (4), 439–47.

Internet exercises

Review some of the sample marketing plans available on these sites.

Sites to visit

1   www.curves.com
     www.shapexpress.com
     www.starbuccutsfitness.com
     www.thelittlegym.com

Exercise

Visit these websites and discuss the target market and competitive strategy of each company.

Sites to visit

2   www.bplans.com
     www.knowthis.com/general/marketplan.htm
     www.howstuffworks.com/marketing-plan.htm

Study questions

1. Discuss some of the difficulties that can be encountered in making marketing planning work in an organization. How can these difficulties be overcome?

2. Using Porter's five forces framework, assess the attractiveness of an industry of your choice.

3. Under what circumstances may incremental planning be preferable to synoptic marketing planning, and vice versa?

4. Compare and contrast a cost leadership strategy with a differentiation strategy. Is it possible to pursue both strategies simultaneously?

5. What is meant by value chain analysis? What role does it play in the planning process?

Key terms

marketing planning the process by which businesses analyse the environment and their capabilities, decide upon courses of marketing action and implement those decisions

strategic business unit a business or company division serving a distinct group of customers and with a distinct set of competitors, usually strategically autonomous

business mission the organization's purpose, usually setting out its competitive domain, which distinguishes the business from others of its type

marketing audit a systematic examination of a business's marketing environment, objectives, strategies and activities, with a view to identifying key strategic issues, problem areas and opportunities

customer analysis a survey of who the customers are, what choice criteria they use, how they rate competitive offerings and on what variables they can be segmented

distribution analysis an examination of movements in power bases, channel attractiveness, physical distribution and distribution behaviour

competitor analysis an examination of the nature of actual and potential competitors, their objectives and strategies

industry a group of companies that market products that are close substitutes for each other

strategic issue analysis an examination of the suitability of marketing objectives and segmentation bases in the light of changes in the marketplace

marketing structures the marketing frameworks (organization, training and internal communications) on which marketing activities are based

marketing systems sets of connected parts (information, planning and control) that support the marketing function

control the stage in the marketing planning process or cycle when the performance against plan is monitored so that corrective action can be taken, if necessary

supplier analysis an examination of who and where they are, their competences and shortcomings, the trends affecting them and the future outlook for them

SWOT analysis a structured approach to evaluating the strategic position of a business by identifying its strengths, weaknesses, opportunities and threats

marketing objectives there are two types of

marketing objective—strategic thrust, which dictates which products should be sold in which markets, and strategic objectives, which are product-level objectives, such as build, hold, harvest and divest

strategic thrust the decision concerning which products to sell in which markets

strategic objectives product-level objectives relating to the decision to build, hold, harvest or divest products

core strategy the means of achieving marketing objectives, including target markets, competitor targets and competitive advantage

target market a segment that has been selected as a focus for the company's offering or communications

competitor targets the organizations against which a company chooses to compete directly

differentiation strategy the selection of one or more customer choice criteria, and positioning the offering accordingly to achieve superior customer value

value chain the set of the firm's activities that are conducted to design, manufacture, market, distribute and service its products

References

1. **Anonymous** (2005) The Giant in the Palm of Your Hand, *Economist,* 12 February, 59–61; **Brown-Humes, C.** (2005) Nokia Shares Fall as Margins Squeezed, *Financial Times,* 22 July, 21; **George, N.** (2005) Nokia Wins Back Market Share to Bolster Top Spot, *Financial Times,* 28 January, 21.

2. **Piercy, N.** (2002) *Market-led Strategic Change: Transforming the Process of Going to Market,* Oxford: Heinemann.

3. **Day, G.S.** (1984) *Strategic Marketing Planning: The Pursuit of Competitive Advantage,* St Paul, MN: West, 41.

4. **Ackoff, R.I.** (1987) Mission statements, *Planning Review,* **15** (4), 30–2.

5. **Hooley, G.J., A.J. Cox** and **A. Adams** (1992) Our Five Year Mission: To Boldly Go Where No Man Has Been Before ..., *Journal of Marketing Management,* **8** (1), 35–48.

6. **Wilson, T.** (1992) Realizing the Power of Strategic Vision, *Long Range Planning,* **25** (5), 18–28.

7. **Porter, M.E.** (1980) *Competitive Strategy: Techniques for Analyzing Industries and Competitors,* New York: Free Press.

8. **Anonymous** (2005) Nose to Nose, *Economist,* 25 June, 77–9.

9. **Done, K.** (2005) The Big Gamble: Airbus Rolls Out its New Weapon in its Battle with Boeing, *Financial Times,* 17 January, 15.

10. **Marlowe, L.** (2005) New Jet Could Carry Up to 800 Passengers, *Irish Times,* 18 January, 10.

11. **Graham, G.** (1997) Competition is Getting Tougher, *Financial Times,* Special Report on Danish Banking, 9 April, 2.

12. **Nakamoto, M.** (2005) Caught in its Own Trap: Sony Battles to Make Headway in a Networked World, *Financial Times,* 27 January, 17.

13. **Piercy, N.** (2002) *Market-led Strategic Change:*

Transforming the Process of Going to Market, Oxford: Heinemann, 259.

14. **Dutta, S.** (2004) eBay Strategy (A), European Case Clearing House, 304-063-1

15. **Madapati, R.** (2005) eBay Under Meg Whitman: From Strength to Strength, European Case Clearing House, 305-114-1.

16. **Waters, R.** (2004) Sparkling eBay Top of the Tree, *Financial Times,* 10 December, 29.

17. **McDonald, M.H.B.** (2005) *Marketing Plans,* 4th edn, London: Butterworth-Heinemann.

18. **Nuttall, C.** (2004) Google Writes its Place in the World's History Books, *Financial Times,* 16 December, 24.

19. **Anonymous** (2004) Champ or Chump?, *Economist,* 11 December, 54–5.

20. **Dickie, M.** and **J. Lau** (2004) IBM Brand Loyalty Holds Key For Lenovo, *Financial Times,* 9 December, 26.

21. **Umaskankar, R.** (2005) Lenovo's Big Opportunity: IBM?, European Case Clearing House, 305-131-1.

22. **Hall, W.K.** (1980) Survival Strategies in a Hostile Environment, *Harvard Business Review,* **58** (Sept/Oct), 75–85.

23. **Day, G.S.** (1999) *Market Driven Strategy: Processes for Creating Value,* New York: Free Press.

24. **Mackintosh, J.** (2004) Volkswagen Misfires: The Carmaker Counts the Cost of its High Spending and its Faltering Search For Luxury, *Financial Times,* 9 March, 19.

25. **Buckley, N.** (2003) Domino's Returns to Fast Food's Fast Lane, *Financial Times,* 26 November, 14.

26. **Fifield, A.** (2003) Kiwibank Can Afford to Hold Critics to Account, *Financial Times,* 24 April, 11.

27. **Anonymous** (2005) Hewlett-Packard: Exit Carly, *Economist,* 12 February, 53–4.

28. **Morrison, S.** (2005) Fortune Favours the Bold in Printer Wars, *Financial Times,* 13 May, 26.

29. **Waters, R.** and **S. London** (2005) A Struggle

Over Strategy: HP Counts the Cost of 'Playing the Other Guy's Game', *Financial Times*, 11 February, 15.

30. **Drucker, P.F.** (1993) *Management Tasks, Responsibilities, Practices*, New York: Harper and Row, 128.

31. **Piercy, N.** (1986) The Role and Function of the Chief Marketing Executive and the Marketing Department, *Journal of Marketing Management*, **1** (3), 265–90.

32. **Leppard, J.W.** and **M.H.B. McDonald** (1991) Marketing Planning and Corporate Culture: A Conceptual Framework which Examines Management Attitudes in the Context of Marketing Planning, *Journal of Marketing Management*, 7 (3), 213–36.

33. **Greenley, G.E.** (1986) *The Strategic and Operational Planning of Marketing*, Maidenhead: McGraw-Hill, 185–7.

34. **Terpstra, V.** and **R. Sarathy** (1991) *International Marketing*, Orlando, FL: Dryden, Ch. 17.

35. **Oktemgil, M.** and **G. Greenley** (1997) Consequences of High and Low Adaptive Capability in UK Companies, *European Journal of Marketing*, 31 (7), 445–66.

36. **Raimond, P.** and **C. Eden** (1990) Making Strategy Work, *Long Range Planning*, **23** (5), 97–105.

37. **Driver, J.C.** (1990) Marketing Planning in Style, *Quarterly Review of Marketing*, 15 (4), 16–21.

38. **Saker, J.** and **R. Speed** (1992) Corporate Culture: Is it Really a Barrier to Marketing Planning?, *Journal of Marketing Management*, 8 (2), 177–82. For information on marketing and planning in small and medium-sized firms, see **Carson, D.** (1990) Some Exploratory Models for Assessing Small Firms' Marketing Performance: A Qualitative Approach, *European Journal of Marketing*, 24 (11), 8–51; and **Fuller, P.B.** (1994) Assessing Marketing in Small and Medium-sized Enterprises, *European Journal of Marketing*, 28 (12), 34–9.

39. **O'Shaughnessy, J.** (1995) *Competitive Marketing*, Boston, MA: Allen & Unwin.

40. **Greenley, G.** (1987) An Exposition into Empirical Research into Marketing Planning, *Journal of Marketing Management*, 3 (1), 83–102.

41. **Armstrong, J.S.** (1982) The Value of Formal Planning for Strategic Decisions: Review of Empirical Research, *Strategic Management Journal*, 3 (3), 197–213.

42. **McDonald, M.H.B.** (1984) *The Theory and Practice of Marketing Planning for Industrial Goods in International Markets*, Cranfield Institute of Technology, PhD thesis.

43. **McDonald, M.H.B.** (1984) *The Theory and Practice of Marketing Planning for Industrial Goods in International Markets*, Cranfield Institute of Technology, PhD thesis.

44. **Abell, D.F.** and **J.S. Hammond** (1979) *Strategic Market Planning*, Englewood Cliffs, NJ: Prentice-Hall.

Turn the page for a Case Study on LEGO

Case 12 LEGO: the toy industry changes

How times have changed for LEGO. The iconic Danish toy maker, best known for its LEGO brick, was once the must-have toy for every child. However, LEGO has been facing a number of difficulties since the late 1990s: falling sales, falling market share, job losses and management reshuffles. Once voted 'Toy of the Century' and with a history of uninterrupted sales growth, it appears LEGO has fallen victim to changing market trends. Today's young clued-up consumer is far more likely to be seen surfing the web, texting on their mobile phone, listening to their MP3 player or playing on their Game Boy than enjoying a LEGO set. With intensifying competition in the toy market, the challenge for LEGO is to create aspirational, sophisticated, innovative toys that are relevant to today's tweens.

History

In 1932 Ole Kirk Christiansen, a Danish carpenter, established a business making wooden toys. He named the company 'LEGO' in 1934, which comes from the Danish words 'leg godt', meaning 'play well'. Later, coincidentally, it was discovered that in Latin it means, 'I put together'. The LEGO name was chosen to represent company philosophy, where play is seen as integral to a child's successful growth and development. In 1947 the company began to make plastic products and in 1949 it launched its world-famous automatic building brick. Ole Kirk Christiansen was succeeded by his son Godtfred in 1950, and under this new leadership the LEGO group introduced the revolutionary 'LEGO System of Play', which focused on the importance of learning through play. The company began exporting in 1953 and soon developed a strong international reputation.

The LEGO brick, with its new interlocking system, was launched in 1958. During the 1960s LEGO began to use wheels, small motors and gears to give its products the power of motion. LEGOLAND was established in Billund in 1968, as a symbol of LEGO creativity and imagination. Later, in the 1990s, two new parks were opened in Britain and California. LEGO figures were introduced in 1974, giving the LEGO brand a personality. The 1980s saw the beginning of digital development, with LEGO forming a partnership with Media Laboratory at the Massachusetts Institute of Technology in the USA. This resulted in the launch of LEGO TECHNIC Computer Control and paved the way for LEGO robots. LEGO introduced a constant flow of new products in the 1990s, and placed greater focus on intelligence and behaviour. The new millennium saw LEGO crowned the 'Toy of the Century' by *Fortune* magazine and the British Association of Toy Retailers. LEGO is currently the fourth largest toy manufacturer in the world after Mattel, Hasbro and Bandai, with a presence in over 130 countries.

Challenges for the traditional toy market

A number of environmental shifts have been affecting the toy market over the past decade. Some of these are described below.

- *Kids getting older younger.* By the time most kids reach the age of eight they have outgrown the offerings of the traditional toy market. A central factor in children abandoning toys earlier is their lack of free time to play. Children today have a lot more scheduled activities and, with greater emphasis on academic achievement, a lot more time is spent studying. Faced with more media and entertainment choices these sophisticated and technologically savvy consumers are favouring electronic, fashion, make-up and lifestyle products. The most susceptible group to this age compression are 'tweens'—children between the ages of 8 and 12—a US$5 billion market, accounting for 20 per cent of the US$20.7 billion traditional toy industry.

- *Intensifying competition from the electronic and games market.* As noted above, today's young consumer is far more likely to be seen surfing the web, texting on their mobile phone, listening to their MP3 player or playing on their Game Boy than enjoying a LEGO set. A survey by NPD Funworld, in 2003, found that tween boys who played video games spent approximately 40 per cent less time playing with action figures when compared with the previous year. Handheld toys with a video and gaming element suit the mobile lifestyle of today's tween. As demand for these more sophisticated toys increases, traditional toy makers are facing more direct competition with the electronic and video games market.

- *Fickleness of young consumers.* The toy market today is very fashion-driven, leading to shorter product life cycles. Toy manufacturers are facing increasing pressure to develop a competency in forecasting market changes and improving their speed of response to those changes. In an effort to get a share of the huge revenues generated by the latest hot toy, many toy manufacturers have left themselves more vulnerable to greater earnings volatility.

- *Power of the retail sector.* Consolidation in the retail sector and the expansion of many retail chains has placed enormous pressure on the profit margins of traditional toy makers. Major retailers can exert tremendous power over their suppliers because of the vast quantities they buy. Many retailers insert a clause in their supplier contracts that gives them a certain percentage of profit regardless of the retail price.

Many traditional toy makers are struggling to keep up with these environmental changes. It appears no one is safe, when even the world-renowned LEGO brand can fall victim to changing market trends. The cracks first began to show in 1998, when LEGO made a loss for the first time in its history. This began a major reversal in the fortunes of a company that had become accustomed to decades of uninterrupted sales growth (see Table C12.1). Ironically, it is the success of LEGO that may ultimately have paved the way for its downfall.

What went wrong for LEGO?

According to Kjeld Kirk Kristiansen, owner of the business and grandson of its founder, following many years of success the LEGO culture had become 'inward looking' and 'complacent' and had failed to keep pace with the changes taking place in the toy market. This lack of environmental sensitivity was evident in the US market in 2003, where LEGO failed to predict demand for its Bionicle figures, resulting in two of its best-selling products from this range being out of stock in the run-up to Christmas. It appeared nothing had been learned from the previous year, when also in the run-up to Christmas the much sought-after Hogwarts Castle sets were out of stock across the UK.

LEGO had also become over-dependent on licences in the 1990s, for products such as Star Wars and Harry Potter, as its main source of growth. This left LEGO vulnerable to the faddishness of these products: the years in which the Star Wars and Harry Potter films were released coincided with profitable years for LEGO, while losses were reported in the intervening years.

The diversification of the brand into the manufacture of items such as clothing, bags and accessories was another mistake for LEGO. The company over-

Table C12.1 LEGO financial information

LEGO financial information (mDKK)	2004	2003	2002	2001	2000
Income statement					
Revenue	6704	7196	10116	9475	8379
Expenses	(6601)	(8257)	(9248)	(8554)	(9000)
Profit/(loss) before special items, financial income and expenses and tax	103	(1061)	868	921	(621)
Impairment of fixed assets	(723)	(172)	–	–	–
Restructuring expenses	(502)	(283)	–	(122)	(191)
Operating profit/(loss)	(1122)	(1516)	868	799	(812)
Financial income and expenses	(115)	18	(251)	(278)	(280)
Profit/(loss) before tax	(1237)	(1498)	617	521	(1092)
Profit/(loss) on continuing activities	(1473)	(953)	348	420	(788)
Profit/(loss) on discontinuing activities	(458)	18	(22)	(54)	(75)
Net profit/(loss) for the year	(1931)	(935)	326	366	(863)
Employees: Average number of employees (full-time), continuing activities	5569	6542	6659	6474	6570
Average number of employees (full-time), discontinuing activities	1725	1756	1657	1184	1328

complicated its product portfolio and it ran close to over-stretching the LEGO brand. Kristiansen, who resumed leadership in 2004 to guide the company out of crisis, is quoted as saying 'LEGO was so busy chasing the fashion of the day that it took its eye off its core brand.'

The phasing-out of its long-established pre-school Duplo brand, to be replaced by LEGO Explore, was another error. Parents were left confused, with many believing the larger-size Duplo brick had been discontinued. This error resulted in a loss of revenues from the pre-school market in 2003. Adult fans of LEGO (AFOLs) were also left disgruntled when LEGO changed the colour of its new building bricks so that they no longer matched the colour of the old bricks.

While other toy manufacturers have moved production to low-cost destinations such as China, LEGO has been reluctant to follow suit. Today it still manufactures the bulk of its product in Billund and Switzerland. The reasons posited for the company's reluctance to move include a strong sense of loyalty to Billund, where one-quarter of the residents work at the LEGO factory, and concerns that a move would affect its brand image. While its loyalty to these sites is admirable, and brand image worries understandable, the question is whether its long-term future is viable without such a move.

A new direction for LEGO

In an attempt to turn around its fortunes LEGO has developed a number of new marketing strategies. These include the following.

- A back-to-basics strategy is seeing LEGO refocus on its core brick-based product range and place more emphasis on its key target group—younger children. In 2003, LEGO relaunched its classic range of brick-based products and many new product lines have centred on eternal themes such as Town, Castle, Pirates and Vikings. LEGO has reinstated the Duplo brand and introduced the Quarto brand, which consists of larger bricks for children under two. Other new lines include LEGO Sports, born from strategic alliances with the National Hockey League and US National Basketball Association. While the traditional audience of LEGO has always been young boys it has introduced a new range, 'Clikits', a social toy developed specifically for a female audience. Clikits consists of pretty pastel-coloured bricks, which provide numerous

options to create jewellery and fashion accessories.

- LEGO has admitted to over-diversifying its brand. In response to this, LEGO has withdrawn many of its manufacturing lines, instead opting to outsource these to third parties via licensing deals. LEGO is also selling its LEGOLAND parks in a bid to refocus efforts on its core product and improve its financial situation.

- In an attempt to create a story-based, multichannel brand, LEGO has engaged in a number of licensing deals, with varying degrees of success, but more importantly it is now developing its own intellectual property. The Bionicle range, launched in 2001, was the first time LEGO had created a story from the start as the basis for a new product range. The Bionicles combine physical snap-together kits with an online virtual world. This toy brand has also been extended into entertainment in the form of comics, books and a Miramax movie: *Bionicle: Mask of Light*. The range has proved a major success for LEGO and, building on this success, it has developed Knights Kingdom.

- Sub-brands that LEGO has neglected, including Mindstorms and LEGO TECHNIC, both aimed at older children and enjoyed by some adults, are being given more attention. With so many adult fans of LEGO, efforts are also being made to further engage the adult market. The company is currently considering whether to market its management training tool, entitled LEGO Serious Play, to a wider adult audience.

- LEGO has overhauled its packaging, and the style and tone of its advertising. The emphasis is now being placed on the LEGO play and educational experience as opposed to product detail. The strap-line 'play on' was introduced in January 2003 to accompany the change. The slogan draws its inspiration from the company's five core values: creativity, imagination, learning, fun and quality. LEGO is also making greater use of more interactive communication tools to promote its products, which it is believed will encourage consumers to interact more with the brand. 2005 has seen LEGO invite fans on a tour of the company. Here they are given the opportunity to meet new product developers, designers and toolmakers, and learn about the company's history, culture and values.

- LEGO is also taking steps to reverse its insular culture. In an attempt to build a more market-driven organization, it is spending more time consulting children, parents, retailers and AFOLs. The company established the LEGO

Vision Lab in 2002 to examine how the future will look to children and their families. A variety of sources are being used to make assessments of future worldwide family patterns, including anthropology, architecture, consumer patterns and awareness, culture, philosophy, sociology and technology.

- Plagued by supply-chain inefficiencies LEGO has improved production time from concept to the retailer's shelf. An example of this is the Duplo Castle, which was developed in nine months.

Conclusion

Having taken its eye off the ball, LEGO is fighting back with a new customer-focused strategic approach. Continuous improvement, in response to changing market trends, is now key if LEGO is to ward off the many challenges it still faces. It is still involved in many licence agreements, making it vulnerable to this cyclical market. Its back-to-basics strategy has been widely praised but it remains to be seen if LEGO can balance this with its increasing activity in software. With children's growing appetite for video games with a more violent content, can LEGO satisfy this target group while still remaining true to its wholesome 'play well' brand values? Will LEGO succeed in its attempts to target young girls and its desire to target a more adult audience? Will it succeed in its attempts to reduce costs and improve efficiencies? Will CEO Jorgen Vig Knudstorp succeed where his predecessors have failed? Only in the fullness of time will these questions be answered but one thing is for sure: no brand, no matter how powerful, can afford to become complacent in an increasingly competitive business environment.

Questions

1. Why did LEGO encounter serious economic difficulties in the late 1990s?
2. Conduct a SWOT analysis of LEGO and identify the company's main sources of advantage.
3. Critically evaluate the LEGO turnaround strategy.

This case was prepared by Sinéad Moloney, University of Limerick, as a basis for classroom discussion rather than to show effective or ineffective management.

The material in this case was drawn from the following sources.

i. **Brown-Humes, C.** (2004) After the Crash: LEGO Picks up the Pieces, *Financial Times*, 2 April, 10.

ii. **Carter, M.** (2003) LEGO's Bid to Rebuild and Keep its Balance, *Financial Times*, 28 October, 8–9.

iii. **Foster, L.** (2004) Toys are Child's Play No More, *Financial Times*, 10 June, 12.

iv. **Goodman, M.** (2004) Lego's Rescue Brick by Brick, *The Sunday Times*, Business Section 1, 14 November.

v. **Mortimer, R.** (2003) Building a Brand out of Bricks, *Brand Strategy*, April, 16–19.

vi. **Tsui, B.** (2001) Toymakers are Geared Up to Showcase Tween Tech, 2 December, *Advertising Age*, 7 (72), 8.

vii. **Widdicombe, R.** (2004) Online: Building Blocks for the Future, *Guardian*, 29 April, 19.

viii. www.lego.com.

Glossary

ad hoc research a research project that focuses on a specific problem, collecting data at one point in time with one sample of respondents

administered vertical marketing system a channel situation where a manufacturer that dominates a market through its size and strong brands may exercise considerable power over intermediaries even though they are independent

advertising any paid form of non-personal communication of ideas or products in the prime media (i.e. television, the press, posters, cinema and radio, the Internet and direct marketing)

advertising agency an organization that specializes in providing services such as media selection, creative work, production and campaign planning to clients

advertising message the use of words, symbols and illustrations to communicate to a target audience using prime media

advertising platform the aspect of the seller's product that is most persuasive and relevant to the target consumer

ambush marketing any activity where a company tries to associate itself or its products with an event without paying any fee to the event owner

attitude the degree to which a customer or prospect likes or dislikes a brand

awareness set the set of brands that the consumer is aware may provide a solution to a problem

beliefs descriptive thoughts that a person holds about something

benefit segmentation the grouping of people based on the different benefits they seek from a product

bonus pack pack giving the customer extra quantity at no additional cost

brainstorming the technique whereby a group of people generate ideas without initial evaluation; only when the list of ideas is complete is each one then evaluated

brand a distinctive product offering created by the use of a name, symbol, design, packaging, or some combination of these, intended to differentiate it from its competitors

brand equity the goodwill associated with a brand

name, which adds tangible value to a company through the resulting higher sales and profits

brand extension the use of an established brand name on a new brand within the same broad market

brand stretching the use of an established brand name for brands in unrelated markets

brand values the core values and characteristics of a brand

business analysis a review of the projected sales, costs and profits for a new product to establish whether these factors satisfy company objectives

business mission the organization's purpose, usually setting out its competitive domain, which distinguishes the business from others of its type

buying centre a group that is involved in the buying decision; also known as a decision-making unit (DMU) in industrial buying situations

catalogue marketing the sale of products through catalogues distributed to agents and customers, usually by mail or at stores

cause-related marketing the commercial activity by which businesses and charities or causes form a partnership with each other to market an image, product or service for mutual benefit

channel integration the way in which the players in the channel are linked

channel intermediaries organizations that facilitate the distribution of products to customers

channel of distribution the means by which products are moved from the producer to the ultimate consumer

channel strategy the selection of the most effective distribution channel, the most appropriate level of distribution intensity and the degree of channel integration

choice criteria the various attributes (and benefits) people use when evaluating products and services

classical conditioning the process of using an established relationship between a stimulus and a response to cause the learning of the same response to a different stimulus

cognitive dissonance post-purchase concerns of a

consumer arising from uncertainty as to whether a decision to purchase was the correct one

cognitive learning the learning of knowledge, and development of beliefs and attitudes without direct reinforcement

communications-based co-branding the linking of two or more existing brands from different companies or business units for the purposes of joint communication

competitive advantage a clear performance differential over the competition on factors that are important to target customers

competitive bidding drawing up detailed specifications for a product and putting the contract out to tender

competitor analysis an examination of the nature of actual and potential competitors, their objectives and strategies

competitor targets the organizations against which a company chooses to compete directly

concept testing testing new product ideas with potential customers

consumer panel household consumers who provide information on their purchases over time

consumer pull the targeting of consumers with communications (e.g. promotions) designed to create demand that will *pull* the product into the distribution chain

continuous research repeated interviewing of the same sample of people

contractual vertical marketing system a franchise arrangement (e.g. a franchise) tying producers and resellers together

control the stage in the marketing planning process or cycle when the performance against plan is monitored so that corrective action can be taken, if necessary

core strategy the means of achieving marketing objectives, including target markets, competitor targets and competitive advantage

corporate vertical marketing system a channel situation where an organization gains control of distribution through ownership

culture the traditions, taboos, values and basic attitudes of the whole society in which an individual lives

customer analysis a survey of who the customers are, what choice criteria they use, how they rate

competitive offerings and on what variables they can be segmented

customer benefits those things that a customer values in a product; customer benefits derive from product features (see separate entry)

customer relationship management (CRM) the methodologies, technologies and e-commerce capabilities used by firms to manage customer relationships

customer satisfaction the fulfilment of customers' requirements or needs

customer value perceived benefits minus perceived sacrifice

customized marketing a market coverage strategy where a company decides to target individual customers and to develop separate marketing mixes for each

database marketing an interactive approach to marketing, which uses individually addressable marketing media and channels to provide information to a target audience, stimulate demand and stay close to customers

decision-making process the stages that organizations and people pass through when purchasing a physical product or service

depth interviews the interviewing of consumers individually for perhaps one or two hours with the aim of understanding their attitudes, values, behaviour and/or beliefs

differential advantage a clear performance differential over competition on factors that are important to target customers

differentiated marketing a market coverage strategy where a company decides to target several market segments and to develop separate marketing mixes for each

differentiation strategy the selection of one or more customer choice criteria, and positioning the offering accordingly to achieve superior customer value

diffusion of innovation process the process by which a new product spreads throughout a market over time

direct mail material sent through the postal service to the recipient's house or business address, promoting a product and/or maintaining an ongoing relationship

direct marketing (1) acquiring and retaining customers without the use of an intermediary;

(2) the distribution of products, information and promotional benefits to target consumers through interactive communication in a way that allows response to be measured

direct response advertising the use of the prime advertising media, such as television, newspapers and magazines, to elicit an order, enquiry or a request for a visit

distribution analysis an examination of movements in power bases, channel attractiveness, physical distribution and distribution behaviour

distribution push the targeting of channel intermediaries with communications (e.g. promotions) to *push* the product into the distribution chain

domain names global system of unique names for addressing web servers; the Domain Name System (DNS) is the method of administering such names. Each level in the system is given a name and is called a domain: gTDL refers to global top-level domain names (e.g. .com, .edu, .org); ccTDL refers to country code top-level domain names of which there are about 250 (e.g. .uk, .fr); domain names are maintained by the Internet Corporation for Assigned Names (ICANN) (www.icann.org)

dynamic pricing an outcome of yield management where prices are frequently adjusted depending on demand for the product or service

e-commerce the use of technologies such as the Internet, electronic data interchange (EDI), e-mail and electronic payment systems to streamline business transactions

economic value to the customer (EVC) the amount a customer would have to pay to make the total life cycle costs of a new and a reference product the same

effectiveness doing the right thing, making the correct strategic choice

efficiency a way of managing business processes to a high standard, usually concerned with cost reduction; also called 'doing things right'

electronic data interchange (EDI) a pre-Internet technology, which was developed to permit organizations to use linked computers for the rapid exchange of information

environmental scanning the process of monitoring and analysing the marketing environment of a company

ethics the moral principles and values that govern the actions and decisions of an individual or group

event sponsorship sponsorship of a sporting or other event

evoked set the set of brands that the consumer seriously evaluates before making a purchase

exaggerated promises barrier a barrier to the matching of expected and perceived service levels caused by the unwarranted building up of expectations by exaggerated promises

exclusive distribution an extreme form of selective distribution where only one wholesaler, retailer or industrial distributor is used in a geographical area to sell the products of a particular supplier

exhibition an event that brings buyers and sellers together in a commercial setting

experimentation the application of stimuli (e.g. two price levels) to different matched groups under controlled conditions for the purpose of measuring their effect on a variable (e.g. sales)

exploratory research the preliminary exploration of a research area prior to the main data collection stage

family brand name a brand name used for all products in a range

focus group a group, normally of six to eight consumers, brought together for a discussion focusing on an aspect of a company's marketing

focused marketing a market coverage strategy where a company decides to target one market segment with a single marketing mix

franchise a legal contract in which a producer and channel intermediaries agree each other's rights and obligations; the intermediary usually receives marketing, managerial, technical and financial services in return for a fee

full cost pricing pricing so as to include all costs, and based on certain sales volume assumptions

geodemographics the process of grouping households into geographic clusters based on such information as type of accommodation, occupation, number and age of children, and ethnic background

global branding achievement of brand penetration worldwide

going-rate prices prices at the rate generally applicable in the market, focusing on competitors' offerings rather than on company costs

group discussion a group, usually of six to eight consumers, brought together for a discussion focusing on an aspect of a company's marketing strategy

hall tests bringing a sample of target consumers to a room that has been hired so that alternative marketing ideas (e.g. promotions) can be tested

horizontal electronic marketplaces online procurement sites that cross several industries and are typically used to source low-cost supplies such as MRO items

inadequate delivery barrier a barrier to the matching of expected and perceived service levels caused by the failure of the service provider to select, train and reward staff adequately, resulting in poor or inconsistent delivery of service

inadequate resources barrier a barrier to the matching of expected and perceived service levels caused by the unwillingness of service providers to provide the necessary resources

individual brand name a brand name that does not identify a brand with a particular company

industry a group of companies that market products that are close substitutes for each other

information framing the way in which information is presented to people

information processing the process by which a stimulus is received, interpreted, stored in memory and later retrieved

information search the identification of alternative ways of problem solving

ingredient co-branding the explicit positioning of a supplier's brand as an ingredient of a product

inseparability a characteristic of services, namely that their production cannot be separated from their consumption

intangibility a characteristic of services, namely that they cannot be touched, seen, tasted or smelled

integrated marketing communications the concept that companies co-ordinate their marketing communications tools to deliver a clear, consistent, credible and competitive message about the organization and its products

intensive distribution the aim of intensive distribution is to provide saturation coverage of the market by using all available outlets

Internet a vast global computer network that permits instant communication, such as the gathering and sharing of information, and that offers the facility for users to communicate with one another

Internet marketing the achievement of marketing objectives through the utilization of the Internet and web-based technologies

just-in-time (JIT) the JIT concept aims to minimize stocks by organizing a supply system that provides materials and components as they are required

key account management an approach to selling that focuses resources on major customers and uses a team selling approach

lifestyle the pattern of living as expressed in a person's activities, interests and opinions

lifestyle segmentation the grouping of people according to their pattern of living as expressed in their activities, interests and opinions

macroenvironment a number of broader forces that affect not only the company but the other actors in the environment, e.g. social, political, technological and economic

manufacturer brands brands that are created by producers and bear their chosen brand name

marginal cost pricing the calculation of only those costs that are likely to rise as output increases

market segmentation the process of identifying individuals or organizations with similar characteristics that have significant implications for the determination of marketing strategy

market testing the limited launch of a new product to test sales potential

marketing audit a systematic examination of a business's marketing environment, objectives, strategies and activities, with a view to identifying key strategic issues, problem areas and opportunities

marketing concept the achievement of corporate goals through meeting and exceeding customer needs better than the competition

marketing environment the actors and forces that affect a company's capability to operate effectively in providing products and services to its customers

marketing information system a system in which marketing information is formally gathered, stored, analysed and distributed to managers in accordance with their informational needs on a regular, planned basis

marketing mix a framework for the tactical management of the customer relationship, including product, place, price, promotion (the 4-Ps); in the case of services, three other elements to be taken into account are process, people and physical evidence

marketing objectives there are two types of marketing objective—strategic thrust, which dictates which products should be sold in which markets, and strategic objectives, which are product-level objectives, such as build, hold, harvest and divest

marketing orientation companies with a marketing orientation focus on customer needs as the primary drivers of organizational performance

marketing planning the process by which businesses analyse the environment and their capabilities, decide upon courses of marketing action and implement those decisions

marketing planning the process by which businesses analyse the environment and their capabilities, decide upon courses of marketing action and implement those decisions

marketing research the gathering of data and information on the market

marketing structures the marketing frameworks (organization, training and internal communications) on which marketing activities are based

marketing systems sets of connected parts (information, planning and control) that support the marketing function

mass customization the opposite to mass production, which means that all products produced are customized to the predetermined needs of a specific customer

media class decision the choice of prime media (i.e. the press, cinema, television, posters, radio) or some combination of these

media vehicle decision the choice of the particular newspaper, magazine, television spot, poster site, etc.

microenvironment the actors in the firm's immediate environment that affect its capability to operate effectively in its chosen markets—namely, suppliers, distributors, customers and competitors

misconceptions barrier a failure by marketers to understand what customers really value about their service

mobile marketing the sending of text messages to mobile phones to promote products and build relationships with customers

modified rebuy where a regular requirement for the type of product exists and the buying alternatives are known but sufficient (e.g. a delivery problem has occurred) to require some alteration to the normal supply procedure

money-off promotions sales promotions that discount the normal price

motivation the process involving needs that set drives in motion to accomplish goals

new task refers to the first-time purchase of a product or input by an organization

omnibus survey a regular survey, usually operated by a market research specialist company, which asks questions of respondents

operant conditioning the use of rewards to generate reinforcement of response

own-label brands brands created and owned by distributors or retailers

parallel co-branding the joining of two or more independent brands to produce a combined brand

parallel importing when importers buy products from distributors in one country and sell them in another to distributors who are not part of the manufacturer's normal distribution; caused by significant price differences for the same product between different countries

perception the process by which people select, organize and interpret sensory stimulation into a meaningful picture of the world

perishability a characteristic of services, namely that the capacity of a service business, such as a hotel room, cannot be stored—if it is not occupied, there is lost income that cannot be recovered

personal selling oral communication with prospective purchasers with the intention of making a sale

personality the inner psychological characteristics of individuals that lead to consistent responses to their environment

place the distribution channels to be used, outlet locations, methods of transportation

portfolio planning managing groups of brands and product lines

positioning the choice of target market (*where* the company wishes to compete) and differential advantage (*how* the company wishes to compete)

premiums any merchandise offered free or at low cost as an incentive to purchase

price (1) the amount of money paid for a product; (2) the agreed value placed on the exchange by a buyer and seller

price escalation the additional costs incurred in taking products to an international market, including transportation costs, distribution costs, taxes and tariffs, exchange rates and inflation rates

price unbundling pricing each element in the offering so that the price of the total product package is raised

product a good or service offered or performed by an organization or individual, which is capable of satisfying customer needs

product features the characteristics of a product that may or may not convey a customer benefit

product life cycle a four-stage cycle in the life of a product, illustrated as a curve representing the demand; the four stages being introduction, growth, maturity and decline

product line a group of brands that are closely related in terms of the functions and benefits they provide

product mix the total set of products marketed by a company

product placement the deliberate placing of products and/or their logos in movies and television programmes, usually in return for money

product-based co-branding the linking of two or more existing brands from different companies or business units to form a product in which the brand names are visible to the consumer

production orientation a business approach that is inwardly focused either on costs or on a definition of a company in terms of its production facilities

profile segmentation the grouping of people in terms of profile variables such as age and socio-economic group so that marketers can communicate to them

promotional mix advertising, personal selling, sales promotion, public relations and direct marketing

prospecting searching for and calling upon potential customers

psychographic segmentation the grouping of people according to their lifestyle and personality characteristics

psychological pricing taking into consideration the psychological impact of the price level that is being set

public relations the management of communications and relationships to establish goodwill and mutual understanding between an organization and its public

publicity the communication of a product or business by placing information about it in the media without paying for time or space directly

qualitative research exploratory research that aims to understand consumers' attitudes, values, behaviour and beliefs

reasoning a more complex form of cognitive learning where conclusions are reached by connected thought

reference group a group of people that influences an individual's attitude or behaviour

relationship marketing the process of creating, maintaining and enhancing strong relationships with customers and other stakeholders

repositioning changing the target market or differential advantage, or both

research brief written document stating the client's requirements

research proposal a document defining what the marketing research agency promises to do for its client and how much it will cost

retail audit a type of continuous research tracking the sales of products through retail outlets

retail positioning the choice of target market and differential advantage for a retail outlet

reverse marketing the process whereby the buyer attempts to persuade the supplier to provide exactly what the organization wants

rote learning the learning of two or more concepts without conditioning

safety (buffer) stocks stocks or inventory held to

cover against uncertainty about resupply lead times

sales promotion incentives to customers or the trade that are designed to stimulate purchase

salesforce evaluation the measurement of salesperson performance so that strengths and weaknesses can be identified

salesforce motivation the motivation of salespeople by a process that involves needs, which set encouraging drives in motion to accomplish goals

sampling process a term used in research to denote the selection of a subset of the total population in order to interview them

secondary research data that has already been collected by another researcher for another purpose

selective attention the process by which people screen out those stimuli that are neither meaningful to them nor consistent with their experiences and beliefs

selective distortion the distortion of information received by people according to their existing beliefs and attitudes

selective distribution the use of a limited number of outlets in a geographical area to sell the products of a particular supplier

selective retention the process by which people retain only a selection of messages in memory

service any deed, performance or effort carried out for the customer

services marketing mix product, place, price, promotion, people, process and physical evidence

shareholder value the returns to a company's shareholders, which grow when the company increases its dividends or its share price rises

social responsibility the ethical principle that a person or an organization should be accountable for how its actions might affect the physical environment and the general public

sponsorship a business relationship between a provider of funds, resources or services and an individual, event or organization that offers in return some rights and association that may be used for commercial advantage

straight rebuy refers to a purchase by an organization from a previously approved supplier of a previously purchased item

strategic business unit a business or company division serving a distinct group of customers and with a distinct set of competitors, usually strategically autonomous

strategic issue analysis an examination of the suitability of marketing objectives and segmentation bases in the light of changes in the marketplace

strategic objectives product-level objectives relating to the decision to build, hold, harvest or divest products

strategic thrust the decision concerning which products to sell in which markets

supplier analysis an examination of who and where they are, their competences and short comings, the trends affecting them and the future outlook for them

SWOT analysis a structured approach to evaluating the strategic position of a business by identifying its strengths, weaknesses, opportunities and threats

target audience the group of people at which an advertisement or message is aimed

target market a segment that has been selected as a focus for the company's offering or communications

target marketing selecting a segment as the focus for a company's offering or communications

telemarketing a marketing communications system whereby trained specialists use telecommunications and information technologies to conduct marketing and sales activities

test marketing the launch of a new product in one or a few geographic areas chosen to be representative of the intended market

trade-off analysis a measure of the trade-off customers make between price and other product features, so that their effects on product preference can be established

undifferentiated marketing a market coverage strategy where a company decides to ignore market segment differences and to develop a single marketing mix for the whole market

value chain the set of the firm's activities that are conducted to design, manufacture, market, distribute and service its products

value-based marketing a perspective on marketing which emphasizes how a marketing philosophy and marketing activities contribute to the maximization of shareholder value

variability a characteristic of services, namely that being delivered by people the standard of their performance is open to variation

vertical electronic marketplaces online procurement sites that are dedicated to sourcing supplies for producers in one particular industry

vicarious learning learning from others without direct experience or reward

viral marketing electronic word of mouth, where promotional messages are spread using e-mail from person to person

website a collection of various files including text, graphics, video and audio content created by organizations and individuals

World Wide Web a collection of computer files that can be accessed via the Internet, allowing documents containing text, images, sound and/or video to be used

Author Index

Subject Index